PRAISE FOR MICHAEL GANNON AND
BLACK MAY

"*Black May*, like everything Michael Gannon has written,
bears the hallmarks of his careful scholarship and thorough
research . . . [and] by all odds will have to be recognized as
the final word on that critical period of the Battle of the Atlantic when the U-boats were vanquished."

—CAPTAIN EDWARD L. BEACH, author of *Run Silent, Run Deep*

"A significant addition to the history of World War II . . .
Black May does the best job I have seen yet of describing in
detail why the U-boats lost the Battle of the Atlantic."

—VICE ADMIRAL JAMES F. CALVERT, USN (Retired),
Naval Institute Proceedings

"In *Black May*, Gannon combines storytelling, scholarship
and analysis about the defeat of the largest submarine fleet
ever."

—KEN MOORE, *Naples Daily News*

"A splendid book . . . Based on a wealth of original archival
sources, *Black May* is a gripping tale of the undersea war by
one of our finest naval historians."

—CARLO D'ESTE, author of *Patton: A Genius for War*

Please turn the page for more extraordinary acclaim. . . .

"Michael Gannon possesses an extremely rare talent. He combines the skeptical eye of the historian, the fastidious care of the researcher and the dash and enthusiasm of the popular writer. He re-creates for us the nightmare conditions of the German U-boat crews, and the harsh and hazardous lives of the men hunting them. He also probes, in a fair but critical way, the decisions of the top brass on both sides."

—LEN DEIGHTON, author of *Blood, Tears and Folly*

"Michael Gannon gives us a look over the shoulder of all the players in the 1943 showdown against the U-boats in the North Atlantic: the tacticians, the grand strategists, and the brave men on the sea and under it. The author of *Operation Drumbeat* has outdone himself."

—BRIAN MCCUE, author of *U-Boats in the Bay of Biscay*

"Gannon is at his best, describing the men and women who used those new weapons of war to reduce U-boats to victims rather than predators."

—*Tallahassee Democrat*

"Gannon's narration is as exciting as any techno-thriller fiction, without either violating the integrity of his sources or sliding into melodrama."

—DENNIS SHOWALTER, *History Book Club Review*

"What is impressive to me about *Black May* is that even after a hundred or so books have been written about the Battle of the Atlantic, Mike Gannon has been able to uncover new material and use it to develop new perspectives and new insights into how the battle was won and lost. . . . Gannon's felicitous style and keen appreciation of the human aspects make it a pleasure to read."

—FRED MILFORD, Battelle Memorial Institute (Retired)

BLACK MAY

THE EPIC STORY OF THE ALLIES' DEFEAT OF THE GERMAN U-BOATS IN MAY 1943

Michael Gannon

A Dell Book

Published by
Dell Publishing
a division of
Random House, Inc.
1540 Broadway
New York, New York 10036

Grateful acknowledgment is given the University of Toronto Press for permission to quote from the poem "Behind the Log" by E. J. Pratt. Copyright © 1989, all rights reserved.

Crown copyright material in the Public Record Office, London, is reproduced by permission of the Controller of Her Brittanic Majesty's Stationery Office.

Copyright © 1998 by Michael Gannon

Dell books may be purchased for business or promotional use or for special sales. For information please write to: Special Markets Department, Random House, Inc., 1540 Broadway, New York, N.Y. 10036.

Dell® is a registered trademark of Random House, Inc., and the colophon is a trademark of Random House, Inc.

ISBN: 0-440-23564-2

Reprinted by arrangement with HarperCollins Publishers, Inc.

Printed in the United States of America

Published simultaneously in Canada

October 1999

10   9   8   7   6   5   4   3

OPM

TO BUZ WYETH

This May the situation was quite out of hand: as I was soon to learn, the number of boats that failed to return from patrol reached 41, more than one a day, and there was talk of "Black May."

> KAPITÄNLEUTNANT
> PETER "ALI" CREMER
> *U-Boat Headquarters Staff, Berlin*

May was a very black month for the U-boats. Sinkings of U-boats probably averaged one a day.

> BRITISH ADMIRALTY
> *Monthly Anti-Submarine Report*

We had lost the Battle of the Atlantic.

> GROSSADMIRAL KARL DÖNITZ
> *Commander-in-Chief, German Navy*

Contents

xii ■ Contents

Acknowledgments

Every book has a beginning. This one began when, in March 1992, I received a letter from Mrs. Stephen (Joan) Raushenbush in Sarasota, Florida, inquiring if I would be interested in seeing certain of her late husband's papers relating to his civilian service in the British-American war against the German U-boats (submarines) in World War II. I immediately said yes, and shortly afterward, my spouse and I visited her in her home. Some months later, I was able to turn up additional documents relating to Stephen Raushenbush in the National Archives in Washington, D.C. Those documents provoked in me strong curiosity about the month of May 1943, which, it was generally known, had been a pivotal thirty-one days during which the U-boats had suffered a substantial defeat in the North Atlantic. It was particularly intriguing to find that not only had the Allies' uniformed naval and air services effectively engaged the U-boat fleet in several notable battles during that May but, prior to that month, a team of civilian scientists and statisticians had contributed significantly to the Allies' operational tactics and capabilities. Raushenbush had been a member of that team.

Other writing responsibilities delayed further inquiry into the May story until, beginning in spring 1995, extended research visits to Great Britain and Germany brought into high relief the major events and personalities of what the Germans called, at its conclusion, "Black May." It quickly became obvious that to understand why, how, and by whom May's battles were won for one side and lost for the other, it was necessary to view that month from both the Allied and German perspectives, as far as the archival documents and recollections of the surviving participants made that possible; particularly in the case of the month's centrally important Battle for Convoy ONS.5. It also seemed desirable to put a human face on the story so that the reader was not confronted simply with steel, aluminum, and high explosives but could come to know at least the names, and sometimes the personal qualities, of the human beings who crewed the U-boats, the warships, and the aircraft; commanded their operations; developed their tactics; or tracked their movements. Nor did I want to neglect the personal stories, not to mention the heroism, of the most numerous contingent at sea in 1943: the merchant mariners. Indeed, there is a large human story behind the principal events of May that can only be hinted at in this volume.

My thanks for assistance in providing me the means for understanding what happened in "Black May" go, in Germany, to the distinguished naval historian Dr. Jürgen Rohwer, in Weinstadt, who favored me with his weighty insights and helpful suggestions; Horst Bredow, the energetic and always helpful director of the U-Boot-Archiv in Cuxhaven-Altenbruch; Thomas Weis, who guided me through two days of selecting maps and photographs from the Marine Archive of the Bibliothek für Zeitgeschichte (Library of Contemporary History) in Stuttgart; the archival staff of the Bundesarchiv/Militärarchiv (Federal/Military Archive) in Freiburg i. Br.; and Horst Einbrodte, Vice-President of the Verband Deutscher U-Bootfahrer e.V. (U-Boat Veterans Association) in Hamburg.

Special thanks are given to Kathi Michalowski, in Barntrup, Germany, my research assistant on this project as she was for an earlier book, *Operation Drumbeat,* whose skills are matched only by her unflagging enthusiasm. Together we arranged interviews with six surviving U-boat commanders who were at sea in May 1943. My gratitude for their participation in that part of the research goes to Horst von Schroeter (U-*123*); Harald Gelhaus (U-*107*); Helmuth Pich (U-*168*);

Klaus-Peter Carlsen (U–732); Klaus Popp (U–522); and Herbert Werner (I.W.O. on U–230 in May, later Commander of U–415). Thanks also are owed two crew members who agreed to be interviewed: Rolf Elebe (U–752) and Kurth Claus (U–552).

In London, England, I had the very good fortune of being allowed to probe the knowledge base and to mine the documentary collections of J. David Brown, Head of Naval Historical Branch, Ministry of Defence, and his colleagues W. J. R. "Jock" Gardner, M. "Mac" McAloon, and Robert M. Coppock. Quite literally, I would not–to use the ocean convoy imperative–have been able to make "a safe and timely arrival at my destination" without their generous escort. The reader of my endnotes will observe the frequency with which I am obligated to Mr. Coppock, curatorial officer, Foreign Documents Section, for his accurate data and searching analyses.

My thanks go as well to the archival staff of the incredibly rich and indispensable primary document source, the Public Record Office (PRO) in Kew, outside London. In that connection, special mention should be made of two historian colleagues who assisted me greatly at the PRO: David Syrett of Queens College of the City University of New York and the late John Costello. Thanks are owed as well to Chris Howard Bailey and her associates at the Oral History Collection of the Royal Naval Museum in Portsmouth; the staff of the Churchill Archive, Churchill College, in Cambridge; David J. Lees, regular researcher at the Naval Historical Branch; Nigel Turner, producer and director, ITN Productions, London, who kindly directed me to RAF Coastal Command veterans; Gillian M. Hughes, record agent, Teddington, Middlesex; and Mr. John Delaney and staff of the photographs archive at the Imperial War Museum, London.

I am grateful to two distinguished gentlemen who gave me interviews: Professor Sir Harry Hinsley, in Cambridge, and Sir Robert Atkinson, in Winchester; as I am also grateful to three accomplished RAF Coastal Command pilots who corresponded with me: the late Air Vice Marshal Wilfrid Ewart Oulton (died October 1997), in Lymington; Air Commodore Jeaff Greswell, in Saunderton, Princess Risborough, Bucks.; and Squadron Leader Terence Malcolm Bulloch, in Burnham, Bucks.

In Ottawa, Canada, I had expert assistance in using the documentary collection at the Directorate of History, National Defence Headquarters, from senior historian Roger Sarty. In this country the same generous help was given me by archivist Michael Walker at the Operational Archives Branch, Naval Historical Center, Washington Navy Yard; and by archivists John E. Taylor, Barry Zerby, and Sandy Smith at Archives II of the National Archives and Records Administration in College Park, Maryland. Sandy Smith set a new benchmark of "beyond the call" assistance. Appreciation is given to the staff of the Interlibrary Loan Office of the University Libraries, University of Florida; the staff of the Reference Desk, Headquarters Library, Alachua County, Florida; and the staff of the University of Florida Computing Help Desk.

I thank my colleagues at the University of Florida: Associate Vice President Catherine A. Longstreth, Associate Dean Elizabeth Langland, and Professor of History and Department Chair Robert McMahon, who made possible a research and writing sabbatical in fall 1996. Numerous individuals have helped me in various ways during the writing of this book, and I express my gratitude to them: Jerry N. Uelsmann, Maggie Taylor, Leonidas Roberts, Florence Goldstein, Roger Thomas, Ken Ekelund Jr., Robert A. Bryan, Raymond Gay-Crosier, Helen Armstrong, Jim Craig, Larry Severy, Sherrel Brockington, Lewis A. Sussman, and veterans of U.S.S. *Bogue* who are acknowledged by name in the endnotes.

Also acknowledged with gratitude are Brian McCue for his assistance in interpreting statistics used in chapter 8 and cartographer Paul Pugliese for his well-crafted maps, three of which are based on graphics supplied by Jürgen Rohwer and Thomas Weis.

Particular thanks go to the distinguished gentleman and my good friend M. S. "Buz" Wyeth Jr., former vice president and executive editor, Adult Trade Division, of HarperCollins. Buz believed in this book and, before his recent retirement, gave it a robust launch. I also thank warmly Paul D. McCarthy, senior consulting editor, who came on board to navigate *Black May* through the remaining rocks and shoals. Barbara Smerage, of Gainesville, Florida, expertly keyboarded the final text.

As a sign of loving gratitude to my spouse, Genevieve Haugen, for her keyboarding of the early draft chapters and the endnotes; for her patient, lonely vigil on the dock while waiting for this ship to come in; and for her unstinting support of the project itself, I do now solemnly swear that I will clean up my study.

A Word to the Reader

This book does not attempt to describe every Allied convoy sailing in May 1943. Neither does it recount every operational patrol by the U-boats, every torpedo launched by them at Allied shipping, every Allied surface ship engagement with the U-boats, or every depth charge dropped on U-boats by aircraft. Rather, it focuses on *those major actions at sea that defined "Black May"* and led to that month's unprecedented number of U-boat losses.

U-boats are referred to here as "it" until identified by number and name of the Commander, after which the pronoun used is *she* or *her*. In keeping with Royal Navy practice, escort vessel Captains are sometimes referred to not by their personal names but by the names of their ships. In place of the abbreviations *A/S* (Anti-Submarine) or *A.U.* (Anti-U-Boat Warfare) customarily used in British documents, the present text uses *ASW* (Anti-Submarine Warfare), which is more familiar to an American readership (though *ASW* also appears in British documents).

The approach taken in this narrative to the surviving record of what happened in May 1943 is both chronological and thematic, the latter usually to give background or to describe one battle separately from others; for example, the Bay Offensive as distinct from the convoy battles.

Any errors of fact or interpretation, though one strives mightily to prevent them, are, of course, the author's own.

Prologue
Winter–Spring 1943

The Battle of the Atlantic was the dominating factor all
through the war. Never for one moment could we forget
that everything happening elsewhere, on land, at sea, or
in the air, depended ultimately on its outcome, and amid
all other cares we viewed its changing fortunes day by
day with hope or apprehension.

WINSTON S. CHURCHILL

The decisive point in warfare against England lies in attacking her merchant shipping in the Atlantic.

KARL DÖNITZ

Whatever efforts are made by the land armies, the Navy
must have the casting vote in the present contest.

GEORGE WASHINGTON, 1781

In the first dark hours of the first day of the forty-fifth
month of the longest armed struggle of World War II–the
Battle of the Atlantic–134 submarines of the German underseas fleet (*U-Bootwaffe*) were at sea, of which 118 were on or
proceeding to operational stations in the North Atlantic
Ocean, where 58 were already deployed in four battle groups.
Most of the U-boats, as they were called, had sortied from
French bases on the Bay of Biscay, the remainder from bases
on the Baltic Sea, from which they rounded the north of Scotland. It was the largest number assembled at sea to that date
in the war, 1 May 1943. Steel-gray spectral presences, they
made an ominous murmuring across the deep, as of the gath-

ering of a host, on the eve of a titanic trial of strength. At issue was control of the ocean's merchant shipping lanes. The enemy was Great Britain's Royal Navy and Royal Air Force, helped by forces of the United States and Canada. Most of the U-boats were ordered to form patrol lines across the expected routes of warship-guarded transatlantic convoys of freighters and tankers that sailed between North America and the British Isles. Others watched for north-south coastwise convoys or for independently sailing vessels along the shores of Spain and West Africa, or for shipping inside the Mediterranean Sea.

Armed with the most recent types of destructive torpedoes, all the Atlantic boats were under the same general order from Grossadmiral Karl Dönitz, Commander-in-Chief of the German Navy (*Kriegsmarine*) and Flag Officer, U-Boats: *Angreifen! Ran! Versenken!*–Attack! Advance! Sink! Their purpose in the transatlantic sea lanes: destroy British and American vessels that, through their deliveries of food, fuel, ferrous and nonferrous metals, other raw materials, and finished weapons, were keeping Great Britain in the war, and making possible a future Allied cross-Channel invasion of German-occupied Europe. As April gave way to May 1943, the Allied defensive war against the U-boat was perceived by many in London and Washington, if not in Moscow, as the single most important campaign of World War II, for upon its outcome rested the success or failure of the Allies' strategies in all other theaters of operation. This was so because victory in Western Europe depended on uninterrupted sea communications across the North Atlantic, which provided aid to the Soviet ally as well as to the British (although Arctic convoys to Murmansk and Archangel had been suspended since March because of the growing crisis in the Atlantic), and because the Allied strategic assumption was that the defeat of Germany ensured the defeat of Japan, but not the converse.

Put in the simplest terms, Admiral Dönitz and his U-boats were engaged in a tonnage battle (*Tonnageschlacht*) with Allied trade, that is, in a campaign to sink more British and American merchant ship tonnage than the Allies could replace with new construction. Dönitz and his staff had calculated in 1940 that in order to accomplish that attrition, his boats (with surface raiders, aircraft, and mines accounting for a small percentage of the total) would have to inflict a monthly loss rate of 700,000 Gross Register Tons (GRT). If successful, Britain's armed forces, industries, and people would be strangled or starved into submission. The British had estimated that 600,000 would be enough to do them in. But so far, by either measure, Dönitz was not winning that battle. Operating during the first half of 1942 in poorly defended waters off the United States East and Gulf coasts and in the Caribbean Basin, the best that he had done was 125 ships for 584,788 GRT, of which only 10 percent was convoyed, in May 1942; and 131 ships for 616,904 GRT, of which only 12 percent was convoyed, in June 1942. The best that he had done where most of the merchant traffic was convoyed under warship and aircraft protection was 118 ships for an impressive (and record) 743,321 GRT, in November 1942. The numbers fell off in the following three months.

Then, in the first twenty days of March 1943, his sharks had gone on another feeding frenzy, sinking seventy-two vessels, sixty of them in fourteen Royal Navy-protected convoys. Twenty-two of the ship losses came on 16-20 March during an attack by three U-boat groups code-named *Raubgraf* (Robber Baron), consisting of eight boats; *Stürmer* (Go-Getter), eighteen boats; and *Dränger* (Pusher), eleven boats, with several other independently operating boats, against three convergent transatlantic eastbound convoys identified by the Allies as SC.122, HX.229, and HX.229A, with a combined 125 merchant ships in orderly columns. The three convoy formations had been protected during their passage by nine destroyers, three frigates, four sloops, nine corvettes, and two cutters, and at various times by fifty-one Royal Air Force and Royal Canadian Air Force aircraft.[1] German radio broadcasts called the engagement "the greatest convoy battle of all time," based on the number and tonnage of ships claimed as sunk for the loss of only one attacker (U-*384*).[2] Allied tonnage lost to U-boats in the month by 20 March amounted to 443,951

GRT. Had sinkings continued at that same pace for the remainder of the month, which they did not, the tonnage harvested (688,124 GRT) would have approached November's record and would have exceeded the original British minimum calculated for a decisive *guerre de course*. The actual monthly total was 105 ships for 590,234 GRT.[3] And more to the point, by spring 1943 neither number would have matched the minimum tonnage now required to keep pace with replacement construction from America's unexpectedly productive ninety-nine shipyards. The bar on the high jump had been raised to 1.3 million GRT.

Still, the numbers for March, particularly the losses from SC.122 and HX.229–HX.229A was unharmed–were of a magnitude to set off alarm bells in the Anti-U-Boat Division of the Naval Staff at the British Admiralty at Whitehall, London, the district where many government departments are located and a term frequently used as a synonym for *Admiralty*. In language committed to writing well after the convoy disaster, one senses the consternation that reputedly swept certain corridors of Whitehall at the time. Though the convoy system had proved in two world wars to be the keystone of Britain's trade protection, for the first time in the second war there were doubters. "It appeared possible," the Anti-U-Boat Division reflected, "that we should not be able to continue [to regard] convoy as an effective system of defence."[4] In a watershed expression, the Admiralty is alleged to have conceded, "The Germans never came so near to disrupting communication between the New World and the Old as in the first twenty days of March 1943."[5] Captain Stephen W. Roskill, R.N. (Royal Navy), official historian of Royal Navy operations in World War II, stated in 1956: "Nor can one yet look back on that month without feeling something approaching horror over the losses we suffered."[6]

One could have countered that there was no need for these expressions, since American shipyards were producing such prodigious numbers of replacement hulls, new Allied "bottoms" had already exceeded in the preceding fall any destruction that the U-boats were then inflicting; further, that 90 percent of all ships in convoys attacked by U-boats were getting through to port safely, even 82 percent of hard-hit SC.122/HX.229. Indeed, well-hidden in the bowels of the "Citadel," a concrete blockhouse on the northwest corner of Whitehall, two relatively junior reserve officers held the contrary and optimistic view that U-boat fortunes were in constant and inevitable decline. A mere glance at the graphs that covered the walls of their Submarine Tracking Room of the Admiralty's Operational Intelligence Centre (OIC) was enough to persuade Tracking Room director Temporary Commander Rodger Winn, R.N.V.R., Special Branch, and his deputy, Lieutenant Patrick Beesly, R.N.V.R., that most of the relevant numbers were going Britain's way: shipping losses alongside replacements; U-boat groups alongside Allied escort vessels and aircraft; U-boat equipment alongside new Allied weapons and detection devices.[7]

But if we may believe the official history, their careful optimism seems not to have passed persuasively up and across to the Anti-U-Boat Division, whose attention, we are led to believe, was focused on quite a different set of facts: (1) that the Germans had the largest U-boat strength yet seen in the Atlantic war; (2) that U-boat construction still exceeded casualties; (3) that 84 percent of the ships sunk in March were sunk while in protected convoy; and (4) that from an average of 39 percent of ships sunk in convoy during the second half of 1942, the average toll for the first quarter of 1943 had risen to a startling 75 percent.[8] Captain Roskill expressed the worry: "Where could the Admiralty turn if the convoy system had lost its effectiveness? They did not know; but they must have felt, though no one admitted it, that defeat then stared them in the face."[9] Would the U-boats succeed at last in severing Britain's lifeline and winning the Atlantic—perhaps the war?

Those fears, amply expressed in the official history written thirteen years later, were not discovered by this writer in any of the documentation from the immediate post–20 March period as far as January 1944. That includes the Most Secret minutes of the War Cabinet Anti-U-boat Warfare Committee

(A.U. Committee), the highest deliberative body to be concerned with such matters. Those fears would seem to be overwrought at best and irrational at worst, assuming that they were actually uttered by Admiralty authorities, as reported. Indeed, on 30 March, in a document prepared for the A.U. Committee, the First Sea Lord, Admiral of the Fleet Sir Dudley Pound, spoke with cautious optimism about anti-U-boat prospects in the months immediately ahead. For one thing, he told the Prime Minister and members of that body, the heavy winter weather, which had caused so many merchant ship stragglers from convoys and had hampered the Navy's high-frequency direction-finding equipment (receivers and antennas that tracked radio transmission from U-boats), was moderating. Second, both Support Groups (destroyers and other warships detailed to reinforce the close escorts of threatened convoys at sea) and auxiliary aircraft carriers had been freed up from operations in the Mediterranean and in North Russian waters, and were now being redeployed in the North Atlantic convoy lanes. Third, and most important, a significant number of new land-based aircraft were becoming available for Atlantic escort patrol. Thus, from the First Sea Lord, no Admiralty hand-wringing here!

And His Lordship might well have added that while during 1942 the at-sea loss exchange rate was 45,000 tons of merchant shipping sunk per U-boat lost, during the first quarter of 1943 the rate had fallen to 28,000 tons per U-boat lost. Other restorative tonics could be found in the facts that during the same first quarter, 270 more merchant ships in convoy made safe and timely arrivals at their destinations than had done so during the last three months of 1942; more U-boats (19) had been sunk in February than in any previous month of the war; and even in woeful March the figures for new shipping construction exceeded sinkings by 300,000 tons. It would seem that the despondency theme voiced by certain members of the Naval Staff's Anti-U-Boat Division and repeated in the Admiralty's official history as well as in much of the historical literature since 1956 did not represent the Admiralty's position and at this date deserves to be consigned overside in a weighted bag.[10]

To the question of where the Admiralty could turn if the convoy system had lost its effectiveness, the only answer had to be, there was *no* alternative, save independent sailing, which had proved so disastrous when tried earlier that only Karl Dönitz would have been comfortable with it now. From January to July 1942 nearly 400 independently routed vessels had been lost to U-boats off the East and Gulf coasts of the United States and in the Caribbean Basin. As late as October–December 1942, 101 independents (including stragglers) were sunk in all sea lanes, as compared with 87 ships in convoy. And the final tabulation of the Atlantic struggle of 1939–1945 would reveal that in the nineteen most productive single U-boat patrols of the war, the losses of independently sailing merchantmen were 79 percent of the total tons sunk.[11] It should have been obvious by spring 1943 that a mass transfer of convoyed ships to the independent column would result in even higher losses, approaching the calamitous. It would have been equivalent, in fact, to giving the order, "Convoy is to scatter," that First Sea Lord Admiral Sir Dudley Pound gave to the Arctic convoy PQ.17 (Iceland to Murmansk) on 4 July 1942: of the thirty-four-ship convoy, twenty-four instantly created independents were sunk by German U-boats and aircraft. In sum, it remains hard to believe that sober minds in the upper reaches of the Admiralty seriously considered casting adrift the doctrine of convoy.

But if they did indeed waver, Their Lordships might have been emboldened in the faith did they know that statistical analyses done by the German Naval War Staff in Berlin at the same time revealed that the tonnage numbers credited to each U-boat per day at sea had been erratic and generally down since the preceding November. In that previously noted record month, the average per boat at sea number for the month was 329 GRT. In December it was 139. In January 1943 it was 129; in February 148; and in March 230.[12] By those numbers, for the U-Bootwaffe to meet the new tonnage minimum of 1.3 million GRT (of which Dönitz may well have been unaware: the Naval Intelligence Division figure given him in 1943 was 900,000 GRT per month) it would have to place at sea no fewer than 433 boats—nearly three and a quarter times the current figure—which was not possible anytime soon given German shipyard production of 19 boats per month, which barely exceeded the monthly loss rate in combat.[13] For the present, a 1.3 million GRT achievement would have to come from greatly increased efficiency in each boat per sea-day, or from a collapse of British escort protection, or both. Neither seemed likely.

In any event, the stage was set in April for a decisive collision of the forces at sea, when Whitehall expected that, once refitted in Biscay bases from their exertions of March, the U-boats would return to the convoy lanes with even greater strength than that seen in the month before. If the ides of March was bad, that of April might be worse. As it happened, though, April was not the cruelest month at all. Sinkings by U-boats actually went down, to forty-eight ships for 276,517 GRT, which was 47 percent of the March losses. And the U-boat per day at sea number was a low 127 GRT estimated, 76 actual.

One reason was a declining number of operational U-boats on North Atlantic stations, owing to longer-than-expected refit time at the Biscay bases, where many boats in need of repair, fuel, food, and armament replenishment had to lie for days in vulnerable berths outside the bombproof service and repair bunkers.[14] By the ides of April (13 April), only thirty-three boats were on operations, and only one battle group, code-named *Meise* (Tit, a small European bird of the family Paridae), was formed, northeast of Cape Race, Newfoundland. Admiral Dönitz's U-Boat Headquarters (called *BdU,* from *Befehlshaber der Unterseeboote* [Commander-in-Chief, U-Boats]) in Berlin considered the problem in its war diary for 16 April:

> Convoy warfare in March has led to a considerable wearing down of U-boats. A large number of boats have returned owing to fuel and torpedo exhaustion

and damage. The gaps thus produced must be filled as quickly as possible, if the monthly sinking figures are to be increased. On 6 April, therefore, all boats of Type IX [large, long-distance IXB and IXC boats not normally employed in convoy operations] about to put out were ordered to proceed to the North Atlantic in order to make up the number of U-boats needed there to intercept convoys.[15]

Not until the latter part of the month was the U-Bootwaffe able to dispatch a sizable fresh stream of boats, and so provide the numbers at sea on 1 May given at the beginning of this prologue. Sinkings of merchant ships declined for another reason as well, namely the larger number and effect of Allied convoy escorts, both surface and air, that Britain was able to deploy at sea in this month. Thus, though eleven convoys were attacked in the month, and all sustained losses for a total of twenty-nine sinkings, a stronger force of Allied ocean escorts, which included new "Support Groups" of emergency-directed escort warships and two auxiliary aircraft carriers, repeatedly drove off the German attackers and sank fifteen of their number, seven in the last week of the month. (U-boats sank twelve independently routed merchant ships in April.) Ten eastbound (234 ships) and nine westbound (182 ships) Atlantic convoys reached their destinations without interception.

There also appears to have been either an unaccountable decline of U-boat aggressiveness during the month, or else a surge in OIC Tracking Room wishful thinking on the subject, since it is here that one first reads an expression that is repeated in various British documents composed in the months thereafter: "It was in April that, for the first time, the U-boat groups failed to press home attacks even when favorably situated to do so."[16] The "failure to press" was detected during Commander Winn's analysis of decrypted wireless (radio) transmissions between the U-boats and their headquarters, particularly with respect to the traffic's frequent mention of Allied aircraft, whose number and threat had increased. "The outstanding impression felt on reading recent U-boat traffic," Winn observed, "is that the spirit of the crews which are at present out on operations in the North Atlantic is low and general morale is shaky."[17]

If true that there was such a holding back, it is difficult to understand why such caution would be credited to a lack of will or morale. There certainly may have been sinking feelings—even despondency—at Berlin, where officers studied doleful statistics; but if Royal Navy frontline morale had not cracked under the unremitting strain of three and a half years of convoy losses, it is hard to conceive that U-boat ranks and ratings (officers and enlisted men), just off a staggering triumph at sea, would have lost heart simply because they sighted additional numbers of aircraft, or because they were failing to keep up with the exceptional sinking rate of the month before, while suffering, it should be added, no more U-boat losses (15) in April than they did in March. Vizeadmiral Horst von Schroeter, who as *Oberleutnant zur See* [hereafter *Oblt.z.S.*] commanded U–*123* on operations during April, told this writer in December 1995 that morale remained high on his boat and that he noticed no special decline among other crews when he returned to base at Lorient. Were there, then, no "low spirits" as detected by Winn?

> I would like to say yes and no, because a lot of good friends of ours had gone down and had been lost. But, on the other hand, we had our duty. We had been in a war, in a world war; we had been soldiers, and we had to do our duty. I could imagine on our side in the minds of the Commanders there was some uncertainty because of the losses. They didn't know what weapons the enemy had at hand, therefore they may have been more reluctant on pressing, on getting through. As for pessimism expressed in conversations with other Commanders at Lorient, I don't remember such talking, because we more or less avoided talking about those things.[18]

If the Tracking Room observation was true that certain U-boats exhibited reluctance to attack targets with the expected dash and initiative, one likely reason was their reduced levels of command experience, owing to U-boat officer casualties that included not only Commanders but First (I.W.O.) and Second (II.W.O.) Watch Officers, who had merited their own boats. The BdU addressed this problem in its war diary for 7 April, and again near the end of the month, on the 25th, when it did a wash-up on a botched attempt by nineteen boats of the *Meise* group to operate against eastbound convoy HX.234 on 21-24 April: Noting conditions of "extremely changeable visibility" on the seas south of Greenland, the diary commented that, "The Commanders, for the most part inexperienced and fresh from home waters, were unable to cope with those conditions."[19] Yet, having said that much in mitigation of the Tracking Room's interpretation, it is also true that BdU found reason, on 19 April, to admonish Commanders at sea for their lack of "warrior and fighter instincts." This astonishing message, decrypted and read by the British, was occasioned by the apparent acceptance among some Commanders of a rumor that Allied escorts left depth charges, with timers, suspended from buoys:

> The enemy has based his defensive measures to a considerable extent on their morale effect. The man who allows his healthy warrior and fighter instincts to be hoaxed and humbugged ceases to have any appreciable powers of resistance to present-day enemy defenses. He is no longer capable of attack but feels universally hunted and persecuted.[20]

Whatever the meaning of April's various mixed signals, it is enough to say that at month's end the pendulum that had swung so far in Germany's favor during March had returned by 30 April to center. For Dönitz the prognosis should have been clear: the tonnage battle was not winnable. Since the previous fall the figures for Allied merchant ship construction had passed and had continued to exceed with ever-increasing plurality the figures for merchant ship losses; and by July 1943 the construction gains would overtake losses caused by U-boats *plus* all other enemy action, e.g., mines, aircraft bombs, surface raiders, and *Schnellboote* (S-boats, 105-foot fast torpedo boats).[21] Despite growing evidence that his U-Bootwaffe lagged behind the curve, with little real chance of catching up, Dönitz persisted in talking as though the struggle for tonnage was still a war-winning strategy. Thus, on 11 April, to Adolf Hitler, at the Führer's Berghof on the Obersalzburg near Berchtesgaden, in Bavaria, Dönitz pleaded that an increased allocation of 30,000 tons of steel be made to the U-boat yards in order to make possible a stepping-up of construction to twenty-seven boats per month. Hitler agreed with Dönitz's argument, which included the following language:

> Submarine warfare is difficult. However, it is obvious that the aim of sinking merchant ships must be to sink more than the enemy can build. If we do not reach this objective, the enemy would continue to suffer severely through loss of his material substance, but we would not be successful in bleeding him to death due to the diminution of his tonnage. I therefore fear that the submarine war will be a failure if we do not sink more ships than the enemy is able to build.[22]

In continuing to promote the tonnage battle, Dönitz may well have thought that his boats and crews were capable of mounting one last transcendent effort, which, while it could not hope to reverse the merchant ship replacement gains, would at least make the rate of ship and cargo losses in convoy unacceptably high to the Allies. If such an effort could be uncoiled and sustained for a month's period–here one can only speculate about his intentions and expectations–perhaps Britain would give up on convoys and scatter her seaborne trade in independently routed vessels–a not unreasonable expectation if certain Admiralty reports and histories were believed. Against such unprotected shipping his U-boats could then prowl and strike at their ease (with one eye cocked for aircraft). Was this the Grand Admiral's desperate hope?

Would he now commit all his boats in one last throw of the dice? *Spes contra spem?*

Then, as though to confirm the plausibility of his continued faith in the tonnage battle, on the night of 30 April/1 May a single German boat, U–515, commanded by thirty-three year-old Kapitänleutnant (hereafter *Kptlt.*) Werner Henke, carried off one of the most spirited and successful actions by a U-boat in the entire Atlantic campaign, sinking seven convoyed ships of 43,255 GRT in the space of eight hours and forty minutes, torpedoing four of them within six and a half minutes! Here certainly was a higher efficiency of boats and perhaps the beginning of a transcendent effort. If what Henke achieved at the opening of May could be extrapolated by his and other boats, at the same pace, until the end of May, Dönitz would have his 1.3 million GRT in a single month's time.

1

Omens
Mayday

Not only must every opportunity to attack be resolutely seized, but it would also be a grave error to depart from the principles which have been hammered into U-boat crews so hard and so frequently: "get to your position ahead just as quickly as you can, launch your attack just as soon as you can, exploit your opportunities at once and as fully as you can."

KARL DÖNITZ

Enemy submarines are to be called U-boats. The term "submarine" is to be reserved for Allied underwater vessels. U-boats are those dastardly villains who sink our ships, while submarines are those gallant and noble craft which sink theirs.

WINSTON S. CHURCHILL

The U–515 was on her third operational patrol since the long-range Type IXC boat emerged from the yards of Deutsche Werft at Hamburg-Finkenwerder and Werner Henke raised the national flag and his Commander's pennant above her conning tower at the *Indienst-stellung,* or formal commissioning, on 21 February 1942. After six months of workup and tactical exercises, she had made her maiden war patrol, and Henke's first as a *Kommandant,* on 12 August–14 October 1942 off Trinidad and Tobago in the southeast Caribbean, netting ten Allied ships sunk, for a total of 52,807 GRT; a not-inconsiderable tally for a single cruise, even given the fact that Henke was operating against mostly independently routed ships in a weakly defended area. It was a score outdone by only a handful of German boats during the war, and matched by only one U.S. Navy submarine in the Pacific (U.S.S. *Tang* in June–July 1944).[1]

The U–*515*'s second cruise, on 7 November 1942–6 January 1943, off Gibraltar and the Azores, resulted in only two sinkings, but one vessel was a Royal Navy destroyer depot ship, H.M.S. *Hecla* (10,850 tons), and the other a passenger liner-troopship, *Ceramic* (18,713 GRT). The loss of life from the two ships had been dreadful: 279 lost from 847 ranks and ratings on the former; all but one of 656 on the latter. By 30 April 1943, U–*515*'s third patrol, begun on 21 February, was already one of the longest of the war, and due to grow longer still. Operating off first the Azores and then Dakar in Senegal, on the bulge of West Africa, U–515's third cruise, like the second, had been mostly a run of bad luck, with only two merchant trophies of 10,657 GRT to show for sixty-nine days of steaming–a poor individual tonnage rate per sea-day of 154 GRT.

The first sinking had come on the evening of 4 March while U–*515* was northwest of the Azores. On a calm sea with little wind and good visibility, Henke sighted a large freighter proceeding independently at 15 knots on a course of 050° (degrees). He advanced on the surface toward the target. What happened next he described in his war diary *(Kriegstagebuch,* hereafter KTB):

Double fan launch [*Fächer*] from [torpedo]Tubes II and IV. [Torpedo] speed 14 knots, range [to target]1,200 meters. [Target's] bows on right, bearing 80 degrees, [torpedo] depth 5 meters, running times 37 and 38 seconds. Two hits amidship and forward [but] the steamer doesn't sink. Coup de grâce [*Fangschuss*] from [stern] Tube VI, depth [set to run below the keel of the target] 9 meters, [torpedo warhead equipped] with Pi 2 [*Pistole–2:* a detonator designed to be activated by the magnetic field of a ship's steel keel], running time 36 seconds. Hit toward the stern, in the engine room—a powerful explosion. The steamer sinks slowly on an even keel, transmits wireless signal. [Another] coup de grâce, this time from Tube I. Depth 10 [meters] with Pi 2, running time 25 seconds. Hit forward—great explosion. Ship goes down after about 10 minutes. It's the *California Star* at 8,300 GRT, [which was sailing] from New Zealand to England with butter, cheese, lard, and meat. The Second Officer was taken prisoner. The Captain and First Officer probably went down with their ship.[2]

The *California Star,* which carried general cargo as well as food, was a motor ship of British registry. Fifty of her seventy-four men on board were killed, fatally wounded, or drowned. The sinking took place at latitude and longitude coordinates 42°32′N, 37°20′W. On 21 March and 1 April U–*515* rendezvoused with two returning boats, U–*106* (Kptlt. Hermann Rasch) and U–*67* (Kptlt. Günther Müller-Stockheim), to take on fuel, provisions, and spare parts. Henke's second success on this patrol came thirty-six days after the first, on 9 April, at night, while steaming off Dakar. This victim, the French motor ship *Bamako,* was a smallish 2,357 GRT, slightly overestimated by Henke:

Advanced on a freighter of 3,500 GRT. Double fan launch from [stern] Tubes V and VI. [Target's] speed 8.5 knots. [Torpedo]depths set to 3 and 4 meters. [Target's] bows on right bearing 80 degrees. Range 800 meters. [Torpedo] running times 60 and 61 seconds. Hits fore and aft. Ship capsizes and sinks very quickly.[3]

Twenty of the ship's thirty-seven crew and passengers went to watery graves at position 14°57′N, 17°15′W.

The wages of war were not only bottoms and cargoes—a reminder, if one were needed by affronted humanity, that the fragile tissue of men was no equal to the violent and deadly instruments that roamed the spring Atlantic seeking whom they might devour. In that connection, it bears mention that if there has been a general fault with histories of the Atlantic war it has been their tendency to concentrate on the uniformed fighting services of sea and air, while giving scant notice to the civilian British, American, and other Allied merchant seamen who experienced the most danger of U-boat attack at sea and suffered by far the most human casualties.[4]

A summary of wartime losses in the British Merchant Navy makes the point: about 185,000 merchant seamen served aboard freighters, tankers, and motor ships, of whom 32,952, or 17 percent, lost their lives. That was a higher casualty rate than the 9.3 percent suffered during the war by the Royal Navy, the 9 percent by the Royal Air Force, and the 6 percent by the British Army. To the merchant seamen casualties must be added losses suffered by Royal Navy and Army Royal Regiment of Maritime Artillery gunners who served aboard most merchant vessels and were colloquially called D.E.M.S. ratings, after Defensively Equipped Merchant Ships.

Henke's U-boat was a Type IXC *Atlantikboot,* an improved version of two earlier submarine models, IXB and IXA, which had been built in the late 1930s and 1940 to specifications close to those of a World War I boat, U–*81.* The IX series had been envisioned originally as command and control boats, in which tactical group ("pack") leaders could direct operations at sea (an idea abandoned in late 1940); also as reconnaissance and mine-laying boats; and, finally, as long-range high-seas attack boats. In the last capacity, Types IXB and IXC boats had conducted immensely successful torpedo operations against Allied shipping as far distant as the United States East Coast, the Caribbean Basin, and the coast of West Africa.

Because of their large displacement (1,120 tons, surfaced) and wide, flat upper deck, the Type IX boats received the sobriquet *Seekuh* (sea cow), after aquatic herbivorous mammals like the manatee. The IXC was 76.8 meters (254 feet) in length—about 21 feet longer than today's Boeing jumbo jet 747-400—and 6.8 meters (22¼ ft.) across the beam. Surfaced keel depth was 4.7 meters (15½ ft.). Its fuel bunkers, or tanks, had a capacity of 208 tons, allowing for a surface, as against submerged, range of 11,000 nautical miles at an economy speed of 12 knots. (The prior Type IXB, a series produced in fewer numbers, had a smaller fuel capacity by 43 tons and a surface range of 8,700 nautical miles.) Propelled on the surface by two 2,200-horsepower diesel engines (nine-cylinder, four-cycle, supercharged, salt water-cooled) manufactured by Maschinenfabrik Augsburg-Nürnberg AG (MAN), the IXC was capable of 18.3 knots maximum speed (one knot was one nautical mile per hour, about 1.15 statute miles per hour); and it was on the surface, which surprises many modern readers, that U-boats of this period did most of their travel and fighting: The submerged attack by periscope was an exception rather than the rule. In truth, because it could not operate continually under water, the 1943 U-boat was a submersible rather than a genuine submarine. It launched its torpedoes in the manner of a motor torpedo boat, and dived only to avoid enemy ships and planes, to find relief from rough weather, or to make an occasional submerged attack in daylight. Submerged, it could make 7.3 knots maximum (except that in U–515's case, top speed tested out at 7.46), which greatly reduced its maneuverability and effectiveness, particularly in convoy battles.[5]

Underwater propulsion was provided by twin electric dynamotors *(E-Maschinen)*, manufactured by Siemens-Schuckertwerke AG, each rated at 500 horsepower. Power was supplied by sixty tons of storage battery arrays distributed under the interior deck plates. Even at economy speed of four knots, a submerged boat would exhaust its battery power after 64 nautical miles (one nautical mile was about 1.15 statute miles). By clutching a diesel to a dynamotor, which served as a generator, the batteries could be recharged, but that lengthy procedure required that the boat surface. Another kind of power transfer was supplied by compressed air, the product of either diesel-driven Junkers air compressors or an electric compressor that the crew employed for blowing water from the ballast, or diving, tanks when the boat surfaced; for starting the diesels; and for launching torpedoes from their tubes. Like the storage batteries, the compressed air tanks were "topped up" each time the boat surfaced.

In exterior appearance the IXC had the general form of any other boat or ship. It presented a sharp-edged stem at the bow, a rounded hull, a flat upper deck bisected by a superstructure, in this case a conning tower, and a stern. The outer steel casing visible to the eye, which also enclosed the fuel bunkers and the ballast tanks, made the hull more efficient for surface travel. The heart of the U-boat's architecture, however, could not be seen: it was the pressure hull, a long, narrow, cylindrical tube constructed of welded high-tensile steel plates 18.5 millimeters thick. This structure, resistant to fifteen atmospheres of water pressure when submerged, enclosed the U-boat's crew and its engines, motors, compressors, controls, and torpedoes. The normal crew list of a Type IX included four officers and forty-four ratings, but occasionally, on particularly long patrols, the complement would be increased by one or two officers, additional ratings, and perhaps a cameraman-correspondent from the official news service *Propaganda-Kompanie* or a physician. In those cases, the interior of the boat on departure, already constricted by food stores and reserve torpedoes, would be so cramped as almost to prevent human movement.

While the IX boats had the distinct advantage of long-range war waging, and while they performed well against independently sailing or weakly escorted vessels in distant coastal waters, where, in fact, the IXB sank more tonnage *per boat* than did any other U-boat type in the war, and individual IX boats became the third through sixth most productive of the war, they were at a marked disadvantage in the heavily escorted transatlantic sea lanes, where Britain's seaborne trade moved in tight convoy columns protected by Royal Navy close escorts—destroyers, sloops, frigates, and corvettes—as well as by aircraft, both land-based and, from March 1943, escort carrier-based. The IXs had several particular problems that made them less suitable for convoy operations than another U-boat type that was three times more numerous in the Atlantic at this date, namely, the Type VII.

How well-regarded this latter type was by Dönitz and his boat commanders in convoy operations is evidenced by the fact that prior to and during the war 709 VIIs were manufactured and delivered to the U-Bootwaffe (as against 159 IXAs, IXBs, IXCs, and IXC/40s), of which 665 were VIICs or VIIC/41s. Produced in greater numbers than any other design in submarine history, the VIIC boat was arguably the best-integrated combat system developed by German engineers prior to the Type XXI, described later. Smaller than the IX, with a lower silhouette, more maneuverable both on the surface and underwater, the whippetlike VII dived faster than the IX, putting 13 meters (42.6 feet) of water above the hull in thirty seconds, while the larger IX required thirty-five seconds at best to do the same. As has been calculated, during that five seconds' difference an Allied anti-submarine aircraft such as a Consolidated B–24 Liberator could close a target more than a third of a mile on a depth-bomb attack.[6] Furthermore, underwater, the VII boats were more stable in maintaining depth and, because of their smaller size, were less easily located by British detection gear.

During March and April 1943 it was observed by BdU (U-Boat Headquarters) that the losses of IX boats to Allied escorts in the Atlantic was proportionately much higher than the losses of VIIs, leading to a decision on 5 May: "Type IXC boats leaving French ports are to be detailed to remote western or southern operational areas."[7] The same observation explains why it was such a radical step a month before, on 6 April, for BdU to direct IXs "to proceed to the North Atlantic in order to make up the number of U-boats needed there to intercept convoys"; and why the commitment of those resources had to be quickly reversed: though making up less than a quarter of the Atlantic force in April, the IXs suffered twice as many losses (8 to 4) as did the VIIs.[8] Never enthusiastic about the IXs as a U-boat type, Dönitz had energetically opposed the construction figures that the Naval Staff in Berlin had advanced for them. Nonetheless, during the January–July 1942 offensive off the American coast (chapter 3) he had to have been thankful that he had as many IXs as he did, for the long-distance boats accounted for two-thirds of the merchant traffic sunk in those waters.

Essentially, a U-boat's pressure hull existed as a weapons platform, that is, as a means for delivering to the enemy, sometimes overtly, sometimes in stealth, a considerable destructive threat. Although a IXC like U-*515* carried two deck guns on its upper casing, a 10.5 cm forward and a 3.7 cm aft, as well as one or two 20mm anti-aircraft guns on a platform aft of the conning tower, and although some boats (notably the IXB U-*123*) had sunk shipping with gunfire alone, the World War II U-boat's main armament was always the torpedo.[9] A IXC could carry as many as twenty-two torpedoes. Normal stowage on a *Feindfahrt* (operational patrol) was fifteen to seventeen. These cigar-shaped weapons would be stored as action-ready in the launch tubes, of which the IXC had six, four bow and two stern, and as reserves under and over floor plates or in chains or cradles that temporarily displaced sleeping bunks in the fore and aft torpedo rooms.

Additional stowage was provided by six containers under wood slats between the pressure hull and the upper deck casing, but by 1943 U-boats rarely used them because of the length of time it required the crew to winch a torpedo down the open forward hatch, a period during which the boat was critically vulnerable. Concern was spreading by April 1943 that the Allies possessed new, more powerful depth charges, as evidenced by increased cases of damage to the upper deck containers. Should those containers fracture and fill with water, and should weight thereby suddenly increase to offset the trim, a submerged U-boat could fall fatally out of control. For this reason, as well as for the fact that the now constant danger of air attack had deterred boats from reloading at sea, BdU ordered all boats of whatever type preparing to sortie from base to leave their containers behind.[10]

Technically speaking, the action-ready torpedo in a tube was not "fired" during combat, for no explosive powder was ignited to serve as a propellant. Rather, the tube was flooded and the torpedo was "launched," or "released," by a blast of compressed air at about twenty-four atmospheres of pressure. The usual command was *Los!* ("Release!"). (It should be noted, however, that the word *shot* [*Schuß*] was frequently used in U-boat KTBs to indicate a torpedo launch, and the report of a launch filled out by Watch Officers was called a "Shooting Report" [*Schussmeldung*].) Once released, the torpedo became an independent, self-propelled submarine of its own, with guidance system, engine or motor, propellers, rudders, and hydroplanes, which steered its high explosive warhead to immolation against or under the hull of an enemy ship. Its destiny was to tear a hole in that hull, causing the ship to sink. U-boat men called their torpedo an *Aal* (eel).

Henke's U–515 carried two types of eels:

T-I, G7a, "Ato":

This torpedo, standard armament throughout the war and valued for its dependability, was driven by a gassy steam generated by a combustion of alcohol and compressed air. Power was passed through a turbine to a single six-bladed propeller. Speed settings permitted runs of 30, 40, or 44 knots for ranges, respectively, of 12.5 kilometers, 7.5 km, and 6 km at depths below the surface prescribed by the launch officer. In daylight, the G7a left a visible surface wake of exhaust gases (bubbles). The warhead, filled with 280 kilograms of high explosive, was detonated by a Pi3 pistol that was activated either by impact on a ship's hull or by magnetic influence of a ship's keel. The Pi 3-equipped G7a had a tendency to explode at the end of a miss run. The "G" stood for type number; the "7" for length, 7.16 m (7.8 yards); the "a" for air-steam propulsion. Diameter of the G7a was 53.46 cm (21 inches), the same as for the British Whitehead torpedo.

T-III, G7e, "Eto":

This type was propelled by a 100 horsepower electric motor powered by lead-acid wet cell batteries that drove a pair of two-bladed counter-rotating propellers. An improved model of an earlier electric eel (T-II), the T-III, or G7e, was the more common weapon on board U-boats in spring 1943. It had all the same dimensions as the G7a and the same warhead weight. A Pi 2 pistol allowed for both contact and magnetic detonation. The latter was the preferred setting, since, instead of releasing most of its energy upward alongside the hull in a detonation plume, it directed its major force directly upward against the keel, theoretically sinking the target with a single explosion; but see U-515's two coups de grace with *California Star*. The T-III's principal advantage was that it left no bubble wake to give away the U-boat's position. Its main disadvantages were: (1) it was slow (30 knots only) with a short range (5 km), and that only if the batteries were pre-heated to 30°C before launch; and (2) the G7e–the "e" standing for electric–had to be serviced every three to five days in order to maintain its complex innards, particularly the power system.[11]

The U-515 was not yet equipped with the newest operational torpedo type, FAT, for *Federapparattorpedo* (spring-operated torpedo). This weapon, also called the *Geleitzugtorpedo* (convoy torpedo) was a G7a ("Atofat") or G7e ("Etofat") fitted with a guidance system that caused it to take a direct course for a given range toward a convoy's ship columns, then to turn right or left and describe a succession of long or short legs, or loops, the expectation being that a snaking, to-and-fro course through the columns would result in a random *Treffer*, or hit. FATs, which the British called "Curlies," were still not common equipment in spring 1943. The U-515 would not receive FATs until her fourth cruise, beginning 29 August, when she would also carry another new torpedo type, introduced the previous February and March, the acoustic anti-escort T-V, G7es, called *Zaunkönig* (wren), which was designed to home in on the cavitation noise (24.5 kHz) of an escort vessel's propellers running at 10 to 18 knots. This type, which was even rarer than the FAT on U-boats at sea in spring 1943, would have its first success in combat in September.[12]

Most of the officers and crew who launched U–515's eels had served together since the boat was commissioned. In that respect they were unlike the typical crew, some of whose enlisted members normally transferred out of a boat following two patrols in order to take the classwork and training required to qualify them for a new specialty, higher grade, or both, after which they would be assigned to different boats. Somehow, Kptlt. Henke had avoided that rotation, with the result that he commanded an unusually high number of experienced twenty-two-year-olds at a time when the average age of non-petty officer crewmen was a year or two younger.[13] Furthermore, at the date of commissioning, Henke had inherited a cadre of petty officers (23 years old and older) who had had prior experience on Type IX boats.

This veteran crew, most of them U-boat volunteers, was motivated, we may believe, not only by the usual inducements of proud service in an elite arm; education in the latest technology; specially high pay rates, including combat patrol bonuses; the best rations to be found in any of the German services; generous leaves; and the near-certainty of medals, including Iron Crosses first and second class; they were also motivated by the success of their Commander in sinking ships, for *that* was the particularly energizing tonic on a U-boat. Many negative distractions could be set aside, for example, lack of promotion opportunities because of the crew's continuity of service on this particular boat, Henke's sometimes severe disciplinary responses to minor crew infractions, or the festering personality conflict between the Chief Engineer and his senior engine room machinist—all of that mattered little if the boat was going from success to success with her torpedoes. When, at last, U–515 succumbed to U.S. Navy destroyers on 9 April 1944, American interrogations of her survivors disclosed that even at that date, when the Atlantic war was long before lost, morale aboard U–515 remained high.[14]

The thirty-three-year-old man who commanded *Fünf-fünfzehn* (515) was one of the most enigmatic and troubled

Commanders in the U-Bootwaffe. Hardly the one-dimensional German type, he was an amalgam of conflicting traits. On the one hand impetuous, even hotheaded, in his performance of duty he was the model of professional cool. Uncomfortable under naval discipline himself, he was quick and rigorous in imposing it on others. Outgoing and gregarious by nature, he was viewed by his fellow officers as a vainglorious loner. Respectful of the Nazi state, which, among other things, punished Germans who listened to American popular music, he loved jazz and kept an impressive collection of Cole Porter songs on phonograph records. In stature he was five feet nine inches in height, 175 pounds. Good-looking, blue-eyed, he was always the impeccably attired *schöner Henke*–"Handsome Henke."[15]

Disciplinary problems dogged the young officer during a career which, from his entrance into the Navy as an officer cadet in 1934 up to the outbreak of war, was spent mainly on shore assignments, except for two tours amounting to fourteen months on the pocket battleship *Admiral Scheer*. In March 1940, he was ordered to the U-Boat School *(U–Schule)* at Pillau, East Prussia (now Baltiysk, Russia). Pausing in transit at Berlin to visit a girlfriend, Henke ended up late on arrival–Absent Without Leave–by two days. Though the AWOL charge resulted from a misunderstanding of his due date, he was court-martialed and sent to duty with a punishment company. Finally allowed to complete his studies, he was assigned in November 1940 as a Second Watch Officer (*Zweiter Wachoffizier*, or II.W.O.) to the Type IXB U–*124,* based at the newly occupied port of Lorient on the Brittany coast of France. It was there that he learned that because of his spotty disciplinary record, he had lost all seniority and would have to rebuild his career from the bottom.

In four patrols on U–*124,* during which he advanced to First Watch Officer (I.W.O.), Henke not only redeemed his reputation but proved himself an excellent candidate for Commander's School at Danzig (now Gdansk, Poland), to which he was assigned in November 1941. Following two months of intensive instruction in command responsibilities, simulated attack procedures, and the newest torpedo technology, Henke reported to the Deutsche Werft yards in Hamburg-Finkenwerder to assemble his crew and take command of U–515. The successes achieved during his first two command patrols with the new IXC earned him restoration of his seniority on the career list, promotion to *Kapitänleutnant* (Lieutenant), and the award of Germany's highest decoration, Knight's Cross of the Iron Cross.[16] He was the seventieth U-boat officer to win the coveted *Ritterkreuz*.

Henke, his crew, his boat, and his torpedoes were fully primed for the steamy equatorial night of 30 April/1 May off West Africa.

On 13 April, after finding little else off Dakar besides *Bamako*, which he sank on the 9th, Henke steamed southeast past Portuguese Guinea (now Guinea Bissau) to take up a new position southwest of the busy port of Freetown, in Sierra Leone, which he reached on the 16th. But for nine days after that date, no ship traffic appeared either shoreward or seaward–a "sour-pickle time." Nor did the conning tower bridge lookouts sight so much as an aircraft during that same period. Then, on the 25th, two British Royal Air Force (RAF) Short Sunderland flying boats came into view. Two days later, lookouts sighted a merchant vessel's smoke, but another flying boat, this time a RAF PBY–5 Catalina flying boat, of American design and manufacture, forced the boat to dive and fall behind the contact. Better luck, it seemed, came in the late morning of the 28th, while U–515 was submerged to avoid possible morning air reconnaissance. The hydrophone *(Gruppenhorchgerät,* or GHG), which was an underwater passive sound detection device, picked up the sound of explosions from two series of depth charges, as well as the *swish-swish-swish* of warship propellers. Henke came to periscope depth and made an observation of one "London" type cruiser, four destroyers, and two passenger ships, which he assumed were filled with troops, steaming on a course of 340° (toward the northwest) at 12 knots.

Since it was daylight, he decided to make a submerged attack. The range was 5,000 meters. That would be a stretch for his Eto wakeless eels, but Henke ordered a double fan-launch (*2er Fächer*) from forward Tubes I and IV, with depths set to 3 and 5 meters. Both eels missed and, after eight minutes, detonated at the ends of their runs. The sour-pickle time continued. And, on the 29th, U–*515* had the unpleasant experience of being surprised by an RAF Catalina that dived on the boat out of dark cloud cover. The 20mm anti-aircraft gun abaft U–*515*s tower gave a good account of itself with about ten hits on the Catalina, which, thrown off its stride, dropped five depth bombs harmlessly astern. After which–*ALAARMM!*– the boat dived, as it would have to do twice more that evening when probing Catalinas came again.[17]

Daytime on the 30th passed uneventfully. The morning was spent submerged. Crew members who were not asleep went about their usual duties, tending to the Eto mechanisms, checking the battery arrays for chlorine gas buildup, monitoring the wireless telegraph (W/T) receivers and hydrophone, oiling the rocker-arm hinges on the nine-cylinder MAN diesels, filling out report forms, studying for qualifying exams, cooking the midday meal, or shaving–Henke was one of the few commanders who forbade beards. No man wore more than shorts because the tropical temperature inside the boat exceeded 100 degrees Fahrenheit.

At 1345 German Summer Time (GST), which all boats observed no matter what their position at sea, and which was two hours ahead of Greenwich Mean Time (GMT), U–*515* blew tanks and surfaced to air out the noxious and foul-smelling interior. The lookouts searched the ocean's edge for smoke plumes, but there were none. After fifteen minutes, the boat resumed an underwater listening station, until 2041, when Henke ordered the boat surfaced again so that he and the bridge watch could survey the horizon in the day's last light. Twenty-one minutes later, a lookout seized like a bird dog and exclaimed, *"Herr Kaleu!"* the diminutive of Henke's rank. Following the lookout's point, Henke drew into the lenses of his Carl Zeiss 7 x 50 binoculars the murky images of smoke clouds where the ocean met the sky shoreward to the southeast. He estimated the smoke at range 15 nautical miles, bearing 145°. Gradually, the images sharpened and mast tops became visible, then funnels and bridge screens. Henke counted fourteen large, fully laden merchant ships in convoy, average tonnage 6,000–7,000 GRT, proceeding northwest, guarded by what appeared to be three destroyers and five other escort vessels.[18] Actually, the convoy, designated TS.37, was composed of eighteen merchant vessels protected by only three escorts, the smallest in the Royal Navy's inventory: the corvette H.M.S. *Bellwort* and two trawlers. The convoy's five columns had originally included a nineteenth merchant ship, but two days before she had left the formation to proceed independently, accompanied by a third trawler.

Destined for Freetown, the convoy had originated on 26 April a short distance to the east-southeast, at Takoradi, on the Gold Coast (today's Ghana). The run between those two ports had been made many times without losses: only eight ships sunk out of 743 sailing since September 1941. It was hoped by the British Admiralty's Flag Officer Commanding West Africa, headquartered at Freetown, that RAF overflights along the route would be a sufficient supplement to the small Royal Navy (hereafter RN) surface escort to deter U-boat attacks. The aircraft available for that purpose were one Hudson (an American Lockheed passenger plane converted to bomber) squadron and two Sunderland flying boat squadrons operating from Bathurst (Banjul, Gambia), one Catalina squadron at Freetown, and a half-squadron of Wellington bombers at Takoradi, with detachments of Hudsons at Port-Étienne (Nouâdhibou, Mauritania) and Lagos, Nigeria.

There were two sea/air escort failures, however. An interception of a W/T (radio) transmission in Morse code from Henke's boat was made by the Senior Officer, Escort, but that fact (not the message itself, which was unknown because it was encrypted) was not forwarded or relayed directly to Headquarters, Flag Officer, with the result that three destroyers at Freetown that might have been sent out at once to reinforce the escort did not sortie until it was too late. Furthermore, at 1820 GST (1620 GMT), which was two

hours and fifty-one minutes before civil twilight in the area,
the one aircraft assigned to dusk patrol over TS.37 ran into
line squalls and electrical storms that forced it to leave the argosy and return to base. The continuing bad weather, combined with an absence of moonlight, caused the RAF to
scratch a planned all-night escort. As a consequence, by
nightfall Convoy TS.37 was near-naked to its enemy.[19]

The night was black with flashing sheet lightning across
the horizons. The sky was overcast with heavy rain squalls,
but visibility was good. There was a moderate sea with swell
and a light westerly wind, force 3-4 on the Beaufort scale. As
Henke advanced to his work, a radar detection device on
board (*Funkmessbeobachter* [*FuMB*], or "Metox," after the
name of the first French firm, based in Paris, to manufacture
the equipment) sounded a high-pitched alert tone through
the U-boat's loudspeaker system. Metric radar pulses from
one or more surface escorts not yet equipped with 10-centi-
meter radar (which was outside the FuMB's frequency range)
were searching for an enemy signature. Henke continued his
advance regardless and, after two hours and fifty-four minutes, still on the surface, passed under the cover of a rain
squall into the rear of the convoy columns.

When he had proceeded forward as far as the convoy center without having been sighted, and there took up a position,
at steerageway (the minimum speed required for helm to
have effect), canted northeast across the convoy's base
course, his First Watch Officer (I.W.O.) Oblt.z.S. Ernst
Sauerberg brought up to the conning tower bridge the UZO
(*U-boot-Zieloptik*), target-aiming binoculars with fourteen-inch
barrels, and attached them to the rotating UZO post bracket.
With these 7x50 lenses, reticle-etched for degrees of elevation
and deflection, the I.W.O. obtained bearing, range, and angle-
on-the-bow for a *Mehrfach*, or multiple launch, against two
target ships in one of the port columns astern and transmitted
the data to the Siemens-made deflection calculator (*Vorhaltrechner*) manned by the Second Watch Officer (II.W.O.),
Leutnant Heinrich Niemeyer, in the tower below. Mean-

while, the aft torpedo room crew opened the exterior caps of Tubes V and VI, to flood them for launch.

When the aim-off heading had been established by the calculator and transmitted to the guidance systems of the two stern torpedoes, and a depth of five meters, as decided by the I.W.O., had been handcranked into the eels by the torpedo room crew, Henke gave permission to launch. At 2256 GST the I.W.O. shouted *Los!* and hit the electromechanical launch button. *PISSSHH! PISSSHH!* Blasts of compressed air 1.2 seconds apart sent the two eels seaward and, 0.4 seconds after launch, the rudder vanes, directed by inboard gyro compasses, began to steer the warheads toward their targets. Simultaneously, Henke began counting the seconds from launch on his stopwatch; the aft torpedo room ratings vented the excess air inboard to prevent exterior surface bubbles; in the Control Room (*Zentrale*), the Chief Engineering Officer (*Leitender Ingenieur,* or L.I.) began taking water into the stern regulator tanks to compensate for the lost weight on board of the two eels; the sound man reported the torpedo runs as hot, straight, and normal; and the I.W.O. began setting up aiming triangles for four target ships forward in the convoy's starboard columns. Henke's war diary records:

> First shot *(Schuß)* at 2256 from Tube V at a 6,000 GRT freighter, bows left bearing 70°. After a running time of 58 seconds, the torpedo hit amidships causing the ship to sink immediately.

> Second shot at 2256 from Tube VI at a 7,000 GRT tanker, bows left bearing 60°. After a running time of 59 seconds, the torpedo hit abaft the bridge, breaking the ship apart. The crew sent up white rockets and went quickly into lifeboats. We observed the sinking.

One minute after the first launches, the I.W.O. and deflection calculator had a trigonometric solution for a torpedo in the bow tubes. Again, Henke's KTB:

Third shot at 2257 from Tube I at a 6,000 GRT freighter, bows left bearing 80°. After a running time of 51 seconds, the torpedo hit amidships and the vessel sank quickly.

Within the next four minutes, the I.W.O. would have aiming triangles for three more ships:

Fourth shot at 2258 from Tube IV at a 7,000 GRT freighter, bows left bearing 80°. After a running time of 52 seconds, the torpedo hit amidships and the vessel burst apart.

Fifth shot at 2259 from Tube II at a 5,000 GRT freighter. After a running time of 60 seconds, the torpedo hit amidships and the vessel sank immediately.

Sixth shot at 2301 from Tube III at a 6,000 GRT freighter. After a running time of about 90 seconds we heard a [magnetic exploder]hit at 10 meters depth, and we thoroughly believe the ship sank.

White rockets signaling Hit By Torpedo went up in the dark night, to be joined by brilliant starshell illuminants fired by the convoy's tiny escort in an attempt to sight the surfaced U-boat. In the same light Henke's lookouts descried a small patrol vessel and a "destroyer" to port, and then, to starboard, another "destroyer" coming at them bowson! Henke ordered an Alarm dive to 170 meters (562 feet). Depth charges dropped by what must have been the corvette *Bellwort* exploded a fair distance away. In the U-boat's sound room the hydrophone operator heard the noises made by bursting bulkheads in the sinking ships. The torpedo crews reloaded three Etos.[20]

Henke erred in stating that he had scored six hits and had observed five sinkings. Both his stern shots missed, despite his observations. But the rapid fusillade from his boat did result in four starboard column ships being hit, all of which would sink. First to take a torpedo was the motor ship *Kota Tjandi,* a 7,295 GRT Dutch vessel in British service sailing from Haifa, Table Bay, and Takoradi for Freetown and the United Kingdom. Hit on the port side, as were the three victims to follow, this ship carried 7,453 tons of general cargo, including potash, rubber waste, and 1,000 tons of tea. Of her crew of 91 plus eight Navy and Army gunners, six men were lost.[21]

The second vessel, struck on the starboard hand of *Kota Tjandi,* was the British freighter *Nagina,* 6,551 GRT, carrying a general cargo of 4,886 tons that included 2,750 tons of pig iron. Her crew numbered 103, including eight Navy and two Army gunners. Next hit was the British steamer *Bandar Shahpour,* 5,236 GRT, sailing from Abadan, Mormugao, and Takoradi for Freetown and the U.K., with 6,768 tons of general cargo, including 3,000 tons of manganese ore, together with oil seeds, rubber, copra, and 2,002 bags of mail. Her crew, with four Navy and four Army gunners, numbered 62. She carried eight passengers: two women, one child, and five Merchant Navy officers. The last victim was the British motor ship *Corabella,* 5,681 GRT, with a cargo of 8,035 tons of manganese ore. The crew, including six Navy and two Army gunners, who, like the gunners on the other torpedoed vessels, never got a shot off at their attacker, numbered forty-eight. The four ships were all hit within six and a half minutes, and all in or near the position 07°15′N, 13°49′W.[22]

From the Masters of *Nagina, Bandar Shahpour,* and *Corabella* we learn what happened to the crews on board those three vessels (there being no report found from the Master or crew of *Kota Tjandi*). Captain W. Bird stated that *Nagina* sighted a single torpedo approaching the ship from abeam on the port side. Its warhead exploded loudly but without a flash between Nos. 1 and 2 holds in the vicinity of the 'twin decks and threw up a large column of water that, when it fell, crushed the fore part of the bridge. The No. 2 lifeboat and a raft were destroyed by the blast, but little other damage could be seen in the very dark night. Immediately, the ship listed about 10° to port and Captain Bird ordered engines stopped. Three minutes after the explosion, when the list increased, Bird ordered Abandon Ship. The five running lifeboats were lowered, one of which capsized. Three rafts were also launched, Bird joining the last of them.

Everyone was clear of the ship within seven minutes of being torpedoed, and from their boats and rafts they watched the holed *Nagina* go down, bow first, at 2113 GMT. Bird's raft, with ten aboard, was overloaded, with the result that when three other men in the water grabbed hold of its sides, the raft capsized. The survivors managed to get purchase on the raft again, and a quarter-hour later, No. 6 lifeboat rowed over and took the thirteen on board. At 2230, H.M. Trawler *Birdlip*, part of the convoy escort, rescued the occupants of that boat and those of No. 5 boat. Five more survivors were found by a destroyer from Freetown but not until 3 May, and No. 3 boat with its survivors was not found, by an aircraft and a motor launch, until 4 May. Notwithstanding the exposure suffered by these last two groups, casualties were light: the Second Wireless Operator was killed by the explosion and a Chinese carpenter was missing. To Admiralty authorities, Captain Bird complained: "I do not consider that this convoy was sufficiently protected. There were three destroyers lying in Freetown Harbour; the Naval authorities must have known that this convoy was passing through this dangerous area where submarines were known to be operating, yet these destroyers were not sent to our assistance."[23]

Captain W. A. Chappell reported that the torpedo that struck his ship, S.S. *Bandar Shahpour,* was also sighted before it hit, by one of the gunners at his action station, but not in time to give a warning. The explosion, when it came, was dull and flashless, but it sent up a large column of water that then cascaded over the ship. Much of the 2,002 bags of mail, too, went skyward and came down like snowflakes over the deck and surrounding sea. Captain Chappell received reports that the mainmast had collapsed on the wireless room, destroying it and its equipment; that the engineers' accommodation on the port side was destroyed; that the deck on the port side was twisted and fractured; and that the settling tanks in the engine room had burst, spewing oil and forcing the Fourth

Engineer, who was on watch, to flee the engine room without stopping engines. Fortunately, because of the damage to the settling tanks, the engines gradually stopped on their own. Chappell fired white flares and transmitted an emergency message that was acknowledged by the Convoy Commodore. Then, deciding that the freighter's condition was hopeless, he ordered Abandon Ship. Though the vessel was still slightly under way, three lifeboats sufficient to carry all the passengers and crew were successfully lowered; No. 4 boat became fouled and capsized on becoming waterborne. Chappell and the Chief Engineer, J. R. Black, were the last to leave, and, after a half-hour, all the survivors, with but one loss, were taken aboard *Birdlip,* making a total of 253 convoy survivors packed onto that small vessel. From the trawler's gunwales the *Bandar Shahpour* party watched their ship go down at 2300 GMT.

When the trawler delivered her human cargo to Freetown at noon on 1 May, Chappell discovered that the dangers of being sunk were not all nautical. The accommodations provided his officers and his Goanese crew were appalling. The so-called Grand Hotel rooms assigned to his officers were so stinking and unhygienic, it was a wonder, he stated, that they did not all die from dysentery or typhoid; and the Sabars Hotel, which housed his native crew, was so foul that every man among them became sick. "They were simply wallowing in filth," he reported, "and the food provided was uneatable; some were only given a piece of bread, with jam, after being without food for 36 hours." No baths were available. It was worse, he said, than the boardinghouses in Bute Street, Cardiff.[24]

The last to be struck by one of U–*515*'s six torpedoes was the British motor ship *Corabella*. While steaming at 8½ knots on a course 295°, she was struck in No. 2 hold on the port side. "It was not a violent explosion, just a dull thud," her Master, Captain P. Leggett, reported. In his cabin at the time, he found it difficult to make his way to the bridge because of piles of wreckage and debris in the corridor. On finally making the bridge, he found it in a collapsed state, with jagged ce-ment and iron everywhere. Looking out, he saw that the foretop mast and wireless aerial were down; worse, that the cabin containing the emergency wireless had been stove in, making it impossible to send out an S.O.S. There was no sign on deck that any sea water had been thrown up by the explosion (indicating that a magnetic exploder had detonated beneath the hull).

Rather quickly, the vessel listed to port and settled by the bow. Leggett ordered Abandon Ship. About twenty-five men made it off in the starboard boat, but as the starboard raft became waterborne its painter (the bowline used for tying up) carried away and the raft was lost. There was trouble with the small port boat as well: it got hooked upside down to the davit for the accommodation ladder, and could not be forced loose. Leggett therefore shouted, "Every man for himself!" and the remaining crew, with the exception of the Third Officer, who was injured and would not be seen again, jumped over the side. Just before Leggett himself jumped, the ship shuddered, throwing him against hatch coamings, but he made it safely into the water, from which he watched his ship sink within twelve to fifteen minutes of being torpedoed. With a great amount of wreckage floating about him, Leggett was able to grab hold of a wood plank for buoyancy. He was soon joined by Gunner Stuart Carnelly, "but for whose strenuous efforts in keeping me afloat until help came, I should undoubtedly have drowned."

Help arrived after two hours in the form of *Birdlip*, which, with the addition of Leggett and Carnelly, had thirty more souls aboard her narrow decks. Five crewmen were rescued just before sunset on 1 May, and, about the same time, four more were sighted clinging to wreckage by an RAF aircraft, which dropped a rubber dinghy close to their position. Two of the men, Donkeyman William Kelly and the Cook, J. Brown, were badly injured. When the inflated dinghy splashed nearby, the other two men, Radio Operator Stuart Byatt and Second Steward George Newton, swam to retrieve it, and gave up their own places in the dinghy so that the injured men could rest more comfortably. Byatt and Newton took turns swimming and splashing around the dinghy to keep sharks and barracuda clear. And, thus, they passed the night of 1/2 May, until picked up the next morning and taken to Freetown. Altogether, nine crew members from *Corabella*, including the Cabin Boy, were dead or missing.[25]

At 0130 GST on 1 May, Henke surfaced to search the area of his attacks. What he saw in the lightning-lit night was sea wrack and deck debris stretching across the swells east to west, numerous lifeboats and rafts showing lights, and then a large *Bewacher* (the trawler *Birdlip*) picking up survivors. Un-accountably, because it was not U-Bootwaffe practice to target survivors, Henke attacked the rescue vessel; exactly how, he did not say in his KTB. Also unaccountably, he failed to sink her, though she was probably stationary in the water.[26] Documents presented after the war to the International Military Tribunal at Nürnberg disclosed that Hitler had several times insisted that U-boats should kill survivors by shooting up their lifeboats, as a means both of denying those crews to new ships and of intimidating other crews from going to sea.

No formal order to that effect was ever traced to Admiral Dönitz, although, where "rescue ships" were concerned, in autumn of 1942 he had stated in an order: "In view of the desired annihilation of ships' crews their [rescue ships'] sinking is of great value."[27] Apparently, to sink a warship containing survivors was understood by Dönitz to be of a different moral character from the sinking of survivors in a lifeboat. Not exactly a directive to do so, his ambiguously worded order could nonetheless be interpreted by a Commander as permission to sink a rescue vessel, if the opportunity presented itself, and that may have guided Henke with respect to *Birdlip*. On balance, Dönitz seems to have resisted Hitler's pressure to engage in *Schrecklichkeit* (terribleness, dreadfulness), on the grounds that it violated international conventions governing sea warfare, that it compromised the honor and integrity of the U-Bootwaffe, and, more practically, as the German Naval Staff expressed it on 16 December 1942, that: "The killing of survivors in lifeboats is inadmissible, not just on humanitarian grounds but also because the morale of our own men would suffer should they consider the same fate as likely for themselves."[28]

At Nürnberg the only documented incident of incorrect behavior toward survivors presented by the Allied prosecutors was a machine gun attack on the merchant crew of S.S. *Peleus,* a Greek vessel, in the Indian Ocean on 13 March 1944. The boat responsible was U–852, commanded by Kptlt. Heinz Eck. Captured after the war and placed on trial together with his officers by a British court-martial, Eck denied that he had received any orders, directly or ambiguously, from Dönitz to shoot at shipwrecked survivors. The Commander, his I.W.O., and the ship's doctor, both of whom had joined in the shooting, were executed by firing squad on 30 November 1945.[29] (An example of "inadmissible" behavior exhibited by United States Navy submarine officers toward Japanese survivors in the Pacific is provided by the historian of That undersea war. Particularly relevant is the incident on 26 January 1943 when the submarine *Wahoo* [Lieut.-Cmdr. Dudley Walker Morton, U.S.N.] spent an hour shooting Japanese survivors of a torpedoed troopship as they floated in the water.[30]) In the main, existing records support the contention that German U-boat conduct toward survivors was correct, even on many occasions solicitous when crews provided them food, water, medical supplies, compasses, position, and course to land. Werner Henke's biographer describes his subject as similarly "humane," though in the particular case at hand Henke may be said to have backed into the compliment by his failure to destroy the rescue vessel *Birdlip* and her human cargo.[31]

That incident closed, and with three new Etos in the bow tubes, Henke called for *A.K. voraus*–"Both ahead full!" He would pursue the convoy north and see what damage he could do to its remaining ships. At 0513 he sighted its trailing edges, and twenty-seven minutes later, with the air still very dark and visibility down to medium, he nosed his way into the convoy columns, as before, from astern. First Watch Officer Sauerberg took a reading on three separate ships to port that

were steaming, he estimated, at 7 knots. Three Etos in the
bow tubes were set to run at 7 meters depth, Pi 2 pistols fixed
for magnetic detonation. Henke's KTB:

> First shot from Tube IV at a 6,000 GRT freighter, bows
> right bearing 100°. After a running time of 68 seconds
> the torpedo hit below the aft mast causing a very wide
> detonation column containing ship fragments. The
> steamer burned. We assume it sank.

> Second shot from Tube I at a 6,000 GRT freighter,
> bows right bearing 90°. After a running time of 65 sec-
> onds, this ship, too, put out a wide detonation column.
> It burned immediately. We assume it sank.

> Third shot from Tube III at a 7,000 GRT freighter,
> bows right bearing 90°. After a running time of 35 sec-
> onds, the torpedo hit toward the stern causing a large
> detonation and flames that shot very high. Apparently,
> artillery ammunition went up. We observed the burn-
> ing stern sink.

By 0549 the sky was alive with starshells and white rockets that illuminated two nearby "destroyers." There were
three RN destroyers that had come on the scene belatedly
from Freetown: H.M.S. *Rapid, Malcolm,* and *Wolverine.* Henke
crash-dived in the shallow (80 meters, 250 feet) coastal water,
seeking temperature gradients and varying density layers that
abounded there as a protection against the inevitable British
sonar detection pulses (called asdic). Taking a southwesterly
course toward deeper water, U–*515* again succeeded in elud-
ing her pursuers. The sounds of depth charges and of ship
hulls fracturing receded astern.

Henke's rampage was over.[32] And this time his observations were all correct. During one remarkable night he had
equaled the record seven sinkings [plus one damaged] in a
single twenty-four-hour day achieved by U-boat "ace" Kptlt.
Joachim Schepke (U–*100*) against Convoy SC.11 on 23 November 1940. And he had exceeded the earlier *best night* of six

sinkings (one damaged) posted by Kptlt. Otto Kretschmer (U–99), the "tonnage king," on the night of 18/19 October 1940, one of three nights (17-19 October) during which nine U-boats savaged Convoys SC.7 and HX.79 off Rockall Bank near Ireland–nights that came collectively to be called in Germany *die Nacht der langen Messer,* "The Night of the Long Knives."[33] (This phrase, earlier used to describe Hitler's bloody purge of Ernst Röhm and his SA ["storm troopers"] leadership in 1934, originated in a medieval legend, known in both Germany and Britain, that told how Saxons who invited the British king Vortigern and his leaders to a banquet slaughtered three hundred of the leaders with their long knives.)

There was no glory for the merchant seamen, of course. Though their cost in lives was less in Henke's second fusillade, the newly afflicted seamen of Convoy TS.37 experienced anyone's full share of "peril on the sea," which, it must be added, they managed with commendable composure. First hit this time was the Belgian freighter *Mokambo,* 4,996 GRT, out of Matadi and Takoradi for Freetown and the United Kingdom with a cargo of *1,139* tons of palm oil, *1,520* tons of kernels, 440 tons of copal, 2,000 tons of cotton, 2,000 tons of copper, and 38 tons of wolframite.[34] Other than that the weather at the time was cloudy and showery, that the sky was still very dark, and that there was a slight sea with a west wind, Force 3 on the Beaufort scale, there are no surviving details of her sinking.

Henke's second victim was the British steamer *City of Singapore,* 6,555 GRT, which was sailing from Calcutta and Takoradi for Freetown and Liverpool. Her cargo was 9,000 tons, which included 2,750 tons of pig iron, 2,750 tons of general cargo and mail, and, the remainder, jute, linseed, and groundnuts. The ship was hit by a torpedo that exploded just abaft the mainmast on the starboard side, throwing up a tall column of water but showing no flash. The hatches and beams from No. 5 hold were crushed; No. 4 hold flooded; the deck gun was blasted off its platform onto the deck; one of the six lifeboats was rendered useless; and the remaining boats, like the ship as a whole, were completely covered with oil from the tanks.

The Master, Captain A. G. Freeman, followed the book: He stopped engines; sent out wireless messages, which were acknowledged; fired two white rockets and showed the red light; and, when the ship had almost lost headway so that boats could be lowered without fear of their capsizing, he threw the Confidential Books overboard and ordered Abandon Ship. Freeman left last in No. 2 boat after making certain that no one remained on board. By that time, the ship was quickly sinking aft and the poop was awash. Fourteen minutes after the torpedo hit, Freeman heard a loud report, which he assumed was the No. 4 deep tank bulkhead collapsing, following which the vessel folded in two and disappeared. An hour and a half later, the survivors were picked up by *Birdlip* and by the convoy's second trawler, H.M.T. *Arran*, and taken by them to Freetown. Not one of the eighty-seven-man crew and two gunners had been lost. Freeman reported: "I consider this Convoy was inadequately escorted."[35]

The last ship to be hit by Henke, who had expended only nine eels to cause seven sinkings—an unusually successful economy of firepower—was the British freighter *Clan Macpherson,* 6,940 GRT, out of Calcutta, Durban, and Takoradi for Freetown and the United Kingdom with 8,421 tons of general cargo that included 2,750 tons of pig iron, plus zinc, mica, jute, linseed, tea, and groundnuts.[36] His crew, including gunners, numbered a large 140. No one saw the track of the torpedo, which exploded, "not violently," in No. 2 hold on the starboard side. Knowing that the hold was 100 feet in length and 134,000 cubic feet of space, and fearing that it would fill quickly, the ship's Master, Captain E. Gough, immediately ordered Abandon Ship. He switched on the red light, fired two white rockets, sent out a W/T message, and threw overboard the Confidential Books.

"All my men lined up like soldiers," Gough reported, "no one attempted to do anything without orders, and within ten minutes the five lifeboats and the one small boat were clear of the ship," which, they *saw,* did not go down as expected. The men on the small No. 2 bridge-boat were taken on board a freighter, *Silver Ash,* and the occupants of the other five boats, keeping in contact with each other by means of flashlights, had the opportunity of being rescued by *Arran*; but, instead, Gough asked the trawler to stand by them until daybreak, when he and the crew from the five boats reboarded their still floating vessel. The pumps were put on and all the engineers went below to raise steam. By 0920 the ship was under way doing twenty revolutions, and Gough had her under helm on a course of 047° toward Freetown, some 67 nautical miles distant. But, after a short while, it became apparent that No. 1 hold was filling, and some measure had to be taken to balance the ship.

Accordingly, Gough ordered the Chief Engineer in the engine room to fill tanks Nos. 4 and 5 in an attempt to bring the boat down by the stern. When that action was completed, though, the ship was listing to starboard, and the sea was lapping at the fore deck. Gough rang the engine room. "Finish With Engines." He thought he might take a tow, stern first, from *Arran.* But it was no use. *Clan Macpherson* was not going to make it. He again ordered Abandon Ship and personally phoned the engineers and engine room crew to order them out. Unfortunately, two minutes after the boats were away, the ship suddenly upended, hung there in that state, quivering, then sank in a frothy gulp, and there was no sign in the boats of Chief Engineer Neil Robertson, or of the Second, Fourth, and Fifth Engineers, "who were just a little slow in leaving the engine room."

In his report Gough complimented a half-dozen Lascars (East Indians) in his crew who had gone into No. 1 hold and, working up to their waists in water, tried to build up a bulkhead with bags; had the bulkhead collapsed, "all would have most certainly been drowned." The boarding party reached Freetown Harbour at 2015 GMT on 1 May, where the Europeans, including Masters and Officers, were assigned to the ghastly Grand Hotel and the native crew were placed in even grimmer boardinghouses. By 10 June, so far as Gough knew, the natives were still housed in squalid conditions, with awful food, if any, and no water for bathing, most of them afflicted with boils and diarrhea. The extent of the suffering caused by U-boat warfare was simply unknown to its perpetrators.[37]

In London, Prime Minister Winston Churchill called the heavy sinkings "deplorable."[38] His Anti-U-Boat Warfare Committee invited an explanation for the lack of air cover provided Convoy TS.37 from Sir Archibald Sinclair, Bt., M.P., Secretary of State for Air. Sinclair responded that, "Bad weather was responsible for the absence of air escort during the night on which the 7 ships had been sunk."[39]

Inside U–515, as the opening day of May drew to a close, Werner Henke received a *Funkspruch* (wireless signal) from BdU in Berlin acknowledging his report of the sinkings. It consisted of one word: BRAVO. Henke recorded his and the crew's reaction to it: *Große Freude im Boot*–"Great elation in the boat."[40]

At midnight GST on 30 April/1 May, twenty-seven-year-old Kptlt. Harald Gelhaus, Commander of the Type IXB U–107, was on the surface pursuing a fast ("15 to 16 knots"), zigzagging, independent steamer on a northeasterly course in 47°49'N, 22°02'W, about 560 miles southwest from Cape Clear, Ireland. He was on his thirteenth *Feindfahrt* (war cruise), his tenth as a Commander. This steamer was his first target sighted since departing base at Lorient, France, on 24 April, and he still had his full complement of torpedoes fore and aft. If he had had to attempt this pursuit from astern, he might not have overhauled the target while it was still dark, since his own maximum speed under diesel power was only marginally better than the steamer's. Fortunately, though, he stood at bow ahead position, and his only real problem would be in figuring out the steamer's zigzag pattern. He writes in his KTB:

> So I run in front of him with two engines at full speed, and I can just keep him in sight. Because of the high

swell the bridge and funnel are often well out of the water. I hope he won't see me.

As the steamer zigzagged to the west, the swell made it hard to keep him in the binoculars. Gelhaus made up his mind to attack with a three-eel fan shot (*Fächer*) when he next zigzagged east. But when that altered course came, it was so sharply to the east that Gelhaus's bow was out of position, and he had to use his stern tubes, V and VI. Those two torpedoes were released at 0300 GST on a bearing of 70°, but with a variance of 6.4° between them; speed of target 16 knots; range 1,500 meters; running time 80 seconds:

A hit amidships, apparently in the engine room. There's fumbling with flashlights on deck. It seems that the lifeboats are being readied for lowering. The steamer turns to port, slows, and loses steam. But to make sure he doesn't get away, we point the bow at him at short range and launch a coup de grâce from Tube II. After 29 seconds there's a hit under the bridge. The steamer sinks a bit deeper and stops. Boats are lowered into the water. But because the ship still shows no sign of drowning, we give him another coup de grâce, from Tube III, set at 7 meters depth. After 51 seconds there's a hit in the forward hold behind the mast. The ship sinks only a bit more and lists 15° to starboard. While waiting for it to sink, we maneuver up to a lifeboat to find out the ship's name. It turns out to be the 12,000 GRT heavy refrigerator ship *Port Pictory* [actually *Victor*], out of Glasgow, built just last year in Newcastle, heading from Buenos Aires to England, the specific port of destination not yet known. Its cargo consists of 10,000 tons of frozen meat and skins. Additionally, there were 60 passengers on board, including women and children.

Gelhaus learned that the ship carried one 4.7-inch gun and two 12-pounders, though none was fired, and that the Captain was, apparently, still on board. "We took no prisoners," he wrote, "because we had no room on board." Because the vessel was still floating after an hour–its position having been sent out repeatedly by the ship's radio operator together with the distress call SSS . . . SSS . . . SSS (Struck By Torpedo)–Gelhaus put yet another eel into her hull, hitting the waterline below the front edge of the bridge after a 42-second run. This time the vessel broke apart and the midship descended below the surface, leaving only the bow and stern visible. "I consider the steamer as having been sunk," he wrote, "because its chances of making port are extremely unlikely, but complete sinking will still take a while due to the amount of insulation." He reported as much to BdU, adding that he still had nine Etos and six Atos together with 161 cubic meters of fuel remaining.[41]

More precise information about M.V. *Port Victor* and her ordeal comes from her Master, Captain W. G. Higgs, who, with the Chief Officer, was the last to leave her. The 12,411 GRT motor vessel had actually sailed from Montevideo on 17 April with a refrigerated cargo of 7,600 tons and a general cargo of 2,000 tons. The crew numbered 99, including nine Naval and three Military Gunners, who, like so many other D.E.M.S. gunners, never got off a shot either for lack of time or because they never saw their assailant. The passengers, sixty-five in number, included twenty-three women and children. The first of Gelhaus's torpedoes struck in the engine room on the port side while the ship was steaming at $16^3/4$ knots, on a mean course of 055°, Zigzag Pattern No. 11. The explosion was accompanied by a brilliant flash that illuminated the whole ship for a split second and a large column of water that cascaded over the upper deck. The No. 4 lifeboat collapsed in the chocks and the No. 6 boat, which was "swung out," disappeared from view. Electrical power failed, and with the engine room flooding, the port engine stopped. With no one in the engine room answering the telephone, the Chief Engineer stopped the starboard engine using remote controls on the upper deck.

Captain Higgs had a distress message sent by wireless, which was acknowledged, while he personally threw the

Confidential Books and Wireless Books overboard in weighted boxes. He then went to the embarkation deck, where the passengers were assembling at boat stations. When the remaining boats were lowered to that deck, Higgs ordered them loaded and lowered. The first to go down was No. 2 boat on the port side with about fourteen women and an Able Seaman in charge. Just as it was being lowered down the falls, however, the second torpedo struck just under it. The blast and the column of water discharged flung most of the boat's occupants into the sea, where they had to swim vigorously against being sucked into the large hole made in the hull by the explosion. Most of the younger women managed to overcome the suction and reach a nearby raft. Two middle-aged women did not.

When the passengers had been lowered, Higgs gave orders for the crew to abandon ship. The third torpedo to hit the ship exploded under No. 8 boat and completely wrecked it, the Second Officer being the only survivor ("injured and badly shattered") of the eight or nine crew who were in it at the time. The rest of the crew were able to abandon on the other boats and four rafts, after which Higgs and the Chief Officer went down the starboard ladder and jumped into the sea, where they were hauled on board No. 5 boat. From that heaving perch Higgs watched the U-boat approach No. 1 boat, which was in the charge of the Bosun. (The U-boat, Higgs said, was "freshly painted dark gray with no distinguishing marks on the conning tower"—although Gelhaus said in an interview in 1997 that the conning tower bore the device of four aces.)

While he hid his cap and prepared to remove his uniform coat, Higgs listened to the conversation between the Commander and the Bosun. Asked where was the ship's Captain, the Bosun answered that he was probably still on board. In answer to further questions, the Bosun gave the name, tonnage, age, route, and cargo of the ship. Hearing women's voices, the Commander expressed surprise. On being told that there were women and children passengers, the Commander said that they "had no business to come to sea."

Then, after apologizing for not being able to take anyone on board and wishing the survivors a "good voyage," he steamed off. Higgs later described the Commander as physically a "big man," and said that while he interrogated the Bosun, a U-boat crewman kept a handheld machine gun trained on the lifeboat.

When the Bosun's boat encountered No. 2 boat, he found that it held several gravely injured men and that the morale of the occupants generally was very low. The Bosun transferred into it Able Seaman Daniels, a tall strong Irishman with a keen sense of humor. Though Daniels had been a bit of a problem to Higgs on several occasions during the voyage, he quickly redeemed himself in No. 2 boat, where he threw overboard two dead bodies and made the wounded as comfortable as possible, including the Second Steward, who had an arm broken in three places, and a 74-year-old Church of England Canon, who had a deep cut on his head. To everyone in the boat, his cheerfulness and good nature were an inspirational lift. "In a time like this," Higgs said, "I could not have wished for a better man." When daylight came and No. 2 boat brushed by No. 5, containing the Chief Officer, Daniels asked him if the Official Log had been lost. When told yes, it had, Daniels said, "Good, the Old Man won't be able to fine me when we get back now."

At 0700 GMT, with five lifeboats and three rafts collected, and, on Higgs's order, a tot of rum being passed around to each person, someone cried, "Aircraft!" Higgs called to the crew of each boat to throw over a red smoke flare. Within minutes the aircraft, a B–24 Liberator of RAF Coastal Command, turned in their direction and circled the lifeboats and their clouds of red smoke. After signaling that help was coming, the aircraft departed, but returned every two hours to give reassurance. In the early afternoon the Liberator dropped a package containing food, water, and a note saying that a destroyer should reach their position about 1750. The note ended: "Best of luck and drop us a line when you get back," signed by the eight men of the air crew. Shortly after 1700, H.M.S. *Wren* hove into view, made a wide circle around the lifeboats listening with her asdic for any U-boat that might be lurking below, then began taking the survivors on board, a process completed by 1730. When the destroyer made port at Liverpool on 4 May, Higgs reported his fatal casualties: seventeen in number, including the old Canon, who couldn't make it. "All my Engineers, Officers and men behaved extremely well," he stated, "and I cannot speak too highly of the magnificent conduct of all my passengers."[42]

Interviewed in 1997, Gelhaus said that he received a letter from Captain Higgs in 1948, asking how U-107 had been able to hit him since his ship was traveling at high speed and zigzagging. Higgs also wrote that the first coup de grâce torpedo had hit on the port side just as a lifeboat on that side holding women and civilians was being lowered. Gelhaus expressed regret at learning that, and explained simply, in his interview for this book, *"Aber da hätte ich nichts dafür gekonnt, denn es war ja dunkel"*—"I could not have done anything about it because it was dark." He said that in 1955, during a business trip to England, he intended to visit Higgs, who had invited him to do so, but found there that he had died, and that his wife had moved to an unknown address.[43]

On the same 1 May, U-659, commanded by Kptlt. Hans Stock, was patrolling 380 nautical miles west-northwest of Cape Finisterre ("land's end"), the rocky promontory at the most westerly point of Spain. A Type VIIC, U-659 was one of eleven boats that had been formed by BdU into *Gruppe Drossel* (Group Thrush).[44] Stock's orders called for him eventually to break through the Strait of Gibraltar into the Mediterranean, but his first duty since the boat slipped her moorings at Brest on Easter Sunday, 25 April, was to form part of the *Drossel* disposition in a controlled operation against Allied coastwise traffic on the U.K.-Gibraltar-West Africa run. At night on 1/2 May the *Drossel* boats were advised by BdU that a British cruiser-minelayer, H.M.S. *Adventure*, was somewhere in their neighborhood. Stock decided against pursuing the faster vessel.

No smoke plumes appeared on the second day, but early

on 3 May, following her regular forenoon exercise dive to correct trim, U–*659* received an F.T. (*Funktelegraphie,* wireless message) that a reconnaissance Focke-Wulf 200 Kondor aircraft of *Fliegerführer Atlantik* based in western France had sighted a southbound convoy of eleven cargo ships and six escorts in position approximately 44°N, 14°W. Stock moved eastward at full (flank) speed (*äußerste Kraft*) to the attack. About 1400 GST, he learned from BdU of the presence of a second southbound formation, consisting of twenty-seven vessels, in nearly the same position as the first. Stock decided to go after the second set of targets instead. Before midnight, as the sea state was deteriorating, he ordered another dive to adjust trim.[45]

"Clear the bridge!" The dive order sent the bridge watch scrambling down the conning tower hatch. The Watch Officer, last man through, pulled the hatch closed and wheeled the spindle home in its bed. Meanwhile, in the *Zentrale* (control room) below, the Chief Engineering Officer (L.I.) had ordered, "Vent main ballast!" and slammed the ball of his hand against the dive bell, which shrilled throughout the boat. At once, two dozen pairs of hands in the control room and aft in the engine and maneuvering rooms whirred among banks of red and black valve wheels, overhead vent levers, and panel switches to open the external ballast tanks to water, cut off the outside air intakes and exhaust valves for the diesel engines, and engage the E-motors for underwater running.

Stock probably instructed the L.I. to level off at periscope depth, while he himself checked a stopwatch against both the column of mercury in the periscope elevation indicator and the needle on the *Tiefenmesser,* or depth manometer, expecting to see thirteen meters of water put above the hull inside thirty seconds. Facing the hull on the starboard side, two planesmen operated brass buttons, up and down, that controlled protruding bow and stern hydroplanes, which, like an aircraft's horizontal stabilizers, caused the submerging U-boat to pitch at a certain angle. Soon, with the diesels' roar and vibrations stilled, only a faint hum heard from the E-motors aft, and every crew member silent at his diving station, the sea closed over U-659.

The senior planesman reported when the mercury column showed 13.5 meters, periscope depth, and the L.I. ordered the planes brought to neutral and jockeyed to maintain as much as possible a constant level attitude while he went about the critical business of adjusting the boat's weight and tilting movement. This he did by pumping water by the hundreds of kilograms fore or aft between trim tanks at the extreme bow and stern. Maintaining trim was crucial, lest in an emergency dive the boat either plunge to the seabed or broach the surface, bow- or stern-first. Meanwhile, the Helmsman (*Rudergänger*), stationed on the forward starboard side bulkhead, steered the boat by compass, using brass rudder buttons for "port" and "starboard," and the Navigator (*Obersteuermann*) at his high table plotted the boat's position.

Just forward of the amidships control room, and reached through a watertight circular hatch offset to port, were the Commander's felt-curtained bunk and desk space on the port side of a narrow fore-and-aft gangway, and, on the starboard side opposite, the wireless (*Funkraum*) and hydrophone (*Horchraum*) rooms. Continuing forward, one came upon the bunk-long accommodation of the I.W.O., II.W.O., and L.I. (*Offizierraum*), where a mess and worktable along the port side enabled this compartment to serve as a wardroom. Beyond, through another hatch, was bunk space for four men of Chief Petty Officer rank (*Oberfeldwebel*), though U-659 carried only three, and, farther still, past a portside head, one reached the forward torpedo room (*Bugtorpedoraum*), home not only to the four bow torpedo tubes but also to the majority of the ratings, popularly called "Lords" (*Pairs*).

Here the hull narrowed markedly, accentuating the cramped interior of the smaller Type VIIC boat, made all the more confined by the conditions attendant to a just-commenced *Feindfahrt:* two of the room's spare torpedoes, hung by hoist rings suspended from an I-beam, displaced sleeping bunks; food crates, sacks, and cans occupied every nook and cranny of floor space; while overhead hammocks bulged low with hams, sausages, fruits, and *Kommissbrot,* the hard navy black bread. The only way to get about was by hands and knees. Every man yearned for early attack successes, so that the two spare "eels" in the bunk areas could be placed inside the white-painted tubes, and the lashed-up bunks, with their blue-and-white-checked gingham sheets and pillowcases, could be brought down for sleeping and sitting.

None of the Lords would be nearly as anxious, however, about getting rid of the brow-bruising fresh food hammocks. They knew that once the perishable fresh food was consumed they would have only tinned food to eat, and that by the time that exchange came to pass, every bucket of food hauled down the passageway from the galley would take on a taste compounded of the boat's accumulated vapors of stale, humid air, diesel oil, battery gas, bilges, oven fumes, soiled trousers, unbrushed teeth, urine, vomit, semen, smegma, and Colibri cologne. By then, too, the gingham sheets and pillowcases of the "hot bunks"—so-called because they would be constantly occupied day and night by seamen and technicians coming off their various watches—would be making their own gamy contributions to the putrescent atmosphere.

Returning to the control room through the constricted steel cylinder (though not a perfect cylinder for its whole length) that was the VIIC's pressure hull, one walked over a storage area almost as large as the working and living space above. Beneath the floor plates were lead-acid storage battery arrays whose dead weight counterbalanced the diesel engines and a second battery compartment in the after section of the boat. Here, too, was stored ammunition for the deck and anti-aircraft (*flak*) guns.

The rolled galvanized sheet steel skin that formed the pressure hull itself thickened as one approached the control room, from 1.6 cm at the bow and stern to 1.85 cm amidships, and to 2.2 cm where the conning tower joined the hull. Passing through the control room, which was 6.2 meters (20 1/3 feet) across the beam, one came to a circular hatch that led into the Petty Officers' accommodation (*Unteroffizierraum*) and, after that, the galley (*Küche*) with its little Vosswerke stove, short refrigerator, sink, and pantry that served the single cook (*Smutje*). From there the boat's one central, single-level gangway opened to the oily and smelly, but now silent, engine room (*Dieselmotorenraum*), where twin MAN 6-cylinder, 4-cycle engines of 1,160 horsepower each provided surface propulsion.

The humming dynamotors were in the next compartment aft, the *E-Maschinenraum*, or maneuvering room. Here, by contrast to the appearance of the engine room, two clean E-Motors that sparkled beneath equally gleaming control panels drove the boat's two propeller drive shafts underwater. There was other equipment in this room as well, including an electricity-driven air compressor on the port side and a Junkers diesel-driven compressor on the opposite side, which were used for filling containers of the compressed air that the control room required for blowing water from the ballast tanks when the boat surfaced and for launching torpedoes. Here, too, was an auxiliary steering wheel for use in moving the double rudders in the event the electrical steering buttons in the control room were disabled. From the maneuvering room it was then just a few steps into the aft torpedo room with its lone white-faced launch tube. Every three days the Eto that occupied that tube, or the one spare stowed beneath the E-motors, would be opened up and inspected by the torpedo mates, called "mixers." Under wire-shielded lights the mixers would unscrew inspection plates and test the eel's battery level, electric motor, guidance system, and depth-keeping mechanism.[46]

The mixers and other crew members who occupied the interior space of U–*659* were, like the crewmen of all U-boats, a selective, highly trained group. The four officers were all graduates of the Naval Academy (*Marineschule*) in Flensburg-Mürwik, a cadet training establishment through which the future officer passed after a year of practical experience that included three months at sea. Following the Academy curriculum, they would have spent eight to twelve weeks at *U-boot-Schule* in Neustadt in Schleswig-Holstein or Pillau (after 1940). Twenty-seven-year-old Stock, the Commander, had been a member of the 1935 entering class (*Crew 35*). After receiving his commission and completing several operational training courses, he had served as I.W.O. with Kptlt. Heinrich Lehmann-Willenbrock on U–*96*. (It was on the cruise of U–*96* in late 1941 to the North Atlantic and Mediterranean that Lothar-Günther Buchheim, a twenty-three-year-old war correspondent who accompanied the crew, based his much later novel [1973] followed by a motion picture, both named *Das Boot* ["The Boat"].) After Commander's Course with the 26th Flotilla at Pillau, Stock was given the new boat U–*659*, which he commissioned on 9 December 1941 and took on four patrols prior to this one.

By 1943, with most of the surface Navy frozen in port, the majority of young officers, such as Stock's I.W.O., II.W.O., and L.I., were assigned to U-boats. By contrast, most of the boat's petty officers and lower ratings were volunteers. Twenty to twenty-four years in age, they had entered the Kriegsmarine from hometowns situated largely in northern and central Germany: Hamburg would be an example of the former, the Ruhr and Saxony districts examples of the latter. Their formal schooling prior to trade schools did not exceed the requisite eight primary grades, and their religious affiliations were roughly three-quarters Protestant, one-quarter Roman Catholic. Some crewmen had volunteered directly from civilian life for the U-Bootwaffe; others had served previously on light surface vessels.

Generally speaking, the crewmen fell into two categories: seamen (*Seemänner*), which included helmsmen, planesmen, lookouts, gunners, the deck force, cook, and stewards; and the engineering/technical personnel (*Techniker*), who operated the boat's seagoing and torpedo attack equipment, such as the diesels, E-motors, torpedo mechanisms, radio, hydrophone, and the diving and surfacing systems. The second category had a high representation of nonspecialized entry-level metalworkers from the industrial regions of central Germany—young men who might be expected to feel comfortable in an all-metal environment, who had a common vocational experience to bind them together as comrades, and who possessed the canny skills to contrive emergency repairs when the boat was far from base. All hands would have received three months of basic naval training, followed by three to six months of intensive course work at U-Boat School, either at Neustadt prior to May 1940, or at Pillau from May to November 1940, or at Gdynia after the latter date.[47]

Whatever their backgrounds, categories, or ratings, the crewmen of U-659, like all U-boat men, shared certain communalities. Everyone ate the same food, used the same head (a second head aft was usually employed as a pantry for canned foods), and breathed the same foul air. Nor was there any dress code to distinguish ranks from ratings, petty officers from mates. Except for the tropical white cover worn on the Commander's *Schirmmütze*, or peaked cap (for visual identification at night), every man's attire had a dull sameness. Most wore standard blue-gray fatigues, perhaps with a *Schiffchen*, or forage cap, made from blue wool with black lining. In cold weather one saw sweaters knitted by grandmother and other unconventional mufti.

On the bridge in cold weather the watch officer and lookouts wore gray-green leathers, and, in heavy weather, sou'westers. When in warm waters, on the other hand, short pants of varying hues were the dress of the day. In one other particular, too, the crewmen were aware of their societal cohesion: at sea every man depended absolutely on the performance of every other. In no other war machine was the integral participation of every team member so vital. Any one man of them could sink the boat. One hatch uncovered, one valve unturned, one battery array unchecked for gas, one enemy aircraft unspotted, one vessel on collision course unsighted, and the mission, boat, and crew were doomed.

The trim secured, Stock took a careful look around the horizon and sky with the wide-angle sky periscope, whose shaft dominated the forward center space of the control room, and, seeing no enemy ship or aircraft, he ordered: "Surface!" The L.I. accordingly instructed his ballast tank operators, "Blow main ballast!," listened approvingly as the hissing compressed air expelled water from the ballast tanks (diesel exhaust would finish the task on the surface), and called out the upward cant angles on the fore and aft planes. When the E-motors had driven the boat dynamically forward to the water's surface and the conning tower bridge hatch had broken clear (*"Turmluk ist frei, Boot ist raus!"*), the diesels were lit, and Stock pounded up the aluminum ladder that ran up through a hull hatch into the tear-shaped conning tower (*Turm*) that housed the fixed attack periscope eyepiece, the torpedo deflection calculator, and a compass repeater with rudder buttons.

After opening the upper tower hatch, Stock stepped up onto the dripping open bridge, where he was followed by the I.W.O., commanding the midwatch, a seaman Petty Officer, and two seamen. Since the seas were heavy, with waves breaking against the tower, the boat was now pitching and rolling sharply in the riled-up water, and the men at once attached their safety harnesses to brackets extending out from the bridge's wood-slatted enclosure. From the bridge, Stock and the lookouts could see, fore and aft, the full length of the boat's deck casing, 67.1 meters (221⅓ feet), with its hardwood planking, and along the waterline to either side the long, bulging "saddle tanks," which contained, among their various bunkers, the main fuel oil and ballast tanks. Under diesel propulsion the boat threw up frothy bow and stern wakes, all the more pronounced because of the shuddering dark rollers.

Movement on the bridge was constrained by the periscope shafts, the sky scope forward, the attack scope aft, and the UZO post with its bracket for the surface attack optics set above a ring marked off in compass degrees. Other equipment on the bridge included a gyrocompass, magnetic compass, engine telegraph dial, extendable radio antenna, and voice pipe. The space was enclosed front and two sides by double-plate steel cladding that rose to a height of 1.5 meters above the bridge deck, as a protection against hard seas and small-to medium-arms fire. Aft of the bridge was a circular, railed-in flak platform for the 20mm anti-aircraft gun—and for cigarettes and pipes in calmer weather, when crewmen thought of it as a *Wintergarten*.

With the bridge set only seventeen feet above the water, Stock and his lookouts had limited vision of the horizon, acquiring through their 7 x 50s about twelve kilometers range in ideal visibility conditions on a clear day, and much less on a night like this night, when visibility was poor. An additional one or two kilometers might be gained by shinnying up the extended sky periscope standard. As a result of the VIIC's low silhouette, its visual search rate was never more than 2,350 square nautical miles per day, in good conditions, as compared with the larger and faster U.S. Navy fleet submarine's 7,000 to 10,000 square nautical miles per day: the U.S. sub had brackets built on the periscope shears (supports) that enabled it to place eyes thirty-five feet above water. But for Stock and the midwatch later this night, 3/4 May, at 0325 GST to be exact, distance vision proved not to be a factor. In the event that now unfolded it would have been better had they all been nearsighted, as—

CRUUUNCH!!

The boat careened hard to port from a ramming amidships on the starboard side. The lookouts were startled by what they now saw: the crushed bows of another U-boat! Below, water and fuel oil poured into the control room and other compartments. The L.I. called up the voice pipe to inform Stock that the inrush was so great it could not be stanched, and the boat could not long be kept afloat. Stock and the I.W.O. went below, where Stock, finding the L.I. up to his chest in oil, ordered the crew to don life jackets and abandon the boat: *"Alle Männer aus dem Boot!"*

Men scrambled up the tower ladder, then down the tower sides, and mustered on the tossing upper deck—though not all of them, since it appears that some of the engine room personnel and radiomen remained on duty too long to make their escape, and that both Stock and the I.W.O. similarly got trapped below. Among the officers, in fact, only the L.I. made it out. Survivors stated that the radio operators got off a short signal reporting both the boat's loss by ramming and her position, 43°32′N, 13°30′W. Five minutes after the collision, a towering wave broke over the mortally wounded frame of U–*659*. The men on deck went flying into the water, and the boat, heeling over to starboard, sank from view.[48]

The other boat was U–*439*, a Type VIIC commanded by Oblt.z.S. Helmut von Tippelskirch (Crew 37). A native of Cuxhaven, the twenty-five-year-old Kommandant had earlier served as I.W.O. on U–*160*. The U–*439*, his first command, had departed Brest on 27 April, and on the night of 3/4 May occupied a station adjoining U–*659* in the *Drossel* line, from which she was proceeding this night at the highest speed that the sea state permitted, to intercept the first of the two reported southbound convoys. By 0100 GST she sighted the convoy and by 0325 she was positioned ahead of it, making seven knots. At that instant, survivors from his boat said, Tippelskirch altered course slightly to port and his bows rammed the starboard side of U–*659*, which no one had seen. Tippelskirch immediately ordered both engines full astern, but the maneuver in rough seas caused the diesel exhausts to drown and the interior of the boat to fill with blue fumes. Because the collision had caused heavy leakage through the two port bow torpedo tubes, the bow compartment had to be closed off.

Meanwhile, the L.I. tried to adjust the surface trim by blowing the forward ballast tanks, but these, it was discovered, had been damaged in the collision. He compensated by flooding some of the after tanks, but this brought the boat dangerously low in the water, and the L.I. recommended abandonment. Tippelskirch, thinking the boat might yet be saved, ordered the engine room personnel and radio operators to remain at their stations and the remainder of the crew to go up on deck with their life jackets. There they saw that their boat was down by the bows and already half-submerged. Survivors doubted that the radiomen's distress signals were heard, since most of the forward transmitting antenna wire was underwater. Said one:

The Commander sent a W/T [radio] message: "Boat rammed, boat sinking, crew abandoning ship." Messages should be ciphered if possible, so that the English shouldn't understand; and they [the radiomen] calmly ciphered the whole message and tapped it out to the last letter, and the water had already reached their feet. The message went out. Perhaps they [BdU] received it, perhaps they didn't.[49]

They did not receive it.

From the bridge Tippelskirch could see the other U-boat not far distant. Though it appeared to be in a sinking condition, he asked it by signal lamp for assistance; but U-659 replied by lamp that she, too, was going under. Then a huge rogue wave, probably the same that swamped Stock's boat, drove U-439, still carrying inside about twenty-four engine machinists and radiomen, into the 2,761-fathom deep, a bourn from which none returned. Those men who had been on deck, thrown off violently from their tenuous footing, swam off with flashing signal lights, hoping to attract either other *Drossel* boats or, just as well given the circumstances, the enemy.

At 0500, British Motor Torpedo Boat 670, leading the starboard column of the first reported southbound operational Coastal Forces convoy, ran into diesel smoke and fumes, and afterwards sighted men swimming in the water. The starboard column stopped and rescued twelve survivors, three from the forty-five-man crew of U-659, and nine from the forty-eight-man crew of U-439. The only officer among them was the L.I. of U-659. Taken first to Gibraltar and then on 13 May to the Combined Services Detailed Interrogation Centre, U.K., at Latimer House, Chesham, Buckinghamshire, England, the survivors underwent the usual interrogation by RN officers. The nine from U-439 proved particularly intractable, and the interrogators reported, "They were mostly more security-conscious than has been the case among recent U-boat prisoners of war."[50] All they would say about their Commander, Tippelskirch, was that he was adventurous and very popular with his men, but that, having teethed on a Type IXC (U–*160)*, he always had difficulty handling a VIIC. About the I.W.O., Oblt.z.S. Gerhard Falow, they had mixed feelings: on the one hand, they found him easy-going and well-liked; on the other, they thought him lazy and personally responsible for the loss of their own boat, and of U–*659* as well.

Apparently, Falow himself, before his watery death, agreed with that last judgment, as the British learned in detail from the secret bugging of twenty-one-year-old Herbert Apel, a U–*439 Maschinengefreiter* (the U.S. Navy equivalent: Fireman, third class; the Royal Navy: Stoker, second class). The interrogators housed Apel in a POW hut with a *Steuermann* named Schultz from SS *Regensburg,* a German blockade-running freighter that had been sunk by the cruiser H.M.S. *Glasgow* off the north of Iceland on 30 March. The interrogators knew that a man from one boat or ship would want to relate his experiences, knowledge, and thoughts to someone he did not know from another U-boat or ship.

Accordingly, on 21 May Apel described to Schultz (and through hidden microphones to the British listening post) how Tippelskirch erred by placing a man on lookout duty who had no previous experience of watchkeeping in that boat; and how the I.W.O. Falow erred by taking more interest in events occurring in the port quarter than in the seascape on the starboard sector which was his responsibility–though Falow did take the ultimate responsibility for the dereliction, as Apel explained:

APEL: Do you know what our First Officer of the Watch did? Anyone else would have fetched it [a lifebelt] for him, and someone else did fetch it, and brought it to him. He said: "I won't take anything." Well, of course, we were absolutely staggered that he wouldn't take the lifebelt. Then he went and stood forward on the bridge. He gripped the bridge with both hands and went down with the boat like that. At the time of the mishap he was on the bridge. The boat which we had rammed appeared in his sector. Of course, he would have been definitely held responsible in

Germany. To be quite honest, it was our fault—or rather it was the fault [of those] on the bridge. We had a new *Bootsmaat* [Petty Officer Third Class (USN)] on the patrol. He'd never been on watch at all. At six o'clock in the evening, the Commander sent for him and said: "You've been on watch on the bridge in the other boat, haven't you?"—"Yes."—"Can you see well at night, too? Have you sighted anything yet? You're sure you can do it?"—"Yes." "Good, you can do watch on the bridge tonight." He [the *Bootsmaat*] stood forward. . . . And suddenly on the port side of the boat, aft, tracers were seen, so there must have been some firing—so [the port quarter lookout] naturally thought that must be the convoy, and reported it at once. The Officer of the Watch was interested, turned round and had a look. The Commander was on the bridge and looked, too. The [new *Bootsmaat*] forward, who should really have continued to look straight ahead, looked round too, and the Commander said to the two look-outs [forward]: "Pay attention, don't look over there, that doesn't concern you. Something may come from any side." Until now that [policy] had always been so, and had always been successful, and this time apparently he didn't say that to the new [*Bootsmaat*]. He should have known it himself. There was more firing. The others kept their eyes glued to their sector, when suddenly the Officer of the Watch turned round and yelled: *"Verdammte Scheisse—A.K. zurück!"* ["Hell and damnation!—full speed astern!"] But it was already too late.

SCHULTZ: Perhaps the boat didn't sink at all. You can't possibly tell.

APEL: She definitely went down. She heeled over almost vertically and went down like that. The diving tanks were still full of air. She probably stopped sinking at two hundred meters, three hundred meters, or even three hundred fifty meters for about half an hour, and then, in time, she would get heavier and heavier as more water came in.

SCHULTZ: Yes, but they can still blow the tanks or—

APEL: No, no. Our whole bow compartment was under water.

Forward in the bow compartment the bulkhead was closed. It was a watertight bulkhead but will not stand up to heavy pressure. The lower bulkhead will certainly have caved in. Even before, it was never quite watertight, water already came. . . .

SCHULTZ: There's no proof at all that the men are dead.

APEL: Oh yes. Just think, where could they blow the tanks? First, the diving tanks were still full of air, but there was water in the boat. . . . We were unlucky. We started up both pumps immediately and we were unable to get rid of a single drop of water that had broken in.[51]

Another closemouthed survivor, but from the other boat involved in the collision, was Bruno Arendt, a twenty-three-year-old *Bootsmann* (the U.S. Navy equivalent: Petty Officer, First Class; Royal Navy: Chief Petty Officer). Quartered with Helmut Klotzsch, the *Obersteuermann* (Navigator) of U–*175*, sunk on 17 April, Arendt was heard to say (and recorded) on 13 May:

ARENDT: The Interrogation Officer wanted to know the number of the boat, but I won't tell him that.

KLOTZSCH: What number did you have?

ARENDT: Six-fifty-nine.

KLOTZSCH: Some two hundred boats have been sunk already.

ARENDT: They will make a fine mess of things this summer. There is no question of there being more boats operating now. As soon as they come out they're sunk. . . . By the time you've sailed for three years you're just about finished.

KLOTZSCH: Yes, I know an Obersteuermann who is now on his sixteenth patrol.

ARENDT: Well, let him get that over safely, and then he'll go on his seventeenth and that will be the end of him! Twelve men [from our two boats] were saved altogether.

KLOTZSCH: Twelve men from two boats?

ARENDT: Yes. There were forty-eight in our boat. That's ninety-six in the two boats.

KLOTZSCH: It's a tragedy. The whole business of U-boat sailing has simply become a job for convicts.[52]

Two sets of omens. Which would prevail? The triumphant
auguries of Henke (U–*515*) and Gelhaus (U–*107*)? Or the
woeful auguries of Stock (U–*659*) and von Tippelskirch
(U–*439*)? But pantomancers were probably few on either
side. More dully, the slogging procession of May would tell.

2

The War at Sea
Detection and Attack

In all the long history of sea warfare there has been no parallel to this battle, whose field was thousands of square miles of ocean, and to which no limits of time or space could be set.

CAPTAIN STEPHEN W. ROSKILL, D.S.C., R.N.

On certain naval histories:
They are primarily accounts of what happened, and do not, in my view, adequately explain why it happened.

SIR STUART MITCHELL

The months of July and August [1941] saw the North Atlantic U-boat operations sink to their lowest level of effectiveness, and it looked almost as though the defense had won the race against the attack.

DR. JÜRGEN ROHWER

By the date of the events described in this narrative the major forces, directions, and trends in the Atlantic campaign had long been established. There is no need to review all the operational details of the war at sea from the outbreak of hostilities on 3 September 1939 to the beginning of May 1943, since these have already been essentially addressed in the historical literature. But before considering developments in Allied armed countermeasures to the U-boats, which is the intent of this chapter, it might be helpful to tease out of the previous forty-four months of data several findings that are surprising and provocative.

The first of these relates to numbers. At the outset of war, Dönitz had only thirty-nine operational U-boats, including twenty-two Type VIIs and Type IXs–instead of the 300 he had stated was the minimum number he would require to conduct a successful war against Great Britain's Atlantic trade, and instead of the 162 oceangoing boats he had been promised by Hitler in the naval construction program scheduled for completion in 1948(!). Of these twenty-two, only six to eight could be deployed on operational stations at any one time, the remainder being in transit or in repair yards. Through February 1941 his available force declined in number rather than grew, despite the successes of the first year and five months, which included the sinking of the battleship *Royal Oak* by U-47 (Korvettenkapitän [hereafter Korv. Kapt.] Günther Prien) on 14 October 1939 and a five-months-long U-boat spree in waters adjacent to the United Kingdom and Ireland from June to October 1940 that added 1,395,298 enemy GRT to Dönitz's bar graphs and became known among U-boat crews as *glückliche Zeit*–the "Happy Time."

Those successes, gained mainly against nonconvoyed, independently routed ships, unquestionably impressed Hitler, but the Führer's favor was not reflected in his allocations of steel and workers for U-boat construction, with the result that, owing to combat losses, in February 1941 Dönitz commanded fewer operational boats (22) than he had on the first day of war. In that month, however, the delivery rate improved, and by the end of July 1941 the number of operational boats surpassed Dönitz's original number. The increase would be sustained thereafter with occasional slight diminutions (May–June 1942, October 1942–January 1943, and March–April 1943) until May 1943, when Dönitz would have no fewer than 433 boats in commission (207 operational in the North Atlantic theater).

One might have expected that after mid-1941 the U-boats' success rate would increase at the same rate as that of new commissionings. But such was not the case. From July 1941 forward, sinkings decreased markedly. From 305,734 GRT of Allied shipping sunk in June 1941 the totals fell to

61,471 in July and 67,638 in August. Whereas in September 1940, when an average of thirteen operational U-boats were at sea, Dönitz's commanders had sunk 265,737 GRT, for an average of 753 GRT per boat per day at sea, one year later, in September 1941, when an average of 36.5 boats were at sea, his commanders sank only 208,822 GRT for an average of 186 GRT per boat per day. The tonnage sunk in October 1941 dropped to 182,412 GRT, that in November to 91,628 GRT, and the total in December was 101,687 GRT, with correspondingly low GRT averages per boat per day. In other words, during 1941 the more operational boats there were, the fewer their successes.

And 1941 is not the only period in which we notice that discrepancy. As indicated in the prologue, the greatest monthly toll of Allied shipping lost to U-boats in the war (743,321 GRT) was taken in November 1942, a month in which the U-Bootwaffe had 95 operational boats at sea. Their average sinkings per boat per day were 220 GRT. Two years earlier, in November 1940, when there were only 11 operational boats at sea, the average sinkings per boat per day were 430 GRT. With nearly nine times the number of boats, the U-Bootwaffe in its best month of the war scored slightly more than half the successes per boat of those achieved by their forerunners.

In January, February, and March 1943, which are closer to the special focus of this narrative, there were 92, 116, and 116 U-boats, respectively, operating in the Atlantic, where sinkings were, again respectively, 218,449, 380,835, and 590,234 GRT. Taken alone, these were impressive figures, augmented in no small part by the mauling of SC.122/HX.229 in March; but considered in terms of the large operating force at sea in those months we find that the tonnage numbers credited to each boat per day at sea were 65, 99, and 147 GRT, which, taken together, represented no improvement over the figures posted during the second half of 1941.[1] Dönitz was still sinking fewer merchant ships per investment of U-boat days.

Returning to 1941, where we first notice a sharp falloff in U-boat productivity, we can ask, how may it be explained?

One reason that has been offered is the sudden loss of three individual U-boat "aces" in March: Prien (U–47) and Kptlt. Joachim Schepke (U–100,) both of whom were killed, and Korv. Kapt. Otto Kretschmer (U–99,) who was captured. These commanders, who had first made their reputations in the "Happy Time," had achieved tonnage totals ranging from Schepke's 156,941 GRT to Kretschmer's 257,451. All were *Ritterkreuzträger,* winners of the Knights Cross of the Iron Cross, with Oak Leaves, and, as such, were inspirational role models for the rest of the officer corps.

Fregattenkapitän (hereafter Freg. Kapt.) Günter Hessler, Dönitz's son-in-law and a member of his operations staff, stated after the war that the U-boat successes prior to July 1941 were not "due only to the skill of such men as Prien, Kretschmer and Schepke, for there were equally competent commanders in 1941, who however had to contend with much greater difficulties."[2] He may have had in mind such men as Kptlt. Engelbert Endrass (U–46, U–567), Korv. Kapt. Reinhard Suhren (U–564), and Kptlt. Adalbert Schnee (U–201). Endrass would be lost in December 1941. Postwar analysis, however, would place an emphasis on how important for the U-Bootwaffe's overall success was the performance of certain individual commanders, whose loss would be a pronounced negative. No more than thirty-commanders (2 percent of the whole), it was found, accounted for some 30 percent of Allied shipping sunk by U-boats during the war; and, significantly, for what it said later about replacement commanders, all had entered the Kriegsmarine before 1935. Only fourteen commanders accounted for nearly 20 percent of all sinkings. Only 131 boats sank or damaged six or more ships. Meanwhile, 850 boats, which represented three-quarters of all boats commissioned during the war, failed so much as to damage a single merchant vessel.

With these figures in hand, Günter Hessler notwithstanding, the argument that the loss of three proven performers in Prien, Schepke, and Kretschmer had an adverse effect on U-boat fortunes in July-December 1941 is, though not decisive, persuasive. As has been written, "One cannot leave the subject of human factors without re-emphasizing the importance of the aces on both sides. . . . Kretschmer, Prien *et alia* were good enough to distort all statistics. The difference was that [Allied] escort commanders lived to improve their skill and to pass it on, whilst U-boat aces had a short life."[3]

Another reason more frequently, and convincingly, offered is the acquisition by the British, in February-June 1941, of access to secretly encrypted radio traffic between Dönitz and his boats. The story is now a familiar one. For secret radio communications the three German armed forces, land, sea, and air, employed a once commercially available electrical-mechanical encryption machine. Called Enigma, it resembled a typewriter with a standard keyboard, which was used for punching in the message to be encrypted. Above the keyboard were three (later four) rotors, and below the keyboard facing the operator was a plug board. By altering the rotor settings and plug pairings each day, it was estimated that the possible permutations created by the machine approached one hundred and fifty million million million, a number maintained by German cipher experts to be beyond solution. But in 1934 Polish Intelligence Service mathematicians, by yoking six Enigma machines together, did find a partial solution. They managed to pass on their findings to French cryptanalysts, thence, after France, too, fell, to the cryptanalysis establishment at the (mostly) fictitious Government Code and Cipher School (GC&CS) in England.

Housed in a red-brick mansion in pseudo-Tudor-Gothic style at Bletchley, halfway between Oxford and Cambridge, GC&CS had already made substantial progress against Enigma on its own. Under the direction of academics, notably the Cambridge mathematician Alan Turing, GC&CS constructed an electromagnetic scanning machine called the *Bombe.* Fed to the Bombe's innards, intercepted German signals traffic began to shed its veils. First to be read was Luftwaffe (Air Force) Enigma, on 22 May 1940. Shortly afterward, the machine decrypted Wehrmacht (Army) traffic. Single-story white-frame Nissen huts sprang up behind the mansion to house academics who translated and interpreted the in-

coming German messages. Hut 8, however, which was
assigned to naval traffic, was frustrated by the Bombe's inability to penetrate the Kriegsmarine's more complex U-boat
cipher, generated by the marine version of the Enigma machine, *Schlüssel M* (*Marine-Funkschlüssel-Maschine M*). Naval
Enigma, in fact, would resist for a full year until finally forced
to submit in winter-spring 1941.

What Hut 8 had needed to resolve the impasse were operational wired rotors and operators' handbooks that gave daily
Schlüssel-M settings and pairings. In a series of "pinches"
conducted from February through June 1941, the Royal Navy
obliged. On 12 January, off a captured crewman of the sunken
U–33 in the North Channel between northern Ireland and
Scotland came rotors. On 4 March, from the wrecked German whaling trawler *Krebs* off the coast of Norway, came key
tables and settings. Armed with these materials, Hut 8 could
then read U-boat traffic in the *Heimische Gewässer* (Home Waters) key for the entire month of April. More pinches were to
follow. From the captured weather ship *München* east of Iceland on 7 May came settings and keys for June. And, the *pièce
de resistance*, two days later, destroyer H.M.S. *Bulldog* boarded
U–110 (Kptlt. Fritz-Julius Lemp) in mid-Atlantic and came
away with a Schlüssel-M including spare rotors, a Home Waters handbook with daily settings and pairings, special settings
for *Offizier*, officer-only, signals, and short-signals (*Kurzsignale*) code books, all valid to the end of June.

Included also was the first captured naval grid chart of the
North Atlantic and most of the Mediterranean. This chart, Nr.
1870G *Nordatlantischer Ozean*, with land surfaces in green and
water surfaces in white, was divided into blue-lined squares,
each identified by a digraph; for example, going west to Newfoundland a U-boat would pass through naval squares BF,
BE, BD, BC, and BB. Each artificial square, about 486 nautical
miles per side (along 50° latitude) was subdivided into nine
smaller squares identified by double-digit numerals, from 11
to 99. Each smaller square was then subdivided nine times,
then nine times again to form a fine screen that could take positions at sea down to a *Marinequadrat* (naval square) no

larger than six nautical miles to a side. Typically, a U-boat's position in radio messages and war diaries would read as follows: ET 6278, which was Werner Henke's position in U-*515* when he sank his first four ships southwest of Freetown on the night of 30 April/1 May. The naval square coordinates would be used by the U-Bootwaffe throughout the war in the place of latitude and longitude. A square was usually cited as *quadrat,* or *qu.*

When this godsend was received at GC&CS, Hut 8 began reading the other side's mail much closer to the grain. More help was to come. In a tightly planned operation on 28 June, British cruisers and destroyers boarded a second weather ship, *Lauenburg,* in the Norwegian Sea and captured the Home Waters key for July, allowing for continued Hut 8 penetration during that month. By mid-August 1941 Hut 8 had no further need of pinches and was able on its own to decrypt the key within fifty hours of transmission (41 hours in September, 26 in October). There had been brief blind spots on 1–4 August and 18–19 September, but from November forward the key would be read daily with virtual currency until war's end.[4] The only downside to that success was that beginning in February 1942, Home Waters' use for U-boat operations would cease, to be replaced by a new, more intricate cipher key named Triton. Employing a fourth rotor in the Enigma machine, Triton would remain impenetrable for nearly eleven months.

In the meantime, from July forward, GC&CS was able to send U-boat decrypts by secure circuit to Commander Winn and Lieutenant Beesly in the Submarine Tracking Room of the Operational Intelligence Centre of the Admiralty, where U-boat positions for the first time could be established confidently on the Main North Atlantic Plotting Table that depicted latitudes and longitudes 73°N to 5°S and 100°W to 60°E. When received there, the decrypts were given the designation "Special Intelligence," or "Z." When the essential information contained in the decrypts, though never the raw decrypts themselves, was signaled by OIC to headquarters, base, and fleet commanders, it became known as "Ultra."

The confidence and authority of the Tracking Room advanced dramatically. By Winn's order, a large photograph of Admiral Dönitz looked down upon what Winn fancied was a shadow BdU.[5] Now, as he and Beesly observed the proceedings of individual U-boats, as revealed in their daily position reports back to BdU, and followed the organization of anticonvoy patrol line groups, as ordered by the BdU Operations transmitter, the two RN Reservists could do for British trade convoys what had not been possible in any reliable way before: provide evasive routing around known U-boat concentrations. Noting this watershed in anti-U-boat warfare, numerous historians have credited the newly acquired signals intelligence with causing the precipitous decline in merchant ship sinkings that occurred in July and the remainder of 1941.[6]

Before considering a third possible reason for the U-boat failures of July–December 1941, it would be well to remark that Germany's own radio monitoring and cryptanalysis service, *B-Dienst* (*Funkbeobach-tungsdienst*), was not itself idle during this same period. Since before the war, in fact, its staff–500 in 1939, 5,000 in 1942–at Tirpitzufer 72-76 in Berlin had been busily attacking various of the British codes and ciphers, gaining entry early on to the Royal Navy Administrative Code, Auxiliary Code, Merchant Navy Code, and Naval Code No. 1. It also had modest success against Naval Cipher No. 2, adopted on 20 August 1940. But it was Naval Cipher No. 3, introduced at the start of October 1941, that most engaged the energies of the B-Dienst cryptanalysts, since its content dealt specifically with Allied convoys. Originated in June 1941 for use by the British, United States, and Canadian navies in the Atlantic, and popularly called the Anglo-American Convoy Cipher, it quickly became the conduit for information about convoy departures, routes, diversions, and arrivals, as well as about stragglers.

By December 1941 B-Dienst was making its first breaks into the cipher, and two months later it was reading as much as 80 percent of the transmitted signals.[7] This was a perilous development for the convoy system, since Admiral Dönitz, often with movement and diversion information ten to twenty hours in advance, could place his U-boat patrol lines directly athwart convoy courses. Since the same intelligence source conveyed to him the Admiralty's daily U-boat dispositions signal, Dönitz also knew what (in general) Winn's Tracking Room knew about his U-boat positions, though he never tumbled to the conclusion that the accurate Admiralty signals on the point were based on cracked Enigma.

There were occasions when U-boats were lost under suspicious circumstances, or when German surface refueling tankers were swept from the sea in a flash (as five were in 3–15 June 1941), or when a convoy suddenly altered course around a patrol line, or when an ocean-full of U-boats failed to sight targets and Dönitz became sufficiently troubled about cryptographic security that he consulted Konteradmiral Ludwig Stummel, whose Second Department (Operations) of the Naval Staff in Berlin superintended naval ciphers. Stummel always assured Dönitz that Admiralty information had to have come from shore-based radio direction finding, from air reconnaissance, or from surface ship sightings. The Enigma cipher, with its variable range and changes of settings, was invulnerable to enemy penetration by all known methods of mathematical analysis, Stummel insisted, and even if an entry should be made by accident, the information developed would be long out of date and operationally useless.

Dönitz's own staff analyzed the suspicious cases and came to the same conclusion that ordinary noncryptographic means could account for them. Nonetheless, Dönitz took the precaution of introducing a series of complex position-disguising devices into the cipher transmissions, all of which were eventually solved by GC&CS. He also restricted the number of staff who had authorized access to U-boat positions information as well as the number who were permitted to tune in the U-boat wavelength.[8]

As a result of each belligerent having the other side's key, sea warfare in the Atlantic during the winter and spring of 1943 became in part a backroom chess game as the Tracking Room, playing Ultra, sought to outwit BdU, playing B-Dienst, and no doubt on numerous occasions one side was able to neutralize the other's advantage. After the war, in a secret report ("three copies only") dated 10 November 1945, Paymaster Commander WGS Tighe, R.N., of the Signals Division, Admiralty, presented a report titled "German Success Against British Codes and Ciphers." It exists today in nineteen-page summary form.[9] In it Tighe described the Signals Division as "shocked" to have learned after the war from captured documents and interrogations of German cryptanalysts that Naval Cipher No. 3 had been thoroughly compromised, and that this security failure "not only cost us dearly in men and ships, but very nearly lost us the war." That extravagance was matched by Tighe's subsequent claim that "all successes obtained by U-boats against convoys HX229 and SC122 in March 1943, when 22 ships were sunk, can be directly traced to the information obtained by reading our signals."[10]

Certainly B-Dienst was at concert pitch prior to that battle of 16–20 March—called by the RN official history the "biggest convoy disaster of the war"—and Tracking Room records show that B-Dienst, hence Dönitz, had prior information about the ocean course of SC.122 and about both the original route and a diversion of HX.229. What the Germans did not know was how far along their courses the two convoys had proceeded by 15 March. That was the date, at 1918 GMT, when U–91 (Kptlt. Heinz Walkerling), en route to a refueling rendezvous, sighted and followed a destroyer that was proceeding on a northeast course in qu BC 3486 (49°33′N, 40°35′W). Thinking that it might be overhauling a convoy, Walkerling trailed it and was rewarded with the chance sighting of HX.229.[11]

Various sources state that knowledge of the German reconstruction of Naval Cipher No. 3 was smelled out by American Naval Intelligence in March and May 1943.[12] But GC&CS had learned from Enigma solutions as early as December 1942 that B-Dienst was reading the cipher.[13] This is confirmed by Francis Harry (now Sir Harry) Hinsley, O.B.E., M.A., F.B.A., who was a team member of Hut 8 from its beginning, where his long tousled hair and worn corduroy trousers caused him to become known to Commander Winn, a frequent contact, as "Professor Corduroy." Four decades later, in 1981–1984, Hinsley published the official history of British Intelligence in World War II. In June 1996, when the writer brought the Tighe Report to Hinsley's attention, the quondam cryptanalyst, later President of St. John's College and Professor of the History of International Relations at Cambridge University, recalled how dismayed Hut 8 was to learn that B-Dienst was looking over the Admiralty's shoulder and that no one there was doing anything about it!

"We had a watch on to see if the Germans were reading Allied ciphers," he told the writer. "It was awkward for OIC and Bletchley Park to know the Germans were reading the Anglo-American Convoy Cipher from December to August." The responsible person for doing something about it was Paymaster Captain D. A. "Willie" Wilson, R.N., in charge of naval cipher security under the Director of the Signals Division, Admiralty. "Wilson was slow to conclude that the Germans were reading the cipher, for which he was criticized at the time and after the war." When he finally acknowledged the security breach, Wilson dawdled in replacing the compromised cipher. "His argument was that there was a large number of holders of the cipher spread all over the yard, that it couldn't be replaced partially, and that he couldn't replace it any faster than he was doing. Well, there was a certain amount of muttered criticism about the delay at Bletchley Park and at the OIC. The delay is an extraordinary story."

As for Tighe, unlike Wilson he probably was not "indoctrinated," that is, "in the know" about Ultra, "thus accounting for his naiveté." His report "was probably an attempt [by the Signals Division, Admiralty] to defend themselves, to cover-up and justify themselves." A temporary modification of the cipher was introduced, finally, in June, and the cipher was completely changed to a secure key in August 1943, after which there were no further German entries. With that closure the Allies won the cryptographic war.[14]

The paper victory did not mean, however, that Ultra was the one decisive factor either in the improvement of Allied fortunes at sea after June 1941 or in the pivotal defeat of the

U-boats to come in spring 1943, despite the "Ultra Myth's" persistence in claiming so.[15] Several features of Sigint (signals intelligence) work against that judgment. For one thing, there were frequent time delays between the interception of an Enigma transmission and its decryption. As we have seen, the average intervals in August, September, and October 1941 were fifty, forty-one, and twenty-six hours, respectively. Following the decryption of the Triton key in December 1942, the delays in decryption were frequently longer than those. When one reflects that a fast convoy might cover 240 nautical miles in a twenty-four-hour period and that U-boats might proceed between 320 and 370 nautical miles in the same period, it becomes evident that a much-delayed Ultra message might have little or no operational value.

Too, at some critical times when the Germans changed Enigma settings, GC&CS went completely blind so far as decryption was concerned (though it and the Tracking Room had other, less accurate resources to fall back on, as discussed below). Such was the case during the eleven-month drought following introduction of the fourth rotor. During the critical months January through May 1943 there were numerous failures of shorter duration, including ten days in January, seven days in February, the periods of 10–19 March, when the battle of SC.122/HX.229 was fought, and 26 April–5 May, when the protracted and definitive battle for Convoy ONS.5 was waged across 720 miles at sea (see chapters 4 through 7). And even when Triton decrypts were in hand, they were "not uncommonly" seventy-two hours old, making their operational value marginal. For all the above reasons, one has to look for another component reason for the Allies' post–June 1941 success in protecting merchant shipping.

Here Sir Harry Hinsley helps us and in so doing sets aside any pro-Sigint bias he might be expected to have. Though he does say that "The difference between what the U-boats now [post-June 1941] achieved over-all and what they might have achieved—and, indeed, expected to achieve—was due to the great improvement in the evasive routing of the convoys that took place when GC and CS began to read the naval Enigma," he stresses the fact that:

> For the reduction in actual shipping losses the main cause was a change in the Admiralty's policy. From 18 June it raised the minimum speed limit for independently routed ships from 13 to 15 knots, and there followed a dramatic decline in losses of "independents," from 120 ships in the three months April to June to 25 ships between the beginning of July and the end of September.[16]

Cryptanalyst and historian David Kahn agrees that Sigint was not the main cause for the reduction in shipping losses:

> . . . Intelligence did not always rule in the war against the U-boats. Other factors outweighed it. The July-August loss of tonnage fell to under a third of the May-June figure for reasons unrelated to B[letchley] P[ark]. More escorts were available and were accompanying convoys uninterruptedly across the Atlantic. The escorts' experience made them more efficient. The minimum speed of ships sailing independently was raised from 13 to 15 knots. Air cover was increased.[17]

It appears that all three factors examined above–loss of the U-boat aces, Allied signals intelligence, and improvements in the convoy system, especially the inclusion of 13–to–15-knot ships–had a cumulative effect in producing the turnaround of 1941; but that the last-named factor had the single most pronounced effect, as discussed below.

Whereas in World War I it took Great Britain nearly three years to institute a convoy system, thus finally stanching a trade hemorrhage that sorely threatened the island nation, in September 1939 she had in place detailed plans in the event of war for the immediate deployment of RN vessels to escort merchant ships in convoy. The first formation of ships in column sailed on 6 September. By the end of the first month of war, 900 ships had sailed in convoy without a loss, while thirty-nine Merchant Navy vessels that had been independently routed were sunk by U-boats. In the beginning there were few available escort ships—destroyers, frigates, sloops, and corvettes—that were equipped for anti-submarine warfare. The majority of destroyers were assigned to the Home Fleet for use against the Kriegsmarine's high seas fleet. Still, the Trade Division of the Admiralty was able in September 1939 to develop three major convoy routes that could be protected with the naval assets at hand:

1. OA and OB: Outward bound from Britain to North America and Africa
2. HX: Homeward bound to Britain from Halifax, Nova Scotia
3. SL: Homeward bound from Sierra Leone

During the first four months of the war, 5,756 individual ship sailings were made in convoy, suffering only four sinkings by U-boats. The German opportunities to attack the convoys were greatly improved in the following summer, however, by their not having to sortie any longer from Baltic and North Sea bases, which required a lengthy roundabout the north of Scotland before reaching the North Atlantic sea lanes. With the surrender of France to German ground forces in June 1940, Admiral Dönitz was able to base his boats on the Brittany peninsula and Western French coast directly abutting the Bay of Biscay and the Atlantic. There, at Brest, Lorient, St.-Nazaire, La Pallice, La Rochelle, and Bordeaux, the Organisation Todt erected bombproof U-boat shelters, some of them with steel-reinforced walls three meters thick and even stouter carapaces seven meters in depth.

Outside Lorient harbor, at Kernével, Dönitz established his headquarters, BdU, in a requisitioned chateau. Kptlt. Fritz-Julius Lemp, later of the ill-fated U–110, was the first commander to put in at Lorient, in U–30, on 7 July 1940. With establishment of the Biscay bases in close proximity to Allied shipping, not only that which moved east-west but also north-south convoys and independent shipping to and from Gibraltar and Freetown, and with replenishment and repair facilities readily available to the operational fleet, Dönitz effectively multiplied both his force and their time at sea by a factor of three.

In these circumstances, a year later Dönitz was able finally to institute full-scale a tactic that he had first conceived while commander of the submarine UB–*68* in the Mediterranean in 1918. Instead of individual operations against convoys and independents, he envisioned group operations led by a flotilla commander employing the new technology of radio telegraphy. Twenty-one years later, in May 1939, when a Rear Admiral in Hitler's Kriegsmarine and Führer der Uboote (FdU), Dönitz tested his concept in sea exercises, which proved the feasibility of radio-controlled mass attacks, what he called *die Rudeltaktik* (pack tactics, later known to the British as wolfpack operations).[18]

In the original theory, pack attacks would be directed by a Type IXB command boat at sea, but soon after war operations began, Dönitz abandoned that plan and established the principle of shore direction in its stead: At headquarters, it was thought, where contact could be maintained with every boat, and where intelligence was readily available, Dönitz and his operations staff could best command the formation of U-boat patrol lines (or "rakes") that would stand at right angles to convoy courses, with average spacings of 8 to 15 miles between boats, and vector them toward known or suspected targets.

First attempts at this battle management system in October and November 1939 were unsuccessful, in part because the U-boats were too few in number to form effective packs. Subsequent efforts in 1940 were little better in practice and result. By spring 1941, however, when the number of boats had increased and the high degree of coordination required by the management plan was more precisely fixed in the minds of U-boat Commanders, Dönitz launched the *Rudeltaktik* in earnest. The plan called for the first boat on a line that sighted a convoy to report its position, course, and speed to BdU by radio. That boat thereafter would not normally attack the convoy but rather shadow it, constantly updating its position and course as the contact-keeper.

From BdU, radio orders would direct the other boats in line to converge on the convoy and attack it in concentration at night on the surface, when the U-boats could take advantage of the darkness, of their low nap-of-the-water silhouettes, and of their high speed under diesel engine power. The strength of the *Rudeltaktik* was that it enabled U-boats to fall upon a convoy all together like a pack of wolves on a flock of sheep. Its weakness was that the high-frequency radio signals of both the shadowing boat and of BdU were vulnerable to interception, to radio direction-fixing, and, after May–June 1941, to decryption. But it was the system that Dönitz would stick to like paste up to and through the climactic events of May 1943.

Typically, a transatlantic convoy crossed 3,000 miles at sea in nineteen to twenty days westward, fifteen to eighteen eastward. The average number of ships sailing in each convoy by May 1940 was forty-six, and the forties range remained the rule until 1943, when the optimum convoy size was raised in number. Until May 1941, the U-boats operated east of 40°W longitude in the Western Approaches north and south of Ireland. It was possible for the RN to give adequate surface escort to that distance from bases in Britain, Northern Ireland, and Iceland.

When in May 1941, however, the U-boats moved farther to the west outside the escorts' radius of action and sank nine ships for 54,451 GRT from Convoy HX.126 in qu AJ (40°52′ to 41°36′W longitude), on the 20th/21st, the Admiralty decided that the time had come to provide complete transatlantic—what came to be called "end-to-end"—escort. Here the Royal Canadian Navy (RCN), then in the middle of a huge expansion, played a central role. An RCN escort group out of St. John's, Newfoundland, covered HX convoys as far as 35°W, where they were relieved by a British group from Iceland, which in turn was relieved by a U.K.-based group for the final leg from 20°W to the North Channel. The number of RN escorts rose from 108 in June 1941 to 134 in November. The number of RCN escorts in the western Atlantic similarly increased.[19] Also, beginning in September, U.S. Navy (hereafter USN) destroyers escorted Britain-bound convoys as far as a midocean meeting point (MOMP), or "chop" (Change of Operational Control) line, south of Iceland, where RN escorts took the guard. And by August the Germans were remarking on a higher efficiency of escorts on both the transatlantic and Gibraltar runs: "Not only had the numbers of escort vessels and aircraft risen, but their methods of keeping the U-boats at a distance had improved. Where a few months ago one U-boat had been adequate for shadowing, a whole group was now required."[20]

The Admiralty introduced oilers to enable the escorts, particularly short-legged destroyers whose fuel bunkers had been designed for close-in warfare in the North Sea and English Channel, to extend their range and stay with their convoys. Also, as earlier noted, in what historian J. David Brown has called one of the most important decisions taken by the Admiralty at this time, on 18 June 1941 the Trade Division required all ships with speeds of 13–15 knots, which previously had sailed independently, to form up with slower-moving convoys; only those ships whose speed exceeded 15 knots would be routed independently thereafter on the expectation that at that and higher speeds, those ships could evade U-boats, whose maximum sustained speeds were in the range of 17–18 knots. Whereas in the second quarter of the year 120 ships proceeding independently were lost to U-boats, during the second half of 1941 only 49 independents went down, because fewer independents were being sailed.[21]

All the while, the U-boats were not going unscathed. By 31 December 1941 sixty-seven boats had been sunk in the year, forty-five by RN ships, one by an RCN vessel, three by Allied submarines, five by mines, four (and another shared) by RAF aircraft, and the remainder by miscellaneous causes. Where in 1940, when there was a monthly average of 13–5 U-boats at sea, there was a yearly total of 22 U-boat casualties, for a monthly average loss of 1.8 percent, in 1941, when there was a monthly average of 25.5 boats at sea, there was a total of

67 casualties, for a monthly average loss of 5.5 percent. During the last quarter of 1941, one Atlantic boat was lost for every three ships in convoy sunk—an insupportably poor exchange rate. By any measure, at year's end the Allies were ruling the convoy lanes. The improvement in the performance of surface escorts was due to higher experience levels, better skill in the use of detection gear and weapons, tighter training programs, and closer coordination by voice radio with RAF Coastal Command aircraft—though it must be said that that Command had not yet come into its own as an antisubmarine force.

The principal weapon of the surface escort against a submerged U-boat was the depth charge, a canister of high explosive, first Amatol, then Minol, and finally, in the summer of 1942, Torpex—though Minol fillings continued in use through 1943. Torpex was a high-explosive mix of Cyclonite, TNT, and aluminum flakes. The standard Mark VII "heavy" D/C weighed 250 pounds, sank at 16 feet per second, and, when detonated by a present-to-depth hydrostatic fuse, caused the formation of a spherically shaped gas bubble with an initial temperature of about 3,000° Centigrade and, on the periphery of the bubble, a pressure pulse, or shock wave, equivalent to 50,000 atmospheres. The pressure pulse rose to peak level within a few milliseconds and moved through the water at the velocity of sound, its energy dissipating directly with the square of the distance traveled. Because of the greater density and incompressibility of water, the shock wave traveled farther and faster underwater than it did in an above-water explosion. Such a wave was considered able to fracture a U-boat's hull if initiated within 20-26 feet of it and to cause damage within 50 feet.

Surface evidence of the shock wave was given by a breaking of the water's top layer and a "dome" of spray. Evidence of the expanding gas bubble was provided by the familiar towering "plume" that broke through later.[22] An escort vessel both "fired" and "dropped" D/Cs, though the verb *fired* was normally used for both. Firing was done laterally by mortar "throwers," two to each side, port and starboard. The drops came by gravity off racks, or rails, at the stern. In 1941 and 1942 escort Captains used the throwers and rails in various combinations, usually in salvos of five, but by 1943 experience had shown that the most effective D/C attack was made in a "10 Pattern," with four fired and six dropped, five set to explode above the target and five below. In order, the forward throwers fired first, then the aft throwers, after which six D/Cs were rolled off the stern. The resulting pattern formed a fore-to-aft oval.[23]

In December 1942 a Mark X "One Ton" D/C was distributed, usually one to a ship. Filled with a 2,000-pound charge, and theoretically the equivalent of a 10 Pattern, the Mark X was designed to reach deep-diving boats. It was housed in a ten-foot-long cylinder and fired by cordite charge from a torpedo tube. Escorts had still other weapons available to them, including 4-inch deck guns and Oerlikon anti-aircraft guns that, on several occasions, at maximum depression, were used with effect against surfaced boats. A weapon of last resort was ramming and, though this action usually brought damage to the escort's bows, requiring seven to eight weeks to repair, by May 1943 about twenty-four boats had been dispatched by this means.[24]

Detection of a submerged U-boat, whose principal advantage was underwater stealth, was made possible by the development between the wars of a sound-ranging device called asdic (an acronym that grew out of Anti-Submarine Division, the Admiralty department that initiated the system). An asdic apparatus, housed in a dome on the underside of a vessel's hull, sent out sound waves in pulses that, when they struck an undersea object such as a U-boat, returned a pulse echo that gave the object's bearing and range, though not (before 1943) its depth. When the pulses bounced off a U-boat's hull they emitted within the boat a loud, piercing *PING-ping!* A similar system in the U.S. Navy was called Sonar (*So*und *Na*vigation and *Ra*nging), a name later adopted by the RN.

Early wartime Types 123 through 129 had serious limitations, including short range of effectiveness, about 1,300 yards

(1.2 kilometers) in good sea conditions, and inutility above vessel speed of around 15 knots. Range and accuracy improved in 1942 with the introduction of the Types 144/145 series, and depth determination became possible with the Type 147 in 1943, but upgrading in the fleet was slow and erratic: in 1944 58 percent of British corvettes still mounted old equipment. Another failing of early asdic was its inability to hold a target during the final 200 yards of an attack approach, when a U-boat could use the blind zone for evasive maneuvers. This problem would be met later by the development of thrown-ahead weapons such as the "Hedgehog," a bank of twenty-four contact-fused projectiles with Torpex warheads equivalent to 50 pounds of TNT fired from mortar spigots to form ahead of the attacking ship a circle 120 feet across or an ellipse 120 feet by 140 feet. The Hedgehog had teething troubles well into the summer of 1943.

Again, the early asdic series could not track very deep-diving boats. Diving beneath the D/C spread—a submerged boat could alter depth at the rate of one and a half feet per second—was, of course, another defense of boats that were being "pinged." Numerous efforts were made by the British to determine the maximum diving depth of the VIIC, the most numerous U-boat type. In 1942 RN submariners tested the captured U–570 (renamed H.M.S. *Graph*) and found that her thick hull survived the atmospheres of pressure at 200 meters (656 feet). The deepest measurement taken by asdic during the war was 238 meters (780 feet). Günter Hessler, who commanded U–107 until November 1941, then served on Dönitz's BdU staff, wrote after the war that by the summer of 1942 new Type VIICs had been strengthened to a standard of 200 meters, "which in practice meant that in an emergency they could go down to 300 metres without harm."[25]

From interrogations of U-boat prisoners the British learned that most Commanders considered 200 meters the deepest safe depth when under attack, but that "good evidence" indicated that in the summer of 1943 one boat involuntarily dived to 340 meters (1,115 feet) without breaking up.[26] Interesting is the finding that as late as early 1943 the maximum depth setting for British D/Cs was 550 feet. In June of that year both the D/C and asdic recorder settings would be readjusted to 750 feet.[27]

Another defense against asdic was discovered by U-boats that operated in warm waters, such as those around Freetown, where temperature gradients and heavy density layers refracted the asdic sound beam. Boats in those climes frequently carried bathythermographs and thermometers to measure density and temperature. Efforts were made for a time to cover U-boat hulls with sound-absorbing (anechoic) coatings, such as layers of synthetic rubber, but these tended to separate from the hulls underwater. After 1943, the *Pillenwerfer* decoy that mimicked a U-boat's asdic signature came into use. Called by the British SBT, for "submarine bubble target," the decoy consisted of a canister containing metallic calcium-zinc "pills" that on contact with sea water created hydrogen bubbles. These bubbles returned an echo to asdic pulses that represented the dimensions of a U-boat. The canister was ejected through a six-inch-diameter tube (*"Rohr 6"* in Type VIICs) that projected through the pressure hull in the maneuvering room. The device remained suspended at a depth of about 30 meters (98 feet), and its bubble screen lasted for 15–20 minutes. Because it did not move laterally, the asdic operator was usually not fooled by it. More sophisticated decoys that did move were introduced later in the war.[28]

All the while, the best way to defeat asdic was to employ the night surface attack, whether delivered singly or in a pack, since asdic was effectively blind to surface targets. By this means Admiral Dönitz neutralized the early advantage that asdic had given the British, and he might thereby have earned an advantage for himself had not the British and Americans presented him with two other *shipborne* electronic marvels: high-frequency (radio) direction-finding (HF/DF, or "Huff-Duff") and, more widely fitted, radar.

By use of a transformer circuit called a radiogoniometer, HF/DF receivers could determine the direction from which a radio signal was transmitted. Both Britain and the United

States had ground-based HF/DF stations in operation during the early years of the war, and these took bearings around the clock on U-boat radio transmissions. By 1942 British DF receivers and antennas covered the North Atlantic sea lanes at listening posts ranging from the Shetlands around to Land's End; south to Gibralter, Ascension, Freetown, and Cape Town; and west to Iceland, Newfoundland, and Bermuda.

All of the bearings taken by these stations were communicated to the main station at Scarborough, England, and thence to the OIC Tracking Room at the Admiralty, where retired Lt.-Cmdr. Peter Kemp, R.N., headed a plotting team of never more than seven men and women who graphically presented the bearings taken on a particular boat's transmitter by black strings drawn across a chart of the North Atlantic. Where the strings from three or more stations converged, that, it was estimated, marked the position of the U-boat. With as many as six bearings establishing the intersection, or "cut," it was thought that a boat could be "fixed" within 25 nautical miles. Until naval Enigma gave more precise data in June 1941, this was the most reliable information on U-boats at sea that the OIC possessed, and convoys were vectored around estimated U-boat positions on the strength of DF intelligence.[29] The network would play a critical role again during the Triton blackout of February–December 1942.

In the United States the USN had two similar HF/DF networks at work in 1942, one on the Pacific coast to monitor Japanese traffic, and another of seven stations that dotted the eastern seaboard from Winter Harbor, Maine, to San Juan, Puerto Rico. Analysis of U-boat transmission bearings received by the eastern net was done in the Atlantic Section, Intelligence Center (Op–20-G, later F–21), a clone of the OIC Tracking Room in the Navy Department (Main Navy) at Washington, D.C. Exchanges of data took place freely between the two rooms, and they with a similar Canadian Navy room at Ottawa. Early USN DF technology lagged behind that of the British, and the bearing computation experience of operators was so small that USN fixes were often qualified as being within 200 miles of the U-boat targeted.[30] An intense training program improved the performance of the operators. And the equipment deficit was corrected by the gift of two superior systems, one British and one French. In the spring of 1941, an Army-Navy technical mission to England returned with a complete Marconi-Adcock HF/DF installation, which the naval members of the mission judged to be "far ahead of us in these developments."[31] And an even more advanced system, antedating that of the British, instantaneous, automatic-indicating HF/DF, invented by French engineer Henri Busignies and smuggled out of German-occupied France, made its way, along with the inventor, to the United States in December 1940, where it was reconstructed by the International Telephone and Telegraph Corporation (ITT) and first supplied in prototype models to the USN net in the fall of 1941. Busignies's system became the basis for future U.S. development in the field.[32]

There were problems with the usefulness of shore-based HF/DF that were shared with Ultra, namely, that (a) they gave the Allies information at too great a distance for tactical attack purposes, and with a wide margin for inaccuracy since, many more times than not, they gave no indication of the direction in which a targeted U-boat was proceeding; and (b) they suffered time lags of collating and plotting or of decryption that allowed a U-boat Commander to nip out of the area where he had been tagged. What was needed, the RN decided early on, was shipborne HF/DF equipment that permitted *immediate* pursuit at sea of a *close-by* target.

The RN engineers realized the difficulty of reducing an installation to weight and size that would fit on a small escort vessel. So did the engineers of the German Navy, who particularly thought that the antenna required for HF/DF reception was far too large to be fitted to an escort vessel, such as a destroyer or frigate. Lacking apparently the imagination to conceive the impossible, Dönitz's technical advisors persisted in that view long after B-Dienst intelligence, visual observation, and U-boat experience had amply demonstrated otherwise, and, in fact, they remained obdurate on the point up to the end of the war, always explaining Allied detection successes as the work of radar.[33]

The British resolved the weight and size problem in 1940, when they mounted a prototype FH 1 set and antenna on the destroyer H.M.S. *Hesperus* in March of that year. Though the FH 1's performance was disappointing, the experiment proved that seaborne installations were possible. An improved FH 3 set, which gave an aural presentation of target data (requiring earphones) was fitted to two fleet destroyers, H.M.S. *Gurkha* and *Lance,* in July 1941. And in October of the same year, an FH 4 set with visual presentation on a cathode ray tube, having met all test expectations, went into escort service on board the ex-American four-stack destroyer H.M.S. *Leamington,* which accompanied the troop convoy WS.107 to Madagascar in March 1942.

While a single HF/DF set could detect the azimuth bearing of a U-boat transmitting to base or to another boat on a high-frequency wave band, and even determine from the ground wave whether it was near or far (25–30 nautical miles being its maximum range), the crosscut bearing provided by a second HF/DF-equipped escort gave a fairly exact fix, and an escort could be detached to pursue the fix, attack the surfaced U-boat, drive it off, or force it to submerge, after which asdic would be employed. This action would have a particular value if the transmitting boat was a shadower, since underwater its observations and communications were greatly limited. Thus, seaborne detection made possible aggressive tactical operations that were not possible with shore-based detection. Too, HF/DF at sea provided data that even shipborne radar could not deliver, since HF/DF's range was about 25 miles while Type 271 radar's on a surfaced, trimmed-down U-boat was only 3,000–5,000 meters, depending on sea conditions. Production of HF/DF equipment was slow, however, owing to radar's greater popularity as an "active" detection system. The number of sets at sea on RN and RCN escorts in 1942 was very small, but by spring 1943 at least two escorts with each convoy had either FH 3 or FH 4 equipment.

In the United States, production of a shipborne system

called DAQ, based on the Busignies design, trailed the British work by many months. Though a USN decision was taken in March 1942 to build sets for ships, manufacturing delays prevented deployment until 1943. Even midway into that year, the first successful U.S. anti-U-boat attack mounted by an American HF/DF-equipped ship, the escort carrier U.S.S. *Bogue* (CVE–9), on 22 May 1943, was based on bearings taken by a British set just recently installed at Liverpool. The attack, made by *Bogue*'s TBF–1 Avenger aircraft, resulted in the surrender and scuttling of U–*569* (Ober. Hans Johannsen). In his report on the action, Carrier Captain and Commander, Sixth Escort Group, Giles E. Short, U.S.N., stated:

> From the time the BOGUE left Belfast a continuous watch had been maintained on the newly installed HF/DF. Three radiomen from the BOGUE manned this equipment under the supervision of Sub-Lieutenant J. B. Elton, R.N.V.R., who had been assigned . . . to assist on this trip. The HF/DF equipment proved invaluable. . . . An HF/DF bearing was directly responsible for the attack on the sub-marine which surrendered. . . . Without doubt the . . . transmission at 1727Z was made by the U-Boat and wrote its death warrant.[34]

The second successful HF/DF-directed U.S. attack, by aircraft from the escort carrier U.S.S. *Card,* would not come until August 1943, well after the U-boat war had been decided. Meanwhile, from June 1942 through May 1943, British HF/DF-equipped escorts employed their new equipment with great effect, chasing down bearings unknowingly supplied by the loquacious German boats and attacking their surprised crews. Admiral Dönitz was fully aware that the British were attempting to monitor his and the U-boats' communications from shore-based stations, and though he was advised by Naval Staff engineers that no DF bearings of any accuracy could be acquired from high-frequency signals, he warily restricted radio use by his boats.[35] For necessary traffic such as position updates, convoy sightings, and damage reports he had the engineers devise *Kurzsignale* (short signals), letter codes (by which, for example, a damage and position report could be made using only four letters of the alphabet), rapid frequency changes, and electronically compressed messages that went out in bursts, or "squirts." These attempts to elude the shipborne HF/DF receivers generally failed, and the message content in its various forms was successfully unscrambled by the interception stations and GC&CS.

Prior to a convoy engagement, the attacking "wolfpack" patrol line normally observed radio silence, except that on some occasions (see the *Fink* line boats in chapters 4 and 5) the boats gave noon or evening position reports in great proliferation. Once the shadower boat reported a sighting, however, that boat's signals to base became frequent; and with the battle joined, other boats soon joined in the chatter: When on 4–9 February 1943 U-boat Groups *Landsknecht* and *Haudegen* attacked Convoy SC.118, the U-boats made 108 radio transmissions in a period of seventy-two hours, and one boat alone, U–*402*, sent forty-one signals during the four-day battle, all of which were detected by shipborne HF/DF.[36]

Although Dönitz was prepared to take some risks of DF detection with his high-volume command and control communications net, he never realized during the war how thoroughly his boats at sea were being exposed by that system; just as, of course, he never knew that his own "rudder commands from the beach" were being read by GC&CS and Rodger Winn. Because it brilliantly exploited the German reliance on radio control, Britain's mostly unheralded shipborne HF/DF deserves to be recognized as one of the principal tools employed by the Allies against the U-boats up to May 1943—hence its extended treatment here—and it would play a particularly significant role in the two May battles for transatlantic Convoys ONS.5 and SC.130 (described in chapters 4, 5, 6, 7, and 10).

During the crossing of ONS.5 the destroyer H.M.S. *Duncan* (Senior Officer Escort Group B7, Commander Peter Gretton), which was equipped with FH 4, counted 107 DF contacts on U-boats before having to leave the convoy because of fuel depletion. The frigate H.M.S. *Tay,* equipped with FH3, counted 135 transmission intercepts, many of them shared as cross-cuts with *Duncan* before 3 May, when the latter withdrew.[37]The same two escorts, again under Gretton, accompanied SC.130 later in the month, when the surface escorts had excellent air cover, and collected 104 DF bearings between them. Later, Gretton described how *Duncan* and Tay were "able to get fixes on U-boats transmitting near us with great accuracy and to send aircraft quickly after them."[38] In his analysis of the battle from the other side of the hill, Admiral Dönitz, of course, attributed the British success to radar:

> These attacks could only be attributed to a very good radar location device which enables the aircraft to detect the boat above the clouds even, and then to make a surprise attack from the clouds. The amazing thing is that apparently at the time only 1 to 2 machines [aircraft] in all were escorting the convoy, according to intercept messages of aircraft operating. Each machine, however, detected during the whole day one boat more frequently than every quarter-hour, from which it must be concluded that the enemy's radar hardly missed a boat.[39]

German historian Jürgen Rohwer has concluded: "If we analyze the great convoy battles between June 1942 and May 1943 . . . the remarkable fact is that the outcome of the operation always depended decisively on the efficient use of HF/DF."[40] Although effective use of radar detection by escort ships and aircraft was also progressing from strength to strength during that same period, and while granting that it was the new shipborne centimetric radar operated by the escorts of ONS.5 on the fogbound night of 5/6 May 1943 that made possible that most pivotal Allied victory in the U-boat war (chapters 6 and 7), still, in normal visibility conditions, more U-boats in the convoy battles of 1942–1943 were first detected by HF/DF than were by radar.[41]

What the British at this time called RDF (for Radio Direction Finding, which was a deliberate cover) and what the

Americans called Radar (for *Ra*dio *D*etection *A*nd *R*anging), an acronym coined by USN Lieutenant Commanders Samuel M. Tucker and F. R. Furth, is an electronic tool understandable to modern readers familiar with its use in air traffic control, weather forecasting, and police speed guns. Instead of passively receiving radio signals, as in HF/DF, a radar set actively generates a stream of short radio energy pulses that, once transmitted through an antenna, return echoes from any physical objects the stream encounters—objects as solid as an airplane and as gossamer as a cloud. The presence of these objects is displayed on a cathode ray tube (CRT) in such a way that the radar operator can determine mass, bearing, and range.

The technology was co-invented in 1934–35 by the British (Scottish-born) engineer Robert Watson Watt, superintendent of the Radio Department of the National Physical Laboratory near the Berkshire town of Slough, and by American engineers, notably Robert Morris Page, Albert Taylor, and Leo Young, at the Naval Research Laboratory at Anacostia in Washington, D.C. Thanks to the original research of Watson Watt, who is customarily called the "father" of radar, British engineers were able to erect the famous Chain Home radar network that, by providing range, course, and altitude of incoming Luftwaffe bombers and fighters, helped the RAF to win the Battle of Britain in 1940.

Quickly miniaturized, RDF sets were installed in RN escort vessels beginning in fall 1940. This first equipment, Type 286 (1.5 meter wavelength), could obtain echoes on a trimmed-down U-boat at no more than 1,000 meters; hence, except in moonless nights or in fog, it was frequently outperformed by a human lookout. By March 1941 about ninety escorts were so equipped. In the same month and year Type 271 (10-centimeter, or S-band) radar was fitted to an escort, the corvette H.M.S. *Orchis*. When 271 entered general service with the escort fleet in 1941–42, U-boat detection range jumped to 3,000–5,000 meters. By May 1942, 271 was mounted on 236 RN ships of all categories.

The 271 was made possible by a remarkable device called

the resonant multi-cavity magnetron valve. The invention of two British physicists at the University of Birmingham, John Randall and Henry Boot, the cavity magnetron's central feature was a cathode and anode structure built into a block of copper through which either six or eight symmetrical holes were bored. The high-frequency radio oscillations produced by the device enabled a radar apparatus to operate on a wavelength of 9.7 centimeters–rounded out in popular usage to "10-centimeter," or "centimetric" radar.[42] This represented an extraordinary advance in power, range, and accuracy over the previous "metric" radar, and constituted, in the words of Britain's most accomplished air and naval operations research scientist, physicist Patrick M. S. Blackett, "one of the most decisive technical developments made during the war."[43]

Its narrow horizontal beam width enabled a single escort to find, fix, and hold a nearby U-boat on the surface at night and in fog. And from its first operational use until the fall of 1943, its beam was not detectable by any German search receiver then at sea. A U-boat Commander proceeding on the surface at night near a convoy escort had no way of knowing that he was being "painted." But in the plot, or operations room, of the nearby escort, that U-boat was exposed starkly on the 271's plan position indicator (PPI), where a sweeping radial line from the center of the circular CRT screen rotated in synchronization with an outside antenna and, each time it passed the U-boat's position, displayed it as a bright phosphorus-lit spot.

In September 1940, a seven-member British Technical and Scientific Mission to the United States, headed by physicist Henry Tizard, arrived in Washington, D.C., with a black solicitor's box containing, among other scientific objects and blueprints, a hand-sized eight-cavity magnetron. The gift was not entirely magnanimous: the British knew that to win their war they would need American technological assistance and industrial capacity. Members of Tizard's mission, which was conducted at the height of the Battle of Britain, were mindful, too, that their homeland might soon be invaded; if the war was lost in the Old World, this means for continuing the fight would be in the hands of the New.

Grateful U.S. radar specialists acknowledged that the gift put them two years ahead of the curve, and James Phinney Baxter III, official historian of the U.S. Office of Scientific Research and Development, was moved to write in 1947, "When the members of the Tizard Mission brought [a cavity magnetron] to America in 1940, they carried the most valuable cargo ever brought to our shores."[44] The encomium should not be accepted uncritically to mean that centimetric radar alone, or even principally, won the war at sea. By itself it was not a war-winner, though one could certainly say it was a *battle* winner, as in the final stage of the surface battle for Convoy ONS.5 (chapter 7), where centimetric radar was the triumphant technology. In the regular structure of surface engagements between escort vessels and U-boats, centimetric radar fell into place as one of five technological innovations that, taken together, swept the field. The first four were, in the order in which they were employed: (1) HF/DF; (2) radar; (3) hydrophone effect (using asdic to listen for underwater noise such as cavitation from a U-boat's propellers); and (4) asdic echo contact. (Close in, one must not discount the Mark I eyeball.) The fifth innovation was TBS (Talk Between Ships), an American-developed very high frequency (VHF) voice radio-telephone (R/T) system, introduced in early 1941 and universally fitted on escorts a year later. At low power and short range it was immune to DFing. TBS enabled an escort commander to give instantaneous direction to the movement of his ships and to converse with overhead air cover. It also enabled the individual surface escorts to coordinate attack maneuvers between and among themselves. It is clear that by the date of the May 1943 battles, an Atlantic escort was an electronics platform of daunting authority.

RAF Coastal Command began the war with a fleet of Avro Ansons (301), Lockheed Hudsons (53), Vickers Vildebeests (30), Short Sunderlands (27), Saro Londons (17), and Supermarine Stranraers (9). The most numerous aircraft, the

Anson "Annies," which entered RAF service in 1936, were obsolescent, and by the close of 1941 had been replaced by Wellingtons, Halifaxes, Whitneys, and other advanced designs; so, too, the Vildebeests, Londons, and Stranraers were struck off the inventory. The Hudsons, an American passenger plane refitted as a bomber, continued to be purchased and used in large numbers.

But the principal survivors among the original list, which in fact soldiered on to the end of the war, were the Sunderland flying boats. Admirably equipped for long-range antisubmarine patrols, the "Queens," as air crews called them (U-boat crews, noting their languorous flight maneuvers, called them *müde Bienen,* "tired bees"), would score the second-highest U-boat tally of the war. Third in ranking would be the Vickers Wellington, a two-engine bomber never designed for maritime operations, but greatly effective in the Bay of Biscay (see chapter 8). Two American designs that came on the scene in 1941 and performed well were the Boeing B–17 Flying Fortress, a four-engine heavy bomber, and the Consolidated PBY–5 and PBY–5A (amphibian) Catalina twin-engine flying boat.

The overall favorite aircraft in Coastal Command and the most successful sighter and destroyer of U-boats was the four-engine Consolidated B–24 Liberator heavy bomber. Though somewhat harder to handle, more demanding in maintenance time, and certainly more drafty than the Fortress, the Liberator was esteemed for its range. In a V.L.R. (for Very Long Range) modification, where weight reduction was achieved by removing self-sealing liners (if present) to the fuel tanks, most of the protective armor plating, the turbo-superchargers, and the belly gun turret, the Liberator had a low-altitude operational range of 2,300 nautical miles at an economical 150 knots, while carrying, on takeoff, 2,000 gallons of high-octane fuel and eight 250-pound depth charges (gravity bombs with hydrostatic fuses). This was the aircraft that would give overhead coverage to threatened convoys in distant midocean lanes, force shadowing U-boats to submerge (which until May 1943 they uniformly did on sighting a reconnaissance bomber), and thus retard their speed, maneuverability and visibility, hence, their potential for organizing packs. This was the aircraft that, operating from both shores of the Atlantic, would eventually plug the Air Gap between Iceland and Newfoundland in May 1943–assisted by newly introduced carrier-borne aircraft.

No. 120 Squadron received the first Mark I Liberators in June 1941 and in September began flying nine of them southwestward from bases in Northern Ireland and Iceland to their Prudent Limit of Endurance (PLE), governed by fuel remaining. But the numbers of these aircraft in Coastal remained depressingly few, as American Admiral Ernest J. King, Commander in Chief, United States Navy (after 30 December 1941), hoarded most Navy-assigned Liberators (designated PB4Y-1) for the Pacific theater, while almost all of the RAF-assigned Liberators that made it to the U.K. were claimed by Bomber Command. By September 1942 Coastal still had only one squadron (No. 120) containing V.L.R. Mark Is, six in number. The V.L.R.s were "being allowed to die out," Coastal complained to the Under-Secretary for Air. The squadron list also included two Mark IIs (range 1,800 miles) and three Mark IIIs (1,680 miles). Other squadrons had PBY-5 Catalinas (1,840 miles) and PBY-5As (1,600 miles), but the V.L.R. was the most desperately needed long-distance performer. (There were none in Newfoundland, Canada, Gibraltar, or West Africa.) And Coastal's Atlantic operations were being denuded of other essential resources, including, between October 1941 and January 1942, 166 air crews and whole squadrons of Catalinas shipped to overseas bases.

Penetration by GC&CS of the German naval cipher and the development of a fairly accurate plot in the OIC Tracking Room made it possible, on 9 May 1941, for the Admiralty to draw a distinction between threatened and nonthreatened convoys. Coastal thereafter concentrated its forces on threatened convoys, thus making more efficient use of its air assets, but without V.L.R. aircraft, sorties directed to threatened convoys outside a radius of 450 miles from air bases could not be sustained beyond a short period of time, and Coastal began to worry about "the lavish expenditure of engine hours in order to get, at most, two or three hours with the [threatened] convoy."

Even on as late a date as February 1943, when Air Marshal Sir John Slessor took over as Air Officer Commanding-in-Chief (AOC-in-C), Coastal Command, No. 120 still remained the lone operating V.L.R. squadron. Based at Aldergrove in Northern Ireland with a detachment at Reykjavik, Iceland, it then counted among its assets five Mark Is and twelve Mark IIIAs modified to V.L.R. requirements. A new squadron with modified Mark IIIAs was forming at Thorney Island, near the Isle of Wight on the southern coast of England, but it was not yet operational; neither was No. 502 at nearby Holmsley South, which was awaiting V.L.R.-modified Halifax IIs. And still, by Admiral King's decision, there were no Liberators in Newfoundland. When Convoys SC.122/HX.229 were pummeled in the following month, President Franklin D. Roosevelt pointedly asked King where all the Navy Liberators had been.

That more of the Liberators then in the U.K. had not been allotted to ASW work was owed to the fixation of RAF Air Staff (abetted by Churchill) on night bombing of Germany. Contention between Coastal and Bomber Commands over the question of which targets, U-boats or factories, would more effectively create a matériel advantage for the Allies' cross-Channel invasion of the Continent simmered all through the first six months of 1943. The doctrinal dispute, which, particularly in March of that year, involved heavy-handed wrestling over bomber allotments, extended to the question, Was the U-boat force better destroyed at sea (Coastal) or at its construction and assembly yards (Bomber)?

Historians who incline to the Coastal position in that debate can only wonder how much earlier and more thoroughly the U-boat threat might have been brought to an end had the majority of V.L.R. Liberators not been concentrated on land warfare, where postwar analysis showed that overall German war production had not been substantially reduced by Allied bombing and that "de-housed" civilians—a Bomber Command term—had not faltered in morale. In a recent book, Clay Blair writes: "A number of studies would show that a Coastal Command ASW force of merely a hundred B–24S could well have decisively crushed the U-boat peril in the summer of 1941, sparing the Allies the terrible shipping losses in the years ahead." That might be pitching it a little high, since the essential improvements in attack procedures described in the following chapter were not all in place during 1941, but the point is well taken.

A smaller number than a hundred V.L.R. bombers is proposed as sufficient in 1942–1943, when Coastal attacks were far more lethal than before, by a historian of the maritime air war, Alfred Price. He holds that three squadrons, comprising about forty aircraft, "would have gone—and later did go—a considerable way towards nullifying the threat to convoys in mid-Atlantic." And the transfer of that number to Coastal from Bomber Command would not have appreciably weakened the bombing offensive over Germany. After all, Price points out, many times Bomber Command was losing that number of bombers in a single night.[45]

By the end of 1942 none of Coastal's aircraft was equipped with centimetric radar. Not until February 1943, after resolution of numerous technical problems and intense competition between Coastal and Bomber Command for the equipment, was the Telecommunications Research Establishment (T.R.E.), of the Ministry of Aircraft Production, at Malvern in Hereford and Worcester (after May 1942), able to fit ASV (Air to Surface Vessel) Mark III 10-centimeter radar to Coastal Liberators, Wellingtons, Sunderlands, and other reconnaissance bombers. In the meantime, since 1940, Coastal aircraft operated with metric (1.5 meter) ASV Mark II equipment, which was unsatisfactory for several reasons: limited range, approximately 10 miles maximum; unclear returns because of sea clutter; a hard-to-read light-bar graph display; poor construction resulting in numerous failures and difficult servicing; chronic shortage of parts; and poor training of operators.[46]

When in December 1941 Coastal Command Headquarters at Northwood in Middlesex reflected on the maritime air war to date, it could count fewer than a handful of kills and one capture, most of them shared with surface vessels. A force that was projected from the outset to have an offensive, not defensive, purpose, as yet Coastal was not meeting its mark. At fault was not a lack of commitment. Coastal had responsibilities other than the anti-submarine war, for example, protection of the United Kingdom's coastal waters and destruction of enemy shipping, but by 1941 its main effort was clearly directed at the U-boats. Kills had not materialized in the expected number because of aircraft shortages, particularly in the long-range category, inadequate search tactics, poorly executed attack procedures, and the above-mentioned radar deficiencies, but since May 1941 Coastal air was performing at least one indisputable service by concentrating "scarecrow" patrols over threatened convoys, while leaving unthreatened convoys on their own.

Aircraft shortages would be made up gradually as Prime Minister Churchill's cabinet became more attuned to the gravity of the Atlantic struggle, Churchill saying that what was most needed were new air tactics and *time* to train.[47] The latter would be provided by a totally unexpected *coup de main* that led to a diminution of U-boat operations in the convoy lanes. The former would be provided not, as might be expected, by an increase in hardware, by astute command judgment and leadership, or even by air crew proficiency and gallantry, though each of these factors was an essential precondition. The improvement would come from a band of civilian physicists, mathematicians, and other academics, "Boffins" as they came to be called—"gentlemen in grey flannel bags"—who took on a myriad of complex search and attack problems and, to the astonishment of the uniformed service, solved them. But first, the events of 7 December 1941 and following.

First Charge
To Defend or to Hunt?

Probably the anti-submarine campaign in 1943 was waged under closer scientific control than any other campaign in the history of the British Armed Forces.

PROFESSOR PATRICK M. S. BLACKETT

Gaily the backroom boys
Peddling their gruesome toys,
Come in and make a noise,
Oozing with science!
Humbly their aid we've sought;
Without them we're as nought,
For modern wars are fought
By such alliance.

ANTI-SUBMARINE WARFARE
DIVISION NAVAL STAFF, ADMIRALTY

The defeat of the U-boat must remain a first charge on the resources of the United Nations.

THE CASABLANCA CONFERENCE

The Japanese attack on Pearl Harbor caught Hitler and Dönitz just as much by surprise as it did the Americans. Dönitz reacted swiftly when on 9 December Hitler lifted all previous restrictions on attacks against both USN warships and merchant vessels under U.S. flag. His Commanders had long bridled under those restrictions, since U.S. destroyers had been escorting Britain-bound convoys as far as Iceland,

and it seemed to Dönitz that the Americans had long been belligerents in everything but name. Not surprisingly, there had been several incidents involving U-boats and USN vessels, including the sinking of the destroyer U.S.S. *Reuben James* by U–552 (Kptlt. Erich Topp) on 31 October 1941. Unknown to Dönitz, another Admiral, Ernest J. King, then Commander in Chief Atlantic Fleet (CINCLANT), was also itching to shake off the fetters of formal nonbelligerency.

When war between the two nations came formally on 11 December, King pulled all his destroyers home to the U.S. Atlantic seaboard expressly to defend it against the U-boats, stating that, "The imminent probability of submarine attack in that area, and the weakness of our coastal defense force, make it essential that the maximum practicable number of our destroyers be based at home bases."[1] The move seemed all the more sensible since U-boat activity had slackened in the east-west convoy lanes, Dönitz having been compelled by the Naval Staff in Berlin to withdraw boats from those waters for stations off Gibraltar to attack Mediterranean-bound supply transports during the British winter offensive against General Erwin Rommel's *Afrika-Korps.*

Dönitz was pleased to meet King's expectations. He immediately requested that twelve boats be made available for an operation along the North American coast, but Naval Staff allowed him only six, of which one, the newly commissioned U–128, had to be withdrawn because of mechanical problems. The other five were U–123, Type IXB (Kptlt. Reinhard Hardegen), U–125, IXB (Kptlt. Ulrich Folkers), and U–66, IXC (Korv. Kapt. Richard Zapp), which were to form *Gruppe Hardegen* for attacks in U.S. waters; and U–109, IXB (Kptlt. Heinrich Bleichrodt) and U–130, IXC (Korv. Kapt. Ernst Kals), which were to form *Gruppe Bleichrodt* for attacks southeast of Halifax and in Cabot Strait off Cape Breton Island. To their joint operation Dönitz gave the code-name *Paukenschlag*–"beat on a kettledrum"–or "Drumbeat." What was meant here was not "drumroll," as some would have it, but a single percussion of a timpani stick on the stretched head of a brassbarreled kettledrum; a sudden blow–*einen kräf-*

tigen Paukenschlag–since, as Hardegen, Commander of U-123, insisted to the writer, the aim was to deliver a simultaneous surprise attack on a given day, later signaled to be 13 January. Though many waves of additional U-boats were to follow the first five to North America, their latter operations were not called *Paukenschlag*. None of the original five boats would make their assigned positions by the 13th, but, two days before the deadline, U-123 sank the 9,076-GRT British freighter *Cyclops* 300 miles east of Cape Cod, effectively beginning the campaign.

News of the Drumbeat fleet's coming was flashed by Rodger Winn to the U.S. Navy Department (Main Navy) in Washington, D.C. From there the Tracking Room's U-boat position estimates were sent, day by day, to the appropriate USN eastern seaboard defense commands.[2] The sinking of *Cyclops* on the 11th was all the confirmation anyone required. But Hardegen gave further notice of his coming, sinking the 9,577-GRT former Norwegian motor tanker *Norness* 60 miles southeast of Montauk Point, Long Island, on the night of the 14th.

Twenty-one of the destroyers Admiral King had brought home to defend U.S. coastal waters were stationed at ports that bracketed Hardegen's approach, from Casco Bay, Maine, in the north to Norfolk, Virginia, in the south. All were battle-ready. Four other destroyers in the same districts were ready "only in an emergency." But no emergency was declared. Nor were the ready-category destroyers deployed by Admiral King or anyone else to meet the invasion. By this date, effective 30 December 1941, King was Commander-in-Chief, United States Fleet (COMINCH), with headquarters at Main Navy, but he maintained direct personal command over all anti-submarine warfare (ASW), requiring the various Atlantic commands in the U.S. Strategic Area to clear all such operations through him.[3]

As it happened, by King's order or compliance, most of the destroyers that he had assembled on the seaboard to defend against "submarine attack in that area" were sent off or held in port for other missions instead.[4] Even when, at 10:00

P.M. Eastern Time on the 15th, Hardegen stood at the Ambrose Channel Lightship station marking the entrance to New York Harbor (which he had reached in 22 days of transit, 98 percent of the distance on the surface), with the tip of Sandy Hook, New Jersey, to his port and Coney Island to starboard, none of the seven ready-status destroyers in the harbor that night–U.S.S. *Gwin, Mayrant, Monssen, Rowan, Trippe, Roe,* and *Wainwright*–sallied forth to meet him. Hardegen then leisurely withdrew and sank the 6,800-GRT British tanker *Coimbra* on his way out of the harbor approaches. The worst was yet to come.

For three weeks Hardegen and the other two boats in his group savaged Allied independently routed shipping along the East Coast as far south as Cape Hatteras and into the deeper waters of the U.S. Strategic Area. They were joined there eventually by the two Gruppe Bleichrodt boats, which, harried by Canadian destroyers and aircraft and impeded by freezing weather, made revolutions south to friendlier U.S. waters where coastwise shipping was steaming without surface or air escort, advancing along the buoys in straight line ahead, as though in peacetime, and mercilessly outlined by shore lights. Not only were buoy lights and lighthouses undimmed, but coastal communities, amusement parks, and beach resorts were still brilliantly lit, providing a luminous backdrop to merchant ship silhouettes as they passed north and south.

This was particularly true along the Jersey shore, where even the headlights of automobiles could be seen from U-boat bridges. Commanders learned that they could save fuel by bottoming out during the daytime, and then surfacing at night to wait in stationary bow attack position, like Prussian deer hunters in camp chairs waiting for game to be driven in front of their guns. And there was little in the way of defenses to concern them. An occasional destroyer or aircraft would be sighted, and at dusk on the 15th one aircraft chanced across U-123's course and dropped four bombs to starboard, but continued without circling or returning. Neither the USN nor the U.S. Army Air Corps made a single planned attack or a "scarecrow" effort to keep the U-boats down.

At Kernével, Admiral Dönitz was enthusiastic about the early reports, which showed, he said, "that activities of U-boats can be successful much longer than was expected."[5] Though it was being waged at a great distance, the tonnage battle remained the same battle. Only the venue had changed. The transportation of the sinews of war was an endless chain, whether in the Western Approaches to Britain, or in midocean, or off the Carolina Capes. The chain could be pulled apart at any point. It was immaterial where. And now, the most vulnerable link of it—Dönitz's new *Schwerpunkt* (focus)—was the American coast.

Altogether, the five Paukenschlag boats sank twenty-five ships for a total tonnage of 156,939 GRT, a number that compares favorably with the 152,000 GRT sunk by nine boats in the famous "Night of the Long Knives" in October 1940. While the simultaneously delivered drumbeatlike strike that Dönitz had envisioned did not happen as scheduled, the operation was a triumph nonetheless, and in the weeks and months that followed, an exultant Dönitz sent out wave after wave of additional Type IX boats to pursue the advantage. The first blood drawn by Drumbeat soon became a hemorrhage, staining the waters off Florida, in the Gulf of Mexico, and throughout the USN-protected Caribbean basin, including the Panama Sea Frontier. Not only American flag ships but scores of British bottoms sank beneath the torpedo onslaught.

Complained RN Commander-in-Chief Western Approaches Admiral Sir Percy L. H. Noble: "The Western Approaches Command finds itself in the position today [8 March] of escorting convoys safely over to American eastern seaboard, and then . . . finding that many of the ships thus escorted are easy prey to the U-boats . . . off the American coast or in the Caribbean."[6] Even some Type VIIC boats, by filling their torpedo compensating tanks and freshwater tank with fuel oil, managed to make the voyage over (and back) to participate in the "Second Happy Time." A new set of U-boat "aces" emerged, including Hardegen (U–*123*), Kptlt. Johann Mohr (U–*124*), Kptlt. Erich Topp (U–*552*), Kptlt. Rolf Mützelburg (U–*203*), and Oblt.z.S. Georg Lassen (U–*160*).

Beginning in April, boats operating in the Gulf and Caribbean were able to extend their time on station thanks to the deployment of a new large (1,688 tons surface displacement) U-boat type, the XIV, which carried no torpedoes but, instead, 700 tons of oil as well as spare parts, ammunition, food, other supplies, a physician, and replacement specialist ratings. Popularly called *Milchkuh* (milch cow), the U-tanker's capacity to refuel and revictual extended the patrol time of a Type IX boat by eight weeks, that of a Type VII by four, thus becoming for Dönitz a long-distance force-multiplier. The U–*459* (Kptlt. Graf Georg von Wilamowitz-Moellendorf) was first on station, refueling the IXB U–*108* (Kptlt. Klaus Scholtz) on 20 April, and then fourteen more boats in April and May. By the beginning of summer three more milch cows were tending pump at assigned naval square positions in the Western Atlantic.[7] (By the end of summer the British would have to contend with their ministrations in the transatlantic lanes, particularly in the Greenland Air Gap.)

As the number of ships sunk mounted into the hundreds, King's Navy came under heavy pressure from various quarters to do something about shore lighting and to institute coastwise convoys. In March, a month when oil tankers went down at an average of more than one a day, the Petroleum Industry War Council persuaded the Navy and War departments, which to that date had shared responsibility for coastal lights, to suppress them. The two departments formally agreed that thenceforth control of coastal lights would be "a Navy function."[8] Admiral King quickly exercised his sole authority, ordering that, despite the understandable protests of amusement parks, resorts, and other business interests, all shore lights must be "dimmed"–blackouts, he said, "were not considered necessary."[9] Although both the German and British coasts practiced total light elimination, dim-out was as far as King would ever go during the war. Tragically for the freighter and tanker crews, U-boat Commanders were able to

silhouette shipping traffic about as well under dim-out regula-
tion as under full illumination, especially in conditions of haze
and low-lying cloud banks.[10]

As for convoy, King would have none of it, arguing that he
did not have sufficient escort vessels to make convoying possible and safe. When King thought of escorts he thought of
destroyers, and with most of that class ship needed either in
transatlantic work or in the Pacific (always King's overriding
concern), he considered ships of lesser draft and tonnage as
useless for escort. "Stout hearts in little boats," he said, "cannot handle an opponent as tough as the submarine"[11]–this in
spite of the fact that the British had been doing quite well with
205-208-foot "Flower" class corvettes; and in spite of the fact
that later, in May and June, 165-foot Coast Guard cutters,
U.S.C.G. *Icarus* and *Thetis,* sank two of the first three U-boats
destroyed in U.S. waters.[12] King's doctrine became: "Inadequately escorted convoys are worse than none."[13] This was
the exact opposite of all that British experience had taught
since 1939, and, indeed, since 1917, when the Royal Navy of
World War I learned the value of convoy under USN tutelage.[14]

Gradually, however, King was forced to change his mind,
not least because of the remonstrations of Rodger Winn, who,
though a lowly Commander and a reservist at that, was dispatched to Washington by an exasperated Admiralty to reason with the obdurate USN chief.[15] By mid-March it was
clear that King was undergoing a mind-change. The "little
boats" he had disparaged before he now began assembling for
convoy escort duty: 173-foot-class patrol craft, 165-foot-class
cutters, 147-to-162-foot RN trawlers on loan from the Admiralty, 110-foot-class subchasers, down to 83-foot-class cutters,
which, though originally considered "of very limited usefulness," proved, once convoy was instituted, to be an effective
guard on the short-leg run between New York and Delaware
Bay.

With these and other small craft, joined by nine destroyers, King and his subordinates sailed the first southbound
convoy, KS.500, from Hampton Roads on 14 May; and a

northbound formation, KN.100, steamed out of Key West the next day. Later in May, links were established to New York and Halifax; and in August-September a Galveston-Mississippi-Key West link gave protection to tanker traffic out of Texas ports. The Caribbean basin was last to come into the convoy system.

In U.S. East Coast waters the good effects of convoy practice were almost immediately apparent. Whereas in the U.S. Strategic Area between the latitudes of West Quoddy Head, Maine, and Jacksonville, Florida, there had been forty-two sinkings in March and twenty-three in April, the number fell to four in May, rose to thirteen in June, fell to three in July, and then to zero for the remainder of the year. Figures for sinkings around the Florida peninsula showed a similar decline, as the Gulf figures would, too, after convoy became the routine mode of traffic there in late summer. As a result, Admiral King began saying, on 21 June: "Escort is not just *one* way of handling the submarine menace; it is the *only* way that gives any promise of success."[16]

As another result, in July, King's counterpart Admiral Dönitz transferred the main U-boat effort back to wolfpack tactics in the transatlantic sea lanes. He had known that it would be only a matter of time before his independently operating boats would have to give up the American coast, but he had never imagined that the shooting season would last as long as it did: six months, if one reckons it from U-*123*'s sinking of *Cyclops* on 13 January to mid-July, when the U-boat withdrawal began. Left behind on the seabeds from Maine to Galveston to Panama were the hulks of 397 Allied ships and the bones of no fewer than 5,000 souls—U.S., British, Norwegian, and other merchant seamen; USN and RN officers and men; and civilian passengers. The human casualties were twice those suffered at Pearl Harbor. Many other ships, not sunk, were damaged, some with death and injury resulting.

Overall, the six-months-long entombment of ships and men constituted one of the greatest maritime calamities in history. In terms of ships, raw resources, and matériel, it was the American nation's costliest defeat of the war. On 19 June

U.S. Army Chief of Staff General George C. Marshall lamented: "The losses by submarines off our Atlantic seaboard and in the Caribbean now threaten our entire war effort."[17] For the Germans the operation on the American littoral was the most successful sustained U-boat campaign in the whole course of the war. In exchange for negligible losses—nine U-boats sunk—the U-Bootwaffe carried off a triumph that was fully the equivalent of victory in a major battle on land. One may agree with historian Gerhard L. Weinberg that the offshore battle also "must be regarded as the most disastrous defeat ever suffered by American naval power."[18]

The U.S. Navy might well be grateful that it was not worse than it was, which one may assume it would have been if Dönitz had been allotted the twelve boats he sought for the opening blow; and had Hitler not in February diverted twenty operational boats to reconnaissance duty off the coast of Norway, where he expected imminent British landings; and had not a particularly severe European winter frozen the Southern Baltic parts where scores of new boats were trapped while working up;[19] and had not thirteen boats, including the now much-sought-after Type IXs, been lost in the ill-starred attempt to stop North Africa-bound convoys in the vicinity of Gibraltar.

If there were any consolations that the Allies could draw from the massacre on the American Main, it would seem that they were three in number: First, it occurred at just the time when the new Kriegsmarine four-rotor cipher Triton came into service fleet-wide, and as a result, except for three days, 23 and 24 February and 14 March, GC&CS went blind for eleven months.[20] For the Allies to possess Enigma information during the period February-July would have granted them no special advantage, since the majority of U-boats, operating independently and transmitting infrequently, could not have been located regularly by cryptographic intelligence; nor could shipping have been diverted around them on the strength of Sigint. Of course, when the U-boat offensive returned to midocean convoy routes starting in August, and radio-directed patrol lines began forming again, the absence of Enigma was keenly felt.[21]

Even then, Commander Winn's Tracking Room was not without resources, which included access to the *Heimische Gewässer* (Home Waters) key, which continued to be used by the Kriegsmarine for *Räumboot* (motor minesweeper) escorts that shepherded U-boats in and out of the Biscay bases; penetration of the *Tetis* key used by new boats working up in the Baltic; RFP, or radio fingerprinting, which could identify an individual U-boat's transmitter; TINA, an oscillographic operator signature device that displayed the specific keying style, or "fist," of each U-boat Morse sender; HF/DF; and knowledge long assembled in the Tracking Room about BdU's operating theory, characteristics of particular Commanders, U-boat routes, average speed of advance, and endurance at sea. From these remaining sources, plus Winn's canny intuition, the Tracking Room developed daily an estimate, or "working fiction," of U-boat operations.

The second consolation, to British strategists as much as to any like-minded officers in the USN, was the convincing demonstration in American waters of the value of convoy as a battle-winning expedient. And why was it so? Because either (1) the convoy drew U-boats to warships: instead of fruitlessly searching for the elusive craft–"hunting the hornets all over the farm"–the escorts had the U-boats in close proximity, where they could be attacked; or (2) the U-boats, unnerved by the hazards of attacking protected shipping, withdrew to more congenial waters, as happened in the American experience; or (3) attack opportunities declined mathematically, since if a U-boat was not correctly positioned to attack a convoy, it missed all the ships that formed it, and had to wait a long while for another chance.[32]

The third consolation that the Allies could take from the first half of 1942 was that the sea war in the west bought time for RAF Coastal Command and RN escorts to enlarge forces, improve training, and perfect tactics. It is to that opportunity, and to the role of the boffins, that our narrative now turns.

When in June 1941 Air Marshal Philip Joubert de la Ferté took command at Northwood, succeeding Air Chief Marshal Frederick Bowhill as Air Officer Commanding in Chief (AOC-in-C) Coastal Command, he decided that he needed an advisor at his elbow in the operations room who was not a member of the uniformed service: a civilian scientist, privy to every operation and every command secret, who could give him objective, disinterested guidance on the day-by-day anti-U-boat war. In Joubert's radical concept this civilian would advise on matters normally understood as being exclusively within the province of the RAF officer. His choice fell on Patrick M. S. Blackett, one of the most accomplished and versatile physicists of his day–"wonderfully intelligent, charming, fun to be with, dignified and handsome . . . married to one of the most delightful women in the world who did much to prevent him from becoming too serious."[23] An RN veteran of World War I, Blackett had given scientific advice to the Air Ministry during the mid–1930s when serving as a member of the short-lived "Tizard Committee," chaired by physicist Henry Tizard. Other members of that body, which was largely responsible for the initiation of Britain's radar network, were physiologist A. V. Hill and physicists H. E. Wimperis, A. P. Rowe, and F. A. Lindemann, later Lord Cherwell. This was a prototype "Operational Research Section," a term that radar pioneer Watson Watt would later claim to have coined in 1940.[24]

With Lindemann, whose presence on the Tizard committee was owed to pressure exerted by the then Mr. Winston Churchill, Blackett had a difficult relationship up to and throughout the war. In 1939–1940 Blackett worked with the Royal Aircraft Establishment (R.A.E.) at Farnborough, where he designed bombsights and other equipment that he personally flight-tested. With physicist Evan James Williams (1903–1945), whom he recruited to Farnborough, he worked on magnetic field detection of submarines. Blackett served seven months in 1940–1941 at the Anti-Aircraft (A.A.) Command at Stanmore, where he worked on gun-laying radar sets, until March 1941, when he received the call from Joubert.

Taking Williams with him, Blackett made it clear to

Joubert that he had severed all connections to the design, manufacture, and testing of weapons. "From the first," he wrote later, "I refused to be drawn into technical midwifery." Instead, he would hold himself free for non-routine investigations of a purely scientific nature; he would encourage numerical thinking on the conduct of operations; he would subject every assumption to quantitative analysis and empirical test; and thus he would "help to avoid running the war on gusts of emotion."[25] He rejected, too, the constant clamor of all the services for "new weapons for old." What was needed at Coastal, he concluded, was for commanders, air crews, and maintenance personnel to make "proper use of what we have got."

To that end he and Williams began scrutinizing every aspect of Coastal's operations and asking or recognizing the importance of questions about even the blindingly obvious. To give an example: There had to be measurable explanations for what was then Coastal's very low U-boat sighting rate and mere 1 percent kill rate of those boats sighted. A month after assuming his new position, Blackett paid a visit to Admiral Percy Noble's Western Approaches operations room at Derby House, Liverpool, from which all British surface and air escorts were controlled; indeed, it should be pointed out that since March 1941, Coastal, while remaining an essential arm of the RAF, had been under the operational command of the Admiralty, the two services sharing responsibility for the air war against U-boats. The positions of escorts as well as the estimated positions of U-boats were displayed on an immense wall plot. A quick glance at Coastal aircraft positions and examination of their numbers of hours flown led Blackett to calculate on the back of an envelope the number of U-boats that should be sighted by the aircraft. Back at Northwood he checked actual sightings for that day and found them to be four times fewer than what he had calculated.

The reason eluded him until one day a Wing Commander asked casually, "What color are our aircraft?" Blackett recognized at once that that was the right question. Coastal bombers, designed originally for night action over land, were painted black—a paint that made them stand out starkly against a North Atlantic cerulean blue or overcast sky, thus enabling an observant U-boat to dive before being sighted. Using first models and then aircraft, Blackett found that a white-painted bomber was sighted at 20 percent less distance than that at which a black aircraft was seen. Williams then calculated that a white aircraft would sight a surfaced U-boat on 30 percent more occasions than a black one, which should lead to an increase in sinkings. Within a few months all Coastal aircraft used on anti-U-boat patrols were repainted with matte white leading edges and under-surfaces.[26]

A less simple problem, and one that became a classic in the early history of operations research, was that of depth charge (D/C) settings. The prevailing assumption at Coastal and the Admiralty was that on average, U-boats that sighted approaching aircraft could dive to a depth of about 100 feet before an attack could be delivered. Accordingly, depth charges were set to explode at that depth. The reasoning seemed flawless until Williams discovered (1) that if a boat had gotten that deep, it would also have traveled a certain distance horizontally, with the result that a bomber would not know where to drop his D/Cs; and (2) that in about 40 percent of attacks to date the boat was on the surface or had been submerged for no longer than 15 seconds, in which case 100-foot fuse settings rendered the D/Cs useless.

After some difficulty on Williams's part in persuading Coastal officers that if the depth-setting adjuster was turned down to the 25-foot mark, the average number of U-boats sunk per given number of attacks would increase by two and a half times, the shallower setting was gradually introduced, starting with 50 feet in July 1941, progressing to 33 feet in January 1942, and reaching 25 feet in July of that year. The changes in setting were accompanied by a corresponding increase in lethality. Commented Blackett: "There can be few cases where such a great operational gain had been obtained by such a small and simple change of tactics."[27]

Under Blackett the Operational Research Section (O.R.S.) at Coastal grew into a tightly knit and formidable band of scholars, which included two future Nobel Prize winners (Blackett and John C. Kendrew), five future Fellows of the Royal Society (Blackett, Kendrew, Williams, C. H. Waddington, G. W. Robertson), and one future Fellow of the National Academy of Sciences of Australia (J. M. Rendel). With the exception of Blackett, who was forty-five in 1942, all were in their twenties and thirties. These and other O.R.S. members took on a wide range of problems affecting Coastal's performance. Nine times out of ten the O.R.S. analysis found that existing operational assumptions and procedures were soundly based. Joubert's staff had concluded, for example, that it was a better tactic to force a U-boat pack's convoy shadower under the surface and thus disrupt the pack's operation while it was being organized than to wait until after an attack was made to intervene.

O.R.S. analysis was able to confirm and refine this tactic by showing that in order to do this, patrols must not be laid on too close to the convoy's position. Studies had found, ironically, that most U-boat sightings had been made by aircraft that failed to meet their convoys. This led to the conclusion that most of a U-boat pack assembled more than twenty miles distant from the threatened convoy, and air patrols were vectored accordingly. During the period August 1942–May 1943, patrol at a distance yielded 40 percent more air attacks than continuous close escort (which was the American doctrine), greatly reduced sinkings by day, halved losses on the first night of a convoy battle and halved them again on the second, and detected a high density of boats *behind* the convoy, indicating that the work of the shadower had been frustrated and that the cohesion of the pack had been unhinged.[28]

Blackett undertook additional studies of depth charge attacks (later continued by Dr. E. C. Baughan), which, like the 25-foot D/C setting, led to considerable improvement in lethality. Although Coastal personnel engaged in much discussion about bomb weight, some proposing D/Cs of 35, 100, or 600 pounds, Blackett was convinced that the current 250-pound weapon, with its 19–20 foot killing range, was perfectly serviceable if it was used correctly. He investigated its use under two categories: (1) aiming accuracy and (2) stick spacing. (A *stick* was a group of four to eight individual D/Cs dropped either all together as a salvo or, more often, in a series. In a series drop, an electromechanical intervalometer was used to establish the distance between the D/Cs, that is, "stick spacing." The overall length of the D/C string was the "stick length.")

For accuracy studies Blackett had a rear-facing mirror camera fitted to bombers and examined what the attack photographs showed, which was that pilots were placing the center of the stick length at a point 60 yards ahead of a surfaced U-boat's conning tower. When asked why, pilots told him that it was "aim-off" to allow for the forward travel of the boat during the interval when the D/Cs were falling. This was in the manual; it was how they had been trained. But the photographs showed that the aim-off was not working. Blackett advised Joubert to have the pilots aim bang-on at the conning tower, even though it seemed to violate common sense. When they started doing so, kills increased by 50 percent.

The optimum stick spacing was a more complex problem, the resolution of which was not reached until after Blackett's departure from Coastal in January 1942. Current practice of pilots was to set for 36 feet between charges, but mathematical analysis suggested that this was too short. The O.R.S. recommendation that the spacing be increased to 100 feet was accepted by the Coastal staff in March 1943, after which straddles of a U-boat with 100-foot spacing were increasingly lethal.

O.R.S. attacked many other problems, some as mundane as what came to be called Planned Flying and Maintenance, pursued by Dr. C. E. Gordon, whose aim was to make maximum possible use of crewmen and aircraft. Gordon found that in a typical squadron of nineteen aircraft only 6 percent of the time (in hours) was spent in the air; 23 percent on the ground even though crews were available and aircraft were operational; 30 percent in repair or maintenance; and 41 percent waiting on spare parts or manpower. If efficient use could be made of Coastal's already existing resources, the force at sea could be greatly enlarged. Gordon's "efficiency study," as one would call it today, led to a tripling of flying hours—a squadron of nineteen increasing from 1,300 to 4,000 hours—and proportionately greater peril to U-boats. The O.R.S. system was eventually adopted throughout the RAF and the Naval Air Division.

Other O.R.S. members, particularly the mathematicians, worked on more arcane problems, such as aircraft operational sweep rate and width; sighting ranges of various aircraft and of the various sighting positions within an aircraft; optimum altitudes for visual and radar searches; eye rest requirements for crew; probability-of-kill-given-sighting; open water navigation technique; the average number of convoys sighted by a U-boat during its lifetime (seven and a half), the average life expectancy of a U-boat (14 patrols), and development of what today would be called a "macro-model" of U-boat circulation in the North Atlantic.[29] In January 1942, as earlier noted, Blackett left Coastal. His place as Officer in Charge was taken by Professor Williams. The section's work continued as before, with what might be called even closer association of uniformed Command and civilian scientist after 6 February 1943, when Air Marshal Sir John Slessor succeeded Joubert as AOC-in-C.

Waddington testified that "At least in the sphere of my experience, I have rarely met such critical generosity of mind as was shown to us civilian 'intruders.' " At no time, it appears, was there the slightest concern on the part of Joubert or Slessor that the "suck it and see" scientists sought an unwarranted prominence for themselves or ever considered themselves as anything other than members of a team.[30]

In citing the contributions to Coastal of non-RAF personnel, special mention should be made of the senior Naval Liaison Officer, Commander, later Captain, D. V. Peyton Ward, R.N., who was the very embodiment of the close and fruitful relationship that existed between Coastal and the Admiralty. An invalided-out submariner, "P.W.," as he was affectionately known at Northwood, volunteered for tasks not normally required of his position, and after Joubert's arrival he took it upon himself to interview all returning aircrews who had sighted and/or sunk a U-boat. By writing up and analyzing each such incident, he greatly enlarged the attack data available to O.R.S. A navy-blue in the midst of RAF slate-blue, he represented Coastal on the important interservice U-Boat Assessment Committee, which judged the success of surface and air attacks. After the war, he wrote the official four-volume history of air operations in the maritime war.[31]

All the while O.R.S. and P.W. were bending their minds, the air-crews practiced their own difficult art of air search, hundreds of miles out over the Atlantic's gray flannel, noisily patrolling 1,000 to 5,000 feet off the deck, in every kind of weather, dirty and cold, rarely if ever in their entire flight careers sighting a single U-boat to reward them for their protracted and boring hours. Said one crewman:

> It is difficult to describe the intense boredom of the sorties we undertook: hour after hour after hour with nothing to look at but sea. I am sure that when they found U-boats many crews pressed home their attacks regardless of what was being thrown at them, merely because it was a welcome relief from the boredom.[32]

And many crews would be shot down, in distant positions where no assistance was near or possible. And many other crews were lost to the sea not through enemy action, but through engine failure, adverse weather, navigational error, and fuel depletion.

Coastal Command's motto was: "Constant Endeavor."

The Bay of Biscay is a roughly triangular body of water bordering the Atlantic that is formed on the north by the Brittany peninsula of France, where it does an arabesque toward Land's End on England's Cornwall coast, and on the south by the northern provinces of Spain. About 86,000 square miles (223,000 square kilometers) in size, and 15,525 feet (4,735 meters) deep at its center, it was the body of water traversed by U-boats operating out of bases at the western French ports of Brest, Lorient, St.-Nazaire, La Pallice, and Bordeaux. Normally, outbound and inbound boats transited through a zone, or "choke point," about 300 miles north to south and 200 miles east to west. Here, more than at any other sea position, U-boats could be found in high concentration: traffic ranged from forty-five boats per month in June 1942 to a figure that, in early 1943, passed 100 (expected to increase to 150 by spring). The Strait of Gibraltar was another choke point, but far fewer boats attempted its passage; and the northern route from Germany around the north of Scotland was another transit area, but one that was used almost exclusively by new boats coming into Atlantic service. If one wanted to find a large number of U-boats bunched up in any one place, it would be in the transit zone of the Bay of Biscay.[33] In March 1943, the Admiralty said of the enemy:

> Apart from modifying his tactics, or disengaging from an attack, he can withdraw altogether from any given convoy area as he had done to a large extent in the areas off the American coast. He cannot withdraw from the Bay.[34]

Whether U-boats were bound to and from the midocean transatlantic convoy lanes, where the most intensive pack battles were fought, or to and from what the British called the Outer Seas—Freetown, Cape Town, the Indian Ocean, the Atlantic Narrows, Brazil, the Caribbean, and the North American seaboard—the swept channels of the Biscay minefields were the narrow funnel through which every boat had to pass. To an adversary with marksman instincts, the Bay presented an irresistible bull's-eye.

From the date he assumed command at Northwood in 1941, Air Chief Marshal Joubert cast a malevolent glare in that direction. Like many at Coastal before him, he could not understand why Bomber Command with its heavy bombardment squadrons had not destroyed the steel and concrete U-boat bunkers while they were still under construction and vulnerable. As a matter of fact, Bomber Command did attempt to disrupt construction, making twenty nighttime raids on the Lorient base in 1940, sixteen in 1941, and twelve in early 1942. The U.S. Eighth Air Force made ten daylight raids on St.-Nazaire between November 1942 and June 1943. Other raids were mounted against Brest. All such raids were ineffectual, owing to poor bombing accuracy and to intense anti-aircraft fire that caused heavy bomber losses. The only result on the ground was the flattening of the towns where the bases were situated. Of Lorient and St.-Nazaire, Admiral Dönitz said that not a cat or a dog survived. Left with the problem of nearly completed bomb shelters, Joubert decided that since Coastal Command was envisioned to be an offensive instrument and the hunter role suited his nature, he would direct as much of its power as he could spare from convoy escort to that of offensive patrol against U-boats transiting the Bay. In making that decision, he entered a debate that would never be completely resolved, either in Coastal or the Admiralty: whether 'tis nobler to *defend* convoys and so win the Atlantic by seeing merchantmen to safe and timely arrivals at their destinations, or to take up arms against a sea of U-boats, and by *hunting*, kill them?

What came to be called the First Bay Offensive, launched by Joubert in the summer of 1941, was a daytime operation flown by Sunderlands, Wellingtons, Whitleys, Hudsons, and Catalinas, all of them equipped with 1.5-meter wavelength ASV Mark II radar. It yielded very disappointing results. O.R.S. analysts discovered that 60 percent of the U-boats sighted the approaching aircraft before being spotted themselves, and thus were able to dive out of harm's way. As the campaign wore on into autumn, it became clear that transiting U-boat commanders, alerted to the increased presence of aircraft in the Bay, were charging their batteries on the surface at night and traveling as much as possible submerged during the day. Sightings of boats decreased accordingly, and the record shows that the year ended without a single U-boat kill by aircraft in the Bay.[35]

What was needed, argued Professor Blackett of O.R.S., who chaired a specially organized Night Attack Sub-Committee under the ASW Committee on Aircraft Attacks in the Admiralty, was an effective means of delivering attacks during darkness when the U-boats were on the surface charging. And that meant an illuminant that could display to the pilot's eye targets detected first by radar. In early 1942 combat experiments were run using 4-inch flares towed by radar-equipped Whitleys, but these proved unsuccessful. Another, more promising illuminant was waiting in the wings.

When in September 1940 the then AOC-in-C Air Chief Marshal Bowhill sent around a memorandum asking officers and airmen to submit ideas for improvement of ASW operations, he received back a detailed proposal for an airborne searchlight for use in night attacks on surfaced U-boats. It came from a nontechnical source, a World War I pilot who had flown ASW patrols over the Mediterranean in that conflict, named Squadron Leader Humphrey de Verde "Sammy" Leigh, now serving as Assistant Personnel Officer in headquarters administration. Leigh proposed that the so-called DWI Wellingtons, which had earlier, but no longer, been used to explode magnetic mines from the air by generating a powerful electrical charge, be refitted with a belly-installed retractable carbon arc lamp. The DWIs recommended themselves for this use because they were already equipped with auxiliary engines and either 35- or 90-kilowatt generators.

Bowhill was so impressed by the idea that he relieved Leigh of his desk duties and set him to work full-time on the project. There were numerous obstacles to overcome, starting with the technicians at RAE, Farnborough, who argued the case for towed flares as preferable to the searchlight scheme. The nontechnician Leigh pressed on regardless, and ingeniously solved every problem that he encountered, among them ventilation of the carbon arc fumes, steering control of the lamp's beam in azimuth and elevation, prevention of back glare, or "dazzle," and reduction of weight. In March 1941 the Vickers plant at Brooklands completed a prototype installation employing a naval 24-inch (61 cm) narrow-beam searchlight, giving a maximum 50 million candles without a spreading lens, powered by seven 12-volt 40-ampere-hour type D accumulators (storage batteries); and on the night of 4 May, with Leigh himself operating the light controls in the

nose, the first Leigh Light Wellington repeatedly detected, illuminated, and "attacked" the British submarine *H–31* off
Northern Ireland. Bowhill was no less gratified at this success
than Leigh, but only one month later, when Bowhill was relieved by Joubert, the whole project was canceled and Leigh
found himself reassigned to a desk.

It happened that Joubert had been associated with the development of a competing airborne light system called the
Helmore Light, after an RAF Group Captain, which had been
designed for illuminating enemy bombers at night, and the
new AOC-in-C thought it should be used against U-boats as
well. But the Helmore Light was quickly shown to be unsuitable for Coastal work: its massive array of accumulators occupied the entire bomb bay; the light could not be steered, or
aimed, except by moving the entire aircraft; and the bright-
ness of the light, which was mounted in the nose, dazzled
both the operator and the pilot. "After some two months I
found, as I do not mind admitting," Joubert wrote later, "that I
had made a mistake."[36] Leigh cleaned out his desk a second
time and returned to the hangar.

Months of redesign, flight testing, crew training, and what
Peyton Ward called "difficult to explain" administrative delays
followed, until finally, at the beginning of June 1942, a "penny
packet" of five Leigh Light (L/L) Wellingtons of No. 172
Squadron entered operational service in the Bay. The first
L/L-assisted attack was made on 4 June against the Italian
submarine *Luigi Torelli* (Tenente di Vascello [Lt.-Cmdr.] Au-
gusto Migliorini), resulting in severe damage.[37] The attack
was made by Squadron Leader Jeaff Greswell, flying Wellington "F" of 172 Squadron. During June and July the Wellingtons, showing what the surprised and helpless Germans
came to call *das verdammte Licht*–"that damn light"–made altogether eleven sightings and six attacks, resulting in one kill–
the Type IXC U–*502* (Kptlt. Jürgen von Rosenstiel) en route
home from the Caribbean, sunk by Wellington VIII "H" flown
by Pilot Officer Wiley Howell, an American serving with the
RAF–and two boats damaged.

Before the Wellingtons could improve on that record, Admiral Dönitz ordered his boats in the Bay: "Because the danger of attacks without warning from radar-equipped aircraft is [now] greater by night than by day, in future U-boats are to surface by day. . . ."[38] In a month and a half's time the Leigh Light had taken the night away from U-boats in the Bay, but that, it turned out, would be for now their major contribution. The air war in the Bay returned to daylight hours, and with slightly better returns than before, as between mid-July and the end of September, conventionally equipped aircraft made over seventy sightings and sank three additional boats.

Still, the great opportunity that the Bay presented eluded Coastal's grasp. The ratio of kills to daytime sightings remained disappointingly low throughout the remainder of 1942 and well into the new year. Whereas Coastal had expected that with increased time given to practice attacks, with, at last, 25-foot depth pistols, and with Torpex fillings, the percentage of lethal attacks would rise to 20 percent, it hovered instead at 6 percent. The lethality problem prevailed everywhere in waters that the U-boats infested, even where attacks were made from unseen cloud approaches on Class A targets, that is, those in which the U-boat was on the surface or had been submerged fewer than 15 seconds. Coastal was divided on the question of where blame should be placed: on poor weapons or on poor aim? Rear gunner reports and photographs suggested that the 250-pound Torpex D/C did not seem to injure boats even when perfect straddles were achieved. The O.R.S., however, defended the weapon, and, after intense study, determined that, photographs seemingly to the contrary, the problem was aiming, which could be corrected by more and better training.

In support of this conclusion the O.R.S. produced evidence that three outstanding squadrons, No. 120 (6 kills, 10 damaged), No. 202 (4 kills, 5 damaged), and No. 500 (4 kills, 9 damaged) also had solid records in practice bombing. It pointed as well to certain individual pilots, such as Squadron Leader Terence M. Bulloch, of No. 120 Squadron, with three boats sunk and three damaged, and Flying Officer M. A. "Mike" Ensor of No. 500, with one sunk and three damaged.

In each case, the former in a Liberator, the latter in a Hudson, painstaking practice had translated into successful performance in combat.[39] There was nothing wrong with the weapon. O.R.S.'s findings set in train intensive drills in marksmanship.

Another problem that the daylight bombers had to face was an increase in opposition from the Luftwaffe, which in the summer and fall of 1942 attempted to interdict Coastal patrols in the Bay, employing Focke-Wulf 190s, Heinkel 115s, Junkers 88s, Messerschmitt 210s, and Arado 196s. Some aircraft and crew casualties resulted, but No. 235 Beaufighter Squadron at Chivenor in Devon successfully fought the attackers off, and the enemy air effort died away.

The nighttime bombers, which continued busy in the Bay Offensive, had problems of their own. The first was the French tunny (tuna) fleet, which followed the shoals of tunny into the middle Bay where most of the Leigh Light aircraft were operating. Numerous A.S.V. blips, when illuminated, turned out to be tunny craft. Their radar signature was indistinguishable from that of a U-boat. Use of the searchlight in these cases not only caused a 25 percent waste of effort and ran down the electrical power in the batteries, it gave fair warning to U-boats nearby that an L/L Wellington was in the area. In August the problem was so severe that L/L missions were considered futile and Coastal attempted to warn off the fishing craft by BBC broadcasts, leaflets, and threats to shoot, but nothing worked and the interference remained intractable until the end of the tunny season in October.

In the meantime the L/L flights, indeed all flights, were confronted by a far more serious problem. Admiral Dönitz's technical staff had concluded, correctly, that the illuminated attacks in the Bay had been made possible by airborne metric radar. Helped by an A.S.V. Mark II set captured in Tunisia, BdU technicians developed a radar receiver (Type R.600) that could detect the presence of 1.5-meter pulses and give a U-boat time to dive out of danger. In fact, it produced a warning signal at a greater range than that at which an aircraft could acquire the blip (plus or minus 10 miles). Manufactured by the Paris firm Metox (also later by Grandin), the equipment was put to sea in August on three boats, U-*214*, U-*107*, and U-*69*. Except for problems encountered with the antenna, which was affixed to a crude wooden crosspiece *(Biskayakreuz,* the "Biscay cross," as it came to be called) that had to be carried up and down the tower ladder when surfacing and diving, causing troublesome delays, the three boats reported favorably on the device's effectiveness. Dönitz then ordered the equipment fitted to every boat in the fleet, a process that was nearly complete by the end of the year. This logical German countermeasure enabled the boats to resume surfacing by night.

A dramatic falloff in Coastal sightings, both day and night, together with intelligence drawn by Winn and Beesly from naval Enigma, gave Northwood a strong clue to what had happened. The value of the Bay campaign in these circumstances came under strong questioning, and AOC-in-C Joubert pressed London hard for 10-centimeter equipment with which to defeat the German Search Receiver (G.S.R.). But the first squadron to be so equipped did not become operational until the following March. In the meantime, Coastal relied on the only expedient available: flooding. In this tactic all the aircraft over the Bay except the L/L Wellingtons, which, it was hoped, might catch a U-boat off its guard, were to use their A.S.V. continuously. The expectation was that with the G.S.R. alarm ringing without stop, U-boats would not know when they were being targeted—an alarm that rang all the time was as useless as one that rang not at all—and so might become complacent or careless. But the tactic did not lead to additional sightings and attacks. In fact, during January 1943 a total of 3,136 day hours led to only five sightings, and 827 hours of combined L/L and conventional night patrols produced only three sightings.[40] These were a new low record in the Bay.

During the U-boats' six-month-long picnic on the North American seaboard, overstretched and weary RN surface escorts had a respite in which to fit new detection gear, practice use of weapons, including, on some ships, the new Hedgehog, and train ranks and ratings. The ratings' first training experience, and in many cases, their first glimpse of the sea came when newly commissioned escort vessels received their working up at H.M.S. *Western Isles* in Tobermory harbor on the Isle of Mull off the west coast of Scotland. There the legendary (and quirky) Commodore Gilbert "Puggy" (or "Monkey") Stephenson took callow "Hostilities Only" land-lubbers—1,132 groups in all during the war—and, within two to three weeks' time, shaped them into disciplined, semiskilled seamen who went directly into convoy escort service.[41]

While Stephenson's work with new crews did not require a respite from combat to carry on, the efficiency training of Captains and Watch-Keeping Officers did. This was particularly true of the Western Approaches Tactical Unit (WATU), an operational ASW analysis facility established at the suggestion of Churchill in January 1942, coincidentally the beginning month of the U-boats' American campaign. The facility was erected on the bomb-damaged top floor of the Tate and Lyle Exchange Buildings to the east of Commander-in-Chief Western Approaches (CinCWA) in Derby House, Liverpool. To organize and direct the WATU, Churchill sent an RN Commander (later Captain) named Gilbert Howlands Roberts who, like Peyton Ward at Northwood, had been invalided out of the Navy, in his case because of tuberculosis.

A former destroyer Captain who was trained as a gunnery officer, Roberts modeled his facility on the floor plot used at gunnery school. He divided off a large linoleum-covered floor representing the open sea with lines ten inches apart indicating miles, and placed on that "Tactical Table" wooden models of convoy ships, escort vessels, and U-boats. Then, with canvas and string, he screened off any view of the ocean except for small apertures that gave only restricted views of an operational situation, akin to the restrictions prevailing at sea, particularly at night. Twenty-four "players" could work at the full floor plot, or three groups of eight players each could work at partitions of the plot. They sat at plotting tables around the viewscreens.

While a staff mainly of seventeen- to twenty-year-old Wrens (Women's Royal Naval Service, or WRNS) manipulated both the models and the views allowed of them, combat situations were simulated and escort group Captains and Watch-Keeping Officers were asked to make decisions about appropriate actions to take in the circumstances shown—the circumstances being based on intensive interviews Roberts had conducted with Senior Officers of Escort Groups. Every movement was tracked, those of the U-boats in green chalk, those of the escorts in white, so that at the conclusion of "The Game," as the exercise was called, the participants could inspect their successes and failures in pursuit and attack. The tactical course lasted six days, and as the months progressed, the teenage Wrens gained sufficient competence to be able, discreetly, to advise sea-hardened officers on what might be their next best course of action—as remembered by a Lieutenant (later novelist) named Nicholas Monsarrat, who allowed in his *The Cruel Sea*, "Rather unfairly they seemed to know all about everything. . . ."[42]

Numerous innovative attack procedures evolved from these exercises, the first of them based on reports of U-boat attack behavior during the passage of Convoy HG.76 from Gibraltar to the U.K. in December 1941 that were given Roberts by an offensive-minded Senior Officer Escort (SO) named Commander (later Captain) Frederic John Walker, who commanded the convoy's Escort Group 36. Whereas Walker's escorts thought that a U-boat that attacked HG.76 was about a mile outside the convoy, Roberts deduced from a simulation on his plot that the boat attacked from within the convoy columns, having infiltrated from astern. He thereupon devised a countermeasure to catch such a boat as it attempted escape. Since one of the Wrens suggested that the new tactic would give a "raspberry" to Hitler, Roberts assigned it that name. CinCWA Admiral Noble informed Churchill of this correction to "a cardinal error in anti-U-boat tactics" and within twenty-four hours signaled instructions for Raspberry to the Fleet.[43] This tactic and a modification called Half-Raspberry were the first universally prescribed escort counterattack maneuvers; prior to their decree each SO was free to devise his own maneuvers. Soon, after trials on the Tactical Table, other fruit-named tactics were developed: "Pineapple," "Gooseberry," and "Strawberry"; to be joined by "Beta Search," "Artichoke," and "Observant."[44] Meanwhile, sea training in these maneuvers went on at Londonderry, Greenock, Birkenhead, Freetown, Bombay, St. John's, Newfoundland, and Sydney, Nova Scotia, where escort groups practiced as teams under their own SOs.

It was these finely honed escort teams who met the U-boat men when the latter returned in force to the mid-Atlantic in early August, 1942. The slugging match between these two old enemies from that date until the start of May 1943 was fierce and relentless, but, as already indicated in this chapter and in the prologue, neither side was able to deliver a knockout blow. Nor was the renewed German effort against convoys limited to the major transatlantic trade routes. Admiral Dönitz probed for soft spots in the Outer Seas where Allied defenses might have been attenuated by the need to reinforce the northern lanes; thus, he deployed boats to Freetown, Cape Town, and Madagascar, to the Atlantic Narrows between West Africa and Brazil, to the Brazilian and Panamanian coasts, and to the traffic area eastward of Trinidad in the Caribbean.

In raw numbers the U-boats enjoyed commendable successes. During August, with 86 boats at sea, the U-Bootwaffe made an impressive number of convoy contacts per boat and sank 105 ships for 517,295 GRT; and in November, as noted earlier, the boats scored their highest monthly total of tonnage sunk in the entire Atlantic war. But throughout the period August 1942 to April 1943, their ever-increasing number of operational boats at sea generated *diminishing returns in tonnage sunk per boat per day at sea*–this despite the fact that U-tankers in midocean were multiplying their days at sea, deferring their maintenance, alleviating operational delays caused by the backlog of boats needing fuel at base, and frustrating Coastal Command's Bay Offensive by eliminating the need for two transits per boat through the Bay. (In the twelve-month period prior to the end of May 1943 the supply U-boats replenished 220 U-boats operating against Atlantic convoys as well as 170 boats assigned to Outer Seas.[45])

All the while, the experience and proficiency levels of the U-boat crews were declining, owing both to losses and to rapid expansion, while those of the escort crews were waxing, thanks in great part to the intense training regimen of January–July 1942, and to the fitting during the same period of new equipment such as HF/DF and 10-centimeter radar. From August through April 1943 the U-boats were being sunk at a monthly rate of 9.7, including February's record 19. In the same period, three out of four ocean convoys made port without loss and 90 percent of those convoys that were attacked similarly reached their destinations. German intelligence and BdU completely missed the military convoys of the Anglo-American expeditionary force (Operation Torch) that sailed from the U.K. and the U.S. beginning on 18 October and effected landings on 8 November in French Northwest Africa, at Casablanca in Morocco, and at Oran and Algiers in Algeria. Only one of the 334 ships that participated was attacked by a U-boat, and it by accidental encounter. German records do not disclose a single sighting, even inkling, of that armada as such.[46]

Dönitz, who had expected a possible Allied action at Dakar, and had stationed boats in the Freetown and Cape Verde Island zones as a precaution, found himself on 8 November completely out of position. His rushed disposition of boats to the Moroccan Atlantic coast and to the western approaches of Gibraltar to attack new supply shipping and thus strangle the invasion buildup led to the sinking of ten merchant ships, four transports, and five warships–including Werner Henke's fleet repair ship H.M.S. *Hecla* on 11/12 November–but at terrible cost: eight U-boats sunk, 19 damaged, and one Italian submarine sunk. With such thin results attended by disproportionately high losses, Dönitz pulled his boats in early December for assignment to more productive areas of the Atlantic.

CERTAIN TITLES FOR TRADE AND MILITARY CONVOYS

CU	New York-Curaçao-United Kingdom.
GU	Alexandria-North Africa-U.S.A.
HG	Gibraltar-United Kingdom.
HX	Halifax-United Kingdom.
KMF	United Kingdom-North Africa-Port Said (Fast).
KMS	United Kingdom-North Africa-Port Said (Slow).
KX	United Kingdom-Gibraltar (Special).
MKF	Mediterranean-North Africa-United Kingdom (Fast).
MKS	Mediterranean-North Africa-United Kingdom (Slow).
OG	United Kingdom-Gibraltar.
ON	United Kingdom-North America.
ONS	United Kingdom-North America.
OS	United Kingdom-West Africa.
SC	Halifax-United Kingdom (Slow).
SL	Sierra Leone-United Kingdom.
UC	United Kingdom-Curaçao-New York.
UG	U.S.A.-North Africa.
UGF	U.S.A.-North Africa.
UGS	U.S.A.-North Africa.
UT	U.S.A.-United Kingdom (Military).
WS	United Kingdom-Middle East and India (Military).
XK	Gibraltar-United Kingdom (Special).
EC	Southend to Clyde, Oban or Loch Ewe (Coastal Convoys, North about).
WN	Clyde, Oban or Loch Ewe to Methil (Coastal Convoys, North about).

Three notable command changes took place in the fall and winter of 1942–1943. On 17 November, Admiral Sir Max Horton, since December 1939 Vice-Admiral (later Admiral) Submarines, succeeded Percy Noble as CinCWA. Noble was named Chief of the British Admiralty delegation (BAD) in Washington. Horton had earlier turned down C-in-C Home Fleet because he thought that post to be too much under the thumb of Whitehall. At Submarine Command in Northways, Hampstead, he had forged close working ties with Coastal Command at nearby Northwood, and during three years of war became convinced "that fleets cannot operate without the close cooperation of air power"–a conviction that he would translate into deeds at Western Approaches.[47]

Upon his arrival at the large gray block of buildings that was Derby House, he inspected its facilities, including the armored and gasproof Operations Room in its basement, and called for the principal officers to explain their duties. To Gilbert Roberts of the Tactical School he said, "What do you think you do?" Roberts replied, "Why don't you come up and see properly?" Horton did, and at 9:00 the next morning he returned unattended to begin the six-day course.[48] Not everyone so impressed Horton, however, and more than a few officers fell victim to deadwood cutting.

Horton's mandate as CinCWA was: "the protection of trade, the routing and control of all convoys and measures to combat any attack on convoy by U-boats or hostile aircraft within his Command." (Military convoys and fast troopships remained under the control of the Admiralty.) He also saw as his responsibility the improvement and intensification of training. Early in February 1943 he received a yacht, H.M.S. *Philante*, and a submarine, sometimes two, with which, in effect, to take Roberts's Tactical School to sea. At Larne in Northern Ireland each Escort Group prior to joining its convoy was put through exercises designed by Captain A.J. Baker-Creswell, R.N., to represent actual combat conditions to be encountered. What was more, the exercises were conducted in close cooperation with Coastal Command aircraft, in order to perfect navigation and rendezvous, TBS and signal code communications, and joint attack procedures. Furthermore, surface-air collaboration was to be practiced even while with the convoys en route. And the surface Escort Groups, a Percy Noble innovation, were to be kept together as teams.

Another Noble innovation that, except for one prototype, had not been possible to implement in his predecessor's time for lack of assets was Support Groups—small, highly trained, and offensively minded flotillas of destroyers, sloops, frigates, and cutters that would ride to the rescue of convoys and Escort Groups directly menaced or under attack. In Noble's vision such groups would include, when they became available, auxiliary aircraft carriers. Horton embraced the concept and wrote almost daily to the Admiralty begging for ships to make the forces possible, eventually succeeding in obtaining the loan of a number of Home Fleet destroyers. To these he took the risk of adding sixteen warships obtained by reducing the strength of each Escort Group by one vessel. The result was, at the end of March, five Support Groups fully trained and ready to fulfill their sole mission: hunt down and kill U-boats.

Meanwhile, in his glass-fronted office facing the Operations Room, Horton had constant access in an adjoining office to Air Vice Marshal Sir Leonard H. Slatter, commanding No. 15 Group, whose squadrons covered the North Atlantic convoy lanes from bases on the West Coast of Scotland, in the Hebrides, and in Northern Ireland, with a detachment at Reykjavik. Both men lived on the premises, though Slatter did not follow Horton's somewhat eccentric daily schedule, which had him on the golf course all afternoon, at the bridge table after dinner, and in his office by 2330, usually in "worn and split" pajamas, drinking barley water while directing convoy battles on the huge wall plot opposite, and with, as one observer said, an "uncanny prevision" of what the U-boats would do next. Different in manner from the urbane and kindly Noble, for whom everyone at Derby House had affection as well as respect, especially the Wrens, Horton's behavior prompted such descriptions as "ruthless," "determined," "selfish," "intolerant," "perfectionist," and "maddening."[49] Apparently the flinty old submariner was just the type Churchill thought should lead the surface and air escorts into the dangerous new year—"a thief to catch a thief," as it were.

The second major command change affected that other thief, Karl Dönitz at BdU. When in December Adolf Hitler harangued Grossadmiral Erich Raeder, Commander-in-Chief Navy (*Oberbefehlshaber der Kriegsmarine*), over the failure of a surface force led by two heavy cruisers to advance successfully against an RN Arctic convoy escort screen, and went on to threaten the scrapping of all big ships in the fleet, the proud Hamburger veteran of the Imperial Navy and Battle of Jutland tendered his resignation, which the Führer, though surprised, accepted. On 30 January 1943 Dönitz was named Grossadmiral and C-in-C in his stead, while retaining his command as Flag Officer U-Boats. Now Dönitz had direct access to Hitler, whom he could importune for steel and shipyard workers; he had authority over the Naval Staff, *Seekriegsleitung* (Skl), whose approvals he need no longer seek; and he had freedom to prosecute the Tonnageschlacht without diversion of his forces to unprofitable waters. Just the preceding month he had written in his war diary: "The tonnage battle is the main task of the U-boats. . . . It must be carried on where the greatest successes can be achieved with the smallest losses."[50] But the new appointment also had its disadvantages, principally, as Raeder, who nominated him for the post predicted, that as C-in-C Dönitz "would not be able to dedicate himself to the immediate conduct of the U-boat war to the same extent as formerly."[51] The "Lion," as U-boat men admiringly called him, had already suffered physical distancing from his underseas fleet and their crews, when in March 1942 a British raiding party attacked St.-Nazaire; alerted to how easily such a raid might be made on BdU itself, Dönitz reluctantly abandoned Kernével and established his headquarters in an apartment complex on the Avenue du Maréchal Maunoury in Paris. Now, to consolidate BdU with his new post as C-in-C, he moved U-boat headquarters even farther east, to the Hotel am Steinplatz in the Charlottenburg suburb of Berlin (losing two railroad cars filled with equipment and papers in the process), where BdU became opera-

tional on 31 March 1943. It had been Dönitz's presence on
the dock at Lorient and the other bases, where he attended to
his crews' leavings and returnings, that cemented his standing
as a father figure to his men and elicited a depth of loyalty
from ranks and ratings that was unprecedented in the Kriegsmarine. Now his inspiring figure and voice were far from the
bases, with what negative impact it is impossible to calculate.

With his longtime Chief of Operations Branch
(BdU-Ops), Konteradmiral Eberhard Godt, Dönitz incorporated BdU into the Naval Staff as its Second Section, with
Godt, Chief of Staff, overseeing day-to-day conduct of U-boat
operations—although in the war diary, where major convoy
battles are described and where strategies or policies are declared, one continues to hear the voice of Dönitz, with the result that in the chapters that follow in this narrative the
citations of passages from the diary assume their authorship
by a Dönitz/Godt duumvirate. The entire BdU operations
staff numbered barely more than a dozen officers, most of
them in their early thirties (Dönitz was 51, Godt 42). Though
it could draw upon the much larger Naval Staff for such things
as Intelligence (3/Skl), Communications Service (4/Skl), Radar Countermeasures (5/Skl), and Meteorology (6/Skl), it remained a thin blue line for trying conclusions with the
combined staffs of the Admiralty and Coastal Command, not
to mention GC&CS. (Western Approaches alone had a staff
of over a thousand officers and ratings.)[52]

The third major change in command came in RAF
Coastal, where Joubert was succeeded as AOC-in-C by Air
Marshal Sir John Slessor on 5 February 1943. A Royal Flying
Corps pilot in the Kaiser's war, Slessor had fought off Zeppe-
lins over London and flown artillery observation missions
over the trenches of France. His most recent posts in the Führer's war were Commander of 5 Group of Bomber Command
and Assistant Chief of the Air Staff (Policy). With Air Chief
Marshal Sir Charles F. A. Portal, Chief of the Air Staff, he attended the Casablanca Conference, actually held in a residential suburb of the city called Anfa, where, from 14 to 23
January, Churchill, Roosevelt, and their Combined Chiefs of

Staff conferred on the priorities to be established for future operations. He was present when the conferees approved their final Memorandum, "Conduct of the War in 1943," with, at its head, the now well-known "First Charge" declaration: "The Defeat of the U-boat must remain a first charge on the resources of the United Nations."[53]

Slessor wrote after the war that the person responsible for having that strategic imperative given first ranking was Admiral Ernest J. King, though King's biographer does not mention it, except to say that, "Everyone agreed that the Battle of the Atlantic took first priority."[54] Slessor did not think that the "First Charge" declaration had much practical influence on the anti-U-boat war, except to prod the Air Ministry to divert some of the newly available centimetric radar sets from Bomber to Coastal Command. It was not until March, however, that the first Coastal squadron equipped with 10-centimeter ASV Mark III became operational.[55] That squadron, which flew L/L Wellingtons, was then in a position to defeat the Metox receiver, and so surprise the surfaced U-boats at night as L/L aircraft had done up to six months before. The pure hunt was on again. Or was it?

The Admiralty pressed Slessor to make immediate and maximum use of the centimetric aircraft in the Bay of Biscay, and to take full advantage of the interval of time before the Germans developed a new search receiver to detect 10-centimeter pulses. But Slessor balked at going back to the Bay Offensive, as he stated in a Note to the Prime Minister's Anti-U-Boat Warfare Committee, of which he was a member. The A.U. Committee, as it came to be called, had been formed subordinate to the War Cabinet on 13 November and thereafter met weekly at No. 10 Downing Street under the Chairmanship of the Prime Minister. Its membership was composed of (with varying attendance and occasional visitors) twenty-two Ministers, Admirals, and Air Marshals, together with the scientists Blackett, Watson Watt, and Lindemann (now Lord Cherwell), and Mr. Averell Harriman, President Roosevelt's personal envoy to the United Kingdom.[56]

To this top-level body, on 22 March, Slessor sent his five-page Note accompanied by a twenty-five-page statistical analysis of the Bay Offensive from June 1942 to February 1943 and of the air cover given threatened convoys from September 1942 to February 1943. The analysis had been done by Coastal's O.R.S., then headed by Professor Waddington, which Slessor valued and supported no less than Joubert. The analysis showed, wrote Slessor, that whereas on the Bay patrols there had been one sighting of a U-boat for every 164 hours flown in the period June to September, and one sighting per 312 hours from October to February, there had been one sighting per only 29 hours flown over threatened convoys. While the Bay patrols of No. 19 Group (Air Vice Marshall Geoffrey Bromet) had resulted in a certain number of kills, the lethal rate was a low 7 percent of attacks made, hardly justifying the disproportionate and uneconomical effort employed. Slessor therefore proposed reducing the scale of the Bay Offensive. "Our policy," he concluded, "should be to concentrate the greatest practicable proportion of our available resources on close cover of threatened convoys, the Bay patrols assuming the position of a residuary legatee."[57]

When on 24 March this recommendation was placed on the table by the A.U. Committee for discussion one week hence, the Admiralty found themselves rebuked in their desire to pass from the defensive to the offensive in the U-boat war by going full-bore in the Bay. This was all the more vexing since Slessor's Command was technically under the operational control of the Admiralty. One week later, however, as shown in chapter 8, Their Lordships would be back with a counter-strike—and the Americans alongside them.

Professor Blackett left the O.R.S. of Coastal in January 1942 to become Chief Advisor on Operational Research (C.A.O.R.) to the Admiralty. In that capacity he recruited a prestigious scientific team similar to that at Coastal—Evan Williams would follow him to Whitehall in January 1943—and cast his practical intellect across the whole range of naval operations, including, in a notable study, the optimum size of convoys.

For years the number of ships in convoy had hovered at around forty-five, though the origin and rationale for that rule could not be found by Blackett. A formation larger than that was assumed to be dangerous, since it presented so many targets.

When in late autumn 1942 Blackett investigated convoy statistics for the two-year period 1941–1942, he was startled to find that convoys averaging thirty-two ships had 2.5 percent losses, but that convoys averaging fifty-four ships suffered only 1.1 percent losses. Those figures offended common sense, and Blackett knew that his team would have to develop convincing reasons to explain them. One reason was readily apparent: while the fifty-four-ship convoy occupied a larger sea area than a thirty-two-ship convoy, the guarded perimeter of the area did not expand by the same proportion. And several weeks of hard analysis produced these findings:

> It was found: (a) that the chance of a convoy being sighted was nearly the same for large and small convoys; (b) that the chance that a U-boat would penetrate the [escort] screen depended only on the linear density of escorts, that is, on the number of escort vessels for each mile of perimeter to be defended; and (c) that when a U-boat did penetrate the screen, the number of merchant ships sunk was the same for both large and small convoys—simply because there were always more than enough targets. These facts taken together indicated that one would expect the same *absolute number* of ships to be sunk whatever the size of convoy, given the same linear escort strength, and thus the *percentage* of ships sunk to be inversely proportional to the size of the convoys. Hence the objective should be to reduce the number of convoys sighted by reducing the number of convoys run, the size of the convoys being increased so as to sail the same total number of ships.[58]

Even with these data in hand, Blackett had difficulty convincing the Naval Staff to enlarge the size of convoys, since the staff worried about the vulnerability of a sixty-ship convoy to frontal attacks, an increasingly popular U-boat tactic, as well as about communication and control problems. He eventually won them over, however, and the Admiralty, in turn, at the 3 March meeting of the A.U. Committee, gained that body's approval to start running sixty-*or-more*-ship convoys on a case-by-case basis, as would be done.[59] A sixty-one-ship convoy, HX.231, departed Halifax on 29 March escorted by one frigate (SO), one destroyer, and four corvettes (Escort Group B7; see chapter 4). Helped by a Support Group and Liberators, it arrived at Londonderry 95 percent intact. Blackett wrote later that it was unfortunate he had not appreciated the importance of the convoy size question much earlier than he did. During the preceding year alone 200 ships might have been saved.[60]

In a report to the A.U. Committee dated 5 February, Blackett threw himself into the defense versus offense debate that was then brewing in all the pertinent Commands. Without taking sides, he presented the "defensive values" of saving ships and the "offensive values" of attacking U-boats. Briefly stated, the defensive value of the surface escorts was found, first, by noting that shipping losses in the North Atlantic during the last six months of 1942 were at a rate of 210 ships per year, while the average number of escorts was 100. Since the statistics showed that the number of ships torpedoed per submarine present in an attack decreased as the escort force increased, and that an increase of the average escort strength from six to nine would be expected to decrease the losses by about 25 percent, had there been an additional 50 escorts available in the time period cited losses should have been reduced by fifty-two ships (25 percent). Or, expressed differently, each escort vessel would have saved about one ship a year.

In determining the offensive value of surface escorts, the assumption was made that the sinking of a U-boat saved the shipping it would have sunk in subsequent months. If the escorts sank seven and damaged eight U-boats, and the eight damaged could be considered the equivalent of two additional boats sunk, since the statistics showed that about 0.4 ships were sunk per month by each operational boat, an average of 3.6 ships were saved by the sinking of a U-boat. In their offensive role the 100 escorts saved about 0.7 ships per escort vessel per year. A comparison of the defensive and offensive numbers gave the edge to the defense. Where aircraft were concerned, Blackett made similar assumptions and calculations. Using air cover over threatened convoys in the period cited, for defensive value, he calculated that each long-range aircraft in its average life of forty sorties saved about thirteen ships by defensive action. By contrast, where aircraft conducted hunting operations independent of convoys, for example, the Bay Offensive and other search and attack sweeps, the offensive value obtained from the maximum number of sorties flown by one aircraft was about three ships saved. Again, the results favored the defense.[61]

All through March and April the defense-offense question was debated at Western Approaches, where there was increasing criticism that the current policy–"The safe and timely arrival of the convoy at its destination is the primary object of the escort"–was insufficiently bold. Even the role of the Support Groups as ancillary to the close escorts was thought by some to be a waste of their aggressive potential. Admiral Horton, whom no one could accuse of lacking in offensive spirit, and who longed for the day when he could simply "attack and kill," nonetheless approached the question carefully, mulling over what was known of recent enemy contact and behavior.

During April sixteen convoys were attacked and suffered loss, in no case severe, however; the largest number of ships torpedoed in any one convoy was four. Of those, seven were transatlantic convoys (HX.231–234 inclusive, ON.176 and 178, and ONS.3). The typical U-boat Commander still preferred to attack on the surface at night despite the fact that radar and snowflakes (illuminants) had made that a more hazardous action than it was the year before. The U-boats now strove to get ahead of a convoy, apparently so that they could attack submerged if success on the surface seemed unlikely. In making follow-up attacks, U-boats took advantage of the disturbance created by first attacks, and they displayed a tendency to follow one another in from the same direction, from a mile or two back. Boats detected and driven off by the escorts at night frequently made no additional attempts to attack during the remainder of the night; thus, the boats had only to be detected for the battle to be half-won.

With present enemy policy, most attacks developed in front of the beam of the convoy. The U-boats were attacking more eastbound than westbound convoys, no doubt because the latter carried no cargo and were under first-class air protection for the first 600 miles of their run. Their tendency was to operate primarily in the area between 500 and 700 miles to the northeast of Newfoundland, presumably to be outside the range of aircraft based in Iceland and Ireland, air cover from Newfoundland not apparently being much of a concern to them.

Horton then considered various aspects of escort work: Practically every U-boat sunk during the past year was destroyed *prior* to its attack on a convoy, not afterward. U-boats were most effectively dealt with when they were on the surface, now that asdic was no longer the escort's only weapon; therefore, forcing a U-boat to dive was not always the best policy. Analysis of asdic figures on lost contact for the last six months of 1942 showed that sixty-four percent of boats were at depths of less than 200 feet when lost. And since the morale of the Merchant Navy was showing signs of strain, it was undesirable to use convoy ships as "bait," that is, to accept the sinking of merchant ships as a way of indicating the presence of a U-boat so that it might be attacked.

With that, however, Horton in effect threw up his hands. None of the recent data were any help in resolving the defense-offense question. To defend or to hunt? He finally decided that the Tactical Policy "must still be the safe and timely arrival of the convoy." But there was no reason he could not have it both ways. He left the Escort Groups open to "exercise their initiative under all circumstances," thus giving them authorization to take such offensive action as seemed prudent, necessary, and opportune, while making certain that the convoys under their care were not unduly exposed to enemy attack. "The matter was largely a question of numbers," he wrote in a signal sent on 27 April to all British and Canadian Escort and Support Groups under CinCWA. "Whatever form of warfare is considered, the question of the strength of the opposing forces must play a very large part in deciding whether an offensive or defensive role can be adopted."[62] The defense-offense question, then, would not be decided at Derby House. It would be decided at sea.

4

To Defend

The Battle for ONS.5

> The safe and timely arrival of the convoy at its destination is the primary object of the escort. Evasion attains the primary object, and should therefore be the first course of action considered. At the same time, it must be borne in mind that if enemy forces are reported or encountered, the escort shares with all other fighting units the duty of destroying enemy ships, provided this duty can be undertaken without undue prejudice to the safety of the convoy.
>
> ATLANTIC CONVOY INSTRUCTIONS

Forty-three merchant ships that would make up Outward North Atlantic Slow Convoy Five, abbreviated ONS.5 and code-named MARFLEET, assembled for their voyage on 21–22 April. Destination: Halifax, Nova Scotia, with detachments to Boston and New York. Mostly gray in color, their names painted out, they had sailed from five different ports–Milford Haven, Liverpool, the Clyde, Oban, and Londonderry–and now had rendezvoused off a lighthouse-crested rock called Oversay that rises from the sea at the North Channel entrance between northeast Ireland, the southern isle of the Inner Hebrides, and the Mull of Kintyre. There, over a twenty-four-hour period, the convoy Commodore J. Kenneth Brook, R.N.R., formed his charges, three and four deep, into a broad front of twelve columns. At the center, in column six, Brook stationed himself ahead in the Norwegian ship *Rena,* with only the New York-bound American oiler *Argon* astern.

Most of the ships were elderly tramp steamers. Most were British, but *McKeesport, West Madaket,* and *West Maximus,* as well as *Argon,* were of United States registry; *Bonde, Rena,* and *Fana* were Norwegian; *Berkel* and *Bengkalis* were Dutch; *Agios Georgios* and *Nicolas* were Greek; *Ivan Topic* Yugoslav; *Isabel* Panamanian; and *Bornholm* Danish. Two ships, *McKeesport* and *Dolius* (British), had been with SC.122 when that convoy was savaged by U-boats on 17-20 March. There was not a ship at R/V Oversay that had not sailed in convoy before. The majority were steaming in ballast, bound eventually for North and South American ports where they would load up food, fuel, raw materials, and finished weapons. Seven ships carried coal ("coal out, grain home"), four had general cargoes, and one listed general cargo and clay. Three ships in addition to those at Oversay were to join the formation at sea from Reykjavik, Iceland, on 26 April: *Gudvor, Bosworth,* and the U.S. Navy tanker U.S.S. *Sapelo,* which was returning to the States in ballast. Most of the convoy vessels were Defensively Equipped Merchant Ships (D.E.M.S.) with single four-inch guns manned by Navy and Army gunners. Gross Register Tonnage varied greatly, from tiny *Bonde* at 1,570 tons to the largest freighters at plus or minus 10,000 GRT.

Whatever their size, the merchantmen were expected, once underway, to maintain a speed of seven and a half knots, though their Masters knew, with gale-force seas forecast along the westward course, that was not a likely prospect. The ships' crews also varied in composition, most of them British Merchant Navy, some U.S. Navy and Merchant Marine, others East Indian or Asian in whole or in part except for officers. Most crew had small canvas "panic bags" for carrying their most valued possessions into the lifeboats, if that became necessary; the Americans' bags were more the size of railroad luggage.

By 1200* on 22 April this unexceptional, businesslike merchant fleet was formed up at Oversay with 1,000 yards sepa-

---

* All times are expressed in Greenwich Mean Time (GMT) unless otherwise noted.

rating the columns and 800 yards between each ship ahead and astern. The entire formation occupied eight and three-quarter square nautical miles. The shepherd, Commodore Brook, had gathered his flock. Now he awaited the sheepdog, who, he hoped, would hold the sea wolves at bay. At 1400 the sheepdog arrived in the person of Commander Peter Gretton, R.N., Senior Officer Escort, aboard the destroyer H.M.S. *Duncan*, accompanied by the frigate H.M.S. *Tay;* the corvettes H.M.S. *Loosestrife, Pink, Snowflake, and Sunflower;* two rescue trawlers, *Northern Gem and Northern Spray;* and the tanker *British Lady*.

Together, the warships made up Escort Group B7, the midocean close escort screen charged with seeing convoy ONS.5 to a "safe and timely arrival" at its assigned destination on the opposite shore.[1] A second destroyer, H.M.S. *Vidette,* had been sent ahead to escort the two freighters and the USN tanker from Iceland to a midocean rendezvous with the main body. *Vidette's* Captain, Lieutenant Raymond S. Hart, R.N., was the only regular officer besides Gretton in the group. Two corvette Captains were Australians, one was Canadian; several officers were New Zealanders.

Thirty-year-old Peter William Gretton was educated at the Dartmouth and Greenwich Royal Navy colleges, and, rather than select a career specialization, which was the usual route to promotion, he chose to remain a general seaman officer, or "salt horse." In a nod to specialization he learned to fly and amassed fifty hours of solo time, though he pronounced himself "not a good pilot." In 1936 he earned a Distinguished Service Cross (DSC) leading a landing party at Haifa during the Arab rebellion in Palestine. Three years later, as war with Germany loomed, he did a week's course in anti-submarine warfare at Portland, H.M.S. *Osprey*. That experience, together with his flying, would give him a leg up in understanding the U-boat war when it came. His hankering had always been for destroyers, and he counted himself lucky to be appointed First Lieutenant of the famous destroyer *Cossack,* on which he served in the Second Battle of Narvik, where he was mentioned in dispatches. In 1941 he received his own destroyer command on *Sabre,* and entered convoy escort duty full-time. Transferred to command of the destroyer *Wolverine* in 1942, he helped escort the celebrated Malta convoy in August of that year and, while steaming in the Mediterranean at 26 knots, rammed and sank the Italian submarine *Dagabur,* with the loss of all hands, for which action he was awarded the first of three Distinguished Service Orders (DSOs).

During the weeks when the crumpled bows of *Wolverine* underwent repair, Gretton took the anti-submarine warfare course devised by Captain Roberts at the Tactical Unit in Derby House, Liverpool. The schooling was a turning point for Gretton in several ways. First, he learned how unaware he had been of German submarine tactics and of the best means for frustrating them by use of the latest shipborne detection and weapons technology. Under Robert's tutelage, he quickly filled in the knowledge gaps.

Above all, Roberts stressed, effective ASW seamanship meant learning how, perhaps for the first time, to *think.* War at sea had changed. Courage and endurance were no longer enough. Victory over the U-boat required the intelligent use of technical aids, particularly HF/DF, 10-centimeter radar, and asdic, in that sequence. Second, Gretton realized at Derby House how much convoy duty had been denigrated by the regular Navy, which esteemed big ship–big gun fleet actions and considered the passive tending of seaborne trade as beneath their dignity, with the result that all the best officers went to the Home and Mediterranean fleets, while the failed careers and incompetents ended up in Western Approaches— with certain very notable exceptions, for example, Captain Frederic John Walker, R.N., and Captain Donald Macintyre, R.N., salt horses like Gretton. There was a desperate need in the Atlantic of more good regulars, he concluded (and when, belatedly, in 1943–44, the Home Fleet regulars realized that the Atlantic was where the war was, they climbed over each other to get Escort Group commands). Third, Gretton determined that if ever he received an Escort Group command of his own, he would bring his regular and reserve officers up to Roberts's—and now his—exacting high standards.

That brass hat came in December 1942 when he was advanced to command of Escort Group B7, based at Londonderry. There he embarked in the new twin-screw River class frigate *Tay*, while the destroyer assigned to him, the eleven year-old, 329-foot, *D*–class flotilla leader H.M.S. *Duncan*, was refitting in Tilbury docks prior to recommissioning. The B7 Group had just come off a rough convoy engagement in which the Senior Officer Escort (SO) and his ship had been lost, but Gretton found his ships to be "in great heart." Throughout January, February, and March, a period of expanding U-boat activity, he led them on cross-Atlantic passages that were, ironically, eventful for their lack of U-boat contacts. "For three months the group ran hard but had nothing to show for it but rust," he wrote later. "We seemed always to steer clear of the wolf packs, which were then at the height of their success."[2]

Aboard *Tay* he had his first sea experience with an HF/DF set. The Type FH3 equipment could identify the general position of a U-boat transmitting to base or to another boat on a high-frequency wave band, even indicate whether the U-boat was near or far. More exact "fixing" of a U-boat's position required the "cross-cut bearing" provided by a second HF/DF-equipped ship, as *Duncan* would be when recommissioned. Between sailings Gretton worked his officers and technical ratings hard at Londonderry's asdic and depth charge trainers, radar and HF-DF detection simulators, and the new Night Escort Attack Teacher, where all ranks and ratings who manned detection and communications equipment, the plotting table, or the bridge received intensive and realistic attack drills in nighttime conditions. Time and again they practiced on land the tactical maneuvers they would have to carry out at sea, which bore such code names as Raspberry, Half-Raspberry, Observant, and Artichoke.

Gretton was relentless in the conduct of these exercises and he was quite prepared to sack anyone who flagged in the effort. Among his Captains he had the reputation of an egotist but a gentleman, a hard man but a fair man. "Kindness to incompetents seldom provided a dividend," he wrote after the war, "whereas severity invariably paid. As [German Field Marshal Erwin] Rommel said, 'The best form of welfare is hard training.' . . . But the sailor will never admit it."[3] Gretton had no need as yet to purge this group, however, and the men of B7 seemed to have welded into a tautly skilled team.

Group B7 finally got its blooding in early April when it relieved a Canadian group escorting the fast (nine knots) Convoy HX.231 from New York to the United Kingdom. Entering the mid-Atlantic Air Gap on 4 April, B7 soon had more than enough U-boat contact to make up for its sterile months, as for over four days and nights it battled a pack of fourteen boats. *Tay,* commanded by Lieutenant-Commander Robert Evan Sherwood, R.N.R., made asdic contact with one of them, U–*635,* and sank her with a well-placed pattern of depth charges. Another boat, U–*632,* had been sunk earlier by a Liberator aircraft from Iceland. And U–*294,* badly damaged by depth charges, was forced to return to base. But six merchantmen were lost in the exchange: three in convoy and three stragglers.

The first loss, that of the British motorship *Shillong,* was the worst for Gretton. Loaded with zinc concentrate and wheat in bulk, the 5,529-GRT vessel sank from view within two minutes of being torpedoed, casting her entire crew into the sea. On her search for the U-boat, *Tay* passed slowly through the bobbing survivors, their life jackets aglow with red lights. Gretton shouted encouragement to them, but knew that pursuing the U-boat was his most urgent duty, lest others be attacked, and that *Tay* must not lie hove to lest a torpedo remove her from the screen. But, as late as 1964, when he wrote about the men he left to die, he called the moment "my most painful memory of the war. . . ."[4]

. . . The triple task–
To screen the convoy, counter-attack, and then,

The human third of rescuing the sailors,
Seemed far beyond the escort's hope or effort.

> To save to kill, to kill to save, were means
> And ends closely and bloodily allied.
>
> . . . High strategy
> Demanded of the brain an execution
> Protested by the tactics of the heart.
>
> E. J. Pratt

Finally, a mist descended on the ocean swells and ruined the visibility of the U-boats. On 7 April aircraft roared overhead in great numbers. Eventually, landfall was made off the north coast of Ireland, and B7 reentered its home port at Londonderry. Ninety-five percent of the convoy had come through the pack battle unharmed, and B7 had acquitted itself well in its first real trial of pluck and mind. Gretton was pleased—except with the performance of *Loosestrife,* whose Captain, in his view, had not shaped up to standards, and whom he promptly replaced.

Waiting for Gretton was the recommissioned *Duncan,* which not only gave him a destroyer to go with the frigate *Tay,* but also gave him a second HF/DF set (Type FH4), which made possible cross-cut bearings in combination with *Tay*'s FH3, which alone during HX.231 had proved "worth its weight in gold."[5] *Duncan* was also reequipped with the latest asdics, Type 271 10-centimeter radar, and radio transmitters and receivers. On deck she mounted two guns, two torpedoes, and the new forward-firing impact-fused "Hedgehog." Extra depth charge stowage had been created. His complement of 175 officers and men was unknown and untried, however, and he immediately set them to work jousting with last war-type submarines in the Londonderry exercise area, except on those days when he was asked to review HX.231 with Admiral Horton (CinCWA) in Liverpool, address a large audience of officers on the same operation, and huddle with RAF Coastal Command pilots on how better surface and air escort cooperation might be promoted.

Then came the date, long predetermined, for ONS.5.

As he pulled alongside the Commodore's ship, *Rena,* Gretton exchanged documents with Brook, whose orders had come from the Trade Division of the Admiralty, and advised him by loud-hailer of the disposition of his forces. Gretton stationed *Duncan* in the center behind *Argon* and formed up the rest of his force on the port bow, beam, and quarter, and on the starboard bow and quarter, with the tanker and rescue trawlers astern. The screen in place, Brook signaled his convoy to gather way on course 280°. Notwithstanding the confidence B7 had gained from HX.231, Gretton had every reason at this moment to be apprehensive. He was sailing northwestward into what forecasters told him was atrocious weather with gale-force winds. That meant that his convoy ships, light on the water because they were in ballast, would be buffeted about like so many champagne corks, and that would work havoc with stationkeeping, throw some ships out of control, and leave others stragglers. Maintaining seven and a half knots would be impossible under those conditions. Furthermore, their course, northwest to 61°45'N, 29°11'W, a position east of Ivigtut on Greenland, and thence southwest along the Great Banks of New-foundland, would engage his fleet with pack ice and bergs.

Gretton knew that Western Approaches thought that the northern route was worth the hazard, since aircraft could provide cover south and to the west. Even so, while bombers could fly along much of his route from bases in Northern Ireland and Iceland, ONS.5 eventually would enter the Air Gap longitudes below Greenland that most of those aircraft could not reach. And that was where he assumed the majority of U-boats would be lurking. Were they perhaps already stationed directly athwart his course? Western Approaches had assured him that it had routed ONS.5 through waters that were least expected to be U-boat-infested. It may have informed him, furthermore–the surviving records do not say–that Admiral Dönitz had a record number of boats at sea (27 on return passage) and that probably as many as 36 boats were formed into two operational patrol lines, *Meise* and

Specht (Woodpecker), positioned along an arc 500 miles east of Newfoundland.

It could not give him the source of these data because Gretton, like other commanders of his duty and rank, was not "indoctrinated," that is, in the know about "Z," or "Special Intelligence," which was distributed through one-time pad ciphers to a tightly restricted list of recipients in the source-disguising from called "Ultra." Nor could Western Approaches inform him that the German communications monitoring and cryptographic service, B-Dienst, had possibly discerned ONS.5's course from decrypts of the Anglo-American Naval Cipher No. 3 ("Convoy Code"). If that was so, it is not known on exactly what day such information might have been communicated to BdU. B-Service messages to BdU no longer exist. Weekly summaries of B-Service information do exist, in the Bundesarchiv-Militärarchiv in Freiburg im Breisgau, but the summary for the week of 19-25 April contains no mention of ONS.5. Decryptions of the convoy code were not always current.

An example of the time lag between interception and decryption is the mention of ONS.5 that occurs in the Weekly Summary of 10-16 May, which begins: "The Iceland detachment of ONS.5 consisting of at least three merchant ships [escorted by H.M.S. *Vidette*] was to leave port at 0715 hours on 23 April in order to rendezvous with the main body [of the convoy] during the daytime of 26 April. . . ."[6] Obviously, with such a delay this information had no operational value. The first mention of ONS.5 in the weekly summaries dates from 26 April–2 May, and relates to Third Escort Group (EG3), which will be considered below.

The first week of the voyage went about as Gretton expected. There was the usual mechanical mishap. At 2200 on the first night, the Polish *Modlin* (3,569 GRT), beset by engine trouble, parted company with the eighth column and returned to the Clyde. At daybreak on the 23rd the weather worsened. High waves and strong winds forced numerous ships out of position. B7 busied itself chivvying stragglers back into line all that day and night. As much as he could, *Duncan* kept to the center column, No. 6, and maintained the convoy's slow speed as a means of saving fuel, since the refitted destroyer had been improved in every way except in fuel consumption, for which she was notorious. Her daily consumption at slowest possible speed was 8 percent. At 1630 on the 24th, despite continued heavy seas, *Duncan* closed with *British Lady* in an attempt to top up his bunkers, but after the tanker discharged only two of her 600 tons the buoyant wire and rubber hose streamed astern parted, and *Duncan* had to withdraw and wait for calmer seas. Refueling from *Argon* was impossible, he discovered, except in mirror-flat water, since the positioning of the American oiler's canvas hoses would require *Duncan* to come alongside—too dangerous a maneuver in high seas. The uselessness of *Argon*'s precious cargo was foreboding.

Duncan and *Tay* made regular HF/DF sweeps for U-boats transmitting to BdU or to others boats, but heard nothing. Actually, there was a U-boat not far ahead on their course, but for some reason, still unclear, it had not made a transmission to BdU since sortieing from Kiel, Germany, on 15 April. B7 would not learn of its presence until later in the evening of the 24th, when the boat was attacked by Boeing Flying Fortress "D" of No. 206 Squadron based at Benbecula in the Outer Hebrides. RAF Flying Officer Robert Leonard Cowey was piloting eight miles northwest of ONS.5 on a plan devised by Coastal Command to give the convoy cover from the afternoon of the 24th to midnight on the 27th.

At 1725 one of his crew sighted a fully surfaced U-boat ten miles distant. It was U–*710*, a newly commissioned Type VIIC, on her first war cruise, under an untried commander, Oblt.z.S. Dietrich von Carlowitz, who was probably unaware of the convoy's proximity. Instead of alarm-diving at the appearance of Cowey's aircraft, which was normal U-boat behavior, Carlowitz sent a crew to man the anti-aircraft guns on the platform aft the tower. Inaccurate tracers brushed by as Cowey dove the four-engine bomber to the deck and released a stick of six depth charges (D/Cs) that straddled the U-boat at right angles to her track. The brand-new bows heaved ver-

tically from the explosions and the rear gunner watched the
hull sink stern-down in a forth of debris. Cowey circled back
and dropped another stick into the wreckage, after which he
counted twenty-five survivors flailing in the water. There was
nothing anyone could do for them. Low on fuel, and his
home base closed in by weather, Cowey headed for Reykjavik.[7]

For ONS.5, dawn broke on the 25th with the ocean surface in a state of upheaval. Commander Brook struggled to
keep his ships in station as howling winds and fierce wave action forced numerous vessels out of line. Brook recorded:
"Convoy making 2–3 knots, steering badly."[8] These conditions continued into the night when, at one point, Brook and
Gretton could see seven different sets of "two red lights vertical" from ships that were Not Under Control. The inevitable
happened, as *Duncan* signaled Western Approaches: DURING
GALE LAST NIGHT NO. 93 BORNHOLM COLLIDED WITH NO. 104
BERKEL. BOTH DAMAGED. 104 IS CONTINUING BUT BORNHOLM
LEFT UNESCORTED FOR REYKJAVIK AT 1400. The collision occurred at 2355 when the convoy was proceeding at no more
than 2 knots on course 301°. Brook, who did not learn of the
accident until the next morning, reported that *Bornholm* was
holed in the Engine Room about 10 feet above the waterline.
He commented that progress made against the stormy seas
that night was so slight that the convoy was "to all intents and
purposes hove-to."[10]

A moderate gale continued through the morning hours of the
26th, when all ships were sighted but scattered. B7 managed
to whip in all but No. 81, *Penhale,* lead ship of column 8, which
straggled astern so badly Gretton detached her to Reykjavik,
escorted by *Northern Spray.* During the forenoon hours convoy speed was 3 knots. At 1400 Gretton was cheered by the
arrival of the Iceland contingent–B7's second destroyer,
H.M.S. *Vidette,* with the British *Bosworth,* the Norwegian
Gudvor, and the empty U.S. naval tanker *Sapelo*–which had
been homed to ONS.5's position by HF/DF and an RAF
PBY Catalina. *Vidette* gave Gretton a destroyer not only faster

(25 knots) than *Duncan* but the twenty-five-year-old V&W (Long-Range Escorts) Class vessel also had "longer legs," owing to the removal of one of her boilers and the installation in the vacated space of extra oil stowage. *Vidette* was equipped with asdic and Type 271 radar, though not with HF/DF; hence she could not join *Duncan* and *Tay* in acquiring cross-bearings on U-boat transmissions. Gretton continued to fret about *Duncan's* ability to continue at sea. Unless the weather cleared, he signaled Western Approaches, he might have to separate and refuel in Greenland.[11]

Fortunately, the seas subsided the following morning, long enough for *Duncan* to top up successfully from *British Lady,* completing the process at 1100. He was followed by *Vidette* and the corvette *Loosestrife,* while RAF Hudsons from Iceland provided cover overhead. Later that day *Northern Spray* rejoined the convoy. Gretton recorded his position as 61°25′N, 23°49′W, south of Reykjavik and due east of Cape Discord on Greenland. So far there had been no sightings or electronic detections of U-boats. Except for the boat sunk three days before by Fortress "D," there seemed to be no boats around. If there were, perhaps they were concentrated on a mid-Atlantic convoy known to be on the reciprocal of the same northern course that swept the southern tip of Greenland: The heavily laden SC.128, which departed Halifax on 25 April for the United Kingdom, had been routed to pass north and west of the U-boat groups known to the OIC Tracking Room as of its sailing date.

Between the 22nd and the 25th the *Specht* and *Meise* groups, together with new boats just arrived in the area, had been reshaped by BdU to form three Groups: *Specht, Meise,* and *Amsel* (Blackbird). The *Specht* line, with seventeen U-boats, ran from 54°15′N, 43°15′W to 51°15′N, 38°55′W. An augmented *Meise* line, with thirty boats, ran from 59°15′N, 32°36′W to 56°45′N, 28°12′W. The *Amsel* line, with eleven boats, ran from 54°51′N, 32°00′W to 53°45′N, 29°35′W.[12] The BdU orders establishing these dispositions originated as part of a plan to catch westbound ONS.4, but that convoy arrived at New York safely and intact. Two other convoys on northern courses, SC.127 (departed Halifax 16 April) and ON.179 (departed Liverpool 18 April) successfully eluded the patrol lines, SC.127 being diverted to a more northerly course on the 26th after the order enlarging *Meise* was decrypted nearly fourteen hours after its interception[13]—and just under the wire, as will be shown below. Convoy ON.180 (departed Liverpool 24 April), which trailed ONS.5, similarly would evade the patrol lines. With the majority of U-boats in northern latitudes, two other U.K.-bound convoys that were at sea in this period, HX.235 and HX.236, were safely directed along southerly courses.

Two entries in the BdU war diary for this period are significant for revealing German operational failures and intelligence misjudgments. The first entry, dated 25 April: An earlier eastbound convoy, HX.234, which sailed the northern route and made port in the U.K. with two ships sunk and one damaged, had been pursued for four days (21–25 April) by no fewer than nineteen boats. The investment of that much energy and time had yielded disproportionately small success. In explaining the failure, Admiral Dönitz and Chief of Staff Godt enumerated unfavorable weather, particularly snow and fog; changing visibility conditions; the shortness of the nights on the northern route; strong air cover from Greenland and Iceland; and (cited twice) "the inexperience of the large number of new Commanders who were not equal to the situation."[14]

The second entry, dated 27 April: the BdU reflected on the fact that on the day before, convoy SC.127 had suddenly changed to a more northerly heading and had passed untouched through a temporary seam between Groups *Meise* and *Specht,* which at the moment were maneuvering to new positions. Furthermore, an intercepted American U-boat Situation Report revealed that the Allies knew exactly where the U-boat groups were deployed as well as their current movements, and had the capability to reroute convoys accordingly. How had the enemy gained such knowledge? The BdU answered: "This confirms, more than ever, the suspicion that the enemy has at his disposal a radar device especially effective in aircraft, which our boats are powerless to intercept."[15]

Of course, it is true that the Allies had 10-centimeter airborne radar, undetectable by any equipment with which the U-boats were then supplied, but its average range sweep was fifteen miles, hardly what would be required to descry the positions of even one wolfpack. Apparently Dönitz and Godt more readily believed in the existence of a (for then) preternatural eye in the sky that laid bare anything that moved across thousands of square miles of ocean than that Allied cryptographers had simply done what B-Dienst had done: cracked the other side's cipher. That commonsense conclusion—a kind of Ockham's Razor—never swayed BdU's mind, and Dönitz himself obstinately refused to entertain the likelihood throughout the war and after it. (He similarly refused to believe at this time, as earlier noted, that the Allies possessed shipborne HF/DF capability.) But *had* he been aware that cryptographic intelligence was the source of the Allies' uncanny knowledge, Dönitz would have been greatly encouraged by something else that happened on the day that SC.127 slipped past harm's way: the Allied cryptographers went blind.

At 1200 on 26 April, owing to changes unexpectedly introduced by Berlin in naval Engima settings, GC&CS and the OIC Submarine Tracking Room abruptly ceased reading U-boat traffic, and would not read it again until the afternoon of 5 May, a critical period in ONS.5's westward voyage, since it was during those nine days of cryptographic intelligence blackout that Commander Gretton's convoy would enter the longitudes where U-boat packs were known to be maneuvering in strength.[16] With what Rodger Winn called "no precise information," the most that he and Patrick Beesly in the Submarine Tracking Room could tell CinCWA Admiral Horton after 26 April was that three U-boat groups were still thought to be "in the general area off Newfoundland." As Winn wrote later, "Thus [where ONS.5 was concerned] it was not possible to attempt any evasive routing although the convoy had in the first place been routed as far north as possible to avoid U-boats."[17] Three westbound convoys earlier in April, ON.178, ONS.3, and ONS.4, also had been routed north by the tip of Greenland, with small losses to the first two and none to the third.[18] Perhaps ONS.5 would be as lucky.

The OIC Tracking Room was not without alternative sources of information, as noted earlier. Wireless transmissions from the U-boats could be DFed by a shore-based HF/DF network that supplied Cross-bearings in the Atlantic theater; the U.K. had twenty stations, the U.S. sixteen, and Canada eleven.[19] Furthermore, short signals (*Kurzsignale*) in the old, still readable *Hydra*cipher (as *Heimische Gewässer* had been renamed on 1 January 1943) transmitted by *Räumboote* (motor minesweepers) escorting U-boats in and out of their Baltic and Biscay bases enabled Winn and Beesly to calculate daily the number of boats at sea; and they took into account the fact that by 26 April BdU had three Type XIV tanker and supply boats—*Milchkuhe*—U–487, U–459, and U–461, on station in mid-Atlantic, which could extend the time some of the attack boats, after refueling, could remain on operations. No alternative source, however, could give Winn and Beesly the same confidence that their Main North Atlantic Plotting Table represented actual conditions at sea as that provided, when readable, by crisply accurate "Z," particularly at those times when U-boat groups were regularly forming, re-forming, or shifting their operational areas.

The consequences for ONS.5 were immediate, and dangerous. Unknown to Winn and Beesly, hence unknown also to Horton and Gretton, on 27 April BdU established *Gruppe Star* (Starling), consisting of sixteen newly assembled boats, along a north-south patrol line, or "rake," at 30°W between latitudes 61°50′ and 57°00′N about 420 nautical miles east of Greenland. On the Kriegsmarine grid chart the new patrol line ran from AD 8731 via AK 3523 to AK 0329. The boats were to be in place by 0900 GST on the 28th.[20] The line's northernmost wing just brushed the course of ONS.5. At 0800 on the 28th the convoy was at position 61°45′N,

29°11′W, turning southwest. By 0800 the next day it would pass through 30°W to 34°51′W.[21] Group *Star* had been created expressly to catch the next westbound ONS convoy departing on the eight-day cycle, which was ONS.5.

Winn and Beesly were unable to recommend evasive routing because the order creating *Star*, unknown to them, went out the day after GC&CS's reading of naval Enigma ended. Commander Gretton could not have had that piece of information. Nor could he have known that while GC&CS's eyes were shut, the eyes of B-Service were still open. The German radio monitoring and cryptographic service was reading, though not always in real time, the Anglo-American Naval Cipher No. 3 used for convoy routing. The encrypted transmissions included the daily Admiralty or USN U-Boat Situation Reports (which should have been another clue to BdU that its own cipher had been compromised).

When data from B-Service on the composition, sailing date, course, and speed of a convoy reached the green baize table in BdU's situation room in Berlin/Charlottenburg, it was assigned a number. Convoy ONS.5 was assigned No.33. We do not know the exact form in which information about ONS.5 was first communicated to BdU because that daily or hourly message traffic no longer exists; but the B-Service's extant summary for 26 April–2 May discusses the convoy by name in connection with both the Third Escort Group (EG3), which will appear as a Support Group for ONS.5 later in this narrative, and a USN U-Boat Situation Report:

> The Third Convoy Escort Group was positioned at 47°20′N, 50°03′W on 29 April at 2100, course approximately 100°–200°, speed 15 knots, heading toward ONS.5; it should have changed course at 47°00′W by 11–13 degrees. The American U-Boat Situation Report of 30 April identified up to 20 boats in the general area 59°61′N, 30°43′W as a result of various wireless direction finding methods, and that a few of those boats continue to be positioned near ONS.5.

From this entry it is not possible to pinpoint the day when ONS.5 was first identified to BdU. The dates given, 29 and 30 April, relate to events reflected on after a week's decryption effort. Was word of ONS.5 passed to BdU as early as 26 April, when the week began? We may never know the answer. What *is* known is that in establishing the position of the *Star* line, the BdU war diary of 27 April stated: "The object of this is the interception of the next ONS convoy at present proceeding in the North. . . . A slow southwest-bound convoy is expected there on 28 April."[22]

Advantage: Germany.

At 0900 on the 28th, a time when some late-arriving boats were still maneuvering to their *Star* stations, Oblt.z.S. Ernst von Witzendorff had U-650 on the surface in naval square [qu] AD 8761. Conditions were a moderate sea, wind from the southeast Force 3, and visibility 12 nautical miles. One of the lookouts with binoculars on the conning tower bridge sighted, *"Mastspitzen!"* Von Witzendorff wrote in his KTB: "Mastheads sighted. I am closing them to see what we have. It's a convoy proceeding southwest." At 0942 he transmitted an *Ausgang F.T.* (outgoing wireless message) to BdU: CONVOY AD 8758. Seventeen minutes later he sent again: CONVOY STEAMING AT 8-10 NAUTICAL MILES, COURSE 270°. At 1040 Witzendorff was heartened to see another U-boat of Group *Star* surface a short distance away on the port side. Three minutes later, he received a message from BdU directed to all *Star* boats: GROUP STAR SHOULD ATTACK ON BASIS OF WITZENDORFF'S REPORT. WITZENDORFF IS FREE TO ATTACK AS SOON AS ANOTHER BOAT HAS CONTACT. At 1110 U-650 updated her first report: WESTBOUND CONVOY NOW IS AD 8728, SPEED 8 KNOTS.[23] The 1110 transmission was picked up and DFed by *Duncan* and *Tay*, as well as by escorts supporting eastbound Convoy SC.127, about 60 nautical miles due south of ONS.5.[24] Gretton now knew that ONS.5 was being shadowed—but on behalf of how many boats? He sent the corvette *Snowflake* to search down the bearing for the transmitting U-boat, which Gretton calculated, based on its strong signal, was "close ahead." Meanwhile, he altered course of the convoy 35 degrees to starboard and maintained 296° until 1600, when he returned to the original course. Snowflake's search was fruitless, as was a ten-mile high-speed sweep ahead of the convoy by Duncan. Visibility declined to three miles.

At 1650 a U-boat signal detected from astern at 085 degrees indicated that the course alteration, which placed ONS.5 north of the Star rake, had been successful, for the time being. Tay hunted down that bearing and Vidette tracked another, but made no contact. Gretton worried that the U-boat shadower was part of a large pack–one wholly unanticipated–and that it would not divide its forces between his convoy and SC.127 but concentrate them solely on him, and at night, when the U-boats had 17–18-knot surface speed. As dusk came he worried, furthermore, that he could expect no help from aircraft. The air escort given ONS.5 from 24 April had been discontinued at midnight on the 27th/28th, since there were no OIC reports of U-boats in the vicinity. The convoy had been sighted in the late afternoon by a distant USN Catalina, but the possibility of air cover this night, if requested, was remote, since Iceland was socked in by weather.

At 1838, as a heavy head sea formed, Duncan DFed a U-boat close on the port bow, bearing 210°. He chased it at maximum speed and ordered Tay to make a parallel search to port. At 1920 Duncan's bridge sighted a cloud of spray thrown up around a U-boat's conning tower, about two miles bearing 146°. Gretton altered course to pursue the boat, but at a range of about 3,000 yards it dived. In the rough sea Duncan's asdic failed to make contact, but Gretton fired a ten-charge pattern of D/C by plot. Duncan and Tay then carried out operation "Observant" for an hour. Observant was an asdic square search of two-mile sides with the "Datum Point" (contact point) at the center; one of the escorts could either reinforce the square (sometimes called box) or operate within it. Leaving Tay to sit on the submerged boat while the convoy passed, Duncan returned to establish night stations with the convoy at 2130.[25] The merchantmen, now beginning a southwest leg, were on course 240°, speed 7.5 knots. The wind was freshen-

ing from the southeast at 16–20 miles per hour and the sea
was rough, with moderate long swell.

Knowing that U-boats preferred to attack down sea, so
that spray did not betray their approaches, and knowing, too,
from HF/DF that the U-boats were on the port bow beam,
and quarter, and astern, Gretton "placed his field" with
strength to that side, leaving the starboard bow uncovered.[26]
Attack abaft the port beam was most probable. Where the
Germans were concerned, by nightfall only four of *Star's*
other U-boats had rallied to *U-650*'s reports: *U-386, U-378,
U-532,* and *U-528.* That more had not assembled on the convoy's course, despite BdU's urging to do so, was owed in part
to the "hazy weather" and "strong wind" against which the
boats "had to struggle during their pursuit of the enemy."
This, at any rate, was the assessment of BdU on 1 May, after
all the excuses were in.[27] If only five boats were on the scene
by darkness on the 28th, the rest were not unheard from,
however, as every Commander made his evening position report to Berlin. The W/T traffic–"like a chattering of mag-
pies"–was DFed in England as well as by B7's two HF/DF
sets.

For Gretton there were two immediate good results from
this chatter. In view of the concentration around ONS.5,
CinCWA detached destroyer H.M.S. *Oribi* from the escort of
SC.127 and sent her, at 20 knots, to his assistance. And since
this convoy was likely to be targeted by the western U-boat
packs, when it reached those longitudes a Support Group
(EG3) of four Home Fleet destroyers, H.M.S. *Offa* in command, was ordered to steam out of Newfoundland at 15 knots
to meet ONS.5[28] With those pledges of reinforcement to
brace their spirits, Gretton and his Captains prepared for the
night battle sure to come.

In an interview conducted fifty years later, Lieutenant
[now Sir] Robert Atkinson, R.N.R., Captain of the corvette
Pink, remembered the night of 28 April:

> Well, I remember once getting a fantastic signal. I will
> give you an example–in H.M.S. *Pink.* We were about a

hundred and fifty miles west-southwest of Iceland, approaching Greenland, and there was a moonlight night–going to be a moonlight night, a very nasty night, windy. And we received a signal from the Commander in Chief [Horton]: "You may expect attack from down moon at approximately 0200." Now they knew and were able to interpret in Whitehall [the Admiralty] the various radio activity and signals by the German U-boats–great activity. They knew where the moon would be and when it would rise and where the U-boats might attack from–he liked a profile. And by the feverish increased activity of the radio signalling, they knew attacks were imminent. Now we didn't know that, of course, but the fact that we had a signal telling us to be ready for attack about 0200 made all the difference. And Admiral Gretton, who was Commander Gretton then, we were so highly trained he sent a signal round to our escort group, and do you know what that signal said?–one word, "Anticipate," that's all he said. Didn't get excited, and didn't tell the men to do this, or not do the other. It wouldn't have been any good. We were trained; we knew what to do. And do you know what I did? It was about five o'clock, pitch black, windy as hell, and I said, "Hands to tea, six o'clock." Cleared lower deck and said, "There's going to be a hell of a battle tonight. I'm not sure how many of us will see daylight. I intend to see it if I can." So it was up to us.[29]

The night battle began earlier than Horton, or Atkinson, expected, at exactly 2358 when one of the four *Star* boats in the sea to port made the first of six attempted attacks that took place between that hour and daybreak on the 29th. Gretton wrote up his report of the action in unadorned telegraphic style:

The *first attempt* was made at 2358, when SUNFLOWER on the port bow got an RDF [radar] contact bearing 170°, range 3000 yards. She ran out towards, but the U-Boat dived, and as no A/S [asdic] contact was obtained she dropped two charges and resumed station. TAY was in station by 0300 [29 April] and at 0045 (the *second attempt*) DUNCAN got an RDF contact bearing 100°–3500 yards and turned to attack. The U-Boat dived at 2500 yards and A/S contact was picked up at 1500 but almost at once lost. I dropped one charge, ran out and back over the firing position and was resuming station when at 0114 (the *third attempt*) I obtained an RDF contact bearing 296°–2500 yards. I chased at best speed until at 0119 at range 1100 yards, the U-Boat dived and I reduced to operating speed. RDF plot gave U-Boat's course as 320° and at 0122 A/S contact was obtained on last RDF bearing, her wake was sighted, and an accurate ten-charge Minol [explosive charge] pattern was dropped. At 0130, while running out after this attack another RDF contact was obtained bearing 146°–4800 yards (the *fourth attempt*). I turned towards, chased and at 0140, the U-Boat dived at range 3000 yards. No A/S contact was obtained so one charge was dropped by plot. The chasing course was into the wind and seaspray was flying mast high and the U-Boat saw us coming earlier than when we had chased down sea.

As I was turning to resume station after this attack, yet another RDF contact was picked up bearing 210°–4000 yards at 0156 (the *fifth attempt*) and again I turned and chased at best speed. The U-Boat was heading for the convoy at about twelve knots, but at 0204 at range 1500 yards, he dived and I reduced to fifteen knots. At 0203, the ship passed through a patch of oil about fifty yards diameter, so this U-Boat may have been previously damaged. Good A/S contact was obtained and an accurate ten-charge Minol pattern fired. At the moment of the firing, his wake was clearly seen under the port bow. Contact was regained astern, but lost at 800 yds each time I attempted to attack, so that the idea of

The course of Convoy ONS.5 and the positions of U-boat patrol lines. *Star*, *Specht*, and *Amsel* are shown on the German grid chart. Nautical positions courtesy of Jürgen Rohwer. Cartographer: Paul Pugliese a hedgehog [impact-fused bombs fired forward] attack had to be abandoned. I dropped two deep charges on him by plot and resumed station at high speed. At 0054, I had ordered TAY to take position R [port quarter] in my absence. I was back in station by 0310, and TAY ordered to resume position S [astern].

SNOWFLAKE in position P [port beam] drove off the *sixth attempt*, at 0339, sighting a U-Boat on her port bow, range 1100 yards, steering towards the convoy. SNOWFLAKE attacked and fired two ten-charge patterns, a torpedo narrowly missing her in return. By 0348, SNOWFLAKE had dropped astern into the port quarter position so I moved up to the port beam in her place. At 0354, TAY, in position S, gained and attacked a good A/S contact—a possible but unlikely seventh attempt. By then, dawn was starting to break, and at 0416 I ordered day stations, so that ships would have plenty of time to gain bearing into the ahead stations for the expected dawn attack submerged. The night had been a busy one, the convoy unscathed, and I felt that the U-Boats must be discouraged by our night tactics and might try day attack.[30]

It was a good night's work, and Gretton was elated. Against what he estimated were "five or six" U-boats the B7 team had performed splendidly. Not a single ship in the convoy had been sunk or damaged. But he was sure that the U-boats had suffered, and he was right: of the four boats that actually participated in the attacks, two, U–386 (Oblt.z.S. Hans-Albrecht Kandler) and U–528 (Oblt.z.S. Georg von Rabenau) were heavily damaged and forced to withdraw to base, though it is not possible to determine whether it was *Duncan* or one of the corvettes, *Sunflower* or *Snowflake,* that was responsible for either or both. The Type VIIC U–386 limped into home port at St.-Nazaire on 11 May. On the same day, the Type IXC/40 U–528, also struggling to return from what was her first combat patrol, was approaching the Bay of Biscay when she was bombed by Halifax II "D" of 58 Squadron and finished off by H.M.S. *Fleetwood* and *Mignonette,* escorting convoy OS.47, with the loss of eleven killed, forty-five captured.[31] Gretton certainly thought he had a kill on the third U-boat attempt, which he called "an accurate attack," and this may have caused damage to one of the two boats cited. In any event, it was, as he said, "a most successful night."

On her maiden escort with the Group, *Duncan* had detected and attacked four separate U-boat advances in the space of one hour and fifty minutes, and in weather conditions where the ship was pitching and rolling wildly, and seas washing down the quarter deck made the work of loading and reloading the heavy D/Cs both difficult and dangerous.[32] Gretton used the loud-hailer to praise the behavior of his ship's company during their first baptism of fire. The two corvettes had also given a good account of themselves, although each committed an error: In dropping two D/Cs at 2208 to scare off any U-boats in her vicinity, *Sunflower* inadvertently dropped a calcium flare that lit up the entire seascape–"rather an unnecessary advertisement," as her Canadian Captain, Lt.-Cmdr. J. Plomer, R.C.N.V.R., dryly put it. *Sunflower* turned back to extinguish the light and, on a second attempt, by going hard to starboard, drew it through the propeller stream.[33]

Snowflake had a dicier experience, which Gretton called "an unusual slip in the drill." During the sixth U-boat attack, *Snowflake* followed a radar contact at 0332 and sighted an approaching boat in the process of diving. When about 200 yards astern of the boat's swirl, the wheel was suddenly put hard-a-starboard, though no such order had been given. As a result, the U-boat passed on a reciprocal bearing 200 yards down the port side and no D/Cs were fired. *Snowflake's* Captain, Lieutenant Harold G. Chesterman, R.N.R., dropped three D/Cs between the U-boat and the convoy as scare tactics. At 0336 he gained an asdic bearing at range 2,000 yards and turned to the attack. As he did so, at 0338, ship's hydrophone first detected, then lookouts sighted, a torpedo pass 20 yards down the port side.[34]

This was the only torpedo seen the night of 28th/29th. It

was launched by U–532 (Korv. Kapt. Ottoheinrich Junker), but it was not the only eel in the water. Just three minutes before, by periscope, Junker had launched a four-torpedo *Fächerschuss* (fan shot) from his bow tubes at what he called "the third steamer" in a column, estimated by him at 5,000–6,000 GRT. All the eels missed. The depth of run was three meters, which should have been shallow enough to hit a ship even in ballast. Seven and a half minutes later, Junker would hear end-of-run detonations. Meanwhile, using the two stern tubes that a Type IXC/40 boat commanded, he got off a double launch against *Snowflake* (only one of which torpedoes was sighted), missing again, as already noted, and hearing end-of-run detonations seven minutes later.

Junker states in his KTB (war diary) that as he placed the escort in his crosshairs, he could see convoy steamers in the background. His six misses in that crowded seascape were perhaps ineptitude, or just bad luck. The fault could not have been inexperience: the thirty-eight-year old native of Freiburg im Breisgau had commanded U-boats since 1936, though it bears mention that he did not have a single ship to his credit. With U-532 having to reload all tubes, the initiative now passed to *Snowflake*, which Junker's periscope displayed steaming toward him at high speed, only 1,200 meters distant. "Alarm!" his KTB records, as U-532 opened flood valves and dived to greater depth–and just in time, as *Snowflake* dropped a ten-charge pattern over him at 0343. When the noise and turbulence subsided at 0345, *Snowflake* regained asdic contact. With the recorder marking well, Chesterman came round to port, and at 0351 fired a ten-charge pattern set to 100 and 225 feet. This second attack, Chesterman noted, "is considered to be accurate." Then, with only "doubtful" asdic contact showing on the recorder, and concerned that he should husband his D/Cs remaining for battles to come, Chesterman shaped course to rejoin the convoy.

Deeper than 225 feet, U–532 was still alive, but wounded. Junker wrote in his KTB:

The entire hull of the boat vibrated violently. Before each depth-charge series we could hear the asdic sound pulses [Ping-*tongg!* Ping-*tongg!*] . . . We found major damage done to the forward hydroplanes. They ran quite laboriously and made strong knocking noises. They tended to stick in the "hard up" position, but could be freed again. For the time being we are limiting them to "up 15'". . . . A large number of manometers, lamps, and electrical equipment have gone out, though without any restrictive effect on the boat's operation. . . . Battery array No. 1 was badly cracked, with the result that acid leaked into the bilges. . . . The magnetic compass broke, which is a nuisance because, unable to use the noisy gyrocompass when in creep, or stalking speed [*Schleichfahrt,* about 2.5 knots] we have no means for checking the course of the boat. . . . I don't want to end up running into the hands of the enemy.

Junker records that he remained submerged, experiencing or hearing various series of D/Cs–five more ten-patterns– "additional series or single drops"–"new depth charge attacks"–"three more series"–as far as 0140 (2340 GMT on the 29th) on 30 April, when he surfaced, the last hours having been spent breathing through potash cartridges because of the 3 percent level of CO_2 in the boat. Troubled by intolerable noises inside the boat, he set course back to base. The BdU gave U–*532* credit for "two hits" and duly noted the boat's ordeal: "She was hunted for fifteen hours." The problem with the fifteen-hour story is that the D/Cs heard by U–*532* after *Snowflake's* two drops were not meant for her but for the U-boat involved in the *McKeesport* event, described below. The sum of U–*532's* patrol was: no hits, six misses, and one badly bent boat forced back to base.[35]

The BdU did not learn of U–*532's* alleged hits until 2 May. At the time of the night battle it was dismayed that not a single *Treffer,* or hit, had been scored. In rationalizing the failure, it argued first that the boat's messages to Berlin were inaccurate. They overestimated the convoy's speed—certainly that was the case with U-650's initial estimates—and the reports from U-386 and U-378 on the enemy's position were too far distant from each other to make any sense. Second, atmospheric or magnetic interference apparently was preventing BdU's operational orders from getting through, since no acknowledgments were coming back, and no messages of any kind were received from the boats during the period from 0300 GST on the 29th to 1200 on the 30th. Third, Force 6 winds, heavy seas, and limited visibility greatly hampered surface operations.[36] For the first time in a long while, Admiral Dönitz's command and control system had been frustrated and bootless on the night of the 28th/29th. But an enterprising individual commander, operating on his own initiative, could break the string.

In the early daylight of the 29th, fulfilling Gretton's expectation that, unable to overcome B7's night tactics, the U-boats might try submerged attacks in daytime, U-258 (Kptlt. Wilhelm von Mässenhausen) slipped inside and under the convoy formation, where he took a position at periscope depth starboard of the convoy's No. 4 column. In doing so, he somehow avoided the asdic sweeps by the escorts on day stations as well as by *Tay,* which was searching astern for damaged or shadowing boats, and by *Vidette,* which returned to her station at 0725 after searching out 15 miles. It was broad daylight. At exactly 0729 1/2, the furtive U-258 scored a hit on the 6,198-GRT American Moore-McCormack freighter *McKeesport,* ship No. 42, the second ship in No. 4 column, which was on a return voyage from having delivered to Manchester, England, a cargo of grain, steel tanks, foodstuffs, and chemicals.[37]

Gretton was asleep in his sea cabin when the alarm bell rang. Dashing to the bridge, he ordered "Artichoke" at 0730. In this operation the ship in position "S," astern, closes the torpedoed ship at maximum asdic speed, and ships in the "forward line," that is, "A," ahead, "B," starboard bow, and "L," port bow, turn immediately outward to a course reciprocal to the course of the convoy and sweep in line abreast at 15

knots or at the maximum asdic sweeping speed of the slowest
ship, the wing ships passing just outside the convoy wake, the
inner ship(s) between the columns of the convoy, until reaching a line 6,000 yards astern of the position the convoy was in
when the ship was torpedoed. All other escorts continue on
the course of the convoy.

Five minutes later, Gretton saw a torpedo, which had
passed through several columns without a hit, explode at the
end of its run on the convoy's port quarter, indicating an attack from starboard, probably along 180 degrees. The rescue
trawler *Northern Gem* acquired an asdic contact astern of
McKeesport and made an attack with three D/Cs. There was
no result. And an "Observant" carried out by *Duncan* proved
fruitless. Admiringly, Gretton called U–258's action "a bold
effort," and, what was more, the attacker got away–for now.[38]

On board *McKeesport* the torpedo's explosion had come as
a complete surprise. The Chief Officer, Junior Third Officer,
and two seamen-lookouts on the bridge made no periscope
sighting. Neither did the U.S. Naval Armed Guard who
manned a four-inch gun on the afterdeck. Nor did the sea-
man-lookout on the fo'c's'le, although on the starboard side
he did see a long, dark, round object leap across a trough of
the choppy sea, which he thought was a fish. He correctly
identified a second torpedo that ran astern, but it was too late
to warn about the first. When the warhead detonated with an
awesome bang, it not only shook the whole ship; it opened a
hole at the collision bulkhead of No. 1 hold, which, like holds
2, 3, and 5, was filled with sand ballast; put the steering apparatus out of order; flooded the forepart up to twin decks; and
twisted plates, beams, and hatches. Fire spread through
wooden grain fittings, but the inrushing sea put it out.

McKeesport lurched to port, causing the British *Baron Graham* on that side to consider evasive action. Incredibly, the
listing merchantman maintained convoy speed in her station
for fifty minutes, until, with her engine room flooding, she
started to sink at 0815, and the Master ordered Abandon
Ship. Life nets were thrown over the side and the boats were
lowered. Unfortunately, the boats became entangled in the

nets, and so did some of the men who used them to climb
down to rafts. Several seamen fell into the water, one of
whom would later die from exposure, the only fatality from
McKeesport's complement. Last to leave were the Master and
the crew of the Naval Armed Guard, under command of Ensign Irving H. Smith, U.S.N.R., who gallantly stood by their
gun until ordered to leave. The rescue ship *Northern Gem*
came alongside and picked up the survivors: forty-three
seamen, one critically injured, and twenty-five naval crew.

While the Master had cast overside his Confidential
Books, including his codes, in a weighted container, he had
neglected to jettison his ship's log and charts, on which future
rendezvous positions were marked. Accordingly, *Northern
Gem* made an effort to sink *McKeesport* with her ship's gun, but
the derelict ship remained afloat. It was U.S. Navy Department policy, stated by Secretary of the Navy Frank Knox on
30 March 1942, that "no U.S. Flag merchant ship be permitted to fall into the hands of the enemy." Since that was the
policy and *McKeesport* could be boarded by a U-boat crew,
Gretton ordered *Tay* to go back and hole the wreck, which
she did with depth charges.

The steel shell went down with all her relics of human
habitation, including eight decks of playing cards and other
games: cribbage, dominoes, checkers, and acey deucy; as well
as sports equipment: darts, deck tennis, two pairs of boxing
gloves, and one medicine ball; and divertissements: one por-
table radio, one Victrola, and twelve records. The Master had
no complaint about his escorts. The sinking was, he said, "just
one of those things." *Tay* then pursued a U-boat contact 49
miles astern and did not rejoin B7 until 0600 the next day, the
30th. At 1100 that morning the convoy half-masted colors for
the burial at sea of *McKeesport*'s lone fatality, John A. Anderson, a Swedish national, who had died on board *Northern
Gem*.[39]

No attack on ONS.5 developed during the night of the
29th/30th, although HF/DF and asdic contacts led *Duncan*
and *Snowflake* to drop "scare tactic" charges. The destroyer
Oribi, homed from astern by HF/DF, arrived during the

night, at 0100, from EG3. In the southwesterly wind and sea she had only been able to make 11 knots.[40] Her HF/DF equipment (Type FH3) lent additional detection ability to the screen. Coastal Command, alerted to ONS.5's peril on the 28th but delayed by weather conditions at 120 Squadron's air base at Reykjavik, finally was able to reestablish air contact when a VLR Liberator arrived overhead the convoy at 0645 on the morning of the 30th. Soon afterward, however, owing to a drop in visibility, the aircraft returned to base in Iceland.

The U-boats would remain at bay all that morning, and at 1045, the short-legged *Oribi* took advantage of the respite to oil from *British Lady*. Unfortunately, the destroyer, which was unaccustomed to refueling at sea, fouled the oiler's gear. That fact, plus a new deterioration in the weather that had already been, in Gretton's words, "astonishing even in the North Atlantic," made it impossible for other escorts to top up—with ultimately grave consequences for *Duncan*.[41] By 2100 another gale was blowing from ahead, the wave heights were rising steeply, and the escorts were rolling gunwales under.

At 0105, in the first highly visible sign that some of the U-boats had maintained contact during the past forty-one hours, *Snowflake* acquired a U-boat's radar signature at 3,300 yards, ran down the bearing, fired a starshell at about 10 o'clock three miles from convoy, sighted the boat at 3,000 yards, fired "near misses" at her with both the four-inch deck gun and 20mm Oerlikon anti-aircraft (AA) guns at maximum depression, and forced it to dive. To discourage it further, *Snowflake* dropped a D/C on the swirl—which was a hazardous thing to do given the rough sea, which prevented an attacking ship from getting much beyond the blast effect—as *Duncan* discovered himself when he dropped two on another contact at 2345: with maximum speed up sea only 8 to 9 knots, the D/C pressure waves lifted his stern clean out of the water, opened leaks, and, what was worse, smashed all the gin glasses in the wardroom.[42] There were two other "scare tactic" D/C drops that night, and no general attack on the convoy developed.

The morning weather on 1 May was atrocious. By afternoon a Force 10 gale was dead in the convoy's teeth, preventing all but the most modest progress forward. Convoy speed was 2.7 knots and dropping. In the tempest, columns as well as ships within columns separated from each other. Commodore Brook's log noted: "Half convoy not under command, hove to and very scattered."[43] Gretton, whose *Duncan* was hove to with winds pushing alternately against one bow and then the other, marveled that an entire convoy could be brought to virtually stationary condition. On *Pink*, Lt. Atkinson placed a chair on the raised platform at the fore part of his open bridge and went into half-sleep, rocking with the motion of the corvette. Nearby were a gyro compass and voice pipes to helmsman and navigator. Compass repeaters were on both wings port and starboard. Ahead and several feet below was the asdic hut (or office). Aft and a deck lower was the helmsman. On the port quarter of the bridge was the tall radar hut (office, house). Aft of the bridge were the ship's mast and funnel. For protection against the cold gale Atkinson wore a heavy sweater, a cloth, not very warm, duffel coat with hood, a Balaclava helmet (knitted wool head sock), naval cap, seaboot stockings, and mitts. Like the rest of the crew, he was the recipient of wool clothing articles knitted by women volunteers in Australia, New Zealand, and Canada, with whom correspondence was exchanged and lifelong friendships forged.[44]

Aircraft flew over the dispersed merchantmen during the day, including two RAF VLR Liberators from 120 Squadron in Iceland who gave valuable assistance by identifying the positions of stragglers, and by warning of icebergs, growlers, and pack ice starting thirty miles ahead. Less helpful were two U.S. Army B–25 Mitchell bombers from Ivigtut, Greenland, which made no contact whatever with the convoy either by wireless (W/T), voice radio (R/T), or light signals (V/S), although one of them, as Gretton learned later, made an unsuccessful attack on a U-boat some 60 miles to the south; and one of them further helped to confuse BdU by forgetting to switch off its navigation lights: The flashing beacons, which, of course, announced the bomber's position and course to any

U-boat that might be watching, caught the attention of U-*381* (Kptlt. Graf v. Pückler), which at once signaled BdU about an apparent secret weapon. In Berlin, where Grossadmiral Dönitz and Konteradmiral Godt were at this time unusually accommodating of the notion of secret devices, the BdU war diary for 1 May noted: "The [U-*381*] observed what was probably a new type of location gear. The Commander repeatedly noticed planes approaching at great height and carrying a light like a planet that went on and off."

What is more interesting to learn from the 1 May diary entries concerning convoy "No. 33" is that BdU decided that with only six of sixteen *Star* boats reporting contact with the convoy, the rest having failed to gain purchase, with three survivors of those six now submerged to avoid both the weather and the aircraft, and with so little to show for four days' effort, further pursuit of ONS.5 was not worth the candle. At dusk the longwave antenna array at Calbe, 43 kilometers south of Magdeburg, sent the order, which could be heard by the submerged boats to a depth of 25 meters: break off the operation. BdU's rationalization of the failure read: "This attack failed only because of the bad weather, not because of the enemy's defenses."[45] No doubt a different appreciation of the battle was entertained on the bridge of *Duncan*.

By dawn the next day, the weather had moderated somewhat, and the speed of the convoy was back up to 5 knots. During the previous twenty-four hours only 20 miles had been made. Gretton and his escorts took advantage of the settling seas to round up stragglers, of whom there were many, some at a distance of 30 miles from the Commodore. In this B7 and *Oribi* were helped by a VLR Liberator from the Reykjavik squadron that flew over 1,000 miles to assist in locating ships. Eventually, most of the flock was gathered, except for two parties taken under charge by *Pink* and *Tay* some miles astern, and two laggards that peeled off to sail independently. In the forenoon of 2 May, Gretton and Brook began negotiating the first ice pack on their route. Small growlers and floes now became the hazard rather than high seas. *Duncan* thought this a good time to top up from *British Lady,* but the oiler's constant alteration of course to avoid the ice made the maneuver impossible; and by the time ONS-5 was clear of ice the wind and sea were making up again from the west-south-west, frustrating Gretton once more.

In the evening B7's transmitters vectored in the EG3 Support Group destroyers of Home Fleet, H.M.S. *Offa, Penn, Panther,* and *Impulsive,* which joined at 2040. Unfortunately, like *Oribi,* these were all short-legged ships that had expended a good amount of their fuel making rendezvous. Gretton's *Vidette* was the only destroyer in the enlarged screen that had been designed for or, as was the case, modified for long-range escort duty. There was a brief awkward moment when Gretton, who was junior in rank to the Support Group senior officer, Captain J. A. McCoy, R.N., in *Offa,* "made requests of" (gave orders to) his senior in grade; but Gretton found McCoy more than willing to accept the subservient role, and very friendly in his cooperation.

That night McCoy's ships took up extended screen stations assigned to them by Gretton, which changed from first dark to midnight, from midnight to dawn, and from daybreak to sunset.[46] There was no sign of the enemy during the night, and the morning of 3 May was similarly quiet, except that gale-force winds from the southwest continued to howl around the main body of the convoy, which now numbered thirty-two ships together. The close escort and support ships spent the forenoon searching for stragglers.

Gretton exempted himself from that labor and crawled ahead at convoy speed, anxious about his fuel remaining, and deciding what to do about it. Because of the still heavy seas, topping up from *British Lady* was out of the question; and the weather forecast did not allow for any calmer surface ahead. What oil he had left in his bunkers was sufficient to make Newfoundland only at economical speed. If he stayed with the convoy, the likelihood was that he would go dry and have to be towed. If the enemy was still in touch, his powerless ship would invite easy attack. As for transferring his command of B7 to another ship and sending *Duncan* and her crew to St. John's, that, too, was not an option: the appalling weather made transfer by boat or jackstay impossible. So *Duncan* would have to go, and Gretton with her–at a time, he grieved, when ONS.5 was still in jeopardy, and just at the beginning of a story that Gretton later would describe as "probably the most stirring of convoy history."[47]

At 1600, by R/T, he handed over command as Senior Officer Escort to Lt.-Cmdr. Robert Evan Sherwood in *Tay,* changed course, and proceeded at best economical speed, which was 8 knots, toward St. John's.[48] Though emotionally depressed–"thoroughly ashamed of ourselves," he would say–Gretton understood rationally that the reason for his withdrawal lay not with any inadequacy of himself or his crew, but with the Royal Navy strategists and engineers who decided in the 1920s what ought to be the fuel endurance of a destroyer. In fact, that night and the next morning three destroyers of the Support Group similarly left the convoy because of fuel depletion, first *Impulsive* to Iceland, then *Panther* and *Penn* to Newfoundland. Also, on the 4th, Sherwood detached *Northern Gem* with her *McKeesport* survivors to Newfoundland. And at the same time, he signaled CinCWA that unless the weather cleared enough to make oiling from U.S.S. *Argon* practicable, he would have to detach destroyers *Offa* and *Oribi* no later than Wednesday morning the 5th.[49]

Helped by unexpectedly fine weather and a boost from the Labrador Current, a disappointed *Duncan* made St. John's with four percent of fuel remaining. Left behind in the sea lanes was a severely diminished convoy escort with four of its once seven-strong destroyer force already removed from the screen, facing now the threat that it would lose two more destroyers on the morrow. That would leave ONS.5's escort a predominantly corvette force. And at just this juncture *Tay's* asdic went out and was pronounced irreparable.

But the new commander Sherwood had at least three reasons for optimism: for one thing, CinCWA ordered First Escort (Support) Group at St. John's, consisting of the Egret class sloop H.M.S. *Pelican;* Commander Godfrey N. Brewer, R.N., Senior Officer; the River Class frigates H.M.S. *Wear, Jed,* and *Spey;* and the ex-U.S. Coast Guard Lake class cutter

H.M.S. *Sennen,* to "Proceed at best speed through position 47 North 47 West and thence to reinforce ONS.5"; for another, the winds subsided to Force 6 and the seas abated somewhat, with the result that convoy speed advanced during a twenty-four-hour period from 3 to 6 knots; and, for still another, ONS.5 incredibly had passed through most of the dreaded Greenland Air Gap without sustaining a single attack.[50]

Yet 4 May was a day when lifted spirits also had their troughs: HF/DF receptions, which had been for a while still, became active again and gradually increased in number, indicating to Sherwood that U-boats, whether from the last group or from a new one, were reacquiring contact from port bow and beam. Convoy ONS.5 was not yet beyond jeopardy.

Sherwood's credentials for leadership were longstanding and well-tested. At sea since 1922, when he served with the Merchant Navy, he joined the Royal Naval Reserve in 1929, became a sublieutenant in minesweepers, and served nine months on the battleship H.M.S. *Warspite.* While continuing a member of the reserves, he resumed Merchant Navy duties with Holyhead-Dublin steamers until the outbreak of war, when he took an asdic course, spent a short stint with the Dover Patrol, and transferred to corvettes, assuming command in 1940 of H.M.S. *Bluebell,* among whose fifty-two-man crew he found only three or four who were "capable of any real action of any kind at all." In time he trained them to a high degree of seamanship and technical proficiency, and of himself he said that it was good training to have held command early of a vessel as difficult to handle as a "Flower" class corvette, a ship type that struggled against every wave and swell. The *Bluebell,* he said, "would do everything except turn over."[51] Advanced to command of *Tay* in 1942, he was assigned to Gretton's escort group, with which he captained the first ship on which B7's Senior Officer Escort embarked.

Described as being of medium height and stocky build, Sherwood framed bright, humorous eyes within a full naval beard. Not very well spoken, one of his fellow Captains said of him, and lacking in the kind of presence that Gretton generated, he was nonetheless a fine seaman whose command decisions were swift and firm. Though he was a reservist and lower ranking than Gretton, the Support Group regulars accepted his orders. On every fighting bridge there was confidence that Sherwood had mastered Gretton's painstaking game plan of search and sink. Now, as ONS.5 groped toward the unknown, with HF/DF contacts growing more numerous, and with all the original B7 group that remained damaged and worn by bitter weather and a running fight, it would take all of that mastery to see the convoy into port. Sherwood's concern would have been all the greater had he known that fewer than 70 nautical miles dead ahead as large a wolfpack as any of the war would assemble to meet him.

Collision of Forces
The Battle for ONS.5

We have fed our sea for a thousand years
And she calls us, still unfed,
Though there's never a wave of all her waves
But marks our English dead:
We have strawed our best to the weed's unrest
To the shark and the sheering gull.
If blood be the price of admiralty,
Lord God, we ha' paid in full!

RUDYARD KIPLING

And two things have altered not
Since first the world began—
The beauty of the wild green earth
And the bravery of man

T. P. CAMERON WILSON

The destroyer, with its speed, armament, maneuverability, and capacity to keep the sea, was the traditional and deadly enemy of the submarine. The even better ASW vessel, the destroyer escort, was not yet available in numbers from American yards, where volume construction began in April. Much good could be said as well for the performance to date of the "River" class frigate (301′6″ long overall, displacing 1,370 tons, speed 20 knots) and the "Black Swan" class sloop (299 feet long overall, displacing 1,300 tons, speed 19 knots). But the surprise of the ASW war was the smaller and relatively slow "Flower" class corvette (205 to 208 feet long, displacing 950 to 1,015 tons, speed 16 knots). These perhaps most famous of British ships of the war–fame engendered in great part by the fictional corvette *Compass Rose* in Nicholas Monsarrat's novel *The Cruel Sea*–owed their name to World War I "Flower" class sloops that were based on a whale-catcher design and used in that conflict for minesweeper and utility duty.

Their namesake successors, produced originally by the same yard, Smith's Dock Company at Middlesbrough, and designed by the same naval architect, William Reed, were produced, beginning in 1939, for minesweeping and ASW work in the North Sea and Channel. Their immediate ancestor was Reed's and Smith's Dock Company's commercial whaler *Southern Pride,* whose specifications were closely followed, though somewhat enlarged, because of that craft's ability to keep the sea. In adapting for naval use an already existing mercantile vessel design, and one that was simple to construct, the Admiralty ensured that the new single-screw "Flower" class "corvettes," as they were to be known, could be produced in non-naval yards throughout the U.K. Altogether 221 "Flowers" and "Modified Flowers" would be built in Great Britain and Canada. (Only one "Flower" exists at the date of this writing: H.M.C.S. *Sackville,* launched in 1941, which helped to escort convoy ON.184 during the fateful month of May 1943; fully restored, she is on display at the Bedford Institute of Oceanography, Halifax, Nova Scotia.)

Corvettes, which, as Monsarrat wrote, "would roll on wet grass," were not designed for deep ocean work, but that, ironically, became their primary service as Britain desperately sought escorts for her trade lifeline, and "Flowers" accompanied all but one of the non-carrier-escorted HX, ON, ONS, and SC convoys that crossed the northern sea lanes during the months of April and May. Though well proven as seaworthy in midocean escort, the corvettes' lively dipping and wallowing in heavy seas placed a pronounced strain on ships' companies. Said seaman Cyril Stephens of H.M.S. *Orchis:* "Sick . . . yes, that was the first baptism of a corvette . . . It was like a corkscrew. About the third dip and you'd get tons and tons of water come over the fo'c's'le . . . You had wet clothes on steam pipes trying to dry, you had water floating around all over the place, people being sick . . . It was awful."[1]

Not restricted to courses that headed into heavy seas, to avoid damage or capsizing, as was the case with built-for-speed destroyers, the corvettes could show their broad beams to hard seas with ease and confidence. Not given to slamming, either, as destroyers were want to do in sea states of 5 and upward, the early short-forecastle corvettes did pitch and heave violently, and it was the resulting vertical acceleration that caused seasickness—in combination with poor ventilation, a dank ambiance, and the unbalanced diet of RN messing. As naval architect David K. Brown pointed out recently, vertical acceleration, which varied linearly with wave height, also led in its severe phases to impaired judgment and performance, hence impaired fighting effectiveness (although Sir Robert Atkinson, who commanded *Pink,* told the writer that he experienced no such adverse mental effects). In an attempt to resolve that problem, later ships of the original class were given a lengthened forecastle deck, extra sheer and flare to the bows, and various bridge improvements. The short length of the corvette had one advantage, and that was a small turning circle, assisted by a good-size rudder in the propeller wash, that enabled the ship to get her stern quickly over a submerged U-boat contact.

The number of D/Cs carried on board increased during the war from twenty-five to fifty. Crew numbers similarly increased, from twenty-nine to over eighty. Endurance was rated at 3,850 miles at 12 knots on 233 tons of fuel, the average convoy run being 3,000 miles, though actual endurance was uniformly less. Throughout the war corvettes appeared in the so-called Western Approaches camouflage scheme, which was an all-white ship that merged with the skyline, on which were painted panels of light sea blue or light sea green that blended with the sea. The flower names that adorned these vessels occasioned some ribaldry among seamen in larger RN ships, but no one could doubt the stamina, fighting spirit, or comradeship of the men who sailed them.[2]

A half-century afterward, Lieutenant Harold G. Chesterman, Captain of *Snowflake*, remembered:

We were asked [when he and other corvette officers were serving as consultants to the head of Smith's Dock] what was a corvette like? We said, "Well, for the first six weeks you know you haven't a hope in hell of getting over that next wave, and then maybe, after the next six weeks, you think, well, maybe we will, and then after that you know nothing the Atlantic can throw at you will hurt you." And he said, "Mr. [William] Reed will be interested in that," and asked his secretary to ask Mr. Reed to come in. A venerable gentleman. And [the head] said, "Will you repeat what you said about the corvettes?" We were puzzled, but we did and this Mr. Reed said, "You're being very kind to me." And we looked a bit blankly at each other and he said, "You know I designed them," which of course we didn't, and he told us the story then of how he had been asked by the Admiralty, I think probably 1939, to design a highly maneuverable, small, anti-submarine vessel for the North Sea, five-day duration. And he was a very successful designer of ketches, and so he designed the "Flower" class corvette for the North Sea, five-day duration. And then they had to go into the Atlantic because the Germans got down the French Atlantic ports as well and he told us that he protested strongly, and said, "You can't send them in the Atlantic, they're far too short, you must put a minimum of thirty [more] feet in them." And the Admiralty apparently said, "We can't, there's a lot of yards in Britain can build a ship two hundred feet long, but no longer, and so I'm afraid they'll have to go in the Atlantic." And so he looked quite surprised, when we told him how good they were. Uncomfortable and lively and wet, but safe. And it didn't matter what the weather was, we could go up the gale, across the gale, down the seas, and when merchant ships were heaved-to with the wind on the port bow, or starboard bow, they could only run with it, we could go anywhere. They were wonderful little ships . . . We never lost a man overboard in the whole of the war, not one man washed overboard from a corvette . . . I had two Newfoundland lumberjacks, powerful men, one was called Charles the other Harold, and very, very strong men, magnificent eyesight. They'd go up on lookout, they'd sit on the cross trees, they wouldn't go in the crow's nest, they'd sit on the cross trees. Anyhow, Charles, I think it was, he was on the after depth charge thrower [one day] when one of the blokes on the for'd depth charge thrower [went overboard . . . *Snowflake*] rolled, the sea came in, the sea went out, he went out with it, and Charles just leaned over the side and grabbed him as he went past and pulled him back in again, one handed. Very strong man.

Chesterman deserves a word more here. Like Lieutenant Robert Atkinson, commanding *Pink,* he had served in the North Atlantic from the beginning of the war, first on an ASW trawler, then on the corvettes H.M.S. *Zinnia* and *Snowflake.* On *Zinnia* he was first lieutenant to Lt.-Cmdr. Charles Cuthbertson, R.N.R., on whom Monsarrat based Lt.-Cmdr. Ericson, one of the principal characters in *The Cruel Sea.* An event involving Chesterman also figured in the novel. *Zinnia* was part of the Escort Group 5 screen for outward-bound Gibraltar Convoy OG.71 in August 1941, when five U-boats, initially directed to the convoy by German Focke-Wulf Kondor aircraft, began a four-day assault on the 19th, sinking eight small ships from the convoy proper, including the S.S. *Aquila,* which went down with twenty-one Wrens and one naval nursing sister. On the 23rd, *Zinnia* herself was torpedoed. Her magazine exploded, and it was reported that she went under in twenty seconds. Cuthbertson and Chesterman were flung overside, where Chesterman swam through oil until he found one of *Zinnia's* smoke floats for flotage. Even then, he despaired of rescue and was about to give himself to the sea when he thought of his wife Caroline and how much he wanted to see her again. Summoning the strength to hold on, he was soon after rescued by a boat from the corvette H.M.S. *Campion.* Of the ship's company of eighty-five, only seventeen, including Cuthbertson and Chesterman, survived. Monsarrat, who was aboard another of the convoy's corvette escorts, stated that the attack on OG.71 was his worst experience of the war, and his description of the loss of H.M.S. *Sorrel* in the novel was based on the *Zinnia* event. When Cuthbertson went on to command *Snowflake,* he requested Chesterman to be his first lieutenant again, and when Cuthbertson was given a destroyer command, Chesterman was promoted from No. 1 to *Snowflake's* Captain. Upon his death at age seventy-nine in February 1997, a eulogist said of him: "Chesterman was a professional seaman to his fingertips. He had tremendous physical stamina, and was able to keep his bridge for days at a time in all weathers."[3]

Howard O. Goldsmith was Leading Sick Berth Attendant on *Snowflake:*

> I suppose the nearest thing we ever came to was on ONS.5. We had probably the worst trip weather-wise of any . . . There were times there when the convoy was literally stationary because some of the merchant ships just couldn't make headway against the wind and the sea. And although the engines were turning, the screws were turning, we were just sitting there stationary. And to give you an idea of what it was like, the upper deck was out of bounds. The skipper put the upper deck completely out of bounds. The only people allowed above decks were the bridge crew, and they were told to use the Captain's companionway, which was inboard, to get to the bridge, otherwise out of bounds completely. This seaman was a Newfoundlander who'd been brought up on schooners, and he said, "Well you don't get weather like this every day. I'm going up the mast, see what it's like." And he did, he went to the top of the mast in that sea, right to the

cross trees, above the crow's nest. And when he came down he said when we were in the trough he couldn't see over the top of the waves. So he was talking, what, seventy foot waves, that's big. And we had this for the whole trip . . . The damage to the ship was incredible. People don't realise the tremendous power of the sea, unless you've seen what it can do. But I mean, for instance, all the fo'c's'le stanchions, which were inch-thick iron stanchions, carrying the guard wires round the fo'c's'le, they were all bent at right angles to the deck. They'd just been as though a giant hammer had hammered them over to a right angle. One ship's boat had completely disappeared. One was stoved in. Just the waves had stoved it in, smashed it in. We used to have meat lockers which were welded to the deck. They were on the upper deck to keep the meat fresh, no fridges, you see, and they were welded on the deck and to a superstructure above the deck, welded top and bottom, with wire mesh sides to them, so that the air could flow through, and after that storm, not only had they gone, all the meat had gone, and there were just the weld spots on the deck and above, that's all that was left. That's just the force of the wind, the force of the sea, carried all that away. Deck lockers that were bolted and welded down just disappeared, just went, we never saw them go. Incredible power.[4]

What now if the power of wind and seas, which B7 and ONS.5 thus far had managed to survive, was replaced by the power of a U-boat armada the size and threat of which were as formidable as any in the history of submarine warfare? At the same time that Sherwood and his convoy were edging past what was left of the Air Gap, Dönitz and Godt, prompted by the failure of *Gruppe Star,* were ratcheting up the offensive by combining *Star's* boats with those of the western Group *Specht.*[5] Indeed, *Star's* thirteen boats, including some replacements (U–*710* having been sunk, and U–*386,* U–*528,* and U–*532* having withdrawn with damage), proceeded south-southwest through the Air Gap alongside and past ONS.5, to the convoy's east. BdU's original intent was to have *Star* join *Specht's* seventeen boats in stalking eastbound Convoy SC.128 (BdU's convoy No. 34), which had departed Halifax on 25 April and was steaming on a northerly course to the west of *Specht*. On 1 May U–*628* had reported smoke clouds that BdU took to be from SC.128. *Specht* was directed to chase it down, but it could not do so. It is possible that what U–*628* sighted was not SC.128 but the EG3 Support Group on its passage to join ONS.5.

By 1800* on 3 May the new *Specht-Star* rake ran from 56° 21′N, 44°35′W (on the German grid AJ 5333) to 54°57′N, 39°35′W (AK 4449). Boats from this formation reported seeing smoke clouds and starshells; one signaled it had been driven off by a destroyer. The supposition in Berlin was that these boats were in contact again with SC.128. With a note of frustration, if not desperation, BdU signaled: DO NOT HOLD BACK . . . SOMETHING CAN AND MUST BE ACHIEVED WITH 31 BOATS.[6] Berlin estimated that the convoy was steaming on a course between 20° and 50°. But it was not. While some of its escorts took a course northeastward, firing starshells to draw off the U-boats, SC.128, alerted to *Specht-Star's* estimated position by Canadian Naval Service Headquarters, Ottawa, which had DFed it, took a jog to the west before resuming a northerly course and then turning east above the north end of the rake. Successfully evading *Specht-Star*, the convoy would arrive at Liverpool on 13 May without mishap. In breaking off the hunt, BdU noted, "Most of the boats are short of fuel, and it is pointless for them to run about after the convoy."[7]

At the same time BdU formed *Specht-Star* it also augmented *Gruppe Amsel*, to the south, and formed it into four subgroups, I, II, III, and IV, of five U-boats each, except for I, which had six. *Amsel* now ran, with gaps between the subgroups, from 51°51′N, 49°05′W (AJ 7933) to 44°15′N, 39°35′W (BC 9646). In a revealing comment about BdU's

---

* All times are expressed in Greenwich Mean Time (GMT) unless otherwise noted.

awareness of the Allies' shore-based HF/DF capability, the
Berlin war diary observed: "This new type of disposition
should avoid the drawbacks that arise when a patrol remains
in one place for a long time so that it is D/Fed, sighted, located, etc. by the enemy, who thus finds out its entire extent."[8]
The boats at the extreme ends of this segmented line were
supplied with dummy F.T. messages with which to create the
impression of a larger line "stretching right around the Newfoundland Banks." That impression was not unlikely to be
made, since the OIC Tracking Room was now estimating the
number of U-boats at sea to be 128, the highest ever known,
representing nearly 60 percent of the Atlantic operational
force. When the Allies DFed the boats forming *Amsel,* Dönitz
and Godt expected they would discover the gaps and attempt
to vector convoys through them. The plan then was to combine the subgroups into a closed line. Before it had a chance to
work, however, that plan was overtaken by a new plan, as
BdU realized, on 4 May, that the *Amsel* boats would be
needed in operations to the north.

At 1602 GST (1402 GMT), Berlin began to reorganize
most of the *Specht* and *Star* boats into a new reconnaissance
line code-named *Gruppe Fink* (Finch). Ordered to be in place
by 1000 GST (0800 GMT) on 5 May, the twenty-seven boats
of *Fink* would occupy stations along a line running from west-
northwest to east-southeast, or precisely, from 56°45′N,
47°12′W (AJ 2758) to 54°09′N, 36°55′W (AK 4944). When
formed, the patrol line would stretch 382.6 nautical miles
(nm), with an average spacing of 14.7nm between the boats.[9]
As these boats were moving into position on the afternoon of
4 May, several (U-*264,* U-*628,*U-*260,* U-*270)* reported sighting destroyers *(Offa* or *Oribi,* or both) on southerly courses.
Then U-*628* (Kptlt. Heinz Hasenchar) in quadrant AJ 6271
(55°40′N, 42°40′W) at the near center of the *Fink* line reported
at 2018 GST the mast tops of a southbound convoy that BdU
had been expecting by dead reckoning, that is, by calculation
based on a convoy's course, speed, and elapsed time from a
previously determined position.

This was ONS.5 (No. 33), except that BdU mistakenly

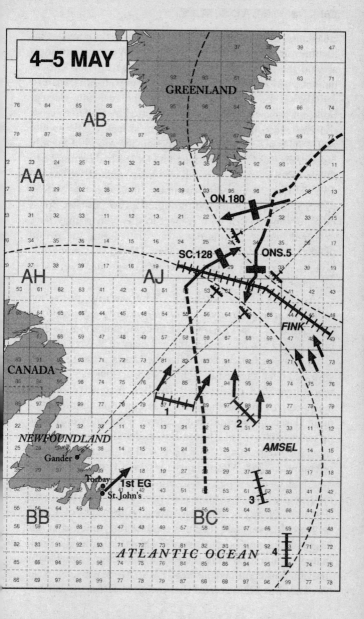

called it ON.180 (convoy No. 36), which was the convoy that had been trailing ONS.5, but which on 4 May was considerably to the north tracking a WSW course through U-boat quadrants AJ 22 and 23, south of Cape Farewell. BdU was also mistaken in both its dead reckoning and real time calculations, for it expected the convoy reported by U–628 to cross the *Fink* recco line on 5 May, when, in fact, ONS.5 would reach the center of that line by the late afternoon of the 4th, before *Fink* was fully formed; and if ON.180 had continued to follow ONS.5's course it would not have reached the line before 6 May. Apparently assuming that convoy No. 33 (ONS.5) had already passed through the *Fink* position, BdU's dead reckoning error with respect to this convoy may have occurred because it was not aware that during the period 0800 GMT 1 May to 0800 4 May, ONS.5 was practically hove to in contrary weather at speeds no greater than 2.7 to 3.1 knots.[10]

As late as 6 May, when BdU did a wash-up (postaction analysis) on this convoy (*Abschlussbetrachtung Geleitz, 36*), it still identified it as ON.180; but in communications to *Fink* boats during 5/6 May and in the war diary of 26 May it called it the "Hasenschar convoy," after the Commander of U–628, who had been the first to sight ONS.5, at 2005 GST, and to report it, at 2018, on the 4th.[11] The BdU practice of identifying a convoy by its shadower was common. Immediately upon Hasenchar's report that a convoy was southwest-bound on course 200°, speed 7 knots, BdU ordered up the northernmost subgroups *Amsel I* and *II,* as well as the independently operating U–258 (Mässenhausen), which had sunk *McKeesport,* and U–614 (Kptlt. Wolfgang Sträter), which had been temporarily hors de combat with engine problems, to join the *Fink* line. Twenty-seven boats strong on the night of 4 May, *Fink* would eventually claim a total of forty-one boats, the largest concentration ever arrayed across and around a single convoy. Dönitz and Godt reinforced this fact in a signal to the massing boats: YOU ARE BETTER PLACED THAN YOU EVER WERE BEFORE.[12] But BdU worried that owing to fuel depletion several of the boats would not be able to operate much longer than they had.

Of these changing U-boat dispositions the OIC Submarine Tracking Room in London and thus Western Approaches had no direct knowledge until after GC&CS made a break back into naval Enigma at noon on 5 May. To that point, as Commander Winn lamented, "Nothing is known from Special Intelligence of the operations during this period."[13] When, however, GC&CS could read German traffic again, the time lag between interception and decryption was so great–from seventeen hours to twelve days, the norm being four days–the information had no operational value in the battle then joined. It is possible at this date to read the GC&CS decrypts crafted afterwards of the traffic that had passed during the blackout period. Similarly, one can consult the American decrypts of the same traffic that date from later in 1943 when U.S. Navy cryptanalysts acquired raw Enigma intercept material as well as their own "bombes" (decryption machines), hence an independent capacity to make penetrations into the German naval cipher Triton.[14] But none of that intelligence was available at the time of battle. The principal value of Ultra in the Atlantic struggle had been its strategic disclosure of U-boat positions, and of their operational instructions from BdU. That value was lost on ONS.5. But not everything was lost. Once a close battle was joined, timely and localized intelligence such as that derived from shipborne HF/DF, radar, and asdic was far the more valuable, and that ONS.5's escorts could collect.

By dusk on 4 May, Sherwood in *Tay* had ample indication that he was in the neighborhood of a large U-boat formation. His FH3 HF/DF was picking up contacts on the port bow, port quarter, starboard beam, and starboard quarter. He was restricted from gaining accurate fixes, however, by the fact that communications failed between *Tay* and FH3-equipped *Oribi*, resulting in *Tay* obtaining only one cross-cut fix in the next three days, 4 to 6 May. If Sherwood needed any confirmation from afar that he was surrounded, it came from the Admiralty, which signaled him at 1920 about the existence of heavy and continuous W/T traffic in his vicinity on 12215 and 10525 kilocycles.[15] Two sweeps by the Support Group destroyers *Offa* and *Oribi* failed to locate any of the sending boats. The convoy was still east of 47°W and north of 40°N, beyond which boundaries, west and south, the new Canadian North West Atlantic (CinC, CNA) Command governed all surface and air anti-submarine escorts, as decided by the Washington Convoy Conference of 1-13 March 1943. (That conference, attended by senior British, Canadian, and American naval and air representatives, also decided, among other things: that the British and Canadians would share command of the northern Atlantic convoy lanes, while the United States would concentrate her forces in the central Atlantic, including the routes of the tanker convoys between the West Indies and Britain; and that [at last] 255 VLR aircraft would be delivered to the airfields on both shores of the Atlantic by July.) In the longitudes where ONS.5 sailed during the critical days of 4-6 May her escorts still remained under British operational control, although the Admiralty's counterpart OIC in Ottawa, employing a high-power, low-frequency transmitter near Halifax, communicated HF/DF-derived U-boat position estimates to convoys, such as SC.128, eastward as far as 30°W.[16]

Whereas SC.128 had been rerouted to evade the DFed *Specht* line, the suggestion has been made that ONS.5 was not similarly vectored around DFed boats before the evening of 4 May because of the escorts' low fuel levels, and their need to continue on the shortest possible route to port.[17] But with so many boats in movement across nearly 400 miles of ocean, there is a question if either Liverpool or Ottawa knew what possibly would have been an evasive route. The shore-based HF/DF accuracy was reported by the Admiralty to be no better than within 120 miles. Even the Admiralty message to *Tay* at 1920 on 4 May expressed itself as being uncertain if it was ONS.5 or SC.128 that was being shadowed, so "very poor" were D/F conditions. Convoy SC.128 at the time was approximately thirty miles north of the *Fink* line, traversing squares AJ 28-29-34 on a course northeast by east.

Escort Group B7 now readied itself to run the gantlet.

With 30 merchant ships present in ten columns, five cables (3,040 feet) apart, on course 202°, speed seven knots, in very clear weather, wind Force 2–a light breeze, four to six miles per hour–and a slight sea with low, long swell, Sherwood placed his night field as follows: *Sunflower* on the port bow, *Snowflake* on the port beam, *Tay* on the port quarter, *Vidette* on the starboard bow, *Loosestrife* on the starboard beam, and *Northern Spray* on the starboard quarter–although the rescue trawler, which was astern, was delayed in taking up her station. Destroyers *Offa* and *Oribi* provided forward cover on the starboard and port bows, respectively, at five miles distance. *Pink* was leeward at 56°32′N, 40°50′W on course 235° with four stragglers, speed 5 knots; Sherwood recommended that she be separately routed, as was done.[18]

No doubt the shore commands that watched this confrontation of forces unfold, whether at Liverpool or London, Halifax or Ottawa, where enemy dispositions could only be guessed at on their wall charts and plotting tables, held their breath as the volume of HF/DF contacts mounted. At sea the incoming Morse traffic was just as omnibus. Said Captain J. A. McCoy, SO, EG3 Support Group, on *Offa:* "During all this time enemy W/T transmissions had become more and more frequent. . . ."[19] There was no doubt on his bridge that a multitude of foes was thickening around them.

One of the *Specht* boats proceeding to form *Fink* never made it to the party. It was taken out of the fight earlier in the day to the north-northeast of *Fink,* or about thirty miles astern of the convoy, by one of two Royal Canadian Air Force Canso A's (as the Canadians called the PBY-5A amphibious Catalinas) that came from Gander, Newfoundland, to give ONS.5 its first real air cover in two days, although neither aircraft met the convoy as such. The Air Gap had greatly narrowed during April and early May, with the result that on no day during its transit of the gap did ONS.5 miss contact of some kind with aircraft: even on 3 May a U.S. Army Air Force (USAAF) B-17 Flying Fortress from Gander rendezvoused with the convoy at 1538, though, at the boundary of its Prudent Level of Endurance (PLE), it could only remain with the convoy for six minutes.[20] Nonetheless, the flyover must have caused the *Specht-Star* boats to keep their heads down.

At 1757 on the 4th, after a seven-and-a-half-hour flight out, the gull-gray-and-white-camouflaged Canso A "W" of 5 Bomber Reconnaissance Squadron was patrolling over position 56°35′N, 42°40′W at 2,000 feet, on course 209° True (T), with wind 20 knots from 270°T, in the base of 10/10 clouds, with visibility 5 miles in haze, when the aircraft picked up a blip on its ASV (10-centimeter) radar. The blip, which went in and out at regular intervals of a few seconds, probably as the result of high swells, indicated a target at seven miles, 25° to port. The pilot, Squadron Leader B. H. "Barry" Moffitt of Toronto, homed onto the blip and, at two and a half miles range, the second engineer, Corporal Harry Knelson of Bladworth, Saskatchewan, made a visual sighting from the port blister. The U-boat was 10° off the port bow, fully surfaced, and proceeding in a rough sea with heavy swell at a speed of 6 to 8 knots on a course estimated at 340°T, or obliquely across the Canso's own course. Its hull and tower he described as being gray in color with patches of green. Ten miles dead ahead of the U-boat, Moffitt and his second pilot could see a straggler vessel from ONS.5.

Moffitt pushed the nose down, opened the throttles, and experienced "the fastest ride I have ever had in a Canso." *Fast* was a word rarely associated with the Canso. Though powered by two thunderous 14-cylinder, 1200-horsepower Pratt & Whitney R1830-82 engines, mounted on a 104-foot-long flexing wing, the flying boat was said by PBY pilots to "climb at ninety, cruise at ninety, and glide at ninety"–an affectionate exaggeration, since the lumbering craft regularly cruised at 110-115 knots, and could build up about 40 more knots in a power glide attack when engines were set to 43 inches manifold pressure and 2,400 rpms. As Moffitt dove out of the cloud base toward the deck, the U-boat sighted him and began an alarm dive. Leveling off at 75 feet with 150 knots indicated, Moffitt attacked from a 12:30 o'clock position, 10° off the submerging U-boat's starboard bow, catching the target with its decks still awash.

By intervalometer, an electromechanical device that enabled a "stick" of D/Cs to be dropped at specified intervals, or spacings, he and his second pilot adjusted their four wing-mounted 250-pound torpex D/Cs, with hydrostatic fuses set to 22 feet, so that they would drop in train at spacings of 46 feet. At the optimum release point the intervalometer was activated, and the stick of D/Cs separated port and starboard from hard points on the wing, severing their arming wires in sequence: one-two-three-four. No hangups. The first D/C entered the water about 80 feet ahead and to starboard of the U-boat, the second about 40 feet from target. The third and fourth fell fewer than 12 feet off the U-boat's port side, one forward of the conning tower, the other aft. Unaccountably, for a dive situation, two crewmen were seen on the conning tower bridge.

Moffitt kicked left rudder and pulled into a climbing turn to port. When the D/Cs detonated in train, sending gray-white water skyward in four violent geysers, Moffitt and his crew watched the U-boat heave to a fully surfaced position for about five to ten seconds, then wallow with no forward motion. After ten more seconds, the boat, still in a motionless horizontal position, sank from view. Immediately, oil appeared in bulk and grew to a slick 200 by 800 feet; four of the Canso crew members could smell its pungent odor through the open blisters. Also sighted were woodplanks with fresh breaks; these would have come from the boat's upper surface decking, where hardwood was used to retard freezing. No survivors or bodies appeared on the frothing surface. Having reached PLE, Canso A "W" departed the scene for Gander at 1828. Back at base, Moffitt submitted photographs and guardedly reported: "U-boat probably damaged."[21] In London, however, the Admiralty's U-Boat Assessment Committee decided, on 28 June 1943, that the U-boat in question, which it identified as U–630 (Oblt.z.S. Werner Winkler), was "known sunk."[22]

Understandably, in the few accounts of ONS.5's passage

that have been written since, that has been the identification and the assessment given. In recent years, however, this and other surface and air attacks on U-boats have received a searching reassessment by Robert M. Coppock, Curatorial Officer, Foreign Documents Section, Naval Historical Branch, Ministry of Defence, London (hereafter NHB/MOD). Through careful examination of such factors as U-boat tracks, W/T communications, damage reports, and fuel reserves, Mr. Coppock has concluded that the boat attacked by Canso "W" was U–209 (Kptlt. Heinrich Brodda), which had sortied from Kiel, Germany, on her first war patrol on 6 April. At 1615 GST on 6 May, with her main transmitter out of commission, U–209 reported to BdU via U–954 (Kptlt. Odo Loewe) that she had suffered extensive damage: AIR-GROUP NO. 2 OUT OF ORDER BECAUSE OF AERIAL BOMBS. PRESSURE CONDUIT NO. 1 OUT OF ORDER. EXHAUST VALVES LEAKING. ONLY PARTIALLY CLEAR FOR SHOOTING. MAIN TRANSMITTER OUT OF ORDER. 29 CBM.

AT 1931 GST BdU RESPONDED, ORDERING BRODDA TO REFUEL, IF NECESSARY, FROM U–119 (Kptlt. Horst-Tessen von Kameke) and afterwards to make for Brest on the Brittany coast, some 1,500 miles distant. The injured boat did not rendezvous with U–119, and nothing was heard from her again. On 23 May the BdU war diary concluded: "U–209 has been on her return passage since the 6th May. On that day U–954 reported that U–209 was damaged by aircraft bombs and unable to send signals. Fuel supplies which were then 29 cbm must have been used up by now . . . so she must be considered lost." The NHB/MOD reassessment concludes that U–209 sank by accident on or about 7 May in the general vicinity of 52°N, 38°W, and that her demise was "almost certainly" the result of the damage she suffered from Canso "W" on 4 May.[23] Winkler's U–630 will be seen later in the narrative.

Another type of engagement was experienced by the second Canso that approached ONS.5 that afternoon. Piloted by Flight Lieutenant J. W. C. "Jack" Langmuir of Toronto, Canso A "E" of 5 Squadron sighted 15 to 18 miles ahead a fully surfaced U-boat proceeding at about 8 knots on a course of

132°T. He later estimated its position as 55°35′N, 43°14′W. The Canso's course was 023° at 5,500 feet. The time was 2045. Langmuir turned on a reciprocal course to the U-boat in order to get the sun at his back, and then, at 8 miles distance, he commenced a dive, going to 20 feet off the deck at 155 knots, and aiming almost directly at the U-boat's bow, hoping for a perfect straddle. During his run in, the "dark brown-green" U-boat, deciding to fight it out on the surface rather than dive, opened up with 20mm anti-aircraft fire from the flak platform aft the conning tower.[24] Pressing on, Langmuir hit the release button and got his perfect straddle, numbers 2 and 3 of the stick entering the water not more than 15 feet to either side of the U-boat's hull, between the conning tower and stern.

As the Canso banked away to port, her crew observed the U-boat's bow lifted above the surface by the explosions, showing daylight between the keel and water for about one-third of the boat's length; yet the boat was still able to maneuver, and did so, making a complete 360° turn to starboard while "pitching and rolling violently" and persisting to offer flak. With all his D/Cs expended, Langmuir moved out of range and ordered the bow gunner, Warrant Officer Clifford Hazlett of Chilliwack, British Columbia, to mount a .30-caliber Browning machine gun in the bow turret, which took about three minutes. Langmuir then made a second run at the boat. Descending from 200 to 50 feet, he called for fire from both the bow gun and the .50-caliber gun in the starboard blister, beginning at 400 yards. Two U-boat crewmen on the flak platform were seen to fall, hit, and to crumble over railings into the sea.

After the pass, Langmuir banked to starboard intending to make a third run, but when he looked back he saw only the U-boat's bow as the craft submerged at an awkward angle. No oil, debris, or survivors were sighted. Having done as much as she could do, Canso A "E" began the long return to base. A large number of photographic negatives were presented at Gander as witness to the action. The assessment from London on 28 June was, "Probably slightly damaged"—a tribute to the integrity of the U-boat's hull, which took at least two D/C charges within close range.[25] The U-boat was identified later from Enigma intercepts as U–438 (Kptlt. Heinrich Heinsohn), out of Brest, which signaled to BdU at 0608 on 5 May that she had had an exchange of fire with an aircraft and received minor damage: 4 BOMBS FROM CATALINA 15 METERS OFF. . . . ATTACKED SEVERAL TIMES BY FLYING BOAT. NO. 40 CYLINDER COVER TORN. OTHER DAMAGES SLIGHT. Later that day she reassured BdU: CAN REPAIR DAMAGES TO ENGINE WITH MEANS ON BOARD.[26]

On the cusp of battle, as a five-hour night fell across the bleak dress of the North Atlantic, Admiral Dönitz's U-Boat Command had every reason to be confident. The initial conditions for a convoy fight had never been so favorable. Forty-one boats were forming the battle line, and a convoy had steamed into their near-middle. At 2213 GST (2013 GMT) Dönitz signaled one last personal exhortation to his commanders:

> I AM CERTAIN THAT YOU WILL FIGHT WITH EVERYTHING YOU'VE GOT. DON'T OVERESTIMATE YOUR OPPONENT, BUT STRIKE HIM DEAD![27]

First out of the box was twenty-eight-year-old Kptlt. Ulrich Folkers, commander of the Type IXC U–125, which sortied on 13 April from her home base with 10th Flotilla at Lorient, a name that soon was to have a curious reprise. On his first patrol Folkers had sailed to the U.S. East Coast in January 1942 as a member of Operation Drumbeat (*Paukenschlag*), during which he sank only one vessel, the 5,666-GRT American freighter *West Ivis*. In three subsequent patrols, however, he put fourteen Allied ships in the locker and received the Knight's Cross in March 1943. His actions on the night of 4/5 May are not known with any accuracy because neither his war diary (KTB) nor his torpedo shooting reports (*Schussmeldungen*) survived the battle. But German message traffic gives him the first trophy of the night, merchantman No. 34 in column No. 3. Her name: *Lorient*.[28] Built in 1921 by Tyne I.S.B. Co. Ltd., Newcastle, the 4,737-GRT *Lorient* was transporting trade for the Continental Coal and

Investments Company of Cardiff. Captain Walter John Manley commanded her merchant crew of forty-six officers and men. On the night of 4 May, without notice or trace, she simply disappeared, with all hands.

Convoy rules specified that upon being torpedoed, a ship should send up two white rockets and key the emergency signal SSS (Struck By Torpedo) on the 600-meter distress band. *Lorient* did neither. Unless she was broken in half, a torpedoed ship in ballast, as *Lorient* was, normally should have had enough buoyancy to stay afloat long enough to make a signal, as well as get her crew away in boats. However, as the next ship to go down demonstrates, that amount of time could be as little as two minutes. In any event, no crewman or debris from *Lorient* was ever found. Commodore Brook commented simply that *Lorient* "parted company," probably indicating no more than that she had become an out-of-sight straggler.[29] The conclusion that *Lorient's* end came at the hands of U–125 is based on a signal from Folkers to BdU, repeated by the latter to all northwest Atlantic boats at 0218 on the 5th: FOLKERS REPORTS ON 36 METERS. ON 4 MAY IN QU AJ 6298 [55°33'N, 41°45'W] INDEPENDENT 4000 TONNER, COURSE 220, SUNK.[30] *Lorient* would be U–125's only victim in the battle. Fewer than thirty hours later, U–125 would be a victim herself.

Significantly, at this same early hour of the battle, Kptlt. Helmuth Pich, Commander of U–168, reported that he was breaking off the line because of fuel shortage. Just as significantly, BdU, which had fretted over the fuel problem from the time *Fink* was organized, signaled back that it would not permit it. Pich was to continue operations, and all boats were to remain engaged until their fuel state reached five tons, when they could disengage to resupply from a *Milchkuh* standing well clear to the east. Pich was back in the line at 2246.[31] The second U-boat to take offensive action was U–707, a Type VIIC commanded by Oblt.z.S. Günter Gretschel. At 2153 Gretschel dived ahead of the convoy, intending to attack at dusk:

[Through the periscope] I can see two destroyers [*Offa* and *Oribi?*] zigzagging regularly ahead of the convoy. Asdic is being used only in short spurts. One destroyer is now only 1000 meters distant, dead ahead . . . ; now it zigzags toward port again. Nothing can be seen of the convoy. I think that all's clear and that I'm through [the screen] when a destroyer heads right for me again. He must have located me [by asdic] because I'm proceeding at a very low speed. Now his asdic is continuous. I dive deeper to A=20 [a prescribed but varying depth such as 30 meters plus 20 meters]. Eight well-placed D/Cs [*Wabos*]. The convoy passes overhead.[32]

The D/C attack was made by *Tay,* which had moved to close ahead of convoy.[33] Gretschel continued:

Surfaced. I am in the rear of the convoy formation. To the front are a few shadows, to starboard a corvette, astern, a large steamer. Battle stations! [*Auf Gefechtsstationen!*] I attack a modern passenger steamer of the type *City of Manchester,* with protruding bow and continuous deck, 7500 GRT, on course 210°. I launch a fan shot from Tubes I, II, and IV, bearing 90°, range 1500 meters. After a run of one minute, 34 seconds, an eel hits abaft the mast, causing a high black detonation column. Immediately, the steamer begins sinking by the stern. The upper deck is awash. The vessel remains floating for awhile, then suddenly stands itself up, the bow vertical, and descends into the sea. Time for sinking: 69 seconds. Secure from Battle Stations! Dive to reload.[34]

This time the sinking was observed by the armed trawler H.M.T. *Northern Spray,* commanded by Lieutenant F. A. J. Downer, R.N.R. The victim was not the type of passenger steamer Gretschel identified, but a 4,635-GRT freighter of the North Shipping Company in Newcastle. Named *North Britain,* she had straggled from the convoy in bad weather on Saturday, 1 May, had rejoined on the 4th, but then had straggled six miles astern again with boiler trouble. The record does not state how many of Gretschel's torpedoes hit home, but is clear that his victim, which was in ballast, sank very quickly, stern first, inside two minutes.[35] The time was 0027 on 5 May. *Northern Spray,* which was nearby, carried out an "Observant" around the spot of sinking but failed to make asdic contact. No boats or life jacket lights could be seen, and the trawler reported to *Tay* that there were no survivors of the crew of over forty. Then, at 0055, some lights were sighted, and ten minutes later the trawler discovered a waterlogged lifeboat and a raft. Repeatedly the lifeboat was brought alongside, but the ten exhausted crewmen inside it made only lethargic efforts to get out. Finally, they and an eleventh survivor on the raft were taken on board, and *Northern Spray* proceeded to the positions of other sinkings.[36]

Hasenschar, the contact-keeper in U-*628,* was next to open a fighting account. With seven other boats of his knowledge in contact with the convoy by dusk (U-*707,* U-*202,* U-*264,* U-*265,* U-*168,* U-*732,* and U-*378*), he thought himself free to shed his shadower's role—*Somit ist für mich Angriff freigegeben.*[37]

> I move toward the convoy columns [on the surface] so I can attack just at the beginning of night. The sea state is 3-4, moderating with a light swell. Visibility is good. As it gets darker the starboard bow escort steams far off to the west and a second destroyer heads south. I'm successful in getting through the hole between them, and now, at first darkness, I'm in contact with the main body of the convoy. Positioned west of the convoy, I start my attack . . . I don't think it's advisable to proceed any closer because escorts on the beam can approach me at short range. In spite of the great distance to target I decide to launch exactly aimed individual shots, because I have precisely calculated target data. All Etos are hot and ready . . . At 0043-0046 I launch from Tubes I through IV at five [*sic*] different

freighters in a row, range 4000 to 5000 meters, torpedo depth set to three meters . . . Then I turn to starboard and make a [single] stern launch, after which I take off on the surface, full speed, toward the northeast because the starboard escorts have moved in my direction again. Calculating from the time of the first torpedo launch, there were four hits, the first after a run of 7 minutes, 58 seconds, the last after 9 minutes, 30 seconds. There was a 3-minute interval between the launch from [bow] Tube I and the launch from [stern] Tube V. We could only observe three hits. The first, which had a high detonation column, was on a large freighter. The others were on two medium-sized freighters. One explosion was very large, so one could assume a sinking. The third freighter hit shoots two white rockets and begins to burn. As we back off from the scene, a muffled explosion is heard at 0105 from the first, large freighter, possibly a boiler explosion. A large black cloud of smoke hangs over the ship for a long time. Then there is nothing more that can be seen of the ship. In the boat we can hear the noises of a sinking ship. The ship sinks. As we continue our withdrawal the rear echelons of the convoy send up illumination flares continuously. Some of the flares are very close, but we are not spotted . . . Because I have one eel left I decide to return to the scene in order to sink a ship that might be damaged . . . At 0225 I observe a shadow with a weak red masthead light. At first it shows little aim-off bearing. For a short while I pursue it with diesels at slow ahead. Now we recognize it to be a corvette, hove-to, bearing 110°. I approach to a range of 800 meters and at 0302 launch a single eel, set at 4 meters depth, from Tube III. After 28 seconds running time there is a huge tongue of flame, followed by spark showers, then nothing more to be seen. A strong shockwave followed. I guess that the entire D/C stowage exploded. The corvette had literally gone up in thin air.[38]

Later, in reporting these attacks to BdU, Hasenschar stated that he had sunk one large freighter, probably had sunk a medium-size freighter, had left a third freighter burning, and had blown a corvette to pieces–*"Atomisiert."*[39] But the twenty-six-year-old Commander was peering through rose-colored binoculars. Only one ship was hit by his torpedo barrage: the 5,081-GRT freighter *Harbury,* with a cargo of 6,820 tons of anthracite coal. As for the vaporized corvette, *Snowflake, Sunflower,* and *Loosestrife–Pink* was on another course–continued rolling and pitching on their assigned stations, unscathed by anything but weather. Some of the explosions reported by Hasenschar may have originated with torpedo hits scored in the same time period by U–*264* (see below). Or they may have been end-of-run detonations.

With a loud explosion, but no flash, one of Hasenschar's wakeless torpedoes struck *Harbury* on the starboard side in No. 5 hold, blowing off its hatches and flooding it. The time was 0046 on 5 May. A fracture in the tunnel door allowed water into the engine room, which began to fill with sea water. The Master, Captain W. E. Cook, made his way to the bridge wings, where he saw that the ship was settling by the stern. Third Officer W. Skinner fired the required white rockets. Only twenty-one or twenty-two years old, Skinner had previously gone down once with a mined ship, a second time with a ship sunk by Japanese aircraft off Ceylon, and, after the latter sinking, he had been sunk yet a third time by a Japanese cruiser that shelled the ship that rescued him. Said Cook later about Skinner's fourth experience, he was "most reliable and cool."

As the well deck went under water, Cook switched on the red lights to mark his position, stopped engines, threw overside the weighted Confidential Books, directed a distress W/T message to be transmitted, placed a W/T set in one of the main lifeboats, and ordered Abandon Ship. The crew succeeded in lowering the two main lifeboats amidships, but the starboard quarter small lifeboat had been rendered useless by the explosion, and the port quarter boat capsized on becoming waterborne. Several lives were lost when a knot of crew-

men stranded aft were forced to jump into the sea. Cook
remained on board with two crewmen and searched the 'midship accommodation to make sure that all fifty-one crewmen,
including seven Navy and two Army gunners, had gotten off.
Near midnight the ship gave a "grinding and wrenching"
sound from aft, leading Cook and the two ratings to think that
Harbury was sinking. They hurriedly boarded the forward
starboard raft, cast off the painter, and drifted away into a
heavy swell and dark night. In the distance they sighted two
white lights, which they assumed belonged to the lifeboats.

Around 0320 they observed a shower of sparks and heard
a loud explosion, which they interpreted to be an end-of-run
torpedo detonation, and an hour and ten minutes later they
sighted *Northern Spray*. Cook attracted the trawler's attention
using a newly issued handheld rocket that threw up five flares.
With some difficulty because of the rough sea and the lack of
ring bolts or cleats on merchant ship rafts to which lines
might have been made fast, the trawler hauled on board the
raft's occupants and, a short time later, those also from the
lifeboats, making a total of forty-four men rescued, six of
whom were slightly injured. Seven were missing.

In the morning (0900), Cook, with his Chief Officer and
the First Lieutenant of the trawler, took a boat to inspect
Harbury and to secure flour and potatoes from her pantry to
replenish the trawler's dwindling stock. They found water ten
feet high in the engine room, above the dynamos, and saw
that the sea was pouring into No. 4 main hold. All indications
were that *Harbury* would sink. At 1000 the boat party returned to *Northern Spray*. A month and a half later, Cook
would say: "I did not see my ship again, but in view of her
condition I am certain that she eventually sank. Aircraft were
sent out the following day to the scene [55°01′N, 42°59′W]
but no sign of the ship could be found."[40]

Hasenschar's KTB, which has not always been reliable,
proved to be correct about the fate of the *Harbury* wreck. At
1230 on the afternoon of 5 May, while proceeding underwater near the position 55°14′N, 43°02′W, Hasenschar sighted a
stopped, presumably damaged, freighter in his periscope lens.

He surfaced, decks awash, long enough to make an observation from the bridge, then submerged again:

> I approach the freighter with full speed underwater. With the periscope I can see that the steamer has been abandoned. It has a slight list to starboard and it's down by the stern. Lifeboats hang out of their davit arms. Stairs and lines hang outboard. At 1451 I surface and clear the guns at a distance of 300-400 meters. With 40 rounds of 8.8 fire from the forward deck gun and 100 2cm armor-piercing shells we get the freighter to sink . . . It lists to starboard and then capsizes . . The vessel displays a repainted shipping company insignia of the "Harrison Line" on the funnel. A drifting cutter with sail nearby carries the name "Harbury." The freighter fits the silhouette of that type. I assume that this is the damaged ship that we torpedoed the night before.

He was right. *S.S. Harbury* was owned by J. & C. Harrison Ltd., of Mark Lane, London. Hasenschar also identified this derelict as *Harbury* in his *Schussmeldungen,* unfortunately the only shooting reports to survive in German archives from any U-boat operating in May 1943.[41] The young Commander would go down with his boat on 3 July 1943 northwest of Cape Ortegal, Spain.

Hard on the heels of *Harbury's* torpedo, two more ships took hits, the work of Kptlt. Hartwig Looks in *U-264.* At 0014, Looks placed his Type VIIC boat ahead of the convoy, on the surface, with the intention of attacking inside the port bow and port beam escorts (*Sunflower* and *Snowflake*). A "destroyer" (*Tay*) visible to the north did not see him in the overcast weather, visibility good but very dark, rough sea with heavy swell, wind from the southwest Force 5. At 0100, 14 minutes after *Harbury* was struck, Looks made his move:

> I have a group of five steamers ahead of me, three at approximately 1500 meters and two behind them at about 2500 meters . . . At 0102 I launch two fan

shots at the larger two of the three nearest ships, one launch of two eels from Tubes II and III at a 6000-tonner and another launch of two from Tubes II and IV at a 5000-tonner. Range 1500 meters, angle on the bow 3.8° and 3.9°, respectively. Torpedo depth set to 3 meters. I then turn hard-a-starboard and launch a fifth eel from the stern tube at a 4500 GRT freighter. All five eels hit home. The first fan launch at the 6000-tonner detonates after runs of one minute, 22 seconds and one minute, 26 seconds, one hitting amidships and the other 20 meters from the stern. Two high smoke columns can be seen. The second fan launch hits the 5000-tonner at the same locations on the hull after runs of one minute, 47 seconds and one minute, 51 seconds. Again there are two high detonation columns. The single launch from Tube V hit the 4500-tonner amidships under the funnel. There is a very high detonation column topped by a large mushroom cloud. I suspect that all three steamers will sink because of the good positioning of the hits. I take off as fast as I can. A destroyer heads toward me from the north at high speed. The steamers I hit shoot up white rockets.[42]

Looks's observations were in the main correct. The larger two steamers were each hit by two torpedoes. But the stern launch at the "4500-tonner" missed, and since no other ship in the convoy was struck within the previous 19 minutes or during the one hour and 17 minutes that followed, there is no accounting for the third explosive scene described by Looks and reported by him to BdU at 0234. The first vessel hit was *West Maximus*, a 5,561-GRT American Hog Islander general cargo vessel in ballast, with 745 tons of slag, ship No. 22 in column 2 on the port side of the convoy. Twenty-five seconds later, a British freighter, the 4,586-GRT *Harperley*, No. 13 on the outside port column 1, took the first of two torpedoes that would puncture her hull.

Neither of the two merchant seamen lookouts on the

bridge nor any of the nineteen U.S. Navy gunners at their stations, sighted a wake from the first torpedo absorbed by *West Maximus*. The explosion, which caused the entire ship to shudder, blew open the port side in the after peak tank and took away part of the stern section. The second torpedo, entering No. 3 hold on the port side, demolished No. 3 aft bulkhead, flooded the fire room, showered the vessel with fuel oil, and buckled the deck plates so badly, said the Naval Armed Guard commander, Lieutenant (jg) J. C. Dea, U.S.N.R., that "it was virtually impossible to walk on the deck." The Master, Captain Earl E. Brooks, immediately ordered Abandon Ship. Of the sixty men on board–thirty-nine merchant crew, nineteen gunners, and two U.S. Army passengers–all but four made it safely down the nets and ladders into four lifeboats, from which, eventually, they were delivered by *Northern Spray*. The freighter went down by the bow at 0135, taking with her the Confidential Books, which Captain Brooks had, for one reason or another, neglected to deep-six. Neither had he gotten off a W/T distress signal nor fired white rockets– though, in Lt. Dea's opinion, "torpedoed ships should not throw out white flares, as they illuminate the area and create visible targets."

On *Harperly*, a sister ship to *Harbury*, the Master, Captain J. E. Turgoose, who was seventeen days into his first command, saw the flashes of the torpedoes that struck *West Maximus* to starboard and slightly ahead in the adjoining column. Moments later, his own vessel was jarred by two torpedoes that exploded through the half-inch-thick hull almost simultaneously, one entering the vicinity of the engine room, the other in the way of the foremast. Turgoose, who was in the wheelhouse at the time, was surprised that the explosions were muffled–more like dull thuds, he said later–and that there were neither detonation flashes nor columns of water that he could see, though survivors from another ship told him afterwards that they saw the flashes. Equally surprising to Turgoose was the fact that at first there was little visible damage–the windows of the wheelhouse were unshattered, for example–but reports came into him thereafter that *Harperly* was listing heavily to port, and for that reason she was hiding broad sea-sucking holes in the ship's side.

Turgoose had the rockets fired—one failed to function—and had an SSS transmitted. The engine room telegraph was jammed, but the engines had already been stopped by the first torpedo, which also took the lives of the Second, Third, and Fourth Engineers. The Second Engineer, W. J. Gilbert, had only moments before volunteered to give up his off-watch time to help with the engines. With the ship's list increasing, Turgoose ordered Abandon Ship. One of the port lifeboats had been destroyed, but the crew successfully launched three serviceable boats and made clear of the ship within the space of eight minutes, Turgoose having to jump to join one of the boats. Ten to fifteen minutes later, he watched his ship disappear by the head. Two men were heard "moaning and shouting" in the water, and by hard pulling on the oars, Turgoose's boat managed to rescue one of them. Two other men clinging to the bottom of a small lifeboat that had capsized went under before they could be reached.

After three and a half hours *Northern Spray* answered the emergency W/T and lights. Thirty-eight survivors were lifted on board the trawler to join fifty-one from *West Maximus,* forty-three from *Harbury,* and two from *North Britain.* Lt. Downer wondered where he would put them if he had to pick up any more. Every open space on his small 150-foot vessel, including the mess decks, ward room, and cabins, was jammed with damp bodies, panic bags, and (from *West Maximus)* American luggage. The trawler's cook, Herbert Arthur Damsell, contrived somehow to serve up meals for everyone, using, among other provisions, the providently salvaged flour and potatoes from *Harbury.* Damsell refused the help offered by cooks from the other ships, saying, "I don't want any strangers in my galley." *Northern Spray* was ordered by Sherwood to St. John's, which was reached without incident at 0750 on the 8th.[43] Any further survivors would have to be rescued by B7's warships.

6

The Fog of War
The Battle for ONS.5

It was the job of the little ships and lonely aircraft, a hard, long and patient job, dreary and unpublicized, against two cunning enemies–the U-boat and the cruel sea.
CAPTAIN GILBERT ROBERTS, C.B.E., R.N.

A war of groping and drowning, of ambuscade and stratagem, of Science and Seamanship.
WINSTON S. CHURCHILL

Both before and during the two and three-quarter hours when five ships of Convoy ONS.5 went to the seabed, Lt.-Cmdr. Sherwood and his escorts were urgently hunting their German adversaries, in line with a principle contained in the Tactical Policy issued by Admiral Horton on 27 April, *viz.*, that U-boats were most successfully detected and destroyed prior to their attacks. Fittingly, it was *Tay* that was first to take the fight to *Fink*. At 2247,* in her night station on the port quarter, *Tay* obtained an asdic contact at 400 yards. She promptly attacked with a ten-pattern. There was no visible result, and Sherwood judged that his contact was not a submarine, since there were "many Non-Sub echoes" in the vicinity. The NHB/MOD reassessment, however, concluded that there had been a submarine present, and identified it as U–*707* (Gretschel), which was not damaged.[1]

---

* All times are expressed in Greenwich Mean Time (GMT) unless otherwise noted.

Second to make an attack that night was Lt. Raymond Hart in *Vidette*. The thirty-year-old destroyer captain had joined the Royal Naval Reserve in 1931 after two years with the Royal Mail Steam Packet Company, and served six months on the battle cruiser H.M.S. *Hood*. When his merchant navy junior officer's position fell victim to Depression-era cutbacks in 1934, he moved to Canada, where he took up lumbering. In 1937 he returned to the sea as a probationary sublieutenant in the RN, and when war broke out he was serving on the destroyer H.M.S. *Hasty*, on which he later took part in the battles of Calabria and Cape Matapan and won the D.S.C. in an action off Tobruk. During Operation Vigorous to revictual Malta in June 1942, *Hasty* was damaged by a German torpedo boat (S-boat) and had to be sunk by another destroyer. From June to October of that year Hart commanded a demolition team called the Hornblowers whose job it was to destroy stores and disable the port facilities at Alexandria should that base be threatened by German occupation. In December 1942, he was given his first sea command in the elderly *Vidette* and assigned to B7. Gifted with intelligence, judgment, and sound seamanship, he has been described as "good-looking" and "dashing."[2]

At 0020 on 5 May, *Vidette* was stationed in position "D," 60° and 5,000 yards on the starboard bow of ONS.5, when her Type 271 radar set picked up a pulse echo bearing 205°, 3,600 yards. Increasing speed to 22 knots, Hart sighted the U-boat five minutes later. At 700 yards the U-boat dived, and at 00301/2 *Vidette*'s D/C team fired and dropped a fourteen-charge pattern at shallow, or ramming, settings over its swirl. The attack damaged the Type IXC U–514, whose Commander, Kptlt. Hans-Jürgen Auffermann, reported to BdU that the charges put his fixed periscope out of order and placed the flange of his starboard stern tube beyond repair; not until the early hours of the 7th, when the battle for ONS.5 was over, would he report that he was capable of further operations.[3]

After opening range to 2,000 yards, Hart returned at a new angle to the attack position hoping to get asdic response, but there was none, and he commenced an operation "Observant." During the second leg of that maneuver, at 0050, another radar contact was acquired bearing 285°, 3,600 yards, and *Vidette* chased up the new bearing, sighting a U-boat known today to have been U–*662* (Kptlt. Heinrich Müller), range 1,000 yards. Electing to attempt an attack before the enemy had a chance to dive, Hart ordered full ahead both engines and Stand By to Ram. The 20mm Oerlikons opened fire, but while their tracers illuminated the U-boat's conning tower, they also temporarily blinded the destroyer's bridge personnel. Oddly, the U-boat appeared to be "reluctant to dive"; that may well have been because U–*662* at that same time was attempting a stern attack on *Vidette*. Finally, she did flood tanks and dive. *Vidette* was able to approach to within 80 yards before the conning tower fully submerged, but not in time to ram. The destroyer proceeded through the swirl and, at 00591/2, fired a fourteen-charge pattern in what Hart thought was "an accurate attack."

Though it was not, it turned out, as accurate as he thought, it had the serendipitous effect of rattling a nearby boat, U–*732* (Oblt.z.S. Klaus-Peter Carlsen), which recorded being depth-charged at the same time. Already nursing earlier injuries, U–*732* was forced by the Wabos to move off for *Rückmarsch* (return voyage) to Brest. Following his procedure in the previous attack, Hart opened the range, this time to 1,700 yards, and returned seeking asdic contact; again there was none, and again he commenced "Observant." At 0125, however, the asdic recorder traced the presence of a U-boat in almost the same position of the last attack, and at 0127 1/2 Hart fired twelve charges (two more intended D/Cs not being set in time). No visible signs of success followed, and at 0150 Sherwood ordered *Vidette* to resume her station *(Offa* had been covering).[4]

Hart's aggressive spirit was matched by that of Chesterman on *Snowflake*. When convoy ships *Harbury, West Maximus,* and *Harperley* were torpedoed within nineteen minutes of one another (0046-0105), Sherwood ordered operation "Half-Raspberry." In a full Raspberry maneuver, all close escorts initiated triangular searches employing starshell illumination rockets. The various triangular patterns to be followed as well as the individual escort sweep speeds and time durations were carefully spelled out in the Atlantic Convoy Instructions.[5] In a "Half-Raspberry" the Senior Officer could modify the maneuver, for example by holding some escorts in place. We know from *Snowflake*'s report that at 0055 she participated in the Half-Raspberry by turning hard-a-starboard to course 335° and proceeding to carry out a 12-knot triangular starshell sweep at the port quarter of the convoy.

At 0104 she fired starshell illuminating an arc 030° to 150°, and at 0108, following the maneuver diagram, she altered course to 210°. One minute later, she received a radar blip bearing 255°, range 3,000 yards, which she pursued at full speed, soon sighting a U-boat on the surface by light of the starshell. At 0111 the corvette's hydrophone picked up the sound (compressed air release) of a torpedo being launched at close range. *Snowflake* continued the chase, but there was little chance of catching up since the Flower's top speed of 16 knots was below that of the U-boats' top surface speeds of 17 (Type VIIC) and 18 1/4 (Types IXB and IXC) knots. Accordingly, when *Snowflake* picked up an asdic bearing of 170°, range 300 yards, indicating a possible submerged U-boat, Chesterman elected to attack that target instead, firing a ten-charge pattern of light D/Cs set to 50 feet and heavy D/Cs set to 140 feet. Fired by stopwatch at 0116, the attack produced no evidence of a hit (it is now concluded by the NHB/MOD reassessment that no submarine was present), and the blast effect of the charges set shallow had the unfortunate effect of fracturing the leads to *Snowflake*'s asdic motor alternators and blowing the bridge fuses.

Instead of returning to the swirl position, Chesterman renewed his pursuit of the surfaced U-boat he had sighted earlier, harrying it with starshell and four-inch gunfire. Finally, he was relieved to see it dive and thus place itself for the time being out of the game. Passing over the swirl at 0127 1/2, Chesterman dropped five light charges set to 100 feet. A minute and a half later, his lookouts sighted a torpedo passing 150 yards ahead from port to starboard. Even though he had forced a dive, Chesterman was not pleased with the surface chase sequence. "Consider I was bluffed by the U-boat into wasting charges," he entered on his report.[6] The boat has been identified by the NHB/MOD reassessment as U-*264* (Looks), which was not harmed.

After having resumed station on the port beam, course 260°, *Snowflake* received a radar return bearing 175°, 3,400 yards, and so informed *Tay* at 0322. The corvette pursued the bearing and when range closed to 2,000 yards she gained the hydrophone effect of highspeed diesels. Chesterman needed faster horses. "Chasing U-boat, unable to overtake," he called to *Tay* by TBS (Talk Between Ships) radio telephone (R/T) at 0339. Sherwood passed the word to Support Group senior officer McCoy, in *Offa*, which resulted in the following exchanges:

OFFA TO *ORIBI* [0341]: If in vicinity assist Snowflake to chase U-boat.

SNOWFLAKE TO *ORIBI* [0345]: My position one-two-zero-Z-Z-nine. Are you joining me?

ORIBI TO *SNOWFLAKE* [0351]: Am proceeding to help you.

SNOWFLAKE TO *ORIBI* [0351½]: Course one-seven-zero. U-boat half-a-mile ahead of me.

At this point *Snowflake* found that she was gaining on the U-boat, which apparently was not proceeding at highest speed, and at 0358 she opened up with starshell, four-inch projectiles, and Oerlikon fire. *Oribi* came up from astern, also firing starshell. At 0359 Chesterman called: "U-boat dived, dropping charges." With "firm contact" by asdic, at 0400 Chesterman fired five light charges set to 100 feet. He maintained asdic contact until 0414, when he dropped four heavy charges set to 225 feet, after which, anxious about running short of D/Cs, he asked *Oribi*'s captain, Lt.-Cmdr. J. P. A. Ingram, to take over the attack. *Oribi*, which earlier, at 0247, had dropped two single D/Cs on what turned out to be a false radar contact, attacked the asdic position held by *Snowflake* with two ten-charge patterns, at 0445 and 0508. The two attacks were handicapped by defective gyro compass repeaters, and at 0417 *Oribi* had had to ask *Snowflake* to be the directing ship, passing ranges and bearings, which she did until 0520, when Chesterman laid course to rejoin the convoy. *Oribi* also abandoned the search at 0554 on orders from *Offa*, without having seen any evidence that would enable him to know that his first ten-pattern had caused heavy damage to the Type VIIC U–*270* (Oblt. z.S. Paul Otto).

In his KTB, Otto described how the first barrage sent his boat plunging toward the bottom with a forward pitch of 20°: "The depth-pressure gauge is maxed out." By running the E-motors at full emergency reverse (*A.K.-zurück*) he managed to slow the descent, and by pumping all available trim water to the stern tanks as well as by sending every crewman climbing into the aft torpedo room he got the boat righted, and was able to begin blowing the ballast tanks to reach a safe depth. As the boat rose, it remained bow-heavy from sea water that was pouring through fractures in the hull forward at a rate of one to two tons per hour. Finally, at 1024 GST, Otto was able to surface. After studying the damage reports, he listed seven categories of *Ausfälle* (breakdowns) in his KTB. There was no alternative but *Rückmarsch*.[7]

Unfortunately for ONS.5, her few defenders could not keep the entire German host submerged and thus for the most part, neutralized. At 0144, Kptlt. Rolf Manke in U–*358* could see several steamers from the bridge of his conning tower. They were on course 200°, passing through the position of a sinking, where, Manke noted, "at least ten lifeboats with lights were floating about." (*West Maximus* and *Harperley* had been torpedoed 42 and 39 minutes before.) "The first of the steamers stopped to take on board the occupants of one of the lifeboats." Manke chose that one for a fan shot from Tubes II and III. The Pi 2 pistols that would detonate the Torpex warheads of the torpedoes were adjusted to accommodate the high swells, and the torpedoes' depth mechanisms were set to run at four meters.

The target ship lay hove-to at a range of 1,500 meters. That number, together with the target's speed, o knots, and bearing, Red [port] 80°, was fed into the electromechanical deflection calculator (*Vorhaltrechner*), and the trigonometric solution of the aiming triangle (a simple calculation, since the target was stationary) was transmitted by it to the torpedo launch receiver (*Torpedoschussempfänger*) in the forward torpedo room, which in turn fed the heading into the guidance systems of torpedoes II and III. When the Petty Officer (*Bootsmaat*) at the torpedo station acknowledged completion of the process by the word *Following!* (*Folgen!*), Manke's first watch officer (I.W.O.) gave the launch order at 0222: "Launch fan shot!" (*"Fächer los!"*)[8]

Manke described the result in his KTB:

> Two explosions were heard in the boat after the 113 seconds run, so perhaps both torpedoes hit. A violent explosion could be seen midships. The steamer broke apart in the middle and sank within one minute. Because of the vessel's length (150 meters) and its 5½ hatches, I judge the steamer to be 8000 GRT. According to *Gröner* [merchant ship silhouette identification handbook] she belongs to the *Port Hardy* class (8700 GRT).

At 0248 Manke ordered the launch of a single eel against the next freighter in line, range 1,600:

> Launch order given. But the torpedo stuck in the tube. A *Mechanikersmaat* [Machinist's Mate] prodded it out with a mine ejector and it hit the target after a run of 118 seconds. A large explosion resulted amidships on the target and the steamer broke apart and sank in a matter of seconds. From *Gröner* we judged the vessel to be of the *Clan Macnab* class, 6000 GRT. . . . Only a destroyer and another escort could now be seen. We pursued the convoy, whose position was obvious from the frequent shooting of flares, but then, because of the sea force and swell, we dived in order to reload in a stable environment.[9]

Manke hit his ships all right, but their tonnages and fates were not as described in the rather inflated account he leaves us, for neither sank "within one minute" (*versank innerhalb einer Minute*) or "in a matter of seconds" (*versank in wenigen Sekunden*). The first vessel hit was the freighter *Bristol City*, bound for New York with a 2,500-ton cargo of China clay (also called kaolin, used in the manufacture of china or porcelain) and general goods. Her GRT of 2,864 tons hardly measured up to Manke's estimate of 8,000. And in her stricken condition she survived well beyond a minute.

At the time of U–*358*'s first torpedo, *Bristol City* was in position 54°00′N, 43°55′W (AJ 6517), heading column No. 1 on the extreme port bow of ONS.5, steering a course of 197° through a sea with heavily confused swell; a southwest wind was blowing Force 5; and the overcast night was very dark, though with good visibility. No one on board sighted the torpedo before it exploded in No. 4 hold on the freighter's port side. Her Master, Captain A. L. Webb, who was on the bridge, stated later that: "The explosion was dull, much quieter than I would have expected. I saw a flash, and a huge column of water was thrown into the air, which cascaded down and flooded the decks." One immediate result of the blast was the collapse of the main topmast and the blowing off of hatches and beams. So much debris fell on the deck that it was difficult for Webb to assess the exterior damage, although he specifically observed that the port lifeboat and after rafts were wrecked. More serious was the flooding below of No. 4 hold and the engine room. Webb rang for the engines to be stopped.

"A few minutes later," he remembered, a second torpedo struck his ship, with no flash, in No. 1 hold. But he also miscalculated times. The interval between torpedoes II and III of Manke's fan shot should have been no more than seconds. A *Fächerschuss,* such as Manke employed, was a simultaneous spread of two or more torpedoes; it differed from a *Mehrfach,* which was a multiple, though not simultaneous, launch. In any event, the second eel compounded the damage to *Bristol City,* collapsing the fore topmast, destroying the windlass, blowing off one of the forward rafts and hatches from Nos. 1 and 2 holds, and flinging China clay into the air. Webb was unable to get rockets off, but M.V. *Dolius* in the adjoining column to starboard sent up two. Nor was Webb able to get an SSS off, since the wireless room had been wrecked. He did see to it that the Confidential Books, which included the Wireless Codes, were secured overboard in weighted boxes. Then, recognizing that there was no hope for *Bristol City,* he ordered Abandon Ship.

Twenty of his crew of forty-four, which included four Navy and two Army gunners who never saw their assailant, jumped from the main deck into the sea to join the starboard lifeboat. A jolly boat with five occupants capsized on reaching the water, casting the crewmen overside; three of them were lifted into the lifeboat, while two floated off and were not seen again, despite the fact that all the crew wore life jackets with red lights. Webb was the last to leave the ship, which was not broken in two, as Manke observed, but had settled by the head and was steaming under; the Master was waist-deep in water before he swam off into the swells, where the lifeboat found him. When the ship finally disappeared it was nine minutes (not one) after the first torpedo had struck. A little more than an hour later, the survivors, three of them injured, were rescued by the corvette *Loosestrife.* Fifteen of the crew were missing, presumed killed by the torpedoes, or drowned, or carried off in the swells.[10]

The second ship, which was hit by Manke's single torpedo launch, was S.S. *Wentworth,* a 5,512-GRT freighter of the Dalgleish Steamshipping Company, bound for New York in ballast. She occupied the third position in column No. 3. Her Master, Captain R. G. Phillips, had learned of *Bristol City*'s misfortune from the Second Officer, and had hurried from his cabin to the bridge. Shortly afterwards, his own vessel was struck by a torpedo on the port side amidships, in the stokehold where the ship's furnaces opened. There was no flash or flame that anyone could see, nor was there much of a noise. Only a modest amount of water was thrown up. But the ship's hull was punctured to form a hole about twelve feet in diameter, with about three feet of its jagged dimensions showing above the water line. The main deck cracked amidships, and both the funnel and wireless room collapsed.

Since the W/T aerial had been carried away, too, the Wireless Operator was not able to send the requisite distress signal. Nor could the rockets be fired, because their sockets had been blown apart. The Third Engineer stopped the engines and Phillips, facing what he thought was certain and imminent sinking, ordered Abandon Ship. By 0330 three of the four lifeboats were waterborne and clear of the ship. Phillips could not get the forward raft to release, but at 0350, when he heard the hull splitting, he abandoned and joined the port motorboat. It was then early morning daylight.

Some of *Wentworth*'s crew were picked up from the sea, but altogether five of the forty-seven-man crew were missing, one from drowning, the rest from the torpedo's blast through the stokehold or engine room. Among the survivors were three Navy and three Army D.E.M.S. gunners, who had been no more able to get a shot off than had their counterparts on *Bristol City*. By 0550 the survivors were lifted on board *Loosestrife*, which Phillips in his report called the *Bluestrife*, and now, by any name, was swollen with bereft humanity. Obstinately, the broken *Wentworth* continued to float well beyond the few seconds that Manke had allotted her. When *Loosestrife*'s Captain, Lt. H. A. Stonehouse, R.N.R., learned that Phillips had failed to toss overside the Confidential Books, he knew he had to sink the derelict. Accordingly, he steamed along her port side and fired a D/C close to the hull. Then, on the starboard side, he put two shells into No. 2 hold. At 0700, over four hours after *Wentworth* was hit, Stonehouse sent word to Phillips, who had gone below, that his ship had finally gone down.[11]

Before *Loosestrife* had steamed to the rescue of the *Bristol City* and *Wentworth* survivors on orders from *Tay,* she had on her own energetically raced after U-boat targets detected by radar and asdic. On one chase she dropped a ten-charge pattern at 0517 on a U-boat that dived after being sighted on the surface, range 1,200 yards; the impact of the charges damaged her asdic recorder. During a second pursuit of a target detected first by radar at 0524, then by eye, *Loosestrife* opened fire with one four-inch high-explosive round (H.E.) and with port and starboard 20mm Oerlikons, scoring what he thought were numerous hits with the 120 Oerlikon rounds fired. No effort was made by the U-boat to offer return fire, and after one minute it dived. At 0527 Stonehouse threw a nine-charge pattern about 100 yards ahead of the diving swirl, the last D/C of an intended ten-pattern getting jammed in the rails. Stonehouse was confident that his pattern was very well placed and a "likely kill." The NHB/MOD reassessment has identified the target of *Loosestrife*'s first attack as U-264 (Looks), which was undamaged; and the target of the second attack as U-413 (Kptlt. Gustav Poel), which received superficial damage. Poel, in fact, says he was not hit by any of *Loosestrife*'s gunfire. As for the D/Cs: "Heavy tremors in the boat, damage is slight, everything can be repaired immediately except for the main transmitter. Everyone breathes a sigh of relief!"[12]

During the dark hours of 4/5 May, Convoy ONS.5 had passed through a Werner Henke Night, as five U-boats accounted for seven ships sunk, matching the number sunk by Henke alone on the night of 30 April/1 May. That the slaughter had not been worse, with (now) thirty-six boats assembled for attack instead of Henke's single U-515, is owed in great part to the spirited and intimidating defense mounted by the B7 defenders. Though Lt.-Cmdr. Sherwood would have no way of knowing it when he and Commodore Brook took stock in the morning–whereas in Berlin Dönitz and Godt were fully aware of it from anxious W/T traffic–his band of escorts had so far damaged three boats so gravely that they made for home: U-532 (Junker), U-732 (Carlsen), and U-270 (Otto).[13] These, it could be argued, were equivalents to kills so far as ONS.5 was concerned.

The escorts had severely handled two other boats, which suffered slight damage, U-514 (Auffermann) and U-413 (Poel), and they had driven off or forced to dive six more: U-264 (Looks), U-707 (Gretschel), U-168 (Pich), U-662

(Kptlt. Heinrich Müller), U-584 (Kptlt. Joachim Deecke), and U-260 (Oblt.z.S. Hubertus Purkhold).[14] To have damaged a U-boat, even in cases where the boat was not forced to retire, was effectively to take that boat for a time out of the convoy battle, since the damaged boat had to tend more to her injuries than to her potential targets, which were passing away at seven or more knots. And to have driven off a boat, or to have forced one to dive, was also effectively to neutralize that boat's usefulness temporarily in a night battle. It is instructive to note that none of the boats damaged, driven off, or forced to dive after 0105, when Looks got lucky, subsequently sank or damaged a ship of ONS.5. In a signal sent to the *Fink* boats during the forenoon of 5 May, Dönitz and Godt showed their impatience at the meager returns obtained thus far in exchange for damage. Urging the boats to use the long daylight hours for submerged attacks and for getting as far ahead of the convoy as possible before nightfall, the two German admirals urged their distant Commanders:

> IMMEDIATELY AFTER NIGHTFALL THE DRUMBEAT [*PAUKENSCHLAG*] MUST BE TIMED TO BEGIN. HURRY— THERE ARE 40 OF YOU—OTHERWISE YOU WILL LOSE THIS CONVOY. THE BATTLE CAN'T LAST LONG SINCE THE SEA SPACE LEFT IS SHORT, SO USE EVERY OPPORTUNITY TO THE FULLEST WITH ALL YOUR MIGHT [*MIT ALLER ENERGIE*.][15]

By 0700 on the 5th, Sherwood had B7 in day stations. The convoy, now twenty-six ships in ten columns, was steering on course 202°, speed seven and a half. The weather was overcast with good visibility, the sea was moderate with swell, and the wind was westerly Force 4. In those conditions *Offa* attempted to oil from *Argon* and *Tay* from *British Lady,* with *Oribi* scheduled to follow *Tay* at the same nozzle. But at 0947, as *Offa* closed the U.S. tanker, the *Argon's* captain signaled that he would not be prepared to discharge fuel for another hour; and when the destroyer returned alongside at 1100 the *Argon's* hose parted after only one gallon had passed! *Tay* had better luck with *British Lady,* and *Oribi* was able to follow at 1420. Not until 1730 in the afternoon was *Offa* able to begin drawing 30 tons from the British tanker, slipping the two at 1930.

These were not the ONS.5 screen's only daylight activities. Numerous HF/DF contacts in all quadrants were acquired beginning at 0654, indicating that ONS.5 was still surrounded. We know from intercepts that the following U-boats were in contact with the convoy or its escorts during the forenoon hours: U-638, U-584, U-438, U-531, U-264, U-260, and U-378.[16] One result was that *Oribi* became particularly busy, followed by *Vidette*. At 1010, *Oribi*, in station bearing 160° 5 miles from the port wing ship of the convoy, was instructed to investigate a first-class bearing of 155° to a distance of 12 miles. Forty-seven minutes later, *Oribi* sighted, first, diesel smoke haze, and then the conning tower of a U-boat. Increasing her speed to 30 knots, the destroyer sighted within the next 13 minutes two additional U-boats proceeding away in what seemed line abreast with the first boat. Apparently aware that they were being overhauled, all three boats dived.

Oribi gained a definite asdic contact at 800 yards and attacked with four charges of a ten-pattern, the remainder being checked when the recorder tracing showed that the U-boat was passing down the port side, hence the six D/Cs left would have fallen progressively astern of it. When contact and a good trace were regained at 1243, a ten-pattern was fired by recorder and stopwatch at 1247, two minutes after which "a slight explosion followed by a heavy underwater explosion was heard, producing a bubbly eruption of water." The quarterdeck then reported what appeared to be a periscope proceeding away from the center of the D/C scum. A third attack with five charges was carried out at 1254, with negative results, after which *Oribi*, thinking it essential "to conserve supplies of depth charges for attacks in the vicinity of the convoy," rejoined to fuel from *British Lady* and, at 1740, to resume station. In this event *Oribi* had been in contact with four U-boats, since identified as U-223 (Oblt.z.S. Karljüng Wächter), U-231 (Kptlt. Wolfgang Wenzel), U-621 (Oblt.z.S. Max Kruschka), and U-634 (Oblt.z.S. Eberhard Dahlhaus).

Vidette was stationed in position "B," off the convoy's starboard bow, when at 1542 she acquired an asdic contact at very close range, bearing 090°. Lt. Hart altered course to intercept the contact, which quickly was classified a submarine. Reaching the target's position at 1544, he fired a five-pattern set to 100 feet. After opening range to about 900 yards, he swept back through the attack position, but received no further contact. *Vidette* conducted an Observant until 1633, when she was ordered to rejoin. Hart's assessment of his action read: "Although there was no evidence of damage to the U-boat, in my opinion the counter attack delivered probably prevented an attack on the Convoy." The NHB/MOD reassessment doubts that a U-boat was present.[17]

Meanwhile, despite these efforts, another convoy ship was torpedoed. The victim was M.V. *Dolius,* ship No. 21 on the port-hand easterly wing. Professor Jürgen Rohwer conjectures that the assailant was U–638, commanded by Kptlt. Oskar Staudinger. A native of Löbau who had earlier (1938-1941) served in the Luftwaffe, Staudinger was one week away from his twenty-sixth birthday. We know nothing of the details of this attack, since the boat's KTB and *Schussmeldung,* if one existed, did not survive the battle. The "KTB" that one does find in the archives for his second Atlantic patrol out of La Pallice, 20 April to 5 May 1943, is a reconstruction done in Berlin on or about 7 May based on his F.T.s (wireless messages), both incoming and outgoing. There is no direct evidence in the F.T.s to show that U–638 sank a ship on 5 May, and the KTB-BdU does not acknowledge receipt of such a report.[18]

Whatever U-boat was responsible, the *Dolius,* a 5,507-GRT freighter of the Blue Funnel Line, was torpedoed on her starboard side at 1240. Since she was the lead ship in column No. 2 on the port-hand easterly wing, the torpedo would have had to come from very slightly ahead or from within the formation. The Master, Captain G. R. Cheetham, judged that the torpedo had been launched from close range between his vessel and the two ships, *Ottinge* and *Baron Graham,* to his starboard. With what Cheetham called a "dull" explosion with no flash, the warhead opened a 30-foot-long hole extending some 15 feet above the waterline. The concussion stopped the engines and the engine room promptly flooded, as did No. 4 hold. The Fourth Engineer and Junior Assistant Engineer were killed at their stations. The ship at first listed slightly, then came upright and began to settle by the stern. Cheetham ordered his crew to stand by the lifeboats. It was an unusually large crew: thirty-nine British and twenty-two Chinese, plus five Navy and four Army gunners.

Some of the Chinese, panicking, began lowering one of the three serviceable boats—No. 3 starboard had been destroyed—but stopped when Cheetham shouted at them. After making a thorough search for any injured, Cheetham disposed of the Confidential Books and gave the command Abandon Ship. Every man behaved with well-ordered discipline, including the Chinese, and the boats were successfully manned and lowered. As the Third Officer's boat pulled away from the vessel, its occupants sighted a crewman still on board waving his arms for assistance. The boat returned to rescue him and another crewman was found lying unconscious below. Twenty-five minutes after the torpedo's explosion, all the known survivors were clear of the wreck. Two engineers and one gunner were dead, one gunner died in the lifeboats, and two gunners were injured.[19]

Two minutes after *Dolius* was hit, Sherwood ordered "Artichoke." *Sunflower* and *Offa* responded, the corvette turning from her port bow station and charging down between columns 2 and 3 at emergency full speed. Slightly astern of the derelict, *Sunflower* picked up an asdic contact in the center of the convoy formation, range 1,200 yards. Lt.Cmdr. Plomer closed the position and dropped a ten-pattern with 150-feet settings. The blasts did some damage to his own ship, but there was no sign that he had done any to a U-boat. Contact was lost, and when *Tay* joined she could not regain, either. From circumstantial evidence, however, the NHB/MOD reassessment has concluded that *Sunflower*'s attack resulted in the sinking of Staudinger's U-*638*, at 54°12′N, 44°05′W—swift retribution, indeed, for the loss of *Dolius*, and proof again of the effectiveness of Artichoke. *Sunflower*'s was the first kill made by the close escort. *Offa*, meanwhile, obtained a doubtful contact at 1301, threw a ten-charge pattern, and rejoined the convoy.[20]

Between 1320 and 1400 *Sunflower* swept a circle around the sinking *Dolius*, then, on orders from *Tay*, began rescuing survivors while *Snowflake* provided cover. Once on board, the *Dolius* officers, ratings, and apprentices did whatever they could to make themselves useful, serving on lookout watches, performing deck tasks of various kinds, and cleaning quarters. Plomer said later, "The ship was sorry to see them go in spite of the overcrowding involved." As *Sunflower* set course to rejoin the convoy, the D.E.M.S. rating who died in a lifeboat was buried overside with a short service.[21]

Since 2244 on the 4th, the corvette H.M.S. *Pink*, rather neglected in this narrative of late, has been trundling along faithfully as lone escort to a separately routed convoy of four stragglers: the American *West Madaket*, the British *Dunsley* and *Director*, and the Norwegian *Gudvor*. At 1150, "*Pink*'s Party," as the tiny fleet came to be called, was in position 54°56′N, 43°44′W, some 80 miles astern of the main body, making about 8 knots on the course, 240°, assigned by CinCWA. Twenty-seven-year-old Lt. (now Sir) Robert Atkinson, commanding *Pink*, was zigzagging ahead, his four charges in line abreast about 3,000 yards astern. With only 30 percent of his fuel remaining, with no chance to overtake the main body and refuel, and with a separate route that increased the distance to be steamed, Atkinson was proceeding on only one boiler, the second being banked, and had shut down one dynamo and rationed water. If an attack situation developed, he knew that the higher speeds required by those maneuvers would make greater than usual demands on his fuel reserves. But he did not quail before that prospect: not having seen any action during the voyage to date, he badly wanted a go at the enemy.[22]

Long experienced in the North Atlantic, Atkinson had served in the Merchant Navy since 1932, and since 1937 as an

officer, beginning as probationary sublieutenant, in the Royal
Navy Reserve. He was called to duty in September 1939 and
given command of the yacht *Lorna,* which, operating off Gibraltar, seized an Italian tanker when that country entered the
war. He took the tanker, which was filled with seven and a
half million gallons of petrol, back to England, where he asked
for a "more active state of war." Accordingly, he was sent for
ASW training at H.M.S. *Osprey* in Portland. That completed,
he was named First Lieutenant of the corvette H.M.S. *Rhodo-
dendron,* which, on 21 November 1940, one month after her
commissioning, became the first ship to sink a U-boat
(U–*104*) at night. His next ship, and first corvette command,
H.M.S. *Snowdrop,* was detached to the "White Patrol" that ran
between the northwest cape of Iceland and the packs and
growlers of Greenland. There, well before *Pink*'s Party, he experienced the trials of a lonely vigil.

The corvette's mission was to travel back and forth across
the Denmark Strait in order to detect a breakout of the German heavy battleship *Bismarck,* though, as he said to the
writer over a half-century later, there was not anything his
"little pea shooter" could have done about it except report.
"There was darkness day and night, wind and cold, a lot of
frostbite, seasickness all the time, poor food." The loneliness
of *Snowdrop*'s solitary watch was deepened by the fact that
"We never went ashore; the Icelanders weren't very hospita-
ble." On another occasion he said: "I was always vulnerable to
seasickness strangely enough, having been at sea all my life,
and I recall on one occasion having so many clothes on and
being so weak from seasickness, I could hardly mount the
companionway to get on to the bridge, I was so physically
weak."[23] After one month of shore duty to help him get over
his seasickness, Atkinson was given command of the newly
commissioned (2 July 1942) corvette *Pink,* named after the
fragrant flowers of the genus *Dianthus.* The corvette joined B7
when Peter Gretton assumed command of the Group.

Now, at 1154 on 5 May 1943, toward the end of the starboard leg of a zigzag, *Pink* obtained a first-class asdic contact
bearing 310°, range 2,200 yards. The echoes, Atkinson said,

were "by far the clearest and sharpest I have ever heard." The event confronted him with two conundrums: (1) Should he expend perhaps an unacceptable amount of previous fuel in making an attack, which might or might not succeed, or should he husband his oil in a simple defensive mode and thus extend his capacity to provide "scare tactic" cover for the stragglers? (2) Should he seize this opportunity to destroy one U-boat, or would his absence in so doing, whether successful or not, expose his small convoy to the torpedoes of another U-boat? The Atlantic Convoy Instructions permitted him to attack, "provided his duty can be undertaken without undue prejudice to the safety of the convoy."[24] Atkinson decided to attack.

At her maximum speed available on one boiler, 11 knots, *Pink* held the contact to 150 yards, and at 1159 dropped three D/Cs, two set to 100 feet and one to 250. More were not dropped owing to Atkinson's concern that at her low speed and with D/Cs set shallow, *Pink* would not get beyond the blast effect. When contact was regained, *Pink* commenced a second run in, during which her hydrophones picked up the sounds of the U-boat's hydroplanes and/or rudder, indicating a depth change or a turn. At 1207, increasing for safety to 15 knots by getting her second boiler "flashed up," she fired ten charges get to 150 and 385 feet. No signs of damage appeared on the surface. One minute later, a "moderately high echo" was obtained again. In setting up for a third attack, Atkinson deduced from the movements of the U-boat that it was endeavoring to put its stern and cavitation turbulence to him. As the target moved to starboard, *Pink* followed, and at 1216, with the range at 250 yards, he ordered the firing of twenty-four Hedgehog bombs with 4° of right deflection because of wind. To his extreme disappointment, the Hedgehog mechanism misfired.

It took eleven minutes of following the plot to acquire a new contact, which was "firm and metallic," at 1227. Two minutes later, the asdic echo was bearing 0°, range 1,400 yards. Good hydrophone effect was also heard on that bearing, and at 1233 Atkinson fired a ten-pattern set to 250 and

385 feet. With no evidence of damage, and not expecting to see any appear right away from that depth, Atkinson's asdic team kept their sound pulses glued to the U-boat's hull, and at 1241 contact was again "sharp and firm." Hydroplane and/or rudder noises picked up by hydrophone suggested that the U-boat might be diving deeper. At 1244 *Pink* made her fourth attack, ten charges set to 350 and 550 feet. This time Atkinson felt confident that he had made an accurate and successful drop. He was confirmed in that confidence during *Pink*'s run out by hydrophone reports of blowing tanks. Then, about 500 yards astern, three huge bubbles followed by numerous smaller ones broke the surface of the water. *Pink* turned back and closed the position to observe the "boiling:"

> . . . The water in the vicinity [was] considerably aer-
> ated in appearance and green and white like shallow
> water. Tangible evidence of destruction was greedily
> and most enthusiastically searched for, but nothing
> further was seen. It was realized that my little convoy
> was drawing away and was now some distance ahead
> and also unprotected, but I decided to risk this and to
> continue with the hunt.[25]

With asdic showing that the U-boat was quite deep and practically stationary, Atkinson decided on a second Hedgehog salvo, which was fired at 1302. But, again, the Hedgehog disappointed as all twenty-four projectiles exploded on striking the water (!) Giving the hunt one last go, Atkinson set up for another deep ten-pattern drop, commencing his run in at 1307, course 110°, speed 13 knots, eight light D/Cs fused for 350 and 550 feet, and two heavy charges with Mark VII pistols to give extra depth fused for 700 feet. (The depths were all guesses, since the Type 145 asdic then in use on corvettes did not indicate the target's depth. The first operational depth-determining asdic, Type 147, would not be available until September 1943. It was not known that a U-boat could dive deeper than 700 feet [213 meters] until June 1943.)

Opening the range to 1,500 yards, *Pink* listened for an echo, but there was none. Nor was there any evidence on the surface, which Atkinson returned to inspect. At 1325 he abandoned the hunt and shaped course for 240° at 15 knots to rejoin his convoy 10 miles ahead. Fourteen minutes later, *Pink* was shaken by a powerful underwater explosion, "like a deep grunt," which left Atkinson "in no doubt as to the fact that the U-boat was destroyed." He was sorely tempted to turn back and see what the surface might reveal, but since his convoy had been unprotected for an hour and a half, he decided that to do so was not prudent.

Atkinson's report on his five-pronged attack was reviewed by the Admiralty's U-Boat Assessment Committee on 28 June 1943, and the conclusion was drawn that "this attack was probably successful and it is assessed as 'Probably sunk.' "[26] By 20 July 1943 the Admiralty was convinced that it knew the identity of the U-boat sunk: "The sinking of this submarine, which was U.192, has since been confirmed."[27] In the subsequent literature from Roskill to Syrett, U-192 (Oblt.z.See Werner Happe) has been identified as the fatal victim of *Pink* on 5 May. We know little about Happe's boat, which had sortied from Kiel on 13 April, because she was lost at some point in the battle and her documents went down with her. A KTB based on messages sent to her was reconstructed in Berlin, but it is not revealing; no response was heard by BdU since 3 May, from qu AJ 3757, and on 6 May (again on 9 May) she was declared a total loss. It is now clear the U–192 succumbed on 6 May (see below), in a sad finish to her first and only patrol.

The better fit as *Pink*'s target is U–358 (Manke), the slayer of *Bristol City* and *Wentworth*. Analysis of the KTBs of the participating boats shows that U–358 was in the approximate same position as *Pink,* astern of ONS.5 (U–358 at 1000: 54°52'N, 43°30'W; *Pink* at 0954: 54°56'N, 43°44'W), and that over a period of one hour and a half she experienced a prolonged pounding from "69 well-placed depth charges." *Pink,* in fact, dropped forty-three D/Cs and twenty-four Hedgehog rockets; the latter may have sounded like D/Cs when they exploded on contact with the surface, but they would have gone off with near simultaneity. In his description of the event,

Manke was not certain about the number of escorts present or about the category of his pursuer, mistaking *Pink* for a destroyer, but he correctly cited a separate "small convoy":

> At 1042 we sighted a small convoy: 3 steamers, 1 destroyer, and 1 corvette. The boat was heard [asdic] by the destroyer. Then 1½ hours of depth charges followed: 69 well-placed depth charges [Wabos]. The destroyer criss-crossed above the boat continuously. He must have a good hydrophone because he used asdic only for a short time before attacking. In addition, he employed doppler effect, and 50 seconds later the depth charges came.

Afterwards, Manke surveyed the damage: diving cells Nos. 1 and 5 were out of service; the tower hatch leaked badly; there were numerous electrical breakdowns; four battery cells were cracked; there was leakage in the cooling jacket of the outer exhaust cutout; torpedo Tube 5 was inoperable for underwater launches; the stern hydroplanes could not be moved beyond 10 degrees; and the boat produced loud noises throughout the interior. After he surfaced to make what repairs he could, Manke discovered that his diesels could not produce more than 10 knots speed. He signaled a report on his condition to BdU, and at 1731 the next day he received a response: RETURN DIRECTLY TO BASE WITHOUT REPLENISHING.[28]

It was not a kill. But it was as good as a kill. In judging U–*358* to have been the U-boat involved, it is useful to note both that no other B7 or Support Group escort made a sustained attack during the time period when *Pink* was attacking, and that no other U-boat reported being attacked during the one hour and thirty minutes when U–*358* was absorbing her punishment.[29]

For Atkinson, elation quickly turned to ashes: "At 1453, my worst fears materialized." About three miles astern of his small convoy, augmented since noon by the arrival of a fifth straggler, S.S. *Yearby,* the corvette Captain saw a "huge column of smoke" rising from the port wing ship, *West Madaket,* which immediately began to settle by the stern. Only one ship was sunk, but it was misfortune enough. The "another U-boat" in Atkinson's conundrum was U-584, commanded by Kptlt. Joachim Deecke. This Type VIIC boat was a veteran of several North Atlantic patrols; had sunk a Soviet submarine (M-175) on 10 January 1942; and on 17 June (GST) of the same year had deposited four German saboteurs (all of whom were captured and executed) on the beach at Ponte Vedra, Florida. Now U-584 was submerged at 1400 on 5 May in qu AJ 5695 (54°47'N, 44°12'W):

> Enemy is in sight [by periscope], course 250°, speed 9 knots, 4 steamers, 3 of them overlapping. Enemy zigzags 20°to 230°. At 1443 I launch a 4-torpedo fan-shot–Tube 4 fails to launch–at 2 overlapping steamers, bearing right 85°, range 2000 meters. The freighter in front is 5000 GRT. The one behind it is larger, and possibly, to judge from its long fo'c's'le, is a tanker. In the foreground is a small vessel, possibly a corvette. After 4 minutes, 48 seconds, and after 4 minutes, 52 seconds, there are 3 torpedo detonations. 5 minutes and 20 minutes later there are two additional detonations, most likely boiler explosions followed by the bursting of bulkheads. After 44 minutes the first steamer sinks, and after 90 minutes the second goes down. The sinking noises are clearly made out [inside the boat]. A corvette drops warning depth charges [*Schreckwasser-bomben*], but they are far off.[30]

By this point the reader may have come to suspect that U-boat Commanders, as a species, were uncommonly given to observation errors, if not to self-deception. With claims of two sinkings instead of one, Deecke was the latest in a line that included Junker (U-532), who claimed two hits (that subsequently were credited him by BdU) when he had made none; Hasenschar (U-628), who made four claims, including a "vaporized" corvette, but had only one actual hit, plus an artillery coup-de-grâce to *Harbury;* and Looks (U-264), with three claims and two actuals. Further, as we have seen, there have been reporting errors in ship types, in times required for vessels to sink, and in the quantity of tonnage destroyed.

Endemic to U-boat claims throughout the war were euphoric tonnage figures, as in Manke's (U–358) claim of 8,000 tons for the 2,864GRT *Bristol City*. Although Dönitz had urged his Commanders to "estimate cautiously and accurately–we are an honest firm!," they nonetheless sometimes inflated their figures either through mistaken observation, or misinterpretation of an end-of-run detonation for a *Treffer* (hit), or old-fashioned wishful thinking.[31] Yet the reader would want to know that all these same defects characterized reporting by U.S. Navy submarine skippers in the Pacific war being conducted at the same time against Japan. A postwar analysis by the U.S. Joint Army-Navy Assessment Committee (JANAC) drastically reduced the number of sinkings and tonnage sunk by U.S. submarines from 4,000 enemy ships and 10 million tons claimed to 1,314 ships and 5.3 million tons actually sunk. In one individual example, the leading U.S. submarine ace of the war, Richard H. O'Kane, had his numbers reduced from thirty-one ships and 227,800 tons claimed to twenty-four ships and 93,824 tons actual.[32]

There was only one ship torpedoed by Deecke on 5 May 1943, and it was *West Madaket*. A sudden jar was felt by those on board the vessel, and the Officer of the Watch and several crew members saw a large geyser of water rise on the port quarter. The torpedo must have penetrated a good distance into the hull, survivors said, because a 5-by-2½-foot hole was torn in the starboard side. Almost at once the stern sagged. Inspection of the deck, where there was a large crack in the plating amidships, convinced the ship's Master, Captain H. Schroeder, that the freighter's back was broken, and he ordered Abandon Ship. The entire crew of sixty-one, including twenty-two D.E.M.S. gunners, who never saw a target, made it into boats safely. In the interim, the other four merchantmen turned to starboard and performed what Atkinson called "some remarkable and spectacular zigzags."

When *Pink* caught up to *West Madaket*, he carried out an Observant, dropping D/Cs intermittently to keep the U-boat down. These were the "warning charges" heard by U-584. The lifeboats were widely scattered and Atkinson endeavored to muster them so that he could make a pickup of survivors while hove-to in the shortest possible time, knowing full well that *Pink* would make an inviting target during the operation. When he approached the boats and found them filled with as much luggage as humanity, he ordered the men out and the luggage left. Then he told the Oerlikon crews to use the boats and luggage for practice fire. Finally, by 1600, without hindrance, he had everyone on board, and could turn his attention to the canted hulk of *West Madaket*.

Although her Confidential Books were safely overboard in a metal container, Atkinson decided to assist the broken merchantman to sink, which he accomplished by firing down her side two D/Cs set to 50 feet from his starboard throwers. "The result was devastating," he stated four days later. "She split as if cleaved by an ax amidships, sinking in two separate pieces and turning turtle as she sank." (To the writer he said, dryly, "That U-boat didn't sink *West Madaket*. I sank her.") Atkinson was surprised that she left no trace of her passing despite the fact that her bunkers contained 540 tons of oil. Now *Pink* set course to catch up with her remaining four charges while her crew busied themselves making room on the tiny corvette for threescore American passengers.[33]

During the daylight hours of 5 May, two functioning merchantmen, *Dolius* and *West Madaket,* were torpedoed. But in exchange, the Germans took a beating of their own. *Sunflower* sank U-638 (Staudinger), and *Pink* mauled U-358 (Manke), which was compelled to move off for return passage. On the same day, in a reprise of the U-439/U-659 collision on 4 May, U-600 (Kptlt. Bernhard Zurmühlen) slammed into U-406 (Kptlt. Horst Dieterichs) at 0905 in qu CG 1746, off the coast of Spain, necessitating the return of both boats, which, like U-439 and U-659, had occupied adjacent stations in Group *Drossel*. The accident took place with the two boats on the surface in good visibility (*gute Sicht*), seas Force 3-4 with medium swell. Unaccountably, U-600 came into view on U-406's port side and took a collision course toward the latter boat, which frantically flashed a recognition signal (*Erkennungssignal*) and turned hard-a-starboard, both engines emergency full (*äußerste Kraft voraus!*). Without deviating, the bow of U-*600* rammed into U-*406*'s hull just forward of the port diving tank. Both boats were compelled by the damages inflicted to make a *Rückmarsch*, U-*600* to La Pallice, U-*406* to St.-Nazaire.[34]

The first U-boat kill by a surface escort had been posted, and the list of damaged and retreating U-boats was lengthening. So, too, was the list of sunk merchantmen, of course, but the ONS.5 hemorrhaging was about to stop, following one last, and spectacular, U-boat success. Three weeks into her second North Atlantic *Feindfahrt,* the Type VIIC U-*266* launched four torpedoes in rapid succession at 1950 on the 5th. We have no details of her attack because the boat, with her documents, was destroyed later in the month. A KTB reconstructed in Berlin based on F.T.s received cites this signal from boat commander Kptlt. Rolf von Jessen:

> Sank one [ship] of at least 5000 GRT and a second, based on sinking noises, probably also 5000 GRT. Two further detonations were definitely heard. At 2150 [GST] the enemy was positioned at AJ 8359, course 200°, speed 7 knots.[35]

Three ships were hit in this action: British steamers *Selvistan* and *Gharinda,* followed by the Norwegian steamer *Bonde,* at 1,750 GRT the smallest ship in the convoy. What Sherwood called "reliable survivors" from the British vessels reported that the torpedoes were seen approaching from port. Since the three victims were positioned toward the starboard side of the convoy, indications were that U-*266* had penetrated inside the columns. That *Bonde* was two columns farther toward the convoy's center, and that her survivors sighted and engaged a periscope on the starboard beam, persuaded Sherwood that the U-boat torpedoed the British vessels with his bow tubes and the Norwegian with his stern.

First hit was the 5,136-GRT *Selvistan,* owned by the Hindustan Steamship Company of Newcastle, whose First Officer, Mr. C. D. Head, was on the bridge at the time. To port side he sighted something moving near the surface that he took to be a porpoise, since it was "spouting water." It crossed in front of *Argon*'s bow in the adjoining column and then, halfway to *Selvistan,* it leaped above the surface, revealing itself to be a torpedo. Head described it as "silvery grey," and thought that because of its slow speed, perhaps 10 to 12 knots, it was nearing the end of its run (G7a torpedoes normally ran at 40 knots, G7es at 30). Though he rang Full Speed Ahead and put the helm hard to port, the ship lacked sufficient speed to swing clear and the torpedo impacted the port side with a dull explosion in No. 5 hold, showing no flash, but sending hatch, beams, and ballast skyward. No more than five seconds later, a second, unseen torpedo punctured the No. 4 hold with exactly the same effects and result.

Quickly, the steamer settled by the stern, and in a matter of only two minutes submerged from view. In that fractional amount of time it was not possible to lower either of the two main lifeboats, but the Master and crew did manage to launch two small bridge boats and the forward starboard raft, on which, or clinging to which, they floated off. Five crewmen were declared missing and one other man, a D.E.M.S. gunner, had a grave head wound from which he would die before rescue. First Officer Head stated later that the Indian firemen, who were the only men to share his boat, "were simply no use at all; they just sat in the boat, praying to Allah to save them, but not attempting to do anything to save themselves." Fortunately, after three-quarters of an hour, the forty men who survived were lifted on board the frigate *Tay.* Since *Tay*'s asdic was inoperable, Sherwood had assigned his own vessel to the rescue mission while directing *Offa* and *Oribi* to carry out Observant around the sinking position.

Second to be hit by U–266 was the 5,306-GRT *Gharinda,* owned by the British India Steam Navigation Company of Glasgow. This freighter, with a large crew of ninety-two, including six Navy and four Army gunners, had straggled on 3 May, owing to heavy weather, and had not regained contact with the convoy until 1100 on the 4th. "About two minutes" after *Selvistan* was torpedoed, *Gharinda*'s Master, Captain R. Stone, estimated, this second British vessel was struck by a torpedo in No. 1 hold on her port side. There was a flash, a very loud explosion, and a towering column of water that rained down on the bridge, carrying with it the hatches of No. 1 hold. The force of the explosion twisted both derricks and blew them over to starboard. Since the ship began to settle rapidly by the head, Stone threw overboard the Confidential Books and rang Abandon Ship. Five of the six lifeboats were successfully lowered except that, owing to a crewman's error, one of the five nose-dived into the sea and swamped.

Stone made a quick inspection of the ship to make sure no one had been left behind, then joined one of the boats. A short time later, he entertained the notion of returning to his ship to see if she could be saved, even though the propeller and rudder were out of the water. The notion, however, was doused by *Tay,* which arrived on the scene and began "hauling up" the survivors; Stone related tersely that he had been "hauled up by the scruff of my neck." Sherwood told Stone that he could not indulge him in his desire to return, because he had to go after the survivors of *Bonde,* which also had been torpedoed. Bereft because of the loss of his ship, Stone could have drawn comfort from the fact, had he known it, that his was one of only two ships torpedoed in ONS.5 that did not lose a single man. If First Officer Head was disappointed with the performance of his Indian crewmen off *Selvistan,* Stone was favorably impressed by his own sixty-eight Indians, of whom he said:

> I am extremely pleased with the native crew, because they showed no sign of panic at any time. I think this is partly due to the fact that on board my ship no English is spoken, all orders are given in the language of the natives, which I consider helps them to understand what is going on, and therefore they are not liable to panic. I would specially like to mention the Indian Quarter Master, Shareatullah, son of Aboth Allee, who in spite of the debris which was falling on the Bridge,

remained at his post at the wheel until ordered to his boat by me.[36]

The thirteenth and final ONS.5 merchantman to die at sea was bantam *Bonde* in column 8. Chief Officer M. MacLellan of S.S. *Baron Graham* remembered:

> The *Bonde* was the little ship we all admired so much in that convoy. In such a vast expanse of sea, she looked so tiny as she courageously battled through the heavy weather, frequently disappearing from view completely in the heavy seas and swells. The first thing I used to do as daylight broke in my morning watch was to look for our little friend, and if she was still bobbing along the day was made.[37]

To Captain Stone of *Gharinda* we owe our knowledge of what happened to *Bonde*. Just after his own ship was torpedoed, Stone was on the bridge about to throw his Confidential Books overboard when he saw the Oerlikon gunners on *Bonde* open 20mm fire against a periscope sighted close on her starboard beam. It was the first time in ONS.5's voyage that D.E.M.S. gunners engaged a U-boat. Stone ordered his own Oerlikons to fire in the direction where *Bonde's* shots were splashing. A few seconds later, he saw and tracked a torpedo wake approaching *Bonde's* starboard side. The nearby *Vidette* also reported seeing torpedo tracks on the steamer's starboard beam. "Then," said Captain John Gates of *Baron Graham*, who was also watching, "there was an explosion and [*Bonde*] seemed to jump up in the water. When the smoke and spray of the explosion had cleared away, the *Bonde* was already standing on her end with her bow and foredeck vertically out of the water. I looked away for a few seconds and in that time the ship sank."[38] There had been no time to lower boats or rafts. When *Tay* came around to pick up survivors she found only twelve men from the crew of thirty-eight.

Alarmed by the sudden loss of three ships, Commodore Brook ordered an emergency turn of 90° to port, which was executed successfully beginning at 1950. He would resume base course at 2045, at which hour Sherwood ordered the escorts to resume station, excepting *Offa* and *Oribi*, which had been conducting Observant around the sinkings. At 2039 *Offa* gained a firm asdic contact and during the next hour and 38 minutes made five large-pattern attacks.[39] *Oribi* joined in the hunt but was unable to acquire contact. McCoy's onslaught resulted in extensive damage to U–*266*, the slayer of *Selvistan*, *Gharinda*, and *Bonde*. Kptlt. von Jessen reported suffering damage to diving tank No. 3, trim cells, Junkers air compressor, and starboard dynamotors. Forced to move off for repairs, the boat never rejoined the *Fink* line, eventually being sunk by an aircraft on 15 May.[40] With no evidence of a kill or damage, *Offa* broke off the action and shaped course for the convoy, taking *Oribi* with her. Explained McCoy: "Heavy W/T activity indicated that the convoy was threatened with annihilation and I considered it imperative to return to it before dark."[41]

In the meantime, at 1954, a VLR Liberator, Aircraft J/120 from Reykjavik, appeared overhead and made R/T contact with Sherwood. Its appearance gladdened everyone in the convoy. Sherwood asked the pilot to search astern for stragglers and wrecks. This the Liberator was able to do for only 45 minutes until, reaching PLE, the pilot and Sherwood had this exchange: Aircraft: "Don't want to go, but have to." *Tay:* "Thank you for your help."[42] Commodore Brook observed that this Iceland-based bomber was the first air escort he had seen since 2 May, "though air support was so sadly needed."[43] (He must have missed seeing the Fortress from Gander on the 3rd; the two Cansos from Gander on the 4th were too distant to be seen.) He might have wondered, though, why he was not seeing aircraft from Newfoundland at this hour late on the 5th, when Gander and Torbay were not far distant. An RCAF Canso of Eastern Air Command did sight four "single vessels," probably stragglers, between 0810 and 0845 earlier in the day but made no contact with ONS.5's main body.[44] A second Canso intended as escort for the convoy crashed on takeoff from Gander, killing five crew members. According to a message from RCAF headquarters in Ottawa on 7 May, a Fortress from Gander met ONS.5 during a ten-hour sweep on the 5th, though its presence was not observed by either Sherwood or Brook. The message containing this information about the Canso and the Fortress was sent to Washington to counter "comment" in the U.S. Navy Department that, "Apparently there was no air support for ONS.5 on 5 May and this [was] assumed to be due to weather." The RCAF response essentially agreed that foggy weather was the reason.[45]

At ONS.5's position the Atlantic surface was calm, there was no wind, and the air was heavy with drizzle and mist. The convoy ships in contact with the Commodore numbered twenty-three in ten columns, on course 202°. As darkness embraced the wrinkled sea and a high volume of HF/DF activity engaged *Tay's* receivers, Sherwood once again deployed his close escort forces for nighttime vigil: *Tay* ahead, his broken asdic on listening watch only; *Sunflower* on the port bow; *Vidette* on the starboard bow; *Snowflake* on the port quarter; and *Loosestrife* on the starboard quarter. The port and starboard beams were uncovered. *Pink* was still occupied with her small flock astern, and the two EG3 destroyers *Offa* and *Oribi* were assigned to positions five miles out on each bow. At BdU in Berlin, Admirals Dönitz and Godt were drawing up their own plans for the night, expressed in four W/T exhortations to the *Fink* boats, of which fifteen are known to have been in contact with the convoy in the evening and early nighttime hours.[46]

HASENSCHAR CONVOY BOATS SHOULD REPORT THEIR CONTACTS AND POSITIONS MORE FREQUENTLY.

ALL ARE TO MAKE THE MOST OF THE GREAT OPPORTUNITY TONIGHT OFFERS.

TO THE MEASURE THAT THEIR ANTI-AIRCRAFT ARMAMENT IS IN ORDER BOATS ARE TO STAY ON THE SURFACE AND FIRE WHEN AIRCRAFT APPEAR. THE AIRCRAFT WILL THEN SOON CEASE TO ATTACK.

IF THERE ARE NO MORE MERCHANTMEN THERE TO BE SHOT UP SINK THE ESCORT VESSELS MAKING FULL USE OF MAGNETIC EXPLODERS.[47]

The mist of early night thickened to fog and drizzle. The U-boats could be seen, phantomlike, mustering on the surface. *Tay* sighted seven boats in close proximity. They may have been the same seven seen by Günter Gretschel in U–*707:*

> I am positioned within sight of seven boats, in front of the convoy. I wanted to make a joint attack in the darkness. Unfortunately, the weather has thwarted our plans. The visibility has gotten very bad, with fog and drizzle, and this makes any attack impossible in the pitch-black night.[48]

Gretschel and the weather notwithstanding, between the hours of 2252 on the 5th and 0947 on the 6th the *Fink* boats made no fewer than twenty-four attempted attacks on the convoy from every direction except ahead. And at battle's end the night did not belong to the U-Bootwaffe, as Berlin had expected. Instead, thanks to a dense fog bank, to shipborne centimetric radar, and to the pluck and skill of the escort Captains, the night belonged to the Royal Navy, which not only protected ONS.5 and *Pink*'s Party from further harm, but sank four of the U-boat attackers and damaged and repeatedly drove off other boats or forced them to dive.

The escorts made twenty attacks of their own during the hours named. Every ship of B7 and EG3 was engaged, churning at full speed across the ocean surface in this direction or that, throwing and dropping D/Cs, firing guns, or ramming, then quickly rejoining the screen. Ships of First Escort (Support) Group, when they came on the scene at 0600, similarly threw themselves at the enemy with great energy. In the midst of which actions Commodore Brook ordered another convoy emergency turn, 90° to starboard at 2310, resuming course at 2336, and evasive turns to 186° at 0100 and to 156° at 0200, in conditions when visibility was one mile by 2202 and 100 yards by 0100! Around and inside the convoy columns, combat was fierce, continuous, and confusing. Proving that sea warfare is one of the most confounding of human activities, the night of 5/6 May proceeded in such seeming disarray that at its conclusion, Sherwood threw up his hands and conceded, "It is quite out of the question to give a detailed account in chronological order."[49]

In the narrative that follows an effort will be made to place a template of order over the tortured seascape by focusing on the principal actions of individual escorts, while leaving aside the parries and thrusts that had no known results. Throughout, it bears keeping in mind that whereas the shipborne Type 271 RDF (radar) oscilloscopes were displaying to Sherwood's men bright, clear U-boat echoes that conveyed enemy positions and ranges, the U-boat Commanders, lacking comparable equipment, were groping about blind. Said Günter Gretschel on U–707: "Surfaced, pitchblack night, fog, can't see your hand in front of your face" [*Hand nicht vor dem Augen zu sehen*].[50]

Advantage: U.K.

Beyond All Praise
The Battle for ONS.5

In the submarine war there had been plenty of setbacks and crises. Such things are unavoidable in any form of warfare. But we had always overcome them because the fighting efficiency of the U-boat arm had remained steady. Now, however, the situation had changed.

KARL DÖNITZ

The seven-day battle fought against thirty U-boats is marked only by latitude and longitude and has no name by which it will be remembered; but it was, in its own way, as decisive as Quiberon Bay or the Nile.

CAPTAIN STEPHEN W. ROSKILL, D.S.C., R.N.

At 2309* on the 5th, *Vidette* was in escort position "C ", starboard bow of a fog-blurred convoy anxiously keeping station by whistle, when she acquired a radar contact nearly dead ahead bearing 200°, range 5,100 yards. Hart sounded action stations, altered course slightly, and increased speed to 18, then to 20 knots. At 2317 a second, smaller echo came in from a radar contact bearing 190°, 7,200 yards. Six minutes later, Hart sighted a U-boat ahead steaming away at high speed. Directly after the sighting, the U-boat commenced a dive and by 2325½ it was fully submerged 700 yards ahead. Hart ran over the still-visible diving swirl and at 2326½ fired the first of a ten-charge pattern; the tenth D/C left the throw-

---

* All times are expressed in Greenwich Mean Time (GMT) unless otherwise noted.

ers 25 seconds later. Nearly a minute after the last gray geyser, the bridge personnel, D/C crews, and engine room ratings heard a large underwater explosion, after which members of the D/C party as well as the Engineer Officer at the top of the engine room hatch observed a dark column of water rising between 300 and 600 yards astern.

Hart considered the U-boat to be seriously damaged if not destroyed. The NHB/MOD reassessment credits him with the destruction of U-531, a Type IXC/40 boat commanded by Kptlt. Herbert Neckel. Launched only nine months earlier by the Deutsche Werke yard at Hamburg, U-531 was on her first war cruise, having sortied from Kiel on 13 April. Two and a half hours earlier, this boat had reported sighting two destroyers in qu AJ 8368. Neckel, a native of Kiel, had earlier served under Kptlt. Fritz-Julius Lemp on U-30, which had sunk the British passenger liner *Athenia* on the first day of the war, with the loss of 112 passengers. Now his war was over, too.

Instead of seeking an asdic confirmation, Hart went after the second radar contact, which was then at range 2,000 yards. Reaching 900 yards, he sighted the U-boat, which soon after appeared to alter course 30° to starboard and to dive. At 2333½ Hart laid a five-charge pattern over the submerged boat's estimated position. After opening range to 1,200 yards, he returned to sweep the area by asdic, but made no contact. While returning to his escort station, he swept the position of his first attack, but there, too, he made no contact. It may well be that one of the U-boats known to have been damaged this night suffered that hurt from *Vidette*'s second attack, probably U-707 (Gretschel), which recorded suffering D/C damage at about that time.[1]

After resuming station at 0125, *Vidette* went an hour without a contact, until at 0226 radar showed a U-boat bearing 230°, range 1,500 yards. Increasing speed to 20 knots, Hart altered course toward the target, but just past range 700 yards the radar echo disappeared into the ground wave. Starshell fired was of little use in the existing fog, but Hart dropped one

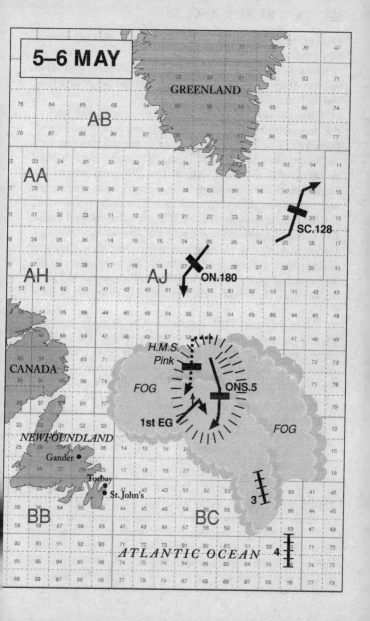

D/C set to 50 feet just to assure the intruder that he was not being ignored.[2]

Back in station, *Vidette* obtained, and pursued, two other radar contacts, at 0310 and 0341, but with no better luck than she had on the 0226 chase.

Then, at 0406, when the destroyer was sweeping back to the convoy screen, her luck changed. The asdic operator reported a contact. One minute later, the contact was classified as "submarine," bearing 097°, range 800 yards. Hart decided to attack with the Hedgehog, and at 700 yards he told the H.H. crew that he would give the order to fire by voice pipe, since, owing to electrical shorts caused by water penetration, the fire buzzer was not reliable. The recorder showed a relative speed of approach to the target of nine knots; it showed, furthermore, that the U-boat was moving slightly to the right, calling for a deflection of 3°right on the projectile pattern. With the last center bearing at 108° and the gun put at 111° to allow for a 3°throw-off to the right, Hart gave the fire order at 0408½.

All twenty-four H.H. bombs were successfully fired and there were no prematures on impact with the water. About three seconds after the last splash, lookouts heard two distinct underwater explosions–H.H. projectiles, which were not fused for depth, did not ordinarily explode unless their nose pistols struck a solid object–and, furthermore, observed flashes. Shortly afterward, the Asdic Control Officer reported "very loud" blowing of tanks and "metallic banging noises." As *Vidette* maintained course and speed, the First Lieutenant and the D/C party reported that the U-boat appeared to be surfacing on the starboard side. It did not do so, but on that side there was a pronounced disturbance on the surface that Hart thought was caused by air escaping the U-boat.

Asdic contact was lost at 120 yards past the point of attack, and though the point and surrounding area were reswept, contact was not regained. No debris appeared on the surface, but Hart was certain on this one: "In my opinion this U-boat was destroyed." And he was right. The boat was U-630, commanded by twenty-eight-year-old Oblt.z.S. Werner Winkler, a native of Wilhelmshaven and a product of the "Olympic" Kriegsmarine officers' class at Flensburg-Mürwik in 1936. A Type VIIC boat, still on her first-ever combat patrol, U–*630* had one merchantman to her credit, the British frozen-meat ship *Waroonga,* sunk with the loss of seventeen seamen during B7's escort of HX.231 in early April. Now U–*630* herself plunged into the locker with twelve unexpended torpedoes and forty-four untold stories of froth-corrupted lungs.[3]

At 2326, while steaming on the convoy's starboard beam, the corvette *Loosestrife* obtained a radar contact bearing green (starboard) 80°, range 4,700 yards. Lt. Stonehouse altered course to pursue and eight minutes later, sighting the contact moving from right to left on the surface, opened up with Oerlikons and one four-inch round at a range of about 800 yards. The 20mm tracers could barely be seen through the fog caroming off the enemy's tower and upper hull, as the U-boat careened like a wraith through a catacomb, and then dived. Asdic contact was gained at 300 yards and the corvette attacked it with a ten-charge pattern by recorder trace. The NHB/MOD reassessment believes that the target was U–*575* (Kptlt. Günther Heydemann), which was undamaged. With no visible result, *Loosestrife* resumed station at 2345. Another radar contact soon after proved to be *Vidette.*

At 0009, in a reshuffle on the convoy screen, Stonehouse was ordered to transfer his vessel to position "H for Harry," starboard quarter in A.C.I.'s screening diagram N.E.6, which was his very good luck, since in that position, at 0030, he detected the boat that he would kill: U–*192,* a Type IXC/40 on her first patrol. Commanded by Oblt.z.S. Werner Happe, a native of Alfeld/Leine, south of Hannover, and a graduate of the "Olympic" class of 1936, U–*192* had sortied from Kiel, Germany, on 13 April, and on 1 May, in qu AJ 3797, had launched a torpedo that missed one of the ONS.5 merchantmen, identity not known. Now, at 0030 on 6 May, U–*192* appeared as a small pulse echo on *Loosestrife*'s radar set, bearing red (port) 95°, range 5,200 yards. Stone-house rang up emergency full ahead and went after it.

Six minutes later, the blurry form of Happe's boat came looming before the lenses of Barr and Stroud Pattern 1900A 7x50 binoculars on board *Loosestrife,* where lookouts called out the range—500 yards—which was a remarkable sighting given the fog. Just as remarkable, Happe's lookouts apparently sighted the corvette at the same instant, since the U-boat abruptly turned to release the venom in her tail, launching two torpedoes from stern tubes, and then commenced a "violent zigzag" ahead. *Loosestrife's* gun crew loaded the four-inch with H.E., but held their fire since Stonehouse's intention was to ram.

At 0040 U-*192* commenced an alarm dive on about the same course very close ahead. As she did so, *Loosestrife* ran directly up her wake. Failing to make ramming contact, Stonehouse fired a ten-charge pattern set shallow. When the D/Cs released their anvil-like blows, the U-boat was observed to break surface, where, seconds later, she shuddered from an interior explosion. The mortally wounded frame was enveloped in a "greenish-blue" flash, which was the description given by several on board the corvette, including two lookout numbers specially posted aft to confirm results. The officer in charge aft watch also saw debris thrown up from the U-boat. Inside the corvette's engine room and boiler room the deck plates lifted in reaction to the explosion, leading some of their occupants to fear that *Loosestrife's* stern had been blown off. After Stonehouse turned to investigate, his First Lieutenant and Yeoman of Signals saw "an immense patch of oil spreading from port hand to starboard bow" as well as floating debris. In combination, the explosion, oil, and debris constituted as definite a confirmation of destruction as Stonehouse was likely ever to get, excepting the retrieval of a Commander's white cap. While his after-action report does not mention it, one may suppose that after so long an ordeal at sea, there was prolonged hearty cheering by ship's company. Certainly we know there was elation among *Loosestrife's* passenger list of twenty-nine survivors from *Bristol City,* whose Master, A. L. Webb, said: "The whole action was extremely exciting, and all my crew thoroughly enjoyed themselves." Stonehouse then set a course of 200° to the convoy, where he resumed station at 0105.[4]

The next success belonged jointly to *Oribi* and *Snowflake.* First, *Oribi.* This EG3 destroyer was in station five miles on the convoy's port bow when, at 0252½, her asdic operator reported, "Echo bearing green thirty–close." Lt.-Cmdr. Ingram had to make an "instantaneous decision" whether this contact was a U-boat or the corvette *Sunflower,* which was thought to be nearby. Since he had no radar contacts to starboard, where *Sunflower* would have shown up as a blip, Ingram swung his ship to that heading, where, with huge relief, he sighted not the corvette but a U-boat sliding out of the fog about one cable (608 feet) on the starboard bow, steering from right to left. It was a perfect plot for a ram, and Ingram's bridge braced for the impact. *Oribi* had been proceeding at 22 knots, but her speed now was somewhat attenuated by the drag met on turning to starboard. As the destroyer bore down, the fo'c's'le hid the U-boat's conning tower, and the stem plowed into the enemy hull probably abaft the tower. The force of the collision slewed the boat around to port side, where, in Ingram's words, "she heeled over with her bows and conning tower out of the water." While a shallow D/C pattern had been ordered, there was no time to get it off; furthermore, the impact of the ramming had broken the light that illuminated the clock and plot.

Worried about damage to his bows, Ingram ordered slow both engines and asked for reports. The forepeak and lower central store were flooded, he learned, but the flooding was contained by a still watertight bulkhead abaft. The asdic dome it was found by trial was slightly damaged, but there was no interior evidence of underwater damage to the hull. At 0310 a still seaworthy *Oribi* turned to port and searched for wreckage from the U-boat. Visibility had improved to about two cables, but lookouts found no sign of the ramming victim except for "a very strong smell of oil over a very wide area," indicating a puncture of the U-boat's portside fuel bunkers. At 0314 the asdic operator reported both asdic and hydrophone contact with a U-boat at green 50°, range 1,100, and Ingram pursued, though at a reduced speed of 12 knots, since the forward bulkheads had not yet been shored. At 0318, by stopwatch, *Oribi* dropped a single charge, set deep, on the last estimated position. At 0332 the search was abandoned, and Ingram shaped course to resume station, at which he had no further actions during the night.

Said Ingram in his report of the ramming: "Taking into account own ship's speed and the damage sustained by herself, together with the force and angle of impact I have no doubt whatsoever that this submarine was sunk."[5] It was a perfectly reasonable conclusion, one that was concurred in by the Admiralty's U-Boat Assessment Committee, on 21 June 1943. In fact, however, the U-boat struck, Type IXC U–*125* (Folkers), survived the ramming, though with serious damage rendering her unfit to dive.[6] At 0331, Kptlt. Folkers reported his plight to BdU: HAVE BEEN RAMMED—AM UNABLE TO DIVE. QU AJ 8652. REQUEST ASSISTANCE. COURSE 90 DEGREES; and heard back assurances from nearby boats U–*552*, U–*381*, U–*413*, U–*260*, U–*614*, and U–*402* that they were proceeding to his succor.[7] Three hours later, at 0625, BdU ordered only the first four boats named above to tend to the needs of Folkers and his crew; the latter two were to remain on operations. The four rescue boats hunted for Folkers until the morning of the 7th, when they reported failure and broke off to refuel from the tanker U–*461* in the adjoining *Marinequadrat* AK 89 directly to the east.[8]

Enter *Snowflake*, which made the BdU rescue order moot. This corvette earlier, at 0231 and 0238, had dropped three heavy charges on U–*107* (Gelhaus) as scare tactics. At 0330, while in station R, on the port quarter, Lt. Chesterman received a radar echo bearing 030°, range 4,100 yards, and, after advising *Tay*, commenced a chase. Fog had closed the visibility to one mile, and starshells were useless, so when he had closed to gun range, Chesterman directed four-inch fire at the target by radar alone. At 0340, the U-boat, which had been working to southward, dived before being sighted. *Snowflake* immediately obtained asdic contact at a range of 400 yards.

Running over the contact at 0341, Chesterman dropped his penultimate D/C, a heavy charge set to 140 feet.

At the moment of dropping, *Snowflake* acquired a second radar contact bearing 170°, range 2,400 yards, moving rapidly left. Chesterman altered course to intercept and again engaged with the four-inch. While firing, *Snowflake* received yet a third radar echo bearing 185°, range 1,000 yards. Fearing a torpedo attack by this third, nearby boat, Chesterman broke off his gun action against the second boat and turned to attack the third, which immediately dived. With asdic contact bearing 160°, range 700 yards, Chesterman began a run in with his last D/C, but for some reason the asdic operator lost the contact before an attack could be made. Meanwhile, at 0349, *Tay,* to whom Chesterman had been reporting his three pursuits, signaled by R/T: "Sunflower assist Snowflake."

Snowflake then began an asdic and radar sweep through the last known positions of the three submerged boats. Chesterman commanded the operation from his action post in the center of the compass platform with, to his left, voice pipes to asdic and plot, and to his right, voice pipes to radar and plot. At 0354, radar picked up a *fourth* boat on the surface, low in the water, and apparently stopped, since the range was closed rapidly. Visibility was bad. At 0400, when range had decreased to 100 yards(!), Chesterman ordered on the starboard search-light. Its sword of white light revealed directly ahead a U-boat heavily damaged about the conning tower, under power though, working rapidly to starboard. Chesterman ordered the wheel put hard-a-starboard with intent to ram, and opened fire with every available weapon that could be brought to bear, scoring a number of hits. The U-boat averted being rammed head-on, but *Snowflake,* maneuvering inside the U-boat's turning circle, came to dead slow alongside its starboard side, where only a few feet separated the two vessels, and illuminated its tower and deck with the port search-light and ten-inch Signal Projector.

That close, Chesterman could see that the enemy boat was down by the stern, the tower was crumpled, the periscope standards were warped, the flak guns were crippled, and the after hatch cover had been blown off. That close, too, *Snowflake*'s guns could not be depressed enough to continue fire, so Chesterman ordered a slow withdrawal. As the corvette drew back, the U-boat settled farther by the stern, causing air bubbles to rise from the submerging after hatch. Some German crewmen abandoned the boat at this point; some others lined the fore-deck; but a few, more determined and belligerent, or perhaps more desperate, made for the forward deck gun. That endeavor was frustrated by *Snowflake*'s port Oerlikon and 40mm pom-pom guns. An officer was seen on what remained of the tower, waving his arms as a sign of cease-fire or surrender. When this was ignored, the rest of the crew went into the sea.

The U-boat's sinking led Chesterman for a time to think that in coming alongside, his port bilge keel had rammed the U-boat's starboard side, but on closer view he found that this was wrong. Suddenly five scuttling charges were heard from the sinking U-boat, the first charge louder than the rest. Sweeping with lights through the survivors, *Snowflake* saw some in a small dinghy, but most swimming singly through a large oil patch. Since *Sunflower* was now present, Chesterman thought that the survivors might be taken on board the two corvettes and delivered to St. John's for interrogation, and he so suggested to *Tay*. Rescue, no doubt, was what the German crew was expecting when they scuttled. Sherwood's reply by R/T was as fatal as it was laconic: "Not approved to pick up survivors." Though Sherwood offered no reason, it is probable that he considered it too dangerous for the corvettes to remain stationary, rescuing survivors in the middle of an ongoing battle.

In the following minutes one of *Snowflake*'s searchlights revealed *Sunflower* dangerously nearby, and both corvettes put wheel hard to avoid collision, which would have been a doubly sad event, since the Australian Chesterman on *Snowflake* and the Canadian Plomer on *Sunflower* commanded "chummy" ships, so much so that in B7 they had become known as *Snowflower* and *Sunflake*. Leaving then the forty-eight-man crew of U–*125,* for it was the same boat that had been rammed by *Oribi,* to bob upon the corpse-ridden sea, *Snowflake,* with *Sunflower,* steamed off to other echoes.[9] The *panische Angst* felt by the U-boat crew, who watched from meager flotage the withdrawal into fog of their only earthly hopes, is, of course, beyond verbal expression.

Snowflake's R/T log for the attack period fairly crackles with the teamwork displayed by the two corvettes:

TO *TAY* FROM *SNOWFLAKE:*
"R.D.F. contact eight o'clock." 0330.
"U-boat dived, chasing another." 0340.
"Second U-boat dived, chasing third." 0345.
"Am attacking with charges–last charge." 0346.
TO GROUP FROM *TAY.*
"Sunflower assist Snowflake." 0349
TO *TAY* FROM *SNOWFLAKE:*
"Not attacking with charges. All three dived. Am not in contact. Resuming station." 0350.
TO *SNOWFLAKE* FROM *SUNFLOWER:*
"Do you wish my assistance?" 0352
TO *SUNFLOWER* FROM *SNOWFLAKE:*
"Yes. R.D.F. contact bearing two-six-zero degrees, three thousand yards from me." 0354.
TO *SNOWFLAKE* FROM *SUNFLOWER:*
"I will pass around you and investigate." 0356.
TO *SUNFLOWER* FROM *SNOWFLAKE:*
"Have rammed U-boat. Please join me." 0401.
"Are you in contact with me?" 0403.
TO *SNOWFLAKE* FROM *SUNFLOWER:*
"Am proceeding in your direction." 0405.
TO *TAY* FROM *SNOWFLAKE:*
"Shall I pick up survivors?" 0407.
TO *SNOWFLAKE* FROM *SUNFLOWER:*
"Am in contact with you, three-one-five degrees, three-five-zero-zero yards." 0410.
TO *SUNFLOWER* FROM *SNOWFLAKE:*
"Investigating another echo and leaving survivors." 0411.

To *Snowflake* from *Tay*:
"*Not approved to pick up survivors.*" 0412.

To *Snowflake* from *Sunflower*:
"*Am in your immediate vicinity.*" 0413 [the time of the near collision].

To *Sunflower* from *Snowflake*:
"*Sorry. Am resuming my station. Glad none of yours hurt. Have one charge for one more.*" 0417.

To *Snowflake* from *Sunflower*:
"*Nice work. Don't mention it. Where shall we go next?*" 0418.

To *Sunflower* from *Snowflake*:
"*Investigating underwater contact.*" 0419.

To *Snowflake* from *Sunflower*:
"*You bear zero-nine-zero, two thousand yards. Am following you.*" 0423.[10]

After that exchange, *Snowflake* dropped the last D/C in her stowage and resumed station.

Since *Offa's* five attacks earlier that night from 2039 to 2218, this EG3 destroyer had rejoined the convoy on the starboard bow; assisted *Vidette*, who was giving three U-boats a headache around the midnight hour; proceeded over to the convoy's port bow to provide cover for an alteration of course to 156° at 0200; gained, regained, then lost a radar contact; and finally, at 0300, regained and held the contact, bearing 258°, range 4,400 yards. The amplitude of the echo received on *Offa's* Type 272 RDF equipment plainly indicated a U-boat, which the destroyer's plot showed to be proceeding at 12 knots on a course of 190°. Captain McCoy increased speed to 20 knots and set a course of 210° to intercept. At 0312, with range at 500 yards, radar contact disappeared in the ground wave, but hydrophone effect picked up the characteristic high-pitched rattle of fast diesel engines on the same bearing. At 0314, the effect grew fainter, leading McCoy to assume that the U-boat had dived. *Offa* altered course slightly to starboard, and soon after, lookouts sighted a wake. The boat had not dived after all, and hydrophone effect became loud again. McCoy hauled out to port clear of the wake, took a course parallel to that of the boat, and at 0315 ordered the twenty-inch Signal Projector switched on.

Brightly illuminated on the starboard bow at 100 yards was a light gray-painted Type VIIC U-boat, trimmed down, with after casing awash. Abaft the tower was "a metal framework," which would have been the *Wintergarten*. Immediately, *Offa* opened fire with the starboard Oerlikons, the main armament and pom-poms being unable to depress enough to gain aim, and several hits were observed against the conning tower. At 0316, when the U-boat began a crash dive, McCoy ordered the wheel put hard-a-starboard to ram. The ship's bows began the turn, but the U-boat's dive, at about eight knots, was very steep and the conning tower was observed to be disappearing safely under the ship about level with the bridge. McCoy himself could see the hull of the U-boat under the surface as *Offa* passed over and ahead. In his after-action report he described what happened next:

> Then I gave the order to fire [D/Cs]. This order most unfortunately miscarried. During the hunt I had twice given orders for the throwers:—in the first instance: "Ready Port," and in the second instance: "Ready Starboard"; but at the moment when I put the helm over it became obvious that the starboard throwers only would be required and I gave the order "Ready Starboard." These were fired correctly but when I followed this up with an order to "fire everything" the man at the pump lever to the traps was so obsessed with the order to fire the starboard throwers only that he failed to fire the traps and so the barrage from the traps, which would have been laid down in a curve over the U-boat, was not dropped and certain destruction was not obtained.

Though the failure to fire was "lamentable," as McCoy stated elsewhere, and whereas Admiral Horton himself lamented later "the failure of a rating to carry out an order at the critical moment," the CinCWA judged McCoy to have conducted this operation "in a very able manner." And while neither man would know it at the time, the detonations of the starboard throwers were sufficient to cause slight damage to the U-boat involved, which, it turned out in a recent reassessment, was U–223 (Oblt.z.S. Karljüng Wächter). That boat, which had a bit of ginger taken out of her this time, would be rammed later, on 12 May, but survive again, until finally succumbing to four British warships on 30 March 1944.[11]

At 2240 on the 5th, *Sunflower* was manning station "M" on the port bow when Lt.-Cmdr. Plomer's radar received a pulse echo from 4,300 yards. *Sunflower* altered course and closed the contact at 14 knots. The U-boat dived and asdic pursued it. At 200 yards from the contact the bearing began moving from left to right. Following, the corvette dropped six and fired four D/Cs in what Plomer called "our best D/C attack–almost exercise conditions." Just before the D/Cs went overside, at 2251, *Sunflower* picked up a second radar contact at 3,400 yards, and Plomer decided to pursue that one at once, in order, we may conjecture, to keep the U-boats off their stride. As he did so, asdic told him that a torpedo was approaching from red (port) 20°. He watched as it passed down the corvette's port side. Immediately, radar picked up yet another contact at 2,800 yards, but now Plomer decided to pursue the U-boat that had attacked him, and at 2258 he sighted it close ahead.

Sunflower's deck gun opened fire, but on the third round the cartridge jammed in the breach. Without an operative main armament, Plomer altered course to starboard at 2305 in an attempt to drive underwater his radar contact of fourteen minutes before. Two minutes later, asdic reported incoming torpedoes–a "full salvo"–from the boat he had just been pursuing. Putting helm hard-a-port, then point back, *Sunflower* managed to be 30° off pointing when the salvo arrived down the port side. Plomer signaled *Tay* at 2312: "Have broken off chase, fired two H.E.s [high explosive rounds], could not gain." Two minutes later, however, his gun reported clear, and Plomer decided he was back in the game. For the next three and a half hours he chased five contacts, firing Hedgehogs at one and a five-charge D/C pattern at another, but all without result. The NHB/MOD reassessment believes it possible that these attacks were delivered against the same target, U–954 (Kptlt. Odo Loewe).

At 0443, while back on station "N," 60° on the convoy's port bow, *Sunflower* received a firm asdic contact at 1,200 yards. The U-boat, it turned out, was in the act of surfacing. Plomer closed at 14 knots in 300 yards visibility and found the German fully surfaced broad on the port beam, on a converging course. He switched on his searchlight, and the U-boat immediately commenced a dive. Plomer then ordered hard to port rudder and double emergency full ahead. In the last seconds before impact hard to starboard was ordered as a course correction, and in Plomer's description, the corvette rammed the U-boat between its conning tower and stern, riding over the U-boat's casing like an icebreaker over ice. As she passed, *Sunflower* dropped two D/Cs set to shallow; a moment before they detonated, the corvette's crew heard another distinct "heavy explosion."

Plomer was persuaded that the U-boat had broken in two, since his two asdic domes underside were undamaged. His last sight of the U-boat, he said, was of her stern projected about 8 feet above the surface at an angle of 45°. All guns that could bear were brought into action. With no further contact showing on asdic, and convinced that the U-boat had sunk, Plomer set course to rejoin the convoy. Among the spectators of this encounter were the Master and sixty-five other survivors of M.V. *Dolius,* who had been picked up by *Sunflower* the day before. Said Captain Cheetham: "I and my crew thoroughly enjoyed ourselves." While the corvette's asdic was still fully operative, she soon discovered defects from the ramming, including leakage in the forepeak. Furthermore, she signaled *Tay* by R/T: "My steering is erratic as gyro is out of action and magnetic compass shaken up a bit. Please give me a wide berth. 0505."

In his after-action report Plomer pronounced the engagement a "kill." Similarly, Captain J. M. Rowland, R.N., Captain (D) Newfoundland, called it a "certainty." In London the Admiralty was less convinced. Complaining that Plomer's report contained no details about exterior damage inflicted on the corvette, or about any wreckage, oil, or survivors seen in the water after the ramming, the U-Boat Assessment Committee expressed doubt that the U-boat had been effectively rammed, much less cut in half. It was much more probable, the Committee argued, "that after a glancing blow the U-boat slid off." And it gave no credence to the suggestion of an internal explosion. As for the two depth charges, it was unlikely that they were in the lethal range. The assessment, given on 21 June, therefore, was: "Probably slightly damaged."[12] But the Committee's finding *may* have been disingenuous, for one of its members always consulted Rodger Winn in the OIC Tracking Room for an opinion. While Winn never transmitted raw Enigma to the Committee, or even divulged to it explicit information drawn from Enigma, it is known that both before and on the date of the Committee's deliberations, Winn held in hand a decrypt of a transmission from U–533 (Oblt.z.S. Helmut Hennig) to BdU, intercepted at 1137 on 6 May and decrypted at 1917 on 9 May:

RAMMED ASTERN BY A DESTROYER [*SIC*] THAT APPEARED OUT OF THE FOG, LOCATING ME BY SEARCHLIGHT. DEPTH CHARGES. AM MOVING OFF TO REPAIR. BOAT WILL BE READY AGAIN IN 18 HOURS. QU AJ 8683 [13]

At 1000, U–533 surfaced and made off to the east on course 90° to undertake repairs. These completed by 1800, she continued east, then northeast on 7 May to join sixteen other former *Fink* boats in forming Group *Elbe* (after the river). That group and a ten-boat Group *Rhein* (after the river), organized from former *Amsel* III and IV boats, were to occupy a 550-mile-long patrol line across the expected courses of two eastbound convoys, HX.237 and SC.129 (see chapter 10). The wounded U–533 successfully took her place in line.[14]

At daybreak on the 6th, four of the five ships making up the First Escort (Support) Group (EG1), the sloop *Pelican* and frigates *Wear, Jed,* and *Spey*–the slower cutter *Sennen* was on a different course to support *Pink*–were closing on ONS.5 from the southwest. In line abreast, four miles apart, their bows cleaving the swells and fog, the warships rode down spur and rein, on 030° at 16 knots, like a seaborne Seventh Cavalry. Numerous R/T signals between busy B7 and EG3 escorts helped the support group home in on the convoy by HF/DF, and at 0550, *Wear* reported the convoy bearing 330°, 8 miles. The group was now inside the *Fink* concentration. Senior Officer, in *Pelican,* was Commander Godfrey N. Brewer, R.N., who, after a year at sea in 1939-1940, had been posted to the Trade Division of the Admiralty as Convoy Planning Officer, where he had the advantage of seeing the "big picture" of convoy warfare. "Escaping back to sea," as he put it, in spring 1942, he returned to Atlantic escort duty with EG1.

At 0552, *Pelican* obtained a small radar contact bearing 040°, range 5,300 yards. When it was classified as "submarine," Brewer closed the contact, keeping it about 10° on the starboard bow to avoid the ship's "blind spot." From the bearing and rate of change in the range, it soon became apparent that the U-boat was on a heading reciprocal to that of the group. Brewer thought that it either had just been driven off after attempting an attack or was proceeding ahead to take up a daylight submerged bow ahead attack position. When the range was 3,000 yards at 0557, *Pelican* began hearing faint hydrophone effect on a bearing of 160°, and several minutes later, when the range had been closed to 500 yards, lookouts sighted a bow wake on the starboard bow.

At 0607, range 300, the U-boat itself became visible on the foggy surface, steering 180°, doing about nine knots, as Brewer judged from the relative speed of approach. It was, he said, "a normal 570 ton type [VIIC] painted a dark colour." When about 100 yards distant, and fine on the port bow, the U-boat crash-dived, turning to port as she sank. *Pelican*'s A and B guns and the port Oerlikon opened fire. Brewer swung to port under full rudder and placed his bows just inside the conning tower swirl. As he passed, he fired a ten-pattern set to 50 and 150 feet. After the explosions, a "very weak and hard to hold" echo was regained, and about a minute later, the Officer in Charge and most of the D/C crew sighted at the explosion area what they described as "two thin founts of water, resembling shell splashes." Brewer came around for a second attack, and during the run-in, with the contact moving very slowly right, hydrophone effect detected various strange noises resembling an Echo Sounder set being switched on and off. This time nine charges set to 150 and 300 feet left the throwers and rails, after which there was no further contact.

A minute and a half later, *Pelican* heard three "small sharp" explosions together with the same switching noises as before; and nine minutes after that, *Pelican* heard two more explosions, the second of which shook the ship. None of the explosions, Brewer remarked, sounded like the detonation of a torpedo or a depth charge. Though afterwards *Pelican* carried out an Observant around the attack position, no wreckage, oil, or survivors were sighted. But based on circumstantial evidence, Brewer's "considered opinion" was that the U-boat was probably sunk. On 28 June the U-Boat Assessment Committee, basing its conclusion largely on tracking evidence and on the fact that there were no further W/T transmissions from this boat (as Dönitz and Godt noticed, too, as early as the end of the day, 6 May), agreed with Brewer's opinion. So does the recent NHB/MOD reassessment. The victim was *U-438* (Heinsohn), which had been damaged by Canso "A" E of 5 Squadron from Gander on the afternoon of the 4th. In good cavalryman fashion, Brewer stated: "This was a good example of a support group arriving at just the right moment to achieve complete surprise."[15]

Brewer might have swept about further, seeking other boats to rend and tear, but for the fact that ONS.5 badly needed reinforcement of the close screen, and defending convoys still had the edge over hunting U-boats in escort doctrine. With EG1's arrival, McCoy on *Offa* decided that he ought to escort the other remaining EG3 destroyer, *Oribi*, out of the endangered area as quickly as possible and see her to safety at St. John's: by daybreak, as a result of her ramming action, *Oribi*'s forepeak and provision room were both flooded. Accord-

ingly, *Offa* detached at 0809, ordering *Oribi* to join and adding
a personal message to Ingram: "I should say you have done
bloody well during the past 24 hours." The two destroyers
made port at 1215 on 8 May.[16]

The B7 flotilla left behind was sore beset by battle fatigue
and fuel depletion from the night's running fight; furthermore,
with *Sunflower* licking wounds from her ramming of U-*533*,
Snowflake lacking D/Cs, and *Tay* with no asdic, *Vidette* and
Loosestrife were the only effective ships on the screen of the
main body. So *Pelican* and *Jed* took up stations ahead and
Brewer detailed *Spey* and *Wear* to sweep twenty miles astern.
Much later, at 2300, slow-gaited *Sennen* would join *Pink* with
her four merchant vessels in company.[17] On her course
toward that rendezvous, which took her to the west of the
main body, *Sennen* acquired two radar contacts, five hours
apart, at 0740 and at 1244, which enabled the 1,546-ton ex-
U.S.C.G.C. *Champlain* and her captain, Lt.-Cmdr. F. H.
Thornton, R.N.R., to participate in the final moments of the
battle. The first contact was obtained bearing 289°, range
4,000, and four minutes later *Sennen* sighted the U-boat diving
at 2,500 yards. When asdic contact was gained three and a
half minutes later, Thornton commenced an attack with a
ten-pattern set to 150 and 300 feet. Following the attack,
which was made at 0753½, *Sennen* regained and lost contact
three times, eventually giving up on it and resuming course.
Thornton judged that the attack was unsuccessful: "Pattern
fired late due to poor recorder trace, and probably too shallow."[18] The NHB/MOD reassessment agrees and identifies
the cutter's contact as U-*650* (v. Witzendorff), which had
been the shadower in Group *Star*.[19]

Sennen's second radar echo at 1244 led to a more persis-
tent effort, as the feisty cutter made no fewer than five separate attacks, two by Hedgehog, and three by D/C, at 1255,
1342, 1405, 1436, and 1522. As in the earlier incident, the
U-boat was sighted in the act of diving, this time at 4,000
yards. By asdic recorder Thornton first fired Hedgehog, with
no explosions; then attacked with D/Cs set to 150 and 385
feet; then fired Hedgehog, with, again, no explosions; then

made two successive D/C attacks, the first of ten set to 150 and 300 feet, the second of five set to 550. With no surface evidence to confirm otherwise, Thornton concluded that the U-boat was "probably not more than badly shaken." The NHB/MOD reassessment concludes that the U-boat received "minor damage," and identifies it as U–575 (Heydemann).[20]

Thornton then proceeded from the area on his original course in order to conserve D/Cs and Hedgehog ammunition, since he had learned that *Pink* was short of both, and "there were still a large number of submarines in the vicinity. . . ."[21]

While trawling astern of the main body, *Spey* obtained a radar contact on the port bow, range 5,200 yards, closing rapidly. The time was 0940. Commander L. G. BoysSmith, R.N.R., rang up full speed and altered toward the contact, which was soon classified as "submarine." At 900 yards the U-boat was sighted in the morning's thick mist, crossing from starboard to port at an estimated 12 knots. To BoysSmith the boat resembled the large "Dessie" Class Italian submarine. He ordered the frigate's four-inch to open fire and altered to port, hoping to ram. The U-boat dived at 400 yards, but not before the gun crew got two definite hits, one on the conning tower base and one on the hull, and a third possible. The second hit threw up a heavy shower of debris. Pom-pom and Oerlikon fire also raked the tower as it slid beneath the waves.

Spey quickly established asdic contact and BoysSmith ordered a tenpattern D/C attack, with lights set to 50 and heavies to 140 feet, carried out by eye over the clearly visible diving swirl and wake; the eyeball order was confirmed by recorder trace. When contact was regained on the port quarter after the attack explosions, *Spey* set up a Hedgehog attack. Asdic showed that the U-boat had turned at about two knots but contact was lost at 500 yards, indicating that the target had gone very deep by the time the H.H. was fired. There were no explosions. With a contact astern at 700 yards, *Spey* launched a third attack, employing ten D/Cs set to 500 and 550 feet, after which contact was not regained.

At this point, *Wear* joined in the sweep, and a less than confident contact was obtained, held to 400 yards. Ten charges set to 150 and 385 feet were delivered by *Spey,* after which all contact was lost. In BoysSmith's opinion, his four attacks were "inconclusive." The U-Boat Assessment Committee decided: "Probably slightly damaged." The NHB/MOD reassessment is that U–634 (Oblt.z.S. Eberhard Dahlhaus) suffered damage from four-inch gunfire but none from D/Cs. Dahlhaus's KTB reveals that he was wounded in the neck by a splinter. His F.T. to BdU reads: A FULL HIT BY DESTROYER ARTILLERY AFTER SURFACING. PORT AIR SUPPLY TRUNK BRIDGE TORN AWAY. HEAVY D/C AND RADAR PURSUIT. BoysSmith's target was not a large boat, after all, but a standard VIIC, with 114 more days of life.[22]

It was after *Spey*'s attack that the battle's fever broke. At 1140, having sensed the dimensions of what Germans later would call *die Katastrophe am* ONS.5, Dönitz and Godt ordered the *Fink* boats to break off operations. *Amsel* I and II boats were to head for qu BC 33 (50°33′N, 39°15′W) and the remainder were to move off to the east, some for replenishment of fuel and supplies from U–461 in AK 8769.[23] The order was a recognition that Dönitz and Godt had lost what could have been a drawn battle had they discontinued at dusk on the 5th. In a veiled concession that they had instead reached a night too far, the two German Admirals signaled their Commanders:

> THIS CONVOY BATTLE HAS ONCE AGAIN PROVED THAT CONDITIONS ON A CONVOY ARE ALWAYS MOST FAVORABLE AT THE BEGINNING. HE WHO EXPLOITS THE MOMENT OF SURPRISE ON THE FIRST NIGHT, AND PRESSES HOME THE ATTACK BY ALL MEANS IN HIS POWER, HE IS THE MAN WHO IS SUCCESSFUL. AFTER THE FIRST BLOW IT BECOMES HARDER AND HARDER. IN ADDITION THERE IS THE UNCERTAINTY OF THE WEATHER, AS ON THIS OCCASION, THERE THE FOG RUINED THE GREAT OPPORTUNITIES ON THE SECOND NIGHT. WE APPRECIATE YOUR HARD STRUGGLE, ESPECIALLY ON THE SECOND NIGHT.[24]

In their wash-up on "Convoy No. 36" at the close of 6 May, Dönitz and Godt concluded that six boats had been lost in the *Fink* campaign–U–*638,*U–*192,* U–*125,*U–*531,* U–*630,* and U–*438.* "If none of these boats report later, this loss of 6 boats is very high and grave considering the short duration of the attack. The blame can be laid mainly on the foggy period that began at 2100 [GST] on the 5th May. "If the fog had held off for six hours, they contended, the U-boats would have had "a really good bag that night," but "the fog ruined everything." They did not concede that staff meteorologists, from a year and a half of U-boat experience in the western Atlantic, not to mention book knowledge, should have known that where the Gulf Stream met the Labrador Current, causing warm water to mix with cold air, there was almost always opaque vapor, especially in the spring, and that the Grand Banks were renowned for their milk-white air. Nor did they concede that the same fog that blinded the U-boats made air cover from Newfoundland impossible for the enemy. Curiously, the Naval Staff at Eberswalde, not many kilometers from BdU, *did* anticipate the whiteout: "As the enemy is today entering the heavily fog-bound area, it is to be expected that only a small portion of the boats will be able to maintain contact." This was on the 5th. Whether there was communication with BdU on the point is not disclosed in the extant records.[25]

The U-boat loss count would be even higher, by one, on 23 May, when BdU acknowledged that U–*209,* damaged by Canso "A" W 5 Squadron on 5 May, had foundered with all hands (probably on 7 May in the vicinity of 52°N, 38°W) during her desperate attempt to make base[26] And one could add as well the loss of U–*710,* sunk by Fortress "D" 206 Squadron on 24 April during the first stage of the battle. The exchange rate of U-boats lost for merchant ships sunk in the two stages was alarmingly high, even given the inflated figures of ships sunk that were transmitted by Commanders to Berlin. The actual number of merchantmen lost to U-boats from ONS.5, beginning with *McKeesport* and ending with *Bonde,* was thirteen. The number reported to Berlin was nineteen merchantmen torpedoed and sixteen sunk (90,500 GRT), including Hasenschar's erroneous count of two definites, including a corvette, plus two probables, which led Dönitz and Godt to add to their "hard struggle" message, cited above: HASEN-SCHAR IS CHAMPION SHOT.[27] That honor should have gone to Jessen (U-*266*), with three definites.

In either event, such high losses of one U-boat (using the low figure of six boats) for every 2.16 (using the actual figure of thirteen merchantmen) or 2.66 (using the claimed figure of sixteen) ships sunk was an attrition rate that could not be borne, and as Dönitz stated later, "I regarded this convoy battle as a defeat."[28] More irreplaceable than the boats, and more critical a loss at this period of the war–one remembers the dangerously declining numbers of trained RAF pilots during the Battle of Britain–was the death toll of U-boat ranks and ratings: a total of 364 human casualties.

Also telling, apart from the number of U-boats sunk, was the number of boats damaged by escort action: Seven boats were so severely impaired they were forced back to base: U-*386,* U-*528,*U-*532* (in the first stage of the battle, 28 April–1 May), U-*648,* U-*732,*U-*358,* and U-*270* (in the second stage, 4-6 May). As noted earlier, boats forced home were the tactical equivalents of kills in a convoy battle. Ten other boats were roughly handled, suffering heavy to light damage: U-*413,* U-*514,* U-*438,* U-*226,* U-*223,* U-*533,* U-*634,* U-*266,* U-*707,* and U-*575.* These boats were removed from the scene for a time, either long or short, while they undertook repairs, and thus were not available during those intervals for operations. (Since Professor Blackett considered four boats damaged to be the equivalent of one boat sunk, by that measure 4.5 boats could be added to the tally of those sunk.) Also notable in the defense of ONS.5 were the twenty-odd occasions when U-boats were driven off or forced to dive; submerged, it bears repeating, they were greatly retarded in their ability to make nighttime attacks. And mention should be made of several boats, such as U-*552* (Kptlt. Klaus Popp), that were forced to retire by reason of fuel depletion.

Finally, the records disclose a failing that was endemic to

the U-boats in this period and for some time prior: most were not pressing their *strength in numbers* and most were not *taking their shots*. Although *Fink* boats made approximately forty attacks, the vaunted BdU wireless control system seems never to have directed more than fifteen boats at a time into close contact with the convoy, the usual number brought to bear being no higher than nine. In the late forenoon of the 5th, BdU had expostulated: THERE ARE FORTY OF YOU. And the boats in contact correctly reported the convoy's position and base course all through the battle, as Enigma intercepts disclose. What was the problem? Was it perhaps the low level of command experience, previously noted, that inhibited the effective maneuver and attack of certain boats? Or did low fuel levels in many boats perhaps induce a caution that led those Commanders "to lose the name of action?" Or did the aggressive behavior of the escort screen, which punched as often as it counterpunched, simply succeed tactically in holding the majority of boats at bay? The textual record would support all three possibilities.

In W/T transmissions to Berlin on 5/6/7 May, a significant percentage of the boats reported large numbers of unexpended torpedoes. It is not unusual to read, for example, in the traffic from U–223 and U–378 on 5 May: 12 E TORPEDOES, 2 A TORPEDOES, their full complement for a VIIC boat; or in that from U–514 on 6 May: ALL TORPEDOES, or in that from U–231 on 6 May: ALL EELS. (This was a longtime besetting weakness of the U-boat force, of which only a little more than 50 percent of boats *actually engaged in combat operations* sank or damaged an Allied vessel during the war.)[29] That so large a concentration of boats, deployed in such favorable position, should have come up short in torpedo launches must have cast a pall of doubt over BdU planning for future operations.

Fog was not alone to blame for the defeat. Dönitz and Godt stated, "The operation against Convoy No. 36 also had to be broken off because of enemy radar." It was obvious that in low-visibility conditions the convoy escorts had been able to readily locate the positions of surfaced U-boats, and without the boats learning of their exposure by means of the standard Metox search receivers. The surface escorts, and aircraft, too, it was reasoned, must be equipped with some new kind of detection equipment. Finding an answer to this problem was of "decisive importance" for submarine warfare. "To sum up," they wrote on 6 May:

> Radar location by air and naval forces not only renders the actual attack by individual boats most difficult, but also provides the enemy with a means of fixing the stations manned by the submarines and of avoiding them, and he obviously makes good use of this method. Radar location is thus robbing the submarine of her most important characteristic—ability to remain undetected. All responsible departments are working at high pressure on the problem of again providing the submarine with gear capable of establishing whether the enemy is using radar; they are also concentrating on camouflage for the submarine against [radar] location, which must be considered the ultimate goal.[30]

Dönitz's son-in-law Günter Hessler, who served on Godt's operations staff, wrote after the war that staff thinking at the time was that the Allies were using either a radar wavelength beyond the capacity of the Metox to detect (which was correct) or a nonradar device such as infrared rays. He expressed the dismay of the staff that in the just-completed operation, "surface escorts alone had sufficed to inflict grave losses on an exceptionally strong concentration of attackers." Where the Allies spoke of the "U-boat menace," the Germans now spoke of the "radar menace." Unless that menace could be quickly and effectively countered, Hessler said, the position of the U-Bootwaffe would become "desperate."[31]

In his *Memoirs,* Dönitz, too, stated that in further convoy operations conducted in poor-visibility conditions, which were a common occurrence in the North Atlantic, the U-boats would be helpless. The Allies' radar advances, furthermore, would enable convoys to take effective evasive action.[32] And radar was not the only technical problem the Germans had to face at this juncture. Hessler informs us that there was consternation expressed after Convoy No. 36 about the fact that British warships were now equipped with powerful new deep-plunging D/Cs as well as with Hedgehogs, about which BdU had learned earlier from decryption, agents, and practical experience. The panoply of weapons arrayed against the U-boats was increasingly sophisticated and effective, particularly since new tactical refinements to "under-water location," or asdic, had made possible accurate depth charge pursuits on days and at times "when there was fog."[33]

In their 6 May appreciation Dönitz and Godt also took serious notice of the danger posed to U-boat patrol lines by Allied air escorts, which had "always forced our submarines to lag hopelessly behind" convoys and had prevented them from scoring hits, "especially when naval [surface] and air escorts cooperated efficiently." They predicted correctly that "the only remaining [air] gaps will be closed within a reasonable length of time by land-based planes, or at any rate by using auxiliary aircraft carriers." Finally, the Dönitz/Godt washup deplored the fact that except for the Pi 2 magnetic influence pistol and a few other minor innovations, "as yet we possess no really effective weapon." This was a stunning concession. They concluded: "The submarine's struggle is now harder than ever, but all departments are working full out to assist the boats in their task and to equip them with better weapons."[34]

They gave no hint, at least here, that they feared insecure W/T communications; although, in fact, Allied cryptographic sources played no role in the defense against *Fink*, and most naval Enigma from 5/6 May was not decrypted until the 9th. They made no mention, either, of HF/DF, which, despite ample cryptographic and operational evidence, both BdU and Naval Intelligence analysts continued to believe was limited to shore-based installations. Refusal to admit the possibility of ship- and aircraft-borne HF/DF had yielded substantial tactical advantage to the Allies, and would continue to do so.[35] Nor did they mention that their long-established principle of concentrating the largest possible number of boats on an individual convoy—in this case nearly one-half of the whole Atlantic force–rather than make fewer attacks on a greater number of contacts had let six other convoys pass unmolested, and had immobilized the attacking force for a week afterward, during which time boats had to be refueled or replaced.

Nor was there any mention in the BdU war diary, or in Hessler's recollections of the BdU mind in early May, of a decline in crew morale and confidence resulting from recent reversals. As shown in the prologue, this was a recurring subject of speculation in the OIC Tracking Room in London, where, at least since 19 April, Rodger Winn had observed in W/T traffic what he thought was an increasing anxiety among Commanders.

So far, by the close of 6 May, the beleaguered circle held. Surviving U-boats in the mid-Atlantic regrouped to fight another day, and another night. As the deadly duel continued, there was no question of the fighting spirit exhibited on either side.

> Sailors above the sea, sailors below,
> Drew equally upon a fund of courage.

E. J. PRATT

While they had no way of knowing about BdU's order of 1140 halting offensive action, no doubt the B7 and EG1 escorts were aware during the late forenoon and early afternoon hours of the 6th that an eerie peace had drifted out from the enveloping fog. There had been no known German torpedo attack against a merchant ship or escort since 0527, when U–192 (Happe) launched a brace of stern tube eels at *Loosestrife*. The U-boats were still about, as *Pelican, Sennen,* and *Spey* had proved, detecting three on the surface between 0551 and 1244, but there had been no observations of periscope wakes or torpedo tracks, which one might have expected on the daylit sea, even in its gauzy cover. Most of the boats appeared to be lying doggo below, outside of asdic range. By an ironic twist, which most hands probably noted, during the preceding night it was the U-boats that had become the quarry, and the escorts the hunter. Perhaps no one was more elated to receive that understanding than Commodore Brook, on *Rena*, who entered a condensed account of "this big Convoy Battle" in his final report, and set down the score as he learned it from *Tay*.[36]

What was left to do, besides mopping up attacks by *Sennen* at 1244 and by *Jed*, which would make the final D/C attack on a probable U-boat contact at 2357 that night, was the collecting of merchant ships that had become scattered in the black and the fog, and the refueling of *Vidette* from *British Lady* beginning at 1130.[37] That completed, the convoy proceeded without incident toward the Western Ocean Meeting Point (WESTOMP) at 48°11′N, 45°39′W, east of St. John's, where Canadian warships out of Newfoundland were scheduled to relieve the ocean escort. At 1500, Sherwood's Mid-Ocean Escort Group B7 and Brewer's First Support Group were joined by the Canadian Western Local Escort Force (WLEF), W-4. They were four corvettes, by name: H.M.C.S. *Barrie* (SO), *Galt, Buctouche,* and *Cowichan*.[38] All the assembled forces together with the convoy columns continued toward WESTOMP, the Navy and Merchant Navy crews of B7 and ONS.5 now having every reason to sense the approaching end of a near three week ordeal, during which they reached and surpassed the human equivalent of PLE. Their stained, worn ships, having survived both the lash of a stern, impartial sea and the bitterest convoy battle of two world wars, rose and dipped with a sober gravity.

Behind their weary screws flowed runnels of gray and white Grand Banks wash. Beneath their keels the Atlantic shoaled on the continental shelf. The long billows of the central ocean gave way to a shorter and choppy surface, while on either beam squadrons of gulls parked on the water to announce the impending shore. What was best, we may believe, the scent of victory was in the air. No one yet could let down his guard, and none could forget merchant mariners left behind in the deep transepts of the cathedral sea, but a lightened mood understandably took hold among all ranks and ratings, whether under the white ensign or the red duster. There was occasion now for the concertina, the George Formby song, dominoes, "uckers" (ludo), or cribbage. And a long unburdening sigh.

Game, set, and match: U.K.

That night, at 2357, *Pelican* received a signal from CinCWA directing her, *Wear*, and *Jed* to part company from the convoy at daylight on the 7th, IF CONVOY CONSIDERED NO LONGER THREATENED, and to proceed at economical speed astern of the convoy to search for torpedoed ships that might still be afloat. They would find no derelicts, but on the forenoon of the 8th, in thick fog, they sighted wreckage and empty lifeboats. After several course changes to support convoys ON.181 and ONS.6, as directed by CinCWA, the three support ship vessels returned through heavy broken pack ice to St. John's, arriving on the 12th.[39] At 1650 on the 7th, on orders from *Tay*, *Vidette* and *Loosestrife* disengaged from the convoy to escort three vessels to St. John's: *British Lady, Empire Gazelle*, and *Berkel* (the last of which had survived the collision with *Bornholm* on 25 April). They arrived on the forenoon of the 9th. The remaining ships of B7, *Tay, Snowflake*, and *Sunflower*, parted company for St. John's on the same day, arriving on the 8th. *Pink* with her straggler party made the same port on the 9th. As for the main body of ONS.5, destined for Halifax, Boston, and New York, Commodore Brook's final report read simply (in local time):

> *May 12th*
> 0520 Detached NY and Boston groups with 3 Corvettes escorting.
> 1100 Formed single line ahead.
> 1200 Proceeding up Swept Channel Halifax.
> 1300 Approaching Pilot Station. Convoy completed.[40]

It was twenty days since the departure from Oversay. A few individual stragglers made port in the days that followed.

On shore, the B7, EG3, and First Support Group Captains typed up their proceedings and after-action reports. Several of them offered, in addition, their reflections on such topics as convoy routes, the performance of personnel, the endurance of escort vessels, the usefulness of weaponry and equipment, and U-boat tactics. A preliminary summary of certain of these comments was prepared on 9 May by Flag Officer Newfoundland Force (Commodore H. E. Reid, R.C.N.) for ciphered transmission to Commander-in-Chief North West Atlantic (CinCNA), Rear Admiral L. W. Murray, R.C.N., in Halifax. The summary began with the observation that the convoy battle had been divided into two periods, 28 April to 1 May and 4 May to 6 May, with a three-day gale in between. After noting that scare tactics based on HF/DF bearings had proved successful, the summary continued:

> U-boats were attacking by night in pairs and threes. Possibly 1 day attack delivered by pair. No new tactics in night attacks. By day, U-boats approached from ahead of centre of convoy and fired from between the columns. U-boats were using 2 different H/F frequencies simultaneously during the night of 4th May. Possibly 2 different packs attacked. A.C.I. [Atlantic Convoy Instructions] diagrams and orders used throughout. Experience shows that at night 6 ships is minimum number on [Type] 271 [radar] close screen unless weather permits 1 side of screen to be left unprotected and that 271 fitted ships of Support Group should be stationed at least 8 miles clear of convoy. Cooperation between Escort and Support Group excellent. Little air cover available due to weather which also prevented fuelling of escorts. Tanker "British Lady" did not carry enough fuel. Rescue trawlers proved their use. It is strongly suggested that convoy was routed too far north into ice and bad weather. Only on 1 night after gale had scattered convoy and in rough sea did U-boats gain upper hand. It is thought likely that day attacks will become more and night attacks less frequent as result of this battle.[41]

Among the individual ship reports, *Tay* commented: "All ships worked hard, capably, and with intelligence and considerable humour, and the situation was always well in hand."[42] And again: "All ships showed dash and initiative. No ship required to be told what to do and signals were distinguished both by their brevity and their wit." *Sunflower* stated that his asdic team were "most keen and efficient at all times," and that his D/C team were a close second. The radar operators, with one exception, had no prior sea experience; they compensated for that somewhat by their zeal. The Chief Bos'n's mate and the Coxs'n had shown exceptional leadership in keeping ship's company, many of whom were at sea for the first time, up to the best service traditions.[43]

Snowflake observed that the four-inch H.E. was effective in forcing a U-boat to dive when radar reported a boat dead ahead and the gun was trained with sights set to zero: "This obviated the necessity of a long chase." (The corvette, it is remembered, was slower than the U-boat on the surface.) During a concentrated attack by U-boats, *Snowflake* recommended, priority should be given to the speed rather than to the accuracy of the counterattack, so that the escort could retake position on the screen in the shortest possible time.[44]

Destroyers *Penn* and *Panther* of EG3, which had been with the convoy for fewer than two days (2-4 May) because of fuel depletion, weighed in with comments about their short-legged craft, *Penn* suggesting that support group operations should be so arranged that destroyers heavy on oil fuel were not sent long distances from base, "as their first need on meeting a convoy is a large amount of fuel," and bad weather often made refueling impossible.[45] *Panther* suggested "that Sloops and Frigates (who are not constantly faced with fuel problem) ought to make up support groups and that destroyers should always form part of a definite escort group"—a suggestion fully concurred with by CinCNA, Rear Admiral Murray at Halifax.[46] For his part, Convoy Commodore Brook praised "the splendid work throughout on part of Escorts, not forgetting (SO) HMS 'DUNCAN' who unfortunately had to leave Convoy short of fuel just before Convoy Battle materialized."[47]

Senior Officer Peter Gretton was all too conscious of his

misfortune as he talked in St. John's with the B7 captains and read their reports. That misfortune being that he had missed out on the events of 5/6 May, which were, he said, "probably the most stirring of convoy history." By a combination of "skill, luck, initiative, and sheer guts," his B7 group, helped by EG3 and First Support Group, had brought off one of the epic victories in the story of sea warfare. Twenty-one years later he would still be tending to his "wounded vanity," writing: "I shall never cease to regret that I did not risk the weather and stay with them until the end. . . The weather did improve and I would probably have been able to fuel. . . . I had missed the 'golden moment' which comes but once in a life-time."[48]

Yet Gretton's wounded vanity should have been assuaged by the commendations that came to him on every side for having trained so capable a force as B7, which, as *Tay's* report noted, needed no further instructions on what to do when the hour of maximum danger arrived. Rear Admiral Murray was unstinting in his praise: "The absence of the Senior Officer of B7 on the big night, while unfortunate and inevitable, none-theless speaks volumes for the training he is responsible for in this outstanding Group."[49] Admiral Horton himself com-mented that it was "a credit to the training of the group that in his [Gretton's] absence it was so ably led by his second in command, Lt.-Cmdr.R. E. Sherwood, R.N.R.,H.M.S. TAY."[50]

Gretton had been the first to laud Sherwood's perfor-mance. He had been in *Tay* with Sherwood during the battle for HX.231, and "I knew that he could compete." In his own analysis of the 5/6 May engagement, produced shortly after the arrival of the B7 Captains at St. John's, Gretton wrote that, "Lieutenant-Commander Sherwood of HMS TAY handled a very dangerous situation with ability and coolness. I consider he did exceptionally well, being ably backed up by the group." It is worth adding that the two-and-a-half-ringed reservist won his victory in the presence of two RN Captains.[51]

With the after-action reports in hand, Gretton offered fur-ther comments on the two stages of the battle: He agreed with his Captains that the convoy had been routed too far to the north, where ice and gales retarded forward progress, prevented fueling, and scattered ships. (This view subsequently was endorsed by Rear Admiral Murray. Recognizing that the far northern route had been selected for evasive purposes, Murray concluded, "It is very much doubted if the game is worth the candle.")[52] Since near Greenland W/T ship-to-shore communication was impossible on any frequency, and the U-boats, which had superior wireless gear, were having the same trouble, the Admiralty should not assume, said Gretton, that a convoy in those latitudes was not being shadowed because of an absence of signals. EG3 was a model of cooperation and assistance, and the presence of *Offa* and *Oribi* on 5/6 May made a significant difference in the battle. Aircraft, particularly the Liberators, which flew to the extreme limit of their endurance in appalling weather, deserved great credit for their coverage, as did the RCAF Cansos from Newfoundland that attacked two U-boats on the 4th, though fog prevented further air assistance from that quarter.

Crediting her as exhibiting "the most outstanding performance" in his B7 group, Gretton singled out *Snowflake* for "carrying out at least 12 attacks and finally bagging a U-boat"; though in fact *Snowflake*, which made seven attacks during the voyage, did not actually sink a boat, and the palm might more fittingly have been awarded to *Vidette,* which sank two. His only criticism was reserved for *Pink,* which, he said, made "an incorrect decision" in leaving his straggler station to go after a U-boat (U–*358*) on the 5th, but, he conceded, "I would have made it myself." In his operation against ONS.5, the enemy had been "dealt a blow that may have far-reaching results on their future tactics and which must inevitably increase the proportion of day to night attacks."

In what was perhaps Gretton's most provocative observation—one that would draw comment from the demanding, some would say irascible, Captain G. W. G. "Shrimp" Simpson, R.N., Commodore (D) Western Approaches in Londonderry—he stated that the just–completed convoy battle proved, as had HX.231 before it, that in favorable seas, an efficient close screen in correct station could alone prevent surfaced night attacks on a convoy.[53] Simpson's read on Gretton's confidence in the close screen was more differentiated and searching:

> A point which is brought out is that when a close R.D.F. [radar] ring of well-trained escorts is round the convoy they can defeat the U-boat on practically every occasion, as was proved by the action on the night of 28/29 April, when six attacks were beaten off without loss. It is noted that losses to the convoy did not occur until the close screen had been reduced to five and then to four escorts. It is considered that it is essential for the safety of a convoy that there should be eight escorts stationed on the close screen. On the night of 4th/5th May, five merchant vessels were torpedoed after the close screen had been reduced to five escorts, and it is considered that if *Offa* and *Oribi,* who were on the extended screen, had been brought in to support the close screen, as was done the following night, better protection for the convoy would certainly have resulted. . . . *Offa* and *Oribi,* disposed singly on the outer screen, could not contribute much to the safety of the convoy and were themselves in considerable danger of being torpedoed.

Admiral Horton concurred in this criticism, noting only that a close escort of eight was the minimum required "at night under normal circumstances." Where Simpson went on to criticize *Tay* for taking the ahead station on the screen when her asdics were out of action, Horton thought that under the circumstances her position ahead was the correct one. And where Simpson criticized the escorts for not firing Hedgehog in incidents where its use was appropriate, and for sometimes using inaccurate depth settings on D/Cs–"the errors have been pointed out to the vessels concerned"–Horton countered generously: "The skill and determination of all escorts engaged in this operation leaves little to be desired." In that compliment he specifically included the Third and First Support Groups commanded by Captain McCoy and Commander Brewer, respectively, who "loyally gave complete co-operation with the Junior Officer in command of the close escort." And to all involved he had earlier, on 6 May, sent a W/T message: "My heartiest congratulations on your magnificent achievements."

Even by-the-book Simpson acknowledged the final showing as "a major victory," and the fact that there were only two failures among the 340-odd D/Cs fired or dropped by B7 and its support elements he attributed to "a very high standard of depth charge efficiency in these groups, and [that] is definitely the result of stiff training." In Horton's comments on Simpson's appreciation of the ONS.5 screen operations, the CinCWA judged that not only were those operations "a classic embodying nearly every method and form of tactics current at the time," they probably marked the end of large U-boat pack attacks: "It may well be," he wrote to the Lords Commissioners of the Admiralty, "that the heavy casualties inflicted on the enemy have gravely affected his morale and will prove to have been a turning point in the Battle of the Atlantic."[54] Like Winn, Horton may have been more optimistic than correct about the battle's effect on German morale. But he was proved right on the second point: In the remaining twenty-four months of war no other U-boat group would attack with the same apparent pluck and confidence. The wolfpack mystique lay at ruinous discount.

How much Horton was now beginning to edge from a defensive to an offensive posture, as a result of this battle and subsequent events in May and early June, is exemplified by his relatively open response to a recommendation put forward on 9 May by Captain McCoy, SO, EG3, in *Offa*, who thought that evasive tactics, such as those employed in the long routing of ONS.5 to the north, were wasteful and unnecessary. Echoing Gretton's confidence in the close screen, McCoy argued that, "Escorts that are fitted with radar and which are handled with determination, will always defeat the U-boat at night or in fog." Therefore, he recommended directly to the CinCWA, "Our policy should be to invite the enemy to attack so that he can be destroyed." This was to use merchant ships as bait, which Horton had rejected as "undesirable" in his Tactical Policy signal of 27 April. On 14 June, Horton responded (present writer's emphases): "It is not agreed that it was desirable *at the time this convoy was run* to route convoys–particularly slow ones–so as to invite attack. If the changed situation which now prevails in the Atlantic were to be maintained, the routing of fast convoys when covered by support groups across the end of a patrol line so as to invite attack by a small number of U/Boats *deserves consideration. . . .*"[55] Even at that date, in mid-June, Horton was guarded and hesitant in his expressions, but in retrospect it is clear that his long-established policy of Defender was tentatively yielding primacy to one of Hunter.

On 13 May, the Newfoundland *Daily News* published a front-page article under the headline: 10 NAZI SUBS DESTROYED IN CONVOY ATTACK. The account, datelined London the day before and transmitted by Reuters, was based on an Admiralty communiqué that did not identify the convoy but did give a summary of anti-submarine attacks by escort ships, which were named, and by RCAF aircraft, though the number of U-boats definitely destroyed in the story did not match up to the number in the headline. *The Times* of London ran basically the same story on the same day, but was more discriminating in citing the U-boat casualties as four destroyed, four very probably destroyed, and two probably destroyed.[56] Following these two accounts, however, there was little public attention and even less scholarly notice given to the Battle for ONS.5. Prime Minister Winston Churchill, who was in Washington, D.C., at the time of the communiqué, sent a congratulatory message to the escorts via the Admiralty on 9 May–MY COMPLIMENTS TO YOU ON YOUR FIGHT AGAINST THE U-BOATS–but eight years later, in 1951, when writing the fifth volume of his history, *The Second World War*, the volume that treated of the Atlantic war in this particular period, he did not think the battle noteworthy enough to mention.[57] Similarly, the official historian of Royal Navy operations during the war, Captain Stephen W. Roskill, D.S.C., R.N., devoted a mere page and a

Kptlt. Horst von Schroeter, Commander of U-*123*, who operated off Freetown, West Africa, during April and May 1943. *Vice Admiral von Schroeter*

Kptlt. Werner Henke, Commander of U-*515*, whose seven ships sunk on the night of 30 April/1 May set a U-boat record. *Bibliothek für Zeitgeschichte Stuttgart*

Kptlt. Heinrich Hasenschar, Commander of U-*628*, the shadower boat in the battle for ONS.5. *Bibliothek für Zeitgeschichte Stuttgart*

Kptlt. Ulrich Folkers, Commander of U-*125*, which was rammed by H.M.S. *Oribi* on the night of 5/6 May. *Bibliothek für Zeitgeschichte Stuttgart*

A Type IX U-boat arrives home from base with victory pennants flying. *Bibliothek für Zeitgeschichte Stuttgart*

Kptlt. Harald Gelhaus (in white cover), Commander of U-*107*, which sank *Port Victor* on 1 May, putting out to sea from his base at Lorient. *Bibliothek für Zeitgeschichte Stuttgart*

The U-boat bunkers at Brest.
Bibliothek für Zeitgeschichte Stuttgart

Kptlt. Werner Henke (in white cover) arrives back with U-*515* at Lorient on 24 June. He had sunk only one ship after his strong showing on 30 April/1 May.
Bibliothek für Zeitgeschichte Stuttgart

A Type VIIC U-boat puts out to sea, her diesel exhaust trailing aft, the Biscay coast in the background. The photograph was taken from an accompanying minesweeper.
Bibliothek für Zeitgeschichte Stuttgart

Three crewmen sleep and two work in a U-boat's forward torpedo room. *Bibliothek für Zeitgeschichte Stuttgart*

A pre-sailing convoy conference. The Convoy Commodore briefs the ship Masters. *Bibliothek für Zeitgeschichte Stuttgart*

H.M.S. *Tay. Imperial War Museum*

H.M.S. *Snowflake. Imperial War Museum*

H.M.S. *Duncan. Imperial War Museum*

Crew members of the "chummy" corvettes H.M.S. *Snowflake (left)* and H.M.S. *Sunflower (right)* exchange friendly banter in port. *Imperial War Museum*

WRENS (Women's Royal Naval Service) adjust convoy and escort positions on the plot. *Bibliothek für Zeitgeschichte Stuttgart*

A Hedgehog battery.
Imperial War Museum

The distinctive plumes created by the underwater explosions of depth charges dropped on a U-boat, in this case by an escort vessel.
U.S. Navy

A depth charge fitted to a thrower on H.M.S. *Sunflower.*
Imperial War Museum

A Fairey Swordfish Mark I equipped with searchlight and A.S.V. radar. *Imperial War Museum*

A Vickers Wellington Mark XIII bomber fitted with A.S.V. aerials. *Imperial War Museum*

A Consolidated B-24 V.L.R. Liberator bomber with matte white undersides, as recommended by Professor Patrick M. S. Blackett. *Imperial War Museum*

A Consolidated PBY-5 Catalina flying boat moored to a buoy. *Imperial War Museum*

half to the battle in his three-volume history, *The War at Sea,
1939–1945,* published in 1956. To be fair, he allotted only
twenty-one lines to the big battle of SC.122/HX.229 in the
foregoing March.

Horton seems to have been the first to have grasped the
decisive character of the ONS.5 triumph, suggesting that it
would prove to be a "turning point" in the Atlantic struggle.
Rodger Winn, in the OIC Tracking Room, wrote sometime
within two and a half years of the battle: "This was probably
the most decisive of all convoy engagements. It represented
the extreme and, as it happens, the last example of coordinated pack attacks."[58] The Most Secret documents containing
Winn's appreciation were not released to the Public Record
Office until 1975. In the meantime, Captain Roskill's assessment of the place that this individual battle occupied in the
war against Germany underwent a striking transformation.
Where the most that he was willing to say in 1956 was that
ONS.5's "adventurous passage" had led to "grave losses" for
the U-boats, three years later, in a review of Karl Dönitz's
Memoirs in *The Sunday Times,* he was emboldened to state:
"[Dönitz] considers that the passage of convoy ONS.5 in
April-May 1943 marked the turning point in the long struggle, and I fully agree with him." Comparing Gretton and Sherwood to the likes of Hawke and Nelson, Roskill added this
flourish: "The seven-day battle fought against thirty U-boats
is marked only by latitude and longitude and has no name by
which it will be remembered; but it was, in its own way, as decisive as Quiberon Bay or the Nile."[59] Perhaps, when viewed
on the larger stage of World War II, it would not be unreasonable to say that the set-piece Battle for ONS.5 was the Midway of the Atlantic.

The pendulum of war, which had swung so dangerously
to the German side in March and had reverted to center in
April, now swung sharply to the Allies' side. In reflecting on
the long, bitter combat experienced by both belligerents during the passage of ONS.5, one's attention is particularly
drawn to the B7 flotilla that was the convoy's original escort.
In late April that force of seven warships, of which the major-

ity were corvettes, set out to protect an argosy of forty-three light-ballasted ships whose best speed was seven and a half knots. Their passage would take them through bow-stopping gales and ice infested seas. Their base course would be anticipated by German intelligence, resulting in their being attacked and chased at their northernmost position. They would have to pass through what remained of the Air Gap, with scanty overhead protection. And then they would fall into the fatal embrace of the largest U-boat attack force ever assembled against a single convoy—a force comprising as many U-boats as, at the time, the convoy and escorts had ships, and five times the number of RN defenders. By any objective standard their condition was desperate. Little wonder that Captain McCoy, whose EG3 had joined in support, said on 5 May that "the convoy was threatened with annihilation." And merchantmen did suffer grievous losses. But B7 close escort ships alone exacted a heavy toll from their assailants, and supporting escorts, both surface and air, made additional U-boat kills. Every man who had been on board the B7 vessels, starting with Gretton, who drew up the game plan, and Sherwood, who executed it, down to the lowest ratings in the boiler and engine rooms, deserved the highest credit. Against all odds, the B7 ships and crews survived and prevailed. In the long Atlantic struggle against the U-boats, theirs truly was a sword-from-the-stone triumph. In looking through British naval/military annals for comparisons, one is tempted to recall Rorke's Drift in 1879, where eighty men of the 24th Regiment of Foot defended the mission station against similarly overwhelming numbers. But Captain McCoy of EG3 will have the last word: "The skill, determination, and good drill displayed by all ships of B.7 Group during the time the Third Escort Group was supporting O.N.S.5 was beyond all praise."[60]

8

To Hunt
The Bay in May

The effectiveness of the present sorties over the Bay can be raised from a low to a real killing effectiveness only when they become part of a larger organized and coordinated force, devoted to surprising, hanging on, and killing.

STEPHEN RAUSHENBUSH

If we strike a decisive blow at the trunk in the Bay, the branches will wither.

AIR MARSHAL SLESSOR

. . . take up arms against a sea of troubles, and by opposing end them.

HAMLET, ACT III, SCENE I

The U-boat has no more to fear from aircraft than a mole from a crow.

ADMIRAL DÖNITZ
4 AUGUST 1942

It is not known whether forty-seven-year-old American economist Stephen Raushenbush had ever seen a submarine or a bomber before he was suddenly posted to London in December 1942 to help develop a new battle plan for the Bay of Biscay. Military tactics were not something in which he had had any great interest since 1917–1919, when he and most of his graduating class at Amherst College went to France with the American Expeditionary Force, he to serve as a volunteer ambulance driver. Though in that capacity he pursued his famous father's compassionate ideals, he did not follow the Reverend Walter Rauschenbusch (1861–1918), a leading exponent of the Social Gospel, into the Baptist ministry. Instead, after the Armistice, he studied economics at the University of Rennes in France, worked in the oil industry in Mexico and Venezuela, researched coal and power issues in New York City, taught at Dartmouth College, and served for eight years as advisor on public utilities to the governor of Pennsylvania, while taking time out in 1934–1936 to be chief investigator for the Special U.S. Senate Committee that inquired into the munitions industry. In his spare time he wrote seven books, ranging in subject matter from *The Anthracite Question* (1923) to *The March of Fascism* (1939).

His last pre–World War II position, beginning in 1939, was with the U.S. Department of the Interior as chief of the Branch of Planning and Research in the Division of Power. He was described at that period of his life as a reserved but friendly person; he wore a mustache and smoked a pipe; though a registered Republican, he expressed political views that were liberal and progressive. Shortly after Pearl Harbor, he took a leave of absence from Interior to serve as a civilian economist and statistician in the office of the Chief of Naval Operations (CNO) in the Navy Department. From there, in late 1942, he was plucked by Captain Thorvald A. Solberg, U.S.N., Head of the Navy Technical Station, Office of the U.S. Naval Attaché (Alusna), London, to undertake air operations planning for the Bay of Biscay.[1]

In the U.K., Raushenbush quickly familiarized himself with the attack opportunities in the Bay as well as with Coastal Command's disappointing success rate there. Since June 1942 Coastal had flown about 7,000 hours and lost aircraft at a rate of about sixteen for every U-boat sunk in the Bay. Since October only twenty-two air attacks had been mounted on the estimated 290 boats that had passed through the Bay.[2] The effort was out of all proportion to the meager results obtained. Raushenbush then set about studying the hardware. Near Glasgow on the Clyde he examined the Type

VIIC U–*570*, captured in August 1941 and renamed H.M.S. *Graph*, and learned her operating characteristics, paying special attention to the boat's capacity for remaining submerged (36–41 hours) and the time required on the surface for fully charging her batteries (6.77–7.77 hours).

At various Coastal bases he studied the type of aircraft that were being flown on Bay patrols and took fascinated notice of new centimetric radar equipment that was just then becoming available for airborne use. At both Whitehall and Northwood he availed himself of the vast operations research data that had been accumulated by Professors Blackett and Williams and their scientific teams, whom Raushenbush found "tired and exhausted from too many seven day weeks."[3] From Williams in particular, who had continued Bay Offensive studies at Coastal during the year following Blackett's departure for other ASW challenges at the Admiralty, and who was later quoted by Blackett as saying that while his scholarly specialty was quantum theory, he "found the subtle intricacies of the U-boat war of comparable intellectual interest," the American economist drew generous guidance and support.[4] In the end, not surprisingly, plans put forward to Churchill's A.U. Committee by Raushenbush and Williams would bear a certain resemblance in conception, if not in details.

When he thought he understood the basic problems that the Bay presented, Raushenbush devoted himself to intense deskwork studies and statistical tables. His roommate at Alusna, Commander Oscar A. de Lima, U.S.N.R., remembered the economist's "endless days and nights of complicated computations," though the endless period was just over a month.[5] Raushenbush's interests were most closely focused on the new availability of "Most Secret" 10–centimeter airborne radar, for which the Germans had no search receiver (G.S.R.). According to a report submitted on 22 December by radar pioneer Watson Watt, the Kriegsmarine would probably not figure out the wavelength, develop an answering G.S.R., and install it in the majority of their boats before "two or three months at the most" after first use of the Allied equipment.[6]

"There was great promise in this situation," Raushenbush wrote privately in 1948. "The danger in it was that the new weapon might (like tanks in 1916) be used in too small numbers, with too small effect, and that the Germans would consequently be given ample notice of the new weapon before it could be used against them with telling effect, and would be ready for it." He anguished, he wrote, over the possibility that a centimetric radar installation would first be used in an area such as the Mediterranean or the European mainland, where it might be captured and compromised.[7] As it happened, a few 10-centimeter sets were flown by Coastal aircraft out of Gibraltar in February before their use in the Bay. And Raushenbush's worst-case scenario—though it is not known that he was aware of it at the time—unfolded on 2 February when an RAF Bomber Command Stirling bomber equipped with centimetric radar went down at night near Rotterdam. The radar set was Type H2S, in which the radar pulses were used in a "look-down" mode for picking out coastlines, lakes, waterways, and (less successfully) cities.

Coastal had forcefully opposed that use of 10-centimeter radar prior to its use in the Bay precisely because capture of the equipment, which seemed likely, would ruin Coastal's chances of obtaining surprise in the Biscay transit area. But Bomber Command spoke louder, claiming that for the success of the night-bombing campaign over Germany—always the overriding imperative in the Prime Minister's mind—the bombers desperately needed H2S as a navigational aid. Churchill gave approval for the new radar's use over enemy territory beginning in January, with, as Coastal feared, predictable results. Though the Stirling's radar equipment was badly damaged, German technicians were able to reassemble the *Rotterdam Gerät,* as they called it, at the Telefunken laboratories in Berlin. By chance, the device was badly damaged a second time in an RAF bombing raid. Again, it was reconstructed, this time in a bombproof bunker. After flight-testing the magnetron valve equipment, the technicians realized that the Allies had achieved a major technological breakthrough, and, where the maritime war was concerned, had leapfrogged the Fu.MB (Metox). News of the disclosure was passed at once to BdU, where on 5 March the Dönitz/Godt war diary reported a confirming incident at sea and ruminated on the *Rotterdam Gerät:*

> U–*333* [Oblt.z.S. Werner Schwaff] was attacked by enemy aircraft at night without previous radar [detection by Fu.MB] in BF 5897. Slight damage, aircraft was shot down in flames. . . . [The aircraft was L/L Wellington "B" of No. 172 Squadron, which had just begun Bay patrols with ASV Mark III.] The enemy is working on carrier waves outside the frequency range of the present Fu.MB receivers. The shooting down over Holland of an enemy aircraft apparently carrying an apparatus with a frequency of 9.7 centimeters is the only indication at present of this possibility.[8]

The secret was out, and it appeared likely that the Germans would now neutralize the centimetric wavelength in the same way that Metox had neutralized the metric. But the Telefunken Company experienced problems in replicating parts of the Allied equipment, and administrative muddles further checked what was to have been a crash program to develop a new G.S.R., with the result, astonishingly, that an effective detector called *Naxos-U* was not shipped to the U-boats until October, far later than the two or three months predicted by Watson Watt, and long after the issue in the Atlantic had been decided.

Raushenbush began his calculations with a review of U-boat performance figures. The optimum (as against maximum) speed surfaced for charging batteries was 12 knots. The optimum speed for running submerged was 1.75 knots. The average battery capacity on entering the 200-mile-deep transit channel was 51 miles submerged, after which a U-boat had to surface for maximum recharge for a period of 6.77 to 7.77 hours, during which it would travel 81 to 93 miles. After another 51 miles submerged, it would have to surface for charging at least once again, briefly, until completing the 200 miles (assuming a direct course) in a total traverse time of 76.37 hours.

Thus, a U-boat in transit would be on the surface and vulnerable to air attack for at least one lengthy period. Any attempt to remain underwater beyond 41 hours would exhaust the air supply, although a boat could surface for 5 to 10 minutes to ventilate. A surfaced U-boat forced to dive by aircraft would later have to charge for approximately seven minutes to compensate for the 100 ampere hours used in one cycle of crash-diving and resurfacing. Since the average density of boats in the transit area at any given time was 15.8 boats, that number together would be exposed from 1,280 to 1,470 miles during their passage. Raushenbush calculated that there would be a density of one surfaced boat per 3,800 square miles.

On the air side, Raushenbush called for an additional 160 long-range aircraft, all equipped with ASV Mark III and many with Leigh Lights, to make up a total force of 260 aircraft. Such a large, coordinated force, trained to capitalize on the Allied advantage of centimetric radar, could be expected to make 7.5 sorties per aircraft per month, to make 1.8 attacks on each of 150 U-boats entering the transit channel each month, to make a minimum of twenty-five kills per month, and to cause damage to a further thirty-four boats. Over the projected 120 operational days of this effort, 100 boats would be destroyed and 136 damaged, thus "paralyzing" the U-boat fleet and throwing it on the defensive. The damaged boats would play their role in the paralysis effect by jamming and overloading the Biscay repair bases.

There were two critical factors in the Raushenbush Plan: (1) the attack program must be put into effect *promptly*, before the enemy devised a centimetric search receiver; and (2) the attacking force must be *sufficiently large from the outset;* "no small driblets" of additional aircraft would make the plan work. On the second point he elaborated that a law of increasing returns could be developed to show that up to a certain point, a large but still less than adequate force would produce only minor results; but that once enlarged to and beyond a certain critical mass, the effectiveness of that force was in high progression. He concluded:

> The morale of the remaining U-boat fleet may be broken by such an effort. If in four months (May–August 1943 inclusive) 100 U-boats are killed, and 136 damaged, and every one is attacked 1.8 times in transit, the U-boat fleet based on Biscay would have lost about 36 per cent of its numbers and the crews of an additional 136 would have been shaken up. The unkilled 175 U-boats may thereby be so broken in morale as to impair their effectiveness greatly.[9]

Raushenbush went on to suggest crew "mutiny" as a possibility, which was going somewhat over the top; the suggestion probably showed the degree to which his views were shaped by British associates, among whom the morale war seems to have been a preoccupation. One suspects, knowing how U-boat crews put out to sea unflinchingly in 1945, when certain to near-certain destruction faced every boat, that infidelity to duty in the U-Bootwaffe was never a consideration.

The Raushenbush Plan was endorsed by Captain Solberg, and, upon his recommendation, by Admiral Harold R. Stark, U.S.N., Commander, United States Naval Forces in Europe, who had it printed up for presentation to the Prime Minister's A.U. Committee on 24 March. In the meantime, it received strong support from the operations research team at the Admiralty, though those politically savvy people knew that the Plan would not fly unless it passed the inspection of Churchill's personal science advisor, Professor Lindemann, now Lord Cherwell. Accordingly, Professors Blackett and Williams (the latter now also with the Admiralty) joined Raushenbush to form a special committee under the chairmanship of Sir Stafford Cripps, Minister of Aircraft Production and vice-chair of the A.U. Committee, for the purpose of bringing Cherwell into camp. In that endeavor they were not entirely unsuccessful.

Cherwell was at first dismissive of the Raushenbush Plan as "based upon somewhat speculative foundations," calling it "unduly optimistic." Without directly challenging any of the American's numbers or calculations, he rejected the "largely theoretical" proposals in the Plan as diverging from prior practical experience in the Bay, where the dividends had been very few. Furthermore, he argued, the presumed advantage of 10–centimeter radar would be overcome "very easily" by a new German search receiver; and the probability that the enemy would sprinkle the Bay with radio decoys seemed to have been treated "rather lightly" by Raushenbush. It would be better, Cherwell said, to devote aircraft resources to the more fruitful duty of protecting menaced convoys. In fact, better still would be the allocation of Coastal Command aircraft to the bombing of German cities, which "must have more immediate effect on the course of the war in 1943." All that said, however, Cherwell did allow that it could be an "interesting experiment" to give the Raushenbush advocates a free run to see how they fared.[10]

Two other events transpired before the plan devised by the U.S. Naval Attaché's one-man Bay research branch was formally presented. First, the Admiralty produced its own similar plan for the Bay. Second, a trial of the two plans was flown by Coastal Command from 6 to 15 February under the code name Operation Gondola. Although authorship of the Admiralty's plan was credited to Blackett, he suggested in a eulogy of Williams (who died in 1945) that the calculations had been done by Williams during the winter of 1942–1943, when "he worked out in great detail the best methods of conducting such an offensive by a balanced force of day and night aircraft equipped with the latest forms of 10 cm. radar."[11]

Williams (or Blackett) shared the plan with Raushenbush, who drew up a one-page summary of comparisons and differences between the two sets of numbers. Both plans called for a total force of 260 heavy aircraft. Where Raushenbush estimated that the force required 160 additional aircraft, Williams estimated 190. Where Raushenbush envisioned a four-month offensive, Williams called for a full year's endurance of effort. Both plans anticipated 150 U-boat transits a month in the Bay during spring 1943 (which proved to be too high). The average number of sorties per aircraft per month were approximately the same, as were the ratios of sightings to attacks, attacks to kills, and attacks to damaged U-boats. Where Raushenbush predicted twenty-five kills per month and thirty-four boats damaged, Williams anticipated twenty-two kills and twenty-two damaged.[12]

The nine-day Gondola trial did not exactly replicate either plan, since the aircraft of only three of the sixteen squadrons participating in whole or in part were equipped with 10–centimeter radar: these were United States Army Air Forces (USAAF) Liberator Squadrons Nos. 1, 2, and 224. Altogether, 136 individual aircraft, including L/L Wellingtons and L/L Catalinas, took part in standard patrols that "fanned" southward over the Inner Bay (East), where during the operational period forty U-boats traversed the area, and the Outer Bay (West), where thirty-eight boats transited. Eighteen sightings resulted (only two initiated by centimetric radar), leading to seven attacks. One U-boat was believed sunk by Liberator "T" of No. 2 Squadron, but a recent NHB/MOD reassessment finds that the U-boat attacked, U-752 (Kptlt. Karl-Ernst Schröter), escaped serious injury. Still, the numbers, particularly those of sightings, and of the reduced flying hours required to make them, seemed provisionally to validate the Raushenbush/Admiralty Plans, taking into account the fact that most aircraft, as noted, were not equipped with centimetric radar. After the end of the operation there was a marked drop in the ratio of sightings to flying hours, back to the former low level.

In early March, to Coastal's great regret, U.S. Admiral King requested the transfer of two USAAF Liberator squadrons from St Eval in Cornwall to Morocco. Air Marshal Slessor stated that their crews had shown "intense energy and enthusiasm" in the anti-U-boat war, and "were just getting into their stride."[13] The loss of these centimetric-equipped aircraft as well as No. 405 Halifax Squadron, which had to be returned to Bomber Command, was a blow to both the Raushenbush and Admiralty Plans. Nonetheless, with the aircraft remaining, including this time the newly operational No.

172 Squadron of centimetric-equipped L/L Wellingtons, an-other combat trial in the Bay called Operation Enclose was laid on by Coastal for dusk 20 to dawn 28 March.

Curiously, as will be shown below, this was at just the time that Coastal was officially denigrating the Bay Offensive as an uneconomical use of Coastal assets; and indeed, it was on the 22nd that Air Marshal Slessor sent his Note to the A.U. Com-mittee (seen in chapter 3) recommending that the Bay be consigned to the condition of a "residuary legatee."[14] Yet Pey-ton Ward tells us that his naval liaison staff at Northwood made the suggestion for a new trial and that Slessor supported it.[15] (This was not the last example of Slessor's paradoxical be-havior.) In P. W.'s conception, the Gondola patrol fan (so-called because it spread out slightly to the east and west be-low the south England and Welsh bases) should be replaced by a single patrol "ribbon" 140 miles wide running north and south across the Bay between longitudes 7° and $10^{1}/_{2}$° W. The width of the ribbon represented the probable maximum dis-tance traveled by a U-boat in 24 hours regardless of the ratio of the time spent surfaced or submerged. The scheme called for aircraft to form a constant stream passing south into the ribbon as far as $44^{1}/_{2}$° N and returning on nearly reciprocal courses. P. W. and his staff added a fillip to the nighttime flights that was calculated to sow uncertainty and carelessness among the U-boat crews: in addition to the 10–centimeter pulses, aircraft still fitted with metric equipment should send the old familiar metric pulses.

No. 19 Group stood down for a week beforehand in order to conserve energy for a seven-and-a-half day intensive effort. Then, at dusk on the 20th, 115 individual aircraft–10 cm.–equipped Liberators of USAAF No. 224 Squadron, 10cm. L/L Wellingtons, other Wellingtons, Halifaxes, Fortresses, Sun-derlands, Whitleys, and one Catalina–began patrolling the ribbon. A week and twelve hours later, their expenditure of 1,300 flying hours had produced twenty-six sightings and fif-teen attacks leading to the sinking of U–665 (Oblt.z.S. Hans-Jürgen Haupt) by Whitley "Q" of No. 10 Squadron Opera-tional Training Unit (O.T.U.), and damage to U–332

(Oblt.z.S. Eberhard Hüttemann) by Wellington XII "T" of No. 172 Squadron. Since forty-one U-boats crossed the ribbon—the estimate having been forty-two—the significant numbers were one-half the Gondola hours per sighting and twice the ratio of sightings to U-boats on passage. Though those results were still not up to the Raushenbush/Admiralty projections, they were sufficiently promising that Coastal planners began scheduling Enclose II for April—at just the moment, it bears repeating, that AOC-in–C Slessor was proposing to concentrate his air resources on close cover of threatened convoys "at," he said, "the expense of the Bay patrols."[16]

When sitting for its twelfth meeting at 6:00 P.M. on Wednesday 24 March in the Cabinet Room at 10 Downing Street, S.W.1, the A.U. Committee, with Churchill in the chair, found three Papers on their agenda. The first was a Note proposing the Raushenbush Plan, to which Admiral Stark, who since the previous meeting had been made a member of the Committee, was prepared to speak. The second was the Note by Marshal Slessor proposing emphasis of air cover for threatened convoys in preference to Bay patrols. And the third was a Memorandum by the First Lord of the Admiralty, Mr. A. V. Alexander, M.P., and First Sea Lord and Chief of Naval Staff, Admiral of the Fleet Sir Dudley Pound, urging that Bomber Command launch new heavy raids on the Biscay bases.[17] Because both the U.S. proposal, which the Committee called the Stark Plan, and the Admiralty's called for the diversion of bombers to the Bay or its bases, and the sense of the Committee was that for the moment those aircraft could only come from Bomber Command's operations over Germany, it was decided to defer discussion of the three Papers until the next meeting and to invite the Air Officer Commanding-in-Chief, Bomber Command, Air Chief Marshal Sir Arthur T. Harris, to present a Paper, if he wished, and to attend the meeting.[18] Two days before that meeting, the Secretary of the War Cabinet, Sir Edward Bridges, circulated a Note specifying that only thirteen members directly concerned with the agenda Papers should attend. By the meeting date there were three additional Papers on the agenda: the invited response from Air Chief Marshal Harris; Cherwell's comments on the Raushenbush document; and a new position paper from the Admiralty proposing the Blackett/Williams Plan while supporting the Stark Plan "for its striking and independent support of the Admiralty view. . . ."[19]

Not surprisingly, in the meeting of 31 March as in his Memorandum to the Committee (dated 29 March), Marshal Harris took aim at that section of the Admiralty's latest document that called for the transfer of 190 long-range bombers from the bombing campaign over Germany to the Bay Offensive. The loss of so many aircraft, Harris contended, would mean calling off bomber operations against Germany for the next four months and throwing the whole brunt of fighting Germany upon the Soviet Union—points his Naval opposites no doubt thought exaggerations. The Minutes read: "He did not think it was fully realized what great damage was done by the attacks on U-boat construction yards and accessory factories. There was continuous confirmation that the U-boat construction programme was being considerably interfered with by these attacks and if they were stopped he was certain that the output of U-boats per month would increase."

As for new attacks on the Biscay bases, which the Admiralty's earlier Memorandum advocated, the U-boats and their essential services were sheltered under impenetrable concrete, Harris reminded the Committee, and the 10,000 tons dropped recently on the bases at Lorient and St.-Nazaire had, as the Admiralty themselves conceded, no appreciable effect on U-boat operations.[20] (Slessor, too, was critical of the bombing, at this stage, of the Biscay bases, "which was actually quite useless and resulted merely in spoiling several nice old French towns."[21]) Chief of the Air Staff Portal spoke up in support of "Bomber" Harris, as he was known in the Force, saying of the U.S. Navy and Admiralty proposals that he deprecated the transfer of any of Harris's bombers to Bay patrols on the strength of "a theoretical calculation."

But the Bay Offensive had its own determined champions, including First Lord of the Admiralty A. V. Alexander, who

pointed out that "without the Bay Offensive we cannot hope
to kill sufficient U-boats to get the upper hand in the Battle of
the Atlantic, whilst on the other hand it is believed that we
can with an adequately equipped Bay offensive sink sufficient
U-boats to destroy their morale." Alexander announced that
the Admiralty had revised downward their estimate of the
number of additional long-range bombers required: from 190
to 175 if the U-boats possessed new 10cm detection gear, to
55 if they did not. The First Lord reminded the Committee
that the enemy could run but he could not hide: "He cannot
withdraw from the Bay." First Sea Lord Pound expressed his
conviction that "the provision of additional aircraft in the Bay
of Biscay [was] an absolute necessity and not a luxury in the
anti-U-boat campaign." And U.S. Admiral Stark said that unless the Allies got the better of the U-boat, "we should be in a
bad way." By increasing the Bay patrols, he submitted, "we
should be able, for the first time, to carry out an all-out offensive against the U-boats."[22]

Of course, the Prime Minister had the last word, and it
was not favorable to the Bay proponents. With only limited
forces, he said, it was not possible to devote the maximum
number of aircraft to every theater. The distribution must be
commensurate with the results obtained, and so far air cover
over menaced convoys, as argued by Slessor, and the bombing campaign against Germany, as argued by Harris, were the
most productive theaters for the effort and resources invested.
Granting that "even if the Bay of Biscay patrols resulted in
sinking only three or four U-boats a month and did not reach
the higher figures mentioned in some of the Papers, this must
be regarded as a very important object," Churchill decided
that aircraft for that purpose could not be supplied by denud-
ing the essential missions of Coastal and Bomber Commands.
Taking a cue from Averell Harriman's suggestion that the
Chiefs of Staff in Washington might find it possible to divert
aircraft from other allocations to the Bay, the Prime Minister
charged the Air Ministry and the Admiralty with the responsibility for consulting on an estimate of the balance of
requirements that might be communicated to the U.S. Gov-

ernment.[23] Oddly, the only Committee member to have his nose put out of joint by these proceedings was Slessor, one of the winners in the debate. Displaying what had all the earmarks of a fit of pique, he railed at the Admiralty for blindsiding him with the Williams Plan and its request for 190 additional first-line heavies, "without discussing it first with the man most directly concerned, namely myself." Thirteen years later, he was still annoyed, writing in his autobiography: "I only received my copy of the paper the day before it was down for discussion, and went immediately to the First Sea Lord to tell him that I strongly disagreed with this method of tackling the problem, which I described as slide-rule strategy of the worst kind . . ." Slessor took satisfaction from recording that, "The Admiralty paper met with very little luck in the U-boat Committee the next day, where I remember one light-hearted Minister saying, '*C' est magnifique, mais ce n'est pas la guerre.*"

On 4 April he submitted to the A.U. Committee a set of counterarguments to the Williams Plan, explaining in his memoirs that "nothing could be more dangerously misleading than to imagine that you can forecast the result of a battle or decide the weapons necessary to use in it, by doing sums." He went on to aver that, "The most important factors in any battle are the human factors of leadership, morale, courage and skill, which cannot be reduced to any mathematical formula"; which human factors, the reader will remember, Captain Gilbert Roberts had insisted to Commander Gretton were no longer enough in the Battle of the Atlantic. Taking on William's operations research directly, Slessor wrote: "Summarizing my objections to the principle of strategy by slide rule, I urged that the problem should be tackled from a less scientific but more practical angle."[24]

It is hard to imagine a more tortured position for Slessor to have taken. It was the very science of O.R.S. that had made his angles practical, a fact that he himself recognized by the close working relationship to O.R.S. that he forged straightaway upon becoming AOC-in-C in the preceding month, and by the very science (and "sums") he employed at length in his own Paper before the A.U. Committee on the threatened convoy-Bay patrol option.

Furthermore, in denigrating slide-rule strategy in his autobiography, he seems to have forgotten that in the foreword he wrote to Professor Waddington's 1946 book, O.R. *in World War 2,* he praised "strategy by slide-rule" by name, and acknowledged that "No one who knows the true facts can have any doubt that a great deal of the credit for what is perhaps still not generally recognised as the resounding victory it was, namely the Battle of the Bay and the defeat of the U-boat in 1943, is due to men like Blackett, Williams, Larnder, Baughan, Easterfield and Waddington himself."[25] Raushenbush's name he seems not to have known, although the name appears prominently in the Stark Plan, where he is identified as its author, and that was the Plan whose calculations Slessor acknowledged to the A.U. Committee near the end of May, as will be seen, as having been vindicated by events in the Bay.[26]

Slessor's letter to the A.U. Committee of 4 April was not taken up by that body. Instead, during the days that followed, Slessor was persuaded to make a complete volte-face. It may have been the Air Ministry or the Admiralty, or both, whose heavy hand wrought this singular reversal–the record does not say–but when the time came for the A.U. Committee to petition the U.S. Joint Chiefs of Staff for additional long-range bombers for the Bay, it was Slessor who was tapped to draft the document. With the fervor of a convert, brought to his new faith by either conviction or thumbscrew, Slessor gave the case for the Bay Offensive its most striking language yet. Signed by him, First Sea Lord Pound, and Admiral Stark, the telegram to Washington read, in part:

> The one place where we can always be certain of finding U-boats is the Bay. Setting aside the relatively small proportion that pass into the Atlantic Northabout [from German ports], the Bay is the trunk of the Atlantic U-boat menace, the roots being in the Biscay ports and the branches spreading far and wide, to the North Atlantic convoys, to the Caribbean, to the East-

ern seaboard of North America, and to the sea lanes where the faster merchant ships sail without escorts. . . . It is a strategic problem which can only be solved by an appropriate deployment of our joint resources, designed to concentrate the necessary force at the decisive point in the battlefield of the Atlantic. We are aware that the United States, like Great Britain, has not enough aircraft to meet in full their many commitments and to afford really adequate protection to the coastal shipping on their long coast lines. But if we strike a decisive blow at the trunk in the Bay, the branches will wither.[27]

In their telegram the three signers called the Bay "second only to the convoy routes" as a strategic priority in the Battle of the Atlantic. They noted that 150 "first-line" aircraft were already engaged in the Bay Offensive, and that thirty to forty long and medium-range aircraft could be added to the force through recall of a Leigh Light squadron from Gibraltar, new construction, and borrowing. These new figures led to a revision of the number of additional aircraft needed. Hence, to make up the 260-aircraft requirement stipulated in both the Stark and Admiralty Plans, Coastal sought from the U.S. Joint Chiefs six squadrons totaling seventy-two long-range antisubmarine aircraft, drawn, the signers underscored, "from the forces already allocated [at the Atlantic Convoy Conference in Washington the previous month] to the Atlantic theatre." At that conference the U.S. side predicted that 217 aircraft of suitable type and equipment, including 56 VLR, would be available "in excess of" immediate Atlantic requirements.

It was important, the signers added, that the squadrons be made available "at the earliest opportunity" so as to take advantage of the period when the U-boats were without a 10–centimeter search receiver. (The A.U. Committee Minutes of their 14 April meeting, which contain a first draft of this communication, indicate that the Committee backed the four-month offensive proposed in the Stark Plan as against the twelve-month offensive proposed by the Admiralty.) The six squadrons would be accommodated at bases in southwest England. A reinforcement on that scale, the signers believed, "might well have results decisive to the issue of the Battle of the Atlantic."[28]

But Washington's reception of the British telegram was cool. While sympathetic to the plans for an intensive operation in the Bay, the Joint Chiefs responded on 1 May, they had to report, regrettably, that the aircraft that they had predicted to be "in excess of" immediate requirements did not and would not in fact exist. The number of ASW aircraft cited in the document produced by the Convoy Conference, Admiral King explained, was based on figures "the origin and accuracy of which could not be entirely vouched for and which apparently had raised hopes as to the availability of aircraft which facts did not now warrant."[29] This reply, appearing so casually dismissive of a formal Allied agreement, caused understandable resentment in England, where a new telegram was drafted asking, if the numbers produced by the U.S. to the Convoy Conference were in error, would the U.S. kindly send the correct figures as quickly as possible?

Another and longer interval ensued before King and the other Joint Chiefs replied, in part because these matters were not exactly in the foreground of King's interests at the time, since he was then engaged in one of the most contentious interservice rows of the war over the question, Who would control American anti-submarine air squadrons, the Navy or the Army Air Force Anti-Submarine Command? Slessor, who would personally observe these bitter turf battles during a visit to the States in June, said later: "The whole atmosphere in Washington was poisoned by inter-service jealousy and suspicion."[30]

On a belief that the reader would not want to be wearied by a recital here of that tedious tangle of disputes, which resulted in the Army's withdrawal from anti-submarine work in the fall of the year, we shall leave that to the parti-pris literature and say simply that, try as Slessor did, he never succeeded in obtaining the seventy-two aircraft requested for the Bay; and it was not until October (!) that he could count any appreciable number of reinforcements from the American side.[31] In that month Coastal had three U.S. Army and one U.S. Naval operational squadrons based at Dunkeswell in Devonshire and two U.S. Naval squadrons that were still working up at St Eval.[32] But by October, it must be recognized, the planned Second Bay Offensive was over, having been waged by the aircraft that Coastal already had in hand, and the crisis of the U-boat war had passed.

Before the telegrams began passing between London and Washington, and Army and Navy air interests began crossing swords across the Potomac River (though invited by the Army's War Department in 1942 to occupy all of the second floor and part of another in the newly erected Pentagon, an invitation that Secretary of the Navy Frank Knox readily accepted, the Navy Bureau Chiefs, not wanting to live cheek by jowl with the Army or Army Air Forces, objected strongly to moving there, and would not do so until 1948), Coastal had mounted another Bay trial, Operation Enclose II, which ran from dusk on the 5th to dawn on the 13th of April. With fewer aircraft (86) than were used in the first Enclose (115), but with three more L/L Catalinas of No. 210 Squadron, the operation was positioned over the same ribbon of sea as before and with the same deceptive 1.5-meter A.S.V. flooding at night.

During the period, twenty-five U-boats transited the ribbon (as against twenty-eight estimated). The total of 980 flying hours produced eleven sightings, more of them at night than in daylight for the first time, and four attacks, leading to the nighttime sinking of U–376 (Kptlt. Friedrich Marks) by L/L Wellington "C" of 172 Squadron, and damage to U–465 (Kptlt. Heinz Wolf) by Catalina "M" of 210 Squadron. Fewer aircraft and fewer flight hours had produced the same results as those achieved by the original Enclose. And other U-boat crews, having affected narrow escapes, no doubt experienced what Raushenbush called "sheer funk."

With the demonstration of higher efficiency in the repeat of Enclose, it was decided, even before that operation was concluded, to launch a full-scale, long-term intensive patrol over a larger ribbon between 8½° and 12° W under the code name Operation Derange. A total of 131 individual aircraft, all that were available at the moment, though well below the 260 considered necessary by Raushenbush and Williams, were committed to the new operation, which was to begin at dawn on 13 April and to continue "until further notice." Included in that number were three new squadrons, a 10cm. L/L Wellington squadron, No. 407, an ordinary Wellington squadron, No. 311, and a Whitley squadron, No. 612.

Up to the end of April, eighty-one U-boats crossed the Derange ribbon, either inbound or outbound, and during that period a total of 2,593 day and night flying hours resulted in thirty-six sightings and twenty-two attacks. The percentage of sightings made to hours flown represented no improvement over Enclose II. But one kill was made and two outbound boats were so badly damaged that they were forced to return to Brest and St.–Nazaire, respectively. The 10cm.–equipped Liberator "D" of 224 Sqdn. dropped six D/Cs on the previously damaged U–332 (Hüttemann) 25 seconds after she had dived, sinking her, northwest of Cape Ortegal, Spain, on the morning of the 29th. Damaged were U–566 (Kptlt. Hans Hornkohl), depth-charged by L/L Wellington "R" of 172 Sqdn. on the night of the 26th; and U–437 (Oblt.z.S. Hermann Lamby), depth-charged by L/L Wellington "H" of 172 on the night of the 29th.[33]

The principal effect of the twenty-two Derange attacks in April, however, was to induce exasperation at BdU, where the Operations staff had grown weary of reports from Commanders during Enclose, Enclose II, and now Derange that despite their Fu.MB (Metox) gear, they were being surprised at night like deer in a car's headlights.[34] On 27 April, Admirals Dönitz and Godt made a fateful decision, which they signaled to all Commanders. Standing War Order No. 483 was forthwith revised to require boats (1) to maintain *maximum submergence at night* through the Biscay transit area, and (2) to *fight it out* with aircraft on the surface in the daytime if surprised while charging batteries. This decision would lead to heavy

U-boat losses during May and the summer months–twenty-six kills and seventeen U-boats damaged in ninety-seven days and nights–causing it to be called by historians "a major tactical error," resulting from, as Slessor represented it, "the stupidity of the enemy."[35]

British aviation historian Alfred Price argues that in April only two out of a dozen anti-submarine squadrons in Air Vice Marshal Bromet's No. 19 Group were fitted with both Leigh Light and 10–centimeter radar, and hence were not numerous enough to cause more than the loss of "a few U-boats to air attack without warning." But in April the ratio of nighttime L/L–10cm. hours flown inside the Enclose and Derange ribbons to nighttime hours flown by unequipped aircraft was 777 to 428, and L/L Wellingtons made seven night attacks without Metox warning between 26 and 29 April, resulting in two outbound U–boats seriously damaged, U–566 and U–437 (see above), which had to abort their departures.[36]

No doubt this nighttime coverage got BdU's attention, and the Dönitz/Godt duumvirate decided that placing their battery-charging boats on the surface at night under the sudden surveillance of searchlights was a more perilous course than was deploying them on the surface in daylight, when at least their lookouts had a reasonable chance of sighting the enemy's approach in time to bring anti-aircraft armament to bear. They would then have both a warning and a defense, neither of which they had under the lights. Perhaps Dönitz and Godt were not as "stupid" as Slessor thought. They were simply wrong. If the plan was to surface during the daylight hours, then the U-boats should have been instructed to dive upon sighting aircraft. They did not have the firepower to fight back successfully. And one downside to maximum submergence, whether by day *or* by night, was greatly increased transit time, which translated into reduced opportunities to sink shipping.[37]

In making the decision to spend the battery-charging hours on the surface in daylight, Dönitz and Godt likely were influenced by U–333's flak success against a Wellington (see above) and U–338's success in downing Halifax "B" of 502

Sqdn., both in March; and by U-*191's* protracted machine-gun defense on 12 April that forced Liberator "M" of No. 86 Squadron to break off an attack—details of which BdU transmitted to all boats as an incentive. (Three L/L Wellingtons were unexplainedly lost in the Bay during April.) But these three successes, it turned out, were thin reeds on which to base so dangerous a general policy.

And so, on the cusp of May, the Battle of the Bay entered a phase that had not been predicted by either Raushenbush or Williams, a phase in which the secret use of 10–centimeter radar counted less than either boffin had anticipated, since the night had effectively been taken away from the equation.[38] Though Bromet's No. 19 Group maintained night patrols at about the same level from April through August, night sightings decreased sharply at the end of April and the battle from I May forward became mainly one of *mano-a-mano* combat in daylight, and let the metal fall where it may.[39] The essential point that should not be lost here is: displaced by the German decision as the top-drawer weapon in the Bay, the Leigh-Lighters nonetheless had proved for a second time that they were the controlling threat. Even now, in a passive role as menace-in-being, by slowing the passage of U-boats through the Bay, they saved numerous merchant ships from torpedo-wrought deaths.

Bromet's bombers were ready for this May battle. Based mostly in Devon, Cornwall, and South Wales, they had trained to near-perfect pitch, absorbing the lesson from O.R.S. in 1942 that it was not the weapon but the man that counted. And they had mastered the tactical doctrine long earned by O.R.S. calculations and combat experience. Foremost in anti-U-boat operations was sighting. Two lookouts, the doctrine held, must keep a continuous watch from ahead to 90°on either side of the aircraft, and to prevent errors through fatigue, they should be relieved every half hour.

An efficient A.S.V. watch must also be maintained, except that A.S.V. Mark II (metric) must not be used in daylight unless visibility was under three miles, or the aircraft was flying above heavy cloud, or the gear was required for navigational purposes. No restrictions were placed on A.S.V. Mark III (centimetric). To avoid eye fatigue, radar operators should be relieved every forty-five minutes. The optimum altitude for detecting and surprising a U-boat was judged to be 5,000 feet where there was no cloud or where cloud bases were above 5,000. When cloud density was not more than 5/10ths and below 5,000, aircraft should patrol 500 to 1,000 feet above cloud tops. When clouds were more than 5/10ths and below 5,000, aircraft should seek concealment by flying as near the cloud base as possible. When a sighting was made, altitude should be lost as quickly as possible in order to be no more than 300 to 500 feet off the deck when three-quarters of a mile to a mile from the target.

The pilot should make the decision as to whether flying an indirect course toward the target was required, either to provide time to get the bomb bay doors open (where aircraft were so equipped) or to avoid an increase of speed that would throw off the bomb intervalometer setting. (Squadron Leader Terence M. Bulloch, cited in chapter 3 for his successes–altogether in his career he would sight 28 U-boats, attack 19, sink 4, and severely damage 3, becoming the most decorated ASW pilot in Coastal–deviated from the rule of fast descent by stalking a sighted boat from cloud cover, and only when positioned to make an attack up or down the boat's track at an angle of about 20° would he initiate his dive. Bulloch did not fly patrols in May, but spent the month instead testing a new rocket-propelled weapon, to be used in action for the first time on 23 May, at the Aircraft and Armament Experimental Establishment at Boscombe Down.)[40]

During the final stage of the run-in, aircraft should descend to 50 feet and deliver their attack as nearly as possible along the track of the U-boat, taking their point of aim according to the following data:

(1) The time from the release of a depth charge from 50 feet to detonation at the shallow setting (25 feet) is approximately 5 seconds (2 seconds in the air and 3 in the water).

(2) If the U/Boat is in process of crash-diving, her speed will be approximately 6 knots (10 feet per second). Therefore, if the U/Boat is attacked while some part of the hull is visible, the centre of the stick should be aimed 5 × 10 = 50 feet ahead of the conning tower (or its estimated position) at the time of release.

(If the conning tower is itself in sight, however, at the time of release, it is desirable to make this the aiming point, although theoretically the stick will then fall 50 feet behind it.)

(3) If the U/Boat has dived before the depth charges are released, the stick must be aimed a certain distance ahead of the swirl, the apex of which is made by the foremost end of the conning tower. This distance is, of course, that run by the submarine between its final disappearance and the time of detonation of the depth charges. Assuming that the speed of the U/Boat is 6 knots, the distances are as follows:

Time of Submersion to release of DC's	Distance to aim ahead of swirl
5 secs.	100 ft.
10 secs.	150 ft.
15 secs.	200 ft.
20 secs.	250 ft.
25 secs.	300 ft.
30 secs.	350 ft.

(4) If the periscope only is sighted, the speed of the U/Boat will probably be only about 2 knots, i.e., 3.4 feet per second, hence the stick should be aimed 5 × 3.4 = 17 feet ahead of the periscope at the time of release.

NOTE: An additional allowance must always be made for the underwater travel of the depth charges (40 feet).

If the U-boat had just submerged, the approximate length of its diving swirl (100 feet) could be used as a yardstick for estimating the distance ahead that D/Cs should enter the water. It was unlikely that a D/C attack would be successful, however, if the U-boat had been submerged for more than 30 seconds, in which case *baiting* tactics might be employed: In these maneuvers, the aircraft set course from the position of the swirl to a distance of at least 30 miles and remained outside that range for not less than 30 minutes; then it returned to the same position, taking advantage of cloud, sun, or weather conditions for concealment, in the expectation that the U-boat would have surfaced again. When a surfaced U-boat used its flak against the aircraft–most boats were then equipped with one 20mm cannon and several machine guns on the bridge–the decision on how to respond rested with the aircraft Captain, but the Tactical Instruction made it clear what was expected of him: "He must remember that the primary reason for his existence is, for the time being, to kill U/Boats and that a U/Boat on the surface presents a much better chance of a kill than one submerged."

The point was made that a U-boat's bridge made a very unstable gun platform in any kind of sea and particularly if the sea was beam-on, and that even a large aircraft properly handled and using its forward guns presented a fleeting, dangerous, and difficult target. Aircraft Captains should therefore press home their attacks against enemy fire, preferably from dead ahead, "making full use of the front guns to kill the U/Boat's gun crews or at least to keep their heads down." (The U-boats, for their part, were instructed when under attack to keep the aircraft on a stern bearing in order to present a small target–though, ironically, this helped the aircraft to drop a D/C straddle up track–and to use all available flak and machine gun fire simultaneously. When the aircraft began its final run in, the U-boat should initiate evasive maneuvers at maximum speed using full helm. In cases where a strong crosswind was blowing, the U-boat's avoiding action should be to windward in order to take advantage of the aircraft's drift sideways.)

Aircraft carrying six or fewer D/Cs on hunting patrols or sweeps, such as Derange, should drop the whole load in one stick; aircraft carrying more than six should drop sticks of six. Aircraft on convoy or other escort duty should drop sticks of four, leaving D/Cs for a possible second attack; this rule could be altered at the Captain's discretion, for example when nearing his PLE or while returning to base. After carrying out an attack on a diving boat by day, the aircraft must drop a marker on or beside the swirl. By night the position must be marked by flame floats, usually two dropped at the same time as the D/Cs.

For purposes of assessment and so that every possible lesson could be learned from each attack, a complete and detailed record, for example, of the exact time lapse between submersion of a U-boat and the release of D/Cs, should be kept by members of the crew. "The story should be complete to the smallest detail and even facts which may appear irrelevant should be included." Within twenty-four hours a connected account should be written down and read by the crew.[41]

Not all of these rules were observed to the letter, as will be seen in the after-action reports that follow. Some pilots, following Terence Bulloch's example, fudged the rules and had unorthodox successes. But in the main, Coastal's tactical doctrine proved out not only in the Bay but also in the convoy routes. The mole, it turned out, had a lot to fear from the crow.

At 2055 GMT on 30 April (all times that follow are GMT), L/L Wellington "N" of 172 Sqdn. lifted off from Chivenor in Devon, bound southwest to the Derange ribbon, where the cloud was 4/10ths to 7/10ths with bases at 2,000 feet, the sea moderate to rough, the air bumpy, and visibility 2–4 miles. At 0007 on 1 May, Pilot Flight Sergeant Peter W. Phillips was patrolling in the ribbon at 1,200 feet on course 168° when he obtained an S/E contact (Special Equipment, a code word for A.S.V. Mark III 10cm radar) bearing Green (starboard) 45°, range 6½ miles. Phillips dived on the surfaced U-boat, which was proceeding inbound on a course of 132°at seven knots, and, after reaching 550 feet three-quarters of a mile from the target, he "struck" (switched on) the Leigh Light. The run-in was made on the U-boat's port bow at 80° to track, while the Navigator, Sergeant H. A. Bate, fired about forty rounds from the front gun before it jammed, and at 0100 Phillips released six Mark XI Torpex D/Cs set to shallow depth and spaced 50 feet apart from a height of 75 feet. All were seen by the rear gunner to explode with blue flashes, two to port and four to starboard; Nos. 2 and 3 were thought to have been very close to the U-boat's hull.

During the aircraft's pass over the target a shudder was felt underneath, though no gun fire was observed. (An hour after the attack it was found that the hydraulic system had been damaged; not known until landing was that the port tire had been punctured.) Phillips made a 180° turn to port and, four minutes later, flew back over the attack position, which was marked by flame floats. Except for a patch of foam and bubbles, nothing could be seen, not even a diving swirl. After twelve more minutes in the vicinity, Phillips resumed patrol. At 0452 he and his five-man crew landed at the nearest base, Predannack in Cornwall. As they did so, the port landing gear collapsed, and the aircraft swung off the runway and slammed into a Nissen hut. Beyond scratches, the crew were not injured. The base Medical Officer pronounced them "very lucky."[42]

The U-boat they had attacked, U–415 (Oblt.z.S. Kurt Neide), returning from her first war cruise, was also very lucky. Damaged by Phillips's D/Cs, she would be attacked twice more before the day was out. At 1136 she was visually sighted on the surface in visibility 15 miles, at 44°35′N, 10°37′W, by Sunderland "M" of Royal Australian Air Force (RAAF) No. 461 Sqdn., flying on Derange. Bearing Green 30° at a range of 5–6 miles, the U-boat was estimated at 6 knots on a course of 100°. Seeing the aircraft approach, U–415 dived. Pilot Flight Lieutenant E. C. "Bertie" Smith, DFC, put the flying boat into a dive and attacked the swirl 18 seconds after submergence from the U-boat's port beam, dropping four Mark XI D/Cs set shallow and spaced 200 feet apart from a height of 50–75 feet. The D/Cs straddled the U-boat's line of advance 70–100 feet ahead of the apex of the swirl. No

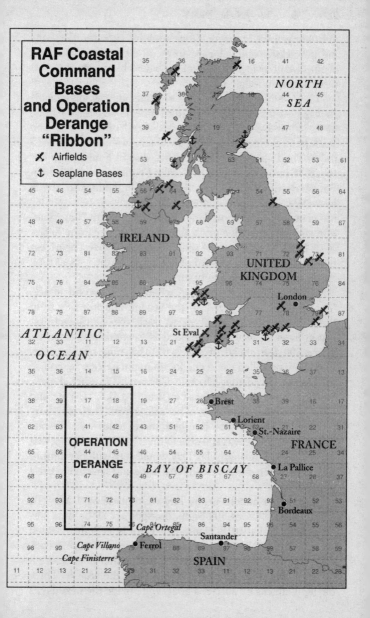

RAF Coastal
Command
Bases
and Operation
Derange
"Ribbon"

✗ Airfields
⚓ Seaplane Bases

NORTH
SEA

ATLANTIC
OCEAN

IRELAND

UNITED
KINGDOM

London

St Eval

OPERATION

DERANGE

BAY OF BISCAY

Brest

Lorient

St.-Nazaire

FRANCE

La Pallice

Bordeaux

Cape Ortegal

Santander

Cape Villano
Cape Finisterre

Ferrol

SPAIN

debris appeared, however. Smith took his aircraft off on baiting procedures and returned in cloud 29 minutes later, but again saw no evidence of damage where his sea marker had disappeared in rough seas.

U–415 had received a severe shaking but was still intact.[43] At 1727 she was sighted for a third time, in position 44°13′N, 10°23′W, by Derange aircraft Whitley "E" of 612 Sqdn. The sea had moderated to a slight swell and visibility was still 15 miles. The U-boat was bearing 180°, distant 5 miles, at a fast speed, 15 knots, on course 090°. Pilot Flight Sergeant Norman Earnshaw descended from 3,000 feet, intending to attack from the U-boat's port quarter at 20° to track. As he began his run in at about 150 knots, U–415 opened fire with 20mm cannon and light machine guns. Earnshaw's release from 90 feet of six Mark XI D/Cs, set to shallow, spaced 200 feet apart, exploded 200 feet to starboard of the target, as the U-boat took hard evasive action in a tight turn.

Kicking rudder, Earnshaw set up for a second attack. Meanwhile, U–415 dived. In the second attack, made from the U-boat's port beam at 90° to track, two D/Cs were released from 70 feet and exploded 28 seconds after submergence 300 feet ahead of the swirl. This time oil was seen. Earnshaw patrolled the scene for 40 minutes, then set course for base at Davidstow Moor in Cornwall.[44] Further shaken, U–415 limped on to her base at Brest. At BdU, Dönitz and Godt were relieved to learn of her safe arrival. Their war diary recorded: "U–415 was bombed three times . . . Despite much damage she was still able to dive."[45] The good luck that carried U–415 through May Day would stay with her until 14 July 1944, when she struck an RAF mine and sank in the Brest approaches.

Two other attacks in the Bay were made on 1 May: At 0825, Halifax "C" of 502 Sqdn. dropped six D/Cs on a surfaced boat, and at 1015, Hampden "L" of 1404 Sqdn. released six on a surfaced boat. Initial contact was made by eye in each case. Return fire was not observed from either boat before it dived. There were no visible results from the attacks. Three daylight attacks on surfaced boats were made the next day, 2

May: by Sunderland "R" of 10 Sqdn. at 0810; by Hudson "W" of 269 Sqdn. at 1437; and by Whitley "G" of 612 Sqdn. at 1531. In the first and third attacks initial contact was by eye; in the second it was obtained by S/E. None of the boats was reported to have fought back.

The first kill in May was made at dusk that day by Flight Lieutenant "Bertie" Smith and his ten-man Australian crew in the same Sunderland "M" they had flown the day before (which deserves mention only because it should be noted that air crews frequently switched aircraft from day to day within a squadron). Smith was trolling in the Derange ribbon at 2,500 feet in the base of 6/10ths cloud. Visibility was 10–12 miles. The darkening sea below was rough in 26–knot winds from 010°. At 1917, eyeballs sighted a U-boat on the surface bearing Red (port) 45°, range 10 miles. Smith estimated it to be traveling at 10–12 knots on an outbound course of 270°. He pushed forward his four engine throttles and climbed into cloud, where he turned to make his approach. At four miles from the target he dove from the cloud. On sighting the flying boat, the U-boat responded with flak and machine-gun fire, and when Smith was down to 300 feet and ½ mile distant, the U-boat abruptly altered course to port. Smith was able to complete his run-in from the U-boat's port beam at 90° to track, while RAF gunner Sergeant R. MacDonald swept the deck with fire from the bow turret. Just before release from an altitude of 50–70 feet, the U-boat gunners were seen scrambling for the conning tower hatch.

Four Mark XII D/Cs straddled the boat just aft of the tower, after which the boat described a tight circle, apparently out of control, then came to a gradual stop with a bad list to port. A large volume of brown vapor blew out from its stern and a white vapor plume rose about three feet from its port quarter. Then a heavy flow of oil was observed pouring from its port side. Meanwhile, Smith was making a climbing turn to 500 feet to set up a second attack, which he delivered at 75 feet with four D/Cs released from the target's starboard bow at 15° to track, again straddling the tower. The now gravely wounded boat settled by its stern. The oil patch spread to 300 yards in diameter. Some fifteen crewmen were seen jumping into the water, where they waved frantically at the aircraft. Then, at 1940, the U-boat's stern sank beneath the waves; its bow followed, reappearing twice briefly at an angle of 30°. The victim was U–465 (Kptlt. Heinz Wolf, 28 years old, from Emmerich/Rhein), on her third war patrol. Smith and crew remained in the area for 30 minutes, then, having reached PLE, returned with their victory photographs to base at Pembroke Dock in South Wales.[46]

Two daylight attacks were made on 3 May against boats sighted on the surface in the Derange ribbon: by Sunderland "S" of 461 Sqdn., at 1044, and by Whitley "R" of 10 Sqdn. O.T.U. In the first instance, the initial contact was made by eye and four D/Cs were released 22 seconds after the U-boat had submerged. In the second, the contact was also made by eye, and five D/Cs (one having hung up) were released while the boat was still on the surface. There were no visible results in either case. On the next day, 4 May, Halifax "S" of 58 Sqdn. was on morning patrol, having lifted off at 0555 for the Derange area, where the seas were very rough under 7/10ths–8/10ths cloud, visibility 8–10 miles. At 1740, the crew made the visual sighting of a creamy wake, bearing Green 90°, which led to a surfaced U-boat, outbound from base at 6–8 knots on a course of 270°, distant 4–5 miles.

Pilot Flying Officer John M. Hartley turned to starboard, lost height rapidly, and approached out of the sun. At 1,400 yards the U-boat opened fire with what Hartley thought was an impressive amount of armament: "heavy guns" from the afterdeck, followed at 1,200 yards by "cannon at the front of the bridge," and later by cannon on the forward deck and two pairs of machine guns on a stepped gun platform in front of the conning tower. He could see about fifteen of the boat's crew, most of them manning the cannons and guns, but two men in black uniform and another in a white sweater, all wearing peaked caps, standing on the deck at the port side of the tower. Hartley ordered answering fire against the pugnacious boat, which scattered some of the men manning cannon and machine guns, the rest maintaining heavy and light flak.

By evasive action Hartley managed to prevent his four-engine Halifax from being hit by that fusillade, and at a quarter of a mile from target, he leveled out to release six Mark XI D/Cs from the U-boat's port quarter at an angle of 60°–70° to track. The navigator firing the front gun saw one man on deck hit and fall overboard. Altitude at the time of release was a relatively high 200–400 feet. The rear gunner reported that the D/Cs straddled aft of the conning tower, two on the port quarter and four on the starboard beam. In addition, the gunner had fired 500 rounds at the tower and hull as the aircraft passed. But the U-boat submerged thirty seconds after the Halifax, turning back, caught sight of it again, and no damage was visible, only the usual D/C scum. Baiting procedure was followed, Hartley returning at 0910, but the marker could not be found. With PLE reached at 1000, the Halifax returned to base, landing at 1258. Subsequent assessment by NHB/MOD has identified the boat as U–*190*, which suffered "slight damage," nothing to prevent her continuing on Feindfahrt.[47]

Three more attacks in the Bay were made later in the day: by Halifax "A" of 502 Sqdn. at 1920, by Catalina "J" of 202 Sqdn. at 2110, and by L/L Wellington "P" of 407 Sqdn. at 2309. In the first, initial contact was made by eye and six D/Cs were released on a surfaced U-boat. In the second, contact was also made by eye and five D/Cs (one hanging up) were dropped 37 seconds after submergence. In the third, contact was obtained by S/E and six D/Cs were dropped 10 seconds after submergence. No results were evident, but minor damage was done to U–*405* (Korv. Kapt. Rolf-Heinrich Hopmann) by the Halifax, and the target of the Catalina was later assessed to be U–*600* (Kptlt. Bernard Zurmühlen).[48]

Three daylight attacks were made on 7 May in the Derange area, the first two on diving boats by Wing Commander Wilfrid E. Oulton of 58 Sqdn. At 0656, just after dawn (Oulton forbade his crew to eat breakfast prior to a morning flight because it put "spots," not U-boats, before the eyes), Oulton sighted a U-boat's wake from the cockpit of Halifax "S," dived on the target, and dropped six D/Cs over its swirl 10–15 seconds after the U-boat's submergence. And at 1015, Oulton dived on another U-boat's wake and released three D/Cs on the submerging boat while its conning tower was still visible. The first attack yielded no visible results. The second, now known to have been against the outbound U–*214,* badly wounded her Commander, Kptlt. Rupprecht Stock, and forced the boat back to her base at Brest. Oulton's aircraft received machine-gun hits during the run in.[49]

The third attack was made by Sunderland "W" of RAAF. 10 Sqdn. Flying on Derange, aircraft captain Flight Lieutenant Geoffrey G. Rossiter and his eleven-man crew had been airborne from Mount Batten in Cornwall since 0635 when, at 1023, they sighted a wake, then the conning tower, of an outbound U-boat on the starboard beam, distant 10 miles. As the flying boat turned to attack, the U-boat, now known to have been U–*603* (Oblt.z.S. Rudolf Baltz), dived and disappeared, making attack inadvisable. Patrol was resumed at 2,000 feet just below 6/10ths cloud base, and at 1220 a fully surfaced U-boat was sighted through binoculars 17 miles away on the starboard bow, in position 47°06′N, 10°58′W. The sea state was moderate, the wind was 235° at twenty-six miles per hour, visibility was twenty miles. Rossiter estimated the U-boat to be making 12 knots on an outbound course of 280°. He made a climbing turn into cloud and broke out of it on course 225°with the still-surfaced U-boat four miles distant on the starboard bow.

As he pushed the elevator column forward into a dive, the U-boat altered course to starboard. Rossiter turned with it and ran in across track 60° on its starboard quarter, the nose gunner opening fire with 100 rounds at 800 yards range, scoring hits on the conning tower, where two men were seen. From a height of fifty feet Rossiter released four D/Cs that straddled the boat just forward of the tower, and the resulting explosion plumes completely obscured the boat. Before the explosions, as the aircraft passed, the tail gunner fired 600 rounds at the tower. Rossiter pushed hard left rudder and turned the ailerons for a quick return to the site. Setting up, he attacked a second time, from the U-boat's port quarter at 45° to track, again releasing four D/Cs from fifty feet. The first

D/C fell within twenty feet of the port side aft of the tower; the three remaining overshot.

The U-boat, plainly wounded, made several complete tight circles to starboard at 4–5 knots, trailing oil and gradually losing way. At 1300 it submerged slowly on course 090°, still putting out oil, and disappeared bows up four minutes later. By 1330 a crescent-shaped oil patch 250 yards in diameter and 500 yards in circumference covered the site. The Sunderland remained in the area for another hour and a half, then shaped course for home with its photographs, becoming waterborne at Mount Batten at 1655. Rossiter received the DFC for this action. The NHB/MOD assessment has identified the stricken U-boat as U–663 (Kptlt. Heinrich Schmid). Seriously damaged, she sank the next day with all hands, probably as the result of these injuries.[50]

An eight-day drought in Bay attacks ensued, owing in great part to heavy pro-German weather that greatly restricted visibility. Then, on the 15th, with visibility improved to as much as 25 miles, there were six attacks in one day, all in sunlight, all resulting from visual sightings in the Derange ribbon. The first, by Liberator "O" of 224 Sqdn., was made at 0936 on a U-boat that had submerged 15 seconds before six D/Cs were released. The boat, now known to be U–*168* (Kptlt. Helmuth Pich), which was returning from its first war cruise during which she participated in the Battle for ONS.5, was not damaged. The second attack, by Whitley "M" of 10 Sqdn. O.T.U., was delivered at 1127 against a boat that took five D/Cs (one hung up) on the surface. It has since been identified as U–*648* and assessed as undamaged.

The third attack, again by Whitley "M," at 1233, was directed at another surfaced boat, outbound from base, since identified as U–*591* (Kptlt. Hansjürgen Zetzsche). Though the Whitley had only the one previously hung-up D/C to drop, which did no damage, the aircraft's nose machine gun wounded the Commander and one crewman, forcing the boat's return to base. The fourth attack, by Whitley "B" of Sqdn. O.T.U., was made at 1314 on another outbound surfaced boat. The six D/Cs released caused slight damage to

U–*305* (Kptlt. Rudolf Bahr). The fifth attack, by Whitley "S" of 10 Sqdn. O.T.U., was delivered at 1403 against the outbound, surfaced U–*211* (Oblt.z.S. Karl Hause), which was not damaged.[51]

The sixth and final attack of the day took place at 1810 when the sun was low and there was a bright glare on the water. Pilot Wing Commander Wilfrid E. Oulton of 58 Sqdn. had lifted off in Halifax "M" from St Eval at 1208 and now was on a routine rectangular creeping line ahead patrol at position 45°28′N, 10°20′W, where he swept the sea below with Polaroid glasses. There was 1/10th cloud at 6,000 feet, the sea was moderate to rough, winds were 080° at twenty-four mph, visibility was 10–15 miles in haze. Ahead a V-shaped wake slowly emerged into view bearing Green 30° distant 10 miles. Realizing that he was up sun where he could stalk, Oulton let down gradually to 2,500 feet, and at four miles range sighted a U-boat on the surface, speed 10 knots on an inbound course of 070°. He circled to starboard and descended through 1,500 to begin the run in. At 1,000 yards the navigator opened fire with the nose gun and saw hits on both the conning tower and hull. At a height of 100–120 feet the Halifax released six D/Cs from the U-boat's port quarter at 10° to track. After crossing, the rear gunner got off additional rounds at the tower and hull and watched for results of the explosions. He reported that two or more D/Cs at the end of the stick fell against the port side of the boat.

When the explosion plumes subsided and the boat could be seen again, the fore part of the hull appeared to lift; then, two to three seconds later, there was a "sudden jerk," and the boat stood up on its stern in a completely vertical position with the bows above water. After Oulton completed a turn for a second attack, he could see a large light blue oil patch and "greenish white water" boiling around the upright 20 feet of bows. The victim's condition was such, Oulton decided, that he could save his remaining D/Cs for another boat. Two minutes following the attack the U-boat's last apparition of "gray with brown patches" slid beneath the waves. At 1827, Oulton set course on the homeward leg and was down at St Eval by

2125. The U-boat sunk was the returning U–266 (Kptlt. Rolf von Jessen), which had been Group Fink's lead scorer in the Battle for ONS.5[52]

With good weather holding, No. 19 Group had another full day on the 16th when five attacks were made in the De-range patrol area, all as the result of visual sightings. The first, by Whitley "E" of 10 Sqdn. O.T.U., was made at 1143 on a diving boat, since identified as U–648 (Oblt.z.S. Peter-Arthur Stahl), which was not damaged. The second attack, by Wellington "H" of 311 Sqdn. (Czech), was delivered at 1410 on a fully surfaced boat, since identified as U–662 (Kptlt. Heinrich Müller), which was not damaged. The third attack, by Liberator "M" of 224 Sqdn. at 1450, was against the same U–648 (Stahl) that Whitley "E" had attacked with six D/Cs three hours before. Now, attacked on the surface with six more D/Cs, the lucky boat escaped again with no damage. The fourth attack, by Liberator "E" of 224 Sqdn., was made at 1650 on a diving boat, which was the same U–662 (Müller) attacked by Wellington "H" two and a half hours before. This time the boat suffered minor damage. Another lucky boat. But, like U–648, she would be sunk within the year.[53]

The killing attack of the day would come at dusk, 2007, when conditions were 1/10th cloud, bases 20,000 feet, sea moderate, wind 110° at 25 mph, and visibility 10 miles in haze. Halifax "R" of 58 Sqdn. made a visual sighting of a narrow brushstroke of a wake across the evening's dark gray surface. The wake was on bearing Red 100°, distant 6–7 miles. Pilot Flight Officer A. J. W. "Tony" Birch immediately altered course to port. The U-boat, when seen, was on an outbound course of 270°, speed 10 knots. Realizing that he could not lose sufficient height in the distance given, Birch made an alti-tude-losing turn, keeping up sun of the U-boat, finally making his run in from due west of the target, out of the sun. Eventu-ally seeing him, the U-boat dived. Birch's six D/Cs dropped while the conning tower was still visible. Because of glare on the water, the rear gunner could not get an exact fix on the stick placement, although, according to the aircraft's after-action report (Form 540), it was thought that one D/C fell 100 feet ahead of the swirl and the remainder in the swirl or wake.

When Birch circled back over the scene, he observed a patch of blue oil. Shortly afterwards, the mid-upper turret gunner sighted what appeared to be a body. Birch dropped a marker and flame floats, then at 2018 set course away on baiting tactics in company with Halifax "B," which had been flying about five miles to the west and had witnessed the attack. When both aircraft returned from baiting, they found a large irregular-shaped patch of blue oil a quarter- to a half-mile in extent. Also seen nearby was a circling Sunderland ("T" of 10 Sqdn.), which reported by R/T that it had seen and photographed wreckage. Shortly afterwards, the Sunderland sighted two bodies and wood planking, although these did not show up in the photographs. Halifaxes "R" and "B," having reached PLE, returned to base, where they sat down at 2345 and 2350. The U-boat was the Type XIVU–463 (Korv. Kapt. Leo Wolfbauer), one of Dönitz's prized tanker boats, under way from Bordeaux on her fifth supply cruise. She was the first Milch Cow to be sunk. There were no survivors.[54]

On the 17th, Halifax "D" of 58 Sqdn. released six D/Cs on U–628 (Kptlt. Heinz Hasenschar), the shadower boat of the Battle for ONS.5, which was returning to base. The U-boat was not damaged. One attack was made at 1721 on the 20th, by Wellington "G" of 172 Sqdn., following an S/E contact. The identity of the target, depth-charged 40 seconds after submergence, is not known. On the 21st there were three attacks, all as the result of visual sightings. At 1459, Whitley "Q" of 10 Sqdn. O.T.U. attacked U–634 (Oblt.z.S. Eberhard Dahlhaus) 21 seconds after submergence. This boat, which had been damaged in the Battle for ONS.5, was not damaged a second time. At 1756, Whitley "H" of the same squadron attacked a boat, thought possibly to have been U–230 (Kptlt. Paul Siegmann), 30 seconds after submergence. And at 2031 Liberator "D" of 224 Sqdn. attacked a boat, thought possibly to have been U–525 (Kptlt. Hans-Joachim Drewitz), 15–20 seconds after submergence.

Three more attacks came on the 22nd. At 1123, Halifax

"O" attacked a boat, unidentified, 30 seconds after submergence; at 1154, Whitley "D" attacked a surfaced boat, unidentified; and at 1227, Whitley "G" attacked an unidentified boat 12 seconds after the conning tower had disappeared. The first of two attacks on the 24th was made by Whitley "J" of 10 Sqdn. O.T.U. at 1122 against a fully surfaced boat, unidentified, that offered no return fire.[55] But such was not the good fortune of Sunderland "L" of 228 Sqdn., based at Pembroke Dock, which four and a half hours later encountered U-441, the first of two VIIC boats converted to anti-aircraft role (Flak-U-boot), the other being U-256.

In this modification a quadruple 20mm cannon was mounted on a raised platform before the bridge, two single 20mm cannon on the after end of the bridge, a 3.7cm gun on a raised platform abaft the bridge, and another "quad twenty" on an extension to that platform. The curtain of fire produced by that amount of armament was formidable. The task given U-441 (Kptlt. Götz von Hartmann), which sortied from Brest on the 22nd, was to operate entirely on the surface in the Bay, attacking Allied aircraft and giving cover to damaged boats unable to dive. When Sunderland "L" made her run in against the boat at 1400 she passed, bleeding, through a hail of fire. Pilot Flying Officer H. J. Debden managed to straddle the boat with his D/Cs before, fatally wounded, his "Queen" plunged into the sea. The entire eleven-man crew was lost. But U-441 was also badly wounded, and had to return to Brest, not to sortie again until 8 July. On the 12th of that month she was dived on by three cannon-equipped Beaufighters of 248 Sqdn., which killed ten U-boat men and wounded fifteen others, including the Commander, forcing the boat back to Brest again. Her sister boat U-256 did not put to sea until October, and, after one less than successful patrol, was reconverted to an attack role.[56] The flak-boat idea was not working.

Attacks were made on a submerged boat on the 29th by Beaufighter "O" of 236 Sqdn., employing a new "R.P." rocket-propelled warhead (see chapter 10); on a surfaced boat on the 30th by Liberator "G" of 224 Sqdn; and on a submerged boat, again on the 30th, by Halifax "E" of 502 Sqdn. All three attacks resulted from visual sightings. None was assessed as causing damage.

The last day of May was one on which, it could be said, No. 19 Group snatched the hood from the falcon. Seven different Derange aircraft made eleven attacks (including second attacks by individual aircraft) resulting in two U-boats destroyed and a third forced back to base. Liberator "Q" of 224 Sqdn. obtained an S/E contact in daylight and dropped six D/Cs on a surfaced boat, causing no visible damage. Fortress "A" of 206 Sqdn. scored the first success of the day, visually sighting a wake and then a surfaced U-boat at 1151. The aircraft attacked from one point abaft the boat's starboard beam with six D/Cs, obtaining a straddle of two explosions on the starboard side and four on the port. During the run in two German crewmen were seen manning a gun on the bandstand (*Wintergarten*), but no fire was observed. Although the Fortress crew saw nothing more than a spot of oil in the explosion mark, British interrogators later learned from captured crewmen from the attacked boat, which was U–523 (Kptlt. Werner Pietzsch), sunk on 25 August 1943, that in A/206's depth-charging she suffered damage to two tanks and had to return to base.[57]

The *coup de théâtre* on the 31st was a joint attack by four aircraft on a U-boat first visually sighted on the surface in position 46°35′N, 10°40′W. Cloud was 5/10ths, bases at 3,000, tops at 5,000. The sea was moderate. Wind was 260° at twenty-five knots. Visibility was fifteen miles. Running parallel to the Biscay coast and creeping westward; Wing Commander Oulton of 58 Sqdn., seen before on the 7th and the 15th, was dipping his Halifax "R" in and out of the cloud base when at 1550 his flight engineer sighted "white horses" bearing 20° Red, distant six miles. Oulton altered course, climbed into the cloud, and increased revolutions per minute (RPMs) and manifold pressure. At four miles from the estimated position of the wake-making U-boat, Oulton dived out of the cloud at a steep angle so as to give the mid-upper turret gunner an opportunity to spray the U-boat's tower and put the German gunners "off their job a little."

After leveling off at 80–100 feet, Oulton made his run in from starboard quarter at an angle of 30° to track, dropping six Mark XI Torpex D/Cs set to shallow depth and spaced 86 feet apart, while the U-boat was still fully surfaced. Photographs later showed a straddle midway between the conning tower and bow. After getting off gun bursts, the rear gunner reported that as the explosion plumes fell away, the U-boat was observed to be "wallowing" in the D/C pool. Oulton circled tightly to port and returned to the scene from dead astern on a westerly course, firing rounds as he came and releasing three more D/Cs. When the spray subsided, the U-boat was seen to be stationary in the center of the D/C scum.

Out of D/Cs, Oulton circled around and made a gun run about 300 yards to port of the injured boat, firing from both the mid-upper and rear turrets. The U-boat was now lying beam on to sea at a northerly heading, surrounded by a large oil patch and considerable wreckage. Twice more Oulton returned to rake the boat with gunfire, now seeing individual crewmen emerge from the tower hatch and run along the deck. Soon there was answering 20mm fire from the boat, but it was inaccurate, and was quickly suppressed. On another weaving, up-and-down pass Oulton saw bodies lying on the bridge. He climbed to 3,000 feet and reported the action to St Eval, suggesting that a reinforcement be sent.

This was done, and at 1710 Halifax "J" of 58 Sqdn. homed in to the position on Oulton's W/T. Since the pilot could not find the U-boat, Oulton led him down to it, then banked off about 200 yards on J/58's starboard to give him covering fire. The U-boat was now circling to port. The J/58 pilot made an attack but dropped his six D/Cs 100 feet off-target. On a second attack run he missed again by the same margin. Oulton later said sympathetically that the pilot, young in age and experience, was "over-anxious." The J/58 stayed around and poured about 200 rounds into the conning tower, on which five crew members were seen; then, at 1275, sighting a Sunderland at 180°, the pilot flew off to attract the flying boat by Aldis lamp signals to the scene. This was Sunderland "E" of 10 Sqdn. At nearly the same time a second Sunderland, "X" of

228 Sqdn., was sighted, and it too was invited to attempt a coup de grâce.

The E/10 swept in from 40° on the U-boat's starboard bow and dropped four D/Cs that straddled the target. Previously able to maneuver, though trailing oil, the U-boat, now badly shaken again, lost way and stopped. The E/10 wheeled around for a second attack, which she delivered at 1747 from the starboard beam. Four more D/Cs descended on the stubborn boat. Three overshot, but one exploded about 30 feet distant from the "yellowish brown" hull, forward of the conning tower.

Sunderland X/228, nearby, watched E/10's two attacks and then, at 1750, made one of her own, from the starboard quarter to the port bow, with four straddling D/Cs. She returned two minutes later with four more D/Cs, which entered the water forward of the conning tower. When the second stick exploded, the U-boat shuddered, and bodies were thrown into the air along with the spray. Shortly afterwards, thirty to forty bodies, some still alive, were seen in the water, suggesting that the crew were on deck in the process of abandoning ship when the last attack was made. Oulton, who was still around, flew over the scene and dropped two rubber dinghies and two Mae Wests. "At that point, I felt very sorry for those poor devils in the water," he said later. "They had only been doing their duty as they saw it and were as brave as any other combatant."[58]

When the boat disappeared from view, both E/10 and X/228 left the scene, satisfied that the thoroughly hammered enemy craft had been destroyed. The U-Boat Assessment Committee agreed with them and gave major credit for the kill to Oulton in R/58, who carried out the first two attacks, causing severe damage, and homed in another aircraft. But it also praised the teamwork exhibited by the other participating pilots. In a rare personal expression, the Committee commented: "A triumph of co-operation and a good party in at the death."[59] Oulton was awarded the DSO and DFC for this and previous actions. Pilot of E/10 Flight Lieutenant Maxwell S. Mainprize and pilot of X/228 Flight Officer William M.

French each received the DFC. The U-boat sunk was later identified as the Type VIIC U–563 (Kptlt. Gustav Borchardt), which had sortied from Brest on her eighth war cruise two days before.

While that remarkable series of attacks was taking place, Sunderland "R" of 201 Sqdn. was patrolling Derange in position 45°38′N, 13°04′W when, at 1711, a surfaced U-boat was sighted visually, bearing 240°T, distant 8 miles, on an outbound course of 250° at 5–6 knots. Pilot Flight Lieutenant Douglas M. Gall immediately headed straight downhill from 5,000 feet at 150 knots. It was his crew's first-ever U-boat sighting after many fruitless and boring 15–hour patrols, and he was not going to let this chance go by if he could help it. The only thought that deterred him was that this submarine might be "one of ours." When he saw light pulses from the boat he feared that they might be Aldis lamp flashes of the recognition Letter of the Day, but a Scottish gunner put his mind at ease: "He's no' flashin,' skipper; he's firin'."

Gall made his run in up the U-boat's track at 50 feet off the deck. In the last seconds of the approach, when it appeared that his four–D/C drop might miss the U-boat to starboard, the U-boat suddenly made a turn to starboard directly into the stick(!). When the explosion plumes subsided, the U-boat was observed to proceed on course for approximately half a minute, then to sink by the stern at a steep angle into the dark malls below.

After making a circuit to port, Gall and his crew saw the surface shimmer from two heavy underwater explosions. One or two minutes later, they watched the sea "effervesce" over an area 200 to 300 feet in diameter and become pale blue and brown in color. A large oil patch appeared and eventually extended a half-mile in diameter. At 1753, Gall's aircraft resumed patrol with the crew cheering loudly at their triumph. But, as Gall said later, his own feelings were the same as those of Oulton after U–563–"the poor devils!"[60] For the action he received the DFC. The boat was later identified as U–440 (Oblt.z.S. Werner Schwaff), which had sortied from St.

Nazaire on the 26th, bound for what she hoped would be her fifth war cruise.[61]

No. 19 Group, and units of No. 15 Group attached to it, did not accomplish May's six sinkings and seven damaged U-boats in the Bay transit area without losses of their own, nineteen aircraft in daytime and two at night. Twenty-eight percent (6) of the losses were to enemy aircraft, mainly JU88C6 heavy fighters based on the Biscay coast at Kerlin Bastard near Lorient and Bordeaux Mérignac. Also active, and possibly responsible for daylight losses to "unknown causes," were four-engine Focke Wulf 200S at Bordeaux and shorter-ranged FW190S at Brest. Another 28 percent of aircraft (6) were lost on takeoff or landing crashes. Twenty-four percent (5) were shot down by U-boat flak. And twenty-one percent (4), including two L/L Wellingtons at night, were lost to unknown causes. (Aircraft occasionally lost engines; the twin-engine Wellington VIII could not maintain altitude on one engine. Some aircraft, as earlier noted, flew into destructive weather systems; some, through navigational error, went down from fuel exhaustion; still others, when close to the sea, hooked a wing on a wave and cartwheeled in.)

The human casualties in the Bay during May were ninety-four crewmen killed, seven missing, and six taken prisoner (from the shotdown Whitley "N" of 10 Sqdn. O.T.U. on 30 May). An additional fifty-two men, two with injuries, were rescued by their countrymen. The number of airmen both killed and missing (101) compares with the number of U-boat crew members killed on six boats, which was 264, figured on the typical Type VIIC crew list of forty-four. The number of U-boat crewmen lost or wounded on damaged boats is not known. The total hours of RAF and RAAF flight time from liftoff to landing required to destroy six boats and damage seven was 6,181 in daytime and 1,314 at night: that is, 1249 flight hours per U-boat sunk, or 576 hours per boat sunk or damaged.

On the strength of the numbers given above it is difficult to assess whether BdU's policy of maximum submergence at night saved more U-boats than would have been saved had most submerged hours been observed by day, as was the practice prior to May. Certainly in favor of the May policy were the five known aircraft shot down in daylight, actions that not only saved the U-boats involved but also inflicted material and human losses on the enemy, which would not have been likely if attempted at night. Without real numbers for comparison the question remains speculative, but the historical judgment continues to be that the Dönitz/Godt policy was mistaken.[62]

Although No. 19 Group was never able to put in the air the full requirement of 260 aircraft specified in both the Stark and Admiralty plans, proportionately, for the number of assets that could be made available, and taking into account the spanner thrown into the plans by BdU's surprise nighttime submergence policy, it was thought by both the Air Ministry and AOC-in-C Coastal Command Air Marshal Slessor that Operation Derange had matched the predictions put forth in Raushenbush's paper. The 103 sightings and 68 attacks in the Bay in May conformed to the numbers crunched in Raushenbush's "slide rule strategy."[63]

Twice Slessor went on record to that effect, first on 12 May in the 18th Meeting of the A.U. Committee, when he stated: "An analysis over the past four weeks of operations in the Bay of Biscay showed that the number of sightings and attacks accorded with the previous estimates that had been submitted to the Committee."[64] And on 23 May, in a "Comparison of Actual and Estimated Results," Slessor reported to the A.U. Committee that his general conclusion, based on a sufficiently long period of operations to permit such a conclusion, was, in the case of Derange, "that the difference between theory and fact is very small—in fact the two can never be expected to approximate more closely in war." (Nor could there ever be a more candid concession to strategy by slide rule.) "The analysis of those operations, therefore, can be taken as bearing out the calculations used in A.U. (43) 84 and 86."[65]

The latter document cited (86) was the Rauschenbush paper (Stark Plan). The former (84), cannily, was Slessor's own "Value of the Bay of Biscay Patrols" Paper, in which he had consigned the Bay offensive to the status of "a residuary legatee." If anyone knew, he did, that while there had been 103 sightings and 68 attacks in the Bay during May, there had been 110 sightings and 67 attacks elsewhere in the Atlantic during the same period; and that, while *six* U-boats had been sunk and seven others damaged in the Bay, during May there had been *nine* sunk and four damaged by Coastal aircraft giving cover to threatened convoys. Slessor had loyally come on board the Raushenbush strategy. But he had been vindicated, too.

Of such judgments it is not thought that Stephen Raushenbush had any direct knowledge. After Enclose I, learning that his permanent position at the Department of the Interior was in jeopardy, he resigned from the Navy and returned to Washington to reclaim it–and to enter an obscurity from which only now he has been delivered. Virtually unknown for the brief but impressive role he played in the making of Black May, he died in 1991 at the age of ninety-five in Sarasota, Florida.[66] Evan James Williams, it was earlier noted, died in 1945. Patrick Maynard Stuart Blackett, Baron Blackett, of Chelsea, died in 1974.

Inside The U-Boat Mind
The Latimer House Discs

HERMANN KOHLER (U–*175*): There are only four things you are allowed to tell as a POW, otherwise you will be guilty of betraying your country. Our Commander read it out to us: your name, rank, number, and home address–you mustn't tell them anything else.

29 APRIL 1943

HELMUT KLOTZSCH (U–*175*): It gets worse and worse, all the U-boat men are grousing.
ADOLF MARCH (U–*175*): Now it practically amounts to this: as soon as one U-boat is put into commission, another is lost at the same moment.

26 MAY 1943

KLOTZSCH: Things look very bad for us. The boats are being sunk one after the other.

13 MAY 1943

WILHELM RAHN (U–*301*): To tell the truth, I haven't much hope. They'll crush us in time.

3 MAY 1943

During the war, approximately 5,000 German prisoners were captured from 181 U-boats. Most of them, ranks and ratings alike, were passed through the Combined Services Detailed Interrogation Centre, U.K., which, in 1943, was situated at Latimer House, Chesham, Buckinghamshire, northwest of London. There, each man was purposely billeted with a POW from a different boat, or a surface ship, or a Luftwaffe bomber or fighter squadron. The expectation was that a U-boat POW who did not previously know his roommate(s) would want to explain in detail his experiences at sea, how his boat was sunk, his boat's operating systems and weapons, the layout of his home base, and his general thoughts about the war. Such raw, contemporaneous accounts, British Intelligence apparently believed, equaled or exceeded in value the often guarded information that the POWs gave to Interrogation Officers in formal debriefings. For that reason, each living space was secretly bugged with hidden microphones that picked up most of what the POWs said to one another, and a team of "listeners"–native German speakers able to identify voices–clandestinely recorded their conversations on shellac-covered metal discs.

The data were then transcribed in both the original German and English translation onto typewritten forms headed with the words: "This report is Most Secret. If further circulation is necessary, it must be paraphrased so that neither the source of the information nor the means by which it has been obtained is apparent." There is no indication in the record that the listeners had any ethical scruples about what a later period in history would call "invasion of privacy." A similar bugging operation was conducted immediately after the war, from July to December 1945, when ten German nuclear scientists were detained in Farm Hall, Godmanchester, near Cambridge. Latimer House, however, was apparently the first large-scale deliberate operation of clandestine recording of ordinary conversation.[1]

The Latimer House transcripts are housed in the Public Record Office, Kew, under Crown Copyright.[2] The extracts given below focus mainly on U-boat men captured in April and May and on conversations of men captured earlier but recorded during May. Several conversations from March, June, and August are included because of the interesting character of the information contained. The writer has endeavored to make a representative and balanced selection of conversations that fall generally into four categories: (1) operational experiences at sea; (2) technical equipment, including torpedoes; (3) the home front and Biscay bases; and (4) questions of morale and the course of the war.

The reader will find that many of the conversations are flat and passionless; some even banal. It is typical sailors' talk, with predictable criticism of superiors and occasional belly-aching–or, as the British translation expresses it, "grousing." One hears exaggerations, misconceptions, and falsehoods, as well as authentic experiences and feelings. There is little that can be called wit or intended humor; and, considering the circumstances, that should not be surprising. How much vital information the Intelligence people drew from the extracts given here is not known. Probably some of the data contributed to the overall interrogation summaries that were printed up periodically.[3]

What, then, are the transcripts' special value to the present narrative? The answer must be that fifty-five years after the events of spring-summer 1943, they provide us the only existing completely fresh, artless, and uninhibited disclosure of the U-boat mind: what these men were thinking and feeling *at the time*. Whereas officers and crewmen interviewed in the 1990s concede that details once green in memory have now gone gray in mind, and that the immediacy of once-intense experiences has dissipated through the wake of years, in these long-ago recorded voices we hear U-boat men as they were, in the months of their testing.

All but one of them cited here are now dead, according to the files of the Verband Deutscher U-Bootfahren e. V. (U–Boat Veterans Association) in Hamburg. On the "listeners" forms they are identified only by number. Walter Köhler, for example, a *Matrosenobergefreiter* (Seaman, first class) captured from U–752 on 23 May, was identified as N 1635; and Helmut Klotzsch, an *Obersteuermann* (Navigator) captured from U–175 on 17 April, was identified as N(Am)15, the "Am" indicating that he was captured as the result of an American action, namely depth charges and gunfire from the U.S. Coast Guard cutter U.S.C.G.C. *Spencer*. At some point in the later history of these transcripts someone (one of the listeners? one of the former POWs?) wrote the prisoners' family names alongside their numbers. The names correspond to names on the U-boat crew lists preserved in the U-Boot-Archiv at Cuxhaven-Altenbruch, where founder and director Horst Bredow was able to supply as well many first, or given, names.

Because not every word or phrase spoken by the POWs was captured on the discs, there are numerous ellipses in the transcripts. Additional ellipses were entered on the following extracts by the writer in order to pass over uninteresting detail or confusing phraseology. Occasionally a word or phrase was added in brackets to identify persons or U-boats or to help the flow of speech: here, as in similar transcripts of unguarded conversation, one learns that people do not always speak in complete sentences. Numerals were written out to conform with speech, *Captain* was changed to *Commander,* and British spellings (e.g., *harbour, defence*) were changed to American forms. Briticisms such as "That's not cricket" were left untouched.

All the speakers in these extracts are identified in the endnotes, where the reader will find each POW's family name, and given name if it is available in the records; the U-boat on which he served; his rank or rating together with the U.S. Navy equivalent; and his date of capture.[4] The first section of the extracts, which focuses on experiences at sea, begins, for example, with conversations between Heinrich Schauffel, a *Leutnant zur See* (Ensign) from U–752, captured on 23 May; Werner Opolka, an *Oberleutnant zur See* (Lieutenant [jg]) from U–528, captured on 11 May; and Karl-Heinz Foertsch, a *Leutnant (Ing.)* (Ensign, engineering duties) from U–659, captured on 4 May. The date of each recording is given below the extract.

SCHAUFFEL: A bomb fell on the after deck of [Kptlt. Heinz]Wolf's boat [U–465] . . . Everything was ripped open, but the bomb didn't explode. We once got a depth charge on deck and were unable to submerge with it, yet they couldn't remove it. It had gone through the woodwork and was so jammed that we couldn't get it out. It happened in the Bay of Biscay and we fought off aircraft for two days.

FOERTSCH: Kapitänleutnant [Heinrich] Schmid [U-*663*] got a direct hit on the metal of his outboard tank, but the thing glanced off.

SCHAUFFEL: Did you hear that the outboard tank of a boat had come off?

OPOLKA: Not the whole outboard tank, but the outer covering was torn off; there are double ribs in it and you couldn't break them down. [Oblt.z.S. Karl] Hauser [U-*211*] once came back with all his compensating tanks smashed. Also, in the Bay of Biscay, he got eight depth charges, four on the surface and four when submerged. The external pressure connection for the quick-diving tank was broken, then the compensating tanks and the oil compensating tanks. . . .

SCHAUFFEL (?): Yes, our boats can take tremendous punishment.

OPOLKA (?): You can do anything you like with them.

Recorded 10 June 1943[5]

FOERTSCH: Not far from the American coast . . . unloaded the two hundred kilogram mines. At first the Commander wanted to see what it looked like there; we rushed off at three-fifths speed, which was reduced to one electric motor at "dead slow." That's how we went along. It wasn't pleasant, sitting right in the harbor entrance.

SCHAUFFEL: Which harbor was that?

FOERTSCH: Over at Jacksonville.

SCHAUFFEL: That's in the south, isn't it?

FOERTSCH: Florida.

SCHAUFFEL: The main thing is that some [merchant ships]ran on to them.

FOERTSCH: Yes. Three of them.

SCHAUFFEL: Does that count?

FOERTSCH: Certainly, they count a tremendous number of points. . . .

Recorded 7 June 1943[6]

OPOLKA: It said on the wireless: "[Korv. Kapt. Hans-Rudolf] Rösing has gone." I bet he laughed!

SCHAUFFEL: He's a smart fellow.

OPOLKA: First-class fellow; he looks very fit, but he's got gray hair.

SCHAUFFEL: He hasn't made many long-distance patrols.

OPOLKA: Three, I think.

SCHAUFFEL: He got the Knight's Cross—what for?

FOERTSCH: He sank one hundred thousand tons.

SCHAUFFEL: Kretschmer was the BdU's favorite, wasn't he?

OPOLKA: The BdU has his favorites, that's quite right. Topp, Kretschmer, Engelbert Endrass, Suhren.

SCHAUFFEL: Endrass was always rather quiet.

OPOLKA: Very quiet, yes; it's a pity that he has gone. It isn't known at all how that happened. We lost five boats there.

SCHAUFFEL: On one convoy?

OPOLKA: Yes, Gibraltar convoy. Endrass, [Eberhard] Hoffmann—

FOERTSCH: Nico [Nicolai] Clausen was nearly lost, too.

OPOLKA: If he hadn't previously rammed the steamer—he still got home.

SCHAUFFEL: His hair has gone gray, too.

OPOLKA: From the last patrol.

SCHAUFFEL: Yes, because of abandoning ship, and water, et cetera.

OPOLKA (?): They did target practice on the U-boat, with flak and ten-point-five [gunfire]. The whole conning tower was shot to bits. Half of the hatch came down on his head. His whole head was full of splinters; his lower jaw was broken, and he was badly cut about below the eye; he couldn't . . . his mouth, he couldn't see. He was picked up by a cutter.

SCHAUFFEL (?): Where did that happen?

OPOLKA (?): In the Atlantic. . . .

Recorded 11 June 1943[7]

SCHAUFFEL: [Werner] Hartmann [U-198] is at sea again, isn't he?

OPOLKA: Yes. He's had some successes, too, and [unclear name] should be *Kapitän zur See* now.

SCHAUFFEL: Hartmann too.

FOERTSCH: Is he *Kapitän zur See* now?

OPOLKA: Yes.

SCHAUFFEL: [Unclear name] has gone, hasn't he?

OPOLKA: Yes. [Otto von] Bülow was very successful!

FOERTSCH: Aircraft carrier . . .

SCHAUFFEL: He's a smart fellow.

FOERTSCH: He was the captain of my training boat–a grand fellow. I know him very well: he couldn't [get on] with [Paul] Büchel, who treated him very badly, very shabbily. I couldn't bear Büchel.

SCHAUFFEL: [Otto] Schuhart was the best of the lot.

Recorded 9 June 1943[8]

APEL: I remember once, the first convoy on my first patrol. The Commander approached–the whole day long we were forced down by aircraft and destroyers; they kept on forcing us to submerge. We were just in contact and wanted to get ahead of it when a destroyer was reported and we submerged. The next time we were ready again– "Aircraft!"–and down we went. The convoy got away every time until one night we had crept up and got well ahead of it. We had gotten right through and had already gone to action stations, ready to attack; the bow caps were open, and we were about to fire. The Commander had picked out a nice eighteen thousand-ton ship that he wanted to sink, when suddenly– *"Pschew, pschew, pschew!"* Starshells! *Bang!* Hell broke loose. The Commander shouted: "Destroyer! Destroyer! Destroyer!" All three were coming for us. "All torpedoes in the tube." All of a sudden we heard the sounds of propellers and *"tsch, tsch, tsch, bang!"* The fun began. It was only a few seconds before we had fired where the ship was lying, and they had located us by radar, which was quite new at that time. They didn't actually see us, the weather was very bad–it was up here between Iceland and England. They fired

starshells and the moment the starshells exploded they
naturally fired their guns of all calibers from two to fifteen
centimeters. They kept on booming away, there were
crashes all round; we submerged immediately; there were
a few depth charges, but not many. They only dropped
eight of them very close to us and a few more farther away
and then they couldn't find us again. Suddenly we surfaced, but the convoy had gone. Then we went after it
again. That day we got another . . . full from the aircraft.
The next day: "Destroyer!" "Crash dive to periscope
depth!" "Action stations!" The Commander said: "I'm going to sink the destroyer. Is everything ready?" Two destroyers; suddenly he zigzagged! The whole . . . made
off. That was another fiasco for us.
Recorded 19 May 1943[9]

NAVIGATOR FROM THE SURFACE SHIP *REGENSBURG:* They
  search the Bay of Biscay, I suppose, don't they?
APEL: They must have a regular sort of patrol there. One formation relieving another, because they know all the
  U-boats have to go through there. For the most part we
  proceed submerged there. You only surface for fresh air
  and in order to charge the batteries and even *then* you are
  disturbed a few times. On our last patrol we were in difficulties on the return trip. We were already near land, we
  could see the French coast, but we were rather far south in
  the Bay of Biscay and we had to proceed northwards
  along the French coast. We still had four hours before getting to the German patrol boat, and then we were located
  by an aircraft. Now the water was only about sixty-five
  meters deep, added to which the whole area was covered
  with wrecks, perhaps even old ground mines, which were
  lying below. In any case, we couldn't dive. It [the aircraft]
  located us continually, but we were lucky right until we
  met the escort, and after that it didn't come back.
Recorded 21 May 1943[10]

APEL: We had followed a convoy across from America. We
  followed it over nearly to England. Then we had warning

of an aircraft; it had been seen rather late. We immediately opened the air vents, that is to say, we dived; the bow and the conning tower were submerged. Do you know how we dive? The English, Italians, and Japanese all come on under power, stop both engines, and let themselves go down. We, the Germans, were the first to hit on the following idea. . . . We are moving along, the alarm is given, and down we go at full speed; you have to hold on to prevent yourself from falling flat. Both hydroplanes right down. Down at three-quarters speed. Occasionally–the Engineer Officer sees to it, that it never occurs too markedly–but this time we had a tremendous list. We were down by the bows, and lying at an extreme angle. And this list is intensified by the fact that the last air vent of the last diving tank is opened up later, and through that the boat goes down still more by the bows. Now the bow and conning tower were submerged; the stern still showed. Then five bombs fell directly over the boat and shook us terribly. Everything flew about. As a result of the fact that we weren't so . . . deep and the bombs were so near; all mechanical and electrical installations failed. The light was out, we were in darkness. Both the engines and the electric motor[s] were put out of action. The main switchboards were blown out, the automatic fuses were burnt out. Our hydroplane motor was out of order. The hydroplanes were still right down. If the engines [electric motors] had gone on working we should inevitably have carried on down with the hydrophones in fixed position until there was a crash. But perhaps we might have been able to crank up the hydroplane at the right moment by hand, but that always takes time and the high speed . . . we should have certainly gone right down out of control. The hydroplane position gauge–we had a mechanical and an electric gauge–was put out of action, too. So we would have had no idea, if the button had been pressed, in what position the rudder would have been. The main rudder was out of action. In short, all sorts of safety installations and everything were not working. The light soon came on again, just switched over. Then the light was on, we let in the main switch, the engines turned again, the motors were repaired; it all went quickly; in any case the boat was again ready to submerge. Just a matter of luck.

Recorded 19 May 1943[11]

APEL: Our boat was sixty-eight meters long. Every conceivable corner was stuffed with provisions. Every few days you're done out of your sleep. Either the torpedoes have to be brought up, or a convoy is reported, or there are destroyers or something about, or the W/T operator reports propeller noises.

My U-boat was the first German U-boat that managed to get through up there between Iceland and Ireland without interference and without being spotted. After that every other boat up there got done in. But we owe it to the extremely bad weather alone that we weren't spotted by any aircraft. A number of U-boats have been destroyed there . . . [Pause] German espionage is very much up to the mark. We knew about practically every convoy, we knew when it put out from New York or wherever it was, and exactly of what it consisted.

Recorded 20 May 1943[12]

APEL: On the last patrol but one we had two destroyers at our heels. They forced us to remain submerged for twelve hours and dropped their depth charges—we counted thirty-six of them, which fell quite close to us—the others were farther off, we didn't count them. He [one of the destroyers] dropped depth charges, which made a terrific noise. The destroyer was sailing at three-quarters speed, and at that moment they couldn't hear anything themselves. Every U-boat always makes good use of that moment if depth-charges are being dropped. We were at three-quarters speed, helm hard over, and above all we made it a habit, when we were depth-charged, immediately to rush to the bilge suction pumps, because they couldn't hear us and we kept trying to get a little water out of the trim regulator. We never had any luck, air kept . . .

in between. . . . Suddenly, after about ten hours, one of the crew and I succeeded. The pump sucked in and we were able to expel a thousand liters of water in all, out of two tanks. The boat became so light again that, without any difficulty and without changing the speed, it could remain at a uniform depth. There was no need to alter the speed now. We proceeded silently, very gently, and he could no longer hear us; he lost us and proceeded in a completely different direction. We made our escape. . . . We once had an alarm owing to aircraft, a Sunderland flying boat. The fellow succeeded in forcing us to remain submerged for seven hours. He dropped a bomb every ten minutes to the second, and always near us. We couldn't surface. Either it was the same aircraft, though I don't imagine so, or it may have been relieved at intervals. A Sunderland. In the middle of the North Atlantic. We were about half-way between North America and Ireland. Exactly every ten minutes he dropped a bomb. It was quite extraordinary. The devil even tracked us from the air. That is an entirely new English discovery and I don't know if we know [about] it, at any rate it was quite unknown to us . . .

NAVIGATOR FROM THE SURFACE SHIP *REGENSBURG*: Did the steamer get away?

APEL: The steamers? Oh, they had all gone! [Pause] I know of one boat where the Commander was absolutely determined to score a proper hit. He approached so close to the ship before he fired that his boat sustained such serious damage from the explosion of his own torpedoes, that he only got home with great difficulty.

Recorded 19 May 1943[13]

KLOTZSCH: . . . The fellows are supposed to defend themselves against aircraft.

ARENDT: Yes.

KLOTZSCH: Proceeding on the surface on a zigzag course is more successful than submerging.

ARENDT: Yes, actual flak cruisers are being built now—U–flak cruisers for the Bay of Biscay.

KLOTZSCH: Well, it's not much good if they are only being built now. They ought to have been ready at the beginning of the war.

Recorded 14 May 1943[14]

ARENDT: We had the cross.

KLOTZSCH: We had the fixed G.S.R.

ARENDT: With the [magic] eye on it?

KLOTZSCH: Yes.

ARENDT: A Funkmaat of our flotilla invented that, at sea. He got the Iron Cross, Class One, for it, and five hundred Reichsmarks.

KLOTZSCH: Good Lord, how stingy!

ARENDT: Well, it doesn't work properly. They've got something else now.

KLOTZSCH: We couldn't locate anything with the [magic] eye, but only listen, in the same way as the old G.S.R. used to work.

ARENDT: When we were on our journey home from our last patrol, on the last night but one, we were suddenly right in the beam of a searchlight. A Steuermann happened to be on watch. He came rushing down.

KLOTZSCH: Did you submerge?

ARENDT: Yes and got away. They had a . . . searchlight. They came from straight ahead. He [the pilot] must have miscalculated, perhaps he hadn't got his bombs quite ready and only the lamps in the petty officers' quarters came down; nothing else was broken. He dropped four bombs. It was just the same when we sailed out there. We submerged and got away and he, too, dropped his bombs quite wide. He didn't hit anything at all. We always got through safely, without any damage, except for the last two times, the last patrol, when we were coming into port, and this time, when we were setting out. Before that we never had any aircraft.

Recorded 13 May 1943[15]

KLOTZSCH: On the trip before, we were at a depth of only eighteen meters. The aircraft was very near. Our present First Officer of the Watch was on duty and he saw it too late, gave the alarm, and the aircraft banked and came towards us and dropped its load and they exploded at eighteen to twenty meters off. We were forced up to the surface by the blast and then the boat went down out of control. We were forced up twenty meters so that the whole boat was on the surface, and then went down again, right down deep, and then we regained control, and then we blew the tanks so that the boat rose, and then we flooded them again, but we couldn't flood them quickly enough, and we remained on the surface for seven minutes with the conning-tower hatch closed down. The Commander went straight back to the periscope and said: "Flood the tanks, he's making another approach, flood the tanks!" It [the diving system] was all out of action. "He's making another approach, flood the tanks!" And he behaved like a madman up in the conning tower, shouting: "Flood them, flood them, he's making another approach, Chief Engineer!" You can't imagine what it was like. I was standing in the control room and thought: "Now one more bomb on us and it will be all up!" He had gotten plenty of time to aim, we were a fine target, floating about on the surface with our conning-tower hatch closed, but he hadn't any bombs left, so he just fired at us with his guns and scored a few hits on the upper deck, in the woodwork and covering of the conning tower. If he had had any bombs we should have been done for, all right. That's the worst of all—when you just wait without being able to defend yourself.

Recorded 3 May 1943[16]

KLOTZSCH: Soon we shall have reached the point where we shall have built a thousand U-boats and if about fifty U-boats go for a convoy—even if it is escorted by twenty destroyers—they will be able to do nothing against them [the U-boats]. They'll exhaust their supply of depth charges, without knowing where to drop them. You saw that in this convoy, when we shot up three hundred thousand tons [*sic*].

CHIEF RADIOMAN FROM THE SURFACE SHIP *SILVAPLANA*: You weren't there yourself, were you?

KLOTZSCH: No. But people who actually participated in this witch's caldron said that not one of the English who had lived through this bombardment would ever sail again. It was such a hell of fire, flames, noise and explosions, dead bodies and screams, that none of all the ships' crews will ever go to sea again. That is definitely one up to us, a clear moral victory, if the enemy's morale should deteriorate to such an extent that he should have no further desire to go to sea. But if they really get short, they will force the crews to sail, exactly as we do.

RADIOMAN: They [the English] are forced to do that already . . .

KLOTZSCH: One U-boat was depth-charged off Finisterre and let in a tremendous amount of water. She sank immediately down to a depth of one hundred fifty meters and settled on the bottom. The crew were standing up to their knees in water and they waited until all was quiet above and then they pumped out the water with bilge pumps and came to the surface again, and in the night they did some welding on the upper deck and got back safely.

On a former patrol we suffered more serious damage than on this one. We remained at a depth of two hundred meters from two o'clock in the afternoon until eleven o'clock at night with battery gas escaping in the boat, which we trimmed only by moving the crew. [Pause]

Near Barbados, off Kingston harbor, we saw English officers strolling on the beach with native women.

Recorded 6 May 1943[17]

KLOTZSCH: We get twenty-five hundredweight of fresh potatoes. Of these I throw ten hundredweight away. Then everything tastes of oil. Fresh vegetables last perhaps eight days. We can't take any more with us, otherwise [they] would go bad. Then fresh bread lasts fourteen days at the most; the stuff lies all over the place in the boat. . . . It is everywhere, in the bilges. The bread lies under the diesel, the sugar and the flour behind the electric motor, everything in tins, flour, rice, eggs, semolina, and everything imaginable. We get about thirty-five hundred tins of milk and about four thousand eggs. We get two eggs every morning and when they begin to go bad, two every evening as well, so that they get eaten up instead of our having to throw all the bad ones overboard. Then the bad eggs smell and they are lying all over the place! Ten cases, each containing three hundred sixty, is three thousand six hundred eggs. Therefore, towards the end, the bad ones are already beginning to smell and then, naturally, one can't find and take out the eggs which are lying right down in the middle, so they too begin to smell. There is always a smell somewhere. Both the "heads" always stink, and everything else, too. There is such a stink, such a fug, such muck and filth, and then on top of all that you start eating this tinned stuff! Then there's all the pill-swallowing business, which nearly lays you out, against scurvy or pyorrhea [inflammation of the gum and tooth sockets causing loosening of the teeth], then against. . . . So that the keenness of his eyesight should not be affected the bridge lookout is given pills to take.

CHIEF RADIOMAN, *SILVAPLANA*: Did you join up voluntarily?

KLOTZSCH: If you can call it that, voluntarily, like everyone else. I didn't want to volunteer, I didn't want to have myself to blame if anything happened to me. So I waited to be called up.

CHIEF RADIOMAN: All the battleships have been put out of service, anyway.

KLOTZSCH: These Petty Officers, third class [*Bootsmaate*] are so completely dumb, [and] those who [are] now . . . noncommissioned officers [*Unteroffiziere*]—never in all my life have I seen such stupidity.

Recorded 3 May 1943[18]

KLOTZSCH: The First Officer of the Watch who left the boat on the last trip, is now in command of a boat himself.

CHIEF RADIOMAN, *SILVAPLANA:* Who is that?

KLOTZSCH: Oberleutnant [unclear name]. He was rather effeminate. In broad daylight once, south of the Azores, he had the port sector [to watch], that is, the sector in which the sun rises—we were on a southerly course—and there he stood on the bridge, singing popular songs and so on. Suddenly the Unteroffizier [in the sector] next to his reported: "Herr Oberleutnant, there is a ship in your sector." There was a twin-funnelled neutral passenger ship lying there, her engines stopped, and she'd already given the recognition signal. Since they had the sun behind them, they'd seen us for a long time and we'd continued to head straight for them, so they said to themselves: "Here's a U-boat, she will probably stop us and demand a recognition signal," so they'd stopped already. All the neutral ships know that, they've all been stopped any number of times. He [the First Officer of the Watch] had allowed them to come within eight hundred meters and hadn't seen them. Just suppose it had been a destroyer or an enemy armed ship—that would have been the end of us, all right! What a peach our First Officer of the Watch was!

CHIEF RADIOMAN: Imagine a fellow like that having command of a boat now!

KLOTZSCH: I'm sorry for his poor crew. All the things we put up with are still in store for them. Everyone in the boat pitied the crew he'd got.

CHIEF RADIOMAN: I shouldn't like to sail under anyone like that.

KLOTZSCH: No more would I but what can you do? . . . Our Second Officer of the Watch, who has now become First Officer of the Watch, once failed to see a flying boat, a huge crate, three hundred sixty miles from land, in broad daylight. We were on a northerly course and it was on a westerly one, which meant that it was at right angles to us, a long way away on the starboard side. The idiot of a Second Officer looked out and saw how the flying boat turned towards us as soon as they saw us, and instead of taking evasive action at high [speed] on the surface, and making off on a zigzag course to allow them to fly over us and drop their bombs, and *then* submerge–because that gives you much more time–he gave the alarm, with the result that everything inside the boat was put out of action and we went down out of control. . . . It was a bad mistake on the part of the bridge watch, the First and Second Officers of the Watch–people like that make your hair stand on end! . . . We were on a homeward course. . . . Suddenly [an aircraft] approached on the starboard side . . . The [helmsman]had . . . the helm to fifteen port and had gone to sleep. I gave him a kick in the pants, all right. It often happens that the helmsman falls asleep, because he sits in the conning tower and for four hours on end has nothing else to do but steer, and if you've got the middle watch, when there's nothing happening in the conning tower and [only a] few smokers join you–smoking is allowed in the conning tower–

CHIEF RADIOMAN: Even when the hatch is closed?

KLOTZSCH: No. In areas where there is danger from aircraft no one is allowed up on the bridge except the four men and the Commander, who sometimes goes up. [In other areas] there are two or three men smoking in the conning tower. When one goes below, the next man may come up; when we're in the middle of the Atlantic or a long way away, some are allowed up on the bridge.

Recorded 7 May 1943[19]

VOELKER: I was going through the Bay of Biscay . . . [and the order was given] to surface: "Look out!" and we submerged again. After about an hour we surfaced again, "Look out!" and down we went again. It went on like that all night long for two nights. We had only just been on the surface for a minute or two and the top of the conning tower was scarcely out of the water when he [the Commander] shouted: "Look out!" and we submerged again and went to action stations. There must have been one aircraft after the other up there. There is always a commotion when we make a crash dive. There was one man in the boat who had his peaked cap on and it got stuck in the conning-tower hatch and when we submerged he couldn't close the hatch. All the water was coming in from above, and the water was pressing down on it and it took two men to pull the cap out!

Recorded 4 May 1943[20]

RADIOMAN FROM THE SURFACE TANKER *GERMANIA:* What else were you attacked by?

KALISCH: Destroyers, corvettes and those fast bombers too.

RADIOMAN: Fast is a slight exaggeration.

KALISCH: At sea they always seem to be fast. Believe me. We detect the aircraft and they're over us in no time. You've hardly started . . . before they reach you.

RADIOMAN: Where would you be now, if you hadn't been captured?

KALISCH: In the North Atlantic. We should be homeward bound now.

Recorded 13 May 1943[21]

VOELKER [Re: sinking of U–*175*]: They had caught sight of our periscope and had also DFed us. We were at a depth of twenty meters and then dived and stayed down. The blast from the depth charges was terrific; we lost control of the boat, everything was smashed. The water was coming in and everything was creaking, groaning, and crackling. We were at a depth of two hundred thirty-forty meters. It was pure chance that we were able to get ourselves up again, pure luck.

When we dived the bow caps were open and we couldn't shut them again. They had been bent by the depth charges, so we went down to two hundred meters.

NAVIGATOR FROM THE *REGENSBURG:* Wouldn't it have been better to have fired them [the torpedoes] out quickly?

VOELKER: That can't be done. You can't get them out.

NAVIGATOR: The water pressure was twenty atmospheres.

VOELKER: We fire at fifteen atmospheres. [Pause] The poor

fellows who are now at sea! In the old days it used to be pleasure trips, even in the little two hundred fifty-ton boats, but now—!
Recorded 9 May 1943[22]

ROSS: In the Bay of Biscay we proceeded submerged during the night. It used to be the other way around. When you've been on duty for four hours in the U-boat and then suddenly come into the fresh air, your strength seems to ebb away. You go quite limp and don't feel like doing anything; you just lie down. When you submerge normally—it's simply called "submerging"—it's exactly like a crash dive and is done just as fast, the only difference being that the bell is not rung. They keep on bringing in something new, until the word *submerge* will simply be forbidden. However, when the command "submerge" [*Tauchen*] or "crash dive" [*Alarm*] is given, or "Action Stations," or some such thing, you know at once, you hear that even in your sleep.

In the Bay of Biscay every day at two o'clock . . . punctually at two o'clock, another day it might be five minutes past or five minutes to, but the fellow [enemy aircraft] was always there about two o'clock. We were proceeding along the coast of Spain and the Commander would say: "We'd better look out, he must be coming soon." The Commander went on to the bridge and then he gave the alarm. They had . . . already seen . . . [the aircraft]. Schultze [Kptlt. Heinz-Otto Schultze, U–*432*] had wonderful eyesight.

MARCH: It was the same in our boat. You might have seen nothing at all, but the Commander would have already sighted something long before.

ROSS: His eyes are keen after years at sea.
Recorded 29 March 1943[23]

PINZER: On the long Africa patrol . . . I was looking round and suddenly I saw a destroyer. You could see her with the naked eye. . . . When we submerged we were forty-five degrees down by the bows. In the electric motor compartment there were sacks of dried potatoes and they suddenly burst. They lay strewn about the Petty Officers' quarters and all over the whole galley; the whole diesel compartment and the bow compartment were full of dried potatoes. In the wardroom as well. . . . All the kitchen utensils got piled up forward in the bow compartment.

RICHTER: . . . On the very first patrol. A devil of a sea. The old hands who were with us said they had never before experienced such seas. It was just about Christmastime. We were proceeding between Iceland and the Faroe Islands on Christmas Eve.

PINZER: When, this last Christmas?

RICHTER: Christmas Eve. I was as sick as a dog.

Recorded 2 June 1943[24]

ELEBE [U–752]: Our morale was about as good as if we were being led to the slaughterhouse. You must remember it was the first patrol and when we saw something we submerged immediately. The Officers of the Watch had a regular slanging match [drag-out quarrel]–it's a wonder they didn't come to blows.

KEITLE [also from U–752]: Yes, that's quite true.

ELEBE: Our officers never dared open their mouths because they knew nothing about it [the boat] and all our Unteroffiziere . . . were old experienced men.

KEITLE: That was the sad part about it: "I'm an officer, you can tell me nothing." Yet what could you say to the lad, he's nineteen–.

GRÄTZ: They wouldn't have got away like that with us.

KEITLE: That was some boat! It was bound to sink! We all said that on the first day.

ELEBE: We said that right from the beginning. *"They* put the boat into commission–*we'll* put it out of commission again." That was obvious from the beginning, first as a joke, and afterwards–my God, how we dreaded this patrol, we older ones. "They should skip this patrol and go straight on to the next." That's more or less how we were talking. And that turned out to be correct, as they introduced a sort of military atmosphere in our mess, with physical training every morning and other such nonsense. We definitely didn't make faulty trials, as normally the engines ran quite well. To think that that damned aircraft had to drop its nice little bomb right where the outer tanks on the pressure hull are! . . . Put out of action immediately as the safety valves in the diesel were smashed, and the fuel began to run out. Up by the outside locker a stream of water came from the Chief Engineer's cabin. Had it only been water which got in, the Chief Engineer could have held the boat, but it was fuel. It was already over the deck plates in the control room–that's practically half the boat–and it began to run into the batteries. Already some of the cells in the battery had broken. And what an atmosphere in the boat! It was icy cold. It felt like minus sixty degrees centigrade, and then we were down by the stern . . . three quarters speed, dead slow. The main air valve was blown off.

Recorded 31 May 1943[25]

SCHAUFFEL: What wonderfully smart boats the [Type] Nine–C boats are!

NOWROTH: That's true.

SCHAUFFEL: They're superb, absolutely superb! What is their diving time like–good?

NOWROTH: It was very good. . . .

SCHAUFFEL: Before you can say Jack Robinson the boat has disappeared.

NOWROTH: . . . But the best time we ever made was thirty-six seconds.

SCHAUFFEL: Good, very good.

NOWROTH: Henke's boat is supposed to have reached thirty-two seconds.

Recorded 1 June 1943[26]

SCHAUFFEL: I'll tell you about us now.

NOWROTH: Who was the Commander?

SCHAUFFEL: [Karl-Ernst] Schroeter [U–752], who has the Knight's Cross. Aircraft forced one boat to submerge.

NOWROTH: Was that in daylight?

SCHAUFFEL: It was at night. We never saw anything, the whole time. We'd already been at sea for five weeks. Afterwards [a message] arrived from a U-boat, I don't know which one. Forced to submerge . . . bearing so-and-so. "The enemy is making off in such-and-such a direction." "We'll see," said the Commander, "I don't believe it, but we can set off now and be there early tomorrow morning." . . . At eight o'clock in the morning aircraft forced us to submerge and we remained submerged until eleven.

NOWROTH: At what latitude was that, roughly?

SCHAUFFEL: It must have been around fifty degrees.

NOWROTH: And the longitude?

SCHAUFFEL: Roughly forty degrees. We surfaced at eleven. I was on watch. . . . When suddenly an aircraft approached on the port side. We didn't stand a chance. . . . . He started dropping his bombs. . . . I went to the machine gun and started firing, but it was too late. It [the plane] was flying at forty meters–just imagine it. I don't know where their eyes were. So we had to submerge. We did so . . . and surfaced again. . . . We should have shot the aircraft down. . . . Two rounds of ammunition misfired. It was impossible to give any sustained fire and then suddenly there was [a]fighter [aircraft] there and he swept our bridge clear . . . everybody killed. I was sitting right in the center. The aircraft fired to the right and to the left of me, but I wasn't hit.

Recorded 31 May 1943[27]

TILLMANNS: We torpedoed an eight-thousand-ton steamer carrying dynamite. It was a surface shot and the ship was blown right out of the water. We were fairly close to it . . . [our]control panel, electric light bulbs, everything was smashed.

Recorded 1 June 1943[28]

[UNCLEAR NAME]: I could distinguish every tree in Russia . . . bushes . . . and in America the coastal road went like this—we could see the houses of the millionaires brilliantly lighted, the lights of the cars shining. You can see the lights at the bends of the road, they shine out over the sea. You can clearly [see] the traffic there. . . .

STOCK: Well, when our U-boat went through the Strait of Gibraltar, I can tell you, it's damn narrow, you could spit across it.

[UNCLEAR NAME]: When you go through with your U-boats, can't they hear you?

STOCK: We go through at night, [and] we're lit up by a searchlight. We slipped through at very slow speed on our electric motor. At that time they hadn't so much D/F gear, et cetera.

Recorded 29 May 1943[29]

LINK: How did they sink you? [Re: sinking of U–752 on 23 May by Swordfish "G" of 819 Sqdn. Royal Navy and Marlet "B" of 892 Sqdn. RN, both from the escort carrier H.M.S. *Archer*]

PINZER: We broke surface and got a bomb from an aircraft.

LINK: How many of you did they rescue?

PINZER: On the destroyer where we were, there were twelve of us. About thirty-five men got out of the boat. We were up near Greenland. Well, we came up with difficulty and they [destroyer crew] hung out ropes, rescue ladders, five in a row—but nobody could get over the railing—it was colder than in Russia. But the men on the destroyer were very decent. We were all given smokes and everything!

Six of our men were aft in the engine room, and couldn't get out. The others all got out. There were very heavy seas running. We were only afraid that the aircraft would fire on us.

LINK: Why?

PINZER: Because they fired right up to the last minute. We could assume that they wanted to fire because we had fired as well. We went on firing to the last round.

LINK: Was it at night?

PINZER: No, about midday. We had submerged on account of aircraft and destroyers, then we broke surface and the Commander kept seeing an aircraft through the periscope, and they told us then that small aircraft had already spotted us under the water, at periscope depth. Then it must have kept right above us. . . . [We]surfaced . . . [son]and suddenly: "Aircraft one hundred meters distant," and instead of opening fire we submerged and were only at a depth of three or four meters when the bomb fell. Immediately a mass of water broke in.

LINK: . . . Where were you based?

PINZER: In St.–Nazaire.

LINK: There's a lot of damage there.

PINZER: The town has been smashed up, but not the shelters.

LINK: No, not the shelters. It is the same in Lorient.

PINZER: The last time they raided there they shot down fourteen aircraft during the night. They dropped bombs and in one night the town became a heap of ruins, but they did *nothing* to the shelters.

Recorded 28 May 1943[30]

WEISSEFELD: Even at sea we had to undergo punishments; we had to do "knee bends" ten times, holding heavy lumps of iron. If one had really committed some bad crime that would have been reasonable, but we were punished for nothing, for forgetting to close a valve or something, which didn't actually endanger the boat at all. The order had been given and if you forgot, you were simply given twenty [knee bends]. I wasn't really upset about it, I knew it was my fault. On the first patrol: when you went through the Petty Officers' compartment at night you were supposed to take off your cap; at night they were asleep in any case, and when they are asleep, why should I take off my cap? One Petty Officer always used to watch out and once he saw a man slipping through with his cap on his head; the next day he had to do knee bends fifty times. The Engineer Officer was just as petty. . . . If we had been able to get home we should have had a fine time lying up for repairs, for at least three months. Everything had been damaged. All the gauges had been smashed. Those lamps, with sort of wire baskets over them, the side lamps were broken, and, of course, most of the bulbs had burst. The emergency lighting was still all right. There were leather bolsters in the bunks which were flying about the bow compartment. In a twinkling the whole boat was devastated [inside] after the first pattern of depth charges. It was only a matter of seconds before the whole boat had been turned upside down.

Recorded 17 March 1943[31]

RADIOMAN FROM THE SURFACE TANKER *GERMANIA*: Is a boat painted each time it sails?

SPITZ: Yes, scraped and repainted.

KALISCH: [Kptlt. Siegfried] Strelow's boat [U–*435*]once came back entirely covered with rust; he had been out for twelve or thirteen weeks. The whole boat was a reddish-brown.

RADIOMAN: What kind of a boat was it, a [Type]Seven-C?

KALISCH: Yes.

RADIOMAN: Twelve or thirteen weeks? . . . needs supplying.

KALISCH: . . . There are also boats which are out for sixteen weeks. . . . They get supplied at sea.

RADIOMAN: Only [Type] Nine boats can stay out for sixteen weeks.

KALISCH: The Seven-Cs too. Why shouldn't a Seven-C remain out for sixteen weeks? Once everything has been used up, it can take on fuel, provisions and, if it needs to, torpedoes as well, at sea. Sometimes they take on torpedoes as well.

SPITZ: That has happened, at the most, two or three times.

KALISCH: But it is possible. The sea must be calm and then they set up the gear.

. . . If you want to take on a torpedo from another boat, when at sea, [the other boat] lowers the torpedo into the water.

RADIOMAN: Simply throw it into the water?

KALISCH: Yes, it floats.

SPITZ: The crane has so much lifting radius that it can pick up [stuff] from another boat?

KALISCH: The boats can't get as close as all that to each other. The swell would bump them against each other. It lowers the torpedo into the water, you pull the torpedo alongside, put a sling round it and haul it up. The only thing is, you mustn't be taken by surprise, or there would be a hell of a mess!

Recorded 16 May 1943[32]

APEL: Corvettes are far the best thing against U-boats, far better than destroyers. We can't get at them because they are built with a shallow draft.

Recorded 21 May 1943[33]

SCHMELING: The good times of U-boat sailing are past.

TILLMANNS: I've been in U-boats since April 1938.

SCHMELING: My cousin was drowned between the twenty-sixth and twenty-eighth of June last year, up there in the "Rose Garden" between Scotland and Iceland. We picked up W/T messages from him and then he was gone; nothing more came through. It was six weeks before his parents got the news: "The boat has been overdue for some time and must be presumed lost." And it wasn't until four weeks after that that they heard he'd died a sailor's death on active service. "He gave his life for Greater Germany."

Recorded 28 May 1943[34]

The second section of extracts focuses on weaponry and detection gear, both German and Allied. There were many more conversations on these and other technical matters than the few extracts reproduced here would suggest, but on the belief that most readers would not want to get caught up too much in the whirring world of machinery and electrons, only six sample conversations on technical matters are extracted here. Less concentrated on May, these conversations stretch from March to August. The favorite subject was the new zigzagging FAT torpedo.

BRÖHL [RE: FAT, OR "CONVOY" TORPEDOES]: It's quite a normal torpedo which has a setting device, so that after traveling a certain distance–FIGHTER PILOT, F.W. 190: What distance?

BRÖHL: It varies. It's adjustable, so that when it goes past the target it doesn't run straight out to the end of its course and then explode, but, after passing the target, it turns round the zigzags, so there is a possibility that after passing it at first, it will still find the target. I can estimate how far away the target is. Then I say it shall be set at twenty-five hundred meters and from there the torpedo makes zigzags.

PILOT: . . . How many zigzags does it make?

BRÖHL: It can go on to the end of its course.

PILOT: How far does such a torpedo run?

BRÖHL: Seventeen thousand meters.

PILOT: I presume they are electric torpedoes?

BRÖHL: Air torpedoes, too.

PILOT: Oh, I see, they're just ordinary torpedoes which run straight. There is this mechanism in them and that's probably what he [Interrogation Officer] meant.

BRÖHL: It's possible he's talking about a different one altogether.

PILOT: The torpedo that you had on board is the "convoy" torpedo, isn't it?

BRÖHL: Yes.

PILOT: And what does that mean?

BRÖHL: Spring mechanism (*Federapparat*).

PILOT: I presume then that this spring mechanism is built into the ordinary torpedo.

BRÖHL: Yes.

PILOT: The spring mechanism is simply a thing which can be set, like my [Luftwaffe] automatic pilot.

BRÖHL: Technically it is rather complicated, making it so that it zigzags and so on. You can set it. For example you usually fire this torpedo at convoys, where several ships are sailing together. Assuming you fire at a particular ship, it [the torpedo]curves around, and if you fire two, three, or

four of these, you can say with ninety percent certainty
that one of them will hit. With a quadruple fan salvo it is
certain, for three or four ships usually sail together.

PILOT: Why did you only have six of these with you?

BRÖHL: They were probably not quite ready, or perhaps they
gave some to each U-boat for practice.

PILOT: How is the setting done?

BRÖHL [DRAWS]: . . . The basic idea is this: . . . I have a
torpedo, it runs for such-and-such a time and for such-
and-such a distance. If I fire at five hundred or a thousand
meters, the remaining sixteen thousand meters are quite
useless. So how can we make use of them somehow or
other?

PILOT: Well, supposing it turns, makes a curve of 180 degrees
when it is ready. What's the setting then?

BRÖHL: I can make the setting according to my own judgment
of what the position is.

PILOT: Let us assume there are three ships at a range of three
thousand meters, a few hundred meters apart—you fire at
the center one—

BRÖHL: I fire at the first ship, which is farthest ahead and lies
in the most favorable position. That is three thousand meters, and I set it for thirty-five hundred, and if it goes past it
begins to zigzag.

PILOT: Yes, how does it zigzag, does it come back on the same
track?

BRÖHL: . . . It makes perfectly ordinary turns on a reciprocal course the whole time. The torpedo travels, we'll say,
one thousand meters back, that is, it travels to and fro
within the area of the steamer's course. You can set it in
several different ways.

PILOT: Is it worked by a spring mechanism?

BRÖHL: That's purely a code name. There probably is a spring
in it.

PILOT: . . . If a torpedo goes past a ship, they think it's all
over and finished with. And then suddenly it comes back
from the other side?

BRÖHL: They can't see the track.

PILOT: Because it's an electric torpedo; that means it can't be an air torpedo.

BRÖHL: It can be built into the air torpedo, and then you simply fire those at night, when you can't see the wake of the torpedoes.

PILOT: The mechanism must be pretty big, mustn't it?

BRÖHL: It's a sort of box, about thirty by thirty centimeters [11.8 by 11.8 inches].

PILOT: It's inside the torpedo; don't you have to take the torpedo out of the tube to set it beforehand?

BRÖHL: It's set by means of a pin.

PILOT: By the Commander or by you?

BRÖHL: By me. There's a pin which goes down into the torpedo and adjusts the setting and then drops out before the torpedo is fired. The torpedoman's mate is responsible for the setting. I give him the data. . . .

PILOT: You must have to take care not to be hit by your own torpedo.

BRÖHL: Yes.

PILOT: How do you do that?

BRÖHL: You make off at three-quarters speed either hard to starboard or hard to port.

PILOT: Immediately after you've fired?

BRÖHL: Yes.

PILOT: How fast does a torpedo like that travel?

BRÖHL: It has a speed of thirty knots. . . .

Recorded 21 March 1943[35]

GASSAUER: [In] the latest innovation, which is already quite old, the torpedo runs towards the target and then makes short loops.

BOMBER PILOT, Ju. 88: Zigzags?

GASSAUER: We've got that too. I can tell you all about that: we call it the FAT. That's a very fine torpedo. You set the preliminary run, that is, you estimate or measure the distance. We'll say the ship is two thousand meters away, so I set the preliminary run for two thousand and I can also set the torpedo to run either to the right or to the left. If I've got the exact range, I set the torpedo for a "short leg"; it can make either short or long zigzags. It then runs straight ahead for the two thousand, allowing for the angle of lead. And supposing it doesn't hit, that it's been fired too short, or too far ahead, then it begins [zigzagging] here. It runs on another three hundred meters and then turns and runs back again.

PILOT: How far?

GASSAUER: Six hundred meters in the reverse direction. Then it runs another six hundred and has another. . . . Supposing the ship is proceeding to port, I set a "left leg" and if it's proceeding to starboard I set a "right leg." I believe it always has a rate of advance of six miles.

PILOT: Per hour?

GASSAUER: Yes, six miles per hour, that is its rate of [zigzagging] advance. That's not the actual [torpedo]speed—that remains the same—but it's the rate of advance. I can do still better now. Supposing there is a convoy there. I fire a quadruple fan salvo. I set one torpedo at two thousand meters, another at twenty-three hundred, and so on, making them all run to the left. It gives me enormous scope for scoring a hit. This so-called FAT torpedo has proved wonderfully good.

Recorded 4 August 1943[36]

BOMBER PILOT, JU. 88 [RE: FAT]: Do the ratings know all about it?

BRINE: They don't know anything about it at all.

PILOT: Then you know about it and the torpedoman's mate?

BRINE: Yes, our torpedoman's mate is an old . . . Let's hope he doesn't say anything. My Commander was a very old hand; he's already made twelve war patrols; he [Interrogation Officer] won't be able to shake him.

It's supposed to travel like this: it can be set in a variety of ways, of course—short zigzags, narrow zigzags, wide zigzags, and in fans. With that torpedo you score a hit ninety-eight or ninety-nine times out of a hundred.

PILOT: Isn't it a question of judgment?

BRINE: No. I aim at a target. Of course, if I hit my target [straightaway], so much the better, the ship is then done for in any case. And if it's a bad shot and the torpedo goes past. . . . [I've] over- or underestimated the range. Usually you underestimate the range, or you underestimate the ship's speed. You're hardly likely to make a mistake in working out the angle of your target, unless the ship passes out of range or zigzags just when you fire. Nearly all the big merchant ships, the fast independent ships, have search gear and, at the moment of firing, they detect it and watch out; they then turn aside and the torpedo goes past. Supposing it goes past here, the torpedo has been set with this preliminary run and it zigzags with the target, so there are always various possibilities of it finally scoring a hit. This torpedo is the right weapon for attacking convoys . . .

Recorded 31 March 1943[37]

KLOTZSCH: . . . Those fellows [the English]have excellent instruments. Have you seen the semicircular thing up aloft, which moves round in a circle? It's a sort of semicircle, about as big as this, which moves round at this speed the whole time; that's the thing which our G.S.R. [German Search Receiver] receives.

MARCH: Yes, that's the radar, that's the same thing; they have the radar, with which they emit a beam. . . .

KLOTZSCH: And then they had a sort of network round the mast, and the thing at the masthead, a sort of network right up aloft. That's for use on the surface. That corresponds to our G.S.R.

MARCH: Yes, they receive with it.

KLOTZSCH: That is *their* receiver; their transmitter is below. They also have excellent hydrophones, and this asdic as well.

MARCH: That asdic must be a marvelous thing.

KLOTZSCH: It is! And recently, of course, there're . . . beams penetrating below the surface from above–as in the case of aircraft. . . . Aircraft can now establish the presence of U-boats when submerged. That's the so-called. . . .

MARCH: . . . Ultraviolet rays.

KLOTZSCH: Yes, it has something—no, not ultraviolet; ultraviolet are rays which can only be rendered invisible, that is, that have such a short wavelength that they are invisible—inaudible. No, that's something else—well, they are frequencies to which the medium of water offers no resistance.

MARCH: But that must be something very special.

KLOTZSCH: They are shorter than—I believe you speak of wavelength zero—from nought to ten centimeters, I believe; thus, they're *extremely* short waves which strike the water with such an impact that the water offers no resistance.

MARCH: They must have absolutely terrific energy.

KLOTZSCH: They have.

Recorded 26 May 1943[38]

BRÖHL: It is a normal receiver, but somewhat specialized for certain wavelengths.

FIGHTER PILOT, F.W. 190: Which wavelengths are they?

BRÖHL: Destroyer wavelengths; they usually work on the one hundred eighty meter band and aircraft on the one hundred forty band. I can't remember the number of kilocycles at the moment.

PILOT: Then that's a receiver and you have someone sitting at it all the time?

BRÖHL: It's a normal receiver and a man sits at it with headphones.

PILOT: And at what distance can he [detect] an aircraft's radar?

BRÖHL: The range is fairly large.

PILOT: Ten miles or so?

BRÖHL: Even at twenty miles.

PILOT: And a destroyer?

BRÖHL: A destroyer as far, too. It depends also on the atmospheric conditions at any given time.

PILOT: You don't have a special aerial or anything, do you?

BRÖHL: Yes, you have a special aerial, which is put up on the bridge; it's a simple cross with horizontal and vertical bars. The destroyer radar wavelengths are vertical and the aircraft radar wavelengths are horizontal; or rather the other way around, the destroyer radar wavelengths are horizontal and the aircraft radar wavelengths are vertical. . . .

PILOT: And is that simply a cross aerial?

BRÖHL: Yes, it's a cross aerial. . . .

PILOT: It can't pick up destroyer and aircraft at the same time, can it, because you are listening in to two different wavelengths?

BRÖHL: You can switch over quickly.

PILOT: Oh, you tune in to a different one?

BRÖHL: Yes.

PILOT: I suppose it is spot-tuned, isn't it?

BRÖHL: Yes.

PILOT: Must there always be a man sitting at it?

BRÖHL: Yes, there's always one there in the areas which are in danger of air attack, especially in the Bay of Biscay and to about twenty to twenty-five degrees West.

PILOT: As far as twenty to twenty-five degrees West. Does the [Allied air] patrol extend as far as that?

BRÖHL: Yes, as far as that. We were in square B[runo] E[mil], I believe that's three hundred fifty sea miles west of Cape Finisterre. That's the northwest corner of Spain. We were rather farther south, and on the same day, another boat, which was to the north of us, about in the latitude of the Bay of Biscay, . . . that is, twenty to twenty-five degrees westward, was bombed by aircraft, suffered serious damage, and had to put back into port. We have to use the search receiver as far out as that. One can say, about two hundred miles west of Portugal, along the whole coast as far as the latitude of Gibraltar, the whole area is in danger of attack from the air.

PILOT: Do you hear it at the same moment as the aircraft begins searching?

BRÖHL: Yes. At first you heard a continuous sound all the

time, starting rather faint and becoming louder, but, later on, the boats evolved a better method. When the aircraft is searching you hear the short continuous sound. Then you switch off. If the sound has become louder, you can tell that the fellows are making their approach, they have found you. If it doesn't recur, you can assume with a reasonable amount of certainty, that it was just an accident. They [G.S.R. operators] always have to search again, as a check, to convince themselves.

PILOT: What would happen if he [Interrogation Officer] found out, for example, that you had something like that [Metox]?

BRÖHL: They know about it. They have noticed that themselves from their lack of success. First, we lost a considerable number of boats . . . in the Bay of Biscay, boats which were putting out to sea and returning to port. Suddenly their [English] successes stopped. Then they knew that we had some countermeasure.

PILOT: Suppose they changed their wavelengths the whole time, suppose each aircraft searched on a different wavelength?

BRÖHL: It wouldn't matter if they did. We can cover the whole scale with our apparatus in any case.

PILOT: Suppose they worked outside the scale?

BRÖHL: In any case, the [G.S.R.]operator always goes over all the wavelengths as a check.

Recorded 21 March 1943[39]

MARCH: Have you been on a G.S.R. course?

RADIOMAN FROM THE *Silvaplana:* Yes, in Le Touquet. I was there as an instructor for six months.

MARCH: Then you are a G.S.R. specialist. The one week we were there we were bored to death.

RADIOMAN: Who was your instructor then?

MARCH: The instructor was good. What was his name—a man with spectacles—Rass, I believe?

RADIOMAN: Yes, Heinz Rass. So he's doing that now?

MARCH: What sort of a course did you have? A short one, too?

RADIOMAN: No, I did the whole thing–

MARCH: They are now training telegraphists simply for the G.S.R. and nothing else, aren't they?

RADIOMAN: Hmm. G.S.R. and radar.

MARCH: That's awful you know, it's so boring. We always have two men on board, one in the W/T compartment and one aloft, who keep two-hour watches. You get absolutely fed up with sitting and turning continuously all the time. On our first patrol, we still had no G.S.R. It was much better then, there was always one Maat and one radio operator] and during the day . . . you were always four [on and] four off, but now, since the arrival of that damned G.S.R., the Commander wanted to have . . . mostly at night–and there were, in all, always three men on watch. Or, even if we had a lot to do, and one fellow got stuck with cipher, three of us had to sit there on account of the damned thing.

Recorded 25 April 1943[40]

In the following section of extracts the POWs speak of the home front as they saw it last, of the war in general, of high-ranking government officials, and of their U-boat bases. Much more could be selected from conversations about the bases with their U-boat bunkers, or shelters, since that was a popular topic, but the descriptions tend to be repetitive and the few reproduced here can stand for the rest.

VOELKER: The last time I was in Germany and my wife and I came out of the cinema, we heard the strangest languages–French, Dutch, Danish, Polish, et cetera, everything but German. The Germans are shedding their blood at the front and these damned foreigners are sitting in our cinemas. Believe me, I'm fed up with National Socialism. If we win the war, we'll rebuild Germany and we won't pay a penny. [We'll see to it that] they [the enemy] are ruined first. They must be bled white.

NAVIGATOR FROM THE *REGENSBURG*: If things go wrong, Adolf [Hitler] will go to Switzerland.

VOELKER: No, he'll do himself in. [Reichsmarschall] Hermann

[Göring] will go to his daughter, who is married and living in Sweden. [Heinrich] Himmler will put on a fig leaf and go to Africa. If things go wrong, the Führer will agree to a negotiated peace.

NAVIGATOR: No, England and America will never agree to a negotiated peace.

VOELKER: If peace is made now, we'll have to go through another war; but I still hope that the Japanese will finish off America.

Recorded 9 May 1943[41]

NOWROTH: You've no idea how many prisoners of war make a getaway in Germany—every day!

SCHAUFFEL: Really!

NOWROTH: When I was on leave at Bonn recently, everything was suddenly barricaded off. I was in civilian clothes with my wife [and] . . . wanted to cross the Rhine by tram, that is, the fast Rhine-bank electric line. I had my naval identity card with me. The tram suddenly stopped on the bridge, all the traffic was held up. The police came in and asked for our identity cards. Everybody who hadn't identity cards had to get out and was taken away. I had my naval identity card with me, with a photograph in it and then he took a good look at me. It was a photograph of me when I was a midshipman. It was still a good likeness. . . . I was stopped twice more on the way. There was a terrific roundup of forty-six English officers who had suddenly gotten away, just imagine it, and they only caught thirty-nine of them. A waiter who was there was in the auxiliary police and in his free time he worked as a waiter and he knew all about it, how many they recaptured and [how]seven of them had completely disappeared. They didn't catch them again. Dirty business . . . There was frightful scandal about it. How on earth is it possible for forty-six officers to escape?

SCHAUFFEL: Germans do it now.

NOWROTH: . . . The whole of Germany is a military machine today. There are Italians, Croats, . . . Belgians. All the races are represented. It's a fact: if we were to lose the war, the enemy would already be in the majority in the country.

SCHAUFFEL: Yes. We're in a sorry state. My wife can shoot with rifle and pistol. I suggested pistol shooting. I said to her: "You know what you have to do if I shouldn't come back, which we hope won't happen, that you at least are. . . . Shoot anyone you see."

NOWROTH: . . . It was always the aim of the Jews to make the Christians their slaves and the only way they could succeed was by means of a war between Christian and Christian.

SCHAUFFEL: We may well thank God that we've got the Führer and Hermann [Göring].

NOWROTH: Yes, yes.

SCHAUFFEL: I have nothing against the English and the English have nothing against us. It's just the Jews who are responsible for the war.

NOWROTH: That's right.

Recorded 31 May 1943[42]

KLOTZSCH: I went with my wife to Weimar, which is the quietest, most idyllic and peaceful town in the Reich, but you keep meeting grousers there. I had several arguments with them, and my wife used to say to me: "Let them talk." I replied: "I can't do that. They are miserable creatures who have never been anywhere near the enemy and here they are, grumbling and grousing. Are we to come from U-boats and listen to that sort of thing?"

I came back from leave. In rather less than a fortnight we sailed. I spent three hundred and four Reichsmarks on drink. Oh my God, how Germany has changed! They aren't National Socialists any longer, they are agitators, nothing but agitators. They just shoot their opponents. I've told my wife that if ever we have a boy, the last thing we must do is to put him in the Hitler Youth. *We* are responsible for the child.

Recorded 3 May 1943[43]

OPOLKA: When guerrillas are captured behind the lines [in Russia] they are naturally shot, but this guerrilla warfare has slackened off there. When it was very bad and people were continually being shot and the miscreants were never caught, they killed one hundred thousand for every German who was shot. That worked.

SCHAUFFEL: Well, I don't know whether that would always work.

OPOLKA: Oh yes.

SCHAUFFEL: What? To kill one hundred thousand people for one German who's shot?

OPOLKA: Well it did work.

SCHAUFFEL: Well, in France at any rate it didn't. Nor in Poland.

OPOLKA: In Poland? It worked in Poland, too. There were no more afterwards. It's quite true what the English say about our having killed masses of them there.

SCHAUFFEL: Well, that had to be.

OPOLKA: I'd like to see the infantry officer here who wouldn't kill a crowd like that if he'd driven into a town in an armored vehicle and a few Poles had come creeping out with their hands up and then thrown in a hand grenade when he opened the roof. That's not cricket! [*Das gehört sich ja nun nicht!*]

FOERTSCH: Things have happened which should never have been allowed to happen.

OPOLKA: However that may be, it's a question of "bend or break." Either the thing goes well–in that case it will have been all right because a problem will have been removed from the Reich with a sudden, momentarily painful brutality, which in the long run will have been a good thing. And if things go wrong, it's all up with us anyway. It's a pity. If we had avoided a war with England, the whole world would have belonged to us.

FOERTSCH: That's the opinion of the English, too.

SCHAUFFEL: Yes, I should only like to know what went wrong that time, with [Prime Minister Neville] Chamberlain.

OPOLKA: Chamberlain was thoroughly friendly towards the

Germans. Perhaps, even if he wasn't that, he at least saw that reason [existed] to cooperate with Germany.

FOERTSCH: The trouble was that something went wrong that time at Munich–that's my opinion for what it's worth.

OPOLKA: Nothing at all went wrong there. Everything was conceded to us except the [Polish] Corridor.

Recorded 10 June 1943[44]

KLOTZSCH: Adolf [Hitler] is unmarried. He hates humanity and he is driving the whole German nation to ruin. He has no normal human feelings. He has a bestial hatred of mankind. We are bleeding to death in Russia–Tunisia has fallen. Here we're well treated; in Germany the English POWs are in chains. I loathe that arch-liar [Propaganda Minister Josef] Göbbels, with his evil tongue, and his twenty-two million tons that have been sunk. Then there's [Labor Front head Robert] Ley with his four or five villas on the Rhine, that villainous blackguard, with his three marriages and his countless illegitimate children; however the war ends, he'll be murdered one day. Here they tell you the truth. Every Englishman can listen to the German radio. Here you can eat in restaurants without coupons. When I was on leave recently, my father warned me about one-sided propaganda. I must admit now that he was right.

Recorded 13 May 1943[45]

CHIEF RADIOMAN FROM *SILVAPLANA:* I was responsible for all the German ciphers in France, the general Enigma and the officer's Enigma machines, all the recognition signals, for the period June to May. I took it as a compliment myself, but I often thought it was quite wrong to give things like that into the keeping of an Other Rank. I could have had the things photographed and no one could have raised a finger against me, no one would have noticed it. And then all the civilians–there are so many of them who sail as wireless officers on merchant ships, and they are all given these ciphers and so on to look after; it's not right at all. And, then, as I said, in France, where espionage activity is even greater.

KLOTZSCH: I also had all our own minefields which we'd laid in the Northern Hemisphere on my grid map, and I used to think: "An Englishman would give me a great deal of money for that map."

Recorded 9 May 1943[46]

FOERTSCH: We went ashore with revolvers, then we shot up the brothel and came back with far more money than we had started out with. They cleared out the brothel later. There were female agents there; there usually are in those bars. A girl working there would earn five Reichsmarks in ten minutes, but there aren't any seamen there; they don't pay anything.

Recorded 8 June 1943[47]

FOERTSCH: In the Royale [a brothel in Paris]there was a spy— an English girl. She was caught. The Germans didn't notice it, but the French girls did. She got into trouble with the French police. Some statements or other were false and she was seized. She hadn't yet done any harm. She was only there together with somebody. [Pause] If we lose the war, it will be [Grand Admiral]Raeder's fault. He didn't build enough U-boats, or didn't switch construction over quickly enough. [Pause]

SCHAUFFEL: One must admit that Churchill is very much on the alert. One has to hand it to him.

Recorded 8 June 1943[48]

SCHMELING: We only experienced one real air raid at Danzig, when they dropped those damned bombs on the town. We had just brought our boat back from tactical exercises, and had put in to Danzig Harbor at three o'clock on Saturday afternoon. At about seven o'clock the sirens went. The flak fired marvelously. That evening there were about twenty-two boats lying there, there were three Type Nines and at that time an order had come out at Danzig that there must always be a watch on board, either the port or the starboard watch, so that they could take the boats in tow. All the twenty-five boats fired—you can imagine the din—and then there was the flak from the Schichau shipyard and the heavy flak on the *Haraldsberg*. They were blazing away all round. Then there were several flak trains there. Twelve aircraft made the attack and four of them they shot down over Danzig itself and two more later when they were flying away; that is exactly half. They dropped incendiaries in the center of the town, mainly in the old town, on dwelling houses. One fell on the children's ward of the Sisters of Charity Hospital and there were forty-eight killed. One fell on the Danzig shipyard, right on the goal of the football field. . . . We had flak guns manned by youths, members of Hitler Youth or schoolboys. They are on the searchlights too.

Recorded 28 May 1943[49]

KALISCH: The U-boat shelter at Brest certainly is a large one.

SPITZ: Does it only take boats from one flotilla?

KALISCH: Yes.

SPITZ: How many pens are there?

KALISCH: There are five pens and ten docks.

SPITZ: Can three U-boats get into each pen?

KALISCH: Yes.

SPITZ: That would be . . . for one flotilla.

KALISCH: Yes. At present the Ninth and the First are together, but they are enlarging the thing now. They are beginning to build again.

SPITZ: Are they in a row now?

KALISCH: Yes, side by side. They are building on another five pens to it now. Just imagine how many boats can get into it.

SPITZ: Five pens, that means fifteen U-boats.

KALISCH: There are more than fifteen U-boats.

SPITZ: Ten docks.

KALISCH: That makes twenty-five and another fifteen.

SPITZ: That makes forty U-boats.

KALISCH: At present they've got a four meter-thick roof. Now they're adding another four meters to it.
Recorded 13 May 1943[50]

GEIMEIER [RE: LORIENT]: The U-boats lie inside in the pens, like cars in a motor garage. When there's an air-raid alarm, the French people and everyone about have to go into the shelters. We then closed the doors there; not a soul could get in or out.

PHILLIPPS: Under what sort of conditions do the fellows live in the one thousand-man shelter?

GEIMEIER: They have their rooms there.

PHILLIPPS: As big as this one?

GEIMEIER: Yes, bigger.

PHILLIPS: How many men to a room like that?

GEIMEIER: It varies, four or five. You spend the first week after you put into port and the last week before you put out, down in the shelter. Everything is in one compartment in the shelter, the noncommissioned officers and ratings are all together. These doors, the movable doors, are all . . . guards outside, wire entanglements, and barbed wire. We lived inside them. . . . The inside of the shelter is lined with wood and there are bunks there. You're together with four or eight men, it all depends. The noncommissioned officers, ratings, and officers all live separately. The last week before the boat puts out to sea and is in the hands of the shipyard, when it is lying in the pen in a dry shelter, we lived in the big shelter all together. It's right on the harbor, we have about ten minutes walk to reach the boat. They're still building shelters; . . . hundreds of Frenchmen are employed there. There are twelve mixing machines where the shelter is being built, all in use. There are two shifts of French workmen–they are building another shelter where we were–who do the shoveling. One shift looks on, smoking cigarettes, while the others work, and then the other relieve them. And then this new lay-out; the concrete is five meters thick, and then there was scaffolding on top; they are adding another meter of concrete on top.

PHILLIPPS: On top of the shelters?

GEIMEIER: Yes. The men now no longer live in the shelters. They live farther outside, about thirty kilometers away, right in the woods. An artificial lake has been installed, and a big mess built, there are hutments there with steam heating and everything in them. They are driven there in buses every day. By the time we were due back from this patrol, the camp would have been ready. There are several flotillas there. I believe the Tenth and the Second are at Lorient, and then there are the ones from St.-Nazaire, too.

PHILLIPPS: Are the U-boat men also supposed to live outside now, no longer inside the shelters?

GEIMEIER: They all live outside.

PHILLIPPS: . . . One flotilla [already] lives up in the woods, doesn't it?

GEIMEIER: Yes, that's the Second Flotilla. When we were there, their camp was already finished.

They were about forty kilometers away from us. We belonged to Tenth and as Tenth wasn't ready, we were still in the shelter; if we'd gotten back we shouldn't have returned to it.

PHILLIPPS: . . . Are the boats [of the Second and Tenth Flotillas] together?

GEIMEIER: The boats themselves are berthed together, but the men are billeted separately, in separate camps; . . . The longest time that any of our boats was at sea was sixteen weeks. Otherwise, the average patrol was five or five and a half weeks if we were not supplied at sea, and eight weeks if we were, or, at most, nine. To which brothel did you go? The one at La Rochelle?

PHILLIPPS: Yes.

GEIMEIER: Do you know the one at La Pallice, too . . . at the top end towards the . . . the petrol store is there.

PHILLIPPS: Yes, I know that [one], too.

GEIMEIER: . . . The layout at Lorient is a sight worth seeing, because the thing has been designed like a wasp's nest. It's like a labyrinth; you can't find your way about in it. All the workshops are inside the shelter, [for example,] the torpedo workshops. . . . Lorient has been smashed up, but that doesn't matter at all. Only the population has suffered, the French population, and no one else. You must imagine the Kiel shipyard . . . [or]the Deutsche Werke, with a large concrete shelter on top, only even more clearly arranged. On one side you have . . . engines, then here are the . . . cleansing workshops where all the pistons are washed down and all that; then here are the . . . workshops, and here are the torpedo workshops; here is the compressor room, where the air compressors are taken off; here is another pen; it is all arranged in pens, and all beside the boat.

PHILLIPPS: Did you actually have a Junkers compressor?

GEIMEIER: Yes.

KUFFNER: You pass through there, the U-boats are in single pens and between the U-boats there are the workshops. It goes right up to the roof. Then there are other things which are separate—Junkers is separate—and that is separate, and all the experimental places are separate.

GEIMEIER: You can't form any picture of it if you haven't seen it yourself.

KUFFNER: Well, the Junkers compressor is damnable!

PHILLIPPS: Is there only one staircase leading to the one thousand–man shelter, is there only one way you can go?

GEIMEIER: There are two proper entrances. But one of them is always closed during the day, it is only opened at coffee and mealtimes . . . otherwise, there's just one way up.

KUFFNER: Inside there you could buy everything in the canteen—cloth, wine, everything you needed. What amount of stuff we took with us on leave! You can buy stockings, cloth, everything.

GEIMEIER: I always bought my wife expensive stockings.

KUFFNER: I used to send my wife a parcel before I put to sea. I

bought her five meters of cloth. It was marvelous blue coat material and cost twenty-four Riechsmarks a meter.
Recorded 11 May 1943[51]

ROSENKRANZ: The English will never find out where the hutments of the Tenth Flotilla are [outside Lorient]. They are inside the woods, right in the middle of them, and they are camouflaged into the bargain! Everything has been camouflaged, even the pond. It is all covered with scrim. You can't see anything at all. They haven't got any landmark there. The huts are covered over with scrim. You can't see them at all. All round them there are meadows. It's all surrounded by woods. They certainly won't find it. They won't see the lake, it isn't really a lake, only a pond. They have no idea where the camp is.

GRÄTZ: Did the hutments belong to the Second Flotilla or the Tenth? Or are both flotillas stationed together?

ROSENKRANZ: No, the camps are perhaps a quarter of an hour apart.
Recorded 15 May 1943[52]

KALISCH [RE: LORIENT]: The roof on the shelters is four meters thick.

RADIOMAN FROM THE *GERMANIA:* And now they are adding an extra four meters. The shelters can only be destroyed by an attempted invasion.

KALISCH: Yes.

SPITZ: But you could destroy the boats lying inside if an aircraft were to fly in front of the opening to the shelters and drop a torpedo?

KALISCH: No, it couldn't do that. It would never get near them.

SPITZ: Why not?

KALISCH: One shelter is here, here is the mole, and up here there are balloons everywhere–shelter balloon barrage; each balloon has three cables. There are about eighteen balloons in front, one next to the other. They form a close wall, so to speak. No aircraft could get through there, and then there are the hills(?) [*die Berge (?)*] everywhere as well, with any amount of flak on them.

SPITZ: There are flak positions on the shelters themselves.

KALISCH: If an aircraft wanted to approach from in front and drop torpedoes there, it would have to come down low, when it would be shot down. They can't do anything there.

Recorded 16 May 1943[53]

ROSENKRANZ: He [Interrogation Officer] asked me about losses. . . .

GRÄTZ: A whole lot of boats are missing from the Tenth Flotilla. There were fifty boats in the flotilla, weren't there?

ROSENKRANZ: I don't know how many the Tenth had, about sixty, I think.

GRÄTZ: Now?

ROSENKRANZ: I believe so. Wait a moment—a fellow who did the officers' pay had sixty-two boats [on his roll].

GRÄTZ: Perhaps he had another flotilla as well.

ROSENKRANZ: No, only the Tenth. The Second Flotilla had its own administration as well. The name of the Commander is supposed to be a secret, but they [Interrogation Officers] know it as well as we do. They are better informed about it all than many U-boat men. . . .

Recorded 9 May 1943[54]

W. RAHN: The Commander hit the First Officer of the Watch over the head with a bottle. They were very drunk, and the First Officer of the Watch retaliated by taking a broom and beating up the Commander.

RADIOMAN FROM THE *Germania:* How are things with the Italians?

W. RAHN: They hate us like poison. When seamen get drunk they open the portholes and throw bottles at the Italians walking by on the street.

Recorded 3 May 1943[55]

GRÄTZ: I believe that all the old Commanders will sail again if the present rate of [Allied ship] sinkings decreases again.

ELEBE: Yes, but the trouble is this: the majority of them haven't been to sea for two years, so that they don't know anything about the very latest methods of defense, and they aren't in a position to voice an opinion.

Recorded 1 June 1943[56]

OPOLKA: We simply must win the war. If things go wrong, presumably the Russians will overrun our country; and even if the Russians don't come right in but confine themselves within certain limits, for the simple reason that they, too, have lost a lot, then all these headhunters will come in, the Poles and the Czechs. I come from the frontier district, from that actual part; I hate the Poles, they're a vile race. I'm anxious about my parents.

Recorded 10 June 1943[57]

The Admiralty's Naval Intelligence Division issued a report on 2 April in which it evaluated morale among U-boat POWs as of mid-March. It had an "on the one hand . . . yet on the other" quality. It reported "no marked deterioration in fighting spirit" among those POWs recently captured. Given the leadership of confident, able, and imaginative Commanders, "even young and raw recruits are resolute in face of the enemy." In captivity, however, the crews recently captured, including officers, had shown a previously unseen tendency to divulge information that they must have known was contrary to their country's interests. The Intelligence people theorized that that talkativeness resulted mainly from Germany's recent reverses on the Eastern Front—the German Sixth Army had fallen at Stalingrad on 2 February—and from the Afrika-Korps' impending collapse in Tunisia, which would occur on 7 May. Other reasons advanced were distaste of Roman Catholic POWs for Nazi treatment of their church, general war weariness, and a mounting feeling that Germany would lose the war. Withal, Intelligence noted, recent POWs continued to believe that they were loyal Germans, and it cautioned that nothing heard from the POWs suggested a decline in the fighting efficiency of U-boat crews still at sea, or that their combative ability would fall "in the near future."[58]

Given the 2 April assessment of talkativeness, it is striking that the secretly recorded POW conversations after March and throughout May and June reveal a studied intention on the part of many recently captured men to stonewall or mislead their Interrogation Officers. Furthermore, among the mass of recorded conversations during that same period, there are relatively few expressions of despondency or of what the British obsessed on, "collapse of morale." There were, of course, a few such fears of inevitable defeat, strongly put, as seen in the epigraphs heading this chapter (which are repeated below together with their serial numbers). As indicated earlier in this narrative, there is little ground for assuming that the U-boat crews ever lost their fighting spirit up to and including the last months of the war. One may argue that morale is a different attribute from courage, and that it, at least, diminishes in the face of inevitable defeat. Perhaps. If ever a distinction could be drawn between morale and courage, perhaps this was the moment. But the morale collapse so long and devoutly sought by the British, and cited so frequently in their documents as a goal, if it ever was achieved in fact, seems not to have had any appreciable effect on the resolute willingness of the German crewman to come back swinging, like one man fighting three. One thinks of Napoleon's army on its way to Waterloo, of whom it was said, they marched without fear and without hope.

MARCH: I don't want to sail in any more U-boats, I've had enough of them.

RADIOMAN FROM THE *SILVAPLANA:* I can well believe that!

MARCH: The anti-U-boat devices are getting too good. They had instruments with which they DFed us exactly. Three destroyers came along, and got us right in the middle. We should never have gotten away again however deep we'd gone. It was hopeless. I believe they sank three U-boats that day.

RADIOMAN: Three U-boats in one day—that's the limit!

Recorded 25 April 1943[59]

OPOLKA: I was with the BdU a whole year at Lorient as Adjutant to the Commander in Chief. [Pause] . . . My father

is a *Kapitänleutnant* on a *Sperrbrecher* [auxiliary mine-sweeper]. But he'd rather sell vacuum cleaners. My brother is a soldier, my brother-in-law is a soldier. . . . I didn't want the war. I'm not a pacifist and I was sorry that I had to remain on the Staff for so long. I kept applying for a transfer. But to say that I enjoy the war–the decisive factor for me is that my parents have to go through the whole damn business a second time. They lost everything and with great labor have struggled to their feet again.
Recorded 9 June 1943[60]

OPOLKA: So you are convinced that we shall win the war?

SCHAUFFEL: Yes, we've both said: "We shall not lose."

OPOLKA: I'll tell you something, no one wins in war.

SCHAUFFEL: When I'm on board, I'm the type of person who likes to start an argument, because the others always said: "We shall win the war." It's nonsense; one must allow logic to play a part. My one fear is that my father's vessel [*Pott*] will go down under him.
Recorded 9 June 1943[61]

LINK: Don't you believe that we will use gas if worst comes to worst?

MARCH: I don't think so. But I think we shall lose the war. Time is no longer our ally. These attacks on Germany now–our losses in the field!

LINK: Two million were killed in the last war; only two hundred thousand have been killed so far in this war!

MARCH: But the English and Americans will hold out longer, and the use of gas would only hasten our downfall.
Recorded 25 May 1943[62]

KOHLER: I have the impression that the English will also keep us on as prisoners, even more than we have the French. If Germany loses the war they will treat us as slaves; if it suits them they will send us to the colonies as slave labor. As outcasts! Who is to stop them? They have certainly no conscience. If there is any justice in the world, we ought to win, especially against England. I hate the English. One is easily inclined here to allow oneself to be influenced by their propaganda. Superficially, the Englishman appears sporting and kind, but really he is as hard as stone; he has no feelings. If a German gives anything, he gives it from his heart. [Pause] . . . Are you also Catholic, or religious [*gottgläubig*]?

GRÄTZ: [I believe] there must be something.

KOHLER: There must be something. If my mother knew! In that second I even confessed. I have never told anyone this, but I believe in God and in the resurrection of the soul. The Church has had a good influence on me. Without the Church I should have become a bad man. I told my wife I would try and remain in the Catholic Church. I said my prayers till I was seventeen years old, and even later, and during this last patrol I prayed three times, in the evening. I prayed that my wife and child should live and that I should come through this patrol. I prayed when I was rescued too. I believe in life after death.

Recorded 29 April 1943 [63]

KLOTZSCH: It's a tragedy. The whole business of U-boat sailing has simply become a job for convicts.

ARENDT: Well, that's just about how you're treated; if you do anything at all, you're locked up.

Recorded 13 May 1943 [64]

ARENDT: I don't want to go to sea anymore. I'm fed up with it. I had intended to get married now.

Recorded 14 May 1943 [65]

KLOTZSCH: Well, I'm not sorry that the damn business is finished.

Recorded 13 May 1943 [66]

KLOTZSCH: It gets worse and worse, all the U-boat men are grousing.

MARCH: Now it practically amounts to this: as soon as one boat is put into commission, another one is lost at the same moment.

Recorded 26 May 1943 [67]

KLOTZSCH: Things look very bad for us. The boats are being sunk one after the other.
Recorded 13 May 1943[68]

RAHN: To tell you the truth, I haven't much hope. They'll crush us in time.
Recorded 3 May 1943[69]

In Peril on the Sea

Tenebrae

The ships destroy us above
And ensnare us beneath.
We arise, we lie down, and we move
In the belly of Death.

RUDYARD KIPLING

Whoever is of the opinion that offensive action against convoys is no longer possible is a weakling and not a true U-boat commander. The battle in the Atlantic is becoming harder, but it is the decisive factor in this war. Be conscious of your great responsibility and be quite certain that you will have to answer for your deeds.

KARL DÖNITZ 21 MAY

There can be no talk of a let-up in the U-boat war. The Atlantic is my first line of defense in the West. And even if I have to fight a defensive battle there, that is preferable to waiting to defend myself on the coast of Europe. The enemy forces tied down by our U-boats are tremendous, even though the losses inflicted by us are no longer great. I cannot afford to release these forces by discontinuing the U-boat war.

ADOLF HITLER 31 MAY

Following the epic battle for ONS.5, nearly 600 Allied merchant ships in fourteen convoys crossed the Atlantic during the remaining three weeks of May. Of that number only six ships were sunk by U-boats. Where the U-Bootwaffe crews were concerned, the startlingly low number did not result from their lack of trying; at Dönitz's urging, they fought desperately to get back into the game. But it was too late. Both the initiative and the numbers had passed to the Allies. There were now too many experienced close escort and Support Group vessels in the convoy lanes. And overhead there were too many shore-based bombers, not to mention at this date carrier-borne British Fairey Swordfish bombers and Martlet (Grumman F4F4 Wildcat) fighters and American Grumman TBF–1 Avenger bombers: it was during these weeks that such aircraft from American-built escort carriers achieved the first singlehanded destruction of a U-boat. These weeks also saw the first successful employments of the American airborne homing torpedo code-named Mark XXIV Mine and of the British "R.P." solid-head rocket projectile. It was all too much for the U-boats, once the aggressors, now left panting heavily in the wake of events. And many went down to sodden deaths. In this chapter our narrative will examine briefly those particular convoys that defined transatlantic traffic during the last three weeks of May, the major aircraft actions outside the Bay of Biscay, and, finally, U-boat losses elsewhere in the Atlantic and Outer Seas.

The surviving U-boats that had operated against ONS.5 moved off to the east and south. Approximately fifteen boats were still capable of operations; ten would shortly be operational after reprovisioning from two milch cows; and nine were on their way back to base. Western Approaches had no information about these movements, since decryptions of German radio traffic were still trying to catch up to events following the cryptographic intelligence blackout from 26 April to the afternoon of 5 May. Suspecting, however, that packs were still operating in the general area of the ONS.5 battle, the next westbound convoy in the eight-day cycle, ONS.6, departing 30 April, was routed to the west of those possible concentrations. Surface protection was provided the convoy by Escort Group B6, consisting of one destroyer, H.M.S. *Viscount* (S.O.), five corvettes, and two trawlers; and air cover flew out of Iceland beginning on 3 May. Despite its evasive route, the convoy did not escape enemy detection. Two

U-boats, U-*418* and U-*952*, from a new *Gruppe Isar* [after the river] forming between Greenland and Iceland, sighted the convoy on the morning of 6 May, when the convoy was at 60°15'N, 24°20'W. Their reporting signals to Berlin were DFed by *Viscount* and shore stations, leading CinCWA to increase the air cover by noon. By 2100,* aircraft had made ten U-boat sightings, two 55 and 73 nautical miles ahead of the convoy columns, seven between 18 and 32 miles abaft the starboard beam, and one 58 miles astern. Several attacks resulted.

Meanwhile, on the surface, one of the corvettes had made a visual sighting on the starboard quarter at 1946. The abundance of air threat, excellent intercommunication between surface and air units, and an evasive alteration of course at 2300 had the desired effect of shaking off the shadowing boats. A second alteration at noon on the 7th avoided boats known to be to the north. The 8th was quiet until dusk, when HF/DF intercepts suggested that the U-boats were closing the convoy again, and *Viscount* sighted a conning tower breaking the surface at a range of 7,000 yards. She pursued, the U-boat dived, and she dropped a ten-charge pattern over the swirl without result. The U-boats backed off, apparently made wary, if not unnerved, by the forces arrayed against them, and the night that followed was uneventful.

At 0700 on the 9th, the convoy's protective screen was enlarged by the arrival of the "cavalry," a Support Group (Fourth Escort Group) made up of destroyer H.M.S. *Faulknor* (SO), two other destroyers, and one of Britain's new escort carriers, H.M.S. *Archer.* But by that time the danger was past and, after 48 hours, the Support Group disengaged to join Convoy ON.182. The ships of ONS.6 then proceeded to their destinations without further incident. The convoy's safe passage through the now-closing Air Gap where *Gruppe Fink* had gathered its predecessor convoy in a deadly embrace was a clear signal of the new dispensation that prevailed.[1]

---

* All times are expressed in Greenwich Mean Time (GMT) unless otherwise noted.

In Berlin, BdU was aware from sailing cycles that a pair of eastbound convoys were due to depart on or about the same date in early May, one a slow-moving SC convoy from Halifax, the other a faster HX convoy from New York. In anticipation of their crossing longitude 42°W at some time on 8 May, Dönitz/Godt formed two patrol lines stretching 550 miles across their probable courses: Group *Rhein* [the river], formerly *Amsel* III and IV, consisting of ten boats spaced at twenty-mile intervals from 47°33′N, 40°55′W to 43°57′N, 40°05′W; and Group *Elbe* [after the river], consisting of seventeen boats, mostly ex-ONS.5 operation, stationed at the same spacing from 52°45′N, 43°55′W to 47°51′N, 41°05′W.[2] Early in the game, the German B-Dienst radio monitoring and cryptanalysis service that so troubled Francis Harry Hinsley in Hut 8 at Bletchley Park learned from decryptions of Allied Naval Cipher No. 3 that on 3 May, eastbound convoy HX.237 was positioned at about 40°50′N, 67°(31–49′?) W, steaming on a course of 056°, speed 9.5 knots; and that on 5 May, eastbound convoy SC.129 was at position 44°50′N, 47°01′W, course and speed unknown.[3] It was likely that the faster convoy HX.237, even if its departure was the later of the two, would be the first to cross the line that Dönitz/Godt had drawn in the sea.

In the evening of 6 May, B-Dienst informed BdU that as of 2130, HX.237 was in BC 7684 (43°56′N, 48°27′W). That information was quickly relayed to the *Rhein* and *Elbe* patrol lines.[4] Further data learned by B-Dienst on the 7th revealed that HX.237 had turned toward the south on a course of 128°, and that SC.129 was on a base course toward the east.[5] This intelligence that the two convoys were taking a more southerly route than expected, which would cause HX.237 to elude the patrol lines altogether and SC.129 merely to brush the southern tip of *Rhein,* had three immediate effects: (1) BdU ordered the *Rhein* boats to move at best speed on a course of 120° so as to position that group's southernmost boat at 39°45′N, 35°02′W; and at the same time, the *Elbe* boats were directed to take the same course of 120° at ten knots in order to intercept SC.129; though BdU conceded that, "No clue to the [present] position of this convoy is in hand."[6] (2) The six boats of Group *Drossel* (Thrush), which had been operating on the coastwise West Africa-Gibraltar-U.K. lanes, were ordered west to reinforce *Rhein* and *Elbe*. And (3) Dönitz/Godt demanded to know "how the enemy was able to intercept our patrol strip" and to divert the two convoys around it.

BdU considered every possible explanation, from detection of the patrol lines by aircraft, to DFing of U-boat radio traffic during the Battle for ONS.5, to the possibility "considered unlikely, that the enemy has cracked our ciphers"—still, BdU ordered an immediate change in Enigma settings. Whatever the reason, BdU stated, "this almost circular detour remains critical."[7] It is ironic that this is one of the few occasions in 1943 when, in fact, decryption of Enigma played no role in the diversion of convoys around wolfpacks. It appears that prior to the movements of the two convoys on the 6th and 7th the Allies had no knowledge of the formation or positions of *Rhein* and *Elbe*. The first British decrypt of German traffic pertaining to the formation of *Rhein* in the existing records is a message intercepted at 1015 on the 7th but not decrypted until 1304 on the 9th; and the first mention of *Elbe* was intercepted at 1320 on the 12th and not decrypted until 1016 on the 14th.[8] Very probably, the two convoys were given southerly routes to evade U-boat concentrations thought to be east of Newfoundland and building up between Greenland and Iceland as well as to provide better flying weather for the aircraft aboard escort carrier H.M.S. *Biter*, which, in the course of events, would offer cover to both HX.237 and SC.129.

Two ocean escort groups were assigned to HX.237: C2, consisting of the destroyer H.M.S. *Broadway* (Lt.–Cmdr. E. H. Chavasse, R.N., SO), a frigate, four corvettes (three of them Canadian), a trawler, and a tug; and Escort Group 5, acting as a Support Group, consisting of *Biter* (Capt. E.M.C. Abel-Smith, R.N., SO) and three destroyers. Owing to heavy fog, C.2 relieved the local escort a day later than planned, at 1400 on 7 May. *Biter* and her escorts were even further delayed, not joining until the 9th, in thick weather unsuitable for flying, but on the 7th and 8th, in better weather, her aircraft had flown out to the convoy to make close patrols ahead and astern and thus "hearten the Masters and their crews." The merchant argosy itself was made up of thirty-eight ships in company and nine stragglers. Two stragglers put back to St. John's, four rejoined the convoy, and three, *Fort Concord, Brand,* and *Sandanger,* continued independently; these three would be sunk on the 12th, the only casualties among the vessels actually or nominally part of HX.237: once again it was proved how vital it was for merchant vessels to keep their stations in a convoy.

At 1300 on the 9th, thanks to BdU's new dispositions, U–*359* (Oblt.z.S. Heinz Förster) of the *Rhein* group sighted the main body in 41°09′N, 26°54′W and, on BdU's order, became its shadower. The U-boat's transmissions were DFed by *Broadway,* who sent the corvette *Primrose* down the bearing, where she got a sighting and, after the boat dived, dropped a ten-pattern, with no evidence sequent. Meanwhile, Chavasse ordered the convoy to alter course 40° to starboard. More HF/DF bearings were acquired later in the day, suggesting that at least two U-boats were in contact with the convoy, but no sightings resulted, and because of the continued milky air, the nine Swordfish and one Martlet of 811 Naval Air Squadron aboard *Biter,* steaming on station astern, could not assist in the hunt. (There had been three Martlets originally, but on the 7th two Martlets had failed to return from patrols, though vigorous efforts were made to home them back. Lost, they both made forced landings alongside ships, a straggler and a trawler, and their pilots were picked up. The two ships were 90 miles northeast of the convoy! Three days later, a Swordfish was lost and its crew rescued in exactly the same way.)

The next morning, the 10th, in slightly more diaphanous air, U–*403* (Kptlt. Hans Clausen), following C2's tug on the surface, sighted the convoy, and at 1647 was sighted herself to starboard by the escort screen. Two corvettes made revolutions after the intruder, and *Biter* was able to launch Swordfish "M," which reached the still-surfaced boat six miles distant before the corvettes. Raked by machine-gun fire when 1,500 yards from the conning tower, the fabric-skinned biplane banked hard out of range; then, as the U-boat dived, it returned to the attack at maximum speed of 120 knots, approaching from the U-boat's port quarter at an angle of 45° to track, and from a height of 60 feet dropped four Mark XI D/ Cs set to 24 feet and spaced 60 feet apart. They missed astern. The surprised U-boat, having survived the attack, signaled BdU that she had been engaged by a *wheeled* aircraft. This was certainly news to BdU, which had just signaled the *Rhein* boats that they need not fear aircraft, since the convoy was out of the range of shore air bases, so BUT LITTLE AIR CAN JOIN THE CONVOY.[9] But *Biter's* flight deck, built on an American merchant hull, had been able to offer the ultimate surprise, a hard-surface landing gear aircraft flying from a midocean runway.

The escort carrier (CVE) was a warship type coincidentally first produced by both the RN and USN in June 1941. In both instances a flight deck was mounted on a merchant ship hull. The RN type, H.M.S. *Audacity*, embarked six Martlet fighters on the converted merchant ship *Hannover* captured from the Germans. Assigned to the U.K.–Gibraltar convoys, she had an outstanding six-month career, destroying five Luftwaffe aircraft, sighting nine U-boats, and on 17 December 1941 sharing in the sinking of U–131 (Korv. Kapt. Arend Baumann) with the 36th Escort Group (Cmdr. Frederic John Walker, R.N., SO), though the attacking Martlet and pilot were lost to the U-boat's gunfire. While escorting Convoy HG.76 on the night of 21–22 December 1941, *Audacity* was struck by three torpedoes from U–751 (Kptlt. Gerhard Bigalk) and sunk.[10]

Her American counterpart, carrier U.S.S. *Long Island*, capable of embarking twenty-one aircraft, would not see action in either the Atlantic or the Pacific theaters but spend her career in ferrying, training, and experimental duties. But beginning in 1942, the USN heavily committed funds to the CVE program, and American shipyards began turning out large numbers of improved carrier conversions from merchant hulls, eventually producing 128 by war's end.[11] British yards produced five. Many of the early U.S. CVEs went to the RN,

which made additional modifications, mainly to the avgas fuel
systems to prevent vapor explosions, and two of these, *Biter*
and *Archer*, were in active service on the Atlantic convoy
routes during Black May. Swordfish "L" from *Biter* had earlier, on 25 April, shared in the destruction of U–*203* (Kptlt.
Hermann Kottmann) along with the destroyer H.M.S. *Pathfinder*, while both ships were with EG5 supporting EG B2, the
close screen of Convoy ONS.4. The aircraft's principal contribution to the kill was two well-placed calcium sea markers,
since her two D/Cs dropped 20 seconds after submergence
apparently did not damage the U-boat. On 10 May, *Archer*,
with Fourth Escort Group, was supporting EG B6 with Convoy ONS.6.

British naval historian David Hobbs has commented on
the relative merits of shore-based and naval-embarked aviation at that period. Most of the flying hours of the former, he
points out, were expended in transit to and from their patrol
areas rather than in patrol itself. Add to that the fact that significant numbers of shore-based bombers and crews had to be
kept in constant rotation on successive legs to and from the
convoy, and the economy of carrier aircraft, which were
based constantly with the convoy, becomes apparent. Furthermore, Coastal Command aircraft did not always successfully rendezvous with their designated convoys; in 1942, for
example, 34 percent of all Coastal sorties were Not Mets. Finally, unlike bombers from afar, the carrier aircraft lent themselves to rapid and flexible tactical use by the escort
commander, the attack on U–*403* being an apt example.[12]
The only problem at this date, apart from pilots' tendency to
get lost navigating, was the inadequacy of the Swordfish aircraft in speed and structural strength.

Following the action against this boat, BdU decided that
the main body of *Rhein* must be 90 miles behind the fast convoy, with little chance to catch up. Accordingly, it ordered
that group, excepting U–*403*, to withdraw from the operation
against HX.237 and to move instead against the slower
SC.129, which was "considered to offer better chances of success." The fast convoy would be left to the shadower U–*403*

and to the six boats of *Drossel* closing from the east.[13] The day-light hours of 11 May were quiet, though HF/DF activity increased, and Chavasse sent two destroyers ahead to probe for threats, and two of *Biter*'s aircraft searched the convoy's perimeter. Later in the day, U–*436* (Kptlt. Günther Seibicke) of Group *Drossel* found HX.237 in BD 9554 (44°15'W, 27°25'W). Another of *Drossel*'s boats, U–*89* (Kptlt. Dietrich Lohmann), reported the presence of carrier-type aircraft circling overhead–either a confirmation or a first disclosure to BdU that the aircraft that attacked U–403 was carrier-borne.

At 2013, another of *Biter*'s aircraft, Swordfish "L," caught U–436 on the surface and attacked her with four D/Cs from 150 feet. During the run in, the "Stringbag," as the frail biplane was called by pilots, took heavy anti-aircraft fire, but the pilot and gunner watched the tracers pass harmlessly between the port upper and lower wings, and the pilot returned fire with his front gun. Following the D/C drop, the pilot climbed to make a return run, but after he got the slow-gaited craft around, the U-boat had disappeared. The pilot dropped a smoke float and resumed patrolling.[14] At 2100 U–*89* reported the convoy on a new course, 000°, or due north.[15] Contact was not resumed until daybreak on the 12th, when the surfaced *Drossel* boat U–*230* (Kptlt. Paul Siegmann) sighted the ship columns in heavy swell astride BD 2826, confirming that the convoy, estimated at 9.5 knots speed, had made an evasive turn to north.[16] Soon afterwards, U–230 found herself under attack by the first Swordfish to make it off *Biter*'s bucking deck that high seas morning, which was the twenty-third birthday of U–230's First Watch Officer (I.W.O.) Herbert A. Werner, a native of the Black Forest region of southern Germany, who was commanding the bridge watch:

> "Aircraft astern!" It was too late to dive. The single-engine plane came in low in a straight line exactly over our wake. I fingered the trigger of my gun. Again the gun was jammed. I kicked its magazine, clearing the jam. Then I emptied the gun at the menace. The mate's automatic [machine gun] bellowed. Our boat

veered to starboard, spoiling the plane's bomb run. The pilot revved up his engine, circled, then roared toward us from dead ahead. As the plane dived very low, its engine sputtered, then stopped. Wing first, the plane crashed into the surging ocean, smashing its other wing on our superstructure as we raced by. The pilot, thrown out of his cockpit, lifted his arm and waved for help, but then I saw him disintegrate in the explosion of the four bombs [D/Cs] which were meant to destroy us. Four violent shocks kicked into our starboard side astern but we left the horrible scene unharmed.[17]

This loss had a sobering effect on *Biter,* who decided that antiquated Swordfish should no longer engage in gunfire duels with U-boats, despite their crews' keenness to do so. Henceforth, the Swordfish were to attack only with D/Cs when the U-boat was seen to be diving or had just dived. In other cases the pilot was to keep the U-boat in observation and, if possible, call in surface ship assistance. *Biter's* next attack would include an excellent example of called-in assistance from *Broadway* and the frigate H.M.S. *Lagan.* At 1230, in good weather, visibility 20 miles, Swordfish "B" sighted a wake, then a U-boat distant four miles, proceeding at 12 knots on a course of 060°. At about the same time, the U-boat–it was U–*89*–sighted the aircraft, altered course, and dived. By the time the Swordfish got down to 50 feet and dropped four D/Cs, U–*89* had been under for 30 seconds. The pilot returned to the position, saw no evidence on the surface, dropped a smoke marker, and reported the action by R/T. *Broadway* received the report and closed the position at 24 knots, while the Swordfish returned to *Biter* short of fuel.

At 1301 *Broadway* reached the marker and, her asdic dome lowered, obtained a contact bearing 045°, range 1,500 yards. Chavasse decided on a Hedgehog attack, which he delivered just as U–*89* accelerated across his bow. There were no explosions. *Lagan,* in the meantime, had arrived to assist and she now made two unsuccessful Hedgehog attacks of her own. Ten minutes later, *Broadway* regained strong echoes on which to fire a second 24-projectile salvo, with a deflection of 15° right. This time, at 1359, there was a single sharp explosive CRACK! that was felt throughout the ship. Twenty seconds later, a second, muffled explosion was heard, and a marker was thrown overside.

Lagan made two Hedgehog attacks on the position without result, but forty-five minutes after *Broadway*'s hit on the U-boat's hull, wreckage appeared on the surface. It consisted of a piece of wood with an electric light switch, two positions for plugs, and the identification *"Schlüssel-M"* (Enigma machine); several pieces of laminated wood varnished on one side and painted white on the other; a woolen jersey with a Nazi emblem; and various other articles of clothing that were not picked up. The single Hedgehog projectile had drilled a fair-size hole. No bodies were seen. They were all entombed below in the Type VIIC iron coffin.[18] And the burying for that day was not over. Within the same hour as *Broadway*'s puncturing hit, another *Drossel* boat was gored; subsequently it would flail about wounded, call desperately for help, then die gamely from the last penetrating effects of a weapon never before used at sea. Ironically, U–*89* was on her way to help that boat when death chose her first.

On 10 December 1941, three days after the attack on Pearl Harbor, the U.S. National Defense Research Committee (NDRC), acting on a proposal made to it sometime before by the U.S. Navy, convened a Top Secret meeting of scientists and engineers at Harvard University to consider the feasibility of a low-weight airborne anti-submarine acoustic homing torpedo. The feasibility agreed upon, the participants met again two weeks later to draw up general requirements and assign responsibilities for design and testing. The requirements in sum were that such a homing torpedo should be able to detect, track, and impact a source of underwater noise, such as the twenty-four-kilocycle sound produced by cavitation–the sudden formation and "popping" of the bubbles created by a high-speed marine propeller; be of a size to fit in existing bomb bays or on a 1,000-pound bomb rack; be droppable from 200 to 300 feet from an aircraft in level flight at airspeeds between 120 and 150 knots; be propelled electrically by a lead acid storage battery at 12 knots for five to fifteen minutes; and be able to carry a 100-pound high-explosive charge.

Bell Laboratories, a division of the Western Electric Company, and the Harvard Underwater Sound Laboratory (HUSL) agreed to pursue independent but cooperative and information-sharing development of the general design. The General Electric Company would design the propulsion and servo motors (and it may also have developed parts or all of the hydrostatic depth-control system). A lightweight 48-volt, shock-resistant, lead-acid storage battery was developed by the Electric Storage Battery Company.[19] HUSL measured the "self noise" made by the torpedo's own propeller and solved the problem of allowing for it; though this was not the problem it might have been, owing to the participation of the David Taylor Model Basin at the Washington Navy Yard. There, Dr. Karl Schoenherr, after discussing prop noise for twenty minutes with Bell Labs visitors, whipped out a large piece of paper and drew a propeller design freehand. "Here is your prop," he said, presenting the sketch of a propeller with a 14³/₄-inch diameter and a 12–inch pitch. When the Bell Labs people protested that these were hardly the precision specifications they required, Schoenherr had a draftsman make a more exact, scaled, dimensional drawing and, after lunch, presented that instead. Not only did the design well serve the prototype acoustic torpedo then under construction, it was not improved upon until five years after the war was over.

The sometimes improvisational character of the torpedo's development was further demonstrated when, for the midsection casings of the torpedo body, Western Electric and Bell Labs engineers turned to a bathtub manufacturer "whose most precise measuring instrument appeared to be a wooden yardstick"; but the company made and shipped interchangeable sections that were remarkably free of defects.[20] In the end, the only significant difference between the Bell Labs and Harvard configurations of the torpedo were the type and placement of the sound-receiving hydrophones. In the Bell Labs model, Rochelle salt crystal hydrophones were arranged symmetrically around the circumference of the torpedo mid-section. In the Harvard model, magnetostriction hydro-phones were mounted on the nose section. While there was no meaningful difference in the performance of the two sys-tems, it was decided by the NDRC to go with the Bell model, since the nose section containing the 92-pound warhead of HBX–1 Torpex high explosive and Mark 142 impact fuse in the forward $14^{1}/_{2}$ inches of the weapon could then be handled independently and, in operations, be attached just before the torpedo was mounted on an aircraft. The four acoustic sen-sors, left, right, up, and down, homed to the noisemaking tar-get by *body shadow*. The hydrophone on the right side, for example, did not hear the noise to the left, or port side, which was shadowed by the torpedo's body, hence the torpedo's guidance system turned the torpedo to port. The up and down sensors acted in the same way along the depth axis.[21]

Prototypes of the torpedo were tested by both boat launches and aircraft drops to measure and verify perfor-mance characteristics. The principal testing was done at Solo-mon's Island on the deepwater Patuxent River in Maryland and at Key West, Florida. At the latter site a USN submarine with a protective cage built around its propellers served as a target for air-launched homing torpedoes loaded with plaster instead of explosive. After the first three of six torpedoes banged into the propeller cage repeatedly until they broke themselves apart, the Captain in command of the exercise called a halt to the testing, reminded everyone present of his secrecy oath, and advised USN personnel involved to stay out of submarines![22]

With testing completed, the design was frozen in October 1942, and production under sole contract was awarded to the Western Electric Company. The first production model was delivered to the USN in March 1943, a remarkable fifteen months since conception. It measured 19 inches in diameter, 84 inches in length, and weighed 683 pounds. Its maximum speed underwater was 12 knots, more than adequate to overhaul a U-boat at its best submerged speed. In fact, its operating characteristics were very close to those first proposed in December 1941. Since the midsection hydrophones had maximum sensitivity in a direction at right angles to the sound source, it was not expected that the Bell model chosen, having reached its present depth, would head directly, nose-first, at the target, even if dropped along the submerged U-boat's track. As a USN operations research study reported in August 1946:

> The torpedo is fitted with a wooden spoiler ring and tail stabilizer to aid its flight in air; these break off when it enters the water. After water entry the torpedo usually circles, with a turning radius of 50 to 150 feet, at a depth below 40 feet, until it comes within the sphere of influence of a sound source sufficiently intense to activate the controls. Thereafter the torpedo proceeds on an approximate pursuit course until it strikes the target (or loses it). At full battery capacity it will run from 12 to 15 minutes, traveling approximately 6,000 yards, after which it will sink, since it has no negative buoyancy.[23]

From this description, it is little wonder that airmen nicknamed the weapon "Wandering Annie." But its official designation, to mask the Top Secret nature and purpose of the device, was Mark XXIV Mine. (Another reason for use of the term *mine,* it has been suggested, was to keep the weapon out of the ponderous USN torpedo establishment with all its baggage.[24]) It also was called FIDO, and when that was thought too closely to suggest "sniffing," the code name was changed to PROCTOR. From the beginning, Mark XXIV was cloaked under the strictest official secrecy, since if word of its function leaked to the Germans, all a U-boat had to do in order to avoid its fatal sting was to proceed at slow submerged speed after diving, when cavitation would fall below the sound sensors' threshold. When a manufacturer's lot of Mk.24s was ready for shipment from Kearny, New Jersey, it was kept hidden and loaded on military aircraft in off-ramp, secure areas.

Usually a guard of one officer and five technicians accompanied the lot until it reached its destination, either USN or RN.

The first RN-destined weapon, however, traveled to the United Kingdom under the guard of only one officer, Acting Group Captain Jeaff Greswell, R.A.F., who had been in the United States on liaison ASW missions to USAAF bases and was asked to escort the Mk.24 on the British liner *Empress of Scotland.* It was Greswell who had worked with Humphrey de Verde Leigh in developing the Leigh Light, who had formed the first operational L.L. squadron, No. 172, and who, on the night of 4 June 1942, had made the first L.L. damaging attack, on the Italian submarine *Luigi Torelli,* while attacking the Italian *Morosini* as well. At a New York dock, Greswell told the writer, he received the weapon from a USN truck heavily guarded by armed sailors, who carried it up the gangway in three separate unmarked boxes, one containing the nose section, one the midsection, and one the tail. Greswell signed off on the USN documents and, after the ship's Captain had the boxes placed in his ship's safe, Greswell asked for and received a receipt. Upon the ship's arrival at Liverpool much the same high-security procedures ensued, and the three boxes were secretly whisked away on a highly guarded RAF lorry. Imagine his surprise, he asked the writer, when, on leave, Greswell received a postal notice from His Majesty's Customs inquiring why he had failed to declare the importation into the United Kingdom of an airborne homing torpedo for use against U-boats![25]

More efficient security attended the first consignment of Mk.24s in number to Northern Ireland on 27 April and to Iceland on 1 May. Originally the weapon was to have been used first against independently operating Japanese submarines in the Pacific, but the British delegation to the Washington Convoy Conference in March had persuaded Admiral King to permit simultaneous use against the U-boats, for which the date 8 May was set, later advanced to 6 May. The greatest secrecy was imposed on USN, Coastal Command, and RN aviation personnel engaged in operational use of the weapon. It was not, for example, to be released except when a U-boat was diving with the conning-tower hatch closed, or when one had already dived (though never beyond two minutes time), so that the nature of the weapon could not be observed. It was not to be used in the presence of any surface ships, both because their propeller sounds might deflect the Mk.24 from its intended target, and because even the crew members of Allied ships without need-to-know clearance were not to observe or learn about the weapon. Nor was the Mk.24 to be used in the Mediterranean or in inshore waters of the Atlantic where it might run ashore. Even the aircrews employing the weapon were not to be told anything about its operation other than the drill required for maintaining, arming, and releasing it, though most crews could figure out Wandering Annie's scheme. These restrictions were so faithfully observed that the Germans did not learn about the Mk.24 until after the war.

In the newly formed second VLR Liberator Squadron, No. 86 at Aldergrove, Northern Ireland, aircrews found that a VLR could carry two Mk.24s plus four D/Cs, and this became the standard load. The first operational sorties with the homing torpedoes took place on 7 May, but there were no attacks. At this stage, it should be mentioned, tactical doctrine was minimal, and only after some operational experience was it learned that an individual Mk.24 aircraft was advised, upon sighting a U-boat, to dive upon it with D/Cs or strafing fire to force a dive so that the Mk.24 could be employed. Later, in USN attacks by CVE aircraft working in tandem, the F4F4 Wildcat induced the dive and the TBM–1 Avenger dropped the Mk.24. It was on 12 May that the first–ever attacks employing the weapon were made, all in support of Convoy HX.237, which was being hounded by the U-boats of *Gruppe Drossel* in 46°40′N, 26°20′W. Three Coastal VLRs from 86 Sqdn. at Aldergrove each sighted a *Drossel* boat and released a Mk.24 after it dived.[26] Two FIDOs wandered off from the scent. But the third hit bang on.

Liberator "B" had lifted off at 0344 with Flight Lieutenant John Wright at the controls. Seven and a half hours later, at 1113, while flying cover for HX.237 in showery weather,

Wright and his seven–man crew sighted a surfaced U-boat at 46°40′N, 26°20′W and initiated an attack. The target was U–456, a Type VIIC boat on her third patrol, having sortied from Brest on 24 April. Her Commander, born at Kiel in 1915, was Kptlt. Max-Martin Teichert, a Knight's Cross holder who had torpedoed, among numerous other ships, the trophy RN cruiser H.M.S. *Edinburgh* on 30 April 1942, while the warship was escorting convoy QP.11 on the Murmansk run; the cruiser had to be finished off by a British torpedo. And, more immediately, on 11 May 1943, Teichert had shared with Clausen (U–403) in the sinking of the HX.237 straggler *Fort Concord*. Now, on 12 May, the *Edinburgh* was about to be avenged.

Lookouts on U–456 sighted the approach of Wright's B/86, and Teichert gave a fateful order to dive. With the conning tower going under, and no ships nearby, Wright's bombardier released a Mk.24 from his bay, and after the torpedo entered the water, B/86 circled while all eyes on board searched the water's rough surface. Two minutes later, within a half-mile of the diving swirl, a "brownish patch" appeared, about 90 feet in diameter. Shortly afterwards, U–456 resurfaced and proceeded at high speed on a zigzag pattern, firing away at B/86 with her Flak armament. The Liberator returned fire and made a D/C run in, but overshot with a stick of three. With no more D/Cs, Wright called up the surface escort on R/T and two destroyers, *Pathfinder* and H.M.S. *Opportune,* raced toward the scene. The Liberator stayed overhead until 1435, when PLE forced it home to base.[27]

Teichert sent a first distress signal to BdU and nearby boats at 1130, following it up with another at 1151:

> AM NOT CLEAR FOR DIVING. QU BD 6646. AIRCRAFT IS KEEPING CONTACT. URGENTLY REQUEST HELP.[28]

The source of his problem was made clear in a signal at 1325:

> AM STEERING COURSE 300 AT HIGH SPEED. BAD LEAK IN AFTER COMPARTMENT, NEED HELP URGENTLY.[29]

The puncture had been made at some point other than at the propeller shafts, since the boat was moving smartly on the surface. From Berlin BdU ordered U-89 (Lohmann) to proceed at maximum speed to Teichert's assistance, and later detailed U-603 (Oblt.z.S. Rudolf Baltz) and U-190 (Kptlt. Max Wintermeyer) to the same task.[30] Teichert may have been heartened to hear the order given to U-89, and he sent out beacon signals for Lohmann to home in on, but it is clear from his message traffic that as time passed, he became more and more anxious about U-89's whereabouts. At 1526 and 1606:

WHERE IS OUR U-BOAT? [*FRAGE WO STEHT EIGENES BOOT U.D.*] . . . LEAK WILL HOLD FOR AWHILE YET.[31]

TO LOHMANN. WHAT IS YOUR POSITION? DO YOU HEAR MY HOMING SIGNAL? MY POSITION IS BD 6569, COURSE 220, SPEED II.[32]

Of course, Lohmann's position was on the seabed, where he no longer heard anything. And soon Teichert would have to fend for his fate alone. At 1640, the destroyer *Opportune*, bearing down at flank speed, had the conning tower of U-456 in sight from 10 miles distance, and no doubt the U-boat had the larger vessel in sight as well. In that extremity Teichert must have thought that there was but one supreme expedient and that was to test the material integrity of his wounded boat against the depths, for at 1645 *Opportune* observed the U-boat dive. Did Teichert think the gamble preferable to surrender? We shall never know. The dive became an irreversible plunge into a bourne from which no hand returned, ranks and ratings closed up at Diving Stations forever.

Though *Opportune*, joined by *Pathfinder*, searched the scene, which was probably BD 6594, or 46°39′N, 26°54′W, no further sign of the U-boat was observed. The Mk.24, unaided by any other agency, had performed its appointed duty, and just seventeen months after its conception. Sole credit for U-456's destruction is given to Liberator B/86.[33] Dönitz/ Godt in Berlin, having, like Teichert, no idea what had really happened to U–456, speculated in the BdU war diary for 13 May that she was "probably sunk by a bomb hit on her stern."[34]

In addition to the sinking of two of the U-boats attacking HX.237, surface and air escorts succeeded on 12 May in damaging several other boats, which had to move off for repairs. At BdU it must have been clear that *Drossel* had taken a beating; accordingly, at 0821 on 13 May, those boats that were operational, unless they were in positions ahead of HX.237, were ordered to abandon that convoy and retire to the southwestward in order to shore up Groups *Elbe I* and *Elbe II,* which had been formed from *Elbe* and *Rhein* three days before to intercept SC.129. Before they got away, however, the *Drossel* boats took one more licking. At 0635, Sunderland "G" of 423 RCAF Sqdn., detailed to a dawn patrol over HX.237, sighted a U-boat at 48°35′N, 22°50′W, ten miles distant from the convoy closing its starboard beam. The Queen made a D/C attack on the surfaced boat, without result, then circled over it, exchanging gunfire. Corvette H.M.S. *Drumbeller* observed the aircraft circling low to the water and sped to the scene, bringing her four–inch gun to bear at 0655. The boat dived, and *Drumbeller,* acquiring an asdic echo, fired depth charges. She was soon joined by the frigate *Lagan,* which made a Hedgehog attack at 0729 that led to two explosions.

Within one minute of the H.H. firing, a large air bubble mushroomed on the surface, followed by smaller bubbles that lasted about ten minutes and then by quantities of diesel oil that eventually formed a patch 600 feet in diameter. Pieces of wood and a rubber eyepiece were recovered by *Lagan.* Definitely sunk was U–753 (Korv. Kapt. Alfred Mannhardt von Mannstein), which had sortied from La Pallice on 5 May. It was her sixth patrol. There were no survivors.[35] Following this action there were a few scattered attacks on sightings by *Biter* aircraft, but by late morning, with the enemy having disappeared from every quadrant, *Biter* and EG5 disengaged to the southwest to support SC.129, about a day's steaming away.[36]

That convoy's close escort EG B2 had had a busy time

since the afternoon of the 11th, when first contact with the enemy was made in 41°N, 33°W, running down HF/DF and radar bearings and dropping D/Cs on various asdic contacts.[37] At 1800 that day, two merchant ships, *Antigone* and *Grado,* were sunk by U–*402* (Korv. Kapt. Siegfried Freiherr von Forstner). Commander Donald Macintyre, SO on the destroyer H.M.S. *Hesperus,* became particularly occupied on the night of the 11th/12th, when he made four D/C, two Hedgehog, and one ramming attacks between 0129 and 0232½ against U–*223* (Oblt.z.S. Karljung Wächter). The reamming resulted after the harried U-boat was sighted surfacing and *Hesperus* opened fire with her 4.7-inch gun and Oerlikons, scoring at least three hits. The boat, which was seen first as trimmed down, or decks awash, then became fully surfaced, and some of the crew came up onto the conning-tower bridge, which was now illuminated by the destroyer's 10-inch signal projector, where some were seen hit by Oerlikon fire and two went overboard (one, a Fireman second class named Zieger, was recovered by U–*359* lt.z.S. Heinz Förster] and later handed back to U–*223).*

The boat then turned under full helm 360° and came beam on across the destroyer's bows. Mindful that he was still ten days' steaming from home and that he did not want to disable himself with two other U-boats known present, Macintyre decided to administer only a "halfhearted ram." With engines stopped and proceeding at about 10 knots, *Hesperus* struck U–*223* just abaft her conning tower. Gunfire delivered at the same moment produced a "blinding red" explosion. As *Hesperus* withdrew, lookouts reported torpedo tracks from another U-boat approaching from astern. The warheads missed. Thinking the rammed U-boat to be in a sinking condition, Macintyre rejoined the screen of SC.129. U–*223,* in fact, did not sink but, extensively damaged, was forced to return to base, which she reached, after limping through the dangerous Bay of Biscay, on the 24th.[38]

By daybreak on the 12th, a considerable number of boats were trying to work their way around to the front, with U–*186* (Kptlt. Siegfried Hesemann) acting as shadower.

Dönitz/Godt urged them onward: DO NOT SLIDE BACK. FOR-
WARD WITH THE HIGHEST SPEED.[39] AT 1133 *Hesperus* obtained
an HF/DF contact bearing 020°, ahead of the convoy about
15 miles, and shaped course to investigate. At 1205, with
speed reduced to 20 knots to allow for an asdic sweep,
Macintyre received a strong echo classified "submarine." Two
minutes later, he made a Hedgehog attack, but there were no
explosions. Then, 30 seconds later, the U-boat showed its
periscope at 50 yards Green 10°, crossing from starboard to
port. Macintyre pursued and fired a ten-pattern, followed by a
second H.H. salvo at 1219, again without result. Asdic contact
was then lost, leading Macintyre to assume that the boat had
gone deep. By hydrophone effect, however, he regained the
target, at 1215½, and made a deep drop of ten Minol and
Amatol D/Cs set to 350 and 500 feet. Eighteen minutes later,
just before a planned deeper drop, *Hesperus* heard a series of
explosions. A fourth and last attack with ten D/Cs set to 550
and 700 feet was carried out at 1233½. Then, at 1245, a single
"sharp" explosion—probably internal—and "peculiar noises"
were heard quite near the destroyer; soon afterwards, wreckage and oil came to the surface. The victim was the shadower
U–*186*, on her second combat patrol.[40]

During the rest of the afternoon there was heavy HF/DF
activity. Between 1530 and 1930 the close escort made six
sightings and two attacks. At dusk, the convoy acutely altered
course 40° to port on to 343° in order to "throw the U-boats
out of position." A large-scale night attack by the *Elbe I* and II
boats—there were twenty-two remaining after one sunk and
two forced back to base with damage—was feared by
Macintyre, but to his surprise it did not materialize; one lone
attack was turned back by *Hesperus* and the corvette H.M.S.
Clematis. By the morning of the 13th, HF/DF traffic had
greatly diminished, and the appearance overhead later in the
day of VLR Liberators no doubt added encouragement to EG
B2's aggressive ahead-of-convoy patrolling. When BdU received a signal from the *Elbe* boat U–*642* that it had sighted a
carrier *(Biter)* proceeding on a southwest course at high
speed, obviously to lend succor to SC.129, BdU concluded,

the decision was made in Berlin to call off operations against the convoy on the 14th. *Biter* joined SC.129 at 1400 on that day, when, because of its threat alone, the U-boats had already been ordered away. Two days later, absent any further contact with the enemy, *Biter* and EG5 disengaged, and four days later still, the convoy arrived safely in home waters.

While "powerful air escort" was named the principal reason for ordering withdrawal, BdU was equally concerned that during the 12th when twelve boats were in contact with the convoy and *no* air escort was yet available, the U-boats still failed to achieve results. It could only surmise that with some unknown shipborne detection devices (actually HF/DF and centimetric radar, primarily the former), "the enemy must have picked up all the boats around the convoy with astonishing accuracy." It observed that "such a rapid detection of the boats has not previously occurred on such a scale."[41] The campaign against HX.237 and SC.129 had sputtered and failed despite excellent intelligence about the convoys' positions, courses, and alterations, and despite the fact that altogether, about thirty-six U-boats operated against the two convoys.

The plain fact was that the U-boats' 1939-period technology (excepting certain torpedo advances) was now no match for the 1943–period sophisticated detection equipment, target plotting tactics, and state-of-the-art weaponry of the surface escorts, not to mention the operational research-developed tactics of the air escorts and their new Mark XXIV Mine. Herbert Werner, I.W.O on *U-230*, complained to the writer that the "May disaster" was owed to the "unconscionable policies of the U-boat Command" that required crews to go to sea that late in the war with "obsolete and inadequate equipment, weapons, and tactics." The BdU staff, he asserted, "had not prepared for this disaster. It discounted what the Commanders were reporting from the field. It didn't want to face reality–the inevitable that was to come."[42]

While that view may be regarded as extreme by other U-boat veterans of Black May, it is beyond serious dispute that by that month, if not earlier, the U-boat, considered as a high seas detection instrument and weapons platform, was outclassed by the *quality* of the Allied forces, sea and air (excluding the Swordfish), arrayed against it. The *numbers* still favored the U-boats, but the disparity in quality was starkly apparent. Add to that the ever-widening gap between the experience and proficiency levels of the human components on either side, and the reasons for what Werner called "the May disaster" were all the more manifest. The material inequalities were reflected in BdU's bar graphs. Since the pivotal Battle for ONS.5, the exchange rate of U-boats lost for merchant ships sunk suffered an ineluctable, if uneven, decline: In the battle for HX.237 the U-boats had exchanged three U-boats lost for four stragglers sunk; and in the battle for SC.129 they exchanged one boat sunk and two severely damaged for two convoy vessels sunk. In Convoy ONS.7 to follow, the loss ratio would be one-to-one, and, strikingly, that one merchant ship lost to enemy action would be the last lost in the Northern transatlantic convoy lanes for the remainder of May and the whole of June.

On 11 and 12 May BdU collected twenty-five U-boats from those just entering the North Atlantic from French, German, and Norwegian bases, as well as from those that were refueling in midocean from the supply boats U–*459,* U–*119,* U–*461,* and U–*514,* and formed them into five small groups, placed southeast of Greenland, named picturesquely after rivers: *Lech, Isar, Inn, Iller,* and *Nab.* Westbound Convoy ONS.7, having departed the U.K. on 7 May under the guard of EG B5, encountered *Iller* on the 13th when U–*640* (Oblt.z.S. Karl-Heinz Nagel) reported sighting its columns in AL 1265. Later on the same day, Groups *Inn* and *Isar* were ordered to combine forces in a new patrol line, Group *Donau* [Danube River] 1, and *Lech* and *Nab* were similarly joined to form *Donau 11,* both new groups charged with the task of interdicting U–*640's* convoy. The *Iller* group, of which U–*640* was a part, was ordered to operate independently against ONS.7.

But shadower U–*640* herself would not be a factor for long, since, early on the next day, she was caught on the surface at position 60°32′N, 31°05′W by Catalina "K" of USN 84 Sqdn. based in Iceland. In 7/10th cloud with bases at 1,700 feet and visibility ten miles, K/84 sighted U–*640* sixteen miles from the convoy and, at 0739, initiated an attack from the still-surfaced U-boat's port beam. At 75 feet off the deck the pilot released three USN 350-pound depth bombs (D/Bs) set to shallow 25-foot depth. Nos. 2 and 3 D/Bs straddled the boat, and following their explosions, the "blue-black" hull slowed from 8 to 2 knots, left a path of air bubbles 20 yards wide, became stationary, wallowed, listed at a sharp angle, and sank.[43]

There were no further incidents during ONS.7's passage until shortly after midnight on the 17th, when *Iller* boat U–*657* (Kptlt. Heinrich Göllnitz), on her first combat patrol (out of Norway), put two torpedoes, two minutes apart, into the 5,196–GRT British steamer *Aymeric,* which had the unhappy distinction of being the last northern transatlantic ship under the red duster to go down in May or in the whole of the month that followed. The ship's foremast collapsed; the hatches from No. 1 hold, the rafts from the fore rigging, and even the derricks were blown over the side; while slag ballast was strewn everywhere. Moments after the second torpedo, the ship's boilers exploded, fracturing both port and starboard sides of the vessel. A number of the Lascar crew panicked while lowering the boats and lives were lost as a result. The ship went under five minutes after the first explosion. Men found themselves swimming in bitterly cold water, where many became stiff and sank. The survivors were rescued by a rescue ship and a trawler. Of the seventy-eight-man crew, fifty-three died. It was one of the worst human tolls of the month.[44] But the drowned and frozen would not go unavenged.

H.M.S. *Swale,* SO of EG B5, ordered "Artichoke" and swept out herself 6,000 yards astern of the victim's position. There, at 0138, she obtained an asdic contact classified as "submarine," bearing 285°, range 900 yards. Three minutes later, *Swale* was on top of the contact with ten D/Cs. When no evidence surfaced, she fired Hedgehogs at 0203. There were no explosions, but the bridge observed patches of light oil in which, peculiarly, small yellow flames appeared. The River-class frigate then fired a second H.H. salvo at 0224 and, 33 seconds later, heard a single loud explosion followed after 107 seconds more by two "muffled" explosions. At 0231, just to be sure, *Swale* dropped a ten-pattern set to 150 and 350 feet over the position, and was rewarded by two loud explosions five and a half minutes later and a second appearance of oil patches. *Aymeric's* slayer would not surface again. The position where forty-four young Germans paid the stern price was 58°54′N, 42°33′W.[45] Convoy ONS.7 continued its passage without further hindrance, joined briefly from daylight on the 18th to 1100 on the 19th by the four-destroyer Third Escort (Support) Group. Close escort B5 was relieved by the Western Local Escort Group at WESTOMP on the 21st and the convoy entered Halifax four days later.

As long before as February, reckoning on the eight-day cycle for departures of ONS and SC convoys, Commander Peter Gretton, SO, Escort Group B7, had set a date at the end of May when he pledged he would be in London to meet a Wren whom he had courted at Gilbert Roberts's Tactical Unit (WATU), and there exchange vows of matrimony with her in St. Mary's, Cadogan Square. At 1330 on the 14th of the month, his prenuptial voyage began, as a now-familiar company of warships—*Duncan, Vidette, Tay, Loosestrife, Snowflake* (her mate, the injured *Sunflower,* to follow), and *Pink*—slipped their moorings at St. John's, Newfoundland, and bore eastward through the inevitable fog. Joining the escort at sea were the rescue trawler *Northern Spray,* also of ONS.5 fame, and an extra corvette, H.M.C.S. *Kitchener.* At 0600 on the 15th, still in fog, B7 met the convoy entrusted to its care, SC.130, consisting of thirty-nine merchant vessels, not including a rescue ship, *Zamalek.*

Heavily laden with grain, sugar, pulp, lumber, fuel oil, gas, and general cargo, the merchant fleet, with many old coal burners, was not expected to exceed seven and a half knots, but Gretton was confident that, *pace* adverse seas and unkindly U-boats, the convoy would reach the U.K. by its due date, the 25th. The first night of passage was spent in thick fog, and when a large iceberg was encountered, *Vidette* positioned herself, fully illuminated and whistle blowing, between it and the advancing columns. That danger past, the rest of the night was spent making steady revolutions on course 081°. With daybreak on the 16th the veil of fog lifted and the columns moved smartly ahead at eight knots. *Sunflower* joined at 1100. Good clear sailing weather continued on the 17th, and five RCAF Fortresses patrolled the surrounding water, though Gretton complained. "The air escort from Newfoundland are not yet trained to convoy work. Their communications are bad and they do not fully understand homing procedure."[46] He particularly regretted that the only day SC.130 was without air cover was the next day, the 18th, when the convoy was sighted by the enemy.

At 2219, in 54°39′N, 36°47′W, rescue ship *Zamalek*, which was equipped with FH3 HF/DF, reported a ground-wave signal to the north. Beginning at 0116 on the 19th the air filled with HF/DF contacts—*Duncan* was fitted with FH4 and *Tay* with FH3—and cross-cuts revealed the presence of four U-boats, one close on each bow of the convoy and one on each quarter. Taking the role of hunter, *Duncan* went after the boat judged to be four miles on the port bow. A radar contact was obtained at 5,000 yards, but the boat dived before being seen on the bright, full-moonlit sea. *Duncan* fired a five-charge pattern in the estimated diving position and started operation "Observant."[47] Though without visible result, this first attack, which kept a U-boat down and out of the game, was representative of the aggressive behavior the B7 escorts displayed thereafter over the next forty-eight hours against an enemy force numbering altogether thirty-three U-boats, though apparently no more than twenty would be in contact with the convoy.

The force was organized by BdU as the result of an intercepted signal in Allied Convoy Cipher No. 3 dated 15 May, which B-Dienst forwarded on the 17th. The signal gave SC.130's position, course, and speed, as well as the identity of its close escort, B7.[48] Here was an opportunity for BdU to gain vengeance for *die Katastrophe am ONS.5*. Accordingly, two patrol lines were established to be in position at 2000 on the 18th athwart the convoy's course: *Donau I,* consisting of thirteen boats (two, U-*640* and U-*657,* had been sunk, unknown to BdU) from AK 4258 (56°03′N, 37°55′W) to AK 8141 (53°31′N, 35°25′W); and *Donau II,* consisting of twelve boats from AK 4944 (53°09′N, 35°15′W) to AK 8734 (50°33′N, 33°35′W). In addition, eight boats coming out from Biscay bases or from at-sea refueling were to take up a patrol line from ED 2181 (50°21′N, 33°25′W) to DD 2769 (48°39′N, 32°35′W) under the name *Oder* (the river). Although BdU's orders creating these dispositions were not decrypted by the Allies until the 19th through the 22nd, according to the Bletchley Park Hut 8 record, thus providing no cryptographic intelligence on the basis of which to divert the convoy from danger, the prescient Rodger Winn in OIC's Tracking Room somehow knew of these dispositions anyway, since on the 17th he wrote in his Special Intelligence Summary:

> The next development will be the establishment of new patrols on an are between 020° and 140° from Virgin Rocks at a radius of 600 miles from Gander, Newfoundland. Twenty or more U/boats are now moving to take these up and the apparent gap through which SC 130 has been routed is rapidly closing: it will be touch and go whether this convoy scrapes through.[49]

But Gretton's first warning did not come until 2219 on the 18th, when the rescue ship *Zamalek* reported HF/DF contact. Later, on reaching port–he knew nothing of B-Dienst's or of Bletchley Park's cryptographic penetrations–he wondered aloud how it happened that so large a concentration of U-boats had been assembled without warning to him from the Admiralty's shore-based HF/DF.[50] The answer no doubt was that the patrol lines were formed under orders of radio silence.[51] Now, at 0300, just before dawn on the 19th, when he knew that he was being shadowed if not surrounded, Gretton turned the convoy 90° to starboard in order to avoid a dawn submerged attack. The stratagem worked, and when the first VLR Liberator (T/120) arrived from Reykjavik and made two attacks on U–731 (Oblt.z.S. Werner Techand), which was undamaged, the enemy boat was approximately where SC.130 would have been had not the foxing course alteration been made. The course 081° was resumed at 0400.

Liberator T/120 went on to sight five additional boats in the vicinity, a record six for one sortie.[52] With so many boats about, Gretton had to be cheered to know not only that aircraft from Iceland and Northern Ireland would watch over him but that a Support Group was on its way to firm up the surface screen: it was the same First Escort Group that had ridden out to assist B7 in the final hours of the ONS.5 struggle. EG1's frigates Wear (S.O.), Spey, and Jed, together with the former U.S.C.G. cutter Sennen (Pelican had to return with engine defects) cleared St. John's at 1930 on the 16th, and in the late morning of the 19th, while closing the convoy 15 miles off from the starboard quarters, Wear sighted a U-boat on the surface bearing 034° 12 miles. At 1135 the boat, identified later as U–952 (Oblt.z.S. Oskar Curio), was seen to dive. At 1209 the crow's nest lookout in Jed sighted a second U-boat, which Jed and Sennen would later hunt.

At 1228 the first boat launched a salvo of four eels that passed between Wear and Jed. Wear then altered course up the torpedo tracks and obtained asdic contact at a range of 1,800 yards. At 1245 she made a Hedgehog attack, but only twelve projectiles fired because a safety ready switch handle retaining spring broke. There were no explosions. What was worse, Wear's helm jammed hard aport and took an hour to fix. In the meantime, Spey closed, obtained contact, and made three D/C attacks, at 1319, 1335, and 1415. The repaired Wear joined Spey in a fourth, barrage-type attack—sixteen D/Cs fired deep from each ship at six-second intervals—at 1533. No evidence appeared on the surface, but U–952 was extensively damaged at 170 meters depth by the last bombardment, and forced back to base.

The second U-boat, meanwhile, was visible to Jed's bridge

by 1227 at an estimated range of 8 miles. Observing *Jed* in pursuit, the boat dived at 1245 when 5 miles intervened. *Jed* made asdic contact at 1312; moments later, the U-boat unaccountably blew tanks, broached the surface, and dived again. *Jed* fired a five-charge pattern at 1316, and a D/C from the starboard thrower fell directly into the swirl, after which an oil patch appeared on the surface. Contact was not regained until a weak echo was received at 1324 and *Jed* reduced speed to 10 knots in order to carry out a Hedgehog attack, which she delivered at 1334. There were no explosions, and subsequent loss of echo led *Jed* to question the contact.

While the frigate started an "Observant" around the position of the first attack, the cutter *Sennen* came on the scene, obtained a contact of her own, and fired a ten-pattern at 1405. The explosion plumes were followed at 1427 by oil and bubbles, then, at 1440, by splintered woodwork and a small red object resembling meat or remains. At 1443 the asdic operator reported strange noises like escaping compressed air, and *Jed* made a H.H. attack on the noise source, with no explosions, at 1447. Oil continued to rise and by 1515, when the two escorts were ordered to rejoin the convoy if no longer in contact, the oil patch was estimated to be over a quarter of a mile wide. In the latest assessment of this engagement, U-*760* (Oblt.z.S. Otto Erich Blum) is thought to have been the target of the first two attacks; she sustained damage to upper-deck containers. The second two attacks were made against U-*954* (Kptlt. Odo Loewe), which was destroyed by *Sennen*'s ten-pattern at 1405.[53] There were no survivors from U-*954,* which was on her first combat patrol, having sortied from Kiel, Germany, on 8 April. Among the dead was twenty-one-year-old Leutnant zur See Peter Dönitz, the Grand Admiral's younger son.[54]

A second U-boat would be sunk in the vicinity of SC.130 that day, though it was not a member of the *Donau* and *Order* groups, and when it was found by Hudson "M" of 269 Sqdn. it was proceeding due west some four degrees latitude north of the convoy's known position. This was U-*273* (Oblt.z.S. Hermann Rossmann), another boat on her first patrol. At 1627 the Hudson pilot dived on the neophyte boat and delivered a four-D/C straddle of the conning tower, No. 3 being observed to enter the water on the starboard side within ten yards of the surfaced hull. Almost immediately afterwards, oil spread from the U-boat's stern, eventually covering an area 100 feet wide and 600 yards long. U-273 remained on the surface for seven minutes, turning continually to starboard, and fighting back with flak. The Hudson returned fire, scoring hits around the tower and causing panic among the lookouts and gunners.

Finally, at 1634, the U-boat attempted a dive, from which she would not resurface, though floating wreckage did. Another forty-four men descended to their deaths while Hudson pilot Flying Officer J. N. F. Bell returned to base (and to a postwar career as a British Airways Captain). It was another of the Atlantic war's fateful exchanges, now almost always unfavorable to the German side.[55] More mysterious was the disappearance of U-381 (Kptlt. Graf von Pückler und Limpurg), which had sortied from St.-Nazaire on 31 March and made her last transmission to BdU at 1502 on 9 May from qu AK 7962. Subsequently, she was ordered, with three other boats, to form Group Inn, and later to join Donau I. Whether she did either is not known. On the 21st, BdU, not having received any further signals from the boat, asked her to report her position. When no response was received, U-381 was posted as missing with effect from that date. Her loss has not been matched to any of the attacks made by the surface ships of EG1 or B7 or by any of the air escorts.[56]

Prior to and following Jed and Sennen's kill of U-954, indeed throughout the 19th and continuing until dawn on the 20th, SC.130's surface escorts made no fewer than twenty-seven individual attacks on U-boats sighted from the cockpit of an aircraft or from an escort's crow's nest or bridge, or detected by HF/DF or radar, and/or tracked underwater by asdic.[57] Each sighting or contact was pursued energetically in keeping with Western Approaches' finding that most U-boats sunk by surface vessels during the year prior to May were destroyed prior to their attacks, not afterward (see chapter 3). As it happened, however, none of B7's attacks and none further of EG1's resulted in a kill.

Duncan and *Snowflake* were certain, because of the accurate placement of the D/Cs and one Hedgehog explosion seven seconds after the pattern struck the water, that they had destroyed a U-boat in a series of six attacks that they carried out jointly between 0755 and 0918 on the 19th, *Duncan* getting in what he thought was the fatal blow. But a recent reassessment finds that *Snowflake*'s contact, U–304 (Oblt.z.S. Heinz Koch), was undamaged except for a tank put out of action, and that *Duncan*'s contact, a different boat altogether, probably U–636 (Kptlt. Hans Hildebrandt), was undamaged.[58] *Wear* and *Spey* severely damaged U–952 at 1245 through 1533 on the 19th, as shown above; *Spey* slightly damaged U–413 (Poel) at 0346 through 0542 on the 20th; and *Jed* lightly damaged U–91 (Oblt.z.S. Heinz Hungershausen) at 0420 through 0439, also on the 20th.[59]

Despite that apparent lack of success in destroying U-boats, the surface escorts achieved a success that, on shore, was more highly valued than U-boat trophies hung on a wardroom wall: they saved every merchant ship in the convoy from harm. They did that, under Commander Gretton's skillful command, by aggressively running to ground every enemy craft sighted or detected, and by directing the VLR Liberators in the cloud cover overhead to every W/T transmission source. The number of HF/DF contacts was striking even by the usual standard of talkative German radiomen: during the 19th and 20th *Duncan* counted fifty-one, *Tay* thirty-one, and *Sennen* twenty-three.[60] As each cross-cut came into his plotting room, Gretton vectored the VLRs to the transmitting boat from their overhead air search patterns, which were called by such code names as "Frog," "Adder," and "Viper." On more occasions than a few, U-boat Commanders were stunned to find that at or before the close of an *Ausgang F.T.* (outgoing W/T transmission), a Liberator was bearing down on their positions. In his war diary entries for 19 and 20 May, Dönitz/Godt complained about the "continual surprise attacks by land-based aircraft out of low-hanging clouds."[61] Of course, BdU attributed them to radar, but the attacks were instead additional evidence of the importance in the Atlantic war of what the Allies affectionately called Huff-Duff.

The final U-boat kill of the SC.130 crossing came from the air at the hands of No. 120 Sqdn. out of Reykjavik, whose aircraft made twenty-seven sightings on the 19th and 20th. Two VLRs struck at U-707 (Kptlt. Günter Gretschel), which like U-413 (Poel) had operated against ONS.5: at 1340 on the 19th, P/120 dropped four D/Cs on the surfaced Gretschel boat without inflicting injury, but at 0810 the next day, N/120, sighting the same boat and attacking ten seconds after Gretschel submerged, caused severe damage, forcing that boat to retire from the field. At 0745 on the 20th, U-418 (Oblt.z.S. Gerhard Lange) was injured by four D/Cs dropped by Liberator "X" of 59 Sqdn. based in Ballykelly, Northern Ireland. The kill was made on the 20th by P/120, whose pilot, Squadron Leader J. R. E. Proctor, lifted off from Reykjavik at 0954 and met SC.130 at 1430 in 55°N, 30°W, where, at Gretton's direction, he began a series of searches, sighting one U-boat at 1448 that he was not able to attack and another at 1710, Red 15° six miles, that he dived on, dropping four D/Cs and obtaining a straddle on the partially submerged boat. It was U-258 (von Mässenhausen), another ONS.5 boat, which had sunk the American McKeesport twenty-two days before.

The Liberator's rear gunner saw the boat's conning tower lifted out of the water for three seconds by the explosions. When the spray of the plumes subsided, the boat was no longer visible, but an oil patch appeared that during the next thirty minutes spread to about 200 feet in diameter, with an "almost white patch" at its head looking like air bubbles. Ironically, at just one hour and eight minutes after this attack, U-258 was sent a signal by BdU ordering her to return to base and to make frequent transmissions over the next three days for purposes of deception. Von Mässenhausen and his crew would not be able to obey that order.[62] Meanwhile, P/120 carried on her patrol, and at 1924 sighted a surfacing U-boat three miles distant. Diving, Squadron Leader Proctor decided to strafe the conning tower with machine-gun fire in an apparent attempt to force the boat back under water so that he could drop a Mk.24 Mine. Six crewmen sighted on the bridge returned his fire and the boat remained on the surface.

Proctor swung the heavy craft around and made another pass, expending 180 cannon rounds against the tower and foredeck. Though his report does not state that the U-boat finally did dive, Proctor released a FIDO at 1931. Three minutes later, he reported, the U-boat could be seen on the surface down by the stern, circling, "in difficulties." At 2143, he began the return flight to base, where he arrived at 0115 on the 21st. Proctor's after-action report in the Squadron's Operations Record Book makes no mention of the Mk.24 but states instead that he released a "600 1b D/C." This was the code for Mk.24, and a cleverly chosen one, since there was a Mark I 600 lb. depth bomb just coming into service. When a weapon was cited in print as a depth "bomb (D/B)" it was in fact a large depth charge; when the citation read "600 lb. D/C" it was the Mk.24. One may have further confidence here that Proctor's weapon was indeed the Mk.24 because No. 120 Sqdn. had not yet been equipped with the 600–lb. D/B.[63] In any event, the Mk.24 was dropped on this occasion without effect: the intended target, U–*418*, made off with no further injury (until 1 June when, homeward bound, she was destroyed by Beaufighter "B" of 236 Sqdn. in the Bay of Biscay).[64]

Among the merchant ship columns of SC.130, stationkeeping was excellent throughout the battle, even during the twenty emergency turns that Gretton ordered in its course. As he commented in his Report of Proceedings, "The convoy was executing blue turns with the precision of a battlefleet."[65] The last such evasive alteration was made at dawn on the 21st, but it was an unnecessary precaution by that time, since, on the evening before, BdU signaled the U-boats to break off the operation and move away westward.[66] The remainder of the passage was uneventful, except that the weather deteriorated and the convoy's speed on the 22nd dropped to 4 knots in an easterly gale. At 1100 that day, on orders from CinCWA, Gretton detached EG1. The major escort work was done. Though heavily beset during its passage, SC.130 arrived unscathed in home waters on the 25th. Some merchant ships entered Loch Ewe escorted by *Loosestrife*, the remainder, with *Vidette*, anchored at the Mull of Kintyre. *Duncan* and the other B7 escorts put into Moville near Londonderry, and, to relieve the reader's suspense, Gretton got himself to the church on time. A "safe and timely arrival" indeed!

In the Admiralty's Naval Staff wash-up on this convoy it was decided that the successful passage was owed to four factors: (1) the heavy air support during the time that U-boats were in contact; (2) the timely arrival of the First Support Group on the 19th; (3) the accurate appreciation of the situation throughout by the Senior Officer escorts; and (4) the successful evasive steering of the convoy both away from known U-boat positions and immediately before dawn each day while in contact in order to hook or slice submerged boats into the rough.[67] What might well have been added was: (5) the efficient use by *Duncan, Tay, Sennen,* and *Zamalek* of HF/DF, which enabled Gretton at considerable distances to vector his air and sea assets economically to fixed targets. Said Gretton in his Comments of Senior Officer, Close Escort: "Directing an escort without reliable HF/DF information is like entering a ring blindfolded."[68]

In the retrospect of a half-century and more, SC.130's was one of the more significant convoy passages of May, since it demonstrated dramatically both how effective Allied escort operations had become and how far the U-boat fortunes, so promising at the beginning of the month, had declined. It is striking also how few of the *Donau* and *Oder* boats dared to run the Allied gantlet. Were their Commanders practicing a caution approaching timidity, or were they simply denied every chance to advance? We shall probably never know, since the few survivors among them today would not be able to speak for all or even most.[69] What is clear is that an already grim exchange rate worsened further, falling from one-to-one in Convoy ONS.7 to a negative balance of three U-boats (counting U–*273* but not U–*381)* lost for zero merchant ships sunk in SC.130. The bar graphs at BdU could be hung with black crepe for the dire tale they told. The mighty U-Bootwaffe, once the scourge of the oceans, only twenty-five days after its strongest-ever month's start, wallowed at worsening discount. *Fortuna secunda, denique adversa, uti.*[70]

On 21, 22, and 23 May the Allies pulled off what might be called a trifecta. On those three days, successively, a British submarine sank a U-boat; an American escort carrier (CVE), U.S.S. *Bogue,* got its first kill; and a U-boat was sunk by the first rocket used successfully in naval warfare. Although it may not seem obvious that one side's submarine might sink another side's submarine, since they were two scorpions that rarely got into the same bottle, it was hardly unknown for that to happen: since the war's start eight U-boats had been sunk by British submarines, the most recent being U–*644* (Oblt.z.S. Kurt Jensen), sunk by H.M.S. (submarine) *Tuna* on 7 April in the North Sea northwest of Narvik. In fact, on the 18th of the same month, the German boat U–*123* (Oblt.z.S. Horst von Schroeter) sank a British submarine, H.M.S. P.615, south of Freetown. On 21 May, H.M.S. *Sickle* was patrolling in the Mediterranean off the southern coast of France when, at 1456, she sighted a Type VIIC boat leaving the port of Toulon on a test run. *Sickle* closed the range to 2,600 yards and, at 1510.29, launched two Mark VIII torpedoes $2\frac{1}{2}$ seconds apart set to depths of 8 and 10 feet. One torpedo struck the U-boat about 30 feet abaft the conning tower, sending up a towering detonation column of water and smoke. The boat settled by the stern and the crew were seen jumping into the sea. The bows of the boat stood up at an angle of 50° and then slid under at 1512.20. *Sickle* made no attempt to pick up survivors, since it would have "unnecessarily hazarded" the submarine. The victim was U–*303* (Kptlt. Karl-Franz Heine). Twenty of the forty-four-man crew were lost.[71]

On 20 May the U.S. Navy created the Tenth Fleet, a paper organization with no warships of its own, which would allow Admiral King, by that date heavily committed to ASW, to bring together all anti-submarine ships, aircraft, weapons, radar and HF/DF, Intelligence, operations research, communications, convoy routing, and tactical attack doctrine and training under one overall command–his own. While a Tenth Fleet chief of staff, Rear Admiral Francis S. "Frog" Low, handled day-by-day administrative duties, and Admiral Royal E. Ingersoll, Commander in Chief Atlantic Fleet (CINCLANT), directed operations at sea, King supervised Tenth Fleet and Low in much the same way that his German counterpart, Dönitz, superintended BdU and Godt. On the date of Tenth Fleet's epiphany–long-awaited, it should be said, by critics, particularly in the Army and USAAF, who thought that the Naval service's approach to the U-boat threat had been too random, reactive, and unstructured[72]–the Tenth Fleet's prize Atlantic weapons platform was in mid-Atlantic steaming toward a pack of twelve wolves. This was U.S.S. *Bogue,* the first American-built escort carrier to fight U-boats under the United States flag.

Converted from a C–3 merchant hull at Tacoma, Washington, named after Bogue Sound in North Carolina, launched on 15 January 1942, and commissioned by Captain Giles E. Short on 26 September of that year, *Bogue* was classified an ACV for Auxiliary Aircraft Carrier (until July 1943, when the classification would be changed to CVE for Escort Carrier). In service she would be designated CVE–9. Popularly, she would be known as a "Jeep" carrier. *Bogue's* flight deck was 442 feet 3 inches long. A narrow "island" (five feet wide, twenty-five long, fifteen high) stood on the starboard side. The vessel's steam turbines and single screw produced a maximum speed in open water of 17.75 knots. Her normal crew complement was 890, but it quickly grew to a crowded 97 officers and 921 men.[73] In November 1942, at San Diego, *Bogue* embarked her aircraft: nine Grumman TBF–1 Avenger torpedobombers and twelve Grumman F4F4 Wildcat fighters. Together they formed the Escort Scouting Squadron Nine (VGS–9), redesignated Composite Squadron Nine (CV–9) on 1 March 1943. Commanding Officer was Lieut.-Comdr. William M. Drane, U.S.N.

In many ways, though not all, the Avenger represented an advance over the *Archer's* and *Biter's* Fairey Swordfish. Where the latter, a fabric-covered biplane, had a weight of 9,250 lbs., a maximum speed of 139 mph, and a range of 546 miles, the aluminum monoplane Avenger had a weight of 15,905 lbs., a top speed of 270 mph, and a range of 1,215 miles. On two counts, however, they were similar: the Swordfish had a crew of two or three and the Avenger a crew of three (pilot, radioman, and gunner); and both had a bomb load capacity of 1,600 lbs.

The Avenger's speed enabled it to deliver an attack before the targeted U-boat could submerge, while exposing the aircraft to flak for the shortest possible time. Again, the Avenger's endurance permitted it to remain on patrol or over a target for an effective period of time. The preferred type of attack, worked out in theory and practice, was a long power glide at maximum speed out of cloud or cloud bases, followed in the final stage by a pushed-over 20° dive with wheels lowered to reduce speed for the D/C drop. While the D/C depth was set to 25 feet in keeping with the doctrine learned at the Fleet Air Arm Anti-Submarine School, Ballykelly, Northern Ireland, which all of *Bogue's* TBF–1 pilots would attend, Squadron Nine chose to reduce the 100-foot spacing recommended there to 75 feet because of the speed of their aircraft.

The purpose of the Wildcats was primarily to provide defense against air attacks, not likely in midocean but possible when operating near the U.K., and secondarily to strafe surfaced U-boats in coordinated attacks with the TBF–1s. In the latter case Lt.-Cmdr. Drane was insistent that the Wildcats restrain themselves by not engaging in highspeed maneuvers that condensed vapor in humid air and gave away the attack, and by not dashing about madly without orders from the accompanying Avenger and thus compromising an attack by driving a U-boat down prematurely. Ideally, a Wildcat should be available on call to strafe the U-boat from three to five seconds before the D/Cs were dropped. The operational endurance of each aircraft type was, for the TBF–1 6 hours at 125 knots, for the F4F4 3.5 to 4 hours at 125 knots. Both types could be launched by the flight deck catapult without the carrier having to turn into the wind, a wind component of only 16½ knots along the track being required by a fully loaded TBF–1, and a component of only 6 knots being required by an F4F4. Without the catapult, wind velocity over the deck necessary to fly off aircraft was 31 and 24 knots, respectively.[74]

Bogue was named the centerpiece of a pioneer aggressive USN sea force called the "Hunter-Killer Group." Her mission, not unlike that of *Archer* and *Biter,* was to hunt down U-boats in the vicinity of convoys and destroy them. It was thought at first by Ingersoll that *Bogue*'s best use was on the Central Atlantic routes to and from Gibraltar, where generally good weather conditions favored aircraft launches and recoveries, but as it happened, *Bogue* found herself from the outset in the thick weather and heaving seas of the North Atlantic lanes. On 6 March 1943, out of Argentia, Newfoundland, accompanied by two "flush-deck" destroyer escorts, U.S.S. *Belknap* and *George E. Badger,* she joined the U.K.–bound Convoy HX.228. Four days later, Avenger pilot Ensign Alexander C. "Goose" McAuslan, U.S.N.R., sighted a U-boat and dove to attack it. Both D/Cs he was carrying hung up in their racks. (In pitching seas the squadron was fitting only two D/Cs in the TBF–1s to assist takeoff.) The U-boat initiated a dive while McAuslan swung around for a second run. Again his D/Cs failed to release. *Bogue* was ordered to return to Argentia; on the way, TBF–1 pilot Lt. H. S. "Stinky" Roberts, U.S.N.R., mistook a gam of porpoises for a U-boat and had yet another bomb rack failure, to the very good fortune of the sea mammals. Something would have to be done about the bomb hangups, and it was.

On 20 March, *Bogue* began a second partial crossing as air escort to SC.123, but rough seas and wet gray curtains caused her aircraft to stand useless in their lashings for most of the voyage. On the 26th she began a return to Argentia, arriving there four days later. On 25 April she joined Convoy, HX.235, which was routed to the southward through better weather. This time, with the addition of three more flush-deck destroyers, U.S.S. *Greene, Lea,* and *Osmond Ingram,* the carrier had a

five-escort screen. The entire support force was designated
Task Group 92.3. Their passage was uneventful until the afternoon of the 28th, when Lt. Roger "Stomp" Santee, U.S.N.R.,
in an Avenger, caught a fully surfaced U-boat about 50 miles
distant from the convoy and attacked it with two D/Cs that
released well enough but ricocheted off the surface, owing to
too much speed on the dive, and went under to explode too
far from the target.

Two days later, TG 92.3 was detached to make for Belfast,
where, during the following two weeks, *Bogue*'s officers
passed through the Anti-Submarine School at Ballykelly, a
British HF/DF set was installed in the carrier's island (see
chapter 2), and VC–9's TBF–1 quota was increased from nine
to twelve, while the F4F4 fighter complement was reduced
from twelve to six.[75] Interestingly, in his comments on the
new aircraft composition, Captain Short suggested that four
slower type-aircraft, such as the Swordfish, be substituted for
three TBF–IS: "The Swordfish, for instance, can be operated
in weather which precludes the landing and take-off (except
by catapult) of the TBF. They could be used for night operations and rough water work when the employment of the
heavy and faster TBF would be unduly hazardous in this class
of vessel. Further, a slow aircraft at night would prove more
effective in spotting submarines than a fast one."[76] The suggestion was not followed.

Bogue departed Belfast Lough at 1837 on 15 May. Three
and a half hours later she rendezvoused with her surface escorts, minus *Lea,* to form the Sixth Escort Group, and proceeded to Iceland. From there, on the 18th, the Group, taking
with it the freighter S.S. *Toltec,* intersected the route of the
westbound convoy ON.184, which it was to accompany in
support of the close screen. Destroyer *Lea* overtook the remainder of the Group on the 18th, and at dawn the next day,
Bogue and her four-stackers took assigned convoy stations,
Bogue in the Commodore's column astern of the escort
tanker. Heavy weather made flying impossible until the 21st
when, coincidentally, ON.184 stumbled on a pack of U-boats
that had been assembled not to meet it, but another, east-

bound, convoy, HX.239 (escorted by *Archer*), crossing 30 miles to the south, which had been betrayed by Naval Cipher No. 3. Again, as in the case of Convoy SC.130 in the middle of the month, B-Dienst had decrypted HX.239's position, course, and speed, and BdU had formed a patrol line of twenty-one boats named *Mosel* (after the river) across it.[77]

Subsequent decryptions by B-Dienst enabled BdU to know the convoy's estimated positions for the 20th, 21st, and 22nd.[78] Since these positions were farther to the south than BdU had anticipated, twelve *Mosel* boats were instructed to proceed southeastward to make contact. Boats of the *Donau* group withdrawing from SC.130 were also vectored to intercept at AK 97 (51°25′N, 30°15′W). None of these orders was decrypted by the Allies before 22 May, and some signals relating to the dispositions of southern *Mosel* were not read until 3 June.[79] On the 20th, B-Dienst intercepted a signal giving the position of convoy ON.184 as 51°01′N, 33°50′W.[80] Ironically, it was the carrier escort of ON.184 that the southern *Mosel* boats would encounter first as the two convoys passed in opposite directions some 520 miles southeast of Cape Farewell.

The morning of the 21st broke CAVU–Ceiling and Visibility Unlimited–and Squadron VC-9 flew continuous search patrols. At twilight on that perfect day, squadron skipper Bill Drane, flying an Avenger with four D/Cs at 3,000 feet 60 miles ahead of the convoy, sighted and pursued a streak of silver with a black splinter at its head. He increased speed to 200 knots, circled, and made his approach from dead ahead, lowering his landing gear on the final run in to reduce speed and avoid the D/C ricochets that had ruined Lt. Santee's chances the month before. This time four Mark 44 flat-nosed D/Cs, released by intervalometer from 50 feet, dug in properly and blanketed the U-boat with explosive geysers. Nothing was seen of the boat thereafter, and no evidence of damage appeared except for some unidentified dark specks in the center of the Torpex slick. Having reached PLE (30 gallons left on return), Drane called for destroyers to investigate and returned to *Bogue*. After the war it would be learned that he had severely damaged U–231 (Kptlt. Wolfgang Wenzel), forcing her back to base.[81]

There was no action overnight, but on the 22nd, which dawned clear with occasional rain squalls, VC–9 made no fewer than five Avenger attacks on three separate U-boats of *Mosel*'s southern wing, beginning at 0635 when Lt. (jg) Roger C. "Bud" Kuhn, U.S.N.R., dropped four D/Cs up the wake of U–468 (Oblt.z.S. Klemens Schamong), which, unable to dive for slightly over an hour, circled slowly, emitting a bluish oil streak. Kuhn's call for backup went unanswered both because he had erred in plotting his position and because he was in a "null" area where ship's radar could not get a fix. Finally, the U-boat sank stern first, and though seriously damaged, managed to make a successful *Rückmarsch*.[82]

Second out of the box, at 1103, was Ensign Stewart E. Doty, U.S.N.R., who found a fully surfaced boat proceeding at high speed almost broad on the convoy's bow 18 miles distant. Just before he mounted an attack the U-boat was DFed by *Bogue*. Coming out of an overcast sky at 1,500 feet, Doty survived incoming flak and released four D/Cs on the U-boat, obtaining one explosion, apparently under the hull between the conning tower and bow, the other three D/Cs falling well to port ahead. As the spray subsided, the U-boat was observed to shake violently to starboard, then to submerge slowly. A bluish oil bubble, about 50 feet in diameter, came to the surface. Shortly afterwards, the boat lifted its bow out of the water at an angle of 45°; then it settled back under at the same angle. Like "Bud" Kuhn's boat, U–305 (Kptlt. Rudolf Bahr) was forced out of the hunt and back to base.[83]

At 1325 Lt. (jg) Robert L. Stearns, flying 26 miles off the convoy's starboard quarter, sighted 5 miles distant a "large dark object" leaving a long wake on a course of 035°, directly opposite to that of the convoy. It was the same U–305, on her way home to Brest with a severe headache. Stearns dove out of a 1,200-foot cloud base and attacked through heavy flak, dropping a four D/C salvo from 125 feet. The charges exploded close aboard U–305, inflicting additional damage (she would spend nearly three months in Brest) and sending her under again to lick her wounds.[84]

Lt. (jg) William F. "Champ" Chamberlain, U.S.N.R., who catapulted off *Bogue*'s deck at 1757, had a daredevil reputation and a record of being hard on aircraft. No one who watched him leave the deck was surprised to see him bank the big Avenger as though he were flying a Wildcat—which is what he used to fly until he complained that the Wildcat pilots were not getting enough flying time. Born in Hoquiam, Washington, he attended the University of Washington, where he studied aeronautical engineering and joined Navy ROTC, eventually entering USN flight school. He was short and stocky, a man of unquestioned courage, without, as an acquaintance said, "a shy bone in his body." Among his adventures: he crash-landed a plane on his parents' farm, ground-looped fighters, and ditched an Avenger at sea when he misjudged the height of waves he was skimming. Aircraft Radioman second class (ARM2c) James O. Stine, who rode with him in May, told the writer: "Our old Chief 'Dusty' Rhodes, who made the crew assignments, couldn't get anybody to ride with Chamberlain. But I said I would. I was older than he was, and sort of a fatalist. I was on board when he went into the drink. But we survived."[85]

Chamberlain was launched to chase down a U-boat bearing that *Bogue* had established at 1723 with her new British HF/DF set. Taking a course of 067°, at an altitude of 1,500 feet in the base of broken cumulus, he bore down the invisible Huff-Duff track at 170 knots, and seven minutes after launch made a visual sighting of the transmitting U-boat 25 miles distant from *Bogue,* proceeding at high speed on a course of 180°. He climbed into cloud cover and circled so as to dive, he hoped undetected, from the U-boat's stern. When properly positioned, he pushed over at 20°, and at 100 feet altitude and still in the dive, he let go four Mark 17–2 flat-nosed TNT D/Cs set to 25 feet that appeared to straddle the U-boat. Two of the D/Cs were captured while still falling in a remarkable photograph taken by Radioman Stine (see frontispiece); at the same time, Gunner Donald L. Clark, AMM2C, swept the

bridge and its startled watch with gunfire. Noting with satisfaction that the U-boat crew had been "completely surprised," Chamberlain watched as the U-boat slowly dived in
the sea of explosive foam.[86] Then, expecting that the Germans, if hurt badly enough, would resurface, he called *Bogue*
for another TBF-1 with D/Cs to relieve him.

On her ninth war cruise, out of La Pallice on 19 April,
U-569 was a singularly unsuccessful boat, with only three
ships to show for twenty-one months on operations. Her second Commander (since 30 January 1943) was Oberleutnant
der Reserve Hans Johannsen, a thirty-two-year-old native of
Hamburg who had been a prewar merchant marine officer
with the Holland America Line. Largely because the boat had
achieved few sinkings, Johannsen had found his new crew
dispirited and listless. On taking command, therefore, he had
had the motto *Los gehts* ("Let's go") together with a compass
rose painted on each side of the conning tower in an attempt
to bolster morale. But there were other crew problems that
were not so easily addressed, such as a general disaffection
from the U-boat arm and a widespread belief that Germany
would lose the war.[87]

On 18 May, U-569 had refueled and revictualed from the
supply boat U-459. On the 22nd she was part of southern *Mosel*, operating ostensibly against HX.239, and in 50°,00'N,
35°00'W when surprised by Chamberlain.[88] According to her
survivors, the Avenger's charges cracked open high-pressure
water lines and water began leaking into the after compartments. The boat dived to 120 meters, but when water reached
the maneuvering room and the boat became very heavy by
the stern, it was no longer possible to maintain trim, and the
crew were ordered to the forward torpedo room in a desperate effort to correct the imbalance. When the boat failed to respond, Johannsen gave the order to surface.[89]

Just as U-569 broke above the waves at 1840, Lt. H. S.
"Stinky" Roberts, U.S.N.R., appeared overhead in Avenger
"7." Sighting the U-boat's bow beneath his port wing from
3,000 feet, Roberts knew that he had little time before the
bridge hatch opened and his presence was discovered. So he

pushed over immediately into a 50° dive-bombing attack, releasing four D/Cs in train at 600 feet and pulling out at 100. As Roberts reported afterwards:

> At the time [the D/Cs] hit the water [the U-boat]had fully surfaced and two distinct explosions were seen half way from conning tower to stern—one on either side of sub—the spray from which merged over U/B. The U/B was seen to rise out of the water—then sink—rise a second time, this time on its side. It sank again and finally rose a third time—this time on an even keel. The gunner opened up at once with 50 cal[iber] turret gun as the crew poured out of conning tower and jumped into water. During this time those on board were frantically waving a white flag. Every effort was made to keep the crew inside with gunfire to prevent scuttling but they kept jumping overboard. Finally all ammunition was expended. . . .[90]

Johannsen had tried to surrender by waving a white napkin, but when Roberts's gunner continued fire, a white sheet was brought up and waved instead. Meanwhile, *Bogue* had called upon the Canadian destroyer H.M.C.S. *St. Laurent* to assist, and Chamberlain, who had flown toward the carrier when Roberts relieved him, returned to the scene after hearing by R/T that the boat had resurfaced, allowing Gunner Clark to get in a few more licks before the white sheet went up. Though it appears that most of the U-boat crew who sprang into the water were wearing life jackets, many were carried away in the heavy sea and lost. One of Johannsen's officers secured a line about his waist and leaped into the water to save two crew members. When at last *St. Laurent* hove into sight, the L.I. descended the tower ladder and opened the sea cock, which scuttled the boat; he did not reemerge. Altogether, the destroyer picked up twenty-five survivors, not including the L.I. and the II.W.O. One crewman, critically wounded, was hospitalized in St. John's. The remainder were turned over to USN authorities in Boston for interrogation.[91]

For the first time in naval warfare, a submarine had surrendered to carrier aircraft. For the first time, too, a U-boat had been destroyed by a CVE's aircraft operating alone. During nineteen months of operations in the Atlantic, Composite Squadron Nine went on to become the highest-scoring ASW squadron in the Navy, with nine U-boats sunk and eight damaged. The *Bogue,* her squadrons, and her surface escorts would together destroy eleven more underseas craft–nine U-boats and two Japanese submarines–during the remainder of the war. "Champ" Chamberlain was awarded the Distinguished Flying Cross and Silver Star for his action against U–*560.* In March 1944, at Norfolk, Virginia, VC–9 boarded CVE–67, U.S.S. *Solomons.* During a cruise in the South Atlantic out of Recife in Brazil, "Champ" showed that his reputation as a plane-buster was still deserved. On making a landing aboard *Solomons*–he was never one, his fellow pilots said, to pay much attention to the Landing Signal Officer–he collided with the edge of the flight deck ramp and split the aircraft in half. "Champ" ended up on deck, but his two crewmen in the tail section careened off the five-inch gun on the fantail into the sea, where, fortunately, they were rescued by the group guardship.

On 15 June 1944, "Champ's" lucky string ran out. Diving on U–*860* (Freg. Kapt. Paul Büchel), which had already been attacked by six VC–9 aircraft, he approached so low–fewer than 50 feet off the deck and into the teeth of heavy flak–that either the flak, or the explosions of his D/Cs, or an internal explosion aboard the damaged U-boat caused his Avenger to be engulfed in flames. Though he managed to make a 180° turn and splash into the water ahead of the U-boat, neither he nor his crew (James Stines had been replaced by his best friend among the ratings) was found by destroyers dispatched to the scene.

That night, a remarkable vigil took place aboard *Solomons,* when one of the carrier's lookouts reported to the bridge that he had heard a sound in the sea that sounded like a human voice. Though it was a dangerous thing to do in U-boat waters, *Solomons* Captain Marion Crist ordered the carrier's speed reduced to two–three knots so that engine, wake, and bow wave noise might be diminished; and all hands–over a thousand–were positioned around the edge of the flight deck to listen for a call from the black, moonless sea. But, though they strained, no one heard a thing other than the pliant waves slapping against the hull, and after a decent, caring interval, the men were returned to normal duties, their only consolation being the knowledge that U–860 had been sunk with half her complement.[92]

Deciding on Sunday the 23rd both that the *Mosel* boats were too far behind ON.184 to continue operations against it and that "it is not possible at present, with available weapons, to attack a convoy escorted by strong air cover," BdU ordered Groups *Mosel* and *Donau* to break off from that convoy and from HX.239 as well.[93] The ON.184 columns proceeded on the remainder of their voyage to New York unmolested, arriving on the 31st. U-boats were still in contact with HX.239 to the south on the 23rd, however, which would prove the undoing of one of their number, U–752 (Kptlt. Karl-Ernst Schroeter). That boat, on her eighth war cruise, made the mistake of surfacing in daylight to make a contact report and encountered a Swordfish from the CVE H.M.S. *Archer* carrying a weapon that was used successfully that day for the first time in combat. It was an airborne rocket fitted with a 25-pound solid steel armor-piercing (A.P.) head called simply "R.P."

Rockets had been fired from Royal Flying Corps aircraft during World War I, though with little success. In the years immediately before the second conflict, their use was considered again in Great Britain as ground-to-air and air-to-air anti-aircraft weapons. As development and trials proceeded in both Army and RAF testing establishments, the rockets came to be called, by the Army, "U.P.s," for Unrotated Projectiles, and by the RAF "R.P.s," for Rocket Projectiles. The RAF developed two types of heads, one a 60-lb. High Explosive (H.E.)/Semi Armor Piercing shell of 6 inches diameter for attacks on U-boats and merchant ships, and the other a 25-lb.

Armor Piercing (A.P.) solid shot of 3.44 inches diameter for attacks on land targets such as tanks, gun positions, and concrete emplacements. In one of those odd paradoxes that characterized some Allied operational research and testing, it was found that the H.E. head worked better against land targets than did the A.P. head; and that, conversely, the latter worked better against submarine and ship hulls. Thus their roles were reversed.

The A.P. head was screwed into a steel tube four feet in length containing cordite that was ignited electrically. The tube and head traveled together, moved forward by the recoil action of gas escaping at high speed from the combustion of cordite in the rocket engine. When launched from an aircraft such as the Swordfish, flying at 120 knots, the rocket reached a maximum velocity of 1,600 feet per second after $1\frac{1}{2}$ seconds. There was no recoil, or "kick," felt by the Swordfish, which could carry a load of eight R.P.s hanging from projector rails, four under each lower main plane. As engineered, the projectiles could be fired in four pairs or as a single salvo of eight. Trials conducted at the Aircraft and Armament Experimental Establishment at Boscombe Down indicated that upon striking a U-boat's hull, the A.P. head fired from 400 yards or less would cause a 3-inch puncture. A perforation that large, it was thought, would prevent a surfaced boat from diving and a diving boat from resurfacing. The introduction of burning cordite into the U-boat's interior was expected to delay a crew's attempt to repair the hole and expel water by pumps. If repair could be effected, the U-boat at the very least would have to return to base.

Remarkably, the R.P. proved to have excellent underwater ballistics. Normally, the pilot's aim should be taken at the base of the U-boat's conning tower. Should the shot fall short and enter the water, and should the firing have been made from an optimum distance of 400 yards, at an angle of 20°, the rocket would travel submerged, reaching a depth of 13-15 feet, for a distance of 100 feet, and retain lethal penetrative power for 70 of those feet. If the angle of shot was less than

10°, however, the rocket on striking the water could be expected to ricochet.

Tactical advice given the first pilots to carry this weapon in May stressed the importance of making the final run in at 400 feet altitude, with slant attack angle on the U-boat of 20°, firing at 400 yards range. Attack should be made as nearly as possible dead on the beam to prevent glancing blows. Attacks should not be attempted when a diving U-boat had reached periscope depth or had completely disappeared. Once rockets had been fired, the pilot should break away at once to left or right, since if the rocket hit the U-boat it would throw up debris, and if it did not hit, but traveled underwater, one-third of R.P.s emerged from the sea at a steep angle, climbing to 200–300 feet.[94]

Before a rocket projectile was fired in anger against a land target or against a merchant ship, Swordfish "B" of 819 Sqdn. embarked on *Archer* struck the first blow, while flying on Sunday, 23 May, in support of Convoy HX.239, about 750 miles west of Ireland. When *Archer* left port she carried the first three carrier aircraft to be fitted with RP. Two of them suffered damage landing in rough weather, however, with the result that "B," piloted by Sub-Lt. Harry Horrocks, R.N.V.R., had sole honors when U–752 made the mistake of traveling surfaced on the port quarter of the convoy in full view of Horrocks and his two-man crew, who were at 1,500 feet 10 miles distant. The time of the sighting was 1015.

Horrocks climbed into cloud cover, where he stayed until he estimated that he was positioned on the U-boat's beam. He then dived and sighted the enemy slightly on his port bow, range one mile. Deciding to fire in four pairs, Horrocks initiated the attack from 800 yards, twice the recommended range. The first pair fell 150 yards short. The second pair was ignited at the optimum 400 yards, but it, too, was short, by 30 yards. The surprised U-boat began a crash dive, and the third pair, from 300 yards, entered the water 10 feet short while the U-boat's stern was still visible. One of these two rockets penetrated the pressure hull. The fourth pair, from 200 feet, cleanly hit the hull about 20 feet forward of the rudders.

The now-punctured boat immediately resurfaced and, after several futile attempts to dive again, circled on the surface while discharging heavy trails of diesel oil. When her crewmen manned the 20 mm flak, Horrocks called for assistance from a nearby fighter. Coming on the scene in less than a minute, Martlet (Wildcat) "B" loosed off a long burst of 600 rounds at the conning tower that killed the Commander, Schroeter, and a midshipman, while sparing the II.W.O., who was standing alongside them. Below, the L.I. ordered the crew out and scuttled the boat. Both the L.I. and I.W.O. went down with her. Eleven survivors were picked up by a destroyer from HX.239's screen, and several more were later pulled from the water by another U-boat, U–*91*.

Aboard *Archer* there was understandable elation in becoming the second escort carrier to bag a U-boat singlehandedly, and the first to get a kill with R.P. It was, states the official British Naval Aviation history, "shooting in the best traditions of the 'Wild West.' "[95]

As stated in A Word to the Reader (page xvii), the focus of this narrative has been on the major convoy battles and on Coastal Command's Bay Offensive, both of which defined the German defeat in May. Still, it must be recognized that Allied operations against U-boats were occurring outside those two contexts throughout the month, and that eleven of those actions led to sinkings. Lest a narrative already heavily saturated with attack detail be further thus burdened, only the essential information about those sinkings is given below.

On 4 May, Coastal Command Liberator "P" of 86 Sqdn., while in 47°10′N, 22°57′W, on passage out to meet Convoy HX.236 northeast of the Azores, received an S/E (10–centimeter radar) contact, soon afterwards sighted a U-boat on the surface, and attacked it with four D/Cs. An oil patch and wood planking announced the result. Sunk with all hands was U–*109* (Oblt.z.S Joachim Schramm).[96] On the 11th, U–*528* (von Rabenau), last seen as a member of Group *Star* on 29 April (chapter 4), where she was damaged and forced back to base by the B7 escort of Convoy ONS.5, was proceeding home in 46°55′N, 14°44′W when she was discovered on the surface by Halifax "D" of 58 Sqdn., which was escorting Convoy OS.47 en route to Africa. Five D/Cs badly wounded the boat, which was then finished off by the sloop H.M.S. *Fleetwood* and the corvette H.M.S. *Mignonette* from the convoy's escort, which picked up fifteen survivors.[97]

On 15 May, a Type IXC boat, U–*176* (Korv. Kapt. Reiner Dierksen), was operating in Outer Seas northwest of Havana, Cuba, when she was sighted by a Vought-Sikorsky OS2U–3 Kingfisher observation plane from USN Patrol Squadron VP–62, which was escorting a two-ship convoy. When the U-boat dived, the pilot marked the swirl with a smoke bomb, then flew over the surface escorts, dipping his wings and directing the Cuban subchaser CS–13 to the scene. The Cuban vessel dropped a three-charge pattern that was followed by *four* explosions. There were no survivors.[98] Similarly, all hands were lost when the flush-deck destroyer U.S.S. *MacKenzie* (DD–175), escorting Convoy UGS.8 200 miles west northwest of the Madeira Islands, encountered and destroyed U–*182* (Kptlt. Nicolai Clausen). The well-proven boat, a type IXD2, was returning to base from patrols off Cape Town and Madagascar. There were no survivors. The date was 16 May.[99]

The next day, at 0830, in the Outer Seas off southeast Brazil, U–*128* (Kptlt. Hermann Steinert) was sighted on the surface by a USN Martin PBM–3C Mariner flying boat (74–P–6) of Patrol Squadron 74 based in Natal and Aratu, Brazil. The U-boat dived, but only 15 seconds had elapsed before the PBM dropped six D/Cs ahead of the swirl. Forced by damage to surface three minutes later, the boat made a run for the Brazilian coast, but another PBM (74–P–5) came on the scene and further crippled the surfaced boat with six D/Cs. At about 0930 the U-boat's bridge lookouts sighted the approach of destroyers U.S.S. *Moffett* (DD–362, Porter class) and *Jouett* (DD–396, Somers class), and Steinert ordered the crew off and the boat scuttled. Seven of the crew died during the attacks, fifty-one were rescued by *Moffett*, and four died aboard her.[100]

On the same day, in the North Atlantic between the

Shetlands and Iceland, Hudson "J" of 269 Sqdn. caught U–646 (Oblt.z.S. Heinrich Wulff) on the surface and released four D/Cs while the diving boat's conning tower was still fully visible. One minute later a 100-foot-high cloud of gray smoke appeared over the D/C scum, followed 30 seconds later by oil and debris. There were no survivors.[101] The Type VIIC U–414 (Oblt.z.S. Walter Huth), on her first patrol, broke through the Strait of Gibraltar and on the 21st was pursuing a convoy in the western Mediterranean when the spanking-new Benson class destroyer U.S.S. Nields (DD–616) destroyed her with D/Cs at 36°01′N, 00°34′E. None of the crew survived.

Five days later, PBY–5A Catalina "F" of USN Patrol Squadron VP–84 from Fleet Air Base, Iceland, sighted a surfaced U-boat southeast of Iceland and attacked it while still surfaced with three 350-pound D/Cs dropped from 100 feet. The U-boat dived, and pilot Lt. R. C. Millard, U.S.N., making a second run, released a Mk.24 acoustic homing torpedo. Its hydrophones correctly fixed on the U-boat's cavitation and brought oil and wreckage to the surface–FIDO's second success of the month. The stern-punctured victim, U–467 (Kptlt. Heinz Kummer), went down with all hands.[102]

At 1356 on the same day, U–436 (Kptlt. Günther Seibicke) was submerged, returning from her third Atlantic patrol, when she was picked up on asdic by the frigate H.M.S. Test, part of the escort of a U.K. to Gibraltar special convoy, KX.10. Test made two D/C attacks, then lost the contact. The nearby corvette H.M.S. Hyderabad joined Test in a box search and at 1434 acquired a contact, which she attacked with a ten-pattern. Eighteen minutes later, having regained contact, Hyderabad dropped a second ten-pattern, which brought to the surface oil, large quantities of wood, a sou'wester, a glove, cigars, and a piece of human flesh. There were no survivors.[103]

On the afternoon of the 28th, northeast of Valencia, Spain, in the Mediterranean, Hudson "M" of 608 Sqdn. based at Blida (El-Boulaïda), Algeria, sighted and sank a U-boat with R.P. It was the first successful use of rockets by the RAF. The victim was U–755 (Kptlt. Walter Göing), from which thirty-

eight crewmen were lost. Nine survivors were picked up by
the Spanish Navy and later repatriated to Germany.[104]

At 2036 on the same day, while on passage out from Reykjavik to meet convoy HX.240 in the mid-Atlantic, Liberator
"E" of 120 Sqdn. sighted U–304 (Koch), seen earlier in the
battle for SC.130, and attacked the partially surfaced boat
with four D/Cs. One minute later, an oil patch and wood
wreckage appeared. All hands went down on this boat's only
combat patrol.[105]

Even before that last date, Grand Admiral Dönitz must have
felt like an infantry company commander whose position was
being overrun by waves of enemy assault troops; for on the
24th day of the month he came, reluctantly, to the conclusion
that the losses in May had "reached an impossible height."
Where "not long ago" one U-boat was lost for every 100,000
GRT sunk, which was an acceptable if not an ideal figure,
now a boat was being lost for every 10,000 GRT. In an analysis prepared by Konteradmiral Godt and the BdU staff, the
RAF was credited with playing a "decisive" role in bringing
about that change in fortunes–attributing to the RAF not
only the land-based aircraft that the U-boats were encounter-
ing but also the carrier aircraft, which were not in fact RAF
but Fleet Air Arm (Naval Aviation). Dönitz concluded that,
"The excessive losses and the lack of success in operations
against the latest convoys now force us to take decisive measures until the boats are equipped again with better defense
and attack weapons."

The decisive measures were to *withdraw U-boats from the
northern transatlantic convoy lanes* and transfer the main effort
to the West African and Brazilian coasts, the Caribbean Basin,
and the traffic between the United States and Gibraltar in the
Central Atlantic. While reminding his boats in a "To All Commanders" signal that the North Atlantic remained the principal operational area, and that operations "must" be resumed
there once new weapons were supplied the boats–he named
an effective radar search receiver, the anti-escort acoustic
homing torpedo *(Zaunkönig),* and the quadruple 20mm anti-

aircraft installations–for now, Dönitz stated, in "a temporary deviation from the former principles for the conduct of U-boat warfare," the boats must in great part vacate the densest convoy lanes because, simply, he would "not allow the U-boats to be beaten at a time when their weapons are inferior."

Of course, he added, the North Atlantic could not immediately or completely be denuded of boats, for a number of reasons. Boats already operating there did not have sufficient fuel to make the Outer Seas and return. It would take time to top them up, and it would be dangerous to bunch them at bases where, because of the limited number of bays in the bombproof shelters, many boats would be exposed to air bombardment. In order to camouflage the general retirement, certain boats would be assigned to stay on Atlantic station and transmit dummy signals to simulate regular patrol line traffic. New boats just coming into Atlantic service from home waters would have to remain on station in the North Atlantic "in spite of the difficult conditions." They would be expected to stand by until the next favorable conditions for attack, that is, the new moon, recurred, the next such period being the end of June. Well-proved, or veteran, boats would be assigned to support the newcomers at that date. In the meantime, Commanders must strive to maintain the good morale of their men in the face of these temporary expedients.[106]

To all officers at sea Dönitz sent an Order of the Day under the same 24 May date. Just the day before, he had signaled them that the development of new defenses against Allied radar and weaponry was receiving "maximum application at all our stations," and that new technology should be ready shortly. The time until then, he told them, "must be passed with cunning and caution," though "with your old inexorable severity in the battle itself."[107] Now, on the 24th, he repeated the theme, more poignantly:

> I know that operations for you out there at the moment are some of the hardest and most costly in losses, since the enemy's defense at the moment is superior in

view of new technical methods. Believe me, I have done everything and will continue to do so in order to introduce means to counter this enemy advance. The time will soon come in which you will be superior to the enemy with new and stronger weapons and will be able to triumph over your worst enemies, the aircraft and the destroyer . . . We will therefore not allow ourselves to be forced into the defensive . . . and we will fight on with still more fortitude. . . We will then be the victors. . . Heil Hitler.[108]

To the Führer personally, at the Berghof on the Obersalzburg near Berchtesgaden on 31 May, Dönitz made the appropriate explanations, identifying Allied aircraft and radar—"We don't even know on what wavelength the enemy locates us"—as the determining factors in his ordering of the U-boat dispersion. A stenographer took down his words:

Our losses have increased during the last month from approximately fourteen U-boats, or thirteen percent of the U-boats at sea, to thirty-six or even thirty-seven, or approximately thirty percent of all U-boats at sea. [In fact, counting U–*439* and U–*659,* which collided during operations on the night of 3/4 May, and the two boats, U–*563* and U–*440,* sunk on the 31st, a total of 41 boats were lost during the month.] These losses are too high. We must conserve our strength, otherwise we will play into the hands of the enemy.[109]

After naming the new detection gear and weapons that he hoped to have on stream soon, Dönitz proposed to Hitler an entirely new remedy: rapid development of a separate Naval Air Force to counteract Allied air with air of their own, with which both to fight off Allied bombers and to bomb convoy vessels.

The naval flyers must learn navigation at sea, celestial navigation, drift computation, how to keep contact with a convoy, cooperation with the U-boats by means of direction-finder signals, how to be guided to the convoy by other planes, and the necessary communications.[110]

The stenographer recorded: "The Führer agrees fully with these views." Obviously, where the threat of Allied aircraft was concerned, Dönitz had come a long distance from August 1942, when he had stated, "The U-boat has no more to fear from aircraft than a mole from a crow." But there is an air of unreality about this Berghof conversation. Even with new detection gear and weapons, there was hardly a chance that obsolete U-boats could again contend with enlarged Allied sea and air forces boasting state-of-the-art equipment operated by undiminished numbers of highly experienced personnel. And the likelihood that at that date, with no experience base and limited material and human resources, Germany could revive its 1930s Naval Air Arm—a fleet of over 700 aircraft was envisioned—was extremely remote, and must have been known to be so to both Dönitz and Hitler. "Just a pipedream" is how the historian of German naval air describes it.[111] And the U-Bootwaffe had to continue functioning under the haphazard, short-range, and generally ineffective umbrella of land-based antishipping warfare aircraft from the Luftwaffe's *Fliegerführer Atlantik* (Air Leader Atlantic) in western France—whose Atlantic grid charts did not even match those carried by the U-boats![112]

Of course, no one liked to recognize defeat when it came, least of all "The Lion" and the Führer: the former because he had invested his life's energies in the U-Bootwaffe, which he had nourished to maturity from its post–1918 beginnings in 1935 and had expanded to the fleet that took to sea on 1 May 1943; the latter because he was aware that even with the reverses suffered in May, the U-boats were still his best weapon against the Allied buildup for an attempt to cross the Channel onto the Continent.

It took Dönitz fifteen years (a ten-year prison sentence adding to the time) to acknowledge in writing the emptiness of his proposals to Hitler and the disingenuousness of his bellicose pledges of final victory to the U-boats. In the pages of his memoirs that address the end of what his staffers called "Black May," the old Admiral acknowledged the cold reality of 31 May:

"We had lost the Battle of the Atlantic."[113]

Epilogue

Though substantially defeated in his campaign to throttle Britain's maritime trade, and frustrated as well by his inability to interdict American military convoys, both to Gibraltar and the United Kingdom, Dönitz continued nonetheless to press the U-boat war in the Central Atlantic and the Outer Seas. He did so, he explained, after carefully considering his options: Should he "call off the U-boat war" in view of the enemy's overwhelming force levels and technological advantage? Or should he "continue operations in some suitably modified form," despite Anglo-American superiority that was likely to increase rather than diminish?

> Germany was on the defensive on all fronts. The Army was engaged in a series of hard-fought defensive battles. The air-raids on Germany itself were becoming increasingly severe. Under these conditions what effect would the abandonment of the U-boat campaign have on our war situation as a whole? Could we afford to abandon it? Were we justified, in view of our inferiority, in calling upon our submarines to continue the unequal struggle?[1]

Dönitz reached the bitter conclusion that he had no alternative but to call for continuance of a sea war that was already lost. And these were his reasons: With only 110 bomb-sheltered berths available at the Biscay bases, many *hors de combat* boats in base would be dangerously exposed to air bombardment. Second, a cessation of U-boat operations would free up hundreds of Allied escort vessels and aircraft that were then tied down by ASW for use elsewhere against Germany. Similarly, a unilateral stand-down would release the vast Allied network of naval and air bases, including ground service personnel and civilian workers, as well as material resources, for employment on other operations. If, for example, the Coastal Command bomber fleet, then consumed in ASW, were permitted to reinforce Bomber Command raids on German cities, the civilian populations of those cities would suffer incalculable casualties and hardships. "Could the submariner stand aside as a spectator, saying there was nothing he could or would do and telling the women and children that they must put up with it?"

Dönitz also considered a compromise strategy in which he would break off the fight until a new-generation boat, the fast electric Type XXI (see pages 414–15), became operational, at which time he would return to sea with enhanced chances of success. But that strategy would not work, he decided, since during such a hiatus the morale of even the best crews would suffer, perhaps irreparably. Furthermore, to have any chance at all, the U-Boat Arm must be in continuous engagement with the enemy in order to know his tools, tactics, and tendencies.

Among Dönitz's reasons for staying in the game, he did not offer Hitler's reason, namely, that fighting a now-defensive battle in the Atlantic was preferable to defending the Third Reich on the beaches of Festung Europa. Furthermore, the U-boat war served Hitler's policy of hamper and delay. Like Frederick II in dealing with his land enemies during the Seven Years War, the Führer hoped that unrelenting attrition at sea would induce one of the Allied powers to lose heart and withdraw, if not from the war, from invasion planning. It was a foolish hope, but after Stalingrad and Black May, it was, we may assume, the only hope he had.

In light of the Führer's Frederician policy, one must wonder if Dönitz, in drawing up his own options, really had a choice in the matter, except at the cost of his Command. By whatever route he reached his conclusions, the Grand Admiral presented them personally to the Flotilla Commanders of the Biscay bases, who unanimously expressed themselves in agreement with them, and went on to pledge the support of their officers and crews.[2] This must have been reassuring to Dönitz. But it must also have been jarring for the Flotilla Commanders to hear their Lion step back from his long-enunciated principle: "Strategic pressure alone is not sufficient, only sinkings count."[3]

In a two-year-long dénouement that has been described extensively in the historical literature, the U-boats failed utterly to inflict further significant pain on Allied shipping, either in the Atlantic convoy lanes or in the Outer Seas. Discounted from the stature of menace to that of problem, they failed also to tie up Allied air and sea forces that might be wanted elsewhere: as early as 24–30 July 1943, Coastal Command aircraft from ASW Groups 15 and 19, with little U-boat threat to occupy them, took part in Bomber Command's horrific firestorm raids on Hamburg.[4] In the Outer Seas, including the U.S. seaboard, the U-boats had occasional successes, mostly against independently sailing traffic, but none at all against American UGS and GUS military convoys in the Central Atlantic. The most sinkings were scored in the Indian Ocean. But everywhere Allied defenses had stiffened, and the boats paid a heavy price: seventy-nine lost in the three months following Black May. Among the losses were seven of the ten available Type XIV milch cows, seriously retarding future long-distance operations.

The new moon periods of June, July, and August 1943 passed without any concentrated return to the North Atlantic convoy lanes. Finally, in September, Dönitz ventured into the latitudes of prior glory south-southwest of Iceland and showed a flash of his old form in a four-day operation by nineteen boats against convoys ONS.18 and ON.202. Nine of the boats were equipped with one of the promised new weapons, T-V, or *Zaunkönig* (Wren), the "antidestroyer" acoustic homing torpedo that responded to the fast cavitation of a warship in the same way that the Allies' Mark.24 Mine reacted to the cavitation of a U-boat. In all, fifteen *Zaunkönig* launches were made against the escorts of the two convoys, which had joined company on the 20th.

In one of the war's more notable examples of overclaiming, the boats reported to Berlin twelve destroyers definitely sunk and three probably, all by T-Vs; also nine merchant ships sunk by conventional torpedoes; for the loss of two U-boats. Their success would have been greater, they added, had they possessed radar, since a dense fog hindered operations for a day and a night, when the boats were blind. The actual Allied losses were three escorts sunk and two damaged, and six merchant vessels sunk. And the U-boat casualties were three sunk (one 160 miles distant before the operation began) and three damaged.[5] Still, the U-boats had achieved a "success," though a Pyrrhic one. It was to be their last convoy "success" of the war. Six more operations against North Atlantic convoys were mounted in September and October, but all were costly failures. In October the exchange rate was one merchant vessel sunk per seven U-boats sunk. The U-Bootwaffe's condition was terminal. After a disastrous run at Convoy ONS.29 during 16–19 February 1944, no more convoy battles were even attempted, the compelling interest of the crews being, it appears, not killing, but avoiding being killed—a peculiar mission to supervene the purely offensive purpose of the craft they crewed.

By that last date, it should be noted, all the promised new weapons and devices had been supplied or fitted to the U-boat fleet. These included, in addition to *Zaunkönig:* quick-firing 20mm anti-aircraft cannon on quadruple mountings; *Naxos*-U, a search receiver capable of intercepting 10-centimeter radar, first introduced (after an incredible delay) in October 1943; and *Aphrodite*, a radar decoy consisting of aluminum foil streamed from a hydrogen-filled india rubber balloon that simulated the radar signature of a conning tower.[6] But, as Günter Hessler conceded, "all the new weapons together could not give back to the old-type boats their striking power."[7] An engineering innovation that did improve the old boats' safety if not their performance was the *Schnorchel* (a dialect word for "nose"), a double-pipe system invented before the war by the Royal Netherlands Navy that enabled a submarine to cruise and charge batteries on diesel power while submerged at, roughly, periscope depth. The "breathing" pipes that extended above the surface brought in air for human consumption and diesel combustion, while at the same time discharging exhaust. The snorkel returned to the U-boat what had once been its principal advantage: stealth, which at this stage meant, in practical terms, protection from aircraft. There were certain offsetting disadvantages, however. Underwater speed on the diesels was not high, and a crew's health and comfort, even life, were threatened when carbon monoxide–laden exhaust gases leaked into the boat's interior, or when the float valve on the intake pipe suddenly closed owing to surface turbulence or miscalculation by the planesmen, and all interior oxygen was sucked away by the engines.

Eventually, the single advantage possessed by snorkel-equipped boats was defeated by American development of 3-centimeter radar that picked up the head of the U-boat's pipes. Snorkel as well as nonsnorkel boats failed miserably to interdict the Normandy invasion fleet of 6 June 1944 or to obstruct the buildup fleets that followed during that month, while RAF Coastal Command's No. 19 Group made easy sport of them. From Normandy to war's end, U-boat effectiveness continued its precipitous decline. A final look at exchange rates reveals how far the numbers plummeted. From July 1943 to the final surrender in May 1945 the exchange rate was 0.5 merchant vessels sunk per U-boat sunk. That was one-eighth the rate for the eight-month period from October 1942 through Black May, and one-thirty-sixth the rate for the eight months preceding that.[8]

The one weapon that stood even a theoretical chance of turning the sea war in Germany's favor was the 1,600-ton Type XXI (and its much smaller 250-ton Type XXIII stablemate) "electro-boat." The first large true submarine (all earlier boats being submersibles), the XXI housed a heavy high-capacity battery array that enabled the boat to proceed submerged at an unprecedented $17\frac{1}{2}$ knots for one hour's time, or at five knots for a full twenty-four-hour day. Such high underwater speed, assisted by a streamlined hull, gave it virtual immunity to the depth charge and Hedgehog, while submergence itself vitiated the probing pulses of airborne radar. Fitted with *Schnorchel,* the boat achieved 10 knots submerged on diesels. It also had remarkable fighting qualities, including the capability of launching eighteen out of its complement of twenty torpedoes inside of 20 minutes. So advanced was the XXI design that it became the template for all immediate postwar submarines commissioned in the U.S., British, and Soviet Union navies. But it never got into the war at hand.

One reason late in the game was RAF Bomber Command, which, in one of its few undisputed successes during the war, created such destruction among the dockyards in Bremen, Hamburg, and Kiel, where the XXIs were being assembled, that production was slowed, workups in the Baltic and Norway were delayed, and U-boat ranks and ratings wondered if they would ever have the chance, before what looked in early spring 1945 to be inevitable surrender, to test the promise of their true submarine. Even at that late date, the German Navy was methodical and conservative. Some "30 to 50" XXIs, according to Hessler, were nearly finished with their trials but were held back for formal completion; six were in Norway finishing snorkel trials; and only *one,* U–2511, was released for operations. Under command of Korv. Kapt. Adalbert Schnee, that precursor boat sailed for the Faeroes between the Shetlands and Iceland. There, on 8 May, Schnee received a "You have fought like lions" surrender signal from Dönitz, who had succeeded the suicided Hitler as Führer:

> U-boat men! Undefeated and spotless you lay down your arms after a heroic battle without equal. . . . Comrades! Preserve your U-boat spirit, with which you have fought courageously, stubbornly, and imperturbably through the years for the good of the Fatherland. Long live Germany![9]

Several hours after reading the long-dreaded message, Schnee sighted a British cruiser and destroyer escort. He decided to make a dummy attack in order to convince himself that the XXI was as good as advertised. Proceeding submerged, with no trouble he inserted himself inside the destroyer screen and made a textbook simulated attack on the cruiser at close range with six torpedoes. It was the first successful "attack" by a new-generation submarine of that size under action conditions, after which U–*2511* returned to base, as instructed. Prior to Schnee's simulated action, the XXI's smaller version, XXIII, proved itself in eight sorties by eight boats between 30 January and 7 May 1945, resulting in seven merchant ships sunk for no losses to themselves. But the promise and the reality were too late to make a difference.

During the two years that followed Black May, no threat to the U-boats was more pervasive or feared than bombs from the air. On 27 April 1943 Dönitz had made a carefully calculated decision that boats transiting the Bay would be safer spending their necessary battery-charging time on the surface in daytime, when they could sight approaching aircraft and defend themselves with flak, rather than at night when, without warning or defense, they might be exposed to the searchlights and bombs of an L/L Wellington or Catalina. Where he erred was in thinking that his anti-aircraft armament was robust enough to provide an effective defense. Most boats had twin 20mm. cannon, but what was needed, at the least, was "Quad Twenties," and those mountings were not fitted fleet-wide until later in the year.

An additional measure of defense was provided starting early June 1943, when BdU initiated U-boat convoys: boats were ordered to depart their bases in groups of three to five, on the surface, in daylight, and to use their combined firepower if challenged by aircraft. The thinking was that an aircraft carried only enough ordnance to take on a single boat. But Coastal pilots responded to this innovation by flying together in loose formations so that one, on sighting a U-boat group, could summon the others for mass attack. Dönitz halted group sailings on 12 June but resumed them at the end of the month. On 17 June, he reduced the U-boats' daylight surface hours to the minimum four to six in every twenty-four required to keep a charge on the batteries.

Meanwhile, on 12 June, AOC-in-C Air Marshal Slessor canceled Operation Derange and ordered the establishment of two new search ribbons, code-named "Musketry" and "Seaslug." Throughout the remainder of June and all of July, Coastal aircraft made those ribbons a killing zone; during July alone eleven boats, sailing either individually or in company, were sunk in the Inner and Outer Bay; two others were damaged. The only relatively safe U-boat transit route that remained was the Piening route, named after Kptlt. Adolf Piening (U–155), who pioneered it. This was a difficult and time-consuming coast-hugging course along the northern coast of Spain.

After four more boats in the Bay were sunk during the first two days of August, Dönitz threw in his hand and declared a retrenchment. He dispersed the groups that were then on passage, recalled six boats that had just sortied, made the Piening detour mandatory, and canceled his maximum submergence at night standing order of 27 April. Boats must thenceforth spend the minimum possible time on the surface day or night when transiting to and from base. There was to be no more seeking out gunfights with aircraft. During the ninety-seven days while the nighttime submergence order was in effect, Coastal Command aircraft in the Bay sank twenty-six U-boats and damaged seventeen–a rate that worked out to one boat destroyed every 3.7 days.[10] The rate was never to be as high again, as Dönitz practiced thereafter a policy of extreme caution. The 97-day slaughter was a great victory for Coastal's No. 19 Group, and Air Marshal Slessor took full credit for it in language that showed that he was still smarting from the impertinence of the "slide-rule strategists" Stephen Raushenbush and Evan Williams in asking for 160 and 190 additional aircraft, respectively, for the Bay Offensive. We won the victory with what we already had, Slessor tartly pointed out:

The most important factors in any battle are the human factors of leadership, morale, courage and skill, which cannot be reduced to any mathematical formula. It was these that won the Battle of the Atlantic, once the irreducible number of the right type of aircraft were made available. And in point of fact it was won with a fraction of the number of long-range aircraft postulated in this scientific study.[11]

There are two assertions here with which one might take exception. While taking nothing away from the leadership qualities of Slessor, Bromet, and other commanding officers in Coastal Command, and certainly nothing from the impressive courage and skill exhibited by the airmen themselves, if the war was to be won on the basis of these attributes alone, the decision just as easily could have gone to Dönitz and his U-boat men. The problem for the Germans was never weak leadership or quailing sailors. It was obsolete equipment and the criminal negligence of their technological establishments to do such things as get a 10-centimeter G.S.R. to the boats immediately upon learning the secrets of the *Rotterdam Gerät*. One remembers what Captain Gilbert Roberts had told Commander Peter Gretton in the Tactical Unit at Liverpool (chapter 4): war at sea had changed; courage and endurance were no longer enough; victory depended increasingly on advanced technology. The Germans were simply too late off the mark with *Naxos-U* and Type XXI.

Again, one may take exception to Slessor's statement that the 160 or 190 additional aircraft were never needed for an effective campaign in the Bay. He overlooks the fact that operations analysts such as Raushenbush and Williams had to take the pessimistic perspective (as in the recent Persian Gulf War, when no analyst came close to predicting the rapidity of the ground campaign). Neither Raushenbush nor Williams could have responsibly assumed that the Germans would take an astonishing six months to get an effective G.S.R. in their boats. Their dereliction was simply not predicted. The victory came easier than assumed and at the expenditure of fewer flying hours because the surfaced U-boats made helpful sightings or radar blips.

Not originally a supporter of the Bay Offensive, which he once consigned to the status of a "residuary legatee," Slessor thought that overall, the protection of threatened convoys offered more opportunities for destruction of U-boats. In principle he was right. In the locating of U-boats, Bay patrols consistently took second place to overflights of endangered convoys.[12] But what must be considered, if killing U-boats was one's first priority, is that there was a finite supply of endangered convoys, given Dönitz's practice of massing U-boats against a few convoys rather than sending smaller numbers of boats against many convoys. Beyond a certain point, allocating more aircraft for convoy protection would not lead to the sinking of more U-boats, though it might have saved more merchant ships by forcing the U-boats down.[13]

In assessing the air war against U-boats in his autobiography, published in 1956, Slessor was eager that the reader know that many more boats were destroyed by RAF aircraft in 1942 and 1943 than were disposed of in that period by Royal Navy surface escorts. He particularly rejected Winston Churchill's characterization of the RAF bomber as "an equal partner with the surface ship."[14] He also separated himself from the Prime Minister's tribute to "M.A.C. ships"–these were Merchant Aircraft Carriers, British conversions from grain ships and tankers that embarked three to four Swordfish each, and were not classified as warships, but gave morale-building air cover to 217 convoys–which, Slessor pointed out, did not sink a single U-boat (although he might have been gracious enough to acknowledge that no merchant vessel was ever lost in a convoy that was protected by a M.A.C. ship). He was similarly dismissive of Churchill's assertion that the hunter-killer groups formed around escort carriers such as U.S.S. *Bogue* were "the most deadly" enemies of the U-boats. While he complimented the "brilliant success" of CVEs U.S.S. *Bogue, Card, Core, Block Island,* and *Santee*–"household words," he called them–he felt constrained to point out that of the 771

U-boats that were sunk by Allied action, only twenty were sunk by the hunter-killer groups, while 255 were dispatched by shore-based air (not including 17 sunk by RAF-laid mines and 66 destroyed by bombing in port).[15] And as for the seventy-two American VLR aircraft that he had tried to obtain, at the A.U. Committee's urging, "we never did get [them]," he wrote. "Actually as it happened it did not much make difference because we were able to defeat the U-boat by ourselves."[16]

A more recent summation of U-boat losses to aircraft has been compiled by Air Commodore Henry Probert. Excluding losses in the Mediterranean and Indian Ocean, he finds that of 772 boats sunk in the Atlantic, Arctic, and British home waters, 305 were destroyed by Allied shore-based aircraft acting alone (Coastal Command's share being 173) and 28 by joint action between shore-based aircraft and naval vessels (Coastal's share being 21). Examining the remainder, he finds that fifty-two boats were destroyed by bombing attacks made on ports by RAF Bomber Command and the U.S. Army Air Force; that seventeen were sunk by RAF-laid mines; and that U.S. and Canadian maritime aircraft accounted for most of the rest.[17]

In a more general listing of causes, Captain Roskill estimated that 288 U-boats were sunk by Allied aircraft (excluding bombing raids), that 246 were sunk by Allied surface craft, and that 50 were destroyed by joint action of aircraft and surface vessels. There are obvious differences between and among these estimates.[18]

Probert numbers the RAF fatalities suffered in the ASW campaign at 5,866, 1,630 of them from the Dominions and European allies.[19] Royal Navy casualties for all theaters were 50,758 killed, 820 missing, 14,663 wounded, and 7,401 taken prisoner. Though it is difficult to establish the breakdown for ASW alone, official RN historian Captain Roskill states that a "very large proportion" of the casualties came from that category. Furthermore, 102 members of the Women's Naval Service (Wrens) were killed in all theaters, and another twenty-two were wounded.

Of the 830 U-boats that saw action in all areas, 480 were sunk in the North Atlantic, the Northern Transit Route, and British Home Waters. Casualty lists give 27,490 as the number of German U-boat men who were killed out of the 39,000 who sailed on operations–a startling 70 percent. (Some 5,000 more were taken prisoner.) It was the greatest mortal loss experienced by any single arm of any of the bellingerent nations. During the final months of the war, when it was near-suicidal for a U-boat even to stand out to sea, crew after crew did so nonetheless, without demurral or complaint. In 1959 Roskill observed: "Whatever one may feel about their methods of conducting war, the morale and stamina of their crews only very rarely wavered, let alone collapsed."[20]

The month of May 1943 has many claims on history, chief among them the epic Battle for ONS.5, which deserves to take a prominent place in the pantheon of naval victories. It was also the month when mastery of both shore- and carrier-based aircraft over the pre-Type XXI submarine was established; when sea warfare was altered by the first successful introduction of airborne acoustic homing torpedoes and rockets; when, arguably, operations research had its greatest impact on actions at sea; when HF/DF and 10-centimeter radar had their efflorescence; and, of course, when the largest number of U-boats to that date in a single month–forty-one–sank into the Atlantic pit.

It would not be prudent, however, to select May 1943 as the first month when the Battle of the Atlantic turned against its makers. The Allied triumphs in May came as the sum of processes that were gradual and cumulative, as we understand when we consider: the intensive training of RN and RAF personnel and the long months of hard experience at sea or in the air that gave them their winning edge; the time-consuming calculations of boffins; the development of new tactics; the invention, manufacture, and installation of new weapons and devices; the sharpening of leadership at all ranks; the tenacity of merchant mariners who, except for the U-boat crews, faced the greatest danger, but never flinched; the growing industrial output of American shipyards and factories; the mines sown by RAF aircraft across the Baltic workup area in 1942 that seriously disrupted the training of many of the U-boat crews that would appear at sea in May; the refusal of Allied warships and crews to grow faint after the setbacks of March; and the resolute spirit of sailors and airmen who fought the U-boats to a draw in April. All those factors from months prior to this month, taken together, conspired to make May the crucible it was. What happened in the black month did not spring suddenly from the brow of Mars.

Nor would it be true to say that May was the start of a descending slope that led the U-Bootwaffe ineluctably to the abyss, for that start could be dated from the summer and fall of 1941, when the U-boats' tonnage per day at sea first began to tail off, never to recover; or, later, from the formal entry of the United States into the war on 7 December 1941, when, with their vast industrial capacity, the Americans doomed Hitler's sea war in the same way that the Russians, with their manpower as well as industry, doomed his land war. Still, the U-boat was a serious threat and had to be beaten, and it *was* substantially beaten, in May, in a victory that, it bears repeating, was the culmination of many months, not days. Similarly, the historian cannot point to any one person who was solely, or even predominantly, responsible for the sea and air successes of that month—not, positively, to Churchill, Horton, or Slessor alone, not to Winn, Blackett, Gretton, or Oulton, on the Allied side; not, negatively, to any individual decisions or actions taken that month on the other side, by Hitler, Dönitz, Godt, or any of their U-boat Commanders. Rather, *team* fought *team*. To the death. And that was what some of the U-boat officers called the month: *das grosse U-boot-Sterben*—"the Great U-Boat Death."[21]

Following the conclusion of May, one individual Escort Group Senior Officer did come dramatically to the fore, and from 1 June forward his name became identified in the popular mind with the mopping-up period. He was Captain Frederic John Walker, R.N., an old salt horse and proven U-boat killer who had spent much of the previous eleven months being "rested" in a staff job. Back at sea as SO of Second Escort (Support) Group in the sloop H.M.S. *Starling*, he commanded three other sloops whose ranks and ratings, like those of *Starling*, were trained to a fine point in his innovative "creeping attack" scheme. In this tactic one sloop, usually *Starling*, positioned herself at 1,000–1,500 yards from a submerged U-boat detected by asdic and stalked it at the U-boat's speed. Eventually, Walker directed one or more sloops to take station ahead and attack with D/Cs–sometimes as many as twenty-six–across the course of the U-boat. No boat that was caught in Walker's vise ever survived the experience, including U–*202* (Kptlt. Günter Poser), which he stalked and attacked from 1213 on 1 June until 1212 on the 2nd, when, with both batteries and oxygen exhausted, the boat surfaced to be destroyed. Under his direction fourteen boats altogether were destroyed before his untimely death by stroke on 9 July 1944. To an adoring British public who acclaimed him Britain's "ace U-boat killer," Walker had modestly answered that that title was owed instead to his "Thousand British Tars."[22]

Those Thousand Tars may stand fittingly as a symbol of the huge numbers of people who were required to defeat and then to mop up the U-boat fleet. It has been estimated recently that it took 100 persons engaged in ASW to match every German U-boat man, and 25 warships and 100 Allied aircraft to match every U-boat.[23] For those millions of British, American, and other Allied personnel, uniformed and civilian, men and women, at least for those who were aware of it as a spinal event on the order of Stalingrad or Kursk, May must have been a source of enormous gratification in exchange for all the operational or work hours they had invested to defeat Bismarckian blood and iron.[24]

Of course, in Berlin, the emotions were quite the converse. Inside BdU, staff member and former Knight's Cross winner on U–*333* Kptlt. Peter "Ali" Cremer surveyed the numbers and listened to official comment: "As I was soon to learn, the number of boats that failed to return from patrol reached 41, more than one a day, and there was talk of 'Black May.' "[25] And May itself was an omen. For the U-boat men, the months thereafter until the end of hostilities would also be as unremittingly black as the bottom of the harsh and remorseless sea.

Notes

Prologue

1. Martin Middlebrook, *Convoy* (New York: William Morrow, 1976), p. 307 and Appendix 3. The Royal Navy ocean escort groups included two United States Navy destroyers, two United States Coast Guard cutters, and two Royal Canadian Navy corvettes. A German study of this convoy battle is Jürgen Rohwer, *The Critical Convoy Battles of March 1943: The Battle for HX.229/SC.122* (London: Ian Allan Ltd., 1977).

2. Ibid., pp. 302–304. The number of ships and tonnage sunk claimed by the U-boat commanders was 32 and 186,000 GRT. The actual losses were 22 and 146,596 GRT. U–*384* (Oberleutnant z. See Hans-Achim von Rosenberg-Gruczszynski) was sunk by Boeing B–17 Flying Fortress "B" of 206 Squadron Royal Air Force on 20 March 1943.

3. The monthly tonnage figures used here for the period May 1942 through March 1943 are given in Jürgen Rohwer, *U-Boote. Eine Chronik in Bildern* (Oldenburg/Hamburg: Stalling o.J., 1962), p. 94. Sinkings of Allied ships by Italian and Japanese submarines are not included in these totals; Prof. Dr. Rohwer to the author, 1 May 1997. Cf. Jürgen Rohwer, *Axis Submarine Successes,* introductory material trans. John A. Broadwin (Annapolis, MD: Naval Institute Press, 1983), pp. 153–160.

4. Cited in Captain S. W. Roskill, D.S.C., R.N., *The Period of Balance,* Vol. II of *The War at Sea 1939–1945,* 3 vols. in 4

parts (London: Her Majesty's Stationery Office, 1956), p. 367.

5. Cited in ibid., p. 367.

6. Ibid.

7. Patrick Beesly, *Very Special Intelligence: The Story of the Admiralty's Operational Intelligence Centre 1939–1945* (Garden City, N.Y.: Doubleday & Company, Inc., 1978), p. 181. Also author's interview with Beesly, Lymington, England, 9 July 1986.

8. Günter Hessler, *The U-Boat War in the Atlantic, 1939–1945* (London: Her Majesty's Stationery Office, 1989), Vol. II p. 100.

9. Roskill, *The Period of Balance*, p. 368.

10. Public Record Office [hereafter PRO], Kew (London), Cabinet [hereafter CAB] 86/4, A.U.(43)103, Memorandum by the First Sea Lord, 30th March 1943. Cf. Michael Howard in N. H. Gibbs, J. R. M. Butler, J. M. A. Gwyer, Michael Howard and John Ehrman, *Grand Strategy,* 6 volumes (London: Her Majesty's Stationery Office, 1956–1972), Vol. 4, August 1942–September 1943, p. 310. The exchange rate for the first quarter of 1943 is given in Professor C. H. Waddington, C.B.E., M.A., Sc.D., F.R.S., *O.R. in World War 2: Operational Research Against the U-Boat* (London: Elek Science, 1973 [though written in 1946]), p. 37. Also see J. David Brown, "The Battle of the Atlantic, 1941–1943: Peaks and Troughs," in Timothy J. Runyan and Jan M. Copes, eds., *To Die Gallantly: The Battle of the Atlantic* (Boulder, CO: Westview Press, 1994), p. 154. As for the reported post–20 March despondency at the Admiralty, the closest expression of that in time found by this writer is PRO, Admiralty [hereafter ADM] 199/2060, "Monthly Anti-Submarine Report" for December 1943, dated 15 January 1944, p. 3, where the Anti-U-Boat Division of the Naval Staff, reflecting on the heavy losses to HX.229/SC.122, stated ". . . that it appeared possible that we should not be able to continue convoy as an effective system of defence against the enemy's pack tactics." This appears to have been a Staff position that neither reflected the Submarine Tracking Room's appreciation nor

percolated up to the First Sea Lord's suite. No doubt it was a source for Roskill's doleful sentences. For a German view of the convoy question, see Rohwer, *Critical Convoy Battles,* 187–188.

11. Timothy P. Mulligan, *Lone Wolf: The Life and Death of U-Boat Ace Werner Henke* (Norman, OK: University of Oklahoma Press, 1995), p. 222, citing Bodo Herzog and Günter Schomaekers, *Ritter der Tiefe: Graue Wölfe* (Wels, Austria: Welsermühl München-Wels, 1976), pp. 308–309.

12. Hessler, *U-Boat War,* Plan 60 (facing p. 113). These Naval Staff U-boat per day at sea estimates were inaccurate on the high side. The true figures, based on postwar analysis of German and British records, were as follows: November, 220 GRT; December, 96; January, 65; February, 99; March, 147.

13. Eberhard Rössler, *The U-Boat: The Evolution and Technical History of German Submarines,* trans. Harold Erenberg (London/Melbourne: Arms and Armour Press, 1981), p. 127, graph: "Deliveries of Types VIIB, VIIC and C/41." See also the information collected by the Operational Intelligence Centre of the British Admiralty on monthly averages of new U-boat construction, commissioning, and first war cruises (19 per month) in the period 1 April 1942–1 April 1943; PRO, ADM 223/16, "Special Intelligence Summary," folio [hereafter f.] 115. The German Naval Intelligence Division figure for minimum tonnage requirement per month in 1943 is given in Hessler, *U-Boat War,* p. 17.

14. Hessler, *U-Boat War,* pp. 101, 103.

15. National Archives and Records Administration [hereafter NARA], Archives II, College Park, Maryland, *Kriegstagebuch des Befehlshabers der Unterseeboote* (War Diary of the Commander-in-Chief of U-Boots), hereafter KTB–BdU, entry for 16 April 1943, record item PG 30348; National Archives Microfilm Publication T1022, Records of the German Navy, 1850–1945, received from the U.S. Naval History Division, roll 4065; National Archives Collection of Foreign Records Seized 1941–, Record Group [hereafter RG] 242. Henceforth in the present narrative U-Boat Headquarters is cited as BdU. All German naval war diaries, including those for individual U-boats, are cited with the prefix KTB.

16. NARA, RG 457, Historic Cryptographic Collection, World War I Through World War II (declassified by the National Security Agency in 1996), Box 94, G.C.&C.S. Naval History, Vol. XVIII, "The Battle of the Atlantic" (typescript), by Lt.-Cmdr. R. J. Goodman, R.N.V.R., Lt.-Cmdr. K. W. McMahan, U.S.N.R., Lt.-Cmdr. E. J. Carpenter, U.S.N.R., and Others (Bletchley Park, n.d., probably 1946), p. 321; it is the wording as given in this manuscript that the present writer has used in the text. The first appearance of the "failed to press home" expression is in Naval Historical Branch, Ministry of Defence, London [hereafter NHB/MOD], Monthly Anti-Submarine Report, Anti-Submarine Warfare Division of the Naval Staff, April 1943, p. 184; the quotation is repeated in F. W. Barley and D. Waters, Naval Staff History, Second World War, *The Defeat of the Enemy Attack on Shipping 1939–1945: A Study of Policy and Operations,* vol. 1A (Text and Appendices) (London: Historical Section, Admiralty, 1957), p. 93. and in many subsequent works, British and American.

17. Beesly, *Very Special Intelligence,* p. 188.

18. Interview with Horst von Schroeter, Bonn, Germany, 26 December 1995. Holding the highest rank in the postwar Bundesmarine, Vice Admiral v. Schroeter, now retired, was NATO Commander Allied Naval Forces Baltic Approaches in 1976–1979.

19. NARA, KTB–BdU, 7, 25 April 1943.

20. U-Boat Headquarters to boats, wireless (W/T) transmission cited in NARA, RG 457, Goodman, McMahan, Carpenter, et al., "Battle of the Atlantic," p. 321.

21. Roskill, *War at Sea,* Vol. II, p. 379, Map 41. See *British Vessels Lost at Sea 1939–45* (first published in 1947 by Her Majesty's Stationery Office; Cambridge: Patrick Stephens, 1948) for daily and monthly listing of losses by enemy action of merchant vessels under the British flag, which includes those on United Kingdom, Dominion, Indian, or Colonial Registers as well as those on Bareboat Charter or on requisi-

tion from other flags. A calculation of these losses from 3 September 1939 through April 1943, excluding losses by capture, seizure, and scuttling, reveals that 58 percent of British losses were caused by U-boats, 17 percent by aircraft, 13 percent by mines, 7 percent by surface warships and raiders, 3 percent by S–boats, and 2 percent by unknown causes. The percentage of losses caused by U-boats as against other causes increased from 1941 (46% by U-boats, 54% by other causes) through 1942 (74% by U-boats, 26% by other causes) to the first four months of 1943 (86% by U-boats, 14% by other causes). Mines were a significant cause of losses in 1939 and 1940, when they were responsible for 32 and 23 percent, respectively; however, their significance declined markedly thereafter (aircraft supplanting them in rank in 1941 and 1942), and by the first four months of 1943 they were responsible for a negligible 5 percent of losses. By this reckoning it would appear that the statement by Professor Geoffrey Till–"Mines were another serious threat to British shipping, and in fact sank more ships than did U-boats–" is in error; Geoffrey Till, "The Battle of the Atlantic as History," in Stephen Howarth and Derek Law, eds., *The Battle of the Atlantic 1939–1945* (Annapolis, MD: Naval Institute Press, 1994), p. 591.

22. *Fuebrer Conferences on Naval Affairs 1939–1945,* Foreword by Jak P. Mallmann Showell (Annapolis, MD: Naval Institute Press, 1990), pp. 316–319. Cf. Rössler, U-Boat, p. 211, Table 34. On 31 March Dönitz had issued twelve "Commandments" to his staff, the second of which read: "The 'Tonnage war' has the first rank. For this every effort must be made." Cited in Peter Padfield, *Dönitz: The Last Führer* (London: Panther Books, 1984), p. 311. Padfield is the best source for Dönitz's early life and naval career.

Chapter 1

1. Mulligan, *Lone Wolf,* p. I50. Mulligan slightly revises the figure of ten ships sunk, pointing out that one sinking

(the American *Antinous)* was shared with U–*512,* commanded by Kapitänleutnant [hereafter Kptlt.] Wolfgang Schultze; p. 220.

2. NARA, KTB–U–*515,* 21.2.43–24.6.43, RG 242, PG 30553/1–6, National Archives Microfilm Publication T1022, roll 3067, p. 4. Additional data are. found in Timothy Mulligan, ed., *Guides to the Microfilmed Records of the German Navy, 1850–1945,* No. 2: *Records Relating to U-Boat Warfare, 1939–1945* (Washington, D.C.: National Archives and Records Administration, 1985).

3. Ibid., 9 April 1943.

4. Notable exceptions to this observation are Vice-Admiral Sir Peter Gretton, K.C.B., D.S.O., C.B.E., D.S.C., *Crisis Convoy* (New York: Kensington Publishing Corp., 1974); and Martin Middlebrook, *Convoy* (New York: William Morrow, 1976).

5. Mulligan, *Lone Wolf,* p. 55.

6. Ibid., p. 62. Off Freetown, West Africa, the Type IXB U–*123* (von Schroeter) once got under in 30 seconds; interview with von Schroeter.

7. NARA, KTB–BdU, 5 May 1943.

8. Ibid., 1 May 1943. The order of 16 April was "lifted with immediate effect" on 5 May. The reason for the Type IX losses was given as "their more complicated structure."

9. For use of gunfire against shipping by World War 1 German submarines, see Anthony Preston, *Submarines* (New York: W.H. Smith Publishers, Inc., 1982), pp. 18–19.

10. NARA, KTB–BdU, 6 May 1943. The Type VIIC had two such external storage containers.

11. Eberhard Rössler, *Die Torpedos der deutschen U-Boote: Entwicklung, Herstellung und Eigenschaften der deutschen Marine-Torpedos* (Herford, Germany: Koehlers Verlags GmbH, 1984). On p. 76 of this work Rössler gives the weight of the G7a and G7e warhead charge *(Ladung)* as 300 kg, whereas in his earlier cited *U-Boat* he gives the weight as 280 kg; p. 344. On the same page of the latter work he gives the ranges of the two torpedo types as 75 and 50 km, respectively, which are obvious typographical errors. In *Die*

Torpedos he gives the range of the G7e as 5,000 meters (5 km). An excellent summary of torpedo types and pistols is Robert C. Stern, *Type VII U-Boats* (Annapolis, MD: Naval Institute Press, 1991), Part Three: "Weapons and Targeting Systems," pp. 78–93.

12. Marc Milner, *The U-Boat Hunters: The Royal Canadian Navy and the Offensive Against Germany's Submarines* (Annapolis, MD: Naval Institute Press, 1994), pp. 62–71. The formal Allied name for the *Zaunkönig* was GNAT, the acronym for German Naval Acoustic Torpedo.

13. Timothy P. Mulligan discusses crew ages in his excellent article, "German U-Boat Crews in World War II: Sociology of an Elite," *Journal of Military History,* Vol. 56, No. 2 (April 1992), pp. 261–281; cf. Mulligan, *Lone Wolf,* pp. 75–76, 80, for U-*515* crew ages, and p. 83 for the information that, "At the time of her [U-*515's*] loss [9 April 1944] 19 of the 54 crewmen had served on all 6 of her patrols; 15 others had served on 3 to 5 patrols."

14. Mulligan, *Lone Wolf,* pp. 85–86.

15. Ibid., pp. 3, 21, 216.

16. Ibid., pp. 26–57, 122–123, 128.

17. NARA, KTB–U–*515,* pp. 14–18, 13–29 April 1943. Cf. Mulligan, *Lone Wolf,* pp. 143–146.

18. NARA, KTB–U–*515,* p. 19, 30 April 1943.

19. Roskill, *War at Sea,* Vol. II, pp. 371–372; Mulligan, *Lone Wolf,* pp. 146–147; PRO, CAB 86/4, A.U.(43)144, Minute from the Secretary of State for Air to the Prime Minister, 5 May 1943.

20. NARA, KTB–U–*515,* 30 April 1943, p. 19.

21. *Lloyd's War Losses, The Second World War, 3 September 1939–14 August 1945,* Volume I, *British, Allied, and Neutral Merchant Vessels Sunk or Destroyed by War Causes* (London: Lloyd's of London Press, Ltd., 1989), p. 667.

22. Ibid., p. 666.

23. PRO, 199/2145, Reports of Interviews with Survivors from British Merchant Vessels Attacked, Damaged or Lost by Enemy Action; from 1st April, 1943 to 30th September, 1943; Shipping Casualties Section, Trade Division, Admiralty

[hereafter Interviews with Survivors], Captain W. Bird, S.S. *Nagina,* 8th June, 1943, ff. 92–93. The order in which the ships were hit is given by Bird; by Captain E. Gough, of S.S. *Clan Macpherson,* f. 97; and by Captain A. G. Freeman, of S.S. *City of Singapore,* f. 105 (except that Freeman, or more likely his interrogator, names No. 12 ship twice).

24. Ibid., Captain W. A. Chappell, S.S. *Bandar Shahpour,* 10th June, 1943, ff. 90–91.

25. Ibid., Captain P. Leggett, S.S. *Corabella,* 18th June, 1943, ff. 87–89.

26. NARA, KTB–U–*515,* 1 May 1943, p. 19.

27. Cited in Padfield, *Dönitz,* pp. 287, 552 n. 135. Cf. John Terraine, *The U-Boat Wars 1916–1945* (New York: G. P. Putnams' Sons, 1989), pp. 467–468.

28. NARA, PG 32173, Microfilm Publication T1022, roll 1724, RG 242, War Diary of the Operations Division, German Naval Staff, *Kriegstagebuch der Seekriegsleitung* [hereafter KTB–1/SK1], 16 December 1942.

29. Padfield, *Dönitz,* pp. 392–396; cf. John Cameron, *The "Peleus" Trial.* Vol. I of the War Crimes Trial series, ed. by Sir David Maxwell Fyfe (London: William Hodge and Co., Ltd., 1948).

30. Clay Blair, Jr., *Silent Victory: The U.S. Submarine War Against Japan* (Philadelphia and New York: J. B. Lippincott Company, 1975), pp. 383–386.

31. Mulligan, *Lone Wolf,* p. 216.

32. NARA, KTB–U–*515,* 1 May 1943, p. 20. The depth charges (D/Cs) came from H.M.S. *Rapid,* which dropped 42 D/Cs on a contact of which she was "fairly certain" initially, but not so certain later on; PRO, ADM 199/434, "Report of Attack on U-Boat," H.M.S. *Rapid,* 0358 through 0559Z, 1 May 1943, at 07°58′N, 14°11′W.

33. Rohwer, *Axis Submarine Successes,* pp. 32–34.

34. *Lloyd's War Losses,* p. 669.

35. PRO, ADM 199/2145, Interviews with Survivors, Captain A. G. Freeman, *City of Singapore,* ff. 105–106.

36. *Lloyd's War Losses,* p. 669.

37. PRO, ADM 199/2145, Interviews with Survivors, S.S.

Clan Macpherson, Captain E. Gough, 10th June, 1943, ff. 97–101.

38. Cited in Roskill, *War at Sea,* Vol. II, p. 372.

39. PRO, CAB 86/2, War Cabinet, Anti-U-Boat Warfare, Minutes of the Meeting held in the Cabinet War Room, on Wednesday, 12th May, 1943, pp. 2–3; CAB 86/4, A.U.(43)144, Minute from the Secretary of State for Air to the Prime Minister, 5 May 1943.

40. NARA, KTB–U–*515,* 1 May 1943, p. 20.

41. NARA, KTB–U–*107,* Roll 3034–3035, 24.4.43–26.5–43, 1 May 1943, pp. 4–5.

42. PRO, ADM 199/2145, Interviews with Survivors, Captain W. G. Higgs, M.V. *Port Victor,* 7th May 1943, ff. 94–96.

43. Interview with Harald Gelhaus, Bochum, Germany, 1 July 1997.

44. Hessler, *U-Boat War,* p. 104 and Diagram 21. One of the eleven boats did not make it on station: U–*332* was sunk in the Bay of Biscay on 29 April by a Consolidated B-24 Liberator bomber "D" of 224 Squadron, Royal Air Force (RAF) Bomber Command.

45. PRO, ADM 186/808, "U 301, U 439 and U 659, Interrogation of Survivors, June 1943," p. 24. The first convoy was an operational formation of fifteen Coastal Forces craft including Motor Torpedo Boats, escorted by three trawlers. The second convoy was probably L.C. Flight "D" consisting of twenty-eight Landing Craft (LCs), escorted by two trawlers and one minesweeper. Torpedoes would have been of little use against these shallow-draft vessels, only the small escorts being minimally vulnerable.

46. For this description of the Type VIIC interior the writer has relied on Stern, *Type VII U-Boats,* passim.

47. See Jordan Vause, *Wolf: U-Boat Commanders in World War II* (Annapolis, MD: Naval Institute Press, 1997), pp. 82–85. Mulligan, "U-boat Crews," passim. After November 1940 the U-boat training school for ratings was changed in name to (in English) U-Boat Instructional Division. Because of the urgency of getting trained men to the front, between 1941

and 1944 the length of courses for officers was cut from twelve to eight weeks and that for ratings from six to three months. A study of U-boat training is given in NARA, RG 457, Historic Cryptographic Collection, World War I through World War II, Box 94, G.C.& C.S. Naval History, Vol. VII, "The U-Boat Arm–Organisation" (typescript), by Lieutenant H. M. Anderson, R.N.V.R., pp. 90–106.

48. PRO, ADM 186/808, "U 301, U 439 and U 659 Interrogation of Survivors, June 1943," p. 24.

49. Ibid., p. 24. PRO, WO 208/4145, Combined Services Detailed Interrogation Centre, U.K. [hereafter CSDIC (U.K.)], Kriegsmarine, March–June 1943; S.R.N. 1802, recorded 13 May 1943. Ibid., S.R.N. 1835. There is no sign in the message traffic decrypted by British and American cryptographers that the distress message from U–439 was intercepted. The BdU war diary indicates that the message was not received there: on 5 May U–439 was ordered to a new position; on 8 May BdU noted that U–439 had not reported since leaving Brest and must be presumed lost "during the last few days in April when air patrolling was very strong." The BdU's knowledge of U–659's fate was even more delayed: on 5 May the boat was ordered (along with U–447) to proceed through the Strait of Gibraltar into the Mediterranean; not until the 19th, when BdU acknowledged that it had heard nothing from the boat, was U–659 "considered lost." NARA, KTB–BdU, 5, 8, 19 May 1943.

50. PRO, ADM 186/808, "U 301, U 439 and U 659 Interrogation of Survivors, June 1943," p. 6.

51. PRO, WO 208/4145, CSDIC (U.K.), Kriegsmarine, March-June 1943; S.R.N. 1837, recorded 21 May 1943.

52. Ibid., S.R.N. 1789, 1803, recorded 13 May 1943.

Chapter 2

1. Hessler, *U-Boat War*, Plan 59, facing Vol. II, p. 112; Plan 60 facing Vol. II, p. 113; Diagram 7, "The U-Boat War in the Atlantic from the Outbreak of War to December 1941"; Dia-

gram 31, "Growth of the U-Boat Arm 1939 to 1945." The reader's attention is invited to the point made in the Prologue, *n*.12, that these are the true figures based on postwar analysis, and are lower than German Naval Staff estimates of the time.

2. Ibid., Vol. I, pp. 71, 73; and Diagram 31 for numbers of operational boats.

3. The statistics are from Mulligan, *Lone Wolf,* p. 221 and *n*.1; Jak P. Mallmann Showell, *U-Boats Under the Swastika* (Annapolis, MD: Naval Institute Press, 1987), p. 18. The quotation is from David K. Brown, "Atlantic Escorts, 1939–45," in Howarth and Law, eds., *Battle of the Atlantic,* p. 468.

4. F. H. Hinsley, et al., *British Intelligence in the Second World War: Its Influence on Strategy and Operations,* 3 vols. (New York: Cambridge University Press, 1981–1984), Vol. I., pp. 337–338, Vol. II, pp. 163, 170–174, 664; David Kahn, *Seizing the Enigma: The Race to Break the German U-Boat Codes, 1939–1943* (Boston: Houghton Mifflin, 1991), pp. 104–184. See PRO, ADM 223/88, Use of Special Intelligence in the Battle of the Atlantic, f. 235.

5. An outline of the process of getting the decrypts from G.C.&C.S. to the Tracking Room and a physical description of the Tracking Room are given in Michael Gannon, *Operation Drumbeat: The Dramatic True Story of Germany's First U-Boat Attacks Along the American Coast in World War II* (New York: Harper & Row, 1990), pp. 153–156. The information comes from interviews conducted by the writer with Beesly on 9 July 1986 and with Kenneth A. Knowles (Captain, U.S.N., Ret.), who served a two-week stint in the Tracking Room during May 1942, on 12 July 1986.

6. E.g., Jürgen Rohwer, "The Operational Use of 'Ultra' in the Battle of the Atlantic," unpublished paper, Medlicott Symposium, 1985; V. E. Tarrant, *The U-Boat Offensive 1914–1945* (London: Arms and Armour Press, 1989), p. 100; Terraine, *U-Boat Wars,* pp. 400–401; and Correlli Barnett, *Engage the Enemy More Closely: The Royal Navy in the Second World War* (London: Hodder, 1991), p. 267 and *n*.19. Professor Rohwer is particularly convinced that the Ultra triumph, leading to evasive convoy routing in the second half of 1941, was "more decisive to the outcome of the Battle (of the Atlantic) than the U-boats sunk in the convoy battles of 1943 or in the Bay offenses"; quoted in Terraine, *U-Boat Wars,* p. 400.

7. Hinsley, et al., *British Intelligence,* Vol. II, pp. 177, 636. A postwar U.S. Navy study estimated that 70 percent of all convoys intercepted by U-boats in the period 1 December 1942–31 May 1943 owed their contacts to Naval Cipher No. 3; see David Syrett, *The Defeat of the U-Boats: The Battle of the Atlantic* (Columbia, SC: University of South Carolina Press, 1994), p. 148, *n*.10. Hessler, *U-Boat War,* says that in February and March 1943, "It was almost entirely due to [B-Dienst] that the U-boats still succeeded in finding convoys"; Vol. II, p. 89.

8. Hessler, *U-Boat War,* Vol. 1, pp. 77–79; Rohwer, "Codes and Ciphers" in Runyan and Copes, eds., *Die Gallantly,* p. 52; Hinsley, et al., *British Intelligence,* Vol. II, Appendix 9, "Devices Adopted for Disguising U-Boat Positions in Enigma Signals," pp. 681–682; Timothy Mulligan, "The German Navy Evaluates Its Cryptographic Security," *Military Affairs,* Vol. XLIX, No. 2 (April 1985), pp. 75–79. Dönitz reported his security concerns to Hitler at the Führer's eastern headquarters, Wolfsschanze, on 8 February 1943: *"The C-in-C Navy* explains with the aid of maps that during this month the enemy, surprisingly enough, found out the locations of our submarines, and, in some cases, even the exact number of [boats]. It was confirmed later on that his convoys evaded the known submarine formation. This detailed information can come from two sources: (a) Treason. (b) Undetected reconnaissance planes locating the formation." *Fuehrer Conferences,* pp. 308–309.

9. PRO, ADM 223/297, "German Success Against British Codes and Cyphers, by R. T. Barrett, based on a report by Tighe," 19 pp. The writer is indebted to the late John Costello for alerting him to the existence of this document. Tighe worked on Anglo-French ciphers before the war. He

was withdrawn from sea duty in 1942 to work in the Signals Division, Admiralty.

10. Ibid., pp. 1, 8.

11. PRO, ADM 223/88, "Admiralty Use of Special Intelligence in Battle of Atlantic," Chapter XV, "Convoys HX 229 and SC 122, March 1943," ff. 258–259. Interview with J. David Brown, Head, Naval Historical Branch, Ministry of Defence, London, 29 May 1997. Brown, furthermore, is reluctant to call HX.229/SC.122 a German "victory," since only 19 of the 40 U-boats involved made contact with either of the two convoys. "That was no way to win a war," he told the writer.

12. See Syrett, *Defeat of the U-Boats*, pp. 117–118 and *n.* 65, 147–148 and *nn.* 9, 10. See also Kahn, *Seizing the Enigma*, p. 263.

13. Kahn, *Seizing the Enigma*, p. 263; Hinsley, et al., *British Intelligence*, Vol. II, p. 554.

14. Telephone interview from London with Sir Harry Hinsley, 19 June 1996.

15. See for example Barnett, *Engage the Enemy*, pp. 276–277: "Yet for all the endurance and professional skill of His Majesty's ships and aircraft and of the Merchant Marine on the High Seas, the decisive instrument of the deliverance lay in the teams of civilians in the quiet huts of Bletchley Park who had broken Dönitz's Enigma cypher. To them for the time being belonged the place of honour 'on the right of the line.'" Also Peter Calvocoressi, *Top Secret Ultra* (New York: Ballantine Books, 1980), p. 97: "The Battle of the Atlantic is the battle which Hitler would have won and nearly won, but which he lost because of Ultra." Terraine, *U-Boat Wars*, quotes approvingly a paper by Jürgen Rohwer, "The Operational Use of Ultra in the Battle of the Atlantic," in which the latter is cited as saying: "There were many factors which influenced the outcome of the decisive Battle of the Atlantic. . . . I would put 'Ultra' at the top of this list of factors," pp. 400–401.

16. Hinsley, et al., *British Intelligence*, Vol. II, pp. 169–170. This point is developed by W. J. R. "Jock" Gardner, "The

Battle of the Atlantic, 1941–The First Turning Point?" *The Journal of Strategic Studies,* Vol. 17, No. 1 (March 1994), pp. 109–123.

17. Kahn, *Seizing the Enigma,* p. 183.

18. Hessler, *U-Boat War,* pp. 64–67; Rohwer, "Codes and Ciphers," in Runyan and Copes, eds., *Die Gallantly,* pp. 39–42.

19. See the excellent studies of RCN escorts and anti-submarine warfare by Marc Milner, *North Atlantic Run: The Royal Canadian Navy and the Battle for the Convoys* (Toronto: University of Toronto Press, 1985); and *U-Boat Hunters.*

20. Hessler, *U-Boat War,* p. 82.

21. J. David Brown, "The Battle of the Atlantic, 1941–1943: Peaks and Troughs," in Runyan and Copes, eds., *Die Gallantly,* p. 140, 151.

22. Robert Hugh Cole, *Underwater Explosions* (Princeton, NJ: Princeton University Press, 1948); T. Benzinger, "Physiological Effects of Blast in Air and Water," in *German Aviation Medicine, World War II* (Washington, D.C.: U.S. Government Printing Office, 1950), Vo. II, pp. 1225–1259; Nelson M. Wolf, Lt. M.C., U.S.N.R., Report Number 646, "Underwater Blast Injury–A Review of the Literature" (Groton, CT: Naval Submarine Medical Center, 1970). The writer is grateful to Captain Claude A. Harvery, M.C., U.S.N., for these citations.

23. Interview with Sir Robert Atkinson, Winchester, England, 2 June 1997.

24. David K. Brown, "Atlantic Escorts, 1939–45," in Howarth and Law, *Battle of the Atlantic,* p. 462.

25. Willem Hackmann, *Seek & Strike: Sonar, Anti-submarine Warfare and the Royal Navy 1914–54* (London: Her Majesty's Stationery Office, 1984), p. 281 and n.46. For asdic technology the writer has relied on this volume throughout. See pp. 216, 279, 281, 283, 296, 337, and 279–280 on the "Q Attachment" for holding contact with deep-diving boats. See Hessler, *U-Boat War,* Vol. II, p. 47.

26. PRO, ADM 186/808, "Interrogation of U-Boat Survivors, Cumulative Edition," June 1944, Chapter IX, "Diving," f. 299.

27. Middlebrook, *Convoy,* p. 69; Vice-Admiral Sir Arthur Hezlet, K.B.E., C.B., D.S.O., D.S.C., *Electronics and Sea Power* (New York: Stein and Day, 1975), p. 229; Hackmann, *Seek & Strike,* p. 280 and n.44.

28. PRO, ADM 186/808, "Interrogation of U-Boat Survivors," f. 295; Hackmann, *Seek & Strike,* p. 321.

29. Beesly, *Special Intelligence,* pp. 20–21, 116; Kahn, *Seizing the Enigma,* pp. 144–145.

30. NARA, RG 457, SRH 149, Lawrence F. Safford, "A Brief History of Communications Intelligence in the United States, March 1952; SRH 305, Safford, "History of Radio Intelligence: The Undeclared War," November 1943; War Diary, Eastern Sea Frontier, July 1942, p. 30.

31. NARA, RG 38, Box 14, Collection of Memoranda on Operations of SIS, Intercept Activities and Dissemination, 1942–45, "Report of Technical Mission to England," 11 April 1941.

32. Kathleen Broome Williams, *Secret Weapon: U.S. High-Frequency Direction Finding in the Battle of the Atlantic* (Annapolis, MD: Naval Institute Press, 1996), passim; Rohwer, *Convoy Battles,* p. 21.

33. Jürgen Rohwer states that by spring 1943 *B-Dienst* had amassed "clear proof" that Allied surface escorts carried HF/DF *(Kurzwellenpeiler).* He reproduces *X-B-Bericht* (cryptographic service report) No. 16/43, dated 22 April 1943, to this effect. Distribution of the proof included Dönitz's Operational and Signals staffs, where apparently it was ignored. From a house near Algeciras in Spain, German photographers of British warships anchored in the roads of Gibraltar recorded the six-sided basket or birdcagelike Adcock HF/DF antennas on the aftermasts of certain ships, but these were interpreted by analysts as being connected to radar. Furthermore, since June 1942, when U–94 (Oblt. z.S. Otto Ites) reported being depth-charged after making a HF transmission, Commanders had frequently voiced their suspicions about the matter. Rohwer, *Convoy Battles,* pp. 199–200 and photographs between pp. 192–193. Axel Niestlé states that the Kriegsmarine became aware of shipborne HF/DF in

June 1944; "German Technical and Electronic Development," in Howarth and Law, eds., *Battle of the Atlantic,* p. 438.

34. NARA, Action Report, Box 855, Serial 026, USS *Bogue* (CVE–9), Report of Operations of Hunter-Killer Group built around U.S.S. *Bogue* furnishing air cover for Convoy ON–184 from Iceland area to Argentia area; from Commander, Sixth Escort Group, to Commander-in-Chief Western Approaches, 29 May, p. 3.

35. Hezlet, *Electronics,* p. 189.

36. Hessler, *U-Boat War,* Vol. II, p. 75; Charles M. Sternhell and Alan M. Thorndike, *Antisubmarine Warfare in World War II,* Report No. 51 of the Operations Evaluation Group (Washington, D.C.: Navy Department, 1946), p. 41; Syrett, *Defeat of the German U-Boats,* p. 12.

37. PRO, ADM 237/113, Convoy ONS.5, Appendix G, HF/DF Report, H.M.S. *Duncan* 24/4/43–5/5/43; HF/DF Report H.M.S. *Tay,* 24/4/43–7/5/43.

38. Vice-Admiral Sir Peter Gretton, K.C.B., D.S.O., O.B.E., D.S.C., *Convoy Escort Commander* (London: Cassell & Company Ltd., 1964), p. 157.

39. NARA, KTB–BdU, "Final Survey of Convoy No. 41 [SC.130]," 20 May 1943.

40. Rohwer, *Convoy Battles,* p. 198.

41. Ibid., pp. 49, 196–197. Rohwer's findings, based on studies of sea and air escort action reports, conflict with those represented in Table 10.4, p. 239 in Hackmann, *Seek & Strike,* where reliance is on the Admiralty's Monthly Anti-Submarine Reports.

42. Robert Buderi, *The Invention That Changed the World: How a Small Group of Radar Pioneers Won the Second World War and Launched a Technological Revolution* (New York: Simon & Schuster, 1996), chap. 4, "A Line in the Ether," pp. 77–97.

43. P.M.S. Blackett, *Studies of War: Nuclear and Conventional* (New York: Hill and Wang, 1962), p. 221.

44. James Phinney Baxter III, *Scientists Against Time* (Boston: Little, Brown, 1947), p. 142. Besides the magnetron, the

Tizard mission brought new weapons hardware and specifications; see Ronald W. Clark, *The Rise of the Boffins* (London: Phoenix House, Ltd., 1962), pp. 138–139.

45. PRO, AIR 41/47, Captain D. V. Peyton Ward, R.N., "The R.A.F. in Maritime War" [typescript], Vol. III, ff. 485, 534; Clay Blair, *Hitler's U-Boat War: The Hunters 1939–1942* (New York: Random House, 1996), p. 319; Alfred Price, *Aircraft versus Submarine: The Evolution of the Anti-Submarine Aircraft, 1912 to 1980* (London: Jane's Publishing Company, Ltd., 1980), p. 146. Also see Terraine, *U-Boat Wars,* pp. 428–429. In Bomber Command's favor, it does appear that bombing of U-boat yards did prevent widespread introduction of the U-boat Type XXI, which could have altered the course of the war at sea in 1945.

46. Price, *Aircraft versus Submarine,* pp. 54–58, 78; Derek Howse, *Radar at Sea: The Royal Navy in World War 2* (Annapolis, MD: Naval Institute Press, 1993), passim.

47. Winston S. Churchill, *The Grand Alliance,* vol. 6 of *The Second World War* (Boston: Houghton Mifflin Company, 1950), p. 127.

Chapter 3

1. NARA, Box 108, CINCLANT, King to CNO Harold R. Stark, U.S.S. *Augusta,* Flagship, undated but after 14 December referred to in the message and before 30 December, when King left *Augusta* to become Commander-in-Chief, United States Fleet (COMINCH).

2. The story of Drumbeat is given in Gannon, *Operation Drumbeat.* The messages referred to are described on pp. 211–212, and one message, together with U.S. Navy Daily Situation Maps, is reproduced between pp. 330 and 331. The documents and maps confirming U.S. Navy receipt of Winn's updated information, as well as the messages themselves, are readily accessible in: PRO, ADM 223/103, "F" Series, Admiralty Signal Messages, October 1941–February 1942, DEFE–3 [hereafter cited PRO, DEFE–3], 2 and 10

January 1942; NARA, RG 457, National Security Agency, "German Navy/U-Boat Messages Translations and Summaries," Box 7, SRGN 5514–6196, 9 January [German Time] 1942; NARA, SRMN–033 (Part I), COMINCH File of Messages on U-Boat Estimates and Situation Reports, October 1941–September 1942, Naval Message 121716, 12 January 1942; NARA [from the Operational Archives, Naval Historical Center], U.S. Navy Daily Situation Maps, 12–15 January 1942.

3. Montgomery C. Meigs, *Slide Rules and Submarines: American Scientists and Subsurface Warfare in World War II* (Washington, D.C.: National Defense University Press, 1990), pp. 46–51, 92.

4. Blair contends that this writer's criticism of King for sending or holding his destroyers for other missions instead is not justified, because King sent or held his destroyers for other missions instead(!); *U-Boat War*, pp. 465–466. The point is that ASW was *the* mission of the moment. The Royal Navy, in the same circumstance, one is confident, would have sent out every ship available–"More of the Dunkirk spirit, 'throw in everything you have,'" Samuel Eliot Morison wrote in another context–if only to *force the U-boats down and out of the bunt.* This was one of the many lessons the British had learned that King and his subordinates chose not to heed. U-*123* was sitting on the surface off Coney Island while seven U.S. destroyers stood inert in New York Harbor. Had the destroyers fulfilled the primary mission for which King had assembled them, the U.S. Navy might well have achieved a *Paukenschlag* in reverse, and possibly have saved the massive expenditure of flesh and steel it went on to lose, as shown below. The mission given most of the destroyers instead was escort of American troopships to Iceland and Northern Ireland. In a new book, British historian Peter Padfield rightfully questions why in early 1942 *that* was the emergency; Peter Padfield, *War Beneath the Sea: Submarine Conflict 1939–1945* (London: BCA, 1995), p. 532, n.61. See Gannon, *Drumbeat,* pp. 238–240, 412–414.

5. NARA, KTB–BdU, 17 January 1942.

6. Quoted in Roskill, *War at Sea,* Vol. II, p. 99.

7. Dönitz, *Memoirs: Ten Years and Twenty Days* (London: Weidenfeld & Nicolson, 1959), p. 219; Beesly, *Special Intelligence,* p. 120. Of its 700 tons of fuel, a U-tanker would have to reserve about 100 for its own operations. The replenishment contacts of each U-tanker during the war are given in Rössler, *U-Boat,* pp. 166–167. The boats' armament was limited to one 37mm gun and two 20mm anti-aircraft guns. Ungainly and slow to dive, none of the tanker Types XIV and XV survived the war.

8. NARA [from the Naval Historical Center], War Diary, Eastern Sea Frontier [hereafter ESF], March 1942, p. 231. The point is one that has been missed by some naval writers who think that after March 1942 the Army continued to share this responsibility with the Navy.

9. NARA, ESF, November 1943, pp. 31–32.

10. Ibid., pp. 32, 37, 38; *Miami Herald,* 8 July 1942.

11. Fleet Admiral Ernest J. King, *U.S. Navy at War 1941–1945: Official Reports to the Secretary of the Navy* (Washington, D.C.: United States Navy Department, 1946), p. 80.

12. Gannon, *Drumbeat,* pp. 382–384.

13. Roskill, *War at Sea,* Vol. II, p. 97; Robert William Love, Jr., "Ernest Joseph King, 26 March 1942–15 December 1945," in Love, ed., *The Chiefs of Naval Operations* (Annapolis, MD: Naval Institute Press, 1980), p. 154.

14. Terraine, *U-Boat Wars,* pp. 92, 413; Rear Admiral William Sowden Sims, U.S.N., *The Victory at Sea* (Garden City, NY: Doubleday, Page and Company, 1921), chap. 3, "The Adoption of the Convoy," pp. 88–117.

15. Beesly, *Special Intelligence,* pp. 113–115; and interview with Beesly, Lymington, England, 9 July 1986.

16. Ernest J. King and Walter Muir Whitehill, *Fleet Admiral King: A Naval Record* (New York: W. W. Norton, 1952), p. 457. Sir John Slessor argues that King erred even in his conversion statement–"proved wrong . . . as much by King's carriers in mid-Atlantic as by Coastal Command in the Bay [of Biscay]." *The Central Blue: The Autobiography of*

Sir John Slessor, Marshal of the RAF (New York: Frederick A. Praeger, 1957), p. 492.

17. George C. Marshall Research Library, Lexington, Virginia, Marshall Papers, Box 73, Folder 12, "King, Ernest J. 1942 May–1942 August," Marshall to King, 19 June 1942.

18. Gerhard L. Weinberg, *A World at Arms: A Global History of World War II* (New York: Cambridge University Press, 1994), p. 378. The argument has been made by U.S. Navy historians Dean C. Allard and Robert W. Love, Jr., and repeated in Blair, *U-Boat War* (p. 692), that the defeat on the American littoral was offset by the "naval victory" achieved by USN warships in safely transporting American troops across the Atlantic to Iceland, Northern Ireland, and the British Isles during January–August 1942. The U.S. Navy's escort of troopships was successful throughout the war, and certainly deserves commendation. But the argument of offsetting victory assumes that because the Navy performed properly in one responsibility it need not be held accountable in another. That principle was not accepted in naval doctrine at the time. Furthermore, it should be noted that during the period cited, the U-boat presence in the transatlantic transport lanes was greatly diminished (Blair himself says that "all available Atlantic submarines including medium-range Type VIIs" were sent to the American coastal campaign; p. 693) and only three small U-boat packs *(Hecht* in May, *Endrass* in June, and *Wolf* in July) could be formed. "Naval victories" are usually won against an enemy at his strength. The argument also assumes that King was "forced to choose" between escorting troopships and escorting merchant ships, Blair, *U-Boat War,* p. 693. That was a false choice in mid-January, when the sailing of a troopship convoy could easily have been delayed in order to take care of *Paukenschlag's* appearance, as such troopship movements were frequently delayed thereafter in Operation Bolero. Blair worries about the possible "wrath of the American Army" (p. 466), should the troopships be delayed; but who, knowing anything about him, seriously believes that the gun-metal eyes of Ernest J. King ever blinked at the emotions of the

Army? (Blair states that troopship escorts were, after all, passing through Canadian waters, "where there were by far the greatest number of Drumbeat boats"; p. 466. There were two Drumbeat boats in Canadian waters at the time, U-*109* and U-*130*; there were three off New York to Hatteras, U-*123*, U-*66,* and U-*124.)* It was a false choice later as well, when other available destroyers, together with multiple small craft, made convoying possible and effective, as demonstrated woefully late in May.

19. Dönitz, *Memoirs,* pp. 207–208; Hessler, *U-Boat War,* Vol. II, p. 16. While the new boats would eventually become available with the Baltic thaw, Hessler writes: "Yet it was the dearth of new boats in the critical early months of 1942 that constituted an irreparable handicap to the whole [American] campaign."

20. *Triton* (called SHARK at GC&CS) was first introduced operationally on 5 October 1941 and overlapped with three-rotor *Heimische Gewässer* (called DOLPHIN at GC&CS) until 1 February 1942. See Ralph Erskine and Trade Weierud, "Naval Enigma: M4 and Its Rotors," *Cryptologia,* Vol. XI, No. 4 (October 1987), pp. 235–244. Triton was introduced not to make decryption more difficult for the Allies–Dönitz had no idea his signals were being decrypted by the Allies–but as an internal security measure: to keep signals traffic out of the hands of German personnel with no "need to know."

21. Hinsley speculates: "Had the U-boats continued to give priority to attacks on Atlantic convoys after the Enigma had been changed, it is likely that there would have been such an improvement in their performance against convoys that the U-boat Command might have concluded that its earlier difficulties had been due to the fact that the three-wheel Enigma was insecure"; Hinsley, et al., *British Intelligence,* Vol. II, p. 230.

22. Donald Macintyre, *The Battle of the Atlantic* (New York: MacMillan, 1961), p. 140; John Keegan, *The Price of Admiralty: The Evolution of Naval Warfare* (New York: Viking Penguin, 1989), pp. 218–219.

23. From an appreciation of Blackett by Sir Edward Bullard, quoted in Sir Bernard Lovell, F.R.S., *P.M.S. Blackett: A Biographical Memoir* (London: The Royal Society, 1976), preface.

24. Clark, *Boffins,* p. 141.

25. Quoted in ibid., pp. 146, 215.

26. Blackett, *Studies of War,* pp. 216–217.

27. Ibid., pp. 214–215. Professor C. H. Waddington, who was a member and later head of the Operational Research Section, provides statistics that show the rise in lethality of attacks following adoption of the 25–foot setting through December 1942. He suggests, however: "Some part in the overall improvement was undoubtedly contributed by the more powerful filling employed [Torpex Mark XI after July 1942] and another part by the gradual increase in the number of heavy aircraft, and thus in the average weight of bomb-load"; Waddington, O.R., pp. 177–178.

28. Ibid., pp. 220–225.

29. Ibid., passim; Brian McCue, *U-Boats in the Bay of Biscay: An Essay in Operations Analysis* (Washington, D.C.: National Defense University Press, 1990), passim.

30. Waddington, O.R., pp. xvi–xvii. In 1942 the U.S. Navy formed a civilian research group corresponding to O.R.S., which it called Anti-Submarine Warfare Operational Research Group (ASWORG).

31. PRO, AIR 41/45–48, "The Royal Air Force in the Maritime War" (typescript), four volumes.

32. Unnamed crewman quoted in Price, *Aircraft versus Submarine,* p. 166. O.R.S. studies found that it took an average of 200 hours of flying time to result in one attack; Waddington, O.R., p. 168.

33. NARA, Box 419, folder marked Command File World War II. Shore Est. Hydrographic Office, "Submarine Supplement to Sailing Directions for the Bay of Biscay," June 1943.

34. PRO, CAB 86/3, A.U.(43)98, The A/S Offensive by Aircraft in the Bay of Biscay, Memorandum by the First Lord of the Admiralty, 28 March 1943.

35. Until recently it was thought that U-*206* (Kptlt. Herbert Optiz) was sunk in the Bay on 30 November 1941 by a Whitley bomber of 502 Squadron, but a reassessment by the Naval Historical Branch, Ministry of Defence, establishes that U-*206* struck a mine off St.-Nazaire on 29 November.

36. Quoted in Price, *Aircraft versus Submarine*, p. 65, which is an excellent source on the Leigh Light. The best source for actual in-flight operation of the L/L is "Leigh Light Wellingtons of Coastal Command" by Air Commodore Jeaff H. Greswell, C.B., C.B.E., D.S.O., D.F.C., R.A.F. (Ret.), typescript, May 1995; letter, Greswell to author, 6 November 1997. Greswell participated in the development and testing of the L/L and made the first damaging attack employing it.

37. An account of the unusual adventures of *Luigi Torelli* is given by Price, ibid., pp. 88–91. The first destruction of a U-boat at night was achieved by a conventionally equipped Swordfish of No. 812 Squadron, Fleet Air Arm, on 21 December 1941 off the Strait of Gibraltar. The victim was U-*451* (Kptlt. Eberhard Hoffmann). A detailed account of the procedures to be followed in making a Leigh Light attack is given in PRO, AIR 41/47, Peyton Ward, "R.A.F. in Maritime War," Vol. III, Appendix VI, ff. 595–596. In the Wellington the Light was mounted in a retractable underturret. Later the Light was mounted on Liberators and Catalinas in a nacelle slung from bomb lugs on the wing.

38. NARA, KTB–BdU, 16 July 1942.

39. PRO, AIR 41/47, Peyton Ward, "R.A.F. in Maritime War," Vol. III, ff. 535–536.

40. Ibid., Vol. III, ff. 495–497.

41. Richard Baker, *The Terror of Tobermory: An Informal Biography of Vice-Admiral Sir Gilbert Stephenson, KBE, CB, CMG* (London: W. H. Allen, 1972).

42. Quoted in Mark Williams, *Captain Gilbert Roberts R.N. and the Anti-U-Boat School* (London: Cassell, 1979), p. III.

43. Ibid., pp. 94–95.

44. "Artichoke" and "Observant" are described in chap.

4. "Beta Search" evolved from the fact that the W/T transmissions of a shadower U-boat began with the Morse B (Beta), or B–bar. The new tactic forced the shadower to dive while, unseen to the enemy, the convoy changed course.

45. McCue, *U-Boats in the Bay,* pp. 30–31; Hinsley, et al., *British Intelligence,* Vol. III, Pt. 1, p. 212. Historian J. David Brown considers August 1942 a more dangerous period for Allied shipping than early spring 1943. Comments to author.

46. PRO, AIR 41/47, Peyton Ward, "R.A.F. in Maritime War," Vol. III, ff. 512, 515. The ship torpedoed, but not sunk, was U.S.S. *Thomas Stone.*

47. Quoted in Rear-Admiral W.S. Chalmers, C.B.E., D.S.C., *Max Horton and the Western Approaches* (London: Hodder and Stoughton, 1954), p. 143.

48. Williams, *Gilbert Roberts,* p. 117.

49. Chalmers, *Max Horton,* pp. 150–155 and passim; Terraine, *U-Boat Wars,* pp. 502–503.

50. NARA, KTB-BdU, 31 December 1942.

51. Quoted in Padfield, *Dönitz,* p. 295. Raeder also nominated Generaladmiral Rolf Carls.

52. Graham Rhys-Jones, "The German System: A Staff Perspective," in Howarth and Law, eds., *Battle of the Atlantic,* pp. 138–157; Chalmers, *Max Horton,* p. 152.

53. Michael Howard, *Grand Strategy,* Volume IV, *August 1942–September 1943* (London: Her Majesty's Stationery Office, 1972), Appendix III(D), "Conduct of the War in 1943," p. 621.

54. Slessor, *Central Blue,* pp. 446, 464; Thomas B. Buell, *Master of Sea Power: A Biography of Fleet Admiral Ernest J. King* (Boston: Little, Brown, 1980), p. 276.

55. PRO, AIR 41/47, Peyton Ward, "R.A.F. in Maritime War," Vol. III, f. 500.

56. The various volumes of A.U. Committee papers are found in PRO, CAB 86/1,2,3,4. After 12 May, when the Atlantic struggle was turning in the Allies' favor, the Committee met several times fortnightly, then, after June, monthly. W. J. R. Gardner, "An Allied Perspective," in Howarth and Law, eds., *Battle of the Atlantic,* p. 524.

57. PRO, CAB 86/3, A.U.(43)84, "The Value of the Bay of Biscay Patrols, Note by Air Officer Commanding in Chief Coastal Command." Slessor made the interesting comment on the O.R.S. analysis: "It will be observed that the proportion of attacks to sightings round the convoys is only about 47% as compared with 75% in the Bay. The reason for this is of course, that only very rarely does an aircraft get more than one sighting on a patrol in the Bay, while round the convoys 3 or 4 is not exceptional, and the number has been known to be as high as 7 on one sortie"; f. 352.

58. Blackett, *Studies of War*, p. 232. The comparison of escort perimeter to convoy size is further elaborated in NARA, RG 38 Chief of Naval Operations, Intelligence Division, Secret Reports of Naval Attachés, 1940–1946, File F–6-e, Stack Area 1oW4, Box 252, Folder "Anti-Submarine Operations, Great Britain, Various, 1943–1944, Intelligence Report, Naval Attaché, London, 12 May 1943": The perimeter of a convoy of 40 ships (4 columns of 10) was 23 miles long when the escort vessels were stationed 4,000–5,000 yards from the outside ships. With 78 ships (6 columns of 13) the perimeter was 27 miles long, which was an increase of only 1/6th. Where the 40-ship convoy required six escort vessels, the 78-ship convoy needed only seven. When the speeds of the two convoys were about the same, the percentage of stragglers from the larger convoys was a little less. The argument for 60-*plus* convoys was the following: If according to operational data six escort vessels lost four merchant ships, nine escorts would lose only three ships per convoy; therefore, 180 ships sailing in three convoys of 60 ships with six escorts each (on the current eight-day cycle) could be expected to result in a loss of 12 ships; the same ships sailing in 2 convoys of 90 ships each with 9 escorts each would lose only 6, cutting losses in half.

59. PRO, CAB 86/2, War Cabinet Anti-U-Boat Warfare, Minutes of the Meeting on 3rd March 1943, f. 125.

60. Blackett, *Studies of War*, p. 233; F. W. Barley and D. Waters, *Defeat of the Enemy Attack on Shipping*, Vol. 1B, Plan 35; Howard, *Strategy*, p. 304 and *n*.

61. PRO, CAB 86/3, A.U.(43)40, Progress of Analysis of the Value of Escort Vessels and Aircraft in the Anti U-Boat Campaign, Report by Professor Blackett, ff. 241–243.

62. PRO, ADM 199/434, "The Commander-in-Chief, Western Approaches to All British and Canadian Escort Vessels Operated by Western Approaches Including Support Groups, 27th April 1943." The Tactical Policy of Coastal Command was overtly offensive: "The Primary object of A/S patrols and A/S escort is the destruction of U-Boats"; Directorate of History, National Defence Headquarters, Ottowa, Canada [hereafter DHIST/NDHQ], Admiralty Atlantic Convoy Instructions (September 1942), Air Operations, p. 201.

Chapter 4

1. The ONS series, which had reached ONS.171, was renumbered beginning with ONS.1 in March 1943, when this series was sailed to Halifax instead of to New York. The restarted ONS convoys sailed every eight days. The principal sources for ONS.5 are: NARA, "Allied Commands, Canadian, Captain (D) Newfoundland, 19 May 1943 (Vols. 1–2)" [hereafter Captain (D) Newfoundland], Boxes 1718–1719; and PRO, ADM 237/113, "Report on Convoy ONS.5." The NARA collection contains Form S.1203 reports of attacks on U-boats, track charts, plotting table diagrams, asdic recorder tracings, and original hand-copied between-ships messages, all of which are lacking in the PRO file. Ship-to-shore messages of ONS.5 are given in NARA, "Tenth Fleet Convoy and Routing Files," Box 113, ON 304–ONS 9.

2. Gretton, *Convoy Escort Commander,* p. 108.

3. Ibid., p. 108. The obituary writer in *The Times* (London) called him "ruthless" in this respect; 13 November 1992, p. 21. One of Gretton's escort group Captains, Lieutenant (now Sir) Robert Atkinson, R.N.R., of H.M.S. *Tay,* described to the writer one of Gretton's practices. Each

morning at sea, at first light, Gretton sent a visual signal to all ships *in Latin*. At voyage's end copies of those signals had to be produced by all ships. Any that got the messages wrong were detailed for extra training in port. Interview with Atkinson, Winchester, England, 2 June 1997.

4. Gretton, *Convoy Escort Commander*, p. 120. The corvette *Pink* was later ordered to search astern for survivors but she found none. Seven men out of the crew of 78 were eventually located by a PBY–5 Catalina flying boat on 12 April and picked up by the rescue ship *Zamalek*. Frostbite forced the amputation of the legs of three men and the feet of a fourth. See Vice-Admiral Sir Peter Gretton, *Crisis Convoy* (New York: Kensington, 1974), pp. 131–134. The U-boats that attacked HX.231 formed Group *Löwenherz*. Most were on their first mission, and only five launched torpedoes. The same choice had been made during the battle of convoys HX.229 and SC.122 on 16–20 March by Lieutenant-Commander Gordon John Luther, captain of the destroyer *Volunteer* and SO of the HX.229 Escort Group B4. On the night of 16/17 March Luther left the convoy undefended in order to rescue survivors from the U.S. Liberty ship *William Eustis*. But later on the same night, realizing that he could not leave the convoy without cover again, Luther ordered the survivors of a second torpedoed American freighter, S.S. *Harry Luckenbach*, to be left in lifeboats, where they died. Middlebrook, *Convoy*, pp. 181–186, 305–307.

5. Gretton, *Convoy Escort Commander*, p. 127.

6. PRO, ADM 223/15, Operational Intelligence Centre, Special Intelligence Summary [hereafter S.I. Summary], for the week ending 19 April 1943; f. 195. Gretton stated in his report on ONS.5 that on 26 April he made "a study of the submarine dispositions"; PRO ADM 237/113, Report of Proceedings–Senior Officer in H.M.S. *Duncan*, p. 1. The X-B-Bericht Weekly Summary of B-Dienst for 10–16 May is found in Bundesarchiv-Militärarchiv, Bestand RM 7/755, X-B-Bericht No. 20/43, Woche vom 10–16.5. 1943, f. 126v. (s.X-B-Bericht No. 19/43).

7. Norman Franks, *Search, Find and Kill: The RAF's*

U-Boat Successes in World War Two (London: Grub Street, 1995), pp. 13–14. The sinking occurred at 61°25′N, 19°48′W, or south of Iceland; Thomas A. Adams and David J. Lees, *Register of Type VII U-boats* (London: Warships Supplement, 1990), p. 40. The loss of U–*710* was acknowledged by BdU on 28 April, when the headquarters war diary observed that, "U–*710* has not reported since it sailed from Kiel on 15.4 [15 April] . . . so that its loss through aircraft must be presumed"; see NARA, KTB-BdU, 28 April 1943.

   8. PRO, ADM 237/113, Commodore's Report.

   9. Ibid., Appendix E, Copy of Naval Messages, p. 2.

   10. Ibid., Report on Collision Between "Bornholm" and "Berkel." *Bornholm* made Reykjavik safely. The time of the collision was 2355.

   11. PRO, ADM 237/113, Appendix E, Copy of Naval Messages, p. 3.

   12. On the Kriegsmarine's grid chart *Specht's* original "patrol channels" ran from AJ 6762 to AK 7791. In such orders to establish channels, or lines, BdU specified the order in which the boats were to array themselves; thus, for *Specht:* U–*203,* 438, 706, 630, 662, 584, 168, 270, 260, 92, 628, 707, 358, 264, 614, 226, 125. The original *Meise* line ran from AK 2386 to 0347. The original *Amsel* line ran from AK 2966 to 6799. See NARA, KTB-BdU 22, 23, 24, 25, 26, April 1943. These lines constantly shifted position and recombined.

   13. Syrett, *Defeat of the German U-Boats,* p. 58.

   14. NARA, KTB–BdU, 25 April 1943.

   15. Ibid., 27 April 1943.

   16. PRO, ADM 223/88, Use of Special Intelligence in Battle of Atlantic, Convoy ONS.5, April-May 1943, f. 270.

   17. Ibid.

   18. Escorts assisting ONS.4 sank two U-boats, U–*191* and U–*203,* the latter with participation by a Swordfish aircraft from the escort carrier H.M.S. *Biter.* Two other boats, U–*174* and U–*227,* were sunk in the last days of April, both by aircraft.

   19. PRO, ADM CO 323/1801/13, OIC and Special Intelligence Monographs, p. 10.

20. KTB–BdU, 27 April 1943. The following boats formed Group *Star*: U–*710*, 650, 533, 386, 528, 231, 532, 378, 381, 192, 258, 552, 954, 648, 209, 413.

21. PRO, ADM 237/113, Convoy ONS.5 8 A.M. Positions British Double Summer Time.

22. Bundesarchiv-Militärarchiv, Bestand RM 7/755, X-B-Bericht No. 18/43, Woche vom 26.4–2.5.1943, f. 55r. NARA, KTB-BdU, 27 April 1943.

23. NARA, Roll 3387, KTB-U-*650*, 10 April 1943 to 28 June 1943; 28 April, p.7.

24. PRO, ADM 237/113, Convoy ONS 5, Report of Proceedings–Senior Officer in H.M.S. *Duncan*, p.2. Convoy SC.127 would safely pass through the northern quarter of the *Star* line.

25. Ibid., p. 2. The description of operation "Observant," as well as of operations "Artichoke" and "Raspberry" that appear later in the text, come from DHIST/NDHQ, 83/761, vol. II, Atlantic Convoy Instructions [A.C.I.], C.B. 04234 (2), Operations Section, Articles 101–149, pp. 51–62.

26. Ibid. Cf. Ronald Seth, *The Fiercest Battle: The Story of North Atlantic Convoy ONS.5, 22nd April–7th May 1943* (New York: Norton, 1961), p. 92. Seth personally consulted Peter Gretton about these details.

27. NARA, KTB–BdU, 1 May 1943.

28. PRO, ADM 237/113, Appendix E, Copy of Naval Messages, p. 4. The order from CinCWA to *Oribi* was sent at 2333 on the 28th. The order to *Offa* and the Support Group was sent at 0026 on the 29th; the other destroyers in this group, to which *Oribi* also officially belonged, were *Penn*, *Panther*, and *Impulsive*.

29. Oral History Collection of the Royal Naval Museum, Portsmouth, England [hereafter OHC/RNM], AC 1993/116, interview with Sir Robert Atkinson, conducted by Dr. Chris Howard Bailey, 11 March 1993.

30. NARA, Convoy ONS.5, Captain (D) Newfoundland, Boxes 1718–1719, Report of Proceedings–Senior Officer in H.M.S. *Duncan*, pp. 2–3.

31. NARA, KTB–BdU, 11 May 1943; Franks, *Search, Find and Kill,* pp. 113–115.

32. PRO, ADM 237/113, ONS.5–Comments of Senior Officer, Close Escort, p. 1.

33. PRO, ADM 237/113, Report of Proceedings–H.M.S. *Sunflower,* May 1943.

34. PRO, ADM 237/113, Narrative of Events During Passage of Convoy O.N.S.5 [by] Commanding Officer, H.M.S. *Snowflake,* p. 1. While the Chief Quartermaster and telegraphsman stated that the steering order was given by the Officer of the Watch, Chesterman concluded that the fault was phonetic: the Officer of the Watch was misunderstood when he was shouting orders through the voice pipes to the Starboard D/C throwers. Cf. Gretton, *Escort Commander,* p. 138.

35. NARA, KTB–U–*532,* Roll 2979, 29–30 May 1943; NARA, KTB–BdU, 1–2 May 1943; ADM 237/113, Commanding Officer, H.M.S. *Snowflake:* Narrative of Events During Passage of Convoy O.N.S.5, 29 April 1943; Ibid., Report of Attack on U-Boat, *Snowflake,* Event 1, 29 April 1943.

36. NARA, KTB–BdU, 28, 29 April 1943.

37. NARA, RG 38, Chief of Naval Operations, Naval Transportation Services, Armed Guard Files, 1940–1945, Mayfield Victory-Mechanicsville, Box 462. Mässenhausen's claims exceeded his results: "At 0924 attacked convoy with three hits on each of four 6000 GRT ships. . . . Two coups de grâce *(Fangschüsse)* on a 7000 tonner." NARA, Roll 2937, KTB–U–*258,* 29-4-43.

38. PRO, ADM 237/113, ONS.5–Comments of Senior Officer, Close Escort, p. 1; Report of Proceedings–Senior Officer in H.M.S. *Duncan,* pp. 3–4.

39. Ibid., Report of Proceedings–Senior Officer in H.M.S. *Duncan,* pp. 4–5. Cf. Seth, *Fiercest Battle,* pp. 99–103. The position of the *McKeesport* sinking was 61°22′N, 35°09′W. The U.S. Navy policy on derelicts is contained in the *McKeesport* folder; NARA, RG 38, Chief of Naval Operations, Naval Transportation Services, Armed Guard Files, 1940–1945, Box 462. The pursuit of a U-boat by *Tay* is de-

scribed in NARA, Boxes 1718–1719, Captain (D) Newfound-
land, Report of Attack on U-Boat, Form S.1203:1959, 29
April 1943. The BdU mentions it on 2 May; NARA, KTB-
BdU, 2 May 1943.

40. NARA, Boxes 1718–1719, Captain (D) Newfoundland, Report of Proceedings–H.M.S. *Oribi,* 29th April, 1943
to 8th May, 1943, p. 1.

41. Gretton, *Convoy Escort Commander,* p. 140. Seth,
Fiercest Battle, says that another reason was *Duncan's* need to
remain stable so that an emergency appendectomy might be
performed on a crewman by the ship's doctor; pp. 105–107.

42. PRO, ADM 237/113, Convoy ONS.5, Report of Proceedings–Senior Officer in H.M.S. *Duncan,* p. 5; Gretton,
Convoy Escort Commander, p. 141. Gretton noted that *Snowflake's* event was the first advance on a convoy at night that
had not been preceded by a HF/DF warning. Use of guns
against a surfaced U-boat had been practiced by Gretton and
his crews off Londonderry following HX.231 in what he
called Exercise Pointblank. An instance was known of a
U-boat forced to dive at 12,000 yards by gunfire from a corvette; DHIST/NDHQ 81/700, J. D. Prentice, R.C.N., Captain (D) Halifax, "Hints on Escort Work," 30 March 1943, p.
3.

43. PRO, ADM 237/113, Brief Narrative of Voyage
(ONS.5), 1 May 1943.

44. Gretton, *Convoy Escort Commander,* p. 141. Interview
with Atkinson, Winchester, England, 2 June 1997.

45. NARA, KTB-BdU, 1 May 1943. An example of
U-boat reports to BdU about weather that made operations
"useless" is that of U–*954* (Kptlt. Odo Loewe) at 1800 GST
on 1 May, 1943; NARA, SRGN 16655. Loewe also reports
the presence of an aircraft "with light like a planet." Information on operation of BdU's long-wave communications system was provided to the writer by Korv. Kapt. Hans Meckel,
A–4 (Communications Officer) in BdU; interview, 20 October 1987.

46. PRO, ADM 237/113, Convoy ONS.5, Report of Proceedings–Senior Officer in H.M.S. *Duncan,* p. 6; Gretton,

Convoy Escort Commander, pp. 141–143; NARA, Boxes 1718–1719, Captain (D) Newfoundland, Report of Proceedings–H.M.S. *Oribi,* 29th April to 8th May, 1943, p. 2.

47. Gretton, *Convoy Escort Commander,* p. 144.

48. PRO, ADM 237/113, Convoy ONS.5, Report of Proceedings–Senior Officer in H.M.S. *Duncan,* p. 6. At this date *British Lady* had only 100 tons of fuel available; ibid., Appendix E, Copy of Naval Messages, p.7.

49. Ibid., Convoy ONS.5, Continuation of Report by Commanding Officer, H.M.S. "TAY"–SO Close escort in absence of H.M.S. "DUNCAN"; Gretton, *Convoy Escort Commander,* p. 144; PRO, ADM 237/113, Naval Messages, 3 May 1943. At 0805 on 3 May CinCWA instructed the convoy's stragglers: "If you are not in contact with an escort proceed directly to Stragglers Route thence to St. Johns keeping as far west as ice permits"; ibid., 3 May 1943.

50. Ibid., 4 May 1943. The order to First Support Group was sent at 0819. At 0800 ONS.5's position was 56°50′N, 42°22′W, convoy course was 196°. Naval Historical Branch, Ministry of Defence, London [hereafter NHB/MOD], "Convoy Positions 1/5/43–30/6/43 Combined Plot"; the writer is indebted to NHB Head J. David Brown for direction to this source.

51. Quoted in Barrie Pitt, *The Battle of the Atlantic* (New York: Time-Life Books, 1977), p. 95. For a half-century *Bluebell* under Sherwood was credited with sinking U–*208* west of Gibraltar in December 1941, but a new assessment gives that sinking to H.M.S. *Harvester* and *Hesperus;* Adams and Lees, *Type VII U-Boats,* p. 11.

Chapter 5

1. Quoted in "Continuous Service," a pamphlet accompanying "An Exhibition Featuring Flowers of the Sea" (Portsmouth, Hampshire: Royal Naval Museum Publications, 1993), n.p. Extracts from an extended interview with Cyril Stephens together with extracts from interviews with other

corvette veterans are given in Chris Howard Bailey, *The Battle of the Atlantic: The Corvettes and Their Crews: An Oral History* (Annapolis, MD: Naval Institute Press, 1994).

2. David K. Brown, "Atlantic Escorts, 1939–45," in Howarth and Law, eds., *Battle of the Atlantic*, pp. 452–475; Peter Elliott, *Allied Escort Ships of World War II: A Complete Survey* (Annapolis, MD: Naval Institute Press, 1977), pp. 12–16, 171–199; Chris Ellis, *Famous Ships of World War 2, in Colour* (New York: Arco Publishing Company, Inc., 1977), pp. 16, 175–177. Artist-naturalist Peter Scott originated the Western Approaches camouflage scheme. Commander James Douglas "Chummy" Prentice, R.C.N. (R), Captain (D) Halifax in 1943 and the Canadian courterpart to Commodore (D) Western Approaches, called the corvette "the handiest anti-submarine ship that was ever built"; cited in Milner, *U-Boat Hunters*, p. 9. Beginning 1 June 1943 Captain Frederic John Walker, R.N., would prove the sloop a worthy competitor.

3. OHC/RNM, AC 1993/174, interview with Harold G. Chesterman, conducted by Chris Howard Bailey, 26 April 1993; "Captain Harold Chesterman," *The Daily Telegraph*, 13 February 1997.

4. Ibid., AC 1993/43, interview with Howard Oliver Goldsmith, conducted by Chris Howard Bailey, 8 February 1993. For a description of the convoy crews, both RN and Merchant Navy, the reader is directed to the excellent chapter "The Convoy Men," pp. 19–55, in Middlebrook, *Convoy*.

5. NARA, KTB–BdU, 1 May 1943.

6. The BdU to *Specht–Star* message is given in PRO, ADM 223/88, Use of Special Intelligence in Battle of Atlantic, f. 271. The number of boats in *Specht–Star* was actually 30. That U–628 sighted not SC.128 but EG3 is put forward in W. A. B. Douglas and Jürgen Rohwer, " 'The Most Thankless Task' Revisited: Convoys, Escorts, and Radio Intelligence in the Western Atlantic, 1941–43," in James A. Boutilier, ed., *The RCN in Retrospect, 1910–1968* (Vancouver and London: University of British Columbia Press, 1982), p. 229. The authors point out that B-Dienst decrypted a position report from SC.128.

7. NARA, KTB–BdU, 3 May 1943. The SC.128 escorts' feint eastward is described as "skillfully executed" in Admiral Karl Dönitz, *Memoirs,* p. 338.

8. NARA, KTB–BdU, 3 May 1943.

9. Ibid., 4 May 1943. In their order of station from WNW to ESE the original 27 boats of *Fink* were to be arrayed thus: U–*438,* 630, 662, 584, 168, 514, 270, 260, 732, 628, 707, 358, 264, 226, 125, 378, 192, 648, 533, 531, 954, 413, 381, 231, 552, 209, 650. The OIC U-boat estimate is given in PRO, ADM 223/15, S.I. Summary, week of 3.5.43 to 10.5.43. The writer is indebted to his friend and colleague Dr. Leonidas Roberts for computation of the length in nautical miles of the *Fink* line.

10. Hasenschar's convoy sighting report is timed at 2018 (GST)–*B Signal* 2018: *Geleitzug qu AJ* 6271–in NARA, Roll 4185, KTB–U–*628,* 8 April to 19 May 1943; 4 May 1943. The "dead reckoning" quote is from NARA, KTB–BdU, 4 May 1943. At 1802 GST on 4 May BdU signaled the assembling *Fink* boats: SOUTHWEST BOUND CONVOY EXPECTED TOMORROW ONWARDS; NARA, RG 457, SRGN 16933. Convoy ONS.5 daily speeds are given in PRO, ADM 237/113, Convoy ONS.5 8 A.M. Positions British Double Summer Time.

11. NARA, KTB–U–*628,* 4 May 1943; NARA, KTB–BdU, 6 May 1943. What Hasenschar sighted was "many mast tops" at 380 true from his position. Thereafter, as contact-keeper, he gave regular reports.

12. NARA, Roll 2886–2887, KTB–U–*264,* 8.4.43 to 1.6.43; 2150 C.E.T., 4 May 1943: *"Ihr steht günstig wie noch nie";* PRO, ADM 223/88, Use of Special Intelligence in Battle of Atlantic, Convoy ONS.5, April–May 1943, f. 272. The BdU war diary states: "In all, 41 boats were stalking the convoy"; KTB–BdU, 4 May 1943. A similar large force of 41 boats had earlier operated against two convoys, HX.229 and SC.122, on 16–20 March 1943.

13. PRO, ADM 223/16, S.I. Summary, Convoy ONS.5, Analysis of U-Boat Operations, f. 85.

14. Bradley F. Smith, *The Ultra-Magic Deals: And the Most*

Secret Special Relationship, 1940–1946 (Novato, CA: Presidio Press, 1992), pp. 105–172. The Bletchley Park decrypts are found in PRO, ADM 223/103, Admiralty Signal Messages, DEFE–3; the U.S. Navy decrypts, including retroactive decrypts of all Kriegsmarine traffic from the beginning of the war, are found in NARA, RG 457, Records of the National Security Agency/Central Security Office: German Navy/ U-Boat Messages Translations and Summaries, SRGN 1– 494668 [hereafter RG 457 SRGN].

15. PRO, ADM 237/113, Naval Messages, 4 May 1943. *Tay's* own HF/DF receptions are recorded in PRO, ADM 237/113, Report on U-Boat transmissions received by H.M.S. *Tay* on HF/DF . . . between 24.4.43 and 8.5.43.

16. Douglas and Rohwer, "Convoys, Escorts," p. 224; W. G. D. Lund, "The Royal Canadian Navy's Quest for Autonomy in the North West Atlantic: 1941–43," pp.138–157, both in Boutilier, ed., *RCN in Retrospect*.

17. Douglas and Rohwer, "Convoys, Escorts," ibid., p. 229. The experienced and accomplished U-boat fighter Donald Macintyre, in his *Battle of the Atlantic,* concluded: "A diversion to avoid it [*Fink*] was impossible"; p. 191.

18. PRO, ADM 237/113, Convoy ONS.5, Naval Messages, 4 May 1943, message sent at 2005; acknowledged and new route for *Pink* given at 2244: ALTER COURSE FORTHWITH FOR (XY) 54 01 NORTH 46 30 WEST THENCE REJOINING CONVOY ROUTE IN (XR). The night stations are given in PRO, ADM 237/113, Convoy ONS.5, Continuation of report by Commanding Officer, H.M.S. "Tay"–SO, Close Escort in absence of H.M.S. "DUNCAN" [hereafter PRO, ADM 237/113, Continuation Report, TAY], No. 3.

19. PRO, ADM 237/113, Report of Proceedings, H.M.S. OFFA, 29th April 1943 to 8th May 1943; 4 May 1943, No. 27.

20. DHIST/NDHQ, Tenth Fleet Records, Box 44, Royal Canadian Air Force Eastern Air Command, Statistics of Anti-Submarine Operations, May 1943, prepared 7 June 1943, p. 3. Earlier, on 2 May, a B–17 attacked three U-boats

in positions ahead of the convoy; W. A. B. Douglas, *The Creation of a National Air Force: The Official History of the Royal Canadian Air Force, Volume* II (Toronto: University of Toronto Press, 1986), p. 553.

21. DHIST/NDHQ, 181.003 (D1341) RCAF HQ file 28-2-52 RCAF a/c attacks on U-Boats re: Attack by Canso A 9747 of 5 Sqn 4 May 43, U630, 43 ff.; Eastern Air Command, Fifty-Second Attack by R.C.A.F. Aircraft (EAC), 4th of May 1943; photographs in File 81/520/8280, Box 7 ONS.5. While still in the area of the attack Moffitt reported his action to *Tay* by R/T, however *Tay* could not make R/T contact in return; PRO, 237/113, Continuation Report, TAY, 4 May 1943.

22. NHB/MOD, Proceedings of U-Boat Assessment Committee, April–June 1943 [typescript], f. 244.

23. NARA, RG 457, SRGN 17295; KTB–BdU, 23 May 1943; R. M. Coppock to author, 13 November 1996.

24. *Flak,* a term commonly used for anti-aircraft gun or fire, was a contraction of *Flugzeugabwehrkanone,* although some say *Fliegerbwehrkanonen.* An excellent discussion of Type VII anti-aircraft weapons and mountings is given in Stern, *Type VII U-Boats,* pp. 100–109.

25. DHIST/NDHQ, 181.003 (D1341) RCAF HQ file 28-2-52 RCAF a/c attacks on U-Boats [hereafter RCAF Attacks on U-Boats]Memorandum, No. 5 (BR) Sqdn, 4th May, 1943; NHB/MOD, Proceedings of U-Boat Assessment Committee, April-June 1943, f. 246. At 2155 CinCCNA sent word of the attack to *Tay,* PRO 237/113, Convoy ONS.5, Naval Messages, 4 May 1943. The NHB/MOD reassessment is "slight damage" to U–*438;* R.M. Coppock to author, 13 November 1996.

26. NARA, RG 457, SRGN 17055, 17090. The attack took place, U–*438* reported, in position qu AJ 6147 (55°51'N, 44°25'W). There is no KTB available from U–*438* because she was sunk on 6 May by H.M.S. *Pelican* (see below).

27. NARA, RG 457, SRGN 16974; PRO, ADM 223/16, Special Intelligence Summary, April 29th-May 5th 1943,

Convoy ONS.5, Analysis of U-Boat Operations [hereafter U-Boat Operations], f. 89.

28. This is also the conclusion of Rohwer, *Axis Submarine Successes*, p. 165.

29. PRO, ADM 237/113, Convoy ONS.5, Report of J. Kenneth Brook, Commodore, R.N.R. in M.V. "RENA" (NOR). Seth speculates that a derelict ship sighted at 1500 on 6 May, position 55°N, 44°W, by U.S.C.G. *Manhassett* was *Lorient.* Near the wreck, with its painted-out name, were empty lifeboats. The wreck sank before it could be salvaged. Seth, *Fiercest Battle,* pp. 192–194.

30. NARA, RG 467, SRGN 17017; KTB–BdU, 4 May 1943; PRO, ADM 223/16, U-Boat Operations, f. 86.

31. Ibid., ADM 223/16.

32. NARA, Roll 3377, KTB–U–*707,* 12 April to 31 May 1943; 4 May 1943.

33. NARA, Boxes 1718–1719, Captain (D) Newfoundland, Form S.1203, Report of Attack on U-Boat, H.M.S. TAY, 4 May 1943. Cf. PRO, ADM 237/113, Commodore Brook, ONS.5, Submarine Attack Report for May 4th/May 5th, 1943 [hereafter Brook Attack Report]. *Oribi* made a visual U-boat sighting at 2130 and was joined by *Offa* in an "Observant" and a sweep along the U-boat's line of advance until 2230. *Vidette* forced a U-boat to dive at 2220.

34. NARA, Roll 3377, KTB–U–*707,* 4 May 1943.

35. PRO, ADM 237/113, Report of Survivors from ONS.5.

36. Ibid.

37. NARA, Roll 4185, KTB–U–*628,* 4 May 1943.

38. Ibid.

39. Ibid., 5 May 1943. The U.S. Navy translation of Hasenschar's F.T. describing to BdU his destruction of the corvette reads: SANK A CORVETTE. (TORPEDO'S) MAGNETIC FUSE ON, DEPTH 4 (METERS). (CORVETTE) BURST INTO ATOMS. See NARA, RG 457, SRGN 17140. Cf. NARA, KTB–BdU, 5 May 1943.

40. PRO, ADM 199/2145, Reports of Interviews with Survivors from British Merchant Vessels Attacked, Damaged or Lost by Enemy Action; from 1st April, 1943 to 30th September, 1943; Shipping Casualties Section, Trade Division, Admiralty [hereafter Interviews with Survivors], S.S. *Harbury,* Capt. W. E. Cook, 16th June 1943. Jürgen Rohwer has the wreck of *Harbury* sunk by U–*264* (Kptlt. Hartwig Looks) at 0707 GST (0507 GMT) on 5 May, *Axis Submarine Successes,* p. 165; but this cannot be if Cook and his party reboarded the wreck well after that hour. Cf. PRO, ADM 237/113, Report of Survivors from ONS.5, where Lieutenant J. Downer, captain of *Northern Spray,* specifies that the boarding party left for *Harbury* at 0900 GMT and returned at 1000. U–*264* did launch two torpedoes at 0707 GST and made a single launch at 0708, but both targets were moving at 7 knots; NARA, Roll 2886–2887, KTB-U–*264,* 5 May 1943: although Looks claimed a sinking with the 0707 launches, no ship under way in ONS.5 was hit by torpedo or gunfire at that time or two hours and 19 minutes before and five hours and 33 minutes after 0707. Syrett, *Defeat of the German U-Boats,* p. 78 and n.55, attributes the sinking of *Harbury* by gunfire to U–*264,* but his endnote does not address the incident; neither does the U–*264* KTB, which makes no mention of it and instead describes torpedo actions against moving targets from 0302 GST (0102 GMT) through 1438 on 5 May.

41. NARA, Roll 4185, KTB–628, 5 May 1943. Cf. Bundesarchiv-Militärarchiv, Freiburg, Case GE 14/3, PG 30659, *Schussmeldung,* U–*628,* 5.5.43, 0243 Uhr; Seite 12: *"S.1a Dampfer 'Harbury' nach 13 Std. mit Artillerie versenkt."* At 2004 on the 5th Hasenschar signaled BdU.: JUST SANK WITH SHELLFIRE IN QU AJ 6543 [55°09′N, 42°35′W] THE HARBURY, PRESUMABLY A SHIP THAT I MYSELF HAD DAMAGED. TORPEDOES EXHAUSTED . . . AM GOING TO PROVISIONER; NARA, SRGN 17156. For *Harbury* see *Lloyd's Register,* ships' names given alphabetically. A few *Schussmeldungen* from May operations can be found appended to KTBs.

42. NARA, Roll 2886–2887, KTB-U–*264,* 5 May 1943. Looks's report to BdU on this attack is in NARA, RG 457, SRGN 17039.

43. NARA, RG 38, Chief of Naval Operations, Naval Transportation Services, Armed Guard Files, 1940–1945, Box 684, S.S. *West Maximus.* The position of the sinking was 55°10′N, 42°58′W; Mr. Thomas Weis to the author, Stuttgart, Germany, 26 February 1997. PRO, ADM 199/2145, Interviews with Survivors, S.S. *Harperley,* Capt. J. E. Turgoose, 16th June, 1943; PRO, ADM 237/113, Report of Survivors from ONS.5. The order for *Northern Spray* to proceed to St. John's was given at 1630 on the 5th.

Chapter 6

1. NARA, Boxes 1718–1719, Captain (D) Newfoundland, Form S.1203, Report of Attack on U-Boat, H.M.S. TAY, 4 May, 2247; R.M. Coppock to the author, 13 November 1996.

2. Seth, *Fiercest Battle,* pp. 123–124; Roskill, *War at Sea,* Vol. II, pp. 70 and *n.*2, 74.

3. NARA, Roll 3067, KTB–U–*514,* 15.4.1943–22.5.1943, 5 May; 0230 GST; NARA, RG 457, SRGN 17189, 17343.

4. NARA, Boxes 1718–1719, Captain (D) Newfoundland, Form S.1203, Report of Attack on U-Boat, VIDETTE (VID ONE, VID TWO), 5 May 1943, 0030 1/2, 0059 1/2, 0127 1/ 2. For U–*732* see NARA, Roll 3398, KTB–U–*732,* 8.4.43– 15.5.43, 5 May, pp. 19ff. In an F.T. at 0515 on the 5th U–*732* claimed to have made a stern tube hit on a "5000 to 6000 tonner," but this was probably Hasenschar's hit on *Harbury.* Because of damage she broke off and returned to base; NARA, RG 457, SRGN 17053. As an aid to researchers it may be emphasized that *Vidette*'s first attacks on the 5th/6th May (VID ONE, VID TWO) were delivered on the day and at the times given above; Syrett, *Defeat of the German U-Boats,* p. 77, and Seth, *Fiercest Battle,* p. 133, construe *Vidette*'s first attacks to be what were actually her fourth and fifth attacks, delivered twenty-three hours later: VID FOUR 2109 convoy time (2309 GMT) and VID FIVE 2117 convoy time (2317 GMT) on the 5th. The correct order is given in the Forms S.1203 as well as in PRO, ADM 237/113, Summary of Attacks and Attempted Attacks on ONS.5, Nos. 15 and 27.

5. See chap. 4, infra, *n*.25.

6. PRO, ADM 237/113, Narrative of Events During Passage of Convoy ONS.5, Commanding Officer, H.M.S. SNOWFLAKE, Incident SNOW 5, 4/5 May 1943; NARA, Boxes 1718–1719, Captain (D) Newfoundland, Form S.1203, Report of Attack on U-Boat, SNOWFLAKE (Event 5), by Sub-Lieutenant R. E. Bennett, R.N.V.R., 4/5 May 1943.

7. Ibid., Incident SNOW 6 and Event 6; PRO, ADM 237/113, Report of Proceedings, H.M.S. *Oribi,* 29th April to 8th May 1943; NARA, Boxes 1718–1719, Captain (D) Newfoundland, Report of Attack on U-Boat, Form S.1203, ORIBI, 1st and 2nd Attacks, 5th May, 1943, by Lieut-Cmdr. J. C. A. Ingram. *Oribi's* second ten-pattern exploded on a decoy bubble target ("Bold") released by U–*270;* R. M. Coppock to author, 13 November 1996. NARA, Roll 2887, KTB–U–*270,* 23.3.43–15.5.43, 5 May 1943, pp. 26–27. Damage sustained by U–*270* is also given in her F.T. of 0959 on the 5th; NARA, RG 457, SRGN 17079. A second corvette, *Sunflower,* made two attacks on an asdic contact at the port bow during the nighttime hours, at 0220, but her Captain concluded that the echo was not from a U-boat; there were two drops of two D/Cs each, one D/C of which on the first drop failed to explode, a rarity in the 40–odd attacks made by ONS–5 escorts in the period 4–6 May.

8. NARA, Roll 3044–3045, KTB–U–*358,* 11.4.43–16.5.43, 5 May 1943.

9. Ibid.

10. PRO, ADM 199/2145, Interviews with Survivors, S.S. *Bristol City,* Capt. A. L. Webb, 9th June, 1943.

11. Ibid., S.S. *Wentworth,* Capt. R. G. Phillips, 24th June, 1943; H.M.S. *Loosestrife,* Report of Proceedings whilst escorting ONS.5, 5 May 1943. Professor Rohwer states that the *Wentworth* wreck was sunk by gunfire from U–*628; Axis Submarine Successes,* p. 165. But two sources, Capt. Phillips and Lt. Stone-house, attribute the coup de grace to *Loosestrife. Harbury* is the better fit for U–*628's* gun action, previously

cited in the text, since that U-boat, which identified the *Harbury* name and shipping line, had just passed through position 55°14′N, 43°02′W, which was near *Harbury*'s last known position 55°or′N, 42°59′W, whereas *Wentworth* was torpedoed at 53°59′N, 43°55′W. Cf. *n.*40 in chap. 5.

12. NARA, Boxes 1718–1719, Captain (D) Newfoundland, Form S.1203, Report of Attack on U-Boat, H.M.S. LOOSESTRIFE, 5 May 1943, 0527; Report of Proceedings, H.M.S. LOOSESTRIFE, 5 May, 0517–0550. R. M. Coppock to author, 13 November 1996. NARA, Roll 2940–2944, KTB–U–*413,* 30.3.43–13.6.43, 5 May 1943.

13. PRO, ADM 223/16; Analysis of U-Boat Operations, f. 86. NARA, Roll 3398, KTB–U–*732,* 8.4.43–15.5.43, 5 May 1943; Roll 2887, KTB–U–*270,* 23.3.43–15.5.43, 5 May 1943; Roll 3387, KTB–U–*648,* 3.4.43–19.5.43, 5 May 1943. Ibid., RG 457, SRGN 17053 (U–*732),* 17079 (U–*270),* 17048 (U–*648).* In the report of the last-named boat, Stahl reported that his damaged Junkers compressor could only be repaired with spare parts from the provisioner boat, which he would meet during his passage to Brest (he had sortied from Kiel on 3 April).

14. PRO, ADM 223/16, Analysis of U-Boat Operations, *f.* 86.

15. The signal in the original German, addressed to *Hasenschargeleit* (the "Hasenschar Convoy"), is given in NARA, Roll 2886–2887, KTB–U–*264,* 5 May 1943, 1242 GST (1042 GMT). Cf. NARA, RG 457, SRGN 17067.

16. PRO, ADM 223/16, Analysis of U-Boat Operations, f. 87.

17. NARA, Boxes 1718–1719, Captain (D) Newfoundland, Form S.1203, Report of Attack on U-Boat, H.M.S. ORIBI, 5th May 1943, 1147, 1243, 1254; PRO, ADM 237/113, Report of Proceedings, H.M.S. ORIBI, 29th April, 1943 to 8th May, 1943; ibid., Report of Attack on U-Boat, Form S.1203, H.M.S. VIDETTE, 5th May 1943, 1341 (VID THREE); R.M. Coppock to author, 13 November 1996.

18. NARA, Roll 3387, KTB–U–*638,* 4.4.43–5.5.43 (reconstruction); KTB–BdU, 5 May ff. 1943.

19. PRO, ADM 199/2145, Interviews with Survivors, M.V. *Dolius,* Capt. G. R. Cheetham, 15th June, 1943.

20. NARA, Boxes 1718–1719, Captain (D) Newfoundland, Form S.1203, Report of Attack on U-Boat, H.M.S. SUNFLOWER, 5th May 1943, 1053; PRO, ADM 237/113, Continuation Report, TAY, No. 13; Report of Proceedings, H.M.S. OFFA, No. 41, 5 May, 1301: the NHB/MOD reassessment finds that U–*226* (Kptlt. Rolf Borchers) reported being attacked at about this time; R. M. Coppock to writer, 13 November 1996.

21. PRO, ADM 237/113, Convoy ONS.5, Report of Proceedings, H.M.S. SUNFLOWER, May 1943. *Dolius* was left taking on water and Plomer sent a signal to Sherwood communicating the Master's opinion that his vessel was beyond salvage.

22. NARA, Boxes 1718–1719, Captain (D) Newfoundland, Narrative of Attack by H.M.S. PINK on U-Boat in Lat. 54–56N Long. 43–44W during the forenoon of May 5, 1943 whilst escorting four stragglers from Convoy ONS.5 [hereafter Attack by PINK], p. 1.

23. OHC/RNM, AC 1993/116, interview with Sir Robert Atkinson, conducted by Chris Howard Bailey, 11 March 1993.

24. DHIST/NDHQ 83/761, Vol. II, Atlantic Convoy Instructions [A.C.I.], C.B. 04234 (2), Operations Section, Articles 101–149, pp. 55–62.

25. NARA, Boxes 1718–1719, Captain (D) Newfoundland, Attack by PINK, p. 4.

26. NHB/MOD, Proceedings of U-Boat Assessment Committee, April–June 1943 [typescript], Précis of Attack by PINK, 5 May 1943, f. 251.

27. PRO, ADM 234/370, Dispatch submitted to the Lords Commissioners of the Admiralty on the 20th July, 1943, by Admiral Max K. Horton, K.C.B., D.S.O., Commander-in-Chief, Western Approaches, 20th July, 1943; "Battle Summary No. 51, Naval Staff History, Second World War, Convoy and AntiSubmarine Reports [hereafter Battle Summary No. 51]," p. 39*n*.

28. NARA, Roll 3044–3045, KTB–U–*358,* 5 May 1943. Handwritten notation by R. M. Coppock on document cited in *n.*26, above. Manke's F.T. to BdU on damages is in NARA, RG 457, SRGN 17085.

29. PRO, ADM 237/113, Summary of Attacks Carried Out by the Escorts of ONS.5, 5 May 1943. The only attack during the period was a single tenpattern (six dropped, four fired) by *Sunflower* at 1253 in the center of the main body; NARA, Boxes 1718–1719, Captain (D) Newfoundland, Report of Attack on U-Boat, Form S.1203, H.M.S. SUNFLOWER, 5 May 1943, 1053 GMT. The identity and fate of U–*358* has been confirmed by the NHB/MOD reassessment; R. M. Coppock to writer, 13 November 1996.

30. NARA, Roll 4188, KTB–U–*584,* 23.3.43–24.5.43, 5 May 1943.

31. NARA, KTB–BdU, 5 May 1943. Dönitz, *Memoirs,* p. 338.

32. Blair, Jr., *Silent Victory,* pp. 877–878.

33. NARA, Boxes 1718–1719, Captain (D) Newfoundland, Attack by PINK, p. 5; PRO, ADM 237/113, Report of Proceedings for ONS.5 (Straggler Portion), 9th May, 1943, No. 4. Ibid., Statement of H. Schroeder, Master of the "Ex" S.S. WEST MADAKET Concerning Torpedoing of Vessel on 5 May 1943: Here Schroeder clearly states that all confidential papers and secret publications were personally thrown overboard by him before leaving the ship. At 1535 *Pink* asked *Tay* for assistance in guarding his flock, but *Tay* replied: "Sorry cannot be done, am beset with U-boats here"; NARA, Boxes 1718–1719, Captain (D) Newfoundland, R/T Log, H.M.S. TAY, Convoy ONS.5, 5 May 1943, 1604. Interview with Sir Robert Atkinson, Winchester, England, 2 June 1997.

34. NARA, Roll 2939, KTB–U–*406,* 25.4.43–11.5.43, 5 May; Roll 3372, KTB-600, 25.4.43–11.5.43; ibid., RG 457, SRGN 17172.

35. NARA, Roll 2887, KTB–266, 14.4.43–Sunk 14.5.43 (reconstructed), 5–7 May; ibid., RG 457, SRGN 17195, at 2232 on the 6th.

36. PRO, ADM 199/2145, Interviews with Survivors, S.S. *Selvistan,* Mr. C. D. Head, 27 July 1943, ff. 116–117; S.S. *Gharinda,* Captain R. Stone, 17 June 1943, ff. 122–124. Information about Indian crewmen, and British attitudes toward them, is given in Middlebrook, *Convoy,* pp. 21–23.

37. Quoted in Seth, *Fiercest Battle,* p. 153.

38. Quoted in ibid., p. 154.

39. NARA, Boxes 1718–1719, Captain (D) Newfoundland, Report of Attack on U-Boat, Form S.1203, H.M.S. OFFA, 5th May 1943, 2042, 2103, 2140, 2153, 2204.

40. The damage to U-*266* is given in Jessen's F.T. to BdU at 2232 on the 5th in NARA, RG 457, SRGN 17195. R. M. Coppock to writer, 13 November 1996.

41. PRO, ADM 237/113, Report of Proceedings, H.M.S. OFFA, 29th April 1943 to 8th May 1943; 5 May 1943, No. 45. Examples of the "heavy W/T activity" detected by McCoy are given in NARA, RG 457 SRGN 17147 through 17183: boats U-*267,* U-*266,* U-*264,* U-*621,* U-*260,* U-*223,* U-*575,* U-*531.*

42. PRO, ADM 237/113, Continuation Report, TAY, 5 May, No. 16. NARA, Boxes 1718–1719, Captain (D) Newfoundland, R/T Log, H.M.S. TAY, Convoy ONS.5, 5 May 1943, 2040.

43. PRO, ADM 237/113, J. Kenneth Brook, Commodore R.N.R., Submarine Report No. 2.

44. DHIST/NDHQ, Tenth Fleet Records, Box 44, Royal Canadian Air Force Eastern Air Command, Statistics of Anti-Submarine Operations, May 1943, pp. 3–4. Ibid., RCAF Attacks on U-Boats, RCAF Message, AFHQ (Air Force Headquarters) to AFCS (RCAF liaison in Washington, D.C.), 7 May 1943.

45. Ibid.

46. These were U-*223,* U-*264,* U-*266,* U-*267,* U-*377,* U-*504,* U-*514,* U-*533,* U-*575,* U-*584,* U-*621,* U-*650,* U-*662,* U-*707,* and U-*438,* the last of which had been wounded by Canso A "E" on 4 May. PRO, ADM 223/16, U-Boat Operations, f. 87.

47. Ibid., f. 87; NARA, Roll 2886–2887, KTB–U–*264*, 5 May 1943; NARA, RG 457, SRGN 17162.

48. PRO, ADM 223/16, U-Boat Operations, f. 87; NARA, Roll 3377, KTB–U–*707*, 5 May 1943.

49. NARA, ADM 237/113, Continuation Report, TAY, 5/6 May 1943, No. 17.

50. NARA, Roll 3377, KTB–U–*707*, 6 May 1943.

Chapter 7

1. NARA, Boxes 1718–1719, Captain (D) Newfoundland, Form S.1203, Report of Attack on U-Boat, H.M.S. VI-DETTE, 5th May 1943, 2326 1/2 (VID FOUR), 2333 1/2 (VID FIVE). This series of attacks by *Vidette* was delivered on the night of 5 May, not on the night of 4 May as given elsewhere. See S.1203 forms and PRO, ADM 237/113, Summary of Attacks and Attempted Attacks on ONS.5, attack no. 27. U–*531* is identified as the victim of *Vidette*'s 2326 1/2 attack in R. M. Coppock to the author, 13 November 1996; the attack position is given as 52°48′N, 45°18′W. For U–*707* see NARA, Roll 3377, KTB–U–*707*, 6 May 1943, p. 10, where times are obscured on the left-hand margin.

2. NARA, Boxes 1718–1719, Captain (D) Newfoundland, Form S.1203, Report of Attack on U-Boat, H.M.S. VI-DETTE, 6 May 1943, 0226 (VID SIX).

3. Ibid., Form S.1203, Report of Attack on U-Boat, H.M.S. VIDETTE, 6 May 1943, 0408 1/2; Report of Proceedings–ONS.5, H.M.S. VIDETTE, 6 May 1943, VID SEVEN; NHB/MOD, Proceedings of the U-Boat Assessment Committee, April-June 1943, Précis of Attack by VI-DETTE, 6 May 1943, 0406, f. 258, and notation by R.M. Coppock. R.M. Coppock to author, 13 November 1996. The words "froth-corrupted lungs" are borrowed from World War I poet Wilfred Owen's *"Dulce et Decorum Est."*

4. NARA, Boxes 1718–1719, Captain (D) Newfoundland, Form S.1203, Report of Attack on U-Boat, H.M.S. LOOSE-STRIFE, 5/6 May 1943, 2336, 0040; Report of Proceedings whilst escorting ONS.5, H.M.S. LOOSESTRIFE, Night of May 5th and 6th, pp. 1–2; PRO, ADM 199/2145, Interviews with Survivors, S.S. *Bristol City*, Captain A. L. Webb, 9th June, 1943. The NHB/MOD reassessment of this attack is "U-*192* sunk" in position 53°06′N, 45°02′W; Coppock to author, 13 November 1996.

5. NARA, Boxes 1718–1719, Captain (D) Newfoundland, Report of Proceedings, H.M.S. ORIBI, 8th May 1943; 6 May 1943; R/T Log, H.M.S. TAY, Convoy ONS.5, 6 May 1943, 0252: ORIBI to TAY–"Have rammed submarine." The Form S.1203 for this attack was not found in the archives.

6. NHB/MOD, Proceedings of U-Boat Assessment Committee, April–June 1943, Précis of Attack by ORIBI, 6 May 1943, 0252, f. 255, and notation by R. M. Coppock.

7. PRO, DEFE–3, No. 552, 6 May 1943; ibid., ADM 223/16, U-Boat Operations, f. 88; NARA, RG 457, SRGN 17231. The F.T. from U-*125* was sent after the ramming by *Oribi* at 0252, not after *Snowflake's* attack on the same boat at 0400 (see below), as given elsewhere.

8. Folkers made no further F.T.s. The futile hunt for U-*125* can be followed in the W/T transmissions from the searchers: NARA, RG 457, SRGN 17231, 17244, 17249, 17292, 17293, 17302, 17329, 17331, 17332, 17333.

9. NARA, Boxes 1718–1719, Captain (D) Newfoundland, Form S.1203, Report of Attack on U-Boat, H.M.S. SNOW-FLAKE, 6 May, 1943, 0330 to 0415; Narrative of Events During Passage of Convoy ONS.5, 8th May 1943, Incident SNOW 11, 6 May 1943; R/T log, H.M.S. SNOWFLAKE. NHB/ MOD, Proceedings of U-Boat Assessment Committee, April–June 1943, Précis of Attack by SNOWFLAKE, 6 May 1943, 0330, f. 257, and notation by R. M. Coppock.

10. NARA, Boxes 1718–1719, Captain (D) Newfoundland, R/T log, H.M.S. SNOWFLAKE: following signals passed and received during events under description, Event 11, 6th May 1943.

11. NARA, Boxes 1718–1719, Captain (D) Newfoundland, H.M.S. OFFA, Report of Proceedings From 29th April, 1943 to 8th May, 1943, Nos. 47–53; Form S.1203, Report of

Attack on U-Boat, H.M.S. OFFA, 6th May, 1943, 0316; Roll 2937, KTB–U–*223*, 15.4.43–24.5.43, 6 May, p. 13; RG 457, SRGN 17255, where Wächter signals 3 HOURS DEPTH CHARGES; R. M. Coppock to author, 13 November 1996; PRO, ADM 237/113, Admiral Horton, C–in–CWA, to The Secretary of the Admiralty, 14th June 1943. Thirteen minutes before *Offa*'s attack, *Loosestrife*, at 0303, attacked a radar/ asdic contact with a ten-pattern; the target is believed to have been U–*621* (Oblt.z.S. Max Kruschka), which was not harmed. Three and a half hours later, *Loosestrife* dropped another ten-pattern on a radar/asdic contact, believed to have been U–*614* (Kptlt. Wolfgang Sträter), with similarly negative results.

12. NARA, Boxes 1718–1719, Captain (D) Newfoundland, Form S.1203, Report of Attack on U-Boat, H.M.S. SUNFLOWER, 6 May 1943, 0450 (with drawings); NHB/ MOD, Proceedings of the U-Boat Assessment Committee, April-June 1943, Précis of Attack by SUNFLOWER, 6 May 1943, 0443, f. 259 (the NHB/MOD reassessment agrees on slight damage); R/T log, H.M.S. TAY, Convoy ONS.5; PRO, ADM 199/2145, Interviews with Survivors, M.V. *Dolius,* Capt. G. R. Cheetham, 15th June 1943.

13. PRO, DEFE–3, No. 609, 6 May 1943; NARA, SRGN 17270.

14. NARA, Roll 2979, KTB–U–*533,* 15.4.43–24.5.43, 6 May, 0655–2400 GST; NARA, KTB–BdU, 7 May 1943.

15. NARA, Boxes 1718–1719, Captain (D) Newfoundland, Form S.1203, Report of Attack on U-Boat, H.M.S. PELICAN, 6 May 1943, 0608 1/2, 0615; PRO, ADM 237/ 113, First Support Group, Report of Proceedings, 4th–12th May 1943, 6th May, Nos. 4–6; NHB/MOD, Proceedings of the U-Boat Assessment Committee, April-June 1943, Précis of Attack by PELICAN, 6 May 1943, 0551, f. 260, and notation by R. M. Coppock; NARA, KTB–BdU, 6 May 1943. Also Coppock to author, 13 November 1996. The "cavalryman" image used here is not simply an American affectation: Winston Churchill stated that the Support Groups were "to act like cavalry divisions, apart from all escort duties"; Churchill, *Second World War*, Vol. 5, *Closing the Ring*, p.8.

16. PRO, ADM 237/113, Report of Proceedings from 29th April, 1943 to 8th May, 1943, H.M.S. OFFA, 6 May, Nos. 56–59. *Offa* and *Oribi* made port in St. John's at 1215 on the 8th. Samuel Eliot Morison, *The Atlantic Battle Won, May 1943–May 1945* (Boston: Little, Brown, 1962), p. 75, n.6.

17. Ibid., Naval Message, 6 May 1943, TAY TO PELICAN, 0800: MY CLOSE ESCORT IS REDUCED TO 1 DESTROYER WHO IF NOT FUELLED TODAY MUST LEAVE FOR ST. JOHN'S N.F. 1 CORVETTE IN ACTION 1 CORVETTE WITH NO DEPTH CHARGES 1 CORVETTE BADLY KNOCKED ABOUT AFTER COLLIDING WITH A U-BOAT AND MYSELF WITH NO ASDICS. REQUEST YOU FORM CLOSE SCREEN. Lieut.-Cmdr. F. H. Thornton, Commanding Officer, H.M.S. SENNEN, To Commanding Officer, H.M.S. PELICAN, 9 May 1943. Naval Message, Immediate to SENNEN and PINK from CinCWA: PROCEED TO SUPPORT PINK WITH STRAGGLERS OF ONS.5. ESTIMATED IN POSITION 53 10 N 46 20 W AT 0800 STEERING FOR 50 N 46 W SPEED 8 KNOTS. At 0800 the main body of the convoy was in position 52°09′N, 44°24′W.

18. NARA, Boxes 1718–1719, Captain (D) Newfoundland, Form S.1203, Report of Attack on U-Boat, H.M.S. SENNEN, 6 May 1943, 0753 1/2.

19. R. M. Coppock to author, London, 13 November 1996.

20. Ibid.

21. NARA, Boxes 1718–1719, Captain (D) Newfoundland, Form S.1203, Report of Attack on U-Boat, H.M.S. SENNEN, 6 May 1943, 1255, 1342, 1405, 1436, 1522.

22. NARA, Boxes 1718–1719, Captain (D) Newfoundland, Form S.1203, Report of Attack on U-Boat, H.M.S. SPEY, 6 May 1943, 0747, 0802, 0815, 0916; NHB/MOD, Proceedings of the U-Boat Assessment Committee, April-June 1943, Précis of Attack by SPEY, 6 May 1943, 0940, f. 261, and notation by R.M. Coppock; Coppock to author, 13 November 1996; NARA, Roll 3386, KTB–U–*634*, 15.4.43–

23.5.43, 6 May 1943 for description of damage and injury to C.O.; NARA, RG 457, SRGN 17310, for U-*634's* F.T.

23. The cease-operations message to *Fink* boats read: BOATS ON HASENSCHAR CONVOY DISCONTINUE OPERATION. GROUP AMSEL 1 AND 2 HEAD FOR QU BC 33 [50°33′N, 39°15′W]. OTHER BOATS GO OFF IN EASTERLY DIRECTION. See NARA, RG 457, SRGN 17278.

24. PRO, DEFE–3, Nos. 512, 6 May 1943: ADM 223/16, U-Boat Operations, f. 88. In underscoring the importance of the first night, BdU repeated a finding of O.R.S. in Coastal Command, which reported in the preceding March: "The engagement between a U-boat pack and a convoy is what scientists would call an unstable equilibrium. If the surface escorts gets a good start, an entire pack can be beaten off with our air assistance: if the U-boats get a good start, the convoy will suffer very heavy losses." PRO, CAB 86/3, The Value of the Bay of Biscay Patrols, Annex II. Air Operations in Defence of Convoys, f. 370.

25. NARA, KTB–BdU, 6 May 1943. NARA, War Diary, German Naval Staff *(Kriegstagebuch der Seekriegsleitung),* Operations Division, Part A, Volume 44 (microfilm), 5 May 1997.

26. NARA, KTB–BdU, 23 May 1943; R.M. Coppock to the author, London, 13 November 1996.

27. PRO, DEFE–3, No. 512, 6 May 1943.

28. NARA, KTB–BdU, 6 May 1943; Donitz, *Memoirs,* p. 339. In his British Admiralty and U.S. Navy Department-sponsored *U-Boat War,* Dönitz's Staff Officer and son-in-law Günter Hessler stated: "The heavy loss of U-boats compelled us to regard this operation as a reverse"; p. 106.

29. PRO, DEFE–3, Nos. 413, 619, 626, 663; NARA, RG 457, SRGN 17189, 17291, 17307. For U-boat success estimates see prologue and chap. 2. Cf. Showell, *U-Boats Under the Swastika,* pp. 16–18; Tarrant, *U-Boat Offensive 1914–1945,* p. 151; and Mulligan, *Lone Wolf,* p. 221 and *n.1.*

30. NARA, KTB–BdU, 6 May 1943.

31. Hessler, *U-Boat War,* p. 106. The term *Metox,* from the first Paris-based French company that manufactured it, was

used interchangeably with *Funkmessbeobachtungsgerät,* "radar search receiver," abbreviated *Fu.M.B.*

32. Dönitz, *Memoirs,* p. 339.

33. Hessler, *U-Boat War,* p. 106. The BdU war diary noted: "The recent increase in cases of damage to upper deck containers [of Type IXB and IXC boats] proves that more powerful depth charges are being used"; NARA, KTB-BdU, 6 May 1943.

34. Ibid.

35. This point is developed in Rohwer, *The Critical Convey Battles,* pp. 199–200; and again in Rohwer and W. A. B. Douglas, "Canada and the Wolf Packs, September 1943," in W. A. B. Douglas, ed., *The RCN in Transition, 1910–1985* (Vancouver: University of British Columbia Press, 1988), pp. 181–182.

36. PRO, ADM 237/113, Submarine Report No. 2, J. Kenneth Brook, Commodore, R.N.R., n.d. Brook erred in stating here that *Gudvor,* which arrived safely at St. John's with *Pink* and *Sennen,* was torpedoed on 5 May, or on any date.

37. PRO, ADM 237/113, Convoy ONS.5, Form S.1203, Report of Attack on U-Boat, H.M.S. JED, 6 May 1943, 2367. The last two escorts to make attacks defending ONS.5, SENNEN and JED, would combine later, on 19 May, in sinking U–954 (Kptlt. Odo Loewe). PRO, ADM 237/113, Continuation Report H.M.S. TAY, 6 May 1943, No. 18; Report of Proceedings, H.M.S. VIDETTE, 6 May 1943, p. 2.

38. PRO, ADM 237/113, Commander in Chief, Canadian North West Atlantic to Secretary, Naval Board, Department of National Defence, Ottawa, Ontario, 9th July, 1943. Here the relieving force is named as WLEF, although, according to Milner, *U-Boat Hunters,* p. xi, the force name was changed in April 1943 to Western Escort Force (WEF). The exact position of WEST–OMP varied slightly from convoy to convoy; see DHIST/NDHQ, Convoy Reports, ONF. 238–ONS.8, 89/34, Volume 23, Directorate of History and Heritage; the writer is indebted to Ms. Gabrielle Nishigushi for this citation. The WLEF force was joined by the de-

stroyer H.M.S. *Montgomery* on the 8th, taking over as SO, and by the corvette H.M.C.S. *Algoma* from the 7th to the 9th.

39. PRO, ADM 237/113, Convoy ONS.5, Naval Message, CinCWA to PELICAN, 6 May, 2357; Report of Proceedings, H.M.S. PELICAN, 6–12 May 1943, Nos. 11–17.

40. Ibid., Convoy ONS.5 Commodore J. Kenneth Brook, R.N.R., in M.V. "RENA" (NOR), Brief Narrative of Voyage, p. 2. On 15 May the Naval Control Service Officer (NCSO), Halifax, signaled Ottawa that S.S. *Lorient* (sunk by U-*125* on 4 May) had not arrived there as scheduled; DHIST/NDHQ, Naval Message, NCSO Halifax to NSHQ Ottawa, 15 May, 1630 (microfilm). Interestingly, there is a German X-B-Bericht interception and summary of an Allied coded message to *Lorient:* "Port of destination for the steamer *Lorient* (4737 tons) was changed on the afternoon of 9 May to Boston"; Bundesarchiv/Militärarchiv, Freiburg im Breisgau, RM 7/755, X–B-Bericht No. 22/43, Woche vom 24.5.–30.5.1943, folio 1941 (s. X–B-Bericht 21/43).

41. DHIST/NDHQ, Naval Message FONF, St. John's, to CinCCNA, Halifax, 9 May 1943, 2225 (microfilm).

42. PRO, ADM 234/370, Convoy ONS.5, Battle Summary No. 51, Continuation Report, H.M.S. TAY, p. 36; Gretton, *Convoy Escort Commander,* p. 145.

43. PRO, ADM 237/113, Convoy ONS.5, Report of Proceedings, H.M.S. SUNFLOWER, "Personnel," p. 5.

44. Ibid., Report of Proceedings, H.M.S. SNOWFLAKE, "Summary," pp. 7–8.

45. Ibid., Report of Proceedings, H.M.S. PENN, 8 May 1943.

46. Ibid., CinCCNA to Secretary, Naval Board, Department of National Defence, Ottawa, 9 July 1943, copy to CinCWA, p. 2.

47. Ibid., Submarine Report No. 2, Commodore J. Kenneth Brook, p. 2.

48. Gretton, *Convoy Escort Commander,* pp. 145–146.

49. PRO, ADM 237/113, CinCCNA to Secretary, Naval Board, 9 July 1943, p. 1.

50. PRO, ADM 234/370, Convoy and Anti-Submarine Warfare Reports, Battle Summary No. 51, Admiral Sir Max K. Horton, K.C.B., D.S.O., CinCWA, to the Lords Commissioners of the Admiralty, 20 July 1943, pp. 28–29.

51. Ibid., p. 38; also NARA, Boxes 1718–1719, Captain (D) Newfoundland, ONS.5–Comments of Senior Officer, Close Escort, n.d. The compliment that immediately follows this quotation in the present narrative is drawn from John Terraine, *U-Boat Wars,* who also states, appropriately, that "this two-and-a half-ringed officer won a battle that an admiral or a general could be well pleased with"; p. 598 and *n.* 162.

52. PRO, ADM 237/113, CinCCNA to Naval Board, 9 July 1943, p. 2.

53. Ibid., pp. 2–4.

54. PRO, ADM 234/370, Convoy and Anti-Submarine Warfare Reports, Battle Summary No. 51, Commodore (D) Western Approaches to CinCWA, Londonderry, 20 June 1943; C–in-CWA to Lords Commissioners of the Admiralty, 20 July 1943, pp. 28–30; ADM 237/113, Naval Message, CinCWA to Escorts ONS.5, 6 May 1943; in ibid. see also CinCWA to Lords Commissioners of the Admiralty 20 July 1943, proposing that an instructional film be made of this "classic" on the basis of track charts and other data, which proposal Their Lordships turned down on 29 September 1943. A congratulatory message was sent to the ONS.5 escorts by CinCCNA Rear Admiral Murray at Halifax, who called attention to RESULTS ACHIEVED WITH MINIMUM OF AIR COVER DUE TO IMPOSSIBLE WEATHER AT [BASES?]; ibid., Naval Message, 6 May 1943. Another compliment for THE BEST EFFORT SO FAR came from NSHQ, Ottawa, on the following day.

55. PRO, ADM 234/370, Convoy and Anti-Submarine Warfare Reports, Battle Summary No. 51, Captain J.A. McCoy, R.N. (SO), EG3, to CinCWA, 9 May 1943, p. 44; ADM 237/113, CinCWA to The Secretary of the Admiralty, 14 June 1943.

56. A reproduction of the St. John's *Daily News* article is

given in Bailey, ed., *Battle of the Atlantic*, p. 64. See *The Times*, Thursday, 13 May 1943, p. 4.

57. PRO, ADM 237/113, Naval Message, Churchill to Escort of ONS.5, 9 May 1943.

58. PRO, ADM 223/88, Use of Special Intelligence in Battle of Atlantic, Convoy ONS.5, April-May 1943, f. 278, n.d.

59. Roskill, *War at Sea*, Vol. II, p. 375. *The Sunday Times* review may be found in the edition of 8 February 1959, p. 13. In more recent years the Horton-Winn-Roskill view has been widely accepted (though perhaps not in Roskill's extravagant expression) by naval historians on both sides of the conflict as well as on both sides of the Atlantic. See, for example, W.A.B. Douglas and Jurgen Rohwer, "Convoys, Escorts," in Boutilier, ed., *RCN in Retrospect*, p. 229; J. David Brown, "The Battle of the Atlantic, 1941–1943: Peaks and Troughs," in Timothy J. Runyan and Jan M. Copes, eds., *To Die Gallantly: The Battle of the Atlantic* (Boulder, CO: Westview Press, 1994), p. 156; Philip Lundeberg, "Allied Co-operation," in Howarth and Law, eds., *Battle of the Atlantic*, p. 360; Syrett, *Defeat of the German U-Boats*, p. 96; and Milner, *U-Boat Hunters*, who concluded: "In a single night the mystique of the Wolf Packs was broken"; p. 38.

60. PRO, ADM 237/113, Convoy ONS–5, Report of Proceedings, Third Support Group (EG3), 9 May 1943.

Chapter 8

1. The writer has relied on a small collection of documents, what may be called the Raushenbush Papers [hereafter RP], in possession of his widow, Joan Raushenbush, in Sarasota, Florida, for the use of which he is greatly indebted. Raushenbush changed his first name from Hilmar Ernst and the spelling of his surname in the 1920s. Solberg (1894–1964) also served at the time as Officer in Charge of Readiness Division, U.S. Naval Forces in Europe.

2. Roskill, *War at Sea*, Vol. III, Part I, p. 263; PRO, AIR

41/48, Peyton Ward, "R.A.F. in Maritime War," Vol. IV, p. 83.

3. RP, "Memorandum for Mr. [Oscar A.] de Lima, " 17 pp., 18 November 1948.

4. Blackett, *Studies of War,* p. 238

5. RP, Commander Oscar A. de Lima, "Subject: Stephen Raushenbush of the U.S. Navy," 7 pp., 25 June 1961.

6. Quoted in Price, *Aircraft Versus Submarine,* p. 116.

7. RP, "Memorandum for Mr. de Lima," p. 2.

8. NARA, KTB–BdU, 5 March 1943. Naval operations analyst Dr. Brian McCue calculates that had *Naxos–U* gone into service in April only seven additional merchant ships would have been lost as a result; *U-Boats in the Bay of Biscay: An Essay in Operations Analysis* (Washington, D.C.: National Defense University Press, 1990), p. 148.

9. PRO, CAB 86/3, A.U.(43)86, War Cabinet, Employment of Aircraft Against U-Boats in the Bay of Biscay. Prepared under instructions of Captain T. A. Solberg by Stephen Raushenbush, 22 March 1943. In an Intelligence Report dated 14 April, called in Washington an "Alusna," Raushenbush advised the Navy Department that in the document cited above he had erred in predicting that each of 150 U-boats entering the transit channel would receive 2.4 attacks. The accurate number was 1.8. See NARA, RG 38, Chief of Naval Operations, Intelligence Division, Secret Reports of Naval Attachés, 1940–1946, File F–6–e, Stack Area 10W4, Box 252, Folder "Anti-Submarine Operations, Great Britain, Various 1943–1944," Intelligence Report (Alusna Report 579), Naval Attaché, London, 14 April 1943 [hereafter Alusna].

10. PRO, CAB 86/3, A.U.(43)99, War Cabinet, Anti-U-Boat Warfare, The Bay Patrol, Note by the Paymaster-General [Cherwell], 30 March 1943. Raushenbush commented in a private note in 1948: "[Cherwell], 30 March 1943. to understand that the estimated number of sightings of U-boats by planes would suddenly jump from the current ratio (about 1 sighting for 100 sorties) to a much better ratio with the new radar"; RP, Memorandum for Mr. de Lima, 18

November 1948. The historian of operational research during the war, Ronald W. Clark, offers a somewhat harsh appraisal of Cherwell; *Rise of the Boffins,* pp. 29–30.

11. Blackett, "Evan James Williams, 1903–45," *Studies of War,* pp. 235–239.

12. The Admiralty's plan and Raushenbush's comparison page are given in NARA, RG 38, Alusna, 11 March 1943. In it Raushenbush identifies the Admiralty plan as coming from O.R.S. Coastal Command, no doubt because it was while still at Coastal that Williams initiated the plan and because in its text he refers to earlier O.R.S. studies. Furthermore, the Admiralty's Memorandum supporting the Williams proposal spoke of it as resulting from "previous investigations by Coastal Command . . ."; PRO, CAB 86/3, A.U.(43)98. When O.R.S. (then under the direction of Professor Waddington) also presented a plan, on 22 March, its numbers were different, as was its conclusion, viz., that the Bay Offensive, by comparison with protective cover given to menaced convoys, was a waste of Coastal's assets. See PRO, CAB 86/3, A.U.(43)84, The Value of the Bay of Biscay Patrols, Note by Air Officer Commanding-in-Chief, Coastal Command. In their two plans Raushenbush and Williams employed fundamentally the same statistical methodology, multiplying the density of surfaced U-boats per square mile by the search rate of Allied aircraft in square miles per hour so as to obtain sightings per flight hour; then using experience-based percentage to predict what fraction of sightings would be converted into attacks, what percentage of attacks would result in damage to the U-boats, and what percentage of damaged boats would be destroyed; then, after finding the number of U-boats destroyed per flight hour, dividing the total of U-boats whose destruction was sought by that number to obtain the number of flight hours required, which flight hours could be turned into a specific requirement for aircraft. Dr. Brian McCue to author, 6 July 1997. Dr. McCue is owed and is given here the warmest of thanks for his expert explanation of the statistical methodology employed by Raushenbush and Williams.

13. Slessor, *Central Blue*, p. 504.

14. See PRO, CAB 86/3, A.U.(43)84 in n.12, above.

15. PRO, AIR 41/48, Peyton Ward, "R.A.F. in the Maritime War," Vol. IV, p. 89.

16. See PRO, CAB 86/3 in *n.* 12 above.

17. PRO, CAB 86/3, A.U. (43)86; A.U.(43)84; A.U.(43)90.

18. PRO, CAB 86/2, Minutes of the A.U. Committee Meeting, 24 March 1943.

19. PRO, CAB 86/3; A.U.(43)96; A.U.(43)99; A.U.(43)98.

20. PRO, CAB 86/2, A.U.(43) 13th Meeting, Minutes, Anti–U-Boat Warfare Committee, 31 March 1943, ff. 152–158; CAB 86/3, A.U.(43)96; AIR 41/48, Peyton Ward, "R.A.F. in the Maritime War," Vol. IV, p. 92.

21. Slessor, *Central Blue*, p.449. Between January and May 1943 Bomber Command lost more than 100 heavy bombers in raids on the U-boat bases; Price, *Aircraft versus Submarine*, p. 146.

22. PRO, CAB 86/3, A.U.(43)98, Memorandum by the First Lord of the Admiralty; CAB 86/2, A.U.(43) 13th Meeting, Minutes, Anti–U-Boat Warfare Committee, 31 March 1943, ff. 152–158.

23. Ibid., Minutes.

24. Slessor, *Central Blue*, pp. 524–526. Without naming Slessor, Blackett wrote about this episode: "During the heat of the controversy over the proposal to transfer some bombers from Bomber to Coastal Command, a leading airman was goaded by the welter of statistics and calculations produced by the Operational Research Groups to remind scientists, 'that wars are won by weapons and not by slide rules.' But in fact 'slide rule strategy' had arrived to stay . . ." Blackett, *Studies of War*, p. 228.

25. Waddington, *O.R.*, pp.xv–xvi.

26. PRO, CAB 86/4, A.U.(43)152, The Bay Offensive: Comparison of Actual and Estimated Results. Note by the Air Officer Commanding-in-Chief, Coastal Command. 23 May 1943, f.136.

27. PRO, CAB 86/4, A.U.(43)126; Memorandum [Tele-

gram] by the First Sea Lord, the Commander U.S. Naval Forces in Europe, and the Air Officer Commanding-in-Chief, Coastal Command; 22 April 1943.

28. Ibid. and PRO, CAB 86/2, A.U.(43) 15th Meeting, Anti-U-Boat Warfare Committee, 14 April 1943, Annex, paragraphs 1 and 12.

29. This is the reading of King's explanation given in Peyton Ward, "R.A.F. in the Maritime War," Vol.IV, p.95. See also PRO, CAB 105, Vol. I; *Principal War Telegrams and Memoranda, 1940–1943, Washington, America, United Kingdom and Europe* (Nendeln, Liechtenstein: KTO Press, 1976), pp. 120–121, 134. King subsequently made an offer of one Catalina squadron and one Ventura squadron to Iceland, but neither would have permitted reinforcement of the Bay patrols; CAB 86/4, A.U.(43)174, Reinforcement of the Bay Offensive, 21 June 1943.

30. Slessor, *Central Blue,* p. 532.

31. For various views of the Army-Navy jurisdictional dispute the reader may wish to consult: Ernest J. King and Walter Muir Whitehill, *Fleet Admiral King: A Naval Record* (New York: W.W. Norton, 1952), pp. 472–471; Wesley Frank Craven and James Lea Cate, eds., *The Army Air Forces in World War II,* Vol. 2 (Chicago: University of Chicago Press, 1949), pp. 402–411; H.H. Arnold, General of the Air Force, *Global Mission* (New York: Harper & Bros., 1949), pp. 362–364; Henry L. Stimson and McGeorge Bundy, *On Active Service in War and Peace* (New York: Harper & Brothers, 1948), pp. 504–517; and Slessor, *Central Blue,* pp. 532–538. Cf. Norman Polmar, "To Be or Not to Be," *Naval Institute Proceedings,* Vol. 123 (September 1997), pp. 62–64.

32. Slessor, *Central Blue,* p. 536.

33. PRO, AIR 41/48, Peyton Ward, "R.A.F. in the Maritime War," Vol. IV, p. 96; Norman Franks, *Search, Find and Kill* (London: Grub Street, 1995), pp. 108–110; Adams and Lees, *Type VII U-boats,* p.19.

34. The U-boats still did not have a 10–centimeter G.S.R., as noted before, but a new visual tuner called the "Magic Eye," when incorporated into the standard Metox gear, not only glowed when the boat was painted by metric radar, but sometimes, if the antenna happened to have exactly the right electrical capacity, it could cause the visual tuner to glow on the harmonics of a 10–centimeter pulse. This happened so rarely, however, that it proved to be an unreliable reed to lean on, and faith in the Magic Eye was shattered during Operation Derange.

35. Price, *Aircraft versus Submarine,* pp. 166–167; Slessor, *Central Blue,* p. 465. Roskill calls Dönitz's decision "perhaps his biggest mistake of the war"; *War at Sea,* Vol. II, p. 371. Historian Philip Lundeberg calls it a "historic tactical blunder"; in Howarth and Law, eds., *Battle of the Atlantic,* p. 361. Peyton Ward also describes it as the first in "a series of tactical blunders" in PRO, AIR 41/48, "R.A.F. in the Maritime War," Vol. IV, p. 96.

36. PRO, AIR 41/48, Peyton Ward, "R.A.F. in the Maritime War," Vol. IV, p. 96 and Appendix VII.

37. This is the recent interpretation of naval operations analyst Dr. Brian McCue; McCue to author, 6 July 1997.

38. In his plan Raushenbush considered six countermeasures that the enemy might take, from diverting U-boat traffic to Norwegian bunkers and German bases to exhausting the endurance of aircraft by bottoming-out in Spanish waters. He failed to consider that Dönitz would go to full submergence at night.

39. Price, *Aircraft versus Submarine,* p. 155, states that Bromet "abandoned the night patrols" so that he could divert the L/L squadrons to daylight work. But Peyton Ward gives the nighttime L/L flying hours in the Enclose and Derange ribbons as follows: 777 (April), 688 (May), 596 (June), 877 (July, including other transit areas), 1,296 (August, including other transit areas), 1,904 and 2,167 (September and October, respectively, including other transit areas). PRO, AIR 41/48, Peyton Ward, "R.A.F. in the Maritime War," Vol. IV, Appendix VII. Peyton Ward does say that from 20 May, L/L Squadrons Nos. 172, 210, and 407 operated "largely by day"; 41/48, Vol. IV, p. 99, *n.*4.

40. Terence M. Bulloch to the author, Burnham, Bucks.,

England, 4 August 1997; Max Arthur, *There Shall Be Wings: The RAF–1918 to the Present* (London: Hodder & Stoughton, 1993), p. 189.

41. This synopsis closely follows the text of PRO, AIR 41/48, Peyton Ward, "R.A.F. in the Maritime War," Appendix VI, Coastal Command Anti-Submarine Tactical Instruction (C.C.T.I. No. 41), 12 June 1943, pp. 1–10; see also 41/48, Vol. IV, p. 99.

42. PRO, AIR 27, Royal Air Force Operations Record Book, Form 540 [hereafter RAF Form 540], April 1943; NHB/MOD, Assessments, May 1943, f. 232. The position of the attack was 44°45′N, 11°57′W.

43. NHB/MOD, Assessments, 1 May 1943, f. 235; Franks, *Search, Find and Kill*, pp. 110–111.

44. RAF Form 540, No. 612 Squadron, May 1943, p. 1; NHB/MOD, Assessments, 1 May 1943, f. 236; Franks, *Search, Find and Kill*, p. 111.

45. NARA, KTB–BdU, 3 May 1943.

46. RAF Form 540, No. 461 Squadron, RAAF, May 1943, p. 1; NHB/MOD, Assessments, 2 May 1943, f. 240; Franks, *Search, Find and Kill*, p. 112. The position of the attack was 44°48′N, 08°58′W.

47. RAF Form 540, No. 58 Squadron, May 1943; NHB/MOD, Assessments, 4 May 1943, f. 243 and notations by R. M. Coppock on ff. 247 and 253.

48. NHB/MOD, Assessments, 4 May 1943, ff. 247, 248, 253, and notations by R. M. Coppock.

49. PRO, AIR 27, RAF Form 540, No. 58 Squadron, May 1943, p. 128; NHB/MOD, Assessments, 7 May 1943, ff. 267–268, and notations by R. M. Coppock.

50. PRO, AIR 27, RAF Form 540, No. 10 Squadron, RAAF, 7 May 1943, pp. 875–876; NHB/MOD, Assessments, f. 269, 7 May 1943, and notations by R. M. Coppock.

51. NHB/MOD, Assessments, ff. 290, 291, 292, 293, 294, 15 May 1943, and notations by R. M. Coppock.

52. NHB/MOD, Assessments, ff. 290, 291, 292, 293, 295, and notations by R. M. Coppock; PRO, AIR 27, RAF, May 1943, p. 12.

53. U-*662* by a USN Catalina of Patrol Sqdn. VP–94 on 21 July, and U-*648* by H.M.S. *Bazely, Blackwood,* and *Drury* on 23 November.

54. PRO, AIR 27, RAF Form 540, No. 58 Squadron, May 1943, p. 13; NHB/MOD, Assessments, ff. 296, 297, 298, 299, 300, and notations by R. M. Coppock.

55. NHB/MOD, Assessments, ff. 302, 313, 315, 317, 318, 319, 320, 321, 323, and notations by R. M. Coppock.

56. PRO, AIR 41/48, Peyton Ward, "R.A.F. in the Maritime War," Vol. IV, pp. 98 and *n.*4, 99 and *n.*1; Franks, *Search, Find, and Kill,* pp. 117–118.

57. NHB/MOD, Assessments, ff. 325, 328, 329, 330, 333. Curiously, the interrogation information on U–*523,* reported in f. 330, does not conform to other details known about that boat: The interrogators informed the Assessment Committee that U–*523* sortied from base outbound on 29 May, when her KTB shows that she sortied on 22 May. Furthermore, when attacked by A/206 the boat in question was on an inbound course of 090°, according to f. 330.

58. Quoted in Norman L. R. Franks, *Conflict Over the Bay* (London: William Kimber & Co., 1986), p. 80. The "yellowish brown" color of the U–*563* hull is unusual, since most color descriptions read "gray," "light gray," or "mud gray." Occasionally, though, one reads of "brown splotches" on the gray, and one other May report described a U-boat as "khaki," which is another way of saying olive brown or yellowish brown; PRO, AIR 27, RAF Form 540, No. 58 Squadron, 31 May 1943.

59. NHB/MOD, Assessments, f. 331. The 58 Sqdn. 504 records that "the U-boat blew up with an orange flash," a detail that is missing from other accounts.

60. NHB/MOD, Assessments, f. 332; Franks, *Conflict,* pp. 77–78.

61. Adams and Lees, *Type VII U-boats,* p. 26.

62. PRO, AIR 41/48, Peyton Ward, "R.A.F. in the Maritime War," Vol. IV, Appendix VII, "Air Operations Against U-boats in the Bay of Biscay Transit Area." Peyton Ward gives 103 as the number of U-boats sighted and 67 as the

number of attacks made in the Bay in May. He counts 7 U-boats sunk in the Bay in May, but he includes U–*332,* which in fact was sunk on 29 April. The Secretary of State for Air Sir Archibald Sinclair, Bt., M.P., stated that there had been 103 sightings and 68 attacks; PRO, CAB 86/4, A.U.(43)161, Aircraft for the Bay Offensive, 5 June 1943. Both sets of figures are higher than the sightings and attacks described in this present narrative, which relies on the U-Boat Assessment Committee documents that considered only those attacks thought likely or possible to have led to a sinking or to damage. For RAF casualties see Peyton Ward, Appendix VII, and Franks, *Conflict,* Appendix IV, pp. 254–259.

63. PRO, CAB 86/4, A.U.(43)161, Aircraft for the Bay Offensive, 5 June 1943; see *n.* 62.

64. PRO, CAB 86/2, A.U.(43), Minutes of the 18th Meeting, A.U. Committee, 12 May 1943, f. 183.

65. PRO, CAB 86/4, A.U.(43)152, Note by the Air Officer Commanding–in–Chief, Coastal Command, 23 May 1943, ff. 134–136.

66. It is not likely that Raushenbush protested his obscurity. A colleague in London, and friend for years after the war, Oscar A. de Lima, said of him: "Stephen Raushenbush is the most self-effacing of men, the most modest of violets. He wouldn't even tell his closest friend what he did in the War." RP, "Stephen Raushenbush of the U.S. Navy," 25 June 1961.

Chapter 9

1. See *Operation Epsilon: The Farm Hall Transcripts,* Introduction by Sir Charles Frank (Berkeley and Los Angeles: University of California Press, 1993); Jeremy Bernstein, *Hitler's Uranium Club: The Secret Recordings at Farm Hall* (Woodbury, NY: American Institute of Physics, 1996). American readers are well familiar with the "Nixon Tapes," but two recent publications serve to remind us that secret

recordings, in the Latimer House model, preceded those tapes: Ernest R. May and Philip D. Zelikow, eds., *The Kennedy Tapes: Inside the White House During the Cuban Missile Crisis* (Cambridge, MA: Harvard University Press, 1977); and Michael R. Beschloss, ed., *Taking Charge: The Johnson White House Tapes, 1963–1964* (New York: Simon & Schuster, 1977).

2. The transcripts for the period March-August 1943 are found in PRO, WO 208/4145 and 4205. Each transcript carries a numeral prefixed by S.R.N., possibly "Secret Recording Number."

3. See, for example, PRO, ADM 86/800, Naval Intelligence Division, Admiralty, "Interrogation of U-Boat Survivors, Cumulative Edition, June 1944," ff. 268–330, which summary was prepared from interrogation "and other information."

4.

HERBERT APEL. U–*439*. Maschinenobergefreiter (equivalent USN rating: Fireman, second class). Captured 4 May 1943.

BRUNO ARENDT. U–*659*. Oberbootsmaat (Boatswain's Mate, second class). Captured 4 May 1943.

(No first name given in the existing records) BRINE. U–*432*. Leutnant z.See (Ensign). Captured 11 March 1943.

JOSEF-M. BRÖHL. U–*432*. Leutnant z.See (Ensign). Captured 11 March 1943.

ROLF ELEBE. U–*752*. Oberfunkmaat (Radioman, second class). Captured 23 May 1943.

KARL-HEINZ FOERTSCH. U–*659*. Leutnant (Ing) (Ensign, Engineering duties). Captured 4 May 1943.

FRIEDRICH GASSAUER. U–*607*. Leutnant z. See (Ensign). Captured 14 July 1943.

ERWIN GEIMEIER. U–*175*. Maschinenmaat (Fireman, first class). Captured 17 April 1943.

FRANZ GRÄTZ. U–*187*. Funkmaat (Seaman [Radioman], third class). Captured 4 February 1943.

HEINZ KALISCH. U-*439*. Matrosenobergefreiter (Seaman, first class). Captured 4 May 1943.

(No first name recorded) KEITLE. U-*752*. Matrosengefreiter (Seaman, second class). Captured 23 May 1943.

HELMUT KLOTZSCH. U-*175*. Obersteuermann (Warrant Quartermaster [Navigator]). Captured 17 April 1943.

WALTER KOHLER. U-*752*. Matrosenobergefreiter (Seaman, first class). Captured 23 May 1943.

(No first name given) KUFFNER. U-*175*. Maschinenmaat (Fireman, first class). Captured 17 April 1943.

ERWIN LINK. U-*659*. Maschinengefreiter (Fireman, third class). Captured 4 May 1943.

ADOLF MARCH. U-*175*. Funkobergefreiter (Seaman [Radioman], first class). Captured 17 April 1943.

LEOPOLD NOWROTH. U-*175*. Oberleutnant (Ing.) (Lieutenant [jg], Engineering duties). Captured 17 April 1943.

WERNER OPOLKA. U-*528*. Oberleutnant z. See (Lieutenant [jg]). Captured 11 May 1943.

OTTO PHILLIPPS. U-*432*. Obermaschinenmaat (Machinist's Mate, second class). Captured 11 March 1943.

ERWIN PINZER. U-*752*. Maschinengefreiter (Fireman, third class). Captured 23 May 1943.

WILHELM RAHN. U-*301*. Oberfähnrich z. See (Senior Midshipman). Captured 21 January 1943.

(No first name recorded) RICHTER. U-*752*. Maschinengefreiter (Fireman, third class). Captured 23 May 1943.

(No first name recorded) ROSENKRANZ. U-*175*. Mechanikerobergefreiter (Seaman, first class). Captured 17 April 1943.

(No first name recorded) ROSS. U-*432*. Funkgefreiter (Seaman [Radioman], second class). Captured 11 March 1943.

HEINRICH SCHAUFFEL. U-*752*. Leutnant z. See (Ensign). Captured 23 May 1943.

GERHARD SCHMELING. U–*439*. Maschinenobergefreiter (Fireman, second class). Captured 4 May 1943.

RUDOLF SPITZ. U–*444*. Funkgefreiter (Seaman [Radioman], second class). Captured 11 March 1943.

HEINZ STOCK. U–*205*. Mechanikerobergefreiter (Seaman, first class). Captured 17 February 1943.

(No first name recorded) TILLMANNS. U–*752*. Maschinenmaat (Fireman, first class). Captured 23 May 1943.

(No first name recorded) VOELKER. U–*175*. Fähnrich (Ing.) (Midshipman, Engineering duties). Captured 17 April 1943.

(No first name recorded) WEISSEFELD. U–*444*. Maschinengefreiter (Fireman, third class). Captured 11 March 1943.

The writer is grateful to Archivist Horst Bredow and his staff at the U-Boot-Archiv in Cuxhaven-Altenbruch for locating the first names of most of these men.

5. PRO, WO 208/4145. S.R.N. 1897.

6. Ibid., S.R.N. 1881.

7. Ibid., S.R.N. 1899.

8. Ibid., S.R.N. 1891. Korv. Kapt. Otto v. Bülow (U–*404*), cited here, was author of one of the war's more interesting acts of overclaiming, when on 25 April 1943 he signaled BdU that he had sunk an aircraft carrier, which he identified as "possibly [U.S.S.] *Ranger.*" The sinking took place, he said, in Qu AK 4737. He had used five torpedoes, including two FATs. "Two tongues of flame observed. Several very heavy shakings when moving away on the surface." PRO, DEFE-3, TOI 1038 GMT, 25/4/43. BdU replied: "Good, good. Report whether in your opinion aircraft carrier was sunk." Ibid., TOI 1237/25/4/43. Bülow reported: "Assume sinking on account of absence of air and sea defense after hits, of severance of contact in spite of very good visibility and of damage which was without doubt heavy. Search proved fruitless." Ibid., TOI 1640/25/4/43.] Within five hours congratulations were transmitted to Bülow from the highest

quarter: "In grateful recognition of your heroic participation in the struggle for the future of our people I award you, as 234th member of the German Armed Forces, the Oak Leaves to the Knight's Cross of the Iron Cross. Adolf Hitler." Ibid., TOI 2150/25/4/43. The next morning Dönitz and Godt conveyed their own kudos. Ibid., TOI 0839/26/4/43. But subsequent intelligence did not support the sinking of *Ranger* or of any other carrier. Hessler wrote: "F.O. U-boats [Dönitz] did not uphold the claim and was irritated at the premature announcement"; Hessler, *The U-Boat War,* Vol. II, p. 103. There is no confirmation of such an attack in British or U.S. records. It may be that Bülow sighted and attacked the nearby RN escort carrier H.M.S. *Biter.* If so, the carrier did not notice it.

9. Ibid., S.R.N. 1833.
10. PRO, WO 208/4205, S.R. Draft No. 3335.
11. PRO, WO 208/4145, S.R.N. 1834.
12. Ibid., S.R.N. 1831.
13. Ibid., S.R.N. 1832.
14. Ibid., S.R.N. 1807.
15. Ibid., S.R.N. 1801.
16. Ibid., S.R.N. 1734.
17. Ibid., S.R.N. 1758.
18. Ibid., S.R.N. 1738.
19. Ibid., S.R.N. 1768.
20. Ibid., S.R.N. 1739.
21. Ibid., S.R.N. 1796.
22. Ibid., S.R.N. 1778.
23. Ibid., S.R.N. 1566.
24. Ibid., S.R.N. 1868.
25. Ibid., S.R.N. 1864.
26. Ibid., S.R.N. 1861.
27. Ibid., S.R.N. 1860.
28. Ibid., S.R.N. 1862.
29. Ibid., S.R.N. 1854.
30. Ibid., S.R.N. 1848.
31. Ibid., S.R.N. 1531.
32. Ibid., S.R.N. 1823.

33. Ibid., S.R.N. 1835.
34. Ibid., S.R.N. 1847.
35. PRO, WO 208/4205, S.R. Draft No. 1905.
36. Ibid., S.R. Draft No. 5470.
37. Ibid., S.R. Draft No. 2220.
38. Ibid., S.R. Draft No. 3495.
39. Ibid., S.R. Draft No. 1977.
40. Ibid., S.R. Draft No. 2802.
41. PRO, WO 208/4145, S.R.N. 1777.
42. Ibid., S.R.N. 1857.
43. Ibid., S.R.N. 1728.
44. Ibid., S.R.N. 1896.
45. Ibid., S.R.N. 1799.
46. Ibid., S.R.N. 1782.
47. Ibid., S.R.N. 1888.
48. Ibid., S.R.N. 1878.
49. Ibid., S.R.N. 1850.
50. Ibid., S.R.N. 1805.
51. Ibid., S.R.N. 1826.
52. Ibid., S.R.N. 1821.
53. Ibid., S.R.N. 1822.
54. Ibid., S.R.N. 1779.
55. Ibid., S.R.N. 1732.
56. Ibid., S.R.N. 1865.
57. Ibid., S.R.N. 1900.
58. PRO, ADM 223/120, N.I.D. UC No. 318, 2 April 1943, "Morale Among U-Boat Prisoners of War." The writer is indebted to W.J.R. "Jock" Gardner at NHB/MOD for sending him a copy of this document.
59. PRO, WO 208/4145, S.R.N. 1695.
60. Ibid., S.R.N. 1890.
61. Ibid.
62. Ibid., S.R.N. 1842.
63. Ibid., S.R.N. 1710.
64. Ibid., S.R.N. 1803.
65. Ibid., S.R.N. 1800.
66. Ibid., S.R.N. 1802.
67. Ibid., S.R.N. 3495.

68. Ibid., S.R.N. 1800.

69. Ibid., S.R.N. 1732.

Chapter 10

1. PRO, ADM 237/114, Convoy ONS.6; ADM 199/2020, An Analysis of the Operation of Support Groups in the North Atlantic (Period 5th May–12th June), 15 July 1943 [hereafter Support Groups]; AIR 41/48, Peyton Ward, "The R.A.F. in the Maritime War," Vol. IV, p. 70.

2. NARA, KTB-BdU, 7 May 1943.

3. The X-B–Bericht Weekly Summary for 3–9 May 1943, Bundesarchiv-Militärarchiv, Bestand RM 7/755, X-B-Bericht No. 19/43, Woche vom 3.5–9.5 1943, f. 87v and f. 88r.

4. Ibid. The information produced by B-Dienst on HX.237 read: "Funkspruch vom 6.5 2330 Uhr [German time] meldete Unbek. aus See die Position des Konvois in 43 56 N 48 27 W."

5. Ibid., f. 87v. The information on 7.5.43 read: "Am 7.5 1600 Uhr befand sich der Geleitzug mit 38 Schiffen in 42 08 N 45 42 W, Kurs etwa 128 Grad, Fahrt 9 sm." See also NARA, KTB-BdU, 8 May 1943.

6. Ibid.

7. Ibid.

8. PRO, DEFE–3, ff. 448 and 449, 745.

9. Ibid., Reel 718, time of interception (TOI) 1730, 9 May 1943, decrypted 21 May 1943; NHB/MOD, Assessments, f. 275.

10. David Hobbs, "Ship-borne Air Anti-Submarine Warfare," in Howarth and Law, *Battle of the Atlantic,* pp. 391–392.

11. Ibid., p. 391. Cf. William T. Y'Blood, *Hunter-Killer: U.S. Escort Carriers in the Battle of the Atlantic* (Annapolis, MD: Naval Institute Press, 1983), Appendix I, "Escort Carrier Technical Data," pp. 279–281.

12. Hobbs, "Ship-borne Air," Howarth and Law, *Battle of the Atlantic,* pp. 389–390.

13. NARA, KTB-BdU, to May 1943.

14. NHB/MOD, Assessments, f. 278.

15. NARA, KTB-BdU, 11 May 1943; NARA, RG 457, SRGN 17844.

16. NARA, KTB-BdU, 12 May 1943.

17. Herbert A. Werner, *Iron Coffins: A Personal Account of the German U-Boat Battles of World War II* (New York: Bantam Books, 1969), pp. 160–161. Although Werner states in his introduction that he wrote this volume "with the aid of notes I took during the war," he told this writer that he consulted no official records such as U–*230's* KTB, accounting for certain events recounted out of sequence and errors in the times given for certain events. Few memoirs of the U-boat war can match Werner's, however, in expressing the grim realities that U-boat men faced in May. "At the end of May all the sea officers at Brest were appalled," he told the writer. "The petty officers and ratings were not fully aware of the extent of the losses. At that level morale remained high. But officers were now criticizing the leadership of the Navy, though only to their close friends." Interview with Werner, Ponte Vedra, Florida, 9 May 1995. A criticism of Werner's book *Iron Coffins* by Jürgen Rohwer is given in *Marine-Rundschau: Zeitschrift für Seewesen*, 67. Jahrgang (Frankfurt a/M: Ver-lag E.S. Mittler & Sohn GmbH bln, 1970), pp. 186–191.

18. NHB/MOD, Assessments, ff. 279, 280, and notations by R. M. Coppock; Coppock to the author, "Loss of U 89 U 456 and U 753 in May 1943," FDS 412, London, by hand, 29 May 1997. Naval Staff History, *The Development of British Naval Aviation* 1919–1945, Vol. II (London: Historical Section, Admiralty, 1956), pp. 119–120.

19. The writer is indebted to Dr. Frederick J. Milford, formerly Vice President for Special Projects at the Battelle Memorial Institute, for sharing with him the impressive body of data that he has collected on the acoustic homing torpedo as well as the careful, balanced analysis that he has made of its use; Milford to the author, Columbus, Ohio, 19 January and 6 May 1996.

20. M. D. Fagen, ed., *A History of Engineering and Science*

in the Bell System: National Service in War and Peace (1925–1975) (Murray Hill, NJ: Bell Telephone Laboratories, 1978), p. 191. See also Mark B. Gardner, "Mine Mk. 24: World War II Acoustic Torpedo," *Journal of the Audio Engineering Society,* Vol. 22, No. 8 (October 1974), pp. 614–626; and Frederick J. Milford, "More on Fido," *Submarines Review* (April 1996), pp. 119–120.

21. Fredrick J. Milford to the author, 19 January 1996; Fagen, ed., *Bell System,* pp. 191, 193.

22. Fagen, ed., *Bell System,* p. 195.

23. NARA, SRH–367, Operations Evaluation Group Study [hereafter OEG] No. 289, "Proctor, A Short History: The Rise and Fall of an Anti-Submarine Weapon," 12 August 1946, p. 5.

24. Fredrick J. Milford to the author, 19 January 1997.

25. Telephone interview with Air Commodore Jeaff Greswell, CB, CBE, DSO, DFC, R.A.F. (Ret.), Saunderton, Princess Risborough, Bucks., England, 28 October 1997. See also Price, *Aircraft versus Submarine,* pp. 133–134, where this story was told first.

26. PRO, AIR 41/48, Peyton Ward, "The R.A.F. in the Maritime War," Vol. IV, p. 63.

27. Ibid. NHB/MOD, Coppock, "Loss of U 89, U 456 and U 753 in May 1943," FDS 412.

28. NARA, RG 457, SRGN 17948.

29. Ibid., SRGN 17965.

30. Ibid., SRGN 17963, 18031.

31. Ibid., SRGN 17980.

32. Ibid., SRGN 17975.

33. NHB/MOD, Coppock, "Loss of U 89, U 456 U 753 in May 1943," FDS 412. F/Lt. Wright made no mention of his use of the Mk. 24 in his after-action report; PRO, Air 27/911, RAF Form 541, No. 86 Squadron, 12 May 1943, p. 4. Earlier published reports that U–456 was finished off by Sunderland "G" of Canadian 423 Sqdn. and two surface escorts are in error, according to Coppock, who concludes that their attack was made instead against U–753 on 13 May; see below. On 14 May the bodies of two crewmen from U–456

were found in BD 6643 by U–448 (Oblt.z.S. Helmut Dauter). From the position given, Coppock concludes that they had been lost overboard.

34. NARA, KTB-BdU, 12, 13 May 1943. Some earlier published accounts indicate that Mk. 24s were used successfully against U–266 on 13 (or 14) May by B/86 and against U–657 on 14 May by a USN Catalina of No. 84 Sqdn. from Iceland. But these are in error, according to Coppock. The U–266 was sunk by D/Cs dropped by Halifax "M" of 58 Sqdn. on 15 May, and U–657 was sunk by the frigate H.M.S. Swale on 17 May. Credit for a successful Mk. 24 sinking of U–954 on 19 May has been given in several sources to Liberator "T" of 120 Sqdn. from Reykjavik, Iceland, but this seems not to have been possible and Coppock gives the credit instead to the frigate H.M.S. Jed and the ex-U.S. Coast Guard cutter H.M.S. Sennen on that date. Following 12 May, the only other successful use of Mk. 24 during the month was by USN Catalina "F" of Patrol Squadron VP–84 against U–467 on 26 May.

35. NHB/MOD, Coppock, "Loss of U 89, U 456 and U 753 in May 1943, FDS 412; Assessments," f. 283.

36. PRO, ADM 199/577, 578, Convoy HX.237. In their summation Dönitz/Godt explained that the operation against HX.237 had to be given up because, "Right from the first day, carrier borne planes were sighted with the convoy, and later on the carrier itself was seen once. These planes and other land-based escorts made the operation very difficult, and on the last day [13th] it had to be given up because this air activity was too powerful." NARA, KTB–BdU, 13 May 1943.

37. During the daytime hours BdU signaled the Elbe I and II boats: BY DARKNESS AS MANY BOATS AS POSSIBLE MUST BE AT IT. OPERATE AT MAXIMUM SPEED TO REACH CONVOY BEFORE THEN. THE FIRST NIGHT IS THE MOST FAVORABLE ONE. EVEN TOMORROW IT WILL BE MORE DIFFICULT. NARA, RG 457, SRGN 17836.

38. NHB/MOD, Assessments, f. 25, and notations by R. M. Coppock, who emphasizes that all the attacks, including

the ramming, were delivered against the same boat; PRO, ADM 199/2020, p. 5. A report of U–*223*'s damage was sent by Wächter to BdU at 1620 GMT. He included mention of the two crewmen lost overboard, the death of the Coxswain, and light wounds suffered by himself and both Watch Officers. NARA, RG 457, SRGN 17989. Förster (U–*359*) went to Wächter's aid, handing over one of the crewmen who went overboard as well as bandages for the wounded. This boat stayed with Wächter until, emergency repairs completed in the evening of the 14th, the rammed boat was able to make a crash dive. Ibid., SRGN 17900, 17992, 18243. Förster also was forced to return to base by an oil track caused by D/C damage to his own boat. Ibid., SRGN 17905, 17943.

39. NARA, RG 457, SRGN 17938. T.O.I. 1031, 12 May 1943.

40. NHB/MOD, Assessments, f. 27, and notation by R. M. Coppock; PRO, ADM 199/2020, Support Groups, Convoy SC.129, pp. 4–5; PRO, ADM 199/577, 579, 580, 2020, Convoy SC.129.

41. NARA, KTB–BdU, 13, 14 May 1943.

42. Interview with Herbert A. Werner, Ponte Vedra, Florida, 9 May 1995. In the introduction to his book *Iron Coffins,* as well as in his interview with the writer, Werner acknowledged that his book was written for a political purpose: to protest that "our lives were squandered on inadequate equipment and by the unconscionable policies of U-Boat Headquarters"; p. xix.

43. NHB/MOD, Assessments, f. 287, and notation by R. M. Coppock. It was probably U–*640* that was attacked at 2043 the evening before by another USN Catalina, I/184; f. 286. This U-boat reported at 0112 that it had been attacked by a Catalina. Some authorities have U–*640* torpedoing the merchant ship *Aymeric* three days later and then being sunk herself by H.M.S. *Swale;* but BdU, Rohwer, and Coppock deduce that *Aymeric* was sunk by U–*657.* That U–*640* was sunk on the 14th, three days before, by K/84 best fits all the available evidence according to Coppock, to the writer, "Loss of U 381, U 640, U 657 and U 258 in May 1943," FDS

442, London, by hand, 29 May 1997. The loss of U–657 is attributed to *Swale* on 17 May; see below. There were three unsuccessful attacks employing the Mk. 24 Mine on 14 May: by Catalina K/84 at 0900; Catalina C/84 at 1337; and Liberator J/120 at 1737. Liberator 0/120 made an unsuccessful Mk. 24 attack at 2159 on the 19th.

44. PRO, ADM 199/2145, Interviews with Survivors, Captain S. Morris, *Aymeric,* 24th June, 1943, ff. 147–148.

45. NHB/MOD, Assessments, f. 32, and notation by R. M. Coppock; also Coppock, "Loss of U 381, U 640, U 657 and U 258 in May 1943," FDS 442.

46. PRO, ADM 237/203, Report of Proceedings– S.C.130. Comments of Senior Officer, Close Escort.

47. Ibid., Report of Attack on U-Boat, H.M.S. *Duncan,* 19 May 1943, 0130.

48. Bundesarchiv-Militärarchiv, Bestand RM 7/755, X–B Bericht No. 21/43 Woche vom 17.5–23.5.1943, f. 159r. Cf. NARA, KTB–BdU, 17 May 1943.

49. PRO, ADM 223/15, Operational Intelligence Centre Special Intelligence Summary, 10.5.43–17.5.43, f. 198.

50. PRO, ADM 237/203, Remarks by Commodore (D), Western Approaches [Simpson], S.C.130., 12 June 1943.

51. NARA, KTB-BdU, 17 May 1943. The first U-boat to sight and report SC.130 was U–304 (Oblt.z.S. Heinz Koch) in Qu AK 4675 early on 19 May.

52. PRO, AIR 27/911, RAF Form 541, No. 120 Squadron, 19.5.43, Liberator III T/120. Gretton was annoyed that this aircraft did not keep in better communication with him, but the pilot's after-action report states that he informed Gretton of each sighting.

53. NHB/MOD, Assessments, ff. 37, 38, 38A, and notations by R. M. Coppock; Coppock to author, "Loss of U 954 and Others in May 1943," London, by hand, 13 November 1996. Most authorities, going back to Peyton Ward, have written that U–954 was sunk by Liberator T/120's attack at 0534 on 19 May in position 55°09′N, 35°18′W. But Coppock has shown that this could not have been the case since U–954 transmitted a (nondistress) signal at 0811 that day,

over two and a half hours after T/120's attack. It should be noted that after EG1 joined the convoy, *Kitchener* was detached to reinforce Convoy ON.184, as per orders from CinCWA; PRO, ADM 237/203, Convoy SC.130, Appendix D.

54. The loss of U–954 was mentioned matter-of-factly in NARA, KTB-BdU, 20 May 1943. Dönitz's older son, Oblt.z.S. Klaus Dönitz, was killed a year later, on 14 May 1943, when an S–boat on which he was a passenger was sunk by a Free French destroyer.

55. NHB/MOD, Assessments, f. 308, and notation by R. M. Coppock.

56. R. M. Coppock, "Loss of U 381, U 640, U 657 and U 258 in May 1943," FDS 442.

57. PRO, ADM 237/203, Reports of Attacks on U-Boats, Convoy SC.130.

58. R. M. Coppock, "Loss of U 381, U 640, U 657 and U 258 in May 1943," FDS 442; NHB/MOD, Assessments, f. 34, and notations by Coppock.

59. NHB/MOD, Assessments, ff. 39, 40, and notations by R. M. Coppock.

60. PRO, ADM 237/203, Convoy SC.130. No count is given in the record of *Zamalek's* HF/DF contacts other than her first at 2219 on the 18th.

61. NARA, KTB–BdU, 19, 20 May 1943. A "Frog" search was astern of convoy to a distance of so many miles. An "Adder" search was ahead of convoy to a distance of 8–12 miles. A "Viper" search was a square flight around the convoy at visibility distance. When an aircraft searched down a DF bearing it was called a "Mamba."

62. NHB/MOD, Assessments, f. 312, and notations by Coppock; PRO, AIR 27/911, RAF Form 541, Liberator I P/120, 20 May 1943.

63. PRO,AIR 27/911, RAF Form 541, Liberator I P/120, 20 May 1943; telephone conversation with R. M. Coppock, 11 November 1997. For a description of the Mark I 600–1b. A.S. *bomb* see CAB 86/4, Report on Progress of Development of Anti-U-Boat Weapons May 1943, f. 130.

64. NHB/MOD, Assessments, f. 312, and notations of R. M. Coppock. On the day before, Liberator T/120 dropped two "600 1b.D.C.'s" in its attack on U–731, as recorded by its pilot Flight Sergeant S.W. Stoves; PRO, AIR 27/911, R.A.F. Form 541, Liberator III T/120, 19 May 1943. For U–418 also see NHB/MOD, Assessments, f. 309, and notation by R. M. Coppock; and Peyton Ward, "R.A.F. in the Maritime War," Vol. III, p. 65. U–418 was destroyed by R.P. (Rocket Projectiles), described below.

65. PRO, ADM 199/2020, Analysis of U-Boat Operations in the Vicinity of Convoy S.C.130. 18th–21st May 1943, p. 3; PRO, ADM 237/203, S.C.130–Report of Proceedings, p. 3.

66. PRO, DEFE–3, Reel 718, TOI 0337, 20 May 1943, decrypted 20 May 1943.

67. PRO, ADM 199/2020, Analysis of U-Boat Operations in the Vicinity of Convoy S.C. 130. 18th–21st May 1943, pp. 2–3.

68. PRO, ADM 237/203, Convoy SC.130.

69. Three Commanders from the *Donau II* line are reported to be still alive on the roster of the Verband Deutscher U-Boot-fahrer, but the writer and his research assistant in Germany have not been able to locate them.

70. "To enjoy fair winds, then foul."

71. NHB/MOD, Assessments, f. 41, notation by R.M. Coppock. The British submarine sunk by U–123 (von Schroeter) on 18 April was P.615, the former *Uluc Ali Reis* built for Turkey and taken over by the RN. Interview with Horst von Schroeter, Bonn, 26 December 1995.

72. A concise presentation of this point is given in Montgomery C. Meigs, *Slide Rules and Submarines,* pp. 90–96. Despite the deployment of "Hunter-Killer Groups"–the pioneer such group centered around the escort carrier U.S.S. *Bogue* is discussed below–Colonel Meigs contends that King never did accept the idea of an offensive strategy; pp. 92–95. The author gives a short account of the Antisubmarine Warfare Operational Research Group (ASWORG), the USN's coun-

terpart to O.R.S. at RAF Coastal Command and CAOR at the Admiralty; pp. 58–62, 195, 216–217.

73. NARA, Modern Military Branch [hereafter MMB], Action Report, U.S.S. *Bogue,* 7 May 1943, Escort of Convoy HX.235, Enclosure "B." Y'Blood, *Hunter-Killer,* pp. 34–35. *Bogue* was the name ship of 44 escort carriers, including 33 that were transferred to the RN; ibid., p. 280. Four other U.S. escort carriers, U.S.S. *Sangamon, Santee, Suwannee,* and *Chenango,* were employed for various tasks during the Torch invasions of North Africa in November 1942, but *Bogue* was "the U.S. Navy's first aircraft carrier used in support of convoys"; pp. 12–28, 35. That the four aforementioned ACVs were not deployed to the transatlantic convoy lanes directly after Torch is criticized by Syrett, *Defeat of the German U-Boats,* who states that "the failure to commit escort carriers to close the Greenland air gap shows, at best, the Allies' lack of understanding of the importance of the Battle of the Atlantic;" p. 17. Perhaps *Americans* would be the better word than *Allies'.* Syrett reports that most of the escort carriers were sent to the Pacific; p. 17.

74. NARA; MMB, U.S.S. BOGUE (CVE–9), Report Escort of Convoy ON.184, Enclosure "A," Discussion of Anti Submarine Tactics; Escort of Convoy HX.235, Enclosure "B."

75. "Wildcats and Avengers: The History of Composite Squadron Nine," typewritten document of the U.S.S. *Bogue* CVE–9 Reunion Association, pp. 3–5; and NARA, MMB, Action Report, U.S.S. BOGUE, Escort of Convoy HX.235, where the correct figure of six (6) Wildcats as the new fighter complement is given; Enclosure C, p. 1.

76. NARA, MMB, Action Report, U.S.S. BOGUE, Escort of Convoy HX.235, Enclosure C, p. 1..

77. Bundesarchiv-Militärarchiv, Bestand RM 7/755, X-B Bericht No. 21/43 Woche vom 17.5.–23.5.1943, f. 158r. Cf. NARA, KTB-BdU, 19 May 1943. The patrol line was established from AJ 6417 (55° 15′N, 44° 25′W) to AK 7559 (52°15′N, 37°35′W), effective 2000 on 21 May; radio silence to be observed. NARA, RG 457, SRGN 18625.

78. These positions as decrypted by B-Dienst were: 49°28'N, 43°47'W at 1700 [GST] on the 20th, 50°27'N, 38°16'W at 1700 on the 21st, and 52°12'N, 33°28'W on the 22nd.

79. NARA, RG 457, SRGN 18695; Syrett, *Defeat of the U-Boats,* p. 135. Some Group *Donau* boats were also directed toward Convoy HX.239.

80. Bundesarchiv-Militärarchiv, Bestand RM 7/755, X–B Bericht No. 21/43, Woche vom 17.5–23.5.1943, f. 159v.

81. PRO, ADM 237/100, Convoy ON.184: Report of Antisubmarine Action by Aircraft, TBF–1 No. 11, 21 May 1943. NARA, Roll 2938 KTB–U–*231,* 13.4.–30.5.43, pp. 22–23. Wenzel recorded that the attack, by a single-engine carrier aircraft, took place at 2120 in AK 7936 (53°15'N, 35°30'W).

82. PRO, ADM 237/100, Convoy ON.184: Report of Antisubmarine Action by Aircraft, TBF–1 No. 2, 0635 22 May 1943. Lt. Richard S. Rogers, flying F4F4 No. 13, made a sighting at 0805, but the boat dived before he could strafe it.

83. Ibid., TBF–1 No. 6, 1103 22 May 1943.

84. Ibid., TBF–1 No. 5, 1325 22 May 1943.

85. Telephone interviews with Captain Frank Fodge, U.S.N.R. (Ret.), Stuart, Florida, 12 September 1996, and Radioman James O. Stine, Walnut Grove, Missouri, 22 November 1997.

86. PRO, ADM 237/100, Convoy ON.184, Report of Antisubmarine Action by Aircraft, TBF–1 No. 6, 1804, 22 May 1943.

87. DHIST/NDHQ, Ottawa, Naval Historical Section Files, 1650-"U-Boats"–U–*569, Report on the Interrogation of Survivors From U–569,* Sunk on May 22, 1943 (Washington, D.C.: United States Government Printing Office, 1943), 17 pp. The writer is grateful to Dr. Roger Sarty, DHIST Senior Historian, for a copy of this report.

88. NARA, KTB-BdU, 21 May 1943.

89. DHIST/NDHQ, *Survivors From U–569,* p. 14.

90. PRO, ADM 237/100, Convoy ON.184, Report of Antisubmarine Action by Aircraft, TBF–1 No. 7, 1840, 22 May

1943. Elsewhere in the same report Roberts states that the white flag first appeared while his gunner was changing ammunition cans.

91. DHIST/NDHQ, Ottawa, Naval Historical Section Files, 1650-"U-Boats"-U 569, "Delivery of 25 Prisoners ex German U-boat to U.S. Authorities." The writer thanks Dr. Sarty for a copy of this document.

92. "Wildcats and Avengers," pp. 29–33, which notes in addition: "There was one more incident, this one involving the officers of the *U-860.* The *Solomons'* Executive Officer brought Commander Buechel [Freg. Kapt. Paul Büchel] and his Exec to the wardroom for a meal. At that point one or more of the ship's Jewish officers walked out in protest, a feeling shared by the squadron's pilots who had lost close comrades. The ship's Exec later explained lamely that they were merely trying to treat the prisoners nicely to gain intelligence from them." Lt. (jg) Stearns and Ens. Doty were both killed in the Pacific. The writer is indebted to *Bogue* veterans Frank Fodge, Ralph Hiestand, David O. Puckett, and James O. Stine, who shared their recollections with him. As pointed out earlier in a discussion of HF/DF (chapter 2), it was Huff-Duff that led to Chamberlain's success. Captain Short of *Bogue* stated that U-*569's* W/T transmission at 1727 "wrote its death warrant"; NARA, Action Report, Box 855, Serial 026, U.S.S. *Bogue* (CVE-9), Report of Operations of Hunter-Killer Group built around U.S.S. *Bogue* furnishing air cover for Convoy ON.184 from Iceland area to Argentia area; from Commander Sixth Escort Group, to Commander in Chief Western Approaches, 29 May 1943, p. 3. PRO, ADM 199/358, Report of Proceedings of Convoy ON.184, The Senior Officer, C.1 Group in H.M.S. *Itchen* to Captain (D) Newfoundland, 1st June 1943.

93. NARA, RG 457, SRGN 18793: TO GROUPS DONAU AND MOSEL: DISCONTINUE OPERATION ON NORTHEAST CONVOY. SET OFF TO WEST; TOI 0934Z, 23 May 1943. Cf. KTB–BdU, 23 May 1943.

94. PRO, AIR 15/210, Coastal Command Tactical Memorandum No. 62, Guide to the Use of RP Against U/Boats;

Tactical Notes on U-Boat Attack with Rocket Projectiles by Swordfish Aircraft; A Brief Survey of the Characteristics of the Aircraft Rocket Weapon. AIR 41/48, Peyton Ward, "R.A.F. in the Maritime War," Vol. III, pp. 61–65, Appendix IV, pp. 1–7.

95. Naval Staff History, *The Development of British Naval Aviation 1919–1945,* Vol. II (London: Historical Section, Admiralty, 1956), pp. 123–124.

96. NHB/MOD, Assessments, f. 245, notation by R. M. Coppock.

97. Ibid, f. 276.

98. NARA, Tenth Fleet, ASW Analysis and Stat. Section, Series VI; ASW Assessment Incidents 3177–3257, Box 102, folder 3208.

99. NARA, KTB-U-*182* (reconstructed), 6.4.43–16.5.43.

100. NARA, Tenth Fleet, ASW Analysis and Stat. Section, Series VI; ASW Assessment Incidents 3177–3257, Box 102, folder 3219.

101. NHB/MOD, Assessments, f. 305, notation by R. M. Coppock.

102. Franks, *Search, Find, and Kill,* p. 194; Less, *Type VII U-boats,* p. 28.

103. NHB/MOD, Assessments, f. 324, notation by R. M. Coppock. Syrett, *Defeat of the German U-Boats,* has U–*436* still operating in patrol lines as late as September and October (pp. 204, 206), but Hessler, Coppock, Mulligan, and Lees all agree that she was sunk on 26 May, certainly no later than 3 June (Mulligan). BdU declared the boat lost as of 4 June; NARA, KTB–BdU, 4 June 1943.

104. Mulligan, ed., *Records Relating to U-Boat Warfare,* p. 160; Lees, *Type VII U-boats,* p. 43.

105. PRO, AIR 27/911, Form 541, Liberator III "E" 120 Squadron, 28 May 1943; Franks, *Search, Find and Kill,* pp. 194–195. The last boats known to have been damaged, as opposed to sunk, during May were U–*552* (Kptlt. Klaus Popp), depth-charged by a Liberator of 59 Sqdn. on the twenty-ninth; and U–*621* (Oblt.z.S. Max Kruschka), depth-charged by Liberator "Q" of 224 Sqdn. on the thirty-first.

106. NARA, KTB–BdU, 24 May 1943.

107. NARA, RG 457, SRGN 18838, 23 May 1943.

108. NARA, KTB–BdU, 24 May 1943.

109. *Fuehrer Conferences on Naval Affairs 1939–1945*, p. 332. The present writer has taken the liberty of changing "submarines" to "U-boats" in the English translation and of spelling out numerals to conform with written speech.

110. Ibid., p. 334.

111. Horst Boog, "Luftwaffe Support of the German Navy," in Howarth and Law, eds., *Battle of the Atlantic*, p. 308.

112. Ibid., pp. 309ff. The present writer was shown the disparities between the Kriegsmarine and Luftwaffe grids at the map collection of the Militärgeschichtliches Forschungsamt in Freiburg im Breisgau.

113. Dönitz, *Memoirs*, p. 341. The original German edition was published in 1958.

Epilogue

1. Doenitz, *Memoirs*, p. 406.

2. Ibid., pp. 406–408; Hessler, *U-Boat War*, Vol. III, p. 8.

3. NARA, KTB–BdU, 13 August 1942. The historian may justly wonder about the moral merits of this decision, as Noah Andre Trudeau wonders about General Robert E. Lee's decision to continue fighting and so lose thousands more lives after he concluded that he could not win the Civil War. See Trudeau, "'A Mere Question of Time': Robert E. Lee from the Wilderness to Appomattox Court House," in Gary W. Gallagher, ed., *Lee the Soldier* (Lincoln: University of Nebraska Press, 1996), pp. 523–558. Writing about another American military tragedy, former U.S. Secretary of Defense Robert McNamara admitted in a recent book that he continued to feed American lives into the killing fields of Vietnam after he realized that that war was not winnable. See Robert S. McNamara, *In Retrospect: The Tragedy and Lessons of Vietnam* (New York: Times Books, 1995).

4. Jürgen Rohwer, "The U-Boat War Against the Allied Supply Lines," in H. A. Jacobsen and J. Rohwer, eds., *Decisive Battles of World War II: The German View* (New York: G. P. Putnam's Sons, 1965), p. 310.

5. Hessler, *U-Boat War,* Vol. III, pp. 25–27.

6. Ibid., pp. 4–5. The *Naxos-U* replaced an interim G.S.R. called *Hagenuk-Wellenanzeiger,* or *Wanze,* the sole virtue of which was that it emitted low levels of radiation. Discovering that the old *Metox* emitted high levels, BdU feared that Allied aircraft were homing on those emissions. It was confirmed in that fear when an RAF prisoner at the German interrogation center Oberursal told his questioners that that was the means used by Coastal aircraft to find U-boats. Though untrue, the POW's lie and the resulting "radiation scare" caused Dönitz to pull the plug on *Metox,* effective 13 August. The *Wanze* that replaced it had no capacity to receive 10-centimeter. The *Naxos-U* worked marginally well against centimetric pulses, but a dependable G.S.R. for that wave band was not available until April 1944.

7. Ibid., p. 51. In the Atlantic war prior to May 1943, U-boats made 1,440 operational patrols amounting to 52,891 days at sea, during which they sank 2,155 ships of 11,551,108 GRT; in the same period, 193 Atlantic patrols, or 13.4 percent, resulted in the loss of the boat and 7,537 fatalities. During the two years that followed, the larger U-boat fleet of that period made 1,027 Atlantic patrols amounting to 36,721 days at sea, during which they sank only 271 ships of 1,363,077 GRT; while 330 patrols, or 32.1 percent, resulted in the loss of the boat and 14,047 fatalities. The futility of U-boat operations after May 1943 is further demonstrated by the marked increase that occurred in Allied ASW assets. Where in May 1943 the Allies could deploy a World War I, between-the-wars, and new construction mix of 131 destroyers, sloops, frigates, and corvettes, in April–May 1945 (exclusive of the central and western Atlantic) they countered the U-boats with 191 destroyers, destroyer-escorts, sloops, frigates, and corvettes, 76 percent of which were new construction since 1943. In April 1943, 293 Allied shore-based ASW

aircraft flew 2,459 missions; in April 1945, 490 ASW aircraft flew 6,314 missions. In April 1943, of the 293 aircraft dedicated to ASW, 98 were four-engined Liberators, Fortresses, and Halifaxes; in April 1945, of the 490 ASW aircraft, 254 were Liberators. The writer is indebted to Thomas Weis for these data.

8. Operations Evaluation Group Study 533, by Carl E. Behrens, "Effects on U-Boat Performance of Intelligence from Decryption of Allied Communications," 28 April 1954, Defense Technical Information Center, Defense Logistics Agency, Cameron Station, Alexandria, Virginia, p. 8. While the U-boats boasted of their *Zaunkönig*, the Allies were not lax in deploying new weapons and devices of their own during the two-year mopping-up period. These included a Magnetic Anomaly Detector (M.A.D.), which picked up the disturbance in the earth's magnetic field caused by the presence of a submerged steel hull and could be fitted to an aircraft such as the Catalina or to a blimp; Expendable Radio Sono Buoys (E.R.S.B.), which, launched from an aircraft, floated on the water's surface and transmitted the noise of a submerged submarine picked up by hydrophones suspended 24 feet below them; more precise 3-centimeter radar to replace or supplement 10-centimeter equipment; Squid, a mortar-fired ahead-throwing weapon similar to Hedgehog except that it was *depth* rather than impact-fused; and Foxer (British) or Cat (Canadian), which were noisemaking devices towed astern of a warship to attract and detonate a *Zaunkönig* at a safe distance from the vessel. Both the Mk.24 and R.P. weapons, first introduced in May 1943, went on to further successes in the two-year period.

9. Quoted in Padfield, *Dönitz*, pp. 462–463.

10. Price, *Aircraft versus Submarine*, p. 165.

11. Slessor, *Central Blue*, pp. 524–525. One example, among many that could be given, of the airmen's "courage and skill" that were praised by Slessor was provided on 28–29 May when Sunderland "O" of 461 Sqdn., Royal Australian Air Force, based at Pembroke Dock, flew out to position 47°50′N, 09°38′W in search of a dinghy containing the crew

of Whitley "P" of 10 Sqdn. O.T.U., which had ditched on the 27th from engine failure. Finding the dinghy, the flying boat attempted a sea landing, but caught a cross-swell, bounced, and then stalled nose down into a tall wave. The impact killed the pilot, F/Lt. W. S. E. "Bill" Dods and seriously injured co-pilot F/O R. de V. Gipps. The rest of the crew managed to get a single serviceable dinghy out through the astrohatch as the aircraft sank, and they rescued Gipps, who was floating helplessly off. The ten Sunderland and six Whitley survivors then tied their dinghies together and spent the night tossing on high waves. Not having heard anything from the flying boat, Pembroke Dock dispatched a second Sunderland "E" the next morning, captained by F/O G.O. Singleton, which found the dinghies at 0630, and made a successful landing alongside them. With the weight of so many rescued men on board, however, Singleton could not take off. Fortunately, other aircraft nearby homed a Free French sloop–*La Combattante*–to the scene. After taking on board all the survivors, including some of the crew from E/461, the sloop took the Sunderland with a skeleton crew aboard in tow. After only four and one-half hours, the tow line parted, and Singleton decided to attempt a takeoff from the heavy sea. For a distance of three miles the flying boat crashed from wave to wave, suffering a hole in the hull seven by four feet, and eventually breaking the surface to become airborne. Singleton realized that with such a large hole it would be suicidal to attempt a water landing. Accordingly, he alerted base that he would put the flying boat down on land at Angle airfield near Pembroke Dock. At 2000 hours he jettisoned excess fuel, unnecessary equipment, and all inflammable materials, while on the ground crash trucks and ambulances assembled at Angle. With his skeleton crew at crash stations, Singleton took aim at the grass bordering the tarmac airstrip. The aircraft's keel plowed noisily into the ground and cut a shallow furrow in the turf 150 yards long before finally slowing to a stop and canting gently over on one wingtip. The squadron record book recorded that it was "believed to be the first time a flying boat has landed on a land drome!" PRO, AIR 27/1913, Operations Record Book, R.A.F. Form 540, No. 461 Squadron, RAAF, May 1943; AIR 41/48, Peyton Ward, "R.A.F. in the Maritime War," Vol. III, p. 103.

12. McCue, *U-Boats in the Bay*, p. 61.

13. Brian McCue to the author, Alexandria, VA, 6 July 1997.

14. Churchill, *Second World War*, Vol. V, *Closing the Ring*, p. 13; Slessor, *Central Blue*, p. 469.

15. Ibid. Slessor, pp. 468–469, 477.

16. Ibid., pp. 535, 537.

17. Air Commodore Henry Probert, "Support from Skies Was Crucial Factor in Eventual Victory," in Chris Heneghan, ed., *Battle of the Atlantic: 50th Anniversary* (1943–1993) (Liverpool: David M. Ratter, Brodie Publishing Limited, 1993), p. 92.

18. S. W. Roskill, *The Navy at War 1939–1945* (London: Collins, 1960), p. 448.

19. Probert, "Support from Skies," p. 92.

20. Roskill, *War at Sea*, Vol. III, Pt. 2, p. 305 and n.2; Roskill, "An Epic Victory," *The Sunday Times*, 8 February 1959.

21. Interview with Klaus-Peter Carlsen, former Commander of U–732, Planegg, Germany, 5 July 1997.

22. For Walker, see Alan Burn, *The Fighting Captain: Frederick John Walker RN and the Battle of the Atlantic* (Barnsley, South Yorkshire: Pen and Sword Books, 1993).

23. *Naval Warfare*, Naval Doctrine Publication–1, 1994, p. 32; cited in Captain Bruce Linder, U.S.N., "ASW as Practiced in Birnam Wood," *Naval Institute Proceedings*, Vol. 122/5/1, 119 (May 1996), p. 65 and n.8.

24. Recently the nationally read German newspaper *Die Zeit* described the naval defeat of May 1943 *as das Stalingrad zur See* ("the Stalingrad at Sea"); 4 June 1993.

25. Peter Cremer, *U-Boat Commander: A Periscope View of the Battle of the Atlantic* (Annapolis, MD: Naval Institute Press, 1984), p. 2.

Select Bibliography

The writer has relied primarily on original archival documents, which are identified in the notes section. He has supplemented those sources with material drawn from interviews with surviving principals and from published works: documentary collections, official histories, technical reports, autobiographies, and other secondary titles. All of the published works consulted are named in the notes. Those books found to have been particularly useful are given in the select list below.

Adams, Thomas A., and David J. Lees. *Register of Type VII U-boats.* Warships Supplement, London, 1990.

Bailey, Chris Howard. *The Battle of the Atlantic: The Corvettes and Their Crews: An Oral History.* Naval Institute Press, Annapolis, MD, 1994.

Baker, Richard. *The Terror of Tobermory: An Informal Biography of Vice-Admiral Sir Gilbert Stephenson, KBE, CB, CMG.* W.H. Allen, London, 1972.

Barley, F.W., and D. Waters. *The Defeat of the Enemy Attack on Shipping: A Study of Policy and Operations,* Vol. 1A (Text and Appendices). Naval Staff History, Second World War. Historical Section, Admiralty, London, 1957.

Barnett, Correlli. *Engage the Enemy More Closely: The Royal Navy in the Second World War.* Hodder and Stoughton, London, 1991.

Baxter III, James Phinney. *Scientists Against Time*. Little Brown, Boston, 1947.

Beesly, Patrick. *Very Special Intelligence: The Story of the Admiralty's Operational Intelligence Centre 1939–1945*. Doubleday & Company, Inc., Garden City, NY, 1978.

Blackett, P.M.S. *Studies of War: Nuclear and Conventional*. Hill and Wang, New York, 1962.

Blair, Clay. *Hitler's U-Boat War: The Hunters 1939–1942*. Random House, New York, 1996.

——. *Silent Victory: The U.S. Submarine War Against Japan*. J.B. Lippincott Company, Philadelphia and New York, 1975.

Boutilier, James A., ed. *The RCN in Retrospect, 1910–1968*. University of British Columbia Press, Vancouver and London, 1982.

British Vessels Lost at Sea 1939–45. Her Majesty's Stationery Office, Cambridge, Patrick Stephens, 1948.

Buderi, Robert. *The Invention That Changed the World: How a Small Group of Radar Pioneers Won the Second World War and Launched a Technological Revolution*. Simon & Schuster, New York, 1996.

Buell, Thomas B. *Master of Sea Power: A Biography of Fleet Admiral Ernest J. King*. Little, Brown and Company, Boston, MA, 1980.

Calvocoressi, Peter. *Top Secret Ultra*. Ballantine Books, New York, 1980.

Cameron, John. *The "Peleus" Trial*. Vol. 1 of the War Crimes Trial series, ed. by Sir David Maxwell Fyfe. William Hodge and Co., Ltd., London, 1948.

Chalmers, C.B.E., D.S.C., Rear-Admiral W.S. *Max Horton and the Western Approaches*. Hodder and Stoughton, 1954.

Churchill, Winston S. *The Second World War*, 6 vols. Houghton Mifflin Company, Boston, 1950.

Clark, Ronald W. *The Rise of the Boffins*. Phoenix House, Ltd., London, 1962.

Cole, Robert Hugh. *Underwater Explosions*. Princeton University Press, Princeton, NJ, 1948.

Dönitz, Karl. *Memoirs: Ten Years and Twenty Days*. Weidenfeld & Nicholson, London, 1959.

Douglas, W.A.B. *The Creation of a National Air Force: The Official History of the Royal Canadian Air Force, Volume II.* University of Toronto Press, Toronto, 1986.

——, ed. *The RCN in Transition, 1910–1985.* University of British Columbia Press, Vancouver, 1988.

Elliot, Peter. *Allied Escort Ships of World War II: A Complete Survey.* Naval Institute Press, Annapolis, MD, 1977.

Ellis, Chris. *Famous Ships of World War 2, in Colour.* Arco Publishing Company, Inc., New York, 1977.

Fagen, M. D., ed. *A History of Engineering and Science in the Bell System: National Service in War and Peace (1925–1975).* Bell Telephone Laboratories, Murray Hill, NJ, 1978.

Franks, Norman L.R. *Conflict Over the Bay.* William Kimber & Co. Limited, London, 1986.

——. *Search, Find and Kill: The RAF's U-Boat Success in World War II.* Grub Street, London, 1995.

Fuehrer Conferences on Naval Affairs 1939–1945. Foreword by Jak P. Mallmann Showell. Naval Institute Press, Annapolis, MD, 1990.

Gannon, Michael. *Operation Drumbeat.* HarperCollins [Harper & Row] Publishers, New York, 1990.

Gibbs, N. H., J.R.M. Butler, J.M.A. Gwyer, Michael Howard and John Ehrman. *Grand Strategy,* 6 vols. Michael Howard, Vol. 4, August 1942–September 1943. Her Majesty's Stationery Office, London, 1956–1972.

Gretton, K.C.B., D.S.O., C.B.E., D.S.C., Vice-Admiral Sir Peter. *Convoy Escort Commander.* Cassell & Company Ltd., London, 1964.

——. *Crisis Convoy.* Kensington Publishing Corp., New York, 1974.

Hackmann, Willem. *Seek & Strike: Sonar, Anti-submarine Warfare and the Royal Navy 1914–54.* Her Majesty's Stationery Office, London, 1984.

Herzog, Bodo, and Günter Schomaekers. *Ritter der Tiefe: Graue Wölfe.* Welsermühl München-Wels, Wels, Austria, 1976.

Hessler, Günter. *The U-Boat War in the Atlantic 1939–1945.* Her Majesty's Stationery Office, London, 1989.

Hezlet, K.B.E., C.B., D.S.O., D.S.C., Vice-Admiral Sir Arthur. *Electronics and Sea Power.* Stein and Day Publishers, New York, 1975.

Hinsley, F. H., et al. *British Intelligence in the Second World War: Its Influence on Strategy and Operations,* 3 vols. Cambridge University Press, New York, 1981–1984.

Howarth, Stephen, and Derek Law, eds. *The Battle of the Atlantic 1939–1945.* Naval Institute Press, Annapolis, MD, 1994.

Howse, Derek. *Radar at Sea: The Royal Navy in World War 2.* Naval Institute Press, Annapolis, MD, 1993.

Kahn, David. *Seizing the Enigma: The Race to Break the German U-Boat Codes, 1939–1943.* Houghton Mifflin Company, 1991.

Keegan, John. *The Price of Admiralty: The Evolution of Naval Warfare.* Viking Penguin, Inc., New York, 1989.

King, Fleet Admiral Ernest J. *U.S. Navy at War 1941–1945: Official Reports to the Secretary of the Navy.* United States Navy Department, Washington, D.C., 1946.

——, and Walter Muir Whitehill. *Fleet Admiral King: A Naval Record.* W.W. Norton & Company, Inc., New York, 1952.

Lloyd's War Losses, The Second World War, 3 September 1939–14 August 1945. Vol.

I, *British, Allied, and Neutral Merchant Vessels Sunk or Destroyed by War Causes.* Lloyd's of London Press, Ltd., 1989.

Love, Jr., Robert William, ed., *The Chiefs of Naval Operations.* Naval Institute Press, Annapolis, MD, 1980.

Lovell, F.R.S., Sir Bernard. *P.M.S. Blackett: A Biographical Memoir.* The Royal Society, London, 1976.

Macintyre, Donald. *The Battle of the Atlantic.* The MacMillan Company, New York, 1961.

McCue, Brian. *U-Boats in the Bay of Biscay: An Essay in Operational Analysis.* National Defense University Press, Washington, D.C., 1990.

Meigs, Montgomery C. *Slide Rules and Submarines: American Scientists and Subsurface Warfare in World War II.* National Defense University Press, Washington, D.C., 1990.

Middlebrook, Martin. *Convoy.* William Morrow, New York, 1976.

Milner, Marc. *North Atlantic Run: The Royal Canadian Navy and the Battle for the Convoys.* University of Toronto Press, Toronto, 1985.

——. *The U-Boat Hunters: The Royal Canadian Navy and the Offensive Against Germany's Submarines.* Naval Institute Press, Annapolis, MD, 1994.

Mulligan, Timothy, ed. *Guides to the Microfilmed Records of the German Navy, 1850–1945,* No. 2: *Records Relating to U-Boat Warfare, 1939–1945.* National Archives and Records Administration, 1985.

——. *Lone Wolf: The Life and Death of U-Boat Ace Werner Henke.* University of Oklahoma Press, Norman, OK, 1995.

Naval Staff History. *The Development of British Naval Aviation 1919–1945,* Vol. II. Historical Section, Admiralty, London, 1956.

Padfield, Peter. *Beneath the Sea: Submarine Conflict 1939–1945.* BCA, London, 1995.

——. *Dönitz: The Last Führer.* Panther Books, London, 1984.

Pitt, Barrie. *The Battle of the Atlantic.* Time-Life Books, Inc., New York, 1977.

Price, Alfred. *Aircraft versus Submarine: The Evolution of the Anti-Submarine Aircraft, 1912–1980.* Jane's Publishing Company, Limited, London, 1980.

Report on the Interrogation of Survivors from U-569, Sunk on May 22, 1943. United States Government Printing Office, Washington, D.C., 1943.

Rohwer, Jürgen. *Axis Submarine Successes.* Introductory material trans. John A. Broadwin. Naval Institute Press, Annapolis, MD, 1983.

——. *The Critical Convoy Battles of March 1943: The Battle for HX.229/SC.122.* Ian Allan Ltd., London, 1977.

——. *U-Boote. Eine Chronik in Bildern.* Stalling, Oldenburg/Hamburg, 1962.

Roskill, D.S.C., R.N., Captain S.W. *The War at Sea 1939–1945,* 3 vols. in 4 pts. Vol. II, *The Period of Balance.* Her Majesty's Stationery Office, London, 1956.

Rössler, Eberhard. *Die Torpedos der deutschen U-Boote: Entwicklung, Herstellung and Eigenschaften der deutschen Marine–Torpedos.* Koehlers Verlags GmbH, Herford, Germany, 1984.

——. *The U-Boat: The Evolution and Technical History of German Submarines.* Trans. Harold Erenberg. Arms and Armour Press, London/Melbourne, 1981.

Runyan, Timothy J., and Jan M. Copes, eds. *To Die Gallantly: The Battle of the Atlantic.* Westview Press, Boulder, Colo., 1994.

Seth, Ronald. *The Fiercest Battle: The Story of North Atlantic Convoy ONS.5, 22nd April–7th May 1943.* Norton Publishing Co., New York, 1961.

Showell, Jak P. Mallmann. *U-Boats Under the Swastika.* Naval Institute Press, Annapolis, MD, 1987.

Sims, U.S. Navy, Rear Admiral William Sowden. *The Victory at Sea.* Doubleday, Page and Company, Garden City, NY, 1921.

Slessor, Sir John. *The Central Blue: The Autobiography of Sir John Slessor, Marshal of the RAF.* Frederick A. Praeger, New York, 1957.

Smith, Bradley F. *The Ultra-Magic Deals: And the Most Secret Special Relation-ship, 1940–1946.* Presidio Press, Novato, CA, 1992.

Stern, Robert C. *Type VII U-Boats.* Naval Institute Press, Annapolis, MD, 1991.

Sternhell, Charles M., and Alan M. Thorndike. *Antisubmarine Warfare in World War II.* Report No. 51 of the Operations Evaluation Group. Navy Department, Washington, D.C., 1946.

Syrett, David. *The Defeat of the U-Boats: The Battle of the Atlantic.* Columbia, SC, University of South Carolina Press, 1994.

Tarrant, V. E. *The U-Boat Offensive 1914–1945.* Arms and Armour Press, London, 1985.

Terraine, John. *The U-Boat Wars 1916–1945.* G.P. Putnam's Sons, New York, 1989.

Vause, Jordan. *Wolf: U-Boat Commanders in World War II.* Naval Institute Press, Annapolis, MD, 1997.

Waddington, C.H., C.B.E., M.A., Sc.D., F.R.S. *O.R. in World War 2: Operational Research Against the U-Boat.* Elek Science, London, 1973.

Weinberg, Gerhard L. *A World at Arms: A Global History of World War II.* Cambridge University Press, New York, 1994.

Werner, Herbert A. *Iron Coffins: A Personal Account of the German U-Boat Battles of World War II.* Bantam Books, New York, 1969.

Williams, Kathleen Broome. *Secret Weapon: U.S. High Frequency Direction Finding in the Battle of the Atlantic.* Naval Institute Press, Annapolis, MD, 1996.

Williams, Mark. *Captain Gilbert Roberts, R.N., and the Anti–U-Boat School.* Cassell Ltd., London, 1979.

Y'Blood, William T. *Hunter-Killer: U.S. Escort Carriers in the Battle of the Atlantic.* Naval Institute Press, Annapolis, MD, 1983.

Glossary

AA. Anti-aircraft.

Abaft. Toward the stern of a ship.

aft. Rearward, or toward the stern of a vessel.

air gap. The mid-Atlantic region that, until spring 1943, was not covered by British or American ASW aircraft.

AK voraus (äußerste Kraft voraus). Engines ahead full.

AK zuruck. Full speed astern.

Alarm! Order for an emergency dive by a U-boat, corresponding to U.S. Navy submarine usage, "Dive! Dive!"

AOC-in-C. Air Officer Commanding-in-Chief (RAF) Coastal Command.

A.P. Armor-piercing.

Asdic. An acronym that grew out of Anti-Submarine Division (of the British Admiralty) standing for a shipborne sound-ranging device that returned a pulse echo indicating a U-boat's bearing and range, though not (before 1943) its depth. The U.S. equivalent system was called *Sonar.*

ASV II. Metric radar.

ASV III. Centimetric radar.

ASW. Anti-Submarine Warfare.

Ato (T–I, G7a). Standard German torpedo with air-steam propulsion system.

A.U. Committee. (British) War Cabinet Anti-U-Boat Warfare Committee.

ballast tanks. Tanks outside the pressure hull of a submarine which, when flooded with water, enabled the submarine to dive.

B-Dienst (Funkbeobachtungsdienst). The German radio-monitoring and cryptographic service.

BdU (Befehlshaber der Unterseeboote). Commander-in-Chief U-Boats (Admiral Karl Dönitz). The abbreviation was also commonly used to identify the Admiral's staff or headquarters.

Beaufort scale. A scale on which wind velocities are registered from 0 (calm) to 12 (hurricane); also from 0 to 17.

Bletchley Park. A mansion and grounds in Buckinghamshire northwest of London, officially called Government Code and Cypher School, where cryptanalysts attacked intercepts of encrypted German wireless (radio) traffic.

bombe. Word used to describe the electromechanical scanning machine devised at Bletchley Park to decrypt the German Enigma cipher.

bow. The forward end of a vessel.

bows. The forward exterior hull of a vessel sloping back from the stem.

bridge. The raised structure from which a power vessel on the surface is navigated.

bulkhead. A wall-like structure inside seagoing vessels used to subdivide space, form watertight compartments, or strengthen the interior framing.

C.A.O.R. Chief Advisor on Operational Research to the Admiralty (Professor Blackett).

CinC, CNA. Commander-in-Chief Canadian North West Atlantic Command.

CinCWA. Commander-in-Chief Western Approaches.

cipher. A secret system of communication ("cypher" in the U.K.) that substitutes letters for letters *(see* code).

code. A secret system of communication that substitutes ideas for ideas *(see* cipher).

conning tower. The low observation tower of a submarine, containing a helmsman's steering controls and topped by an open bridge.

cryptanalysis. The process of "breaking" or "penetrating" a code or cipher by uncovering its key.

cryptography. The science or study of code and cipher systems employed for secret communication.

D/C. Depth charge.

dead reckoning. The calculation of one's position at sea based on course, speed, and elapsed time since the last observed position, taking into account currents, winds, and compass declinations.

decrypt. A deciphered message; to decrypt: to solve a ciphered message.

D.E.M.S.. Defensively Equipped Merchant Ships.

diesel. A compression-ignition type engine; also the combustible petroleum distillate used as fuel.

eel. In German *aal,* a U-boat nickname for torpedo.

E–Maschinen. Battery-powered dynamotors on a U-boat, used for underwater travel.

Enigma. Another name for the *Schlüssel M* cipher machine. The term was also commonly used to denote the machine's encrypted product.

Eto (T–III, G7e). Standard German torpedo with battery-powered electric propulsion system.

Fächerschuss. A simultaneous spread, or fan, launch of two or more torpedoes.

Fähnrich zur See. Midshipman.

Fangschuss. A finishing shot, or coup de grâce.

FAT. (From *Federapparat,* some say *Flächenabsuchender Torpedo*) An anti-convoy torpedo that, after a straight run, made a succession of loops, right or left, through a convoy's columns; called by the British *Curly.*

fathom. Six feet or 1.829 meters.

Feindfahrt. Operational patrol.

I.W.O. First Watch Officer on a U-boat.

flak. (A contraction of *Flugzeugabwehrkanone,* or, some say, *Fliegeabwehrkanone*) A term commonly used for German anti-aircraft gun or gunfire.

flank speed. Full speed.

fore. Forward, or toward the bow of a vessel.

Fregattenkapitän. Captain (junior).

F.T. *See Funk-Telegraphie.*

FuMB (Funkmessbeobachter). A radar detection device, or search receiver, popularly called Metox after the first French firm to manufacture it.

Funk-Telegraphie (F.T.). Wireless Telegraphy (W/T), or radio; the abbreviation *F.T.* stood for a wireless message.

GC&CS. Government Code and Cypher School. *See* Bletchley Park.

GMT. Greenwich Mean Time.

green. Starboard *(Steuerboard);* that is, right.

Gröner. The merchant fleet handbook, with silhouettes of all known freighters and tankers of all nations, compiled by German nautical authority Erich Gröner.

Grossadmiral. Grand admiral, corresponding to fleet admiral (U.S. Navy) or admiral of the fleet (Royal Navy).

gross register tonnage (GRT). The measurement of all the enclosed spaces in a ship expressed in hundreds of cubic feet. As a rule the GRT is more than the weight of a ship alone but less than the weight of the same ship fully loaded.

GRT. *See* gross register tonnage.

Gruppe. Literally, "group"; a patrol line of U-boats with a specific mission, usually given a code name, for example, *Gruppe Star* (Starling).

GSR. German search receiver designed to detect Allied radar.

GST. German Summer Time.

guerre de course. French term meaning a war on seaborne trade or commerce.

H.E.. High explosive. The term is used both for a gun firing high explosive rounds (shells) and for the rounds themselves.

head. Toilet (WC).

Heimische Gewasser **(Home Waters).** A German naval cipher, called DOLPHIN at Bletchley Park.

HF/DF ("Huff-Duff"). High-frequency/direction finding.

H.H. Hedgehog, a code name for mortar spigot-fired contact-fused projectiles employed by escort vessels against U-boats.

Huff-Duff. Nickname for HF/DF (q.v.).

hull. The primary hollow, floatable structure of a boat or ship.

hydrophone. Underwater sound detection device employed by both U-boats and surface warships. In German, *Gruppenhorchgerät,* or GHG.

hydrophone effect. Underwater sound, for example, propeller cavitation of a surface ship or U-boat, detected and shown on instruments as having a certain bearing and range.

hydroplanes. Extended surfaces fore and aft on a U-boat's outboard hull that directed the pitch of the boat underwater.

Kaleu. Diminutive form of the rank *Kapitänleutnant.*

Kapitänleutnant **(Kptlt.).** Rank corresponding to Lieutenant in the U.S. Navy.

Kapitän zur See. Rank corresponding to Captain in the U.S. Navy.

keel. The central structural member of a ship's hull that runs fore and aft along the bottom of the hull for the full distance from stem to sternpost.

Kernével. Residential district bordering the port of Lorient where Admiral Dönitz had his headquarters (BdU) from the fall of France until March 1942.

knot. A unit of speed equivalent to one nautical mile (1.1516 statute miles) per hour.

Konteradmiral. Rear Admiral.

Korvettenkapitän. Commander.

Kriegsmarine. The World War II German Navy, so named from 1935 to 1945.

Kriegstagebuch **(KTB).** German war diary kept by ships and U-boats at sea, also by shore-based headquarters staffs.

KTB. *See Kriegstagebuch.*

Kurzsignale. Short radio (wireless) messages, often to give positions at sea.

Leitender Ingenieur (L.I.). Chief Engineering Officer.

Leutnant zur See. Ensign.

L.I. *See Leitender Ingenieur*. L/L. Leigh Light, the powerful searchlight mounted on certain RAF Coastal Command aircraft.

Marinequadrat (qu). Naval square, an arbitrarily drawn rectangular region of the ocean drafted to Mercator's projection permitting the organization of the ocean surface into a grid chart where the many individual naval squares were identified by letter digraphs and numbered zones.

Mehrfach. A multiple, though not simultaneous, launch of torpedoes.

meter. 39.37 inches.

Metox. *See FuMB*.

MOMP. Mid-ocean meeting point south of Iceland, where U.S. and British naval escorts exchanged responsibility for guarding Atlantic convoys. Also called *chopline* (change of operational control).

Morse code. A message system of dots and dashes, clicks and spaces, or flashes of light that represent letters of the alphabet.

nautical mile. 1.1516 statute miles.

Naxos-U. Code name for FuMB7 German search receiver (GSR) capable of detecting centimetric radar.

NHB/MOD. Naval Historical Branch, Ministry of Defence, London.

Oberleutnant zur See (Oblt.z.S). Lieutenant (Junior Grade).

O.I.C. Operational Intelligence Centre of the Admiralty.

O.R.S. Operational Research Section of RAF Coastal Command.

periscope. An extendable tubelike optical device containing an arrangement of prisms, mirrors, and lenses that permitted a U-boat to view the surface of the sea or the sky from a submerged position.

PLE. Prudent Limit of Endurance.

port. The left-hand side of a vessel as one faces forward.

pressure hull. The U-boat cylinder containing personnel and essential operating systems that was designed to withstand many atmospheres of water pressure when submerged.

quarter. The arc of 45 degrees to either side horizontally from the stern of a vessel.

RAF. (British) Royal Air Force.

RAAF. Royal Australian Air Force.

RDF. Radio Direction Finding, a British cover name for radar.

RCAF. Royal Canadian Air Force.

RCN. Royal Canadian Navy.

R.C.N.V.R. Royal Canadian Naval Volunteer Reserve.

red. Port *(Backbord);* that is, left.

Ritterkreuz des Eisernen Kreuzes. Knight's Cross of the Iron Cross.

RN. (British) Royal Navy.

RNR. Royal Naval Reserve.

RNVR. Royal Naval Volunteer Reserve.

Robr. Torpedo tube.

R.P. Rocket Projectile.

Rudeltaktik. The nighttime "wolf pack" technique of massing U-boats in a patrol line across a convoy's course and of engaging the convoy's formations in a radio-coordinated attack.

Scblüssel–M (Marine-Funkscblüssel-Machine M). Kriegsmarine version of the electromechanical cipher machine used by the German armed forces for telex and wireless (radio) communication. *See Enigma.*

***Schnellboote* (S–boats).** 105-foot fast German torpedo boats, called E–boats by the Allies.

Schnorchel. A valved air pipe that protruded above the water's surface and allowed a U-boat to proceed underwater on diesel power.

Schussmeldung. A U-boat's required "shooting report" on each torpedo or gun action.

sea force (sea state). Seas were recorded in a U-boat's KTB on an ascending scale from zero to ten.

II.W.O. Second Watch Officer on a U-boat.

Special Intelligence. Decrypted German wireless (radio)

traffic from Bletchley Park. Also called Z and, when transmitted as information to operational commanders, *Ultra*.

starboard. The right-hand side of a vessel as one faces forward.

stern. The after (rear) part of a vessel.

Tonnageschlacht. Tonnage battle.

Torpex. A high explosive mix of Cyclonite, TNT, and aluminum flakes.

trim. The balancing of a submarine's weight and equilibrium underwater.

TRITON. A U-boat's cipher key employing four Enigma rotors instead of three, introduced first in October 1941, then fleet-wide in February 1942. It was not solved by cryptanalysts at Bletchley Park (where it was called "SHARK") until December 1942.

U-bootwaffe. The German submarine (U-boat) fleet.

***Uboot-Zieloptik* (UZO).** Surface target-aiming binoculars with luminous graticule. It was attached to a bridge post that automatically fed target line-of-sight bearing and range to the *Vorhaltrechner* (q.v.).

U.K. United Kingdom.

Ultra. The source-disguising form in which the information provided by Special Intelligence ("Z") was conveyed to operational commanders.

USN. United States Navy.

Unterseeboot. Literally, "undersea boat," or submarine, abbreviated as *U-boat* in English.

USAAF. United States Army Air Forces.

USCG. United States Coast Guard.

USNR. United States Naval Reserve.

UZO. *See Uboot-Zieloptik.*

V.L.R. Very Long Range, a term used to describe certain models and modifications of the B–24 Liberator bomber.

Vorhaltrechner. A Siemens-made electromechanical deflection calculator in a U-boat's conning tower that fed attack headings into the gyrocompass steering mechanism of the torpedoes in their tubes.

Wabo. German nickname for *Wasserbombe* (q.v.).

Wasserbombe. German term for depth charge.

WATU. Western Approaches Tactical Unit. way. The motion or speed of a ship or boat through the water.

WESTOMP. Western Ocean Meeting Point, east of St. John's, Newfoundland.

Wintergarten. The open, railed platform on the after part of a U-boat bridge.

WLEF. Canadian Western Local Escort Force.

WRNS. Women's Royal Naval Services.

W/T. Wireless Telegraphy (radio).

X–B-Bericht. Cryptographic service report from *B-Dienst* (q.v.).

Zaunkönig (Wren). An acoustic torpedo designed to home in on the propeller cavitation noise of a convoy escort (warship).

Zentrale. U-boat control room, directly below the conning tower and bridge, containing all dividing controls.

Index

160 sloops 3
160 frigates 1
    destroyer
    destroyer escort
160 Corvette 2
    sub chaser

6 S R 261
   3 5 8 trawler
            tug

138 supply boats
376   "   "
461 tanker p.228